Aeneas to Augustus

A BEGINNING LATIN READER
FOR COLLEGE STUDENTS

The Authors

MASON HAMMOND
Pope Professor of the Latin Language and Literature
HARVARD UNIVERSITY

ANNE AMORY
Associate Professor of Classics
CONNECTICUT COLLEGE

Aeneas to Augustus

A BEGINNING LATIN READER
FOR COLLEGE STUDENTS

SECOND EDITION

REVISED BY MASON HAMMOND

HARVARD UNIVERSITY PRESS
CAMBRIDGE, MASSACHUSETTS
LONDON, ENGLAND

Fifth Printing, 1976

Library of Congress Catalog Card Number 67–12104

ISBN 0–674–00600–3

Printed in the United States of America

PREFACE

Part I of this Reader contains forty-eight prose selections planned to provide a semester of beginning reading for college students who are already familiar with the fundamentals of Latin grammar and have acquired some vocabulary. Part II offers forty-two further selections in prose and verse which have been correlated in length, difficulty, and subject matter with those of Part I. The selections of Part II may therefore be used either along with those of Part I or following them, to allow an instructor to devote a semester to a narrower historical period or to extend the reading over two semesters.

The selections, which deal with the chief characters and events of the history of the Roman Republic, have been chosen with three aims in mind: gradual increase in length and difficulty, continuity of subject matter, and stylistic variety. To help the instructor judge the length of assignments, the number of words (rounded to the nearest five) of each selection is given in the table of contents. The sources from which the selections have been taken range in difficulty from simple late abbreviations of Roman history to authors of the complexity of Sallust, Horace, Lucan, and Tacitus. Both Cicero and Velleius Paterculus have been heavily drawn on. To supplement the indications of sources in the table of contents, there will be found at the back of the book, immediately preceding the vocabulary, a fuller list giving the specific passages used, and a list of authors with their full names, dates, and titles of works from which the selections have been drawn. The selections start with Aeneas and the founding of Rome, to afford background for students who may go on to read Vergil. There follow a few familiar incidents from the Monarchy and early Republic. The main emphasis falls on the history from the Second Punic War, and particularly on the last century of the Republic, culminating in the founding of the Principate by Augustus. Selections have often been adapted or condensed but not so as to interfere with an appreciation of the styles and points of view of the various authors.

The texts generally follow those of editions in the Loeb Classical Library, which are probably the most readily available for further consultation. The full prefaces and notes are intended to satisfy the interest of college students in historical and linguistic matters. The historical information is largely based on articles in the *Oxford Classical Dictionary*.

The notes were originally prepared on the assumption that the book would not contain a vocabulary and that students would be expected to use a dictionary. They therefore afford fuller discussions of the meanings of words than might otherwise have been the case. It may well be, however, that reading an explanation in a note is not only more convenient but also more instructive than looking up a word and selecting an appropriate meaning. In the vocabulary, references are given to many of the notes in which there is discussion of words and meanings, so that to some extent the vocabulary serves as an index to the notes.

In lieu of an index to the grammatical, syntactical, and historical material in the notes, numerous cross-references have been provided. When points once annotated recur in later selections, references are given to the first and the most recent mentions or parallels. In the first edition, such cross-references were given only at the first two or three recurrences, on the theory that students, reading the selections in order and fairly completely, would soon become familiar with often occurring constructions, usages, and other matter. Experience indicates that instructors may prefer to select freely from both parts, so that knowledge of notes on earlier selections cannot be assumed. In this revision more repeated comments and more cross-references have therefore been added to the later selections. Also, forward-looking cross-references, which were formerly avoided on the ground that a student is only confused by citation of material not yet covered, have been introduced to a limited extent, mainly for matters of historical interest rather than for grammatical or syntactical points. The grammatical and syntactical explanations generally follow the statements in Allen and Greenough's *New Latin Grammar*.

In the first edition, no reference numbers to the notes were placed in the texts, in part to avoid interrupting continuity in reading. Those who have used the book, however, have felt that it was an inconvenience to the student not to have references from the texts to the notes. In this edition, therefore, superscript reference numbers have been put in the texts, but so far as possible only at the ends of syntactical or sense units. Where more than one comment is included under the same reference number, the note has been subdivided by small capital letters to facilitate cross-reference. Naturally, in placing the superscript numbers in the text, complete consistency has not been feasible; the run of the sense has occasionally been sacrificed to the need for an immediate explanation of a difficulty, and avoidance of more numbers than necessary in the text has been weighed against avoidance of excessively lengthy notes. It is hoped that, with the help of the lemmata in bold-face type, students will find the notes easy to identify with the texts.

Throughout the texts, notes, and vocabulary, the spellings, forms, definitions, and quantities (where indicated) usually conform to C. T. Lewis, *An Elementary Latin Dictionary*. Both consonantal and vocalic *i* are written *i* but consonantal *u* is written *v*. Genitives singular of second declension nouns ending in *-ius* and *-ium* have been written with *-i* in Republican texts but with *-ii* in texts from the Augustan and later periods and in the titles to the selections. The final consonants of prefixes have been assimilated to following consonants only in certain words in which the assimilated spelling seems more likely to suggest the meaning, as in *collega* for *conlega*, or *illustris* for *inlustris*; the bulk of such words are given the unassimilated spellings preferred by Lewis. The variant spellings are both listed in the vocabulary, with cross-references, as are other variants, such as *vulgus* and *volgus*, or *di* and *dii* for *dei*. In the notes on the verse selections the occasional indications of quantity normally apply to syllables, to assist in scanning; however, proper names and proper adjectives, which are not in the vocabulary, bear long marks over long vowels in their stems when these are final in their syllables, i.e. not "hidden." As an aid to scansion, a brief table of metrical schemes immediately follows the selections. A prefatory note to the vocabulary, on p. 398, explains the procedures followed therein.

Although the notes, metrical schemes, and vocabulary should enable students to translate and scan the texts, it is nevertheless recommended that users of this book consult a dictionary of the completeness of Lewis' *Elementary Latin Dictionary* and a systematic grammar of the scope of Allen and Greenough's *New Latin Grammar*. Systematic grammars usually contain some discussion of the techniques of scansion, namely, syllabification, quantity, and prosody, but students should probably either be instructed in these techniques or have access to a fuller treatment. Among several such, that by Rosenmeyer, Ostwald, and Halporn, *The Meters of Greek and Latin Poetry*, is available in a paperback edition in the *Library of Liberal Arts*, no. 126 (1963); and in hard binding, D. S. Raven, *Latin Metre: An Introduction* (London: Faber, 1965).

This volume passed through several draft versions before the first edition was published in 1962 (second printing with a sheet of corrections, 1963). To express the authors' gratitude to all who assisted at the various stages, and particularly to the many instructors and students whose questions, comments, and corrections have immensely benefited the work, would by now extend unreasonably any specific list of credits. It can only be hoped that those of them who use this revision will realize how much they have contributed to it and how appreciative the authors are. Mrs. Anne Miller Whitman has placed the revising author deeply in her debt for the patience, accuracy, and understanding with which she carried through the exacting correction of the proofs of this revision.

Note to the Third Printing

Significant corrections and additions were made in the second printing on pages 85, 102, 129, 225, 227, 229, 248, 257, 284, 286, 288, 291, 363, and 371 of the text; and on pages 407, 433, 440, 445, 446, 447, 452, and 455 of the vocabulary. Further corrections and additions have been made in this third printing on pages 9, 10, 28, 62, 64, 76, 112, 126, 142, 144, 156, 162, 178, 227, 332, and 371 of the text; and on pages 409, 421, 445, 446, 447, 455, and 457 of the vocabulary. Additions to the vocabulary are listed on page 461.

CONTENTS

PART I

Selections 1–48: Prose

CONTENTS

PART II

Selections 49–90: Prose and Verse

CONTENTS

Aeneas to Augustus

PART I

Selections 1 – 48

Prose

1

The Romans were undoubtedly descended from Indo-European-speaking tribes which occupied Italy during the second millennium B.C. Some, indeed, of their legends emphasized their indigenous, or aboriginal, character. But when, in the third century, they became an important power in the Mediterranean and adopted Greek culture, they found that it was regarded as respectable for a civilized people to have Greek legendary origins. Therefore they (or the Greeks for them) devised stories of Greek heroes who had settled in Italy.

In particular, there was a legend, used by Vergil in the *Aeneid*, that a certain Evander, from Arcadia in the Peloponnese, had settled on the site of Rome. However, because of the rivalry between Rome and Greece during the second century, a legend that the Romans were descended from the Trojan hero Aeneas likewise became popular. Aeneas was supposed to have been the son of Venus and to have had a son Ascanius, also called Iulus. Since the Julian *gens*, to which the family of Julius Caesar belonged, claimed descent from Iulus, and since Julius Caesar made much of the worship of Venus, Vergil chose the legend of Aeneas through which to celebrate the culmination of Rome's rise to world power in Caesar and his adopted son Augustus.

In one of several late Roman summaries of legend and early history, the story of Aeneas is given somewhat differently from the version used by Vergil. The following three passages are summarized and adapted from this fourth-century A.D. account called *Origo Gentis Romanae*.

Aeneas in Italiam advenit

Aeneas, Ilio Achivis prodito ab Antenore aliisque principibus,[1] deos penates patremque Anchisam umeris gestans et parvulum filium manu trahens,[2] noctu ab urbe excessit.[3] Orta luce Idam petiit.[4] Deinde, navibus fabricatis, magnis cum opibus pluribusque sociis Troia digressus,[5] longo mari emenso, per diversas terrarum oras in Italiam advenit.[6]

1. A. **Ilio . . . prodito**: abl. abs.; = "when Ilium had been betrayed to the Greeks"; Ilium was another name for Troy.   B. **prodito**: the verb *prodere* = "to hand over" is used in a number of literal and metaphorical senses, including "to hand over to the enemy" or "to betray."   C. **Achivis**: another name for the Greeks, common in Homer.   D. **ab . . . principibus**: abls. of agent.   E. **Antenore**: one of the few Trojan heroes spared by the Greeks and perhaps for this reason said in some versions of the fall of Troy to have betrayed the city to them.   F. **-que** = "and"; it is an

"enclitic" (Greek; = leaning back on) conjunction, attached to the preceding word. G. **principibus:** adj. = "first" or "chief," here, as often, used as a noun = "chiefs" or "leaders."

2. A. **deos penates:** gods of the pantry (*penus*), i.e. household gods. Their statues, which Aeneas was supposed to have brought from Troy, were housed in the temple of Vesta, goddess of the hearth, in the Roman Forum, to represent the household gods of the whole community.   B. **Anchisam:** Greek names taken over by the Romans are not always completely Latinized. Here the name of Aeneas' father is treated as a 1st decl. noun with a regular acc., but the nom., *Anchises*, retains its Greek ending. C. **umeris . . . manu:** abls. of means.

3. **noctu:** loc. of an old *u*-stem form of *nox*, used adverbially more often than the regular abl. *nocte*.

4. A. **Idam:** a mountain near Troy.   B. **petiit** = *petivit*: in those verbs which have -*v*- (consonantal -*u*-) in the perf. act. system, the -*v*- was frequently slurred in pronunciation and omitted in writing when -*s*- or -*r*- occurred in the ending. Perfs. in -*a*(*v*)*i*, -*e*(*v*)*i*, and -*o*(*v*)*i* then contracted the two vowels into *a*, *e*, or *o* respectively. Perfs. in -*i*(*v*)*i* regularly omit the -*v*-, but usually leave the vowels uncontracted, as here, except before -*st*- and -*ss*- in the ending.

5. A. **magnis . . . sociis:** abls. of accompaniment with *cum*, which is regularly placed between an adj. and a noun.   B. **opibus:** abl. plur. of *ops*.   C. **Troia:** abl. of separation (place from which) without a prep. because it is the name of a town; *a* (*ab*) if used with a town = "from the vicinity of."

6. A. **longo mari emenso:** abl. abs.; = "after a long sea journey," lit. "a long (space of) sea having been measured out."   B. **emenso:** past part. from *emetior*; although deponent verbs are normally act. in meaning, their past parts. often (as here) have pass. meanings.

2

Aeneas proceeded up the west coast of Italy to the mouth of the Tiber. Various omens indicated that here was the site destined by fate for his home. Latinus, the local king, received him hospitably and an alliance was formed between the Trojans and the Latins.

Rex Latinus Aeneam recipit

Latinus, Aboriginum rex,[1] cum ei nuntiatum esset multitudinem advenarum, classe advectam, occupavisse agrum Laurentem,[2] adversum subitos inopinatosque hostes sine mora suas copias eduxit. Priusquam signum dimicandi daret,[3] suspenso certamine, quaesivit qui essent quidve peterent.[4] Deinde cum cognovisset Aeneam, bello patria pulsum et cum simulacris deorum errantem, sedem quaerere,[5] amicitiam foedere iniit,[6] dato invicem iure iurando ut communes hostes amicosve haberent.[7]

1. **Aboriginum:** gen. plur. *Aborigines* (=*ab*+*origo*) was applied to the supposedly original inhabitants of Italy, before the arrival of Greeks, Trojans, Etruscans, Gauls, and other invaders.

2. A. **cum ... occupavisse** = "when it had been announced to him that a crowd of strangers ... had occupied." B. **nuntiatum esset:** pluperf. subj. in a *cum* temporal clause of time antecedent to that of the main verb; since it is pass., its subject is the acc. + inf. in indirect discourse, and, since the inf. clause is equivalent to a neut. noun, *nuntiatum* has a neut. ending. In Eng. such verbs are called "impersonal" and "it" is supplied as the subject. C. **agrum Laurentem** = "the territory of Laurentum," a town southwest of Rome near the coast, of which *Laurens* is the adj.

3. A. **dimicandi:** gen. (objective) of the gerund; = "for fighting." The gen. in Lat. may often best be translated in Eng. by "for." B. **daret:** subj. with *priusquam*, to indicate that the main event anticipates or prevents the subordinate one.

4. A. **quaesivit ... peterent:** *essent* and *peterent* are imperf. subjs. in indirect questions introduced by *quaesivit* (perf. of *quaero* = "ask") + the interrog. pronouns *qui* and *quid*. Following the regular sequence of tenses, the imperf. subjs. are used to represent actions which are incomplete (i.e. pres. or fut.) in relation to that of the main verb, which is secondary or historical (i.e. past). B. **quidve:** *-ve* (= "or") is an enclitic conjunction like *-que* (= "and"); see 1 n. 1F.

5. A. **cognovisset:** introduces the indirect statement *Aeneam ... quaerere.* B. **Aeneam:** for the ending see 1 n. 2B. C. **patria:** abl. of separation without a prep., common in such idiomatic phrases as this. D. **quaerere:** here = "seek," and takes an acc. object (*sedem*); contrast n. 4A above.

6.   **amicitiam . . . iniit:** when the intrans. verb *eo* is compounded with a prep. which would take the acc., the resulting verb may be trans., as here; however, *ineo* may also be followed by *in*+acc.

7.   A.   **dato . . . iure iurando**="when an oath had been exchanged," lit. "given in turn." *Ius iurandum* may be written as two words, as here, or as one (see 9 n. 17A); in either case both parts are declined.   B. **ut . . . haberent:** either a regular purpose clause or a substantive clause of purpose in apposition to *iure iurando* and explaining what they swore. As the names indicate, these two constructions are closely related and it is often difficult to distinguish between them.

3

Protected by their treaty with Latinus, the Trojans began to build their long-sought home in Latium, but were soon interrupted by war. Latinus had betrothed his daughter Lavinia to Aeneas, but her previous suitor, Turnus, aroused his tribe of Rutuli against the foreigner.

In Vergil, Latinus is forced by his people to support Turnus. This account from the *Origo* makes Latinus die in battle on behalf of Aeneas.

Bellum Turni cum Aenea

Itaque ibi coeperunt Troiani munire locum, quem Aeneas ex nomine uxoris suae, Latini regis filiae, quae iam ante desponsa Turno fuerat,[1] Lavinium nominavit. At vero Amata, Latini regis uxor, cum indigne ferret Laviniam, repudiato Turno consobrino suo, Troiano advenae collocatam esse,[2] Turnum ad arma concitavit. Isque mox, coacto Rutulorum exercitu, tetendit in agrum Laurentem.[3] Et Latinus, adversus eum pariter cum Aenea progressus inter proeliantes,[4] circumventus est occisusque. Nec tamen, amisso socero, Aeneas Rutulis obsistere destitit,[5] tandemque Turnum interemit. Hostibus fusis fugatisque, victor Lavinium se cum suis recepit,[6] consensuque omnium Latinorum rex declaratus est.[7]

1. **desponsa ... fuerat**="had been betrothed to Turnus"; past parts. are often treated as simple adjs. and used with the perf. system (instead of the pres. system) of *sum*.

2. A. **cum ... ferret:** a causal clause with the imperf. subj.; = "since she considered it unworthy that ..." *Fero* is often used with an adv. to express a feeling or reaction. B. **Laviniam ... esse:** inf. clause as object of *ferret*; within the clause the abl. abs. *repudiato ... suo* represents a further subordination, which may be rendered in Eng. coordinately: "that Turnus her cousin had been repudiated and Lavinia assigned to a foreigner." C. **suo:** refers back to the main subject, *Amata*, not to the subject of the indirect statement, *Laviniam*.

3. **tetendit:** certain Lat. verbs form the perf. stem by "reduplication" of the initial consonant (compare *dedi, cecidi, etc.*). *Tendo* is both trans. and intrans.; here = "move, go."

4. **proeliantes:** in Lat. a part. alone is frequently used where Eng. would express the noun alone or with the part., e.g. here either "the battling men" or "the fighters."

5. **Rutulis:** dat. with a verb both compounded with *ob-* and meaning "resist."

6. A. **Lavinium** = "to Lavinium," a town near or possibly identical with Laurentum (see 2 n. 2c); *ad* is omitted with names of towns. If *ad* is used with a town, it means "toward the vicinity of"; compare 1 n. 5c. B. **se . . . recepit** = "he returned"; a frequent idiom. C. **suis** = "his (men)," i.e. his troops; possessive adjs. are often used as pronouns to connote friends, family, attendants, soldiers, etc., depending on the context.

7. **Latinorum:** possessive gen. depending on *consensu* and modified by *omnium*. If the gens. were meant to be separated, the order would probably have been *consensu omnium rex Latinorum etc.*

4

The Roman legend that Aeneas had fled from Troy to Italy and had become their founding ancestor raised a chronological problem. The Greeks dated the Fall of Troy about 1184. But the most distinguished Roman antiquarian, Cicero's contemporary Varro, calculated that Rome had been founded in 754/3. To fill this gap, the Romans assumed that Aeneas settled in Lavinium and that his descendants founded Alba Longa, in the volcanic hills south of Rome, where they ruled for four hundred years over the *Albani*.

The legend of the Founding of Rome itself is summarized as follows in another schoolbook roughly contemporary with the *Origo* (see 1 pref.) and called the *Liber de Viris Illustribus Urbis Romae.*

Roma condita

Proca, rex Albanorum, duos filios habuit, Amulium et Numitorem, quibus regnum annuis vicibus habendum reliquit.[1] Sed Amulius fratri imperium non dedit; et, ut eum subole privaret,[2] filiam eius, Rheam Silviam, Vestae sacerdotem praefecit,[3] ut virginitate perpetua teneretur. Quae, a Marte compressa, Remum et Romulum edidit.[4] Amulius ipsam in vincula compegit;[5] parvulos in Tiberim abiecit. Quos aqua in sicco reliquit. Ad vagitum lupa accurrit eosque uberibus suis aluit. Mox Faustulus pastor eos collectos Accae Larentiae coniugi educandos dedit.[6] Qui postea,[7] Amulio interfecto, Numitori avo regnum restituerunt; ipsi, pastoribus contractis, civitatem condiderunt, quam Romulus augurio victor,[8] quod ipse duodecim, Remus sex vultures viderat,[9] Romam vocavit. Et, ut eam potius legibus muniret quam moenibus,[10] edixit ne quis vallum transiliret.[11] Quod Remus inridens transiluit[12] et a Celere centurione rastro fertur occisus esse.[13]

1. A. **regnum . . . reliquit** = "he left the kingdom to be held in turn annually." B. **annuis vicibus**: abl. of manner; lit. = "in annual turns." C. **habendum**: gerundive modifying *regnum* and expressing purpose.

2. A. **ut . . . privaret**: a purpose clause, with imperf. subj. for an incomplete action in secondary sequence. B. **eum subole**: verbs meaning to remove, deprive, strip, etc. take an acc. of the person or thing despoiled and the abl. of separation of that whereof he or it is despoiled; this abl. may often be rendered in Eng. by "of . . ."

3. **Vestae ... praefecit** = "made Rhea Silvia a priestess of Vesta." *Vestae* is probably gen. with *sacerdotem*, not dat. with *praefecit*, although *praefecit* (a verb compounded with a prep.) often takes a dat. of indirect object for the position to which a person is appointed.

4. A. **quae** = *sed ea*; a rel. pronoun often introduces a new sentence or clause, in place of a connective (and, but, for) + a pronoun. Compare *quos aqua, qui postea*, and *quod Remus* below.   B. **a Marte compressa** = "after having been embraced (i.e. raped) by Mars."

5. A. **in vincula**: *in* + an acc. (here neut. plur.) of "place to which" is often used in Lat. where Eng. expects "place in which," as here with the perf. of *compingo*.   B. **compegit; parvulos**: supply "and"; the omission of a connective is common in Lat. in rapid narrative, and is called "asyndeton" (Greek; = not tied together).

6. A. **collectos ... dedit**: Lat. often uses a part. to subordinate the meaning to that of the main verb and still keep clear the temporal relation of the actions; here the order (part., verb) also shows the sequence of the actions. Render in Eng. coordinately: "Faustulus picked them up and gave them to his wife Acca Larentia to be reared" (not "to be educated"); compare 3 n. 2B.   B. **educandos**: gerundive modifying *eos* and expressing purpose; compare *habendum* in n. 1C above.

7. **qui** = *et ei*, i.e. Romulus and Remus; see n. 4A above.

8. **augurio victor** = "as the victor by an augury." Augury, the observation of the flight of birds or other signs, was a regular means of determining the will of the gods. In this case, the twins desired to discover which should give his name to the city; twelve vultures constituted a superior omen to six.

9. A. **quod ... viderat**: in a *quod* causal clause, the speaker or writer uses the ind. when he himself asserts the reality of the cause or reason given, as here, but the subj. when he cites the cause or reason as that of another, without committing himself as to its reality.   B. **ipse duodecim**: supply *vultures viderat*; such condensation is very frequent in Latin.

10. **ut ... moenibus** = "in order that he might protect it (i.e. the new settlement) rather by laws than (simply) by walls." The author attributes to Romulus his own opinion that Rome's law and justice were a more important source of strength than her armed might.

11. A. **ne ... transiliret**: the object of *edixit*; compare the similar construction with *impero*. Such clauses are called substantive *ut* clauses, substantive purpose clauses, indirect commands, or jussive noun clauses.   B. **quis** = "anyone"; after *si, nisi, ne,* or *num*, the pronoun *quis, quid* is indefinite, not interrog.

12. **quod**: object of both *inridens* and *transiluit*; it refers back only to *vallum*, not to the whole prohibition as in 52 n. 11A.

13. **fertur** = "is said" (as often). The late Lat. author takes as authenticated the fact that Remus jumped over the wall but only as report that Celer killed him; see Ovid's version in 52, especially nn. 7A, 11A, 12A.

5

Roman tradition held that the city was ruled by seven kings from its foundation in 754/3 to the final expulsion of the Tarquins in 510/9. The three kings who succeeded Romulus, namely Numa Pompilius, Tullus Hostilius, and Ancus Marcius, are wholly, or mostly, legendary. The last three, however, may well represent a vaguely historical tradition of the domination of Rome by rulers from Etruria. Tarquin the First was supposed to be the son of a Greek immigrant to Etruria and an Etruscan lady. He migrated to Rome and secured the rule. He was succeeded by Servius Tullius, of Latin parentage but married to Tarquin's daughter. The last king, Tarquin the Proud, son or grandson of Tarquin the First, married Servius' daughter and with her connivance murdered Servius to secure the throne. His tyrannical rule culminated in the violation of the chaste Lucretia by one of his sons, the wanton Sextus. Lucretia's husband, Tarquinius Collatinus, and her father, Tricipitinus, joined with Junius Brutus, like Collatinus, a cousin of Sextus, to rouse the people and expel Tarquin and his sons. Collatinus and Brutus were then elected consuls to replace the king, and the Republic was established.

The following account of these last events is based on the *Liber*.

Tarquinii expelluntur

Cum Tarquinius Superbus, ultimus rex Romanorum, Ardeam obsideret,[1] Tarquinius Collatinus, consobrino regis genitus, in contubernio filiorum regiorum erat.[2] Cum forte in liberiore convivio coniugem suam unus quisque laudaret,[3] placuit eis experiri.[4] Itaque equis Romam petunt.[5] Regias nurus in convivio et luxu deprehendunt.[6] Inde Collatiam petunt.[7] Lucretiam inter ancillas in lanificio offendunt.[8] Itaque ea pudicissima iudicatur. Ad quam corrumpendam Tarquinius Sextus noctu Collatiam rediit[9] et iure propinquitatis domum Collatini venit[10] et, in cubiculum Lucretiae inrumpens, pudicitiam expugnavit. Illa igitur postero die,[11] advocatis Tricipitino patre et Collatino coniuge, rem exposuit et se cultro, quem veste texerat, occidit.[12] Deinde Tricipitinus et Collatinus cum Iunio Bruto, sorore regis genito, in exitium Tarquiniorum coniuraverunt,[13] eorumque exsilio mortem Lucretiae vindicaverunt. Tarquinius Superbus ad Porsennam

Etruriae regem confugit,[14] cuius ope regnum recuperare tentavit. Roma pulsus, Cumas concessit,[15] ubi per summam ignominiam reliquum vitae tempus exegit.[16] Tarquiniis in exsilium actis, Brutus et Collatinus primi consules creati sunt.[17]

1.   **Ardeam:** a town not far southwest of Rome, in the territory of the Rutuli, for whom see sel. 3.

2.   A. **consobrino:** abl. of source with *genitus*.   B. **genitus:** serves as past part. of *gigno*, a reduplicated (see 3 n. 3) pres. which replaced an earlier *geno*; with an abl. of source, as here, it is equivalent to "son of."   C. **in . . . regiorum** = "sharing quarters with the king's sons (lit. the royal sons)." *Contubernium* means not only the sharing of quarters (from *taberna* = "tent") but the close relationship established thereby.

3.   A. **forte** = "by chance" or "as it happened"; in origin it is the abl. sing. (of manner) of *fors* (of which only the nom. and abl. sing. occur); it became, like other similar abls., adverbial.   B. **in liberiore convivio** = "at a rather free-and-easy party"; the Lat. comparative often has the connotation of Eng. "rather" + an adj. or adv.

4.   **placuit eis experiri** = "they decided (lit. it was pleasing to them) to test (their wives)." In Lat. *placet* is not a true impersonal verb (compare 2 n. 2B) since the thing or action, here the deponent inf. *experiri*, is the subject and the person is in the dat.; in Eng. it may often best be rendered, as here, by making the person the subject of "decide" with the inf. dependent thereon.

5.   **petunt:** this and the following four verbs are historical pres. in vivid narration; the perfs. resume with *rediit*.

6.   **regias nurus** = "the daughters-in-law of the king"; *nurus* is fem. acc. plur. For the adj. *regias* compare *filiorum regiorum* above; Lat. often uses an adj. in agreement with a noun where Eng. prefers a prepositional phrase.

7.   **Collatiam:** a Sabine town near Rome where Lucretia and her husband lived; hence his surname *Collatinus*. For the omission of *ad* here and below see 3 n. 6A.

8.   **in lanificio** = "(engaged) in wool-working," i.e. spinning and weaving.

9.   A. **ad quam corrumpendam** = "and in order to corrupt (i.e. violate) her"; *ad* + a noun in the acc. with a gerundive in agreement (or *ad* + a gerund in the acc.) is a regular way of expressing purpose; compare 4 n. 1C. For the use of the rel. pronoun at the beginning of a sentence see 4 n. 4A.   B. **noctu:** for the form see 1 n. 3.

10. **iure propinquitatis** = "by right of (his) relationship" (i.e. to her husband); *iure* is abl. of cause. Possessive adjs. often must be supplied in translating.

11. **postero die:** abl. of time when.

12. **occidit:** perf. act. ind. from *occĭdo* (*ob* + *caedo*), not from *occīdo, occīdi* (*ob* + *cădo*).

13. A. **sorore . . . genito:** *sorore* is abl. of source with *genito*, which is abl. in agreement with *Bruto*; see nn. 2A and B above.   B. **in exitium . . . coniuraverunt** = "they formed a conspiracy for the ruin of the Tarquins." *Coniuraverunt* lit. = "they took an oath together."   C. **in:** with the acc., primarily used for motion toward, may less frequently express less concrete concepts of "direction of action" with overtones of feeling or purpose, as here.   D. **exitium** = "ruin" or "destruction"; it should be distinguished from *exitus, -us* = "departure, end, death."

14. **Porsennam:** for this Etruscan chief see 6.

15. A. **Roma . . . Cumas:** for the omission of the preps. see 1 n. 5C (and 3 n. 6A). Cumae lies on the west coast of Italy, just north of the bay of Naples. Names of towns

are often plur. in Lat.   B. **concessit:** perf. act. ind. of *concedo*, which often, as here, is intrans. and = "go, retire, withdraw"; compare *tetendit* in 3 n. 3.

16.   A. **per . . . ignominiam** = "in the utmost disgrace, most dishonorably"; *per* + acc. basically indicates the space or time through which, but came also to be equivalent to an abl. of manner (as here), to an abl. of means, to *ab* + abl. of personal agent, or to an acc. of extent of time.   B. **exegit:** perf. act. ind. of *exigo* (*ex* + *ago*); *ago* and its compounds with expressions of time = "pass" or "spend."

17.   A. **primi . . . sunt** = "were the first (men) to be elected consuls"; *primus* + a verb should regularly be rendered "the first to."   B. **creati sunt:** the verb *creo* frequently = "elect." In the act., the person and the office are both in the acc.; in the pass., as here, the person is subject nom. and the office predicate nom.

6

Two famous incidents of the defense of Rome against Lars Porsenna, an Etruscan chief who was trying to restore the Tarquins (see 5), are related as follows by the *Liber*. The first incident was developed by Macaulay in the most famous of his *Lays of Ancient Rome*.

Horatii atque Mucii res fortiter gestae

Cum Porsenna, rex Etruscorum, Tarquinios in urbem restituere temptaret et primo impetu Ianiculum cepisset, Horatius Cocles (illo cognomine, quod in alio proelio oculum amiserat)[1] pro Ponte Sublicio stetit[2] et aciem hostium, primo cum duobus aliis, tunc, illis regressis, solus sustinuit, donec pons a tergo interruptus est.[3] Cum quo in Tiberim decidit[4] et armatus ad suos tranavit.[5] Ob hoc ei tantum agri publici datum est,[6] quantum uno die ambire vomere potuit. Statua quoque ei in Vulcanali posita est.[7]

Deinde dum Porsenna urbem obsidet,[8] Mucius Cordus, vir Romanae constantiae,[9] senatum adiit et veniam transfugiendi petiit,[10] necem regis promittens. Accepta potestate,[11] in castra Porsennae venit ibique aliquem purpuratum pro rege deceptus occidit.[12] Apprehensus et ad regem pertractus, dextram arae flammis imposuit.[13] Unde cum misericordia regis abstraheretur,[14] quasi beneficium referens,[15] ait trecentos adversus eum similes coniurasse.[16] Qua re ille territus, bellum, acceptis obsidibus, deposuit. Mucio prata trans Tiberim data sunt, ab eo Mucia appellata.[17] Statua quoque ei honoris causa constituta est.

1. A. **illo cognomine:** abl. of description (quality); = "with that epithet."   B. **amiserat:** from *amitto*; for *quod* causal with the ind. see 4 n. 9A. The adj. *cocles* ("one-eyed") occurs in early Lat.

2. **Ponte Sublicio:** the earliest bridge across the Tiber, made of wood and resting on piles (*sublicae*). It probably crossed just below the Tiber Island, where it gave access to a road up the Janiculum and out of Rome to the northwest, toward the Mediterranean.

3.   **interruptus est:** in classical Lat., *donec* and *quoad*="until" are followed by the perf. ind. to indicate an actual event in past time, i.e. here Horatius resisted until the bridge was actually broken down; they (and *dum*="until") are followed by the pres. or imperf. subj. to denote intention or expectancy, i.e. here *interrumperetur* would mean that Horatius resisted to give time for the bridge to be broken down.

4.   **cum quo:** i.e. "with (the fall of) the bridge." Livy II 10.10, followed by Macaulay, has him leap into the river as the bridge collapsed behind him.

5.   **suos**="his own people"; see 3 n. 6c.

6.   **agri publici:** partitive gen. (gen. of the whole) with *tantum.*

7.   A. **ei:** dat. of reference (advantage), i.e. "in his honor"; contrast *ei* as dat. of indirect object in the preceding sentence.   B. **in Vulcanali**="in the Vulcanal," an area in the Forum which contained an altar of Vulcan, god of fire and smiths.

8.   **dum . . . obsidet:** *dum*="while" regularly takes the pres. ind. for an action contemporary with (or inclusive of) a main verb in past time; in Eng. the imperf. should be used.

9.   **Romanae constantiae:** gen. of quality (description), used only when the quality is accompanied by an adj.; it is less common than the abl. of description (quality). The gen. is used rather of essential or abstract traits of character, the abl. of special, incidental, or external characteristics; compare *illo cognomine* in n. 1A above.

10.   A. **veniam transfugiendi**="pardon for desertion," i.e. permission to go over to the enemy; *transfugiendi* is objective gen. of the gerund; compare 2 n. 3A.   B. **petiit**=*petivit;* see 1 n. 4B.

11.   **accepta potestate:** abl. abs.;="when he got permission," lit."with the power (to do so) having been received."

12.   A. **aliquem . . . occidit:** render the past part. *deceptus* coordinately in Eng. (compare 4 n. 6A);="he mistook (lit. was deceived by) someone clad in purple for the king and slew him."   B. **purpuratum:** a noun (perhaps originally a masc. adj.) formed from *purpura*="purple color"; the verb *purpuro* is a rare late form.   C. **occĭdit:** from *occido,* as in 5 n. 12.

13.   **flammis:** dat. due to the *in-* of *imposuit,* not abl. of place where;="on the flames of the altar." *Imponere* takes the acc. of the thing placed, here *dextram* (i.e. *manum*) and either *in*+acc. or the dat. of that on which it is placed. .

14.   **cum misericordia:** the conjunction and an abl. of cause;="when, because of the king's pity," i.e. "because the king pitied him."

15.   **beneficium referens**="repaying a favor."

16.   A. **trecentos:** supply "men"; Lat. adjs. are often used as nouns.   B. **coniurasse**=*coniuravisse*; see 1 n. 4B.

17.   A. **ab eo:** abl. of source (not agent);="after (from) him."   B. **Mucia:** adj., supply *prata;*="the Mucian (meadows)."

7

For more than two centuries following the expulsion of the Tarquins, the internal history of Rome was dominated by a struggle between the hereditary ruling class, called *patres*, or patricians, and the great mass of the citizens, called collectively *plebs*, or plebeians. The well-to-do plebeians were excluded from office and from access to the knowledge of the law, and the poor ones were oppressed by strict enforcement of penalties on debtors and by the arbitrary exercise of magisterial power. In their struggle against these handicaps, the *plebs* were led by their own elective officials, called tribunes, who were at first two in number, but by the mid-fifth century, ten. The patricians were gradually forced to recognize the tribunes as public officials with power to protect the plebeians.

In 452 the plebeians forced the appointment of a board of ten men, *decemviri*, who displaced the regular consuls as heads of the state for 451 in order to codify and publish the laws. In the following year, the ten, led by Appius Claudius, tried to consolidate and continue their power, but the attempt failed. Regular consuls were elected for 449 who passed legislation to guarantee the civil rights of plebeians and published the new code, called the "Laws of the Twelve Tables." These became the foundation of Rome's private law, one of her most important legacies to the civilization of Western Europe and the New World.

The following passage from the *Liber* summarizes the traditional, but suspiciously picturesque (compare the story of Lucretia in 5), explanation for the Decemvirs' fall. Macaulay used this tale also in his *Lays of Ancient Rome*.

Facinus Appii Claudii

Populus Romanus cum seditiosos magistratus ferre non posset,[1] decemviros legibus scribendis creavit,[2] qui eas ex libris Solonis translatas duodecim tabulis exposuerunt.[3] Sed cum pacto dominationis magistratum sibi prorogarent,[4] unus ex his[5] Appius Claudius Virginiam, Virginii centurionis filiam in Algido monte militantis, amare coepit.[6] Quam cum corrumpere non posset, clientem subornavit,[7] qui eam in servitium deposceret,[8] facile victurus cum ipse esset et accusator et iudex.[9] Pater, re cognita, cum ipso die iudicii supervenisset et filiam iam addictam videret,[10] ultimo eius colloquio impetrato,[11] eam in secretum abduxit et occidit;[12] et corpus eius umeris gerens ad exercitum profugit et milites ad vindicandum facinus accendit.[13] Qui, creatis decem tribunis, Aventinum occuparunt,[14] decemviros abdicare se magistratu coegerunt,[15] eosque omnes aut morte aut exsilio punierunt.[16] Appius Claudius in carcere necatus est.

1. **cum . . . posset:** either a temporal or a causal clause.

2. A. **legibus scribendis:** dat. of purpose; = "to write (i.e. codify) the laws." Such a use of a noun and gerundive in the dat. of purpose is regular in Lat. to specify the functions of a magistrate; for other gerundive constructions of purpose compare 4 n. 1c, 5 n. 9A, and n. 13 below.   B. **creavit:** for the meaning "elected" see 5 n. 17B.

3. A. **eas:** i.e. *leges.*   B. **Solonis:** Solon was a famous Athenian legislator of the early 6th cent. B.C. Whether or not Rome would have been closely enough in contact with Greece during the mid-5th cent. to send an embassy to study her laws is disputed. C. **tabulis:** abl. of means; = "by (in Eng., on) twelve 'tables' (notice-boards)."

4. **pacto dominationis:** abl. of means (or cause) and a limiting (defining) gen.; = "by an agreement for rule," i.e. after they had agreed together to rule. The gen. gives the content, or purpose, of the pact.

5. **unus ex his** = "one of these"; *ex* or *de* + abl. is the regular construction with numerals, except with *milia*, which takes a partitive gen.

6. A. **in Algido monte:** one of the Alban Hills south of Rome, which commanded a pass leading to the country of an often hostile tribe called the Hernici.   B. **militantis:** pres. part. gen. masc. sing. with *Virginii*; it is best rendered by a rel. clause (compare 4 n. 6A); = "who was serving as a soldier."

7. **clientem:** in early Rome, since the patricians alone had political rights, many plebeians, particularly the poorer ones, attached themselves as clients to a patrician who was supposed to act for them in need, in return for various services. In later Rome the relation became that between a rich *patronus*, patrician or plebeian, and his usually poor dependent client, either born free or a freed slave.

8. A. **qui . . . deposceret:** a rel. clause of characteristic expressing purpose with the imperf. subj. describing an incomplete action in secondary sequence; = "to sue for her as his slave," lit. "who would ask for her into slavery."   B. **in servitium:** for this use of *in* + acc. see 5 n. 13c. Appius could have his way with Virginia if she was judged to be the slave of his client.

9. **victurus:** fut. part. of *vinco* (not of *vivo, victus*); = "since he would win (his case)"; the part. modifies the subject of *subornavit*, namely Appius Claudius, not the client, who is subject of the intervening clause *qui . . . deposceret*. Appius was, of course, only indirectly the accuser.

10. **iam addictam** = "already adjudged" (to Appius' client).

11. **eius colloquio** = "a talk with her"; *eius* is objective gen.

12. **occidit:** from *occido*; as in 5 n. 12 (and 6 n. 12c).

13. **ad vindicandum facinus** = "to avenge the crime"; for *ad* + gerundive expressing purpose see 5 n. 9A.

14. A. **Aventinum:** one of the "seven hills" of Rome, a center of the plebeians. B. **occuparunt:** contracted form; see 1 n. 4B.

15. A. **abdicare se** = "to give up," lit. "to say themselves out of"; *se* is reflexive to *decemviros*, the subject of the inf., not to the subject of the main verb, *qui* (i.e. *milites*); contrast *suo* in 3 n. 2c. At the end of his term, a Roman magistrate was expected to lay

down his office formally by public pronouncement.   B. **magistratu:** abl. of separation with *abdicare*; compare 4 n. 2B.   C. **coegerunt:** perf. act. ind. from *cogo* = "drive together" (*cum + ago*), either physically, meaning "collect," or, as here, metaphorically, meaning "compel, force."

16. **punierunt:** contracted; see n. 14B above.

8

An event which sank deep into Roman memory was the capture of the city by a tribe of Gauls called the Senones, traditionally dated in 390 or 387. Gallic tribes settled in the Po valley from about 450 until about 350, and the weakening power of the Etruscans exposed central Italy to their raids. These raids were not intended for permanent settlement; nevertheless the thoroughness of the sack of Rome by the Senones endowed the name of "Gauls" with the sort of terror which "Indians" often conveyed in the United States. The Romans later claimed that their city was not again captured by a foreign enemy until it was taken by Alaric and his Visigoths in A.D. 410, after an interval of eight hundred years.

The following account comes from the *Liber*.

Roma a Gallis capta

Cum Galli Senones, relictis ob sterilitatem agris suis, Clusium Italiae oppidum obsiderent, missi sunt Roma tres Fabii qui Gallos monerent ut ab oppugnatione desisterent.[1] Ex his unus contra ius gentium in aciem processit[2] et ducem Senonum interfecit. Quo commoti Galli,[3] petitis in deditionem legatis nec impetratis,[4] Romam petierunt et exercitum Romanum apud Alliam fluvium ceciderunt,[5] die xvi ante Kalendas Augustas,[6] qui dies inter nefastos relatus est, "Alliensis" dictus.[7] Victores Galli urbem intraverunt, ubi nobilissimos senum in sellis curulibus et honorum insignibus primo ut deos venerati sunt;[8] deinde ut homines despicientes interfecerunt. Iuventus cum Manlio in Capitolium fugit,[9] ubi quadam nocte, clangore anseris excitata, Gallos ascendentes deiecit. Tunc Camillus, absens dictator dictus,[10] collectis reliquis Romanis, Gallos improviso impetu occidit. Populum Romanum, migrare Veios nuper captos volentem, retinuit.[11] Sic et oppidum civibus et cives oppido reddidit.[12]

---

1. A. **Fabii:** a prominent family (*gens*) in republican Rome. The leader of these three ambassadors is identified as Marcus Fabius Ambustus. B. **qui ... monerent:** a rel. clause of characteristic expressing purpose; compare 7 n. 8A; a rel. regularly replaces *ut* when *mitto* introduces a purpose. C. **monerent:** regularly takes two accs.

(a double acc.), i.e. of the person advised, here *Gallos*, and of the advice given, here expressed by a substantive *ut* clause; see 4 n. 11A.

2. A. **ex his unus:** for this construction with numerals see 7 n. 5. B. **ius gentium** = "the law of nations," here meaning the generally recognized restriction upon ambassadors from joining in active hostilities.

3. **quo** = "and by this (act)"; for this connective use of the rel. pronoun see 4 n. 4A (and 5 n. 9A).

4. **petitis . . . impetratis** = "after they (the Gauls) had asked for the legates to be surrendered to them and had failed to get satisfaction," lit. "the legates having been asked for into surrender and not having been obtained." For this use of *in* + acc. see 5 n. 13c (and 7 n. 8B).

5. A. **Alliam fluvium:** the *Allia* (also spelled *Alia*) was a small stream flowing into the Tiber eleven miles north of Rome and on the same (east) side. B. **ceciderunt:** from *caedo*, not from *cădo* (*cecĭdi*); compare 5 n. 12 (and 7 n. 12).

6. **die . . . Augustas** = "on day sixteen before the Kalends of August," i.e. on July 17. The Romans reckoned backwards from three fixed days in the month, called Kalends, Nones, and Ides; in Jan., Feb., April, June, Aug., Sept., Nov., and Dec. these fell respectively on the first, fifth, and thirteenth; in March, May, July, and Oct. on the first, seventh, and fifteenth. The Romans also reckoned inclusively the days at both ends, so that the count-back here of sixteen days includes Aug. 1 as the first and July 17 as the sixteenth (since July has 31 days); naturally dates reckoned back from the Kalends are in the month preceding that of the Kalends.

7. A. **qui dies:** the antecedent is often repeated within the rel. clause in Lat.; in translating, it may be omitted or repeated before the rel.: "the sixteenth day—a day which." B. **nefastos** = "of ill-omen, accursed." Surviving Roman calendars mark with *NF* those days on which, because of some religious or other reason, it was not permitted to do public business. The indeclinable Lat. noun *fas*, cognate with the deponent verb *fari* ("to speak"), meant "spoken by the gods," i.e. divinely ordained and permissible, in contrast to *ius*, that which men ordained, or law. Hence *nefas* and the adj. *nefastus* denoted opposed by the gods, i.e. sacrilegious. Of words cognate with *fari*, only *fas* and *fatum* had their significance limited to divine utterance.

8. A. **senum:** from *senex*; partitive gen. plur. with a superlative adj. B. **sellis curulibus:** the Roman consuls, praetors, dictators (all of whom were magistrates *cum imperio*), and curule aediles were entitled to use a sort of folding stool (perhaps of Etruscan origin), made in later days of ivory. They kept this even after their term of office ended and brought it to the senate to use during meetings. C. **honorum:** the original meaning seems to have been any concrete outward sign of rank, and thus it acquired the common meaning of public office or magistracy, as well as that of the more abstract "honor." In addition to the *sella curulis* (see preceding note), magistrates *cum imperio* had a toga with a purple border, *toga praetexta*, which signified that they were particularly under the protection of the gods, and were escorted by lictors bearing the *fasces*. *Fasces* were in Rome simply a bundle of rods, signifying the right to flog; in the field (military command) they contained also an ax, signifying the right to execute without appeal to the assembly, *provocatio ad populum*. D. **insignibus:** neut. plur. abl. adj. used as a noun; the abl. depends on the preceding *in*; = "in the insignia of their offices." E. **ut deos . . . ut homines:** *ut* + a noun = "as." F. **venerati sunt** = "they respected"; perf. ind. (pass. in form, act. in meaning) of the deponent verb *veneror*; the subject is *victores Galli*.

9. A. **iuventus:** fem. sing. abstract for concrete masc. plur. *iuvenes*. B. **Manlio:** a Roman hero whom later tradition presented as a champion of the plebeians. C. **Capitolium:** one of the hills of Rome, called also *Mons Capitolinus*, on which were the chief citadel and temples of the city.

10.   A. **Camillus:** later tradition made him the champion of the patricians. He had been exiled, despite his capture of Veii in 396, but was recalled to rescue Rome from the Gauls.   B. **dictator:** during the early and middle Republic, the consuls might, to meet an emergency, vest a single dictator with the original unshared command (*imperium*) formerly held by the kings. Such a dictator could not hold office for more than six months.   C. **dictus** = "appointed"; contrast *creati sunt* = "were elected" in 5 n. 17B (and 7 n. 2B).

11.   **Veios:** an important Etruscan town nine miles northeast of Rome; its capture removed an old menace to Rome's power and expansion. For the plur. form compare 5 n. 15A.

12.   **et ... et** = "both ... and," correlating the two objects of *reddidit*.

9

During the fourth century, after the Gauls' incursion, Rome re-established her control over the Latins in central Italy and the Etruscans and Umbrians in the north. Then she waged a number of wars against the Oscans and Samnites of southern Italy. From 281–274 the Samnites were aided by Pyrrhus, an adventurous king from Epirus (northwest Greece), but he withdrew, and by 270 Rome was securely established as the leading state of Italy.

Rome was next drawn into conflict with Carthage. This city had been founded by Phoenicians, perhaps as early as 800, on the coast of North Africa. It had secured for itself the trade of the western Mediterranean and had placed settlements along the coasts of North Africa and Spain from outside the Straits of Gibraltar around on the east as far north as the river Ebro (see 10 pref.). Carthage had also placed settlements in Corsica, Sardinia, and western Sicily. In Sicily, however, she met opposition from Greeks who had colonized the eastern and southern parts of the island from around 750 and who were, by 270, under the aegis of Syracuse.

From 264–241 Rome fought in alliance with the Greeks to expel the Carthaginians from Sicily. This First Punic War was waged largely at sea, with heavy losses in ships and men to both sides. However, in 256 the Roman consul Regulus landed in Africa with an army, but was surrounded by the Carthaginians and defeated in 255. Sent to Rome to negotiate a ransom, he was said to have urged the senate not to accept peace on dishonorable terms and to have returned to Carthage to die by torture. Through his heroism he became a stock example of Roman fortitude and selfless devotion to the state.

The following passages on Pyrrhus and on Regulus are from the *Liber*.

A.   *Victoria Pyrrhi*

Pyrrhus, rex Epirotarum, Apollinem de bello cum Romanis gerendo consuluit.[1] Deus ei ambigue respondit: "Aio te, Aeacida, Romanos vincere posse."[2] Hoc dicto incitatus, auxilio Tarentinorum bellum Romanis intulit, eosque apud Heracleam elephantorum novitate turbavit.[3] Victor tandem, cum Romanos adversis vulneribus occisos videret,[4] "Ego," inquit,[5] "talibus militibus brevi orbem terrarum subigere potuissem."[6] Amicis autem gratulantibus,[7] "Quid mihi cum tali victoria," inquit, "ubi exercitus robur amittam?"[8]

Postea, viso altero exercitu Romano, eandem sibi ait fuisse fortunam adversum Romanos quam Herculi adversum Hydram.[9]

B.   *Fortitudo Reguli*

Marcus Atilius Regulus consul, fusis Sallentinis, triumphavit[10] primusque Romanorum ducum in Africam classem traiecit.[11] Ibi de Hamilcare naves longas tres et sexaginta et oppida ducenta et hominum ducenta milia cepit.[12] Absente eo,[13] coniugi eius et liberis ob paupertatem sumptus publice dabantur.[14] Mox, arte Xanthippi Lacedaemonii mercenarii militis captus,[15] in carcerem ductus est. Tunc legatus de permutandis captivis Romam missus,[16] dato iureiurando ut, si non impetrasset, Carthaginem rediret,[17] in senatu condicionem dissuasit,[18] reiectisque ab amplexu coniuge et liberis, Carthaginem regressus est, ubi in arcam ligneam coniectus, clavis introrsum adactis, vigiliis ac dolore punitus est.[19]

---

1.   A. **Epirotarum:** for the declension of Greek names see 1 n. 2B.   B. **Apollinem ... consuluit:** at his famous oracle at Delphi; the topic of consultation is expressed by *de* + a noun + a gerundive expressing (in the pass.) futurity or intention; compare the similar construction in n. 16 below.   C. **bello ... gerendo:** *bellum gerere* is a common idiom = "to wage war."

2.   A. **te ... posse:** a famous example of the ambiguity occasioned in indirect discourse when both subject and object of the inf. are in the acc. The line is a dactylic hexameter verse, the traditional form of oracular responses. Cicero *de Div.* II 116 attributes it to the poet Ennius of the early 2nd cent., for whom see 60 pref.   B. **Aeacida:** voc. masc. sing. of the "patronymic" (Greek; = a name indicating paternity) *Aeacides* = "son" or "descendant of Aeacus." In Greek mythology Aeacus was a judge in the Underworld and the grandfather of Achilles, from whom Pyrrhus traced his descent.

3.   **Heracleam:** a city west of Tarentum near the coast of the Gulf of Tarentum where Pyrrhus defeated the Romans in 280. He defeated them again in the following year at Asculum in south central Italy.

4.   **adversis vulneribus** = "with wounds in front (lit. facing, i.e. toward the enemy)"; abl. of manner or attendant circumstance (not means).

5.   **inquit:** from *inquam*; this verb is used only with direct quotations and is placed after one or more opening words thereof.

6.   A. **militibus:** abl. of means; the troops are considered as instruments, not as persons.   B. **brevi:** supply *tempore*; in this idiom the abl. sing. neut. adj. (abl. of time within which) by itself becomes almost adverbial; compare 5 n. 3A.   C. **orbem terrarum** = "the whole earth," lit. "the circuit of lands"; a common idiom.   D. **potuissem** = "I could have (or, would have) been able." The pluperf. subj. is used

because the clause is the "apodosis" (conclusion) of a contrary to fact ("unreal") condition, in which the "protasis" ("if" clause), "if I had had such soldiers," is not expressed formally, but implied in *talibus militibus*.

7. **amicis ... gratulantibus:** either an abl. abs. or dat. of indirect object with *inquit*.

8. A. **quid ... amittam** = "what (is there) for me with such a victory, where I lose the strength of (my) army," i.e. "what good to me is the sort of victory in which I lose ..." B. **quid mihi:** supply *est*, which is colloquially omitted in this common phrase; *mihi* is dat. of reference (advantage). C. **cum ... victoria:** a colloquial extension of the abl. of accompaniment (or of attendant circumstance), as in Eng. "what have I to do with ..." D. **ubi** = *in qua*, introducing a rel. clause of characteristic, which is general, i.e. "the sort of victory in which I lose," with a conditional implication of "if I lose"; Pyrrhus had in fact already lost the bulk of his men in gaining this particular victory. From this remark, a victory in which the victor's heavy losses make it impossible for him to take advantage of his success has traditionally been called a "Pyrrhic victory." E. **amittam:** subj. in a general rel. clause of characteristic (see preceding note) and pres. to indicate time contemporary with that of the main verb.

9. **Hydram:** the second of the "twelve labors" of Hercules (Herakles) was to slay a many-headed monster called "Hydra" which was ravaging the territory of Lerna in Greece and which had the faculty of growing two heads in place of every one which he cut off. He finally cauterized the neck of each head as he amputated it and thus prevented fresh growth.

10. A. **consul** = "(as) consul," i.e. "when he was consul"; nouns in apposition with proper names are often best translated thus. In the early Republic the two consuls elected yearly were the commanders in any war that arose during their term of office. B. **Sallentinis:** a people of southeast Italy. C. **triumphavit** = "celebrated a triumph." A triumph was a formal celebration of a victory over a foreign enemy, and was an honor much coveted by Roman generals.

11. **primus ... traiecit:** for this use of *primus* see 5 n. 17A. Both as a numeral (compare 7 n. 5) and as a superlative, *primus* may be followed by *ex* or *de* + the abl., but the partitive gen., as here, is more common.

12. A. **Hamilcare:** the head of the distinguished Carthaginian family named Barca, said to mean "lightning." His policy was aggressive and imperialistic, opposed to the more isolationist group of conservative landowners. B. **naves longas** = "warships." C. **hominum:** partitive gen. with *ducenta milia*; compare 7 n. 5.

13. **eo:** i.e. Regulus.

14. A. **liberis** = "to (his) children"; perhaps, but not certainly, the masc. plur. of the adj. *liber, -era, -erum*, used for "children" because they were considered "free persons" as opposed to a man's slaves, although both were under the father's *patria potestas*. B. **sumptus:** masc. nom. plur.; = "(funds for) expenses." Since, in the middle of the 2nd cent., even senatorial Romans were still dependent on their farms for their income, and farms were not yet large, the family of a man long absent on campaign might see the farm run down and themselves impoverished.

15. **Xanthippi:** a Spartan "condottiere" or professional commander, of a type common in the Hellenistic period. The Carthaginians hired him to command their land forces.

16. **de permutandis captivis:** *de* gives the matter concerning which he was ambassador (compare n. 1B above) rather than the purpose for which he was sent; the latter would have been expressed by *ad* + the noun in the acc. with the gerundive in agreement; see 5 n. 9A (and 7 n. 13).

17. A. **iureiurando:** here written as one word; see 2 n. 7A. B. **ut ... rediret:** substantive clause of "purpose" in apposition with *iureiurando* to explain its content;

see 2 n. 7B.   c. **si non impetrasset ... rediret** = "if he did not succeed, he would return." His actual oath would have been a fut. more vivid condition in which the protasis would have been fut. perf. ind. because it was previous in time to the apodosis in the simple fut.: *si non impetravero, redibo* = " if I do not succeed (lit. shall not have succeeded), I will return." Here in the subordinate *ut* clause, the verbs are adapted to secondary sequence in the subj.   D. **impetrasset:** contracted; see 1 n. 4B.

18.   **condicionem dissuasit** = "he argued against (lit. urged away) the term(s)."

19.   A. **clavis introrsum adactis** = "with nails driven inwards," i.e. with the points on the inside of the chest so that he could not rest easy.   B. **vigiliis:** fem. abl. plur.; = "by wakefulness," i.e. by being kept awake. Lat. often uses the plur. of a concrete noun where Eng. uses the sing. of an abstract one.

10

The First Punic War was followed by some twenty years of uneasy peace. During this period Rome organized Sicily and Sardinia/Corsica as her first two overseas provinces, while the Carthaginian general Hamilcar Barca began to establish a quasi-personal control over southern and western Spain. His imperialistic policy was opposed by a "peace party" led by Hanno. But his program in Spain was carried on after his death, first by his son-in-law Hasdrubal and then by his son Hannibal. Rome had forced Carthage to agree not to expand along the east coast of Spain north of the river Ebro, beyond which Rome's ally, the Greek colony Marseilles, controlled the coast of Spain and southern Gaul. South of the Ebro, Rome made an alliance with Saguntum, but Hannibal, in 220, seized this town, as being in his zone. When Carthage would not force Hannibal to withdraw, Rome declared the Second Punic War.

Hannibal made a dramatic march across the Pyrenees, through Gaul, and over the Alps, to descend into Italy in 218. He inflicted a series of overwhelming defeats on the Romans, which culminated in the disaster of Cannae in 216; see nn. 5–11 below. But he never felt strong enough to march on Rome. As time wore on and his home government gave him no support, he was gradually restricted in action. In 203 Scipio Africanus moved an army from Sicily into Africa, and Carthage was forced to recall Hannibal. When the two forces met southwest of Carthage at Zama (202), Hannibal was defeated.

After the defeat of Carthage, Hannibal devoted himself to restoring her political harmony and commercial prosperity. However, the Romans supported his enemies in forcing him to flee from Carthage in 196/5. He took refuge with Antiochus III, called "the Great," king of Syria, and supported him in the war which he waged against the Romans in 192–188; see 12 pref. When Rome defeated Antiochus, she demanded the surrender of Hannibal, but he took refuge with Prusias, king of Bithynia, on the Black Sea. There, in about 183, the implacable Romans finally cornered him and, to escape capture, he took poison.

The following account of Hannibal's career comes partly from the *Liber* and partly from the *Breviarium* of Eutropius, a short history of Rome written, like the *Liber*, in the fourth century A.D.

Hannibalis res gestae

Hannibal, Hamilcaris filius, novem annos natus, a patre arae admotus, odium in Romanos perenne iuravit.[1] Exinde socius et miles in castris patri fuit.[2] Mortuo eo, causam belli quaerens, Saguntum

Romanis foederatum intra sex menses evertit.[3] Tum, relicto in Hispania fratre Hasdrubale, Pyrenaeum transiit et, Alpibus patefactis, in
Italiam exercitum traiecit.[4] Ibi P. Cornelius Scipio consul ei apud
flumen Ticinum occurrit[5] atque, cum proelium commisisset, fugatis
suis, ipse vulneratus in castra rediit.[6] Paucos post dies Ti. Sempronius
Longus alter consulum conflixit apud Trebiam amnem;[7] is quoque
victus est. Proxima aestate Hannibal apud Trasimenum lacum Gaium
Flaminium consulem et Romanorum viginti quinque milia interemit.[8]
Postremo L. Aemilius Paullus et C. Terentius Varro contra Hannibalem missi sunt[9] et, cum in Apulia apud vicum qui Cannae appellatur
pugnatum esset,[10] ambo consules ab Hannibale victi sunt et Paullus
cum Romanorum quinquaginta milibus periit.[11]

Tum Hannibal, cum urbem capere posset, in Campaniam devertit,
cuius deliciis elanguit.[12] Postea, primum a Q. Fabio Maximo frustratus,
deinde a P. Valerio Flacco repulsus, postremo a Ti. Sempronio
Graccho et M. Claudio Marcello e Campania fugatus est.[13] Et cum ad
tertium ab urbe lapidem castra posuisset, tempestatibus repulsus est.[14]
Tandem in Africam revocatus et a Scipione apud Zamam superatus,
ad Antiochum regem Syriae confugit eumque hostem Romanis fecit.[15]
Quo victo, ad Prusiam regem Bithyniae concessit.[16] Unde Romana
legatione repetitus, hausto veneno quod sub gemma anuli habebat,
absumptus est.[17] Positus est apud Libyssam in arca lapidea, in qua
hodie etiam inscriptum est: "Hannibal hic situs est."[18]

1.   A. **annos**: acc. of extent of time; *annos* with a numeral + *natus* is the regular way
of expressing age in Lat.   B. **in Romanos** = "toward (i.e. against) the Romans"; for
the use of *in* + acc. to express purpose or feeling see 5 n. 13c.

2.   **patri**: dat. of reference (advantage); the Eng. idiom is "with his father."

3.   A. **Saguntum Romanis foederatum** = "Saguntum (a town) allied to the Romans";
see pref.   B. **foederatum**: an adj. which takes the dat., not a perf. part., since the verb
foedero is a late formation from the adj.; compare 6 n. 12B.

4.   A. **fratre Hasdrubale**: he held Spain until 207 when he tried to join Hannibal in
Italy; he was defeated and killed in a battle at the Metaurus river in northeast Italy.
He should be distinguished from Hannibal's older brother-in-law, also named Hasdrubal, for whom see pref. above.   B. **Alpibus patefactis** = "when the Alps had been
laid open," i.e. when Hannibal had crossed them.

5.   A. **P. Cornelius Scipio**: Scipio, father of Africanus (see n. 15A below), consul
(see 9 n. 10A) in 218, made the first attempt to stop Hannibal's invasion of Italy.   B.
ei: dat. with *occurrit*, a verb compounded with *ob*-; compare 3 n. 5.   C. **flumen
Ticinum**: the Ticinus was a tributary of the upper Po.

6.   A. **cum proelium commisisset** = "when he had joined battle"; a common idiom for "to fight."   B. **suis:** for the meaning see 3 n. 6C (and 6 n. 5).

7.   A. **Ti. Sempronius Longus:** as Scipio's colleague in the consulship for 218, he made the second attempt to stop Hannibal in the Po valley.   B. **alter** = "the other" here, or often "one of two," takes a partitive gen. (as here *consulum*) or *ex* or *de* + abl.; it may also be used as an adj. modifying a noun.   C. **Trebiam amnem:** another tributary of the Po.

8.   A. **Trasimenum lacum:** Lake Trasimene is in north central Italy.   B. **Gaium Flaminium:** defeated and slain as consul in 217; Fabius Maximus was made dictator for the rest of the year; see n. 13A below.   C. **Romanorum:** partitive gen. with *viginti quinque milia* (25,000); compare 7 n. 5 (and see 9 n. 12C).

9.   A. **L. Aemilius Paullus:** father of Paullus Macedonicus (see sel. 15 B); as consul for 216, he attempted to pursue Fabius' tactics of delay (see n. 13A below), but was later said to have been overridden by Varro; see next note.   B. **C. Terentius Varro:** as Paullus' colleague in the consulship for 216, he was said to have insisted unwisely on fighting the battle of Cannae, from which he escaped alive.

10.   A. **Apulia:** a region along the coast of southeastern Italy.   B. **Cannae:** for the plur. form compare 5 n. 15A (and 8 n. 11).   C. **appellatur:** ind. because the *qui* clause states a fact which is true independently of the circumstances described in the subj. *cum* clause.   D. **pugnatum esset** = "it was fought"; *pugno* is often used in this impersonal passive (contrast *nuntiatum esset* in 2 n. 2B) when it is obvious from the context who the combatants were. Here it may be rendered "there was a battle" or "the Romans and Hannibal fought."

11.   **Romanorum . . . milibus:** compare n. 8C above.

12.   A. **cum . . . posset** = "although he could have taken"; *posset* is subj. in a *cum* concessive clause; otherwise the perf. ind. *potuit* would be used, even though the idea is contrary to fact, i.e. he could have taken, but he did not. In constructions of this sort an ind. form of *possum* denotes a potentiality which is "real" at one time, but is then ended by some other action, here *devertit*; thus the ind. of *possum* may be used where a contrary to fact ("unreal") subj. might be expected.   B. **capere:** Lat. uses a pres. inf. with a past form of *possum* because the actions are contemporary. Eng. does the same with "to be able" (e.g. "he was able to take"), but uses the past with "can" ("he could have taken").   C. **Campaniam:** an area round the Bay of Naples whose fertile volcanic soil made the cities in it, such as Capua, very rich. There Hannibal passed the winter of 216/215, traditionally to the detriment of the condition and morale of his troops.

13.   A. **Q. Fabio Maximo:** appointed dictator (see 8 n. 10B) in 217 (as before in 221), he sought to wear down Hannibal by a strategy of containment and harassment; hence his epithet *Cunctator*, "the Delayer." The policy was at first unpopular with the people, but after the disaster of Cannae proved it to be correct (see nn. 9A and B above), the control of the war in Italy was again entrusted to Fabius. Fabius was the last emergency dictator of the traditional sort; the term was later revived for the much more absolute powers of Sulla (see 26 pref. and n. 13A) and Caesar; see 42 pref.   B. **frustratus:** probably past part. used with pass. meaning of the dep. *frustror* rather than from a rare act. *frustro*; see 1 n. 6B.   C. **P. Valerio Flacco:** held a naval command off south Italy in 215.   D. **Ti. Sempronio Graccho:** great-uncle of the Gracchi (see sels. 18–20) who, as consul in 215, began the recovery of Campania (see n. 12C above) from Hannibal. E. **M. Claudio Marcello:** as consul in 214, he completed the recovery of Campania and then went on to Sicily where (in 211) he captured Syracuse, which had revolted from Roman rule.

14.   A. **ad . . . lapidem** = "three miles from the city," lit. "at the third milestone from the city." Hannibal made a surprise move on Rome in 211, seeking to divert the Romans from the siege of Capua.   B. **tempestatibus:** according to Livy XXVI 11, Hannibal

and the Romans twice lined up to fight outside Rome and on both occasions heavy rain and hail prevented an engagement. The real reason for his withdrawal to south Italy was his inability to take the heavily fortified and defended city or to provision his forces from the hostile countryside.

15.   A. **Scipione:** P. Cornelius Scipio, surnamed *Africanus* for his victory over Hannibal; see pref. above. For his character and career see 12.   B. **Antiochum:** see pref. above.

16.   A. **quo victo**=*et eo victo;* see 4 n. 4A (and 8 n. 3). The Romans defeated Antiochus in Greece and Asia Minor in 191–189; see 12 pref. and 15 pref.   B. **Prusiam:** see pref. above.   C. **concessit**="he withdrew," as in 5 n. 15B.

17.   **legatione:** abl. of means of the abstract noun, instead of *a legatis*; compare 8 n. 9A.

18.   A. **Libyssam:** a small city at the eastern end of the Sea of Marmara (Propontis) near Nicomedia, the capital of Bithynia.   B. **hic:** the adv., = "here," not the dem. pronoun *hic*, in which the *i* is properly short, although it is often considered long.

11

Hannibal's brilliant generalship and ruthless conduct of war left an indelible impression on the Romans. The following passages show both the Romans' respect for his excellence and their hatred for what they regarded as his cruelty and faithlessness. It should not be forgotten that the picture of an enemy's faults is generally created by the bitterness of war, which in the Romans' case was increased by the disgrace of a succession of disastrous defeats and the presence of an enemy on Italian soil for fifteen years.

The first passage below is composed from references to Hannibal in the works of Cicero. The second is from the historian Livy who, in the time of Augustus, wrote a monumental history from the founding of the city to his own day (9 B.C.). Of its 142 *Libri ab Urbe Condita*, 35 survive (I–X, XXI–XLV), as well as summaries of all but two of the lost books.

Hannibalis virtutes et vitia

A. Quis Carthaginiensium pluris fuit Hannibale consilio, virtute, rebus gestis,[1] qui unus cum tot imperatoribus nostris,[2] per tot annos, de imperio et de gloria decertavit? Hunc sui cives e civitate eiecerunt;[3] nos etiam hostem litteris nostris et memoria videmus esse celebratum.[4] Nam callidissimum Hannibalem ex Poenorum ducibus, ut Quintum Maximum ex nostris, accepimus, celare, tacere, dissimulare, insidiari, praeripere hostium consilia.[5] Sed Hannibalem propter crudelitatem semper haec civitas oderit.[6]

B. Numquam ingenium idem ad res diversissimas, parendum atque imperandum, habilius fuit.[7] Itaque haud facile discerneres utrum imperatori Hasdrubali an exercitui carior esset.[8] Plurimum audaciae ad pericula capessenda, plurimum consilii inter ipsa pericula ei erat;[9] nullo labore aut corpus fatigari aut animus vinci poterat; caloris ac frigoris patientia par.[10] Equitum peditumque idem longe primus erat;[11] princeps in proelium ibat; ultimus, conserto proelio, excedebat.[12] Has tantas viri virtutes ingentia vitia aequabant:[13] inhumana crudelitas, perfidia plus quam Punica, nihil veri, nihil sancti, nullus deum metus, nullum ius iurandum, nulla religio.[14]

1.   A. **pluris:** gen. of (indefinite) value; = "of more weight or importance."   B. **Hannibale:** abl. of comparison, which is often used after a comparative adj. instead of *quam* followed by the noun in the appropriate case.   C. **consilio, virtute, rebus gestis:** abls. of specification (respect).

2.   **unus** = "alone, single-handed"; in contrast with *tot . . . nostris.*

3.   **eiecerunt:** the wealthy landowners and merchants at Carthage, who disliked Hannibal's reforms and had Roman support, forced him to flee; see sel. 10.

4.   **etiam** = "even," i.e. "although he was."

5.   A. **callidissimum:** with the infs. *celare etc.* = "most skillful at"; render the infs. by parts. in Eng.   B. **Quintum Maximum:** see 10 n. 13A; for *ut* + a noun = "as" see 8 n. 8E.   C. **accepimus** = "we know," lit. "have received (information)"; *accipere* is often followed by an indirect statement, here *Hannibalem callidissimum (fuisse).*

6.   **oderit:** fut. perf. in form, but fut. in meaning, since *odi*, a "defective" verb, exists only in the perf. system.

7.   A. **numquam . . . fuit** = "never was one (lit. the same) talent more skillful (or, ready) for wholly different things, (for) obeying and commanding"; *ad* + the acc. after adjs. of fitness or use indicates purpose, as with the gerund or gerundive; see 5 n. 9A. B. **parendum . . . imperandum:** gerunds in apposition with *res diversissimas.*

8.   A. **discerneres:** past potential subj.; = "you (i.e. one) would not easily have decided."   B. **Hadrubali:** Hannibal's older brother-in-law, not his brother; see 10 pref. and n. 4A.

9.   **ei erat:** dat. of reference (possession); = "there was to him"; best rendered, as often, "he had."

10.   **patientia par:** supply *ei erat* from above; = "he had just as much endurance of"; for such condensation see 4 n. 9B.

11.   A. **equitum peditumque:** partitive gens. with *primus* (compare 9 n. 11), which here is a superlative adj. meaning "first" in the sense of "most outstanding."   B. **idem:** nom. sing. masc. referring to Hannibal and, as often, equivalent to an adv.; = "likewise, too."

12.   A. **princeps . . . ultimus:** Lat. often uses an adj. modifying the subject where the Eng. idiom uses an adv. with the verb; compare *idem* in the preceding note.   B. **princeps:** here an adj. (not a noun, as in 1 n. 1G); = "first"; it is employed to avoid repetition of *primus*, which would be the natural balance to *ultimus*, i.e. "the first to . . . and the last to . . ."; see 5 n. 17A (and 9 n. 11).   C. **conserto proelio** = *commisso proelio;* see 10 n. 6A.

13.   **has tantas** = "these so great," but it is better Eng. to say "these great" or "such great"; Lat. often uses *hic* (or *is*) and *tantus* together in this way.

14.   A. **nihil . . . sancti** = "no truth, no holiness"; the neut. sing. adjs. are used as abstract nouns in the partitive gen. with *nihil*; compare 6 n. 6.   B. **deum** = *deorum;* it shows the original ending *-um* of the 2nd decl. gen. plur., for which *-orum* was later substituted on the analogy of *-arum* in the 1st decl.   C. **Punica:** adj. from *Poenus*, the Lat. form of the Greek name for the Phoenicians, the founders of Carthage (for which see 9 pref.); *Poenus* itself may be either a noun or an adj. Carthaginian treachery (*perfidia*) became proverbial among the Romans, much as did that of the Indians in the United States; the phrase "perfidious Albion" may also be compared.

12

Publius Cornelius Scipio, given the honorary *agnomen* of *Africanus* after his conquest of Carthage in North Africa (see 10 pref. and n. 15A), displayed in his career and character a mixture of traditionally Roman qualities and unconventional features. By birth he was a member of the important patrician *gens* of the Cornelii. He had, or pretended to have, a mystic strain in his personality which caused, perhaps with his encouragement, stories of supernatural powers and insights to gather around him.

After he had fought with distinction against Hannibal in Italy in the battles at the Trebia and at Cannae (see 10 nn. 7C and 10B), he was elected curule aedile in 213. Three years later, the Assembly voted to him a proconsular command (*imperium*) though he had not yet qualified for one by being either praetor or consul. He was sent to Spain and there eliminated the Carthaginian forces. He was elected consul for 205, although he was still under the legal minimum age (see n. 10B below), in order to deal with Hannibal. After his victory at Zama (see 10 pref.), he urged a policy of generosity and moderation toward Carthage, at a moment when most of his countrymen were hysterically vindictive.

Though Scipio's unusual and rapid advance served later as a precedent for ambitious men to further their careers by exceptional powers and offices, Scipio himself, trained in the Roman ideal of subordination of self to the state, seems never to have extended his powers beyond what befitted a Roman senator and patrician. Censor in 199 and a second time consul in 194, he accompanied his brother Lucius as a legate, when the latter as consul for 190 commanded against Antiochus III, "the Great"; see 10 pref. Yet with all his respect for law and precedent Scipio was personally arrogant, as is shown by his behavior when sentiment at Rome turned against the Scipios, and Cato the Elder (see 13 and 14) brought Lucius (called *Asiaticus* from his victory in Asia) to trial for mismanagement of the war against Antiochus; see n. 14 below. After this incident Scipio Africanus retired to his country villa, where he died in 184 or 183, almost contemporarily with his great foe Hannibal; see 10 pref.

The *Liber* summarizes Scipio Africanus' career as follows.

Scipionis Africani vita

Publius Scipio, ex virtute Africanus dictus, Iovis filius credebatur. Nam antequam conciperetur,[1] serpens in lecto matris eius apparuit, et postea ipsi parvulo draco circumfusus nihil nocuit.[2] In Capitolium intempesta nocte euntem numquam canes latraverunt.[3] Nec hic quicquam prius coepit quam in cella Iovis diutissime sedisset,[4] quasi divinam mentem acciperet.[5] Decem et octo annos natus, patrem apud

Ticinum singulari virtute servavit.[6] Postea, clade Cannensi nobilissimos iuvenes, Italiam deserere cupientes, sua auctoritate compescuit et incolumes per media hostium castra Canusium perduxit.[7]

Viginti quattuor annos natus, cum imperio proconsulari in Hispaniam missus, Novam Carthaginem, qua die venit, cepit.[8] Ibi virginem pulcherrimam, ad cuius aspectum concurrebatur, ad se vetuit adduci patrique eius reddidit.[9] Cum Hasdrubalem Magonemque, fratres Hannibalis, ex Hispania expulisset, victor ex Hispania domum regressus et consul ante annum suum factus, in Africam classem traiecit.[10] Ibi amicitiam cum rege Numidarum Masinissa iam coniunxerat.[11] Cuius auxilio usus, Hannibalem ex Italia revocatum superavit et victis Carthaginiensibus leges imposuit.[12]

Decem post annos, bello Antiochi, legatus fratri fuit atque filium suum a rege captum gratis recepit.[13] Romam reversus, fratre a Catone repetundarum accusato, librum rationum in conspectu populi scidit.[14] "Hac die," inquit, "Carthaginem vici. Quare in Capitolium eamus et diis supplicemus."[15] Inde, populum ingratum indignatus, in voluntarium exsilium concessit, ubi reliquam egit aetatem.[16] Moriens autem ab uxore petiit ne corpus suum Romam referretur.

1. **conciperetur** = "was conceived"; "anticipatory" subj. with *antequam*; compare 2 n. 3B.

2. A. **parvulo**: the word order shows that this is dat. after *nocuit* (= "harmed") and not after the participle compounded with *circum-* (for then the order would have been *draco parvulo circumfusus*); naturally the dat. may be taken with both; = "a snake, though curled around (him), did not harm the baby himself at all." Similar stories of serpents cohabiting with the mother or visiting the child are told of Alexander and Hercules; they suggested divine parentage since snakes were closely connected with various gods.   B. **nihil** = "not at all"; such neut. acc. sings. with verbs (cognate or "of the inner object") are often best represented in Eng. by advs. or adv. phrases.

3. A. **intempesta nocte** = "in the dead of night," lit. "night not divided into times," i.e. continuous or deep night.   B. **euntem**: the verb *latro* = "bark at" may take a direct object.

4. **cella**: the ancient temple was not so much a place of worship as a house for the god, represented by the statue. Hence the *cella* was the enclosed part, where the statue was; the worshipers might go in individually, but ceremonies took place in front. The great temple of Jupiter Optimus Maximus on the Capitol (see 8 n. 9c) at Rome had three shrines at the back of its enclosed part, for Jupiter, Juno, and Minerva. Presumably the center *cella* or shrine of Jupiter is here meant.

5. **divinam mentem** = "the divine intention," i.e. the god's instructions.

6. A. **decem . . . natus**: for this idiom to express age see 10 n. 1A.   B. **Ticinum**: for this defeat see 10 n. 5c.

7. A. **clade Cannensi:** abl. of time when; = "at the disaster of Cannae" (in 216); see 10 pref. and n. 9B.   B. **per media . . . castra** = "through the middle of the enemies' camp"; with superlative adjs. denoting order and succession and with the adjs. *medius*, *reliquus*, and often *ceterus*, Lat. uses the adj. in agreement with the noun where Eng. uses a noun with a partitive gen.   C. **Canusium:** a fortified town just west of Cannae, where the surviving Romans had taken refuge.

8. A. **Novam Carthaginem:** modern Cartagena on the southeast coast of Spain. B. **qua die venit** = (*eadem*) *die qua venit*; i.e. "on the day of his arrival"; *dies* is fem. when meaning a specific day. In Lat. the antecedent often appears only within the rel. clause, agreeing in case with the rel. pronoun. Contrast the repetition of the antecedent within the rel. clause in 8 n. 7A.

9. A. **ibi . . . reddidit:** with Scipio's generosity may be contrasted the story of Appius Claudius and Virginia in sel. 7.   B. **concurrebatur:** imperf. to denote repeated or customary action. The impersonal pass. is used frequently with verbs of motion or whenever the subject is easily deduced; here = "people used to gather (run together)"; compare *pugnatum esset* in 10 n. 10D.

10. A. **Hasdrubalem . . . expulisset:** after defeats by Scipio, first Hasdrubal (see 10 n. 4A) and then Mago tried unsuccessfully to conduct reinforcements to Hannibal in Italy.   B. **ante annum suum** = "before he reached the minimum legal age (lit. before his year)." In the third century it is likely that the minimum ages for holding magistracies had not yet been set by law, but the practice seems to have been not to accept candidates for the consulship younger than 36 years old. Cicero's career shows that in his day the minimum age was 42, i.e. to be held in the 43rd year. This minimum may have been set as early as 180.

11. **ibi . . . coniunxerat:** Scipio had won over Masinissa at the end of his Spanish campaign, and his Numidian cavalry enabled Scipio to win the battle of Zama. In the fifty years after the defeat of Carthage, Masinissa, energetic, ambitious, and long-lived, became the chief power in north Africa. His continual encroachment upon Carthage finally led in 149 to the Third Punic War; see 14 pref. and 16 pref.

12. **victis Carthaginiensibus:** dat. after *imposuit*, not abl. abs.

13. A. **bello:** abl. of time when; = "in the war against (lit. of) Antiochus"; compare n. 7A above; *in bello* is equally common.   B. **legatus fratri:** as Rome's wars necessitated larger armies, the commanders began to appoint older senators (in general, they were at least former praetors) to command legions or groups of legions; such a higher officer was called a *legatus*, with his commander's name in either the gen. or (as here) the dat. of reference (advantage), for which compare 10 n. 2.   C. **gratis** = "as a favor," i.e. without ransom. The abl. plur. of *gratia* is spelled *gratiis* except in this idiom.

14. A. **repetundarum:** gen. of the charge after a verb of accusing; *-undus* is an alternative ending for the gerundive in the 3rd conj. Supply *rerum* or *pecuniarum*; = "property (or, money) to be restored." *Res* or *pecuniae repetundae* was the technical name for an action brought against a Roman general or governor who was accused of extortion in his command or province.   B. **librum rationum . . . scidit** = "he tore up the book of accounts." Africanus had been called to give evidence at the trial, but his speech shows that he thought that he and his brother should be immune from this kind of inquiry because of their services to Rome.

15. A. **inquit:** for its use only in direct quotation see 9 n. 5.   B. **in Capitolium:** see n. 4 above.   C. **eamus . . . supplicemus** = "let us go . . . let us pray"; the hortatory (jussive) subj. is used to give commands in the 1st or 3rd pers. The negative is *ne* and the tense is usually pres.   D. **diis** = *deis;* in classical Lat. *supplicare* usually takes the dat., not the acc. as in later Lat.

16. **egit aetatem:** for this idiomatic use of *ago* see 5 n. 16B.

13

A greater contrast than that between Scipio Africanus and his chief rival, Marcus Porcius Cato "the Elder," is hard to imagine. Scipio, like almost all important figures in Roman history until this time, was a member of an eminent family. He advocated imperialism in Rome's foreign policy and a liberal, philhellene attitude in domestic politics and culture.

Cato, born in 234 as the son of a plebeian farmer, had no senatorial ancestors and was, therefore, what the Romans called "a new man" (*novus homo*). He fought in the Second Punic War and at the same time entered upon his political career. He proved to be a skillful lawyer and orator. Elected consul in 195, he commanded an army in Spain. After a long and active career, he died in 149, shortly after Rome, mostly at his instigation, had declared the Third Punic War.

Throughout his life, and especially as censor in 184, he opposed the luxury, corruption, and Hellenistic culture which were spreading through the Roman upper classes under the patronage of the Scipios. Unlike many social critics, he practiced what he preached by leading a frugal and austere private life which made him, for later times, the embodiment of the "old Roman virtues."

Nevertheless, he is supposed to have learned Greek in his old age and may well be considered the father of Latin prose. In spite of his continuous engagement in the practical activities of farming, war, politics, and law, he found time for a remarkable amount of literary work, including a collection of speeches, which was extant in Cicero's day, a history of Italian communities down to 150 called the *Origines*, now lost, and a treatise on farming (*de Re Rustica* or *de Agricultura*), which is the only one of his works now surviving.

The following passage stresses, as do many comments on Cato, his extraordinary versatility and energy. It is composed from Cicero; from Quintilian, a rhetorician and teacher of the late first century A.D.; from Cornelius Nepos, a Roman biographer and historian contemporary with Cicero; and from the *Natural History* of Pliny the Elder, who died in the eruption of Vesuvius in A.D. 79.

Catonis ingenium

M. igitur Cato idem summus imperator, idem sapiens, idem orator, idem historiae conditor, idem iuris, idem rerum rusticarum peritissimus fuit.[1] Quem virum, di boni![2] Quis illo gravior in laudando,[3] acerbior in vituperando, in sententiis argutior, in docendo edisserendoque subtilior? In omnibus rebus singulari fuit industria.[4] Inter tot operas militiae, tantas domi contentiones, rudi saeculo,[5] litteras Graecas, aetate iam declinata, didicit. Quarum studium etsi senior adripuerat, tamen tantum progressum fecit, ut nihil facile reperiri possit, neque de Graecis neque de Italicis rebus, quod ei fuerit incognitum.[6] Ab adulescentia confecit orationes, quae refertae sunt et verbis et rebus illustribus.[7] Senex historias scribere instituit; earum sunt libri septem. Liber primus continet res gestas regum populi Romani, secundus et tertius unde quaeque civitas orta sit Italica,[8] ob quam rem omnes *Origines* videtur appellasse.[9] In quarto autem est bellum Punicum primum, in quinto secundum; atque haec omnia capitulatim sunt dicta. In iisdem exposuit quae in Italia Hispaniisque aut fierent aut viderentur admiranda;[10] in quibus multa industria et diligentia comparet, nulla doctrina.[11] Reliqua quoque bella pari modo persecutus est usque ad praeturam Servii Galbae, qui diripuit Lusitanos.[12] Atque horum bellorum omnium duces non nominavit, sed sine nominibus res notavit. Elephantum tamen, qui fortissime proeliatus esset in Punica acie, Surum tradidit vocatum, altero dente mutilato.[13]

1. A. **idem etc.**: the pronoun is repeated for emphasis; translate "Marcus Cato was, therefore, at once an outstanding commander, (a) wise (man) etc." For rendering *idem* by an adv. see 11 n. 11B.   B. **historiae conditor**: the gen. is objective. Cato had predecessors in legal studies and in agricultural writing, and earlier Romans had written history in Greek prose or Latin verse (Naevius and Ennius); however, his lost *Origines* (see pref.) seems to have been the first Lat. prose history.   C. **peritissimus**: one of several adjs. followed by the objective gen., here *iuris* and *rerum rusticarum*, rather than by the abl. of specification; = "very skilled (or, experienced) in law and agriculture." Cato's legal writings are lost, though quotations survive from his many forensic speeches; for his work on agriculture see pref.

2. A. **quem virum**: acc. of exclamation.   B. **di**: voc. plural; =*dii*=*dei*; compare *diis*=*deis* in 12 n. 15D.

3. **illo**: abl. of comparison; compare 11 n. 1B.

4. **singulari . . . industria**: abl. of description (quality); the gen. or abl. of description (see 6 nn. 1A and 9) is often best rendered in Eng. by "a man of."

5. A. **militiae . . . domi**: locs.; = "in the field (on campaign) . . . at home (in civil life at Rome)"; this idiom, usually written in reverse order, *domi militiaeque*, is often used to describe the two spheres of a man's public life.   B. **rudi saeculo**: abl. of time within which (or when); = "during (or in) an uneducated age"; it represents a third handicap parallel to the two dependent on *inter* without connective.

6. A. **ut . . . possit**: result clause; *possit* is pres. subj., even though the introductory verb, *fecit*, is past, because the result is still true. Result clauses do not follow the regular sequence of tenses, but take any tense required by the meaning.   B. **nihil . . . neque . . . neque**: although two negatives in Lat. normally cancel each other to make an emphatic positive, a general negative (here *nihil*) is not so canceled by succeeding

negatives which introduce separate subordinate members (here *neque . . . neque* introducing the two prepositional phrases with *de*).   c. **fuerit:** subj., not simply by attraction to *possit*, but in a rel. clause of characteristic (compare 9 n. 8D) after the negative antecedent *nihil*; the perf. is used rather than the pres. (*sit*) because *incognitum* serves as a predicate adj. and not as a past part. in a perf. pass. subj. The perf. subj. in primary sequence indicates past time relative to *possit*, i.e. "so that nothing can (now) be found easily . . . which was unknown to him (when he was alive)."

7. **verbis et rebus:** abls. of means with *refertae*. Expressions of fullness take either the abl. or the gen.

8. **quaeque:** fem. nom. sing. of *quisque*, modifying *civitas*.

9. **videtur appellasse** = "he seems to have called"; *appellasse* (=*appellavisse;* see 1 n. 4B and compare 9 n. 17D) is a complementary inf., not part of a clause serving as the subject of *videtur*. Lat. prefers to use a person or thing as the subject of *videor*, although the impersonal construction with an inf. clause as subject ("it seems that etc.") also occurs.

10.   A. **iisdem** =*eisdem;* compare n. 2B above.   B. **fierent . . . viderentur:** probably imperf. subjs. in an indirect question introduced by the interrogative pronoun *quae* and object of *exposuit*; for the tense see 2 n. 4A. The *quae* might be taken as a rel. with an understood antecedent *ea*, but in that case it seems likely that the verbs would be in the ind. of simple statement rather than the subj. of characteristic, i.e. "those things which happened etc." rather than "those sorts of things which generally happened etc." c. **admiranda:** probably goes with both verbs, i.e. "what (matters), deserving admiration, either happened or were seen"; the second refers to notable sights.

11.   A. **comparet:** pres. ind. of *compareo*, not pres. subj. of *comparo*; it is sing. because *industria* and *diligentia* are considered as a single subject. This use of two words to express a single thought is called "hendiadys" (Greek; = one [idea] through two [words]). Either translate *comparet* by a plur. or render *multa etc.* as "very diligent industry."   B. **nulla:** supply "but" before this; such omission of a connective is called "adversative asyndeton" and is frequently used where the meaning itself suggests a strong contrast; compare 4 n. 5B.   c. **doctrina:** often has a connotation of technical knowledge or training, especially Greek. Cato presumably avoided in his *Origines* anything which smacked of Hellenism, but to Nepos and his contemporaries the lack of conscious erudition may have seemed a mark of the *rude saeculum* (n. 5B above) in which Cato had lived. Some modern scholars, however, feeling that *nulla doctrina* is too harsh a criticism, emend the text to read *nonnulla doctrina* = "with not a little learning."

12.   **Galbae:** as praetor and governor of Further Spain in 151/150, he treacherously massacred the Lusitanians when they sued for peace. In 149, the year of his own death, Cato supported an unsuccessful prosecution of Galba for this act. Cato apparently continued to add to his *Origines* almost until his death.

13.   **Surum . . . vocatum:** with *vocatum* supply *esse* in indirect discourse with *tradidit*. This whole well-known statement raises interesting questions about both Cato's attitude to the *nobiles* and the use of elephants in ancient warfare. It is made by Pliny the Elder (ca. A.D. 77) in a long discussion about elephants in his *Naturalis Historia* VIII 5.11, in which he mentions several elephants which had personal names. The elephants used in ancient warfare were usually the more tractable Indian ones, brought to the Mediterranean via Syria. However, it is indicated by Pliny elsewhere in his discussion and by pictures on coins that the Carthaginians used African elephants despite their more intractable disposition. The objection that it would have been difficult, if not impossible, to bring African elephants across the Sahara desert from central to north Africa is met by Pliny's statement that in antiquity elephants were still to be found in Mauretania (modern Morocco). Since Pliny specifies *in Punica acie*, this elephant did not serve with Pyrrhus, who first brought elephants against Roman troops; see sel. 9 A. In either of the Punic Wars (see prefs. to 9 and 10), he might have been a sole Indian elephant in a force of African ones, obtained in Syria and therefore called *Surus*, "The

Syrian"; the *y* in Eng. "Syria" represents a Greek *u* which is usually also used in early Lat. However, there is an obsolete Lat. word *surus* = "stake" (compare the classical diminutive *surculus* = "twig") quoted from the *Annales* of Ennius, a poet contemporary with Cato who served in the Second Punic War and described it. Thus this word may have been applied by the Roman soldiers of the time as a nickname (or as a translation of a Punic nickname) to an elephant who had only one tusk (*dens*): "Tusker" or "(Old One-)Stake." Pliny implies that Cato deliberately mentioned this brave elephant by name to spite the families of aristocratic commanders whose deeds he passed over in silence. But perhaps in fact Cato singled out the elephant for notice because of his bravery and only incidentally gave the nickname that reflected his having one tusk. Later critics might well have seized on this as an instance of Cato's cantankerous disregard for the aristocratic senatorial families.

14

Cato impressed his contemporaries with his cantankerous vigor and pithy Roman wit. Posterity admired his honesty and patriotism, but was also aware that he had often been narrow-minded, harsh, and quarrelsome. Cicero, however, wrote a dialogue called *de Senectute*, in which Cato appears as a genial and attractive "elder statesman." In the dialogue Cato explains to two young men, Scipio Aemilianus and Laelius (see 16), why he finds old age easy to bear. He cites many examples of men, both Greek and Roman, who had been still useful and active in old age and he interweaves many references to his own life, for which see 13 pref.

The following passage comprises extracts from Cicero's *de Senectute*. Cato is speaking.

Cato senex

Quartum ago annum et octogesimum;[1] et hoc queo dicere, non me quidem eis esse viribus, quibus aut miles bello Punico aut quaestor eodem bello aut consul in Hispania fuerim[2] aut quadriennio post,[3] cum tribunus militaris depugnavi apud Thermopylas, M'. Glabrione consule,[4] sed tamen, ut vos videtis,[5] non plane me enervavit, non adflixit senectus, non curia vires meas desiderat, non rostra, non amici, non clientes, non hospites.[6]

Non enim viribus aut velocitate aut celeritate corporum res magnae geruntur, sed consilio, auctoritate, sententia; quibus non modo non orbari, sed etiam augeri senectus solet.[7] Nisi forte ego,[8] qui et miles et tribunus et legatus et consul versatus sum in vario genere bellorum, vobis cessare nunc videor, cum bella non gero.[9] At senatui, quae sint gerenda, praescribo, et quo modo.[10] Carthagini male iam diu cogitanti bellum multo ante denuntio;[11] de qua vereri non ante desinam quam illam excisam esse cognovero.[12] Quam palmam utinam di immortales, Scipio, tibi reservent, ut avi reliquias persequare![13]

Septimus mihi liber *Originum* est in manibus;[14] omnia antiquitatis monumenta colligo; causarum illustrium, quascumque defendi, nunc conficio orationes; ius augurium, pontificium, civile tracto;[15] multum etiam Graecis litteris utor.[16] Itaque corporis vires non magno opere desidero.[17] Adsum amicis, venio in senatum frequens[18] ultroque adfero res multum et diu cogitatas[19] easque tueor animi, non corporis, viribus. Ita sensim sine sensu aetas senescit nec subito frangitur, sed diuturnitate exstinguitur.[20]

1. **quartum ... octogesimum:** for *ago* in such phrases see 5 n. 16B (and 12 n. 16). Since Cato was born in 234 and says that he is in (lit. leading) his 84th year, the dramatic date of Cicero's dialogue was 151/150, two years or less before Cato's death.

2. A. **non ... fuerim** = "that I am not indeed (a man) of the same strength as (lit. with which) I was." For the abls. of description *eis viribus* and *quibus* (*viribus*) see 13 n. 4. *Vis* in the plur. (*vires*) regularly = "power, strength," often "bodily strength."   B. **fuerim:** perf. subj. in a subordinate clause which is an integral part of an indirect statement.   C. **quidem:** as often, looks forward to the adversative *sed tamen* below. Cato presumably began his military service at seventeen, i.e., if born in 234, in about 217. He served as quaestor, the first of the Roman magistracies, in 204 in Sicily. He became aedile in 199, praetor in Sardinia in 198, and consul in 195; as consul he went out to command in Spain. See further note 4A below.

3. **quadriennio post:** abl. of degree of difference + adv.; = "four years afterwards (lit. afterwards by four years)." An alternative construction for such expressions of time is the prep. with the acc., e.g. *decem post annos* at the opening of the 3rd par. of sel. 12.

4. A. **tribunus militaris:** in 191 Cato served as military tribune on the staff of the consul Glabrio, who defeated the forces of Antiochus the Great (see 12 pref. and 15 pref.) at Thermopylae and drove them out of Greece. It must already have been unusual for a man of Cato's years and distinction to serve as a military tribune rather than as a *legatus*; see 12 n. 13B. In early Roman armies the military tribunes (different from the tribunes of the *plebs*) were young men beginning their senatorial career who served as junior officers of the legions and were in part elected, in part appointed by the consuls. B. **M'. Glabrione consule:** abl. abs.; = "when M'. (= Manius) Glabrio was consul" or "in the consulship of M'. Glabrio." To name the consuls in the abl. (usually both are specified) was the regular way in Lat. of indicating a year.

5. **ut ... videtis:** *ut* + the ind. often = "as"; compare its use with nouns in 8 n. 8E (and 11 n. 5B).

6. A. **curia:** the senate house was adjacent to the Comitium and the Forum, though the senate frequently met elsewhere, in temples or other public buildings as suited the magistrate who summoned it.   B. **rostra:** the speaker's platform between the Comitium and the Forum. The name is derived from the bronze beaks (or rams) which had been taken from ships captured from the Volscians at Antium in 338 and which were attached along its front.   C. **clientes:** for patrons and clients see 7 n. 7.

7. A. **quibus:** the abl. indicates separation with *orbari* (see 4 n. 2B), but means or respect with *augeri*.   B. **augeri:** the pass. of *augeo* is often used figuratively to mean "enriched," with money, offices, or abstract qualities, as here *consilio etc.*

8. **nisi forte** = "unless perhaps"; this phrase regularly implies that the supposition which it introduces is false. For the adv. *forte* see 5 n. 3A.

9. **cum ... gero:** *cum* temporal + the ind. often implies a reason.

10. **quae sint gerenda:** the gerundive with forms of *sum* expresses obligation or necessity; this construction is called the 2nd (or pass.) "periphrastic" (Greek; = a circumlocutionary form) conjugation; for the 1st (or act.) periphrastic conj. see 28 n. 21. *Sint* is pres. subj. in an indirect question dependent on *praescribo*, not in a rel. clause of characteristic with an omitted antecedent *ea* (compare 13 n. 10B); the pres. subj. is

used for an incompleted action in primary sequence. *Sint gerenda* is understood also with *quo modo*; = "I prescribe what (things) are to be done and in what way."

11.   A. **Carthagini ... cogitanti:** dat. of reference (disadvantage); = "against Carthage who has already long been hostile," lit. "thinking in an evil manner." It is unlikely that Carthage was really planning to engage in another struggle with Rome. By the terms of treaty at the end of the Second Punic War (201) she had been forbidden to maintain an army for 50 years. During this period she had suffered much from the attacks of Masinissa (see 12 n. 11) and now that the 50 years were up, was trying to defend herself against him.   B. **bellum ... denuntio** = "I am declaring war long before," i.e. he is trying to get Rome to declare war on Carthage before she attacks Rome. In his effort to precipitate the war, Cato is said to have ended all his speeches in the senate with *censeo Carthaginem delendam esse*. The reasons for Cato's implacable hostility toward Carthage have been variously explained.   C. **multo ante:** for the abl. see n. 3 above.

12.   **ante ... quam:** their separation means that they do not really constitute an anticipatory subordinating conjunction with the subj., as in 12 n. 1; the *ante* is an adv. with the fut. ind. *desinam* and the *quam* is the conjunction after the implied comparison, introducing the second verb, *cognovero*, which is fut. perf. to show that its action will have been completed before that of *desinam* takes place. From this construction develops a use of the ind. in place of the subj. with *antequam* as a subordinating conjunction to emphasize the actuality of the coming event rather than its prospect, i.e. Cato will not cease before he will have learned, but he is sure that he will learn.

13.   A. **quam palmam** = "and this glory," i.e. of destroying Carthage; for *quam=et eam* at the beginning of a sentence see 4 n. 4A (and 8 n. 3).   B. **palmam:** lit. = "a palm branch," often used as a symbol of victory. Cicero, of course, knew that Scipio Aemilianus had in fact destroyed Carthage in 146 (see sel. 16), four years after the dramatic date of this dialogue.   C. **reservent:** pres. subj. with *utinam*, expressing a wish that may be fulfilled.   D. **ut ... persequare:** substantive clause, indicating purpose rather than result, in apposition with *palmam*; = "of completing what your grandfather left undone," lit. "that you should complete the remains of your grandfather."   E. **persequare:** 2nd pers. sing. pres. subj.; *-re* is a common alternative ending for the 2nd pers. sing. pass. ending *-ris*.

14.   **Originum:** for Cato's *Origines* see sel. 13.

15.   **augurium, pontificium:** adjs.; = "augural (contrast the noun in 4 n. 8), pontifical." Roman religion, as a function of the state, was in the charge of several civil boards, or colleges, whose members were senators presumably expert in various aspects of religious lore. Of these boards, the most important were the augurs and the pontiffs. The augurs advised magistrates on how to take auspices and how to interpret omens. The pontiffs were generally responsible for the care of religion and their chief, the *pontifex maximus*, was the head of religious affairs.

16.   A. **multum ... utor** = "I also read Greek literature a good deal"; *multum* is equivalent to an adv.; see 12 n. 2B.   B. **utor:** intrans. and followed by the abl. of means; its Eng. derivative, "use," has become trans. In translating *utor*, render freely by whatever Eng. verb is most appropriate with the abl. noun; hence "read" above, or *aqua utor* = "I drink water," etc.

17.   **magno opere:** abl. of manner which became adverbial; = "greatly." It is often written as one word: *magnopere*.

18.   A. **adsum** = "I am present for," i.e. "I come to the aid of"; especially used of assisting in legal cases; like most compounds of *sum*, it takes the dat.   B. **frequens:** one of several adjs. which are often best rendered in Eng. adverbially; see 11 n. 12A and compare *idem* in 11 n. 11B (and 13 n. 1A).

19.   **adfero res** = "I bring forward proposals (in the senate)."

20.   **sensim ... senescit:** the alliteration suggests that this is a quotation from early Lat. poetry, in which alliteration was common; see 60 sels. H and I.

15

The lifetime of Cato witnessed a great expansion of Rome's overseas empire. Her conquest of Carthage gave her control of the western Mediterranean. To the provinces which she had acquired after the First Punic War (see 9 pref.), namely Sicily and Sardinia/Corsica, she added in 197 the two provinces of Hither and Further Spain. She then turned her attention to the eastern Mediterranean. Even before the Second Punic War (see 10 pref.), she had been drawn into the Adriatic to check the depredations in the Adriatic of pirates from the coast of Illyricum. During the Second Punic War, Philip V, the ambitious king of Macedon, had made an alliance with Hannibal, and the Romans had sent a small force into Greece to wage against Philip the inconclusive First Macedonian War (215–205). After the defeat of Hannibal, Philip's enemies in Greece, seeking to free themselves from him, called in the Romans, thus starting Rome's Second Macedonian War. Titus Quinctius Flamininus was sent as consul in 198 to command the Roman forces. In the following year he defeated Philip at Cynoscephalae in Thessaly, and in 196 he surprised all the Greeks by proclaiming at the Isthmian Games that Rome would withdraw and leave the Greek cities, tribes, and federations free.

Rome's attempt to abstain from interference in Greece was doomed to failure. Only six years after Flamininus' "liberation" of Greece, Rome invaded to repel the attack of Antiochus III; see 10 and 12. After this she withdrew again, but Philip's successor, Perseus, became aggressive, and Rome declared the Third Macedonian War in 171. In 168 her general, the consul Lucius Aemilius Paullus, defeated Perseus at Pydna, in southern Macedonia, and divided the country into four republics. Twenty years later, Macedonia was finally reduced to a province under a Roman governor. At the same time, discontent among the Greeks led to Roman intervention and the sack of Corinth by Lucius Mummius in 146. Though most Greek cities were left "free," the country was placed under the general oversight of the governor of Macedonia.

The first of the following passages is summarized from a more detailed account in Livy by Valerius Maximus, who, in the early first century A.D., made a collection of historical incidents topically arranged and called *Facta et Dicta Memorabilia*. The second is from the *Historiae Romanae* of Velleius Paterculus, a soldier and amateur historian who served under the emperor Tiberius, also in the early first century A.D.

A.   *Graecia liberata*

Philippo Macedoniae rege superato, cum ad Isthmicum spectaculum tota Graecia convenisset, T. Quinctius Flamininus, tubae signo silentio facto,[1] per praeconem haec verba recitari iussit: "Senatus

Populusque Romanus et Titus Quinctius Flamininus imperator omnes Graeciae urbes, quae sub dicione Philippi regis fuerunt, liberas atque immunes esse iubet."[2] Quibus auditis, maximo et inopinato gaudio homines perculsi primo, velut non audisse se quae audierant credentes, obticuerunt.[3] Iterata deinde pronuntiatione praeconis, caelum tanta clamoris alacritate compleverunt,[4] ut certe constet aves, quae supervolabant, attonitas paventesque decidisse.[5]

B.   *Paulli victoria et triumphus*

Perses biennium tali fortuna cum consulibus Romanis conflixerat,[6] ut plerumque superior fuerit magnamque partem Graeciae in societatem suam perduceret. Tum senatus populusque Romanus L. Aemilium Paullum consulem iterum creavit.[7] Filius erat eius Paulli, qui ad Cannas invitus perniciosam rei publicae pugnam inierat, fortiter in ea mortem obierat.[8] Is Persam ingenti proelio apud urbem nomine Pydnam in Macedonia devicit.[9] Ita Paullus maximum nobilissimumque regem in triumpho duxit.

Paullo autem quattuor filii fuere;[10] ex iis duos natu maiores, unum P. Scipioni, Africani filio, in adoptionem dederat, alterum Fabio Maximo.[11] Duos minores natu praetextatos, quo tempore victoriam adeptus est, habuit.[12] Is, cum in contione extra urbem more maiorum ante triumphi diem ordinem actorum suorum commemoraret,[13] deos immortalis precatus est, ut, si quis eorum invideret operibus ac fortunae suae, in ipsum potius saeviret quam in rem publicam.[14] Quae vox, veluti oraculo emissa, magna parte eum spoliavit sanguinis sui;[15] nam alterum ex suis liberis quos in familia retinuerat intra paucos dies ante triumphum, alterum paucioribus post, amisit.[16]

1. A. **signo:** abl. of means.   B. **silentio facto:** abl. abs.

2. **liberas atque immunes:** the first meant that the cities were free to manage their internal affairs without the intervention of a royal or Roman governor; the second, that they were free from any obligation to pay tax or tribute.

3. A. **perculsi** = "smitten"; past part. from *percello*; the verb is often used of strong emotions.   B. **primo:** neut. abl. adj. used as adv. with *obticuerunt*; compare *brevi* in 9 n. 6B.   C. **velut ... credentes:** *velut non credentes se audisse ea quae audierant.*   D. **audierant:** ind. rather than subj. because it is not part of the indirect statement, but a statement of fact put in by the author; compare 10 n. 10c (and contrast 14 n. 2B).

4. **tanta clamoris alacritate**=" with such an immediate outcry," lit. "with such alacrity of clamor." It is common in rhetorical or poetic Lat. to use an abstract noun and a gen. rather than an adj. modifying the noun.

5. A. **ut . . . constet:** a result clause, in which the pres. subj. may follow a secondary tense (here the perf. ind.); see 13 n. 6A. *Certe* (or *satis*) *constat* is a frequent idiom for "it is firmly (or, sufficiently) established that" and in Lat. the subject is the following indirect statement, *aves . . . decidisse.* Despite this, the story is not found in Livy. B. **attonitas paventesque:** in Eng. render coordinately with *decidisse*; compare 4 n. 6A.

6. **Perses:** Lat. regularly changes Greek proper names which end in *-eus* to *-es*; compare *Achilles = Achilleus.* The acc. *Persam* (compare 1 n. 2B), four lines below, instead of *-em*, may result from assimilation of the personal name to the Greek noun *Perses* ("Persian"), which is of the 1st decl.; compare 85 n. 22B and 88 n. 22C.

7. **consulem iterum** = "consul for a second time." Paullus had been consul for the first time in 182.

8. A. **Paulli:** for the elder Paullus see sel. 10, especially n. 9A.   B. **invitus:** an adj. regularly to be translated adverbially; see 11 n. 12A (and 14 n. 18B). Paullus had tried to pursue Fabius Maximus' policy of delay (see 10 n. 9A), but his colleague Varro insisted on meeting Hannibal in a pitched battle; see 10 n. 9B.   C. **inierat, fortiter:** for the omission of "but" (adversative asyndeton) see 13 n. 11B.

9. **Persam:** see n. 6 above.

10. **fuere** = *fuerunt*; *-ēre* is an alternative termination for *-erunt* in the 3rd pers. plur. of the perf. act. ind.

11. A. **natu maiores:** lit. = "greater in birth"; this is the regular Lat. idiom for "older"; *natu* (abl. of respect or specification) is generally identified as the only form in common use of a 4th decl. noun *natus*, but it might equally be the abl. of the supine of *nascor.*   B. **in adoptionem:** for *in* + acc. expressing purpose see 5 n. 13C (and 7 n. 8B). The Romans, partly for religious reasons, attached great importance to the continuity of a family, and adoptions, often, as here, of a boy already related by blood, became very common. See the following genealogical charts for the relations between the families of Scipio, Paullus, Gracchus, and Cato. Such interlocking of families by marriage and adoption played an important role in the history of the last two centuries of the Roman Republic.

12. A. **praetextatos** = "wearing the *toga praetexta*." This toga, worn by boys and magistrates (see 8 n. 8C), had a purple border to signify special protection of the gods; boys changed to an all-white toga at seventeen. *Praetextatus* is an adj. from the past part. *praetextus*; compare 6 n. 12B (and 10 n. 3B).   B. **quo tempore:** for the inclusion of the antecedent within the rel. clause see 12 n. 8B.

13. A. **urbem:** i.e. Rome.   B. **more maiorum:** abl. of accordance (specification); = "according to the custom of (our) ancestors."   C. **ordinem . . . commemoraret** = "he was giving an account"; *commemoro* regularly means "recount, mention," not "remember, commemorate."

14. A. **immortalīs:** acc. plur. adjs. and *i*-stem nouns of the 3rd decl. often have *-īs* for *-ēs* in the acc. plur.   B. **ut si quis . . . invideret . . . saeviret** = "that if any of them (the gods) should begrudge . . . he would vent his wrath (would rage)"; for indefinite *quis* after *si* see 4 n. 11B. Paullus' prayer would originally have had the protasis of a fut. less vivid condition and an apodosis expressing a wish, both pres. subj.: *si quis invideat . . . saeviat* = "if any god should begrudge, may he vent his wrath." But the prayer is here expressed indirectly, in a substantive *ut* clause of purpose or volition (see 4 n. 11A) after a verb of asking (*precatus est*) and in secondary sequence; hence the main verb of the prayer is imperf. subj. and the protasis is attracted into the imperf. subj.; compare 9 n. 17C.   C. **ipsum** = *se ipsum;* the intensive pronoun is occasionally used pronominally in place of the reflexive.

15.   A. **magna . . . spoliavit:** for the abl. of separation see 4 n. 2B (and 14 n. 7A).
B. **sanguinis:** metaphorically for "family" (as often); partitive gen. with *parte.*

16.   A. **liberis:** for its derivation see 9 n. 14A.   B. **paucioribus post:** abl. of degree
of difference + adv.; see 14 nn. 3 and 11C.

Genealogical Charts I–IV

These charts contain only persons mentioned in the text or necessary to understand
their relationships; many members of the families charted have not been included.

I.   Sempronii Gracchi

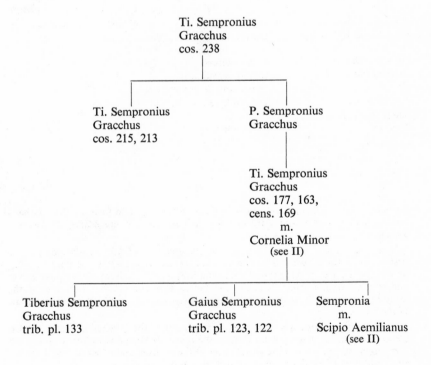

II.   Cornelii Scipiones

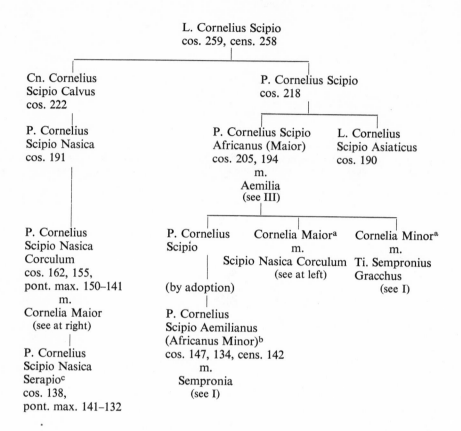

L. Cornelius Scipio
cos. 259, cens. 258

Cn. Cornelius
Scipio Calvus
cos. 222

P. Cornelius
Scipio Nasica
cos. 191

P. Cornelius Scipio
cos. 218

P. Cornelius Scipio
Africanus (Maior)
cos. 205, 194
m.
Aemilia
(see III)

L. Cornelius
Scipio Asiaticus
cos. 190

P. Cornelius
Scipio Nasica
Corculum
cos. 162, 155,
pont. max. 150–141
m.
Cornelia Maior
(see at right)

P. Cornelius
Scipio Nasica
Serapio[c]
cos. 138,
pont. max. 141–132

P. Cornelius
Scipio

(by adoption)

P. Cornelius
Scipio Aemilianus
(Africanus Minor)[b]
cos. 147, 134, cens. 142
m.
Sempronia
(see I)

Cornelia Maior[a]
m.
Scipio Nasica Corculum
(see at left)

Cornelia Minor[a]
m.
Ti. Sempronius
Gracchus
(see I)

[a] Sisters in a Roman family usually all bore the feminine form of their father's *nomen*, here *Cornelia*, and were distinguished by the epithets *Maior, Minor*, and *Tertia*.

[b] Aemilianus was, through his adoption, the grandson of Africanus Maior and the first cousin of the Gracchi. Through his aunt Aemilia (daughter of the elder Paullus), he was the nephew of Africanus Maior, and thus a first cousin of his adoptive father and of the two Cornelias, which made him a first cousin once removed of the Gracchi. Lastly, by his marriage to Sempronia (see chart I), he was the brother-in-law of the Gracchi.

[c] This Scipio Nasica was a maternal first cousin of the Gracchi and also a third cousin through his descent from Calvus, the uncle of Africanus Maior, who in turn through his daughters was the grandfather of the Gracchi and of Nasica, and, by his son's adoption of Paullus' son, also of Scipio Aemilianus.

III. Aemilii Paulli

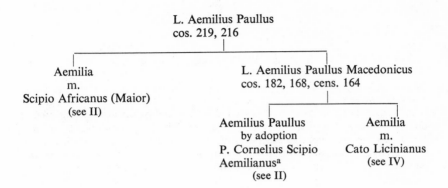

L. Aemilius Paullus
cos. 219, 216

Aemilia
m.
Scipio Africanus (Maior)
(see II)

L. Aemilius Paullus Macedonicus
cos. 182, 168, cens. 164

Aemilius Paullus
by adoption
P. Cornelius Scipio
Aemilianus[a]
(see II)

Aemilia
m.
Cato Licinianus
(see IV)

[a] P. Scipio Aemilianus, Paullus' second son, was adopted by the son of Africanus Maior. Paullus' eldest son was adopted by the son (or perhaps nephew) of Fabius Maximus Cunctator. The two youngest boys died in 167; see 15 B end.

IV. Porcii Catones

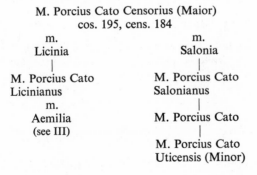

M. Porcius Cato Censorius (Maior)
cos. 195, cens. 184

m.
Licinia

m.
Salonia

M. Porcius Cato
Licinianus
m.
Aemilia
(see III)

M. Porcius Cato
Salonianus

M. Porcius Cato

M. Porcius Cato
Uticensis (Minor)

16

During the years in which Rome extended her power into the eastern Mediterranean (see 15 pref.), she was also involved in military operations in the west. A Third Punic War (149–146) ended in the destruction of Carthage by Scipio Aemilianus. Throughout most of the century, Rome fought against rugged Spanish tribes in wars characterized by brutality, dishonesty, and greed on the part of her commanders. Only a certain Tiberius Sempronius Gracchus (see 18 n. 1A) was a notable exception for his good faith and ability. Finally, in 139, resistance collapsed in southern Spain. In northern Spain, opposition to the Romans was led by the town of Numantia, but this fell in 133 to Scipio Aemilianus after a bitter siege.

Scipio Aemilianus, also called *Africanus Minor* because of his conquest of Carthage, was by birth son of the younger Aemilius Paullus but was adopted by a son of Scipio the Elder (see 15, with its genealogical charts). He not only inherited his adoptive family's traditions of military glory, but grew up in his own father's house in an atmosphere of Hellenism, which was first influential at Rome during the later third century and became prevalent after the conquest of Greece. After his victory at Pydna in 168, the only booty from Macedonia which Paullus kept for himself was the library of King Perseus; see 15 pref. Also, from a thousand hostages whom the Romans required from Greece, Paullus took into his house as tutor for his sons the historian Polybius. After Paullus' death in 160, Aemilianus inherited his patronage of Hellenism and became the leader of those who favored active intervention abroad and at home the enlargement of Roman culture from Greek sources. He surrounded himself with a group of Roman and Greek intellectuals which has become known as "The Scipionic Circle." Noteworthy members were the comic poet Terence (d. 159); the statesman Laelius, called "the Wise" (*Sapiens*), who lived to deliver the funeral oration over Scipio in 129; Polybius, the Greek historian (d. about 120); Panaetius, a Greek Stoic philosopher; and a Roman satirist named Lucilius, the model for Horace's satires.

The first of the following passages is composed from Velleius and Livy; the second from Cicero, Velleius, and Aulus Gellius, who in the second century A.D. published a collection of comments on miscellaneous topics, mostly grammar, literature, and history, under the title *Noctes Atticae*.

A. *Carthago Numantiaque a Scipione deletae*

Eodem tempore statuit senatus Carthaginem exscindere. Itaque Publius Cornelius Scipio, naturalis consulis Aemilii Paulli filius, adoptione Scipionis Africani Maioris nepos, aedilitatem petens, consul creatus est.[1] Bellum Carthagini, iam biennio ante a prioribus consulibus inlatum, maiore vi intulit;[2] eamque urbem, invisam Romanis magis invidia imperii quam ullius eius temporis noxiae gratia, funditus sustulit.[3] Qua re fecit suae virtutis monumentum, quod fuerat avi eius clementiae,[4] et ipse Africanus Minor appellatus est.

Deinde tredecim annis post,[5] multis acceptis circa Numantiam cladibus, Scipio, creatus iterum consul missusque in Hispaniam, fortunae virtutique expertae in Africa respondit in Hispania,[6] et intra annum ac tres menses, circumdatam operibus Numantiam excisamque aequavit solo.[7] Sic nomen suum perpetuae commendavit memoriae; quippe, excisis Carthagine ac Numantia, ab alterius nos metu, alterius vindicavit contumeliis.[8]

B.   *Scipionis virtus et humanitas*

Quorum vero patres aut maiores aliqua gloria praestiterunt,[9] ii student plerumque eodem in genere laudis excellere, ut hic Paulli filius, Africanus Minor, in re militari. Quidam autem ad eas laudes quas a patribus acceperunt, addunt aliquam suam, ut hic idem Africanus eloquentia cumulavit bellicam gloriam.[10] Nam, vir omnibus bonis artibus atque omni virtute praeditus, omnium aetatis suae purissime locutus est.[11] Et certe non tulit ullos haec civitas aut gloria clariores aut auctoritate graviores aut humanitate politiores Publio Africano et amico eius Gaio Laelio,[12] qui secum eruditissimos homines ex Graecia palam semper habuerunt. Scipio enim tam elegans liberalium studiorum omnisque doctrinae et auctor et admirator fuit ut Polybium Panaetiumque, praecellentis ingenio viros, domi militiaeque secum habuerit.[13] Semper aut belli aut pacis artibus serviit; semper inter arma ac studia versatus, aut corpus periculis aut animum disciplinis exercuit.

1. A. **naturalis:** masc. nom. sing. adj. with *filius*.   B. **aedilitatem petens** = "although he was running only for the aedileship"; Lat. parts. are often best rendered in Eng. by a clause; compare 7 n. 6B. Scipio was elected consul in 148 (for 147) and assigned the African command by the assembly; this represents a slight difference from his adoptive grandfather Africanus, who as a private citizen (after his aedileship) was

given a proconsular *imperium* by the assembly in 210, but did not become consul until 205; see 12 pref.

2. **biennio ante:** for the abl. + adv. see 14 n. 3 (and 15 n. 16B).

3. A. **ullius ... gratia** = "on account of any injury of that period (i.e. committed in that period)"; *gratia* is abl. of cause defined by the gen. *ullius noxiae*, and this in turn is limited by the possessive gen. *eius temporis*.   B. **sustulit:** this perf. of the rare compound *sustollo* came to be used, with its past part. *sublatus*, for simple *tollo* because the perf. and part. of the latter, *tuli* and *latus*, were adopted for *fero*; *sustuli* is also used as perf. for the compound *suffero*. *Tollo* basically means "lift up" or "take away," but came to be used with varying connotations; that of "destroy," as here, is one of the most common.

4. **qua re ... clementiae** = "and by this deed (i.e. the destruction of Carthage) he made what had been (a memorial) of his grandfather's mercy a memorial of his own courage." In such comparisons, one or more words must often be repeated in Eng. where the Lat. clause omits them; so here *monumentum* must be supplied with *fuerat*. Africanus Maior could, of course, have destroyed Carthage after his victory over Hannibal at Zama (see 12 pref.), but instead he had urged the Romans to be merciful in their peace terms. The destruction of the city in 146 by Africanus Minor was perhaps a symptom of the increasing ruthlessness of Roman foreign policy in the 2nd cent., but Velleius regarded it rather as a result of Scipio's valor.

5. **tredecim annis post:** abl. + adv. as in n. 2 above.

6. A. **fortunae ... expertae:** the past. part. *expertae* of the deponent verb *experior* is used here with a passive meaning (compare 1 n. 6B); it modifies both preceding nouns, though agreeing grammatically only with the nearest. The phrase lit. means "the fortune and valor which had been experienced," but is best rendered in Eng. by two rel. clauses: "the (good) fortune which he had experienced and the valor which he had shown."   B. **respondit:** with the dat. here = "answered to, corresponded to," i.e. "repeated."

7. **aequavit solo** = "razed," lit. "made level with the ground"; *solo* is dat. sing. of the neut. noun *solum, -i*, after the idea of "likeness" in the verb.

8. **alterius ... alterius** = "of the one ... of the other."

9. A. **quorum vero ... ii** = "truly, those whose"; Lat. often postpones the antecedent, especially when the statement is indefinite or general, as here. Eng. idiom in such statements usually requires the antecedent to be placed immediately before the rel. pronoun.   B. **maiores** = "ancestors"; compare 15 n. 13B.   C. **aliqua gloria:** abl. of specification (respect), regularly used with expressions of excelling.   D. **praestiterunt:** the verb *praesto*, lit. = "stand before," acquired a variety of figurative meanings, among them "surpass, excel." With its synonym *excellere* just below, *in* + abl. is used for variety instead of a second abl. of specification.   E. **ii** = *ei;* compare *iisdem* = *eisdem* in 13 n. 10A.

10. **ut ... cumulavit:** for *ut* + ind. = "as" see 14 n. 5.

11. A. **artibus** = "qualities," as regularly when used of a person; contrast *belli aut pacis artibus* at the end of this passage.   B. **omnium ... suae** = "of all (the men) of his generation"; *omnium* is partitive gen. with the superlative adv. *purissime*; compare 11 n. 11A.   C. **aetatis:** the use of *aetas* as a synonym for *saeculum* or *tempora* is post-Augustan.

12. A. **tulit** = "has produced"; a frequent meaning of *fero*.   B. **gloria ... auctoritate ... humanitate:** abls. of specification with the comparative adjs.; compare n. 9C above.   C. **Publio Africano ... amico ... Gaio Laelio:** abls. of comparison; see 11 n. 1B (and 13 n. 3).

13. A. **auctor**: in classical Lat. *auctor* means "producer, supporter" in a number of contexts; here it means "promoter, patron (in a literary sense)." The meaning "author (of a book)" occurs, but is relatively infrequent. B. **Polybium Panaetiumque**: see pref. above. C. **praecellentis**: agrees with *viros*; for the masc. plur. acc. *i*-stem ending -*is* see 15 n. 14A. D. **ingenio**: abl. of specification; compare nn. 9C and 12B above. E. **domi militiaeque**: for the locs. and the meaning of this idiom see 13 n. 5A. F. **habuerit**: perf. subj. in a result clause, even though the sequence is secondary; compare 13 n. 6A (and 15 n. 5A). Both the imperf. and perf. subj. are used in past result clauses. The imperf. stresses the logical connection of cause and effect; the perf. emphasizes that the result was an actual or historical fact.

17

According to the Greek historian Polybius (see 16 pref.), the acquisition of Rome's overseas empire during the second century caused the breakdown of civic and private morality which, in turn, corrupted the balanced "mixed" constitution which he so admired. Modern historians agree that what has been called "The Fall of the Republic" or "The Roman Revolution" was the result of the problems and tensions created during the second and first centuries by the newly acquired empire. These problems have been variously identified as (1) *moral*: the corrupting opportunities for wealth and power offered to the senatorial and equestrian classes and the pauperization of the urban proletariat; (2) *military*: the gradual change in character of the Roman army from a citizen militia loyal to the state to a professional army, in part of citizens and in part of non-citizen allies, which looked to its generals for rewards; (3) *economic*: the elimination of the small citizen farmers and the increase of large estates owned by rich senators and worked by slaves, and also the emergence of an urban proletariat composed of landless veterans, freed slaves, and the other riff-raff which swelled the population of Rome, where there was no adequate employment for so large a population; and (4) *political and social*: the wide separation of rich from poor, leading to a new type of class conflict, the emergence of a group of rich financiers who did not enter public life by joining the senate and were therefore included in the equestrian class, the use of bribery, either directly or by such handouts as cheap grain and public entertainment, to buy the votes of the assemblies, and the increasing disregard on the part of both upper and lower classes among the Roman citizens of the rights of the more and more heavily burdened Italian allies and provincial subjects.

Among Roman historians, also, the fall of the Republic and the Romans' decline from the high standards of their ancestors were favorite topics. The extent to which the Romans thought of political problems in moral terms can be seen in the following passages. The first is from Sallust, a politician and historian somewhat younger than Caesar and Cicero, who wrote soon after Caesar's death in 44; see 63 pref. The second is from Velleius, and the third from the historian Tacitus, who wrote in the early second century A.D.

Rei publicae Romanae vitia

A. Igitur ante bella Punica domi militiaeque boni mores colebantur;[1] concordia maxima, minima avaritia erat;[2] ius bonumque apud eos non legibus magis quam natura valebat.[3] Iurgia, discordias, simultates cum hostibus exercebant, cives cum civibus de virtute certabant. In suppliciis deorum magnifici, domi parci, in amicos fideles erant. Duabus his artibus, audacia in bello, ubi pax evenerat aequitate, seque remque publicam curabant.[4]

Sed ubi labore atque iustitia res publica crevit,[5] reges magni bello domiti, nationes ferae et populi ingentes vi subacti,[6] Carthago, aemula imperi Romani, ab stirpe interiit,[7] cuncta maria terraeque patebant,[8] saevire fortuna ac miscere omnia coepit.[9] Qui labores, pericula, dubias atque asperas res facile toleraverant,[10] eis otium, divitiae, optanda alias, oneri miseriaeque fuere.[11] Igitur primo imperi, deinde pecuniae cupido crevit;[12] ea quasi materies omnium malorum fuere.[13] Namque avaritia fidem, probitatem, ceterasque artis bonas subvertit;[14] pro his superbiam, crudelitatem, deos neglegere, omnia venalia habere edocuit.[15] Haec primo paulatim crescere, interdum vindicari;[16] post, ubi contagio quasi pestilentia invasit, civitas immutata, imperium ex iustissimo atque optimo crudele intolerandumque factum.[17]

B. Potentiae Romanorum prior Scipio viam aperuerat, luxuriae posterior aperuit.[18] Quippe, remoto Carthaginis metu, sublataque imperii aemula,[19] non gradu sed praecipiti cursu a virtute descitum est, ad vitia transcursum.[20] Vetus disciplina deserta, nova inducta; in somnum a vigiliis, ab armis ad voluptates, a negotiis in otium conversa civitas.

C. Vetus ac iam pridem insita mortalibus potentiae cupido cum imperii magnitudine adolevit erupitque.[21] Nam rebus modicis aequalitas facile habebatur;[22] sed ubi, subacto orbe et aemulis urbibus regibusve excisis, securas opes concupiscere vacuum fuit,[23] prima inter patres plebemque certamina exarsere. Modo turbulenti tribuni, modo consules praevalidi,[24] et in urbe ac foro temptamenta civilium bellorum.

---

1.   A.   **igitur:** Sallust often begins sentences with *igitur*, which in Cicero is usually postpositive. In Sallust's usage it is not strictly logical, but transitional or resumptive after an interruption. It may be rendered freely "well, then," "to resume," "in short," etc. B.   **colebantur:** its subject is *boni mores*, but for the other plur. verbs in this paragraph "the Romans" or "our ancestors" must be supplied as subject.

2.   **concordia . . . avaritia:** Sallust often omits connectives, both "and" and "but," between words, phrases, or clauses; there are a number of instances of such asyndeton

(see 4 n. 5B) in the rest of this passage; compare 15 n. 8C. The sequence noun-adj.: adj.-noun produces the rhetorical arrangement called "chiasmus" (Greek, from the letter *chi*, written X), i.e. crossed or alternating order, a-b: b-a.

3. **bonum**: neut. sing. adj. used as a noun; = "the good" (in a philosophical sense).

4. A. **ubi pax evenerat**: used instead of *in pace* for variety. Sallust often avoids exact parallelism of phrase, but here balances the two parts in chiasmus, for which see n. 2 above.   B. **seque remque publicam**: *-que . . . -que* = *et . . . et* ("both . . . and"), rare in Cicero, is used in poetry and by the historians, especially when one or both of the items paired is a pronoun, as here *se*.

5. A. **sed ubi labore etc.**: the temporal clause extends through *patebant*; for the asyndeton see n. 2 above. The main clause is *saevire . . . coepit*.   B. **crevit**: from *cresco*. Verbs which denote the beginning or progression of an action ("inceptives" or "inchoatives") often have *-sco* in the pres. system; this element properly disappears in the perf. system, which represents actions as already accomplished.

6. A. **domiti . . . subacti**: supply *sunt*; Sallust frequently omits forms of *sum*.   B. **subacti**: agrees in gender with *populi*, the nearer of its two subjects; compare 16 n. 6A.

7. **imperi**: objective gen. with *aemula*, which is here (and in n. 19A below) an adj. used as a noun in apposition with *Carthago*; as an adj. *aemulus* is followed by the dat. In Lat. of the Republican period, the gen. sing. of nouns in *-ius* or *-ium* ended in a single *-ī*, though the accent of the nom. was retained, i.e. *impéri*. The uncontracted ending *-ii* became current in the Augustan age and is used in selections written by authors during the Empire.

8. **cuncta**: agrees in gender with *maria*, the nearer of the two nouns which it modifies; compare n. 6B above.

9. **miscere**: frequently pejorative; = "to disturb, to throw into confusion." In the conservative Roman view, the good state had a place for everyone and everyone should remain in his place.

10. **qui . . . eis**: for the postponement of the antecedent see 16 n. 9A.

11. A. **eis . . . oneri miseriaeque**: *eis* is dat. of reference (possession; compare 11 n. 9) and the *oneri miseriaeque* dats. "of purpose"; thus the two types of dat. constitute a "double dat.," as commonly with forms of *sum*; lit. = "to them . . . for a burden and a misery." However the dat. of purpose in this construction is best rendered in Eng. idiomatically, e.g. "were for them a burden and a misery" or "were burdensome and grievous to them."   B. **optanda alias** = "to be desired otherwise," or "at other times"; i.e. normally leisure and riches are desirable but for the Romans success made them a burden and misery. *Optanda* is neut. nom. plur. of the gerundive. It may be taken either as modifying the two previous nouns of different number and gender, or, since, unlike *cuncta* in n. 8 above, it would then agree fully with neither, it may be used as a neut. plur. noun in apposition with them, i.e. "(things) to be desired."   C. **alias**: adv.   D. **fuere** = *fuerunt*; see 15 n. 10; it recurs in the next sentence, as does *exarsere* = *exarserunt* in sel. C below.

12. **imperi . . . pecuniae**: objective gens. with *cupido*; this is the regular construction in Lat. with words expressing desire and is usually best rendered by "for . . ." rather than by "of"; compare 2 n. 3A.

13. **ea**: neut. nom. plur. referring to the concepts *imperi* (*cupido*), *deinde pecuniae cupido*; compare *optanda* in n. 11B above.

14. **artīs**: the manuscripts of Sallust show *-īs* rather than *-ēs* in the acc. plur. of *i*-stem nouns; compare for adjs. 15 n. 14A (and 16 n. 13C).

15. A. **superbiam . . . edocuit**: the four objects of *edocuit* are the two nouns in the acc. and the two objective infs.; each of the infs. in turn has an object in the acc.   B. **habere** = "to consider," as frequently, lit. "to hold (in the mind)"; it takes with its object

a qualifying adj.; = "to consider all (things) as for sale." For the variation in style compare n. 4A above.

16. A. **crescere ... vindicari:** historical infs. with their subject *haec* in the nom. plur.; the historical inf. is often used in rapid narration by Sallust and other historians instead of finite verbs.   B. **vindicari** = "were punished"; this verb, originally meaning "to be a legal defender (*vindex*) for" (as in 20 n. 13B), came to mean either "to protect" or, by protecting one person, "to punish" another or "to avenge" an act, as in 7 n. 13.

17. **immutata ... factum:** supply *est*; = "was changed ... became"; compare the omission of *sunt* in n. 6A above.

18. **prior Scipio ... posterior** = "the earlier Scipio ... the later (Scipio)." For the career of Scipio the Elder see sel. 12, and for that of the Younger see 16.

19. A. **sublata ... aemula:** abl. abs. explaining the preceding abl. abs. *remoto ... metu*; = "when a rival to the (Roman) empire had been destroyed."   B. **sublata:** past part. of *tollo* = "lift up" or "destroy"; see 16 n. 3B.   C. **imperii:** the gen. sing. is written here with *-ii* because Velleius wrote after Augustus; see n. 7 above.   D. **aemula:** adj. used as a noun (as in n. 7 above) and fem. because referring to Carthage. In this phrase, Velleius echoes that in Sallust's first sentence in the 2nd par. of sel. A above.

20. A. **gradu ... praecipiti cursu** = "step by step (or gradually) ... at a headlong pace, rapidly"; *gradu* and *cursu* are abls. of manner without *cum*.   B. **cursu:** often = "speed, pace" rather than "course."   C. **descitum est ... transcursum (est):** impers. pass.; see 10 n. 10D (and 12 n. 9B); *descisco* and *transcurro* are the regular terms used for soldiers deserting their own side and crossing over to the enemy; they are used metaphorically here.

21. A. **vetus ... cupido:** lit. = "the old and long since implanted in mortals desire for power"; since *insita* is a participle and is modified by the adv. *iam pridem* and has a dat. obj. *mortalibus*, it is best rendered by a rel. clause: "which has long been implanted in men"; compare 7 n. 6B (and 16 n. 1B).   B. **imperii:** for the ending see nn. 7 and 19C above.   C. **cum ... magnitudine:** abl. of accompaniment; = "together with."

22. A. **rebus modicis** = "in (lit. with) modest circumstances"; abl. of attendant circumstance; the underlying meaning of this abl. is either instrumental (= "by") or "sociative" (= "with").   B. **habebatur** = "was maintained"; contrast n. 15B above.

23. **securas ... fuit** = "it was possible (lit. free) to desire undisturbed wealth"; in Lat. the subject of *fuit* is the inf. *concupiscere*, and *vacuum* is a predicate adj. in agreement with the inf.

24. **modo ... modo** = "at one time ... at another"; a frequent meaning.

18

The moral failures discussed in the previous selection were especially prevalent among the ruling class of the Republic. Members of this class, called *nobiles*, were men who came from a narrow group of families within the senatorial order as a whole, families, both patrician and plebeian, who had had consular ancestors. Down to the last third of the second century, these families monopolized the consulship, with its opportunities for command, military glory, booty in slaves and treasure, and the government of wealthy provinces. Two plebeian members of the "nobility," the brothers Tiberius and Gaius Gracchus, were the first to break the stranglehold of the *nobiles*.

The motives of the Gracchi have been much debated both by the Romans and by modern scholars. It is likely, however, that the older, Tiberius, was an idealist with no thought of personal aggrandizement. He became tribune in 133, apparently with the support of a liberal group in the senate, and concentrated his attention on the recovery of public lands from rich senators, who regarded these lands as their own, although technically they held them on lease from the state. When the senate opposed his proposal to distribute this land in small allotments to landless citizens, Tiberius passed a bill directly through the assembly, contrary to the advice of the senate. This threat to the senate's authority further aroused the opposition of the wealthy. When Tiberius stood again for the tribunate of 132, he was murdered by a mob led by a cousin, the conservative Scipio Nasica, and his death seems to have been in some measure approved by his other cousin, Scipio Aemilianus. Nevertheless, the distribution of land appears to have continued at least for some years.

The following summary of Tiberius Gracchus' career comes from Velleius and Valerius Maximus.

Tiberii Gracchi vita et mors

Tiberius Gracchus, Tiberii Gracchi clarissimi atque eminentissimi viri filius,[1] P. Africani ex filia nepos,[2] tribunus plebis creatus est. Vir erat vita innocentissimus, ingenio florentissimus, proposito sanctissimus,[3] tantis denique adornatus virtutibus, quantas mortalis condicio recipit.[4] P. Mucio Scaevola L. Calpurnio consulibus, descivit a bonis;[5] promulgatisque agrariis legibus, summa imis miscuit[6] et in praeruptum atque anceps periculum adduxit rem publicam. Octavioque collegae pro bono publico rogationi intercedenti tribunatum abrogavit.[7] Tunc

triumviros agris dividendis coloniisque deducendis creavit se socerum-
que suum, consularem Appium, et Gaium fratrem admodum iuvenem.[8]

Deinde senatus a consule Mucio Scaevola convocatus censuit ut
consul armis rem publicam tueretur,[9] sed Scaevola negavit se quicquam
vi esse acturum.[10] At P. Scipio Nasica,[11] pontifex maximus, cum esset
consobrinus Ti. Gracchi, patriam cognationi praeferens, omnes hortatus est, qui salvam esse vellent rem publicam, ut se sequerentur.[12]
Tum optimates, senatus atque equestris ordinis pars melior et maior,[13]
et intacta perniciosis consiliis plebs inruere in Gracchum stantem in
area Capitolii cum catervis suis.[14] Is, fugiens decurrensque clivo
Capitolino, fragmine subsellii ictus, vitam, quam gloriosissime degere
potuerat, immatura morte finivit.[15] Postea Scipio Aemilianus a tribuno
Carbone interrogatus quid de Ti. Gracchi caede sentiret,[16] respondit
si is occupandae rei publicae animum habuisset, iure caesum.[17] Nihilo-
minus hoc initium in urbe Roma civilis sanguinis gladiorumque
impunitatis fuit.[18]

1. A. **Tiberii . . . filius:** the father of the Gracchi came from a plebeian family,
the Sempronii Gracchi, who had been "noble" (see pref.) at least since his grandfather,
also named Ti. Sempronius Gracchus, attained the consulship in 238. For the family see
the genealogical charts following sel. 15, and 10 n. 13c. The father of the Gracchi was
twice consul, as well as censor, and commanded both in Rome's eastern wars (see 15)
and in Spain (see 16). He was famous for his austere and honorable character; see 16
pref.   B. **clarissimi . . . eminentissimi:** these and the superlatives in the next sentence
are "polite" superlatives, regularly used in Lat. in complimentary references; they may
be translated by a simple positive.

2. **P. Africani ex filia:** see the genealogical charts following 15. According to tradition, Africanus in his old age betrothed his younger daughter Cornelia to Ti. Gracchus,
father of the Gracchi, but the marriage probably did not take place until after Africanus'
death in about 184. Cornelia was a woman of both character and culture, whose personality and letters were renowned after her death. She bore her husband twelve children,
nine of whom died young.

3. A. **vita . . . ingenio . . . proposito:** abls. of specification (respect) with the superlative adjs.; compare 16 n. 12B.   B. **proposito:** the neut. sing. part. of *propono* is often
used as a noun; it means lit. "(something) put before," but must be variously rendered
according to the context; here, "in (his) intention(s)."

4. A. **quantas . . . recipit** = "as human nature permits"; *quantus*, when correlative
with *tantus*, may regularly be translated simply by "as."   B. **recipit:** often means
"allow, admit," or the like.

5. A. **P. Mucio . . . consulibus:** for dating by consuls see 14 n. 4B. In this idiom *et*
is very often omitted between the names of the consuls when both are specified. Scaevola,
the more important of the two (see below), was one of several Scaevolas who were
eminent jurists.   B. **descivit a bonis** = "he deserted the conservatives"; for the connotations of *descisco* see 17 n. 20c.   C. **bonis:** frequently used at least as early as

Cicero for the "right-minded," i.e. patriotic and conservative men in the state; compare n. 13A below.

6. A. **summa imis miscuit** = "he turned everything topsy-turvy," lit. "mixed high with low." Both *summa* and *imis* (from *imus*) are neut. plur. adjs. used as nouns (compare 17 n. 3); *imis* is probably abl. of accompaniment without *cum*, since the dat. with *misceo* is mostly poetical or late. B. **miscuit:** for the connotation see 17 n. 9.

7. A. **Octavio:** dat. of reference (called "separation") after a verb implying "to deprive." B. **rogationi:** dat. after the concept of "resisting" in *intercedenti*; *rogatio* is a technical equivalent to *lex*, derived from the idiom *rogare populum* or *plebem*, used of a magistrate proposing either a law or the election of a succeeding magistrate to the assembly; see further 56 n. 11B. C. **intercedenti** = "when he interceded"; for rendering a part. in Eng. by a clause see 7 n. 6B (and 17 n. 21A); *intercedo* was the technical term for a magistrate blocking the action of another magistrate, particularly for a tribune interposing his veto. D. **abrogavit** = "abrogated," a technical term, lit. = "ask away," i.e. to ask the people to take away an office or cancel a law; compare n. B. above. Tiberius' step of terminating his colleague's tenure of office by vote of the assembly was unprecedented; for the normal procedure see 7 n. 15A.

8. A. **agris . . . deducendis:** for this use of the dat. of purpose see 7 n. 2A. *Coloniam deducere* was the regular term for founding (lit. "to lead out") a colony. The inclusion of the founding of colonies seems to be a confusion of Tiberius' bill, for land allotments only, with the later program of his brother Gaius, which included colonies; see 19 pref. B. **socerum . . . Appium:** Tiberius had married Claudia, the daughter of Appius Claudius Pulcher, consul in 143, a descendant of the decemvir Appius Claudius, for whom see sel. 7. Senators who had been consuls (*consulares*) retained a great deal of prestige and influence. C. **admodum iuvenem** = "(although he was) merely a youth."

9. **ut . . . tueretur:** substantive clause of purpose, explaining what the senate "resolved," which is a regular meaning of *cerno* or *decerno*. Since the senate was advisory, the consul did not have to follow its resolve and Scaevola refused to put into effect this so-called *senatus consultum ultimum*, or resolve by the senate that the consuls should proclaim martial law. Whether in fact on this occasion the senate passed such a resolve is uncertain; in 121 it did so against Gaius and the then consul Opimius pursued him with a posse and slew him; see 19 pref.

10. **negavit:** *nego* is regularly used in preference to *dico non*, i.e. Lat. puts the negative with the verb of saying rather than in the indirect discourse.

11. **P. Scipio Nasica** (Serapio): a son of Scipio Nasica Corculum (a cousin of Africanus Maior) and Africanus' elder daughter Cornelia; see the genealogical charts following sel. 15. Though he held the religious office of *pontifex maximus* (for which see 14 n. 15), he had no civil magistracy and acted as a private citizen (*privatus*), without support of the senate or authority of the people, in leading the mob which slew Tiberius; contrast on Gaius in n. 9 above. Shortly after, Nasica left Rome to avoid prosecution for murder.

12. A. **vellent:** imperf. subj. in a rel. clause of characteristic; it indicates time contemporary with that of the main verb; see 9 n. 8E (and contrast 13 n. 6C). It may be translated simply "who wished," but the implication is "who (were such as) would wish." B. **ut se sequerentur:** an indirect command after *hortatus est*; see 4 n. 11A (and 15 n. 14B); *se* is reflexive to the subject of the introductory verb *hortatus est*, as regularly in this construction.

13. A. **optimates:** like *boni* above (n. 5C), a political tag applied during the 1st cent. to the conservative "noble" leaders and their followers among the senators and knights. There were many senatorial families whose members seldom rose above the praetorship and who hence were not *nobiles*, yet who generally followed a conservative (optimate) line in politics; see Cicero's discussion in sel. 76. B. **senatus:** probably nom., connected by *atque* with *pars*, rather than partitive gen. like *equestris ordinis*, both limiting

pars. Thus taken, "the senate and the better and larger part of the equestrian order" are closely connected in apposition with *optimates*, and this in turn is connected by *et* with *plebs*, these last two then being subjects of *inruere*. If all three: senate, better part of the equestrians, and unspoiled plebs, were in apposition with *optimates* as the only subject of *inruere*, the connectives would probably have been *et . . . et*.

14.   A.   **intacta . . . plebs** = "(that part of) the plebs which had been untouched by (his) wicked plans," i.e. "which had not been persuaded by (his) radical program." *Plebs* came in the Ciceronian period to be used generally for the urban lower class, rather than in its traditional distinction from "patrician," for which see 7 pref.   B. **consiliis:** abl. either of means or of separation; *intactus* generally has a simple abl. but occasionally *ab* or *de*, which would suggest separation as the basic concept.   C. **inruere** = *inruerunt*; see 15 n. 10 (and 17 n. 11D).   D.   **area Capitolii . . . clivo Capitolino:** the open area on the Capitoline Hill (see 8 n. 9C) in which stood the temple of Jupiter (see 12 n. 4) and other monuments and the steep street which led down from it to the Forum; *clivo* is abl. of means ("way by which").   E.   **cum catervis suis** = "with his followers"; *suis* refers to Gracchus, the subject of the participle *stantem*, and not to the main subject *optimates etc.*; contrast n. 12B above.

15.   A.   **subsellii** = "of a (magistrate's) bench"; these stood on the Capitoline and were presumably broken up and used as clubs in the scuffle.   B.   **degere** = *de-agere*; for the idiom compare 5 n. 16B.   C.   **potuerat:** pluperf. because it denotes a potentiality which existed antecedent to the action of the perf. ind. *finivit*, i.e. "could have spent." Usually the perf. is preferred in this use of *possum* in the ind. to express a potential or unreal condition; see 10 n. 12A.

16.   A.   **Scipio Aemilianus:** for his career see sel. 16. He was Tiberius' cousin and brother-in-law (see genealogical charts following 15), but his conservatism apparently outweighed his family feeling, as did Nasica's (see above), and he opposed Tiberius' political actions. He died suddenly in 129 after a speech opposing the land commission. The cause of his death was never ascertained. Though he may well have died a natural death, gossip suggested that he had been murdered either by his political opponents or by his wife, Tiberius' sister Sempronia.   B.   **Carbone:** C. Papirius Carbo, tribune in 131, was a strong supporter of Tiberius Gracchus.

17.   A.   **si . . . habuisset** = "if he had intended to seize the state," lit. "had had the intention of seizing"; *animum habere* = "to intend" is a common idiom. This was the standard charge made by the optimates against any popular leader. Scipio's direct speech would have used the perf. ind. *habuit* in a past condition stating a simple fact; here the pluperf. subj. *habuisset* is used because it is in a subordinate clause in the indirect statement (*eum*) *iure caesum* (*esse*); compare 14 n. 2B.   B.   **iure** = "rightly," a common idiom; the abl. of manner is used adverbially; see 5 n. 3A.

18.   A.   **in urbe Roma:** with *urbs* and similar words a proper noun is usually in apposition rather than in the gen.   B.   **gladiorum impunitatis** = "of unpunished murder," lit. "of freedom of punishment of swords"; for the use of an abstract noun and a gen. see 15 n. 4.

19

Gaius Gracchus, younger than Tiberius by nine years, was elected to the tribunate for 123. He undertook a much more ambitious program, in which idealism, fraternal vengeance, and political ambition were combined. In broad outline: Gaius revived the distribution of land to the poor. He also provided for the urban proletariat by having the state procure grain from the provinces, especially from Sicily, either by tithes or by purchase, and sell it in Rome at a fixed price, so as to prevent speculation by private grain merchants. He likewise proposed overseas colonies, but the poor were unwilling to leave the fleshpots of Rome for the uncertainty and hard work of new settlements. In order to finance these various projects, Gaius enacted a law by which the censors were required to put up for auction, to companies formed by rich equestrian bankers of Rome, the privilege of collecting the taxes in the recently established (129) province of Asia, formerly the kingdom of Pergamum. He further set the financiers against the senators by transferring membership on the jury courts, particularly on that for the trial of rapacious governors (*quaestio de rebus repetundis*, see 12 n. 14A), from senators, who tended to protect their peers, to equestrians, men who would be hard on a governor who so impoverished a province that it could not meet its taxes.

Gaius held a second tribunate in 122. He failed of election to a third for 121, in part because his recent proposal to extend Roman citizenship to the Italian allies was unpopular with the people as well as with the senate. Lucius Opimius, one of the consuls for 121, suspected Gaius of attempting an armed coup. He secured from the senate a decree advising the consuls to see to it that the state received no harm, and pursued Gaius and his associates with an armed posse. To escape arrest, Gaius had himself killed by a faithful slave. His followers, however, were ruthlessly slaughtered. This was the first certain occasion on which the senate, rather than revive the early practice of appointing a dictator to cope with such an emergency, advised the consuls to impose "martial law" by a decree which came to be called a *senatus consultum ultimum*: see 18 nn. 9 and 11.

The following passage is from Velleius.

Gaii Gracchi tribunatus et exitus

Decem deinde interpositis annis, qui Ti. Gracchum, idem Gaium fratrem eius occupavit furor,[1] tam virtutibus eius omnibus quam huic errori similem,[2] ingenio etiam eloquentiaque longe praestantiorem. Qui cum, summa quiete animi, civitatis princeps esse posset,[3] vel vindicandae fraternae mortis gratia vel praemuniendae regalis potentiae,[4] eiusdem exempli tribunatum ingressus est.[5] Sed longe maiora et acriora petens, dabat civitatem omnibus Italicis,[6] dividebat agros, novis coloniis replebat provincias, iudicia a senatu transferebat ad equites, frumentum plebi dari instituebat.[7] Nihil immotum, nihil tranquillum, nihil quietum, nihil denique in eodem statu relinquebat;[8] quin alterum etiam continuavit tribunatum.[9]

Hunc L. Opimius consul, persecutus armis, morte adfecit. Nam Gracchus profugiens, cum iam comprehenderetur ab iis, quos Opimius miserat, cervicem Euporo servo praebuit,[10] qui non segnius se ipse interemit quam domino succurrerat. Ut Ti. Gracchi antea corpus, ita Gaii, mira crudelitate victorum, in Tiberim deiectum est;[11] crudelesque mox quaestiones in amicos clientesque Gracchorum habitae sunt.[12]

Hunc Ti. Gracchi liberi, P. Scipionis Africani nepotes, viva adhuc matre Cornelia, Africani filia, viri optimis ingeniis male usi, vitae mortisque habuere exitum.[13] Qui si civilem dignitatis concupissent modum,[14] quidquid tumultuando adipisci gestierunt, quietis obtulisset res publica.[15]

1. A. **qui . . . furor:** the antecedent of *qui* is *idem furor*; compare 16 n. 9A (and 17 n. 10).   B. **Gracchum:** the object of *occupaverat*, to be understood from *occupavit* in the main clause; compare 4 n. 9B (and 11 n. 10).   C. **furor:** lit. = "fury, passion," but often denotes radical ideas or actions.

2. **tam . . . similem** = "(Gaius) as like to all his (i.e. Tiberius') virtues as to this error" (i.e. his revolutionary *furor*); *similis* is regularly followed by the dat. The Eng. idiom requires a considerable change, e.g. "who resembled (his brother) not only in his abilities but also in his radicalism."

3. A. **qui cum . . . esse posset** = "and although he could have been"; compare 10 nn. 12A and B.   B. **summa quiete animi:** abl. of manner (without *cum*) + gen.; = "without effort on his part, peacefully," lit. "with the greatest quiet of mind." *Animus* is often used idiomatically in Lat. with a delicate shade of meaning which is hard to reproduce directly in Eng.; compare 18 n. 17A and *mens* in 12 n. 5.   C. **civitatis princeps** = "the foremost (man) in (lit. of) the state"; the adj. *princeps* is often used as a noun to designate outstanding statesmen and leaders of public opinion; compare 1 n. 1G (and contrast 11 n. 12B).

4. A. **vindicandae . . . potentiae:** both gerundive phrases are in the gen. depending on *gratia* (abl. of cause) and indicate purpose; compare *ad* + an acc. and gerundive in 5 n. 9A (and 7 n. 13).   B. **vindicandae** = "avenging"; compare 7 n. 13 (and 17 n. 16B). C. **praemuniendae** = "paving the way to"; for the accusation of kingly ambitions compare 18 n. 17A.

5. **eiusdem exempli:** gen. of quality; = "of the same sort"; compare 6 n. 9.

6. A. **dabat:** this and the following five imperfs., joined without connectives (in asyndeton; see 4 n. 5B and 17 n. 2), are, as often, used of an action attempted or about to take place in past time when something else occurred, often something that blocked the action; the imperf. can thus have a "conative" meaning; = "he was in the process of giving" or "trying to give," etc. Gaius' bill to extend citizenship to the Italian allies

(*socii Italici*) did not pass the assembly since the Roman citizens were jealous of their own privileged status. The other bills were opposed by the senate but enacted by the assembly.   B. **civitatem** = "citizenship." *Civitas* is the material state (citizens, houses, etc.) or its members' rights in it; *urbs* is the geographical city; *res publica* is often somewhat more abstract: the pattern of the state, the commonwealth, or the constitution, although it also has a more concrete meaning of "civil affairs, political life, etc."; see n. 14A below.

7.   **frumentum . . . instituebat** = "he was instituting the distribution of grain (lit. that grain be given) to the plebs." Velleius apparently thought that Gaius set the precedent of free distribution of grain to the poor; actually, he arranged for grain to be sold by the state at a fixed price; see 20 n. 11c.

8.   **immotum . . . tranquillum . . . quietum:** adjs. in agreement with *nihil*, in contrast with the frequent use of the gen. of the neut. adj. with words like *nihil*, for which see 11 n. 14A. As noted there, *nihil* + the gen. = "no truth, etc."; here, as indicated by the final *nihil . . . in eodem statu*, the adj. is predicate, = "he left nothing undisturbed," rather than "no undisturbed thing."

9.   A. **quin:** from *qui* (abl.) + *ne* or *non*; it may be used as a coordinating (as well as a subordinating), contrasting, or emphatic conjunction; here = "rather" or "on the contrary."   B. **continuavit:** the perf. ind. emphasizes a single act completed in past time, as against *relinquebat*, which is imperf. of attempted action in past time, for which see n. 6A above. Gaius succeeded where Tiberius had failed, in continuing his tenure of the tribunate by re-election. It is uncertain whether in Tiberius' time this was actually illegal, or whether the senate's objection was simply because continuation in the tribunate was contrary to custom. If illegal, then the law must have been changed before Gaius' re-election; if contrary to custom, it is hard to understand why the senate made no similar protest against Gaius. A law seems to have existed forbidding successive tenures of the magistracies other than the tribunate as well as fixing the order of and the intervals between tenure of them. This reflected the desire of the office-holding *nobiles* to ensure that the offices circulated among themselves, and that no one person could, by long tenure of office, become independent of the collective control of the senate.

10.   **cum iam comprehenderetur . . . cervicem praebuit** = "when he was about to be arrested . . . he held out (his) neck" (i.e. for his head to be cut off); for the force of the tenses see nn. 6A and 9B above. Romans often enlisted the aid of a slave, a freedman, or a friend to assist them in committing suicide.

11.   A. **ut . . . ita** = "as . . . so"; *ut* and *ita* are often used correlatively to express either parallelism, as here (and in 28 n. 5A), or concession, as in 23 n. 7B.   B. **ita Gaii:** supply *corpus*; compare 16 n. 4.

12.   **quaestiones:** here = "judicial inquiries"; not, as usually, specifically the jury courts, for which meaning see pref.

13.   A. **hunc . . . vitae mortisque . . . exitum** = "this (kind of) end of life, this (kind of) end in death"; object of *liberi habuere*. The first word of the sentence, *hunc*, modifies the last, *exitum*, an extreme example of unusual word order for rhetorical effect, called in Greek "hyperbaton" (= a going over).   B. **liberi:** for the possible derivation see 9 n. 14A (and 15 n. 16A).   C. **habuere:** for the ending see 15 n. 10 (and 18 n. 14c). D. **exitum:** from *exitus*, = "departure" or "result," which should be distinguished from *exitium*, = "destruction," for which see 5 n. 13D. *Exitum* is here somewhat clumsily modified by an objective gen. *vitae*, = "departure from life," and a defining gen. *mortis*, = "the exit (that was) death."

14.   A. **qui si . . . concupissent . . . obtulisset res publica** = "but if they had desired . . . the Republic (i.e. an ordinary political career in it; see n. 6B above) would have offered." Past contrary to fact (unreal) conditions in Lat. regularly have the pluperf.

subj. in both the protasis and the apodosis; compare 9 n. 6D.   B. **concupissent . . . gestierunt:** contracted; see 1 n. 4B (and compare 13 n. 9); *qui* (=*et ei*) serves as subject of both.   C. **civilem dignitatis . . . modum** = "(only) a degree of eminence suitable to a citizen"; *dignitas* often refers to political eminence, reputation, or esteem.

15.   A. **tumultuando:** a gerund in the abl. used as an abl. of means; = "by causing disturbances."   B. **quietis:** Lat. frequently uses a simple adj. where a demonstrative pronoun which it modifies may readily be understood; compare the similar use of numerals in 6 n. 16A; here it = "to (them, being) quiet." It is dat. of indirect object with *obtulisset* and the antecedent of *qui* at the beginning of the sentence; see n. 14A above.

20

Gaius' death was followed by a decade of conservative reaction during which the various Gracchan reforms were either liquidated or reversed. Indeed, the Gracchi had been activated toward reform by only one aspect of the crisis which faced the Roman state, that of the decrease in the number of small citizen farmers. They, like Polybius, were blind to the major issue, the inadequacy of the city-state constitution, in which ultimate authority lay with an assembly of townsfolk, to govern a far-flung empire. Instead of curing the ills of the state, they opened the way for less principled men, whether conservatives or demagogues, to abuse the constitution for their own ends and to subvert the control which the senatorial nobles felt was their right to exercise. The senate, in resorting to violence to oppose the Gracchi, likewise created a dangerous precedent.

Roman literary tradition is, for the most part, hostile to the Gracchi. The first of the following passages, composed from Cicero's writings, represents the ordinary conservative position. Cicero and other optimate senators praised the Gracchi only in political speeches aimed at winning popular support. In the second passage the historian Sallust, an adherent of Caesar, is sharply critical of the nobles who had opposed the Gracchi, though he acknowledges that the Gracchi too were at fault.

A. *Ciceronis de Gracchis sententia*

Tiberius Gracchus, Publi filius et Tiberi Gaique pater, tam diu laudabitur dum memoria rerum Romanarum manebit.[1] At eius filii nec vivi probabantur a bonis, et mortui numerum obtinent iure caesorum.[2] Tiberius enim convellit statum civitatis; sed qua gravitate vir! qua eloquentia! qua dignitate![3] Nihil ut a patris avique Africani praestabili insignique virtute, praeterquam quod a senatu desciverat, deflexisset.[4] Secutus est Gaius; quo ingenio! quanta vi! quanta gravitate dicendi! Ut dolerent boni non illa tanta ornamenta ad meliorem mentem voluntatemque esse conversa.[5]

Hi duo clarissimi, ingeniosissimi, amantissimi plebis Romanae viri plebem in agris publicis constituere conati sunt, qui agri a privatis antea possidebantur.[6] Nam agrariam Tiberius legem ferebat.[7] Grata erat populo;[8] fortunae constitui tenuiorum videbantur. Nitebantur

contra optimates,[9] quod et discordiam excitari videbant et, cum
locupletes possessionibus diuturnis moverentur, spoliari rem publicam
propugnatoribus arbitrabantur.[10] Postea frumentariam legem Gaius
ferebat; iucunda res plebi; victus enim suppeditabatur large sine
labore.[11] Repugnabant boni, quod et ab industria plebem ad desidiam
avocari putabant et aerarium exhauriri videbant.

B.   *Sallustii de Gracchis sententia*

Ubi primum ex nobilitate reperti sunt, qui veram gloriam iniustae
potentiae anteponerent, moveri civitas et dissensio civilis, quasi permixtio terrae, oriri coepit.[12] Nam postquam Ti. et C. Gracchus,
quorum maiores Punico atque aliis bellis multum rei publicae addid-
erant, vindicare plebem in libertatem et paucorum scelera patefacere
coepere,[13] nobilitas—noxia atque eo perculsa—Gracchorum actionibus
obviam iit;[14] et primo Tiberium, dein paucos post annos eadem
ingredientem Gaium ferro necavit.[15] Et sane Gracchis cupidine
victoriae haud satis moderatus animus fuit.[16] Sed bono vinci satius est
quam malo more iniuriam ulcisci.[17]

1.   A. **Publi ... Gaique:** for the gens. with single -*i* see 17 n. 7.   B. **tam diu ...
dum** = "as long as"; prospective *dum* takes the fut. ind.; contrast 6 n. 8.

2.   **numerum ... caesorum** = "are numbered among those justly slain," lit. "obtain
the rank of (those) justly slain"; *numerus* is often used collectively as equivalent to the
Eng. "rank, position." For the thought see 18 n. 17A and for *iure* see 18 n. 17B.

3.   A. **qua ... dignitate:** no verb is expressed in these exclamations. Lat. says "a man
of what dignity!"; Eng. "what a dignified man!" Compare *quo ... dicendi* below;
for the abl. of description see 13 n. 4.   B. **dignitate:** personal; contrast 19 n. 14C.

4.   A. **nihil:** placed for emphasis before the clause in which it belongs as a negative
adv. (stronger than *non*) with *deflexisset*.   B. **ut ... deflexisset:** the result clause
derives from the connotation of the preceding exclamations; "a man of what dignity" =
"a man of such dignity that ..."   C. **desciverat:** ind. even though dependent on a
subj. because it states what Cicero himself asserted to be true (compare 10 n. 10C and
15 n. 3D); its connotation is therefore not contrary to fact, as against *nihil ... deflexisset*. For the meaning of *descisco* see 17 n. 20C (and 18 n. 5B).   D. **deflexisset:**
pluperf. rather than imperf. subj. because of the "contrary to fact" implication of
praeterquam quod; "he would not have fallen away from ... except that he had separated ..." = "unless he had separated etc."

5.   A. **ut dolerent:** result clause derived from the preceding exclamations; see n. 4B
above.   B. **boni:** for the conservative connotation see 18 n. 5C.   C. **illa ... conversa** = "that those great talents (lit. such great adornments) had not been directed
toward a better purpose"; *dolere* and other verbs of emotion may take an objective inf.
clause to indicate that over which one grieves, etc.   D. **mentem:** for the meaning here
compare 12 n. 5.

6. A. **clarissimi . . . amantissimi:** for the "polite" superlatives see 18 n. 1B.   B.
amantissimi plebis Romanae: a regular idiom for "democratic."   C. **qui agri:** for the
repetition of the antecedent within a rel. clause see 8 n. 7A.

7. **ferebat** = "was trying to pass"; *legem ferre* is the regular idiom for "to pass a
law"; here and in *Gaius ferebat* below the imperf. is conative (see 19 n. 6A), whereas the
other imperfs. indicate simply continued action in past time.

8. **grata:** agrees with *lex*, understood from *legem*; if it modified the whole preceding sentence, it would be neut.

9. **nitebantur contra optimates** = "the optimates (see 18 n. 13A) resisted," lit.
"strove against," Tiberius' agrarian law; *contra* is here the adv., not the prep.

10. A. **quod et . . . videbant et . . . arbitrabantur:** the inds. again (see n. 4C above)
give the reasons as Cicero's, not those merely of the optimates; so also in *quod . . .
videbant* at the end of the paragraph.   B. **cum . . . moverentur:** a causal clause, not
temporal.   C. **locupletes:** from *locus + ple-*, a stem meaning "full"; it here connotes
the rich landowning senators.   D. **moverentur:** here followed by a simple abl. of
separation like a verb of depriving such as the following *spoliari*, for which see 4 n. 2B
(and 15 n. 15A).

11. A. **frumentariam legem:** see 19 pref. (and n. C below).   B. **iucunda res:** either
understand *erat*, or take in apposition either with the whole previous sentence or simply
with the *lex*; compare n. 8 above.   C. **victus** (*-ūs*) = "food, sustenance." Cicero here
views Gaius' provision for sale of grain by the state (see 19 pref. and n. 7) in the light
of later developments, when other demagogues steadily reduced the official price in the
face of generally rising market prices and charged the deficit to the treasury (*aerarium*).
Finally Clodius, as tribune in 58, made the distribution a free dole. Cicero, an embittered
opponent of Clodius, delivered the speech from which this statement is drawn in 56.

12. A. **qui . . . anteponerent:** a rel. clause of characteristic with an indefinite antecedent "some" implied in the subject of *reperti sunt*; compare 18 n. 12A. Sallust refers
to the Gracchi as men who, though *nobiles*, placed patriotism ahead of class interest.
B. **quasi permixtio terrae** = "like an earthquake," lit. "as if a mixing up of the earth."

13. A. **rei publicae:** dat., not gen. with *multum*.   B. **vindicare:** takes the acc. of the
person "vindicated," and *in* + the acc. (compare 5 n. 13C) for the aim of the "vindica-
tion"; i.e. here "to set the plebs free" or "to establish the plebs in liberty." With the
meaning here contrast 7 n. 13 (and 17 n. 16B).   C. **paucorum** = "of the nobles";
pauci (lit. = "the few") was often used by the opponents of the optimates (see n. 9 above)
instead of *boni* (see n. 5B above), which the optimates applied to themselves. The concept
was derived from Greek political experience, in which democracies were often under-
mined by oligarchical cliques (Greek *hoi oligoi* = Lat. *pauci*).

14. A. **noxia . . . perculsa** = "guilty (i.e. of the *scelera* just mentioned) and on that
account (i.e. because of their sense of guilt) panicky"; both fems. modify *nobilitas*, which
is a general fem. abstract used collectively for persons; see 8 n. 9A (and 10 n. 17).   B.
eo: neut. abl. sing. of the demonstrative pronoun, referring to the thought behind the adj.
noxia; it is abl. of cause rather than of means and is almost an adv. = "therefore."   C.
perculsa: for the meaning here see 15 n. 3A.   D. **actionibus:** the plur. of this fem. abstract noun is used like Eng. "actions" (as against "acts" or "deeds") and is equivalent
to "conduct." The sing. *actio* may mean "a doing" or "a performing," as *actio gratiarum*
= "a rendering of thanks"; it is also commonly used for pleading a case at law.   E.
obviam iit = "opposed"; this idiom = "meet," either with hostility, as here, or without any implication; it is followed by a dat. of reference (disadvantage).   F. **obviam:**
originally the preposition *ob* + the acc. *viam* = "in the way"; it became adverbial, as in
this idiom; then the Romans made from it an adj. *obvius, -a, -um.*

15. **eadem:** neut. acc. plur. as object of *ingredientem* used transitively; = "entering
(upon) the same (policies)."

16. A. **Gracchis . . . fuit**="the Gracchi had immoderate ambition," lit. "to the Gracchi there was a spirit not at all moderate enough"; for the dat. of reference (possession) see 11 n. 9 (and compare 17 n. 11A). Sallust does not charge the Gracchi with ambitions to seize the state, only with excessive ambition to see their policies succeed; contrast n. 17B below.   B. **cupidine:** abl. either of specification or of cause and limited by the objective gen. *victoriae* (see 17 n. 12); = "in (or, because of) their desire for (lit. of) victory."   c. **animus:** for the meaning here see 19 n. 3B (and compare *mentem* in n. 5D above).

17. A. **bono:** dat. of reference; = "to (or for) a good man"; here *bonus* is used in a moral, not a political, sense; contrast n. 5B above.   B. **vinci:** subject of *est*; infs. used as verbal nouns are considered neut. sing., hence *satius* (= "better"); compare 2 n. 2B. Sallust felt that it would have been better for the optimates to be beaten by the Gracchi than to set a precedent of political murder, which led to so much violence during the later Republic. In fact he exaggerates, since the measures of the Gracchi had already been passed and their murders were due not to an unwillingness to give in but to fear that they would take over the state by violence; see 18 n. 17A (and contrast n. 16A above).

21

In the years following the death of Graius Gracchus in 121, during which the conservatives in the senate regained control, Rome became involved in a war in Africa occasioned by the ambitious intrigues of a Numidian prince called Jugurtha. Though at first Jugurtha secured the support of Rome for his claims by wholesale bribery of Roman senators, public opinion at Rome finally forced the senate to declare war on him in 111. In 109, one consul, a member of the noble family of the Metelli, received the command against Jugurtha. Later writers either admire this Metellus, as do the conservatives Cicero and Velleius, or, like the anti-noble Sallust, somewhat belittle him.

Among Metellus' officers was Gaius Marius, a capable and ambitious man. He was born in 157 at Arpinum, a small hill town sixty miles southeast of Rome, whence Cicero was to come in the next generation; see prefs. to 31 and 64. No previous member of Marius' family had held a magistracy at Rome and thereby entered the senate. Marius had served under Scipio Aemilianus at Numantia in 134/3 (see 16 pref.) and had progressed slowly through the tribunate and, in 115, the praetorship under the patronage of the Metelli. Normally such a man, not of "noble" lineage (see 18 pref.), could not expect to secure the consulship (compare n. 11B below) and thus be recognized as a "new man" (*novus homo*) or the first of a nonsenatorial family to achieve the highest magistracy, as Cato the Elder had done (see 13 pref.) and as Cicero was later to do; see 32 pref. Indeed, Metellus tried to prevent Marius from leaving his staff to campaign for the consulship in 108 but, as the following account shows, Marius rose superior to the optimate opposition and was elected for 107.

This account of Marius' attainment of the consulship comes from Sallust's historical monograph on the war against Jugurtha in North Africa called the *Bellum Iugurthinum.*

Marius consulatum petit

Bello Iugurthino,[1] Uticae forte C. Mario, legato Metelli, per hostias diis supplicanti,[2] magna atque mirabilia portendi haruspex dixit.[3] At illum iam antea consulatus ingens cupido exagitabat,[4] ad quem capiendum, praeter vetustatem familiae, alia omnia abunde ei erant:[5] industria, probitas, belli magna scientia; animus militiae ingens, domi modicus, libidinis et divitiarum victor, tantum modo gloriae avidus.[6] Ubi primum tribunatum militarem a populo petit,[7] plerisque faciem eius ignorantibus, factis notus per omnis tribus declaratur.[8] Deinde ab eo magistratu alium post alium sibi peperit.[9] Tamen is ad id tempus consulatum appetere non audebat.[10] Etiam tum alios magistratus plebs, consulatum nobilitas inter se per manus tradebat.[11] Novus nemo tam clarus neque tam egregiis factis erat, quin is indignus illo honore haberetur.[12]

Igitur ubi Marius haruspicis dicta eodem intendere videt quo cupido animi hortabatur,[13] ab Metello petendi gratia missionem rogat;[14] cui quamquam virtus, gloria, atque alia optanda bonis superabant,[15] tamen inerat contemptor animus et superbia, commune nobilitatis malum.[16] Itaque primum, commotus insolita re, mirari eius consilium et quasi per amicitiam monere ne tam prava inciperet.[17] Postquam haec atque alia talia dixit neque animus Mari flectitur, respondit,[18] ubi primum potuisset per negotia publica,[19] facturum sese quae peteret.[20] Ac postea saepius eadem postulanti fertur dixisse ne festinaret abire;[21] satis mature illum cum filio suo consulatum petiturum.[22] Is eo tempore contubernio patris ibidem militabat, annos natus circiter viginti.[23] Quae res Marium, cum pro honore quem adfectabat tum contra Metellum, vehementer accenderat.[24] Ita cupidine atque ira, pessimis consultoribus, grassari;[25] neque facto ullo neque dicto abstinere, quod modo ambitiosum foret.[26]

1. **bello Iugurthino:** abl. of time when; see 12 n. 13A.

2. A. **Uticae:** loc.; this city, lying just north of Carthage on the coast, was made the capital of the new province of Africa by the Romans after they destroyed Carthage in 146; see sel. 16 A. B. **forte:** for this adverbial abl. see 5 n. 3A (and 14 n. 8). C. **Mario:** dat. of indirect object, primarily after *dixit* but also after *portendi*, for which see n. 3A below. D. **legato:** dat. in apposition with *Mario*. Marius was qualified to be a *legatus* (see 12 n. 13B) since he had been praetor in 115. E. **Metelli:** here gen.; contrast the dat. in 12 n. 13B. Quintus Caecilius Metellus received the command against Jugurtha as consul in 109 and continued as proconsul until replaced by Marius, who was elected consul for 107 and given the command by the assembly against the wish of the senate. Metellus assumed the surname *Numidicus* from this war, conducted chiefly in Numidia, Jugurtha's kingdom. F. **diis:** dat. after *supplicanti*; see 12 n. 15D. G. **supplicanti:** a Lat. part. is often best rendered in Eng. by a clause (compare 7 n. 6B and 18 n. 7C), i.e. "to Marius . . . when he was sacrificing." The occasion for this sacrifice was either to secure good omens at the opening of the campaign in 108 or to render thanks for the successful conclusion of the campaign in 109.

3. A. **portendi:** pres. pass. inf. in indirect discourse after *dixit.* B. **haruspex:** a specialist who interpreted the omens from an examination of the entrails, particularly the liver, of sacrificed animals. The Romans had derived this "science" from the Etruscans; compare 52 n. 3.

4. A. **consulatus:** objective gen. sing. with *cupido*; see 17 n. 12 (and 20 n. 16B). B. **exagitabat** = "had been obsessing (lit. stirring up)." Lat. regularly uses an imperf. for

a continued action in the past which lasts up until the time being discussed, whereas Eng. uses a pluperf. in this situation.

5. A. **ad quem capiendum:** for this construction indicating purpose see 5 n. 9A (and 7 n. 13).   B. **alia . . . erant** = "he had all other (qualities) in abundance"; for the dat. of reference (possession) with *esse* see 11 n. 9 (and 20 n. 16A). The qualities are specified in the list that follows, first by a series of nouns, then by a series of adjs. modifying the last noun, *animus*. For the variation in style compare 17 n. 4A.

6. A. **militiae . . . domi:** locs.; see 13 n. 5A (and 16 n. 13E).   B. **victor:** nouns of agency in *-tor* are frequently used adjectivally, perhaps as a development from apposition; since *victor* here figures in a series of adjs. modifying *animus*, it probably also serves as one; = "(a mind) master over."   c. **tantum modo** = "only (lit. only so much)"; a common expression, sometimes written as one word.   D. **gloriae avidus:** for the gen. compare n. 4A above.

7. A. **tribunatum militarem:** for this office see 14 n. 4A. Marius was probably elected a military tribune sometime between his service as a legionary at Numantia in 134 (see sel. 16 A) and his election as a tribune of the plebs in 119.   B. **petit:** historical pres., which may be translated as past; similarly *declaratur, videt, rogat*, and *flectitur* below; compare 5 n. 5.

8. **factis:** abl. of means (or cause) with *notus*; = "by (because of) his deeds."

9. **peperit:** from *pario*, which lit. = "bear, produce," but often, as here, has the secondary meaning "obtain" or "acquire."

10. **audebat:** for the tense see n. 4B above.

11. A. **plebs:** supply *tradebat* from the next clause and here render it "gave, awarded." *Plebs* is used inaccurately for *populus* (see 18 n. 14A); technically, the *plebs* (in the *concilium plebis*) elected the tribunes, and the *populus* (plebeians and patricians) in the tribal assembly (*comitia tributa*) elected the military tribunes, quaestors, and aediles. But possibly by Marius' day these two assemblies were no longer distinguished in practice. Magistrates with the supreme power (*imperium*), namely praetors and consuls, were elected by the whole *populus* in the military assembly of the centuries (*comitia centuriata*).   B. **consulatum . . . tradebat** = "the nobility (= nobles; see 20 n. 14A) passed the consulship from hand to hand among themselves." The nobles did not bypass elections to the consulship, as Sallust might seem to say, but saw to it that only members of their own group were proposed as candidates.

12. A. **quin** = *qui non* (see 19 n. 9A) = *ut is non*; a rel. clause of characteristic denoting result; render "no new man was so famous . . . that such a man (*is* is expressed for emphasis) was held worthy," lit. "was not held unworthy."   B. **honore** = "magistracy"; see 8 n. 8c. The adjs. *dignus* and *indignus* take an abl. of specification; lit. = "unworthy in respect to that office"; however, this abl., like others (compare 4 n. 2B), is best rendered in Eng. by "of."

13. A. **igitur:** for its opening position see 17 n. 1A.   B. **eodem . . . quo** = "to the same course of action as," lit. "to the same place whither"; advs. of place from the demonstrative and rel. pronouns; the origin (case) of the ending *-ō* is uncertain.   c. **cupido animi** = "his own desire"; on the rendering of *animi* as "own" compare 19 n. 3B; the gen. is here possessive, not objective as in n. 4A above.

14. A. **petendi:** gen. gerund with the abl. *gratia*; compare 19 n. 4A. *Peto* was the regular term for running for office; compare *tribunatum . . . petit* above. If no office is specified, as here, the consulship is meant.   B. **missionem** = "discharge." Candidates for office were required to canvass in person. Marius presumably returned to Rome to stand for the consulship in the fall of 108.

15. A. **cui:** dat. of reference with *superabant*; compare 11 n. 9 (and 20 n. 16A). It serves as a connective, = "for him"; see 4 n. 4A (and 10 n. 16A). But it also carries on to *inerant* (= "in him there were"), which takes either a dat. as a verb compounded with *in-* or *in* + an abl.   B. **optanda bonis** = "(qualities) to be desired by good men";

for *optanda* compare 17 n. 11B.   C. **bonis**: for its connotation here compare 20 n. 17A. The dat. of reference is used instead of the abl. of agent with several constructions: the pass. periphrastic (see 14 n. 10), the gerundive (as here), and often the perf. pass.; though usually called a dat. of agent, it means rather "as far as good men are concerned."

16.   **contemptor**: for the adjectival use of nouns of agency in -*tor* see n. 6B above; this = "a scornful (or, proud) mind (or, spirit)."

17.   A. **mirari . . . monere**: historical infs. (see 17 n. 16A), with Metellus in the nom. (note *commotus*) supplied as subject for both from his mention in an oblique case in the preceding sentence.   B. **mirari** = "express (here, expressed) surprise," as often.   C. **per amicitiam**: for the use of *per* + acc. to express manner or means see 5 n. 16A.

18.   **dixit . . . respondit**: Metellus is the subject of the perfs. *dixit* and *respondit*, but in the intervening clause the subject changes to *animus* and the tense to the historical pres. Such variation is characteristic of Sallust's style; compare n. 5B above.

19.   A. **ubi . . . publica** = "as soon as duty allowed him (to)," lit. "when first he could through public business"; for the use of *per* see n. 17C above.   B. **potuisset**: Metellus continues as subject; it is subj. in a subordinate clause which is an integral part of the indirect statement dependent on *respondit*; compare 14 n. 2B (and 18 n. 17A) and contrast the ind. in 15 n. 3D (and 20 n. 4C).

20.   A. **facturum**: supply *esse* to form the main inf. of the indirect statement after *respondit*.   B. **sese**: a reduplicated form of *se* (acc. or abl.), here acc. subject of the inf. and referring to Metellus.   C. **quae**: rel., not interrog. (contrast 13 n. 10B); understand as its antecedent *ea* as object of *facturum* (*esse*); = "(those matters) which he (i.e. Marius) was seeking"; compare 20 n. 12A.   D. **peteret**: subj. "of integral part"; see n. 19B above.

21.   A. **postulanti**: agrees with *Mario*, to be understood as the indirect object of *dixisse*; for the part. compare n. 2G above.   B. **fertur**: for the meaning see 4 n. 13. C. **ne festinaret** = "that he should not be in a hurry." In a command in indirect discourse the subj. regularly replaces the imperative of direct discourse; the regular sequence of tenses (here secondary) is followed.

22.   **satis . . . petiturum**: still part of the indirect statement introduced by *dixisse*; *suo* therefore refers to the subject of *fertur dixisse*, i.e. Metellus.

23.   A. **is**: Metellus' son.   B. **contubernio patris** = "in the quarters of his father"; abl. of attendant circumstance; see 17 n. 22A. A young man of good family often got his first military experience by being on the staff and sharing the quarters of his father or a relative; see 5 n. 2C.   C. **annos . . . viginti**: for this way of expressing age see 10 n. 1A. Since the youth would probably have had to complete his forty-second year before entering on the consulship (see 12 n. 10B), Metellus was insultingly telling Marius, who was already at least forty-eight, to wait another twenty-two years before aspiring to the consulship.

24.   **cum . . . tum** = "not only . . . but also" (as often).

25.   **grassari . . . abstinere**: historical infs. of which Marius is the subject; see n. 17A above.

26.   A. **quod . . . foret** = "provided only that it (lit. which only) might further his ambition"; *quod* introduces a rel. clause of characteristic equivalent to *dum modo* introducing a clause of proviso.   B. **modo** = "only"; compare n. 6C above.   C. **foret** = *esset*; compare *fore* = *futurum esse*.

22

During the years (111–105) of the Jugurthine War in Africa, Italy itself was threatened from the north. Two Germanic tribes, the Cimbri and the Teutoni, originating just south of Denmark, migrated into Gaul and, as happened to such migratory groups, collected a large number of discontented and footloose Germans and Gauls. They inflicted severe defeats on Roman forces in the recently (121) created province of Narbonese Gaul, the southern or Mediterranean section of modern France. They then split into two groups; the Teutoni approached Italy from the west, along the Riviera, while the Cimbri made a great circuit through Switzerland to enter through the Brenner Pass.

As was customary, the commanders first appointed to repel the Germans were chiefly nobles. In this crisis, however, the successive defeats suffered by the noble consuls and Marius' position as hero of the hour for his victory over Jugurtha combined to overthrow again the conservative leadership of the senate. Marius was elected consul for the second time for 104 and for every year thereafter until his sixth consulship in 100, an unprecedented series. In 102 he defeated the Teutoni at Aix-en-Provence, and in the following year he joined Q. Lutatius Catulus, who had been his colleague in 102, to annihilate the Cimbri near Vercellae in northern Italy. He thus rescued Italy from the threat of barbarian invasions for several centuries.

Nevertheless, when peace was restored, the senate prevented Marius from getting land for his veterans and from being elected to another command. He then (in 100) allied himself with two demagogues, the tribune L. Apuleius Saturninus and the praetor C. Servilius Glaucia, who had undertaken a program of more than Gracchan socialism. But this maneuver proved unsuccessful, for Marius himself was eventually disgusted by their policies of using systematic mob violence to achieve their plans. Finally, he accepted a commission from the senate to restore order and allowed the two to be slain in a riot.

The following passage is composed from Sallust and Velleius.

Marii consulatus multiplicati

Iugurtha Sullae vinctus traditur,[1] et ab eo ad Marium deductus est. Per idem tempus adversum Gallos ab ducibus nostris, Q. Caepione et Cn. Manlio, male pugnatum.[2] Itaque metu Italia omnis contremuit. Nam usque ad nostram memoriam Romani sic habuere alia omnia virtuti suae prona esse, se cum Gallis pro salute, non pro gloria, certare.[3] Sed postquam bellum in Numidia confectum esse et Iugur-

tham Romam vinctum adduci nuntiatum est,[4] Marius consul absens
factus est,[5] et ei decreta provincia Gallia. Isque Kalendis Ianuariis
magna gloria consul triumphavit.[6] Et ea tempestate spes atque opes
civitatis in illo sitae.[7]

Nam cum Germanae gentes, quibus nomen Cimbris ac Teutonis erat,
complures consules fudissent fugassentque[8] atque multos celeberrimi
nominis viros trucidassent, populus Romanus non alium repellendis
tantis hostibus magis idoneum imperatorem quam Marium ratus est.
Tum multiplicati consulatus eius. Tertius in apparatu belli consumptus;
quarto trans Alpis circa Aquas Sextias cum Teutonis conflixit;[9] quinto
citra Alpis ad Vercellas in campis, quibus nomen erat Raudiis,[10] ipse
consul et proconsul Q. Lutatius Catulus fortunatissimo decertavere
proelio; caesa aut capta amplius centum milia hominum.[11] Hac
victoria videtur meruisse Marius, ne eius nati rem publicam paeniteret,
ac mala bonis repensasse.[12] Sextus consulatus veluti praemium ei
meritorum datus, quo Servilii Glauciae Saturninique Apuleii furorem,
rem publicam lacerantium atque gladiis et caede comitia discutientium,
consul armis compescuit,[13] hominesque exitiabilis morte multavit.

1. A. **Sullae:** Lucius Cornelius Sulla was a young patrician senator and noble who
was serving under Marius as quaestor (107) and proquaestor (106–105) and who in
the latter years conducted the treacherous negotiations by which Jugurtha was betrayed
to the Romans. See further 24, 26, and 27.   B. **vinctus** = "in fetters" (lit. "bound"),
past part. from *vincio* (not *vinco*).

2. A. **adversum . . . pugnatum:** Caepio, a noble and conservative, was proconsul in
Gaul in 105 and refused to join forces with the consul Manlius, a *novus homo*; see 21
pref. In consequence, the armies of both were wiped out by the Cimbri near Orange
(*Arausio*).   B. **Gallos:** to make his implied reference to the Gallic sack of 390 (387;
see sel. 8), Sallust identifies the Gauls and Germans.   C. **pugnatum:** supply *est*;
impersonal pass. with an abl. of agent, instead of *duces nostri male pugnaverunt*; see 10
n. 10D (and 12 n. 9B).

3. A. **sic . . . esse** = "thought thus, that all else was ready to yield to their bravery";
for *habeo* = "consider" see 17 n. 15B.   B. **prona:** lit. = "leaning forward," but this
adj. is often used metaphorically.   C. **esse, se cum:** for the omission of "but" see
13 n. 11B (and 17 n. 2).

4. **bellum . . . confectum esse** = "the war was successfully concluded"; a common
idiom. The basic meaning of *conficio* is "make through to the end" or "complete"; as
in the case of *utor* (see 14 n. 16B), the best Eng. equivalent depends on the nature of the
object.

5. **absens:** election to the consulship without personal canvass was almost unprecedented; see 21 n. 14B.

6. **Kalendis Ianuariis** = Jan. 1; see 8 n. 6. In early Rome consuls entered on office
on March 15 (the beginning of spring), but in 153 the date was advanced to Jan. 1 to

permit a consul to get to Spain in time to command a spring campaign. The opening of the civil year then remained fixed at Jan. 1, which in consequence is still New Year's Day. Marius therefore triumphed on the first day of his second consulship in 104; for his first in 107 see sel. 21.

7. **ea tempestate** = "in this crisis"; *tempestas* basically meant "time, season, weather"; then it was used specifically for bad weather, i.e. a storm, either literal (see 10 n. 14B) or, as here, metaphorical.

8. A. **Cimbris ac Teutonis**: dats. agreeing with the dat. of reference (possession) *quibus*, and not, as in Eng., in the predicate nom. in apposition with "name"; a common construction with *nomen est alicui*; see 23 n. 13B.   B. **complures etc.**: see pref. and n. 2A above.

9. A. **quarto . . . quinto** (*consulatu*): abls. of time within which.   B. **circa Aquas Sextias** = "near (round about) Aix-en-Provence," a town in the French Maritime Alps; for this battle and the one below near Vercellae see pref.

10. A. **ad Vercellas** = "near Vercellae"; for *ad* with the name of a town see 3 n. 6A. B. **Raudiis**: for the dat. see n. 8A above. The battle is sometimes known by this name.

11. **amplius**: after *amplius* and *plus, quam* is ordinarily omitted before numbers.

12. A. **ne . . . paeniteret** = "that the republic should not regret his birth," lit. "that it should not repent the republic of him having been born"; the *ne* clause is substantive, serving as the object of *meruisse*.   B. **eius . . . publicam**: verbs of feeling like *paenitet* are impersonal in Lat. and take the gen. of the cause of the feeling (*eius nati*) and the acc. of the person affected (*rem publicam*).   C. **mala bonis repensasse** = "to have counterbalanced (his later) bad (deeds) by (these) good (ones)"; *repensasse* is the contracted (see 1 n. 4B and compare 19 n. 14B) perf. act. inf. of the intensive *repenso, -are*, formed on the stem of the perf. pass. part. of *rependo, -ere, repensus*.

13. A. **quo**: abl. of time within which, referring back to *consulatus*; compare n. 9A above.   B. **Saturninique Apuleii**: his name was L. Apuleius Saturninus (see pref.) but in Lat. the order of proper names is often inverted. For the gens. in *-ii* see 17 n. 19C. C. **furorem**: for the meaning see 19 n. 1C.   D. **lacerantium . . . discutientium**: pres. parts., gen. plur. in agreement with both *Glauciae* and *Saturnini*; they are best rendered as rel. clauses; see 7 n. 6B (and 18 n. 7C). The gangsterism of Glaucia and Saturninus shows the danger of the methods used by the Gracchi when adopted by men of less idealistic aims; see 18–20.

23

Tension mounted in Rome during the nineties, both because of continued demagogic attacks on the privileges of the conservatives and because of growing discontent among Rome's non-citizen Italian allies at the ever heavier burdens and slights put upon them by the Romans. In 91, Livius Drusus the Younger as tribune put forward legislation aimed at relieving both causes of discontent, but the conservatives nullified his laws and assassinated him. Thereupon, in 90, the Italian allies broke into open revolt in what was called the Italic or the Social War, from the Latin word for ally, *socius*. The Romans soon extended citizenship to the allies and by 88 the bulk of the revolt either was suppressed or had collapsed.

The following passage is composed from Florus, who made a summary of Livy in the time of Hadrian (A.D. 117–138), and Velleius.

Bellum Sociale vel Italicum

Sociale bellum vocetur licet, ut extenuemus invidiam, si verum tamen volumus, illud civile bellum fuit.[1] Quippe, cum populus Romanus Etruscos et Latinos Sabinosque sibi miscuerit, corpus fecit ex membris[2] et ex omnibus unus est. Itaque cum ius civitatis, quam viribus auxerant, socii iustissime postularent,[3] quam in spem eos cupidine dominationis Drusus erexerat,[4] postquam ille domestico scelere oppressus est, eadem fax, quae illum cremavit, socios in arma et expugnationem urbis accendit.[5] Quid hac clade tristius? Quid calamitosius?

Quippe, L. Caesare et P. Rutilio consulibus, abhinc annos centum viginti,[6] universa Italia arma adversus Romanos cepit. Quorum ut fortuna atrox, ita causa fuit iustissima;[7] petebant enim eam civitatem, cuius imperium armis tuebantur.[8] Id bellum amplius trecenta milia iuventutis Italicae abstulit.[9] Clarissimi autem imperatores fuerunt Romani eo bello Cn. Pompeius, Cn. Pompeii Magni pater;[10] C. Marius, de quo praediximus;[11] L. Sulla, anno ante praetura functus;[12] Q. Metellus, Numidici filius, qui meritum cognomen Pii consecutus erat.[13]

Tam varia atque atrox fortuna Italici belli fuit, ut per biennium continuum duo Romani consules, Rutilius ac deinde Cato Porcius, ab
hostibus occiderentur,[14] exercitus populi Romani multis in locis
funderentur, utque ad saga iretur diuque in eo habitu maneretur.[15]
Paulatim deinde, recipiendo in civitatem qui arma non ceperant aut
deposuerant maturius, vires refectae sunt, Pompeio Sullaque et Mario
fluentem procumbentemque rem populi Romani restituentibus.[16]

1. A. **vocetur licet** = "although it may be called." *Licet* is often used to introduce a
wish, expressed by an independent (coordinate or "paratactic") hortatory subj., namely
"it is permitted, may you do so and so." This developed into a concessive sense, "granted
that" or "although." The independent subj. is normally retained and *licet* often follows
it (as here), although *ut* is used occasionally. In this sentence, *licet* might keep the basic
meaning "it is permitted," i.e. "one may," and if so, a semicolon might be preferable
to the comma after *invidiam*: "one may call . . .; if, however, we wish . . ."   B. **verum**
. . . **volumus:** supply *dicere*, implied in *vocetur*.

2. A. **miscuerit:** here not pejorative; contrast 17 n. 9 (and 18 n. 6B).   B. **corpus**
. . . **membris** = "it (*populus Romanus*) made a single body out of (separate) limbs." The
reference is to Rome's early incorporation of neighboring peoples into her citizenship, a
precedent which she had ignored during the 2nd cent.

3. A. **ius civitatis, quam** = "the right of citizenship (in that state) which." There is a
conflation of the two concepts covered by *civitas*: "citizenship" and "state"; see 19
n. 6B.   B. **iustissime:** by the end of the Republic, the possession of citizenship by all
inhabitants of Italy as the result of the Social War was recognized as proper, so that
iustissime presumably reflects Livy's text as condensed by Florus.

4. A. **quam in spem:** monosyllabic preps. are often put between their noun and its
adj., *cum* regularly so.   B. **cupidine dominationis:** abl. of cause with an objective gen.;
compare 20 n. 16B. Livy's sources, closer to the Social War and closer in tone to the
optimate point of view, were presumably responsible for the charge that Drusus, like
the Gracchi, was seeking demagogic power for himself. In fact, he, like them, may well
have been sincere; see 18 n. 17A.

5. A. **fax:** lit. = "torch," but the word is often used metaphorically of anything
which incites or causes ruin. Here the image is of a fire spread from the torch which
kindled Drusus' funeral pyre.   B. **urbis:** i.e. Rome; see 15 n. 13A.

6. A. **L. Caesare . . . consulibus:** L. Julius Caesar and P. Rutilius were consuls in
90; for this method of dating see 14 n. 4B (and 18 n. 5A). Caesar (related, but not closely,
to Julius Caesar) was the author of the first law by which citizenship was extended to
those of the allies who had not revolted. Two tribunes of 89 then passed the *lex Plautia
Papiria* by which any allies who surrendered within a short time would also receive
citizenship. This law brought back into the Roman fold all the revolting *socii* except the
Marsi, a strong tribe in central Italy.   B. **abhinc . . . viginti:** Velleius dedicated his
history to M. Vinicius on the occasion of his consulship in A.D. 30, just 120 years after
90 B.C.

7. A. **quorum:** must refer to the Italians (implied in *Italia*), not to the Romans; =
"and . . . their"; for the use of a rel. pronoun as a connective see 4 n. 4A (and 21 n. 15A).
B. **ut . . . ita** = "as . . . so," i.e. "although . . . yet"; *ut* and *ita* are here used correlatively
to express concession; compare 19 n. 11A (and 28 n. 5A).

8. A. **eam civitatem, cuius:** see n. 3A above.   B. **tuebantur:** for the imperf. where
Eng. uses a pluperf. see 21 n. 4B. In the similar sentence above, the pluperf. (*auxerant*)

is used because the increase of the state is regarded as a single action; in *tuebantur* the continuity of protection by the allies is stressed.

9. **amplius:** for the omission of *quam* see 22 n. 11.

10. A. **Romani:** predicate adj. with *clarissimi imperatores*; = "the most famous commanders on the Roman side were etc." B. **Cn. Pompeius:** surnamed *Strabo*, consul in 89. He was a ruthless, self-seeking man who betrayed the optimate cause to Marius and Cinna in 87 (see 25) by not moving quickly enough to the defense of Rome. His son, Pompey "the Great" (see 29 pref.), saved him from assassination by the Marians, but he died soon after, probably in 86.

11. **de quo praediximus** = "whom I have already mentioned," lit. "about whom I have spoken before." This expression (usually in the "editorial we," as here) is often used by Roman writers to remind the reader of a person or subject discussed earlier. Part of Velleius' account of Marius is included in 22; see also 24 and 25.

12. A. **L. Sulla:** see 22 n. 1A. B. **praetura functus:** *fungor* is often used for holding a magistracy; it is a deponent verb and takes an abl. (of means).

13. A. **Numidici:** the Metellus whom Marius replaced in the command of the Jugurthine war; see 21 n. 2E. He went into voluntary exile in 100 rather than take an oath which Saturninus and Glaucia (see 22 pref. and 22 n. 13D) required of all senators to support their demagogic legislation. His son secured his recall in the following year and thus earned the epithet *Pius*; see the next note. *Pietas*, a prime Roman virtue, was not religious piety in the modern sense, but a feeling of obligation, sometimes toward the gods, but just as often toward one's family or country. B. **cognomen Pii:** see the preceding note. After *nomen* or *cognomen*, Velleius and later authors often put the name or epithet in the "defining" gen. (as here); Cicero generally puts it in apposition (particularly if in the nom.); when the person is in the dat., e.g. *nomen ei erat*, Livy and Sallust put the name in dat. apposition with the person rather than in nom. apposition with *nomen* or *cognomen*; compare 22 n. 8A.

14. A. **per biennium continuum** = "in two successive years," lit. "through a biennium"; for *per* + acc. used instead of the acc. of extent of time see 5 n. 16A. B. **Rutilius . . . Porcius:** for Rutilius see n. 6A above. L. Porcius Cato, consul in 89, was a grandson of Cato the Elder. For the inverted order of his name compare 22 n. 13B.

15. A. **utque ad saga iretur** = "and that (*ut* + *-que*) the country went to war," lit. "it was gone to military cloaks"; for the impersonal pass. of a verb of motion see 12 n. 9B. B. **saga:** the neut. acc. plur. is used here to indicate that everybody put on military cloaks, contrary to the usual Lat. practice of using the sing. when each individual wears (or has) only one of the objects mentioned. It is here used by "metonymy" (Greek; = one name for another) for "war"; compare the frequent use of the fem. sing. *toga* for peace, as in 27 n. 13B.

16. **Pompeio Sullaque et Mario:** the first two are closely connected by *-que* as the consuls for 88; *Mario* (*cos.* VII in 86; see 25 pref.) is distinguished from them by *et* as their successor in defeating the revolt. This Pompeius is not Strabo (n. 10B above) but Q. Pompeius Rufus, no relative, who was put to death in 87 by the troops of Strabo when sent to take over command of them.

24

During this same period Rome was threatened in the east by Mithridates, king of Pontus, a small kingdom on the Black Sea. In 88 Mithridates swept through Asia Minor with the full support of the Greek and native populations. An eloquent testimony of the hatred which these people felt toward Roman rule is furnished by the massacre organized by Mithridates in 88, in which 80,000 Italians (both Romans and allies) are said to have been slaughtered in a single day.

The south Italians and the Romans were both eager for Roman rule to be maintained in Asia Minor. Hence the Romans quickly made citizenship available to the Italians (see 23 n. 6A) and ended the Social War in order to move against Mithridates. Unfortunately, at this point there was an internal crisis. Marius had long sought for himself a foreign command (see 22 pref.), but in 88 the command against Mithridates was assigned by the senate to one of the consuls, Sulla; see 23 n. 16. Marius, now aging, violent, and headstrong, wrested the command from him by a bill which the tribune Sulpicius Rufus passed through the tribal assembly. Thereupon Sulla collected his troops, marched on Rome, and drove Marius into exile.

The following passage is composed from Velleius and Florus.

Bellum civile primum, a Marianis atque Sulla gestum

Per ea tempora Mithridates[1]—Ponticus rex, bello acerrimus, virtute eximius, aliquando fortuna, semper animo maximus, consiliis dux, miles manu, odio in Romanos Hannibal[2]—occupata Asia necatisque in ea omnibus civibus Romanis, cum terribilis Italiae quoque videretur imminere,[3] sorte obvenit Sullae Asia provincia.

Hoc deerat unum populi Romani malis, ut iam ipse intra se parricidale telum domi stringeret.[4] Initium et causa belli inexplebilis honorum Marii fames,[5] quippe qui decretam Sullae provinciam Sulpicia lege sollicitaret.[6] Sed, impatiens iniuriae, statim Sulla legiones circumegit et urbi agmen infudit;[7] arcemque Capitolii, quae Poenos quoque, quae Gallos etiam evaserat, quasi captivam victor insedit.[8]

Deinde duodecim auctores novarum pessimarumque rerum, inter quos Marius cum filio et P. Sulpicio, urbe exturbavit;[9] ac, lege lata, exsules fecit.[10] Sulpicium adsecuti equites in Laurentinis paludibus iugulavere,[11] caputque eius erectum et ostentatum pro rostris, velut omen imminentis proscriptionis, fuit.[12] Marius nudus ac limo obrutus, oculis tantum modo ac naribus eminentibus,[13] extractus harundineto circa paludem Maricae, in quam se, fugiens consectantis Sullae equites, abdiderat,[14] iniecto in collum loro, in carcerem Minturnensium iussu duumviri perductus est.[15] Ad quem interficiendum missus cum gladio servus publicus, natione Germanus, qui forte ab imperatore eo bello Cimbrico captus erat,[16] ut agnovit Marium, magno eiulatu expromens indignationem casus tanti viri,[17] abiecto gladio, profugit e carcere. Tum cives, ab hoste misereri paulo ante principis viri docti,[18] instructum eum viatico conlataque veste in navem imposuerunt. At ille, adsecutus circa insulam Aenariam filium, cursum in Africam direxit inopemque vitam in tugurio inter ruinas Carthaginis toleravit,[19] ita ut Marius aspiciens Carthaginem, illa intuens Marium, alter alteri possent esse solacio.[20]

1.   **per ... Mithridates:** this sentence begins as if Mithridates was to be the main subject, but instead, after a series of nouns and adjs. descriptive of him and two abls. abs., he becomes the subject of the dependent clause *cum ... imminere*; the short main clause is the concluding *sorte ... provincia.*

2.   A. **manu** = "in actual combat, hand-to-hand fighting"; it is abl. of specification, like the other abls. in the series *bello ... odio*; compare 18 n. 3A.   B. **odio ... Hannibal:** Hannibal had long since become a symbol of enmity toward Rome and of treachery; see 11.   C. **in Romanos:** for this use of *in* + acc. see 5 n. 13c (and 10 n. 1B).

3.   **terribilis:** an adj. modifying *Mithridates*, but best translated as an adv. with *imminere*; see 11 n. 12A (and 15 n. 8B).

4.   A. **ipse:** i.e. *populus Romanus.*   B. **parricidale:** adj. from *parricidium*, which primarily meant "murder of a father" but extended to the murder of a near relative and then of a fellow citizen; here render "a murderous weapon."   C. **stringeret** = "should unsheathe"; the regular meaning of *stringo* with a word meaning "weapon."

5.   A. **inexplebilis ... fames** = "Marius' insatiable hunger for office"; the gens. are respectively objective (see 17 n. 12 and 21 n. 4A) and possessive.   B. **honorum:** for the meaning see 8 n. 8c (and 21 n. 12B).

6.   A. **quippe qui ... sollicitaret** = "for of course he attempted (to get)"; a rel. clause of characteristic expressing cause, reinforced (as often) by *quippe.*   B. **Sulpicia lege:** abl. of means. Roman laws often took their adjectival definition from the gentile name of the man (normally consul or tribune; compare 23 n. 6A) who brought them before an assembly; they might also be called by the subject, as *lex agraria* in the 2nd par. of 20A. P. Sulpicius Rufus deserted the optimate party when he became tribune in 88 and passed a series of demagogic measures, including this one. For his death see below.

7.   A. **iniuriae:** objective gen. with the adj. *impatiens*, which modifies *Sulla.*   B. **urbi:** i.e. Rome (as in 15 n. 13A and 23 n. 5B); it is dat. after a verb compounded with *in-.*

8. **Poenos ... Gallos:** for *Poenus* = "Carthaginian" see 11 n. 14c. Hannibal had twice marched to the walls of Rome, but withdrew without attacking; see 10 n. 14. The Gauls captured the rest of the city in 390 (387), but the citadel (*arx*) held out; see 8.

9. A. **duodecim ... exturbavit:** Sulla continues as subject of *exturbavit*, of which *auctores* is object.   B. **novarum ... rerum** = "of (a) new and very bad (state of) affairs," i.e. "of this worst of revolutions." For the conservative Roman, *novae res*, lit. = "new things," connoted revolution.   C. **pessimarum:** *pessimus* may often be rendered "this worst of" rather than as a simple adj.   D. **inter quos Marius:** supply *erat*.   E. **urbe:** see n. 7B above; it is abl. of separation ("place from which") without a prep. because of *ex*- compounded in the verb.

10. **lege lata:** for the idiom *legem ferre* see 20 n. 7.

11. **Laurentinis paludibus** = "in the Laurentine marshes." Laurentum (see 2 n. 2c) was connected with the myth of Aeneas' landing in Italy. It lay near the sea close to the mouth of the Tiber, a swampy area in antiquity. Sulpicius was presumably trying to escape by ship.

12. A. **rostris:** the speakers' platform in the Forum; see 14 n. 6B. It became customary to expose the heads of public enemies here.   B. **proscriptionis:** for Sulla's proscriptions see 26 pref.   C. **fuit:** the punctuation in the text regards this as the perf. pass. auxiliary with *erectum et ostentatum*; equally, the parts. may be adjectival and *fuit* may be the main verb with *velut omen etc.* as a predicate nom.: "his head, posted ...., was as if an omen ...."

13. **tantum modo:** for the meaning see 21 n. 6c.

14. A. **harundineto:** abl. of separation; = "from a thicket of reeds" (*harundines*). B. **circa paludem Maricae** = "close to the swamps of Marica," which lay near the coastal town of Minturnae, between Rome and Naples, whence Marius hoped to escape, as he eventually did, by boat to Africa.   C. **in quam:** the acc. of place to which is used, because in Lat. *abdo* involves the idea of motion.

15. **Minturnensium iussu duumviri** = "by order of the duumvir of the Minturnians." The two chief magistrates of a Roman colony, parallel to the consuls at Rome, were called either *duoviri* or *duumviri*.

16. A. **ab imperatore eo** = "by him (i.e. Marius) when he was commander."   B. **bello Cimbrico:** for this abl. of time when see 12 n. 13A (and 21 n. 1); for the war see 22.

17. A. **ut agnovit** = "when he recognized"; *ut* + the ind. often = "when"; contrast 14 n. 5.   B. **expromens ... casus** = "expressing (his) indignation at the misfortune"; *casus* is an objective gen.

18. A. **paulo ... viri:** object of *misereri*, which takes the gen.; = "a man who had been a leader (in the state) a little while before."   B. **principis:** for the meaning of this adj. compare 1 n. 1G (and 19 n. 3C).   C. **docti** = "having been taught"; it modifies *cives* as a simple (not adjectival) past part. and takes the complementary inf. *misereri*. In thus reversing the orders of their duumvir, the citizens of Minturnae risked Sulla's anger.

19. A. **insulam Aenariam:** the island Ischia, at the northern corner of the Bay of Naples.   B. **Carthaginis:** after the sack and cursing of the site by Scipio Aemilianus in 146 (see sel. 16 A), no extensive reoccupation of Carthage occurred until Julius Caesar founded a colony there in 44. Gaius Gracchus had sought to colonize the site in 122 (compare 19 pref.), but the optimates blocked him by stirring up the people's fear of the curse.

20. A. **illa:** i.e. *Carthago*. Though *Carthaginem* is nearer than *Marius* in the sentence, *haec* is not used because the author had his attention fixed on Marius, so that Carthage is the more remote of the two in his thought.   B. **alteri ... solacio:** double dat.; see 17 n. 11A.

25

After defeating the Marian forces, Sulla had to set out on the campaign against Mithridates. The two consuls for the year 87 were Gnaeus Octavius and L. Cornelius Cinna. Sulla bound them both by an oath to abide by his settlement of affairs in Italy, but as soon as he was in Greece, Cinna redistributed the new Italian citizens among all the tribes. Driven out of Rome by his optimate colleague Octavius, he recalled Marius and levied an army of Italians. The Marians, as they were called, recaptured the city and pursued their optimate opponents, killing some (including Octavius), exiling others, and confiscating property. They thus set an example on a small scale for the wholesale proscriptions undertaken by Sulla on his return. Marius (for the seventh time) and Cinna (for the second) assumed the consulship for 86, but Marius died of apoplexy soon after entering office. Cinna, however, continued in control of Rome and Italy for two more years. During this period he, with Carbo as his colleague, put through a series of antisenatorial measures and tried, unsuccessfully, to have Sulla assassinated. He was finally killed (in 84) by troops with whom he hoped to block Sulla's return to Italy; see 26 pref.

The following account is from Velleius, with a small insertion from Florus.

Marii et Cinnae dominatio

Non erat Mario Sulpicioque Cinna temperantior. Itaque cum ita civitas Italiae data esset, ut in octo tribus contribuerentur novi cives,[1] ne potentia eorum et multitudo veterum civium dignitatem frangeret,[2] Cinna in omnibus tribubus eos se distributurum pollicitus est. Qua de causa ex urbe pulsus est collegae optimatiumque viribus, et ex auctoritate senatus consulatus ei abrogatus est.[3] Tum Cinna, retinens insignia consulatus, patriae bellum intulit, fretus ingenti numero novorum civium, e quibus amplius trecentas cohortes conscripserat.[4] Opus erat partibus auctoritate, cuius augendae gratia C. Marium cum filio de exsilio revocavit.[5]

Rediit ab Africa Marius clade maior, si quidem carcer, catenae, fuga, exsilium horrificaverant dignitatem.[6] Itaque ad nomen tanti viri late concurritur,[7] et facile invenit exercitum imperator. Nihil vero illa Marii victoria fuisset crudelius, nisi mox Sullana esset secuta.[8] Non modo mediocres verum excelsissimi atque eminentissimi civitatis viri variis suppliciorum generibus adfecti sunt. In iis consul Octavius, vir lenissimi animi, iussu Cinnae interfectus est. M. Antonius, princeps civitatis atque eloquentiae, gladiis militum iussu Marii Cinnaeque confossus est.[9] Q. Catulus, cum ad mortem conquireretur, conclusit se loco nuper calce harenaque perpolito,[10] inlatoque igni, qui vim odoris excitaret,[11] simul exitiali hausto spiritu, simul incluso suo mortem obiit.[12] Omnia erant praecipitia in re publica.

Secundum deinde consulatum Cinna et septimum Marius, in priorum dedecus, iniit,[13] cuius initio morbo oppressus decessit—vir in bello hostibus, in otio civibus infestissimus quietisque impatientissi-mus.[14] Dominante in Italia Cinna, maior pars nobilitatis ad Sullam in Achaiam ac deinde post in Asiam perfugit.[15] Antequam Sulla, com-positis transmarinis rebus, in Italiam rediret, Cinna, seditione orta, ab exercitu interemptus est—vir dignior qui arbitrio victorum moreretur quam iracundia militum.[16]

1. A. **cum** = "although"; concessive rather than temporal. B. **ita ... cives** = "on the understanding that the new citizens should be enrolled in (only) eight tribes"; *ita ... ut* would normally introduce a result clause (contrast *ut ... ita* in 23 n. 7B) but the sense here verges toward purpose; i.e. the clause gives the aim or understanding of the granting of citizenship to the Italian allies rather than the actual result. In the early expansion of Rome, when new territory was given Roman citizenship, further tribes were created for the new citizens. After 241, when the number of tribes had reached 35, new citizens were enrolled in one or several of the existing tribes. Those who were given citizenship in the Social War (see 23) were enrolled in only 8 tribes to prevent their votes from controlling the state, since votes in the tribal assembly were carried by a majority of tribes (not of individuals). C. **contribuerentur:** a compound of *tribuo*, which basically = "to distribute into the tribes"; hence it and its compounds are often followed by *in* + acc. rather than by a dat. In the next sentence, Velleius uses, after *distributurum* (*esse*), *in* + abl., = "among all the tribes"; the change is perhaps merely to vary his style.

2. A. **veterum civium dignitatem** = "the (political) eminence of the original citizens"; *veterum* is gen. masc. plur. of the adj. *vetus*, which, though 3rd decl., is declined with the consonant rather than the usual *i*-stem endings. B. **dignitatem:** for the political connotation here compare 19 n. 14C.

3. A. **ex auctoritate ... abrogatus est** = "in accordance with a recommendation of the senate, his consulship was abrogated." Since the senate was advisory to the magis-trate consulting it, the abl. of source with *ex* is used instead of an abl. of means (as might be used of a law). Technically a magistrate was supposed to lay down his office voluntarily at the end of his term; see 7 n. 15A. Probably Octavius (see pref.) simply declared Cinna's consulship invalid on the advice of the senate, instead of procuring a vote of the assembly, as Tiberius had done to remove M. Octavius in 133; see 18 n. 7D. Thus Cinna could regard the abrogation as invalid. B. **ei:** dat. of reference (disad-vantage), lit. = "for him" or "as far as he was concerned"; with verbs signifying separation, however, as here, it may be rendered "from him"; compare 18 n. 7A.

4.   A. **ingenti numero:** abl. (of means or locative) after *fretus*, one of several adjs. that regularly take the abl.   B. **amplius:** for the omission of *quam* see 22 n. 11 (and 23 n. 9).

5.   A. **opus . . . auctoritate** = "his party needed prestige," lit. "there was need to (his) party of authority"; in this idiom either *opus est* takes the abl. (probably of means), as here, or the thing needed is nom. and *opus* a predicate nom.   B. **partibus:** dat. of reference (advantage); the plur. *partes* in a political context = "party" or "side."   C. **cuius augendae gratia:** for the gen. of a noun (here a pronoun) + the gerundive dependent on *gratia* see 19 n. 4A (and compare 21 n. 14A).

6.   A. **clade** = "by (because of) his misfortune (lit. disaster)"; abl. of means (or cause), not abl. of comparison after *maior*.   B. **si quidem . . . dignitatem** = "in as much as prison . . . had made his reputation more awesome (lit. terrifying)"; *si quidem* often has a concessive force of "since indeed" or the like, rather than a strictly conditional connotation.   C. **dignitatem:** here more personal than political; compare 20 n. 3B (and contrast n. 2B above).

7.   A. **ad . . . viri:** Eng. idiom might prefer "to a man of so great reputation," but Lat., by placing *nomen* after *ad* and making *viri* the gen., emphasizes the reputation as that which attracted people.   B. **concurritur:** impersonal passive (see 12 n. 9B and 23 n. 15A), and in the historical present (see 5 n. 5 and 21 n. 7B), as is also *invenit* in the following clause.

8.   **fuisset . . . esset secuta:** pluperf. subjs. in a past contrary to fact condition; compare 9 n. 6D (and 19 n. 14A).

9.   A. **M. Antonius:** a distinguished orator (and the grandfather of Mark Antony), whom Cicero made one of the two chief speakers in his dialogue *de Oratore*.   B. **princeps:** often means the first in literature and oratory as well as in politics; see 1 n. 1G (and 24 n. 18B).

10.   A. **Q. Catulus:** the optimate leader who as proconsul won with Marius the victory at Vercellae in 101; see 22.   B. **conclusit etc.:** a charcoal stove or brazier in a closed room will quickly exhaust the oxygen and leave carbon monoxide, which will asphyxiate anyone who stays in the room without ventilating it. Wet plaster, containing only lime (*calx*) and sand (*harena*), would not give out any harmful fumes except in the unlikely case that some poisonous compound, of arsenic or lead for example, had been mixed in. The ancients may have observed that persons who entered rooms closed for drying plaster were asphyxiated and mistakenly concluded that the wet plaster had something to do with it.

11.   A. **igni:** an *i*-stem noun which usually has the abl. in *-i*, not *-e*.   B. **qui . . . excitaret:** a rel. clause of characteristic denoting purpose; compare 7 n. 8A (and 8 n. 1B).

12.   A. **simul . . . simul:** lit. = "at the same time." However, since Catulus obviously could not simultaneously inhale the noxious fumes and hold his breath, translate "first . . . and then."   B. **spiritu:** with *hausto* = "the fume(s)," but also to be supplied with *incluso suo*, = "his own (breath)."   C. **mortem obiit** = "he died, met (his) death"; a regular idiom. For an acc. direct object with a compound of *eo* compare *consulatum iniit* below and see 2 n. 6.

13.   **in priorum dedecus** = "to the disgrace of his former (consulships)."

14.   **quietis:** objective gen. (of *quies*) with *impatientissimus*; compare 24 n. 7A.

15.   **in Achaiam . . . in Asiam:** Sulla drove Mithridates out of Greece in 86, and then pursued him into Asia Minor, where he made peace with him in 84.

16.   A. **vir . . . moreretur** = "a man worthier to die etc."; *dignus* may take a rel. clause of characteristic, as here, which is usually best rendered in Eng. by an inf.   B. **victorum:** gen. plur. of *victor*, not of *victus*. Velleius seems to have regarded Cinna as having been too wicked to have met his end merely in an explosion of the soldiers' wrath; his death should have been reserved for a deliberate decision reached by the victorious Sullans.

26

Sulla, even during his absence in Greece and Asia Minor to wage war against Mithridates, remained the dominant and incalculable factor in Roman politics. His character already showed that curious mixture of ruthless ambition, lack of deep conviction, and yet adherence to the traditional senatorial and optimate conservatism which was to appear so strongly when he became master of the Roman state. He enjoyed the intense loyalty of his troops because of their belief in his uniform good luck, a belief which he fostered by adopting the epithet *Felix*.

In 83 Sulla returned from his victory over Mithridates (see 25 n. 15), but not until late in 82 did he appear before Rome. There, in the "Battle of the Colline Gate" on November 1, with the help of his young lieutenants Pompey and Crassus, he overwhelmed the combined forces of Carbo and of the Marsi, who were still in revolt against Rome; see 23 n. 6A.

Sulla then had himself made *dictator rei publicae constituendae* without limit of time and, with absolute control of the state, put through reactionary reforms aimed at ensuring control by the senate. Among these, he limited the initiative of the tribunes and assemblies, as well as of magistrates and governors, and returned the membership on the juries to the senate (see 19 pref.), whose numbers, however, he increased from 300 to 600 by enrolling worthy and financially qualified equestrians.

But more lasting than any of his optimate reforms was the memory which he left of the ruthless proscription of his opponents of all classes. Since the time of the Gracchi (see 20 pref. and n. 17B), Roman blood had been drawn by Roman swords in civil strife, but now for the first time it was pitilessly let by the victor. Prices were set on men's heads; examples both of betrayal for the collection of blood money and of noble self-sacrifice in the defense of friends were common.

In 79 Sulla retired of his own accord from the dictatorship, presumably believing that he had thoroughly entrenched the optimates in control. In the following year he died.

The following is Velleius' account of Sulla's return to Italy and of his dictatorship.

Sullana victoria et dictatura

Putares Sullam venisse in Italiam non belli vindicem sed pacis auctorem:[1] tanta cum quiete exercitum per Calabriam Apuliamque cum singulari cura frugum, agrorum, hominum, urbium perduxit in

Campaniam; temptavitque iustis legibus et aequis condicionibus bellum componere.[2] Sed iis, quibus pessima et immodica cupiditas erat, non poterat pax placere. Crescebat interim in dies Sullae exercitus,[3] confluentibus ad eum optimo quoque et sanissimo.[4] Felici deinde circa Capuam eventu Scipionem Norbanumque consules superavit,[5] quorum Norbanus acie victus; Scipio, ab exercitu suo desertus ac proditus, inviolatus a Sulla dimissus est.[6] Adeo enim Sulla dissimilis fuit bellator ac victor, ut, dum vincit mitis ac lenis, post victoriam fuerit crudelissimus.[7] Nam et consulem, ut praediximus, exarmatum Quintumque Sertorium (pro quanti mox belli facem!)[8] et multos alios, potitus eorum, dimisit incolumis, credo,[9] ut in eodem homine duplicis ac diversissimi animi conspiceretur exemplum.

Occiso demum Mario Marii filio,[10] Felicis nomen Sulla adsumpsit, quod quidem usurpasset iustissime, si eundem et vincendi et vivendi finem habuisset.[11] Nam videbantur finita belli civilis mala, cum Sullae crudelitate aucta sunt.[12] Quippe dictator creatus, imperio quo priores ad vindicandam maximis periculis rem publicam olim usi erant, eo in immodicae crudelitatis licentiam usus est.[13] Primus ille (et utinam ultimus) exemplum proscriptionis invenit.[14] Nec tantum in eos, qui contra arma tulerant, sed in multos insontis saevitum.[15] Adiectum etiam, ut bona proscriptorum venirent exclusique paternis opibus liberi etiam petendorum honorum iure prohiberentur.[16]

1.   A. **putares:** the imperf. subj. suggests that if the reader had been present on Sulla's arrival, he would have thought; for a similar imperf. subj. of past potentiality, see 11 n. 8A. The perf. inf. *venisse* indicates that Sulla had already arrived in Italy at the time of the supposed thinking.   B. **belli vindicem:** in predicate apposition with *Sullam:* = "as a champion of war."

2.   **legibus ... condicionibus** = "laws ... agreements" (presumably with his enemies); *lex*, however, is occasionally used for the terms of an agreement and may therefore be equivalent here to *condicionibus*, for which see 9 n. 18.

3.   **in dies** = "day by day"; a common idiom.

4.   A. **confluentibus ... sanissimo** = "because all good and reasonable men were flocking to him," lit. "(because men) were gathering to him, (namely) each best and most sane (person)"; superlative adjs. modifying *quisque* are best rendered in Eng. as plurs. in the positive.   B. **quoque:** masc. sing. abl. of *quisque* in apposition with the understood abl. plur. with which *confluentibus* agrees in an abl. abs.; such "partitive" apposition breaks down the plur. group into its separate component individuals. It may often be best rendered in Eng. by "all" and a plur., as in the preceding note.

5.   **Scipionem Norbanumque:** L. Cornelius Scipio Asiaticus, great-grandson of Africanus' brother (for whom see 12 pref.), and L. Norbanus, consuls for 83, were

Marians. Norbanus escaped to north Italy after his defeat and continued fighting against Sulla until the next year, when he committed suicide. Scipio was proscribed in 82, but got away to Massilia (Marseilles), where he lived the rest of his life.

6. A. **acie:** loc. abl. (not means), as commonly; = "in battle."   B. **victus:** supply *est* to make a main verb coordinate with the final *dimissus est*, without connective (in asyndeton). This interpretation—which makes two main clauses, each describing the fate of one of the consuls, as against making both *Norbanus* and *Scipio* subjects of *dimissus est* and the verb sing. in agreement with the nearest—is supported by the statement below that Sulla let one consul, not both, get away safe. Velleius probably thought that the defeat of Norbanus led to his suicide and that Scipio, though proscribed, was allowed by Sulla to escape alive to Marseilles; see n. 5 above.   C. **desertus ac proditus:** past parts. modifying *Scipio* directly.   D. **inviolatus:** past part. as a predicate modifier of *Scipio*; = "was sent away unharmed."

7. A. **vincit:** pres. ind. with *dum*; see 6 n. 8; it is not attracted into the subj. although subordinate to a perf. subj. in the *ut* clause of result.   B. **fuerit:** to be understood also with *mitis ac lenis*; the perf. subj. in secondary sequence in a result clause emphasizes the actuality of the result; see 16 n. 13F.

8. A. **ut praediximus:** for *ut*+ind. = "as" see 14 n. 5 (and contrast 24 n. 17A); for "editorial" *praedico* see 23 n. 11.   B. **Sertorium:** though proscribed by Sulla, since he had fought for Marius and Cinna when they took Rome in 87 (see 25), he escaped by his own efforts (not, as Velleius claims, through Sulla's mercy) to Spain, where he set up an independent state; see 28.   C. **pro ... facem** = "alas, soon (to be) the cause of how great a war!" *Pro* is here not the prep. but an interjection with an acc. of exclamation (for which see 13 n. 2A); it is more often used with a nom. of exclamation, as in *pro di immortales.* For this meaning of *fax* see 23 n. 5.

9. A. **potitus eorum:** *potior* may take the gen. as well as the abl.   B. **credo, ut:** the *credo* is parenthetical and the *ut* clause of purpose depends on *dimisit*; = "let them go, I suppose, so that." The *credo* shows that the attributed purpose is the author's own interpretation; Sulla hardly meant to present himself as a Janus of virtue and vice.

10. **Mario:** Gaius Marius, son (probably natural, not adopted) of the great Marius, was elected consul for 82 with Carbo, who had been consul in 85 and 84 with Cinna; see 25 pref. The younger Marius was slain by Sulla in 82 at Praeneste, just southeast of Rome. Carbo was captured late in 82 by Pompey (see 28–29) and executed.

11. A. **usurpasset ... habuisset:** pluperf. subjs. in a past contrary to fact condition; compare 9 n. 6D (and 25 n. 8).   B. **si ... habuisset:** i.e. if he had died as soon as he won the civil war.

12. **cum ... aucta sunt:** occasionally, as here, a subordinate *cum* temporal clause in past time, though it follows what is syntactically a main clause, actually expresses the main thought in the sentence; in such sentences the main verb is in the imperf. ind. (as here) or the pluperf. ind. and the verb of the *cum* clause is in the perf. ind. (as here) or the historical pres. ind. and not, as usually in *cum* temporal clauses in past time, in the imperf. or pluperf. subj. This construction, called "*cum inversum*," is usually used to indicate a sudden or unexpected occurrence which has anticipated (or prevented) the action indicated in the main clause as about to occur.

13. A. **imperio quo ... eo:** abls. with *usi erant* and *usus est*; see 14 n. 16B. Velleius well distinguishes Sulla's dictatorship from the traditional type held by such heroes as Camillus (see 8 n. 10B) and last by Fabius Maximus (see 10 n. 13A); Sulla was elected (*dictator creatus*; compare 5 n. 17B), and not appointed, as had been earlier dictators (*dictus*; compare 8 n. 10C).   B. **maximis periculis:** abl. of separation without a preposition after *vindicare* = "to save from"; for the meanings of this verb see 20 n. 13B.

14. A. **primus ... ultimus:** here Eng. would use adjs., not advs.; contrast 11 n. 12A. B. **utinam:** supply *fuisset*, pluperf. subj. for a wish that cannot be fulfilled; contrast 14 n. 13C.

15.　A. **tantum**: adv.; = "only" (as often); compare *tantum modo* in 21 n. 6c (and 24 n. 13).　B. **contra**: adv. (not the prep.), as in 20 n. 9.　C. **saevitum**: supply *est*; = "violence was used," lit. "it was raged." For the impersonal perf. pass. see 10 n. 10D (and 22 n. 2c).

16.　A. **adiectum . . . venirent . . . prohiberentur** = "this was added also, namely, that etc."; the *ut* clauses (purpose) are the subject of *adiectum* (*est*). However, *adiectum* (*est*) is often best rendered by a simple connective, "moreover" or "in addition," and the subjs. translated as main verbs in the ind.　B. **bona** = "goods, property" (as often). C. **vēnirent**: from *vēneo, vēnīre* (not from *věnio, věnīre*) which is compounded from the acc. of place to which, *vēnum*, + *eo* and = "to go for sale, to be sold." It is used as the pass. of *vēndo* (from *vēnum* + *do*) = "to give for sale, to sell."　D. **iure**: abl. of separation with *prohiberentur*, not abl. of manner used adverbially, for which see 5 n. 3A (and 18 n. 17B).

27

The first civil wars left deep and bitter memories in Rome. Cicero, born in 106, lived through them as a young man and, indeed, did his military service under Pompeius Strabo, for whom see 23 n. 10B. He makes frequent references to men and events of the period. In Marius' case he was torn between admiration for the home town hero (see 21 pref.) and opposition to him as a flouter of the senate. Moreover, he could not approve of Marius' violence and brutality. Similarly, he made his first important speech against one of Sulla's agents and disapproved of his tyranny, yet as he grew older felt that Sulla's policy of senatorial control of the state was the only wise one.

The first passage, from a speech delivered in 56, shows Cicero's ambivalent attitude; the second, chiefly from his third speech against Catiline (63), emphasizes the horrors of civil war. The third selection, from the Stoic philosopher Seneca the Younger, a century later, shows how lasting was the impression left by Sulla's callousness.

Ciceronis de Mario, Cinna, et Sulla duae sententiae

A. Neque enim ullus alius discordiarum solet esse exitus inter claros et potentes viros nisi aut universus interitus aut victoris dominatus vel regnum.[1] Dissensit cum Mario, clarissimo cive, consul nobilissimus et fortissimus, L. Sulla;[2] horum uterque ita cecidit victus, ut victor idem regnaverit.[3] Cum Octavio collega Cinna dissedit;[4] utrique horum secunda fortuna regnum est largita, adversa mortem.[5] Idem iterum Sulla superavit; tum sine dubio habuit regalem potestatem, quamquam rem publicam recuperarat.[6]

B. Etenim recordamini, Quirites, omnis civilis dissensiones, non solum eas quas audistis sed eas quas vosmet ipsi meministis atque vidistis.[7] L. Sulla P. Sulpicium oppressit; eiecit ex urbe C. Marium, custodem huius urbis, multosque fortes viros partim eiecit ex civitate, partim interemit.[8] Cn. Octavius consul armis ex urbe expulit collegam; omnis hic locus acervis corporum et civium sanguine redundavit.[9] Superavit postea Cinna cum Mario; tum vero, clarissimis viris interfectis, lumina civitatis extincta sunt.[10] Ultus est huius victoriae

crudelitatem postea Sulla—ne dici quidem opus est quanta deminu-
tione civium et quanta calamitate rei publicae.[11] L. Cinna crudelis, C.
Marius in iracundia perseverans, L. Sulla vehemens; atque quid eorum
victoria crudelius, quid funestius?

Senecae de Sullae crudelitate sententia

C. L. Sullam tyrannum appellari quid prohibet, cui occidendi finem
fecit inopia hostium?[12] Descenderit licet e dictatura sua et se togae
reddiderit,[13] quis tamen umquam tyrannus tam avide humanum
sanguinem bibit quam ille,[14] qui septem milia civium Romanorum
contrucidari iussit? Qui autem cum, in aede Bellonae sedens,[15] exau-
disset conclamationem tot milium sub gladio gementium, exterrito
senatu: "Hoc agamus," inquit, "patres conscripti;[16] seditiosi pauculi
meo iussu occiduntur." Hoc non est mentitus;[17] pauci Sullae videbantur.

1. **aut ... aut:** mark the two main alternatives; the following *vel* indicates that
dominatus and *regnum* are merely variants for the second alternative.

2. **clarissimo ... fortissimus:** for the "polite" superlative see 18 n. 1B (and 20
n. 6A).

3. A. **horum uterque ... regnaverit:** Cicero means that first Marius was overcome
(i.e. by Sulla) and fell (i.e. went into exile) and returned to rule; then Sulla did the same;
for these events see the prefs. to 24, 25, and 26.   B. **cecidit:** from *cado*; contrast 5
n. 12 (and 8 n. 5B).

4. **collega:** abl. in apposition with *Octavio*, Cinna's optimate colleague in the consulship of 87; see 25 pref.

5. A. **utrique horum ... mortem:** parallel to *horum uterque etc.* in n. 3A above;
Cicero means that a favorable fortune gave Octavius rule (i.e. when he expelled Cinna)
and then an adverse fortune gave him death (i.e. when Cinna returned); similarly Cinna
ruled from the departure of Sulla until he was killed by troops in 84; for these events
see 25 pref. Cicero exaggerates in the case of Octavius, whose brief supremacy was hardly
a *regnum*.   B. **secunda:** with *fortuna* or *res* regularly="favorable" and is often
balanced against *adversa*, as here.

6. **rem ... recuperarat**="he had restored the Republic," i.e. the outward form of
the traditional senatorial government; for this connotation of *res publica* see 19 n. 6B.

7. A. **recordamini:** in the context of the speech this is better taken as pres. pass.
plur. imperative, rather than 2nd pers. plur. pres. pass. ind. (the same in form), of the
deponent verb *recordor*.   B. **Quirites:** a term for Roman citizens, perhaps of Sabine
origin and meaning "People of the Spear."   C. **vosmet:** an emphatic form of *vos*;
the enclitic particle *-met* may be added to all the personal pronouns except in the gen.
plur.

8. A. **custodem:** by his victory over the Cimbri and Teutoni; see 22 pref.   B.
partim: an adv. often repeated distributively to subdivide a group indicated by a plur.

noun, instead of repeating an appropriate case of *alius* or *pars*. Here the lit. translation is "many brave men he partly cast out of the city and partly slew," but in Eng. it might be rendered "he cast many brave men out of the city and slew others."

9. **omnis hic locus:** the Forum, in which Cicero was speaking.

10. **lumina:** often used metaphorically of notable figures in public life or literature. For the eminent men who perished in the Marian massacres see 25.

11. A. **ne . . . est**="and I do not need to describe," lit. "there is no need either for it to be said." *Ne . . . quidem* often="not . . . either," rather than "not . . . even." B. **opus est**="there is need" often takes an inf.; contrast 25 n. 5A.

12. A. **L. Sullam . . . prohibet:** verbs of hindering, opposing, and preventing may take an acc.+an inf. (as here), or a subj. clause introduced by *quominus*, *ne*, or *quin*. These constructions are usually (as here) best rendered in Eng. by "from"+a part. B. **cui . . . inopia:** *cui* is dat. of reference; *occidendi* is gen. of the gerund of *occido* (contrast n. 3B above) dependent on *finem*; with *inopia*, subject of *fecit*, Eng. idiom would supply "only."

13. A. **licet**="granted that" or "even though"; it introduces a hortatory subj. without *ut* (in "parataxis"); see 23 n. 1A.   B. **togae**="to the status of an ordinary citizen." *Toga* is often used metaphorically (by metonymy) for "peace, civil life, etc."; compare 23 n. 15B.

14. **quis:** often used as an interrog. adj. as well as a pronoun. The adjectival use is especially frequent with words denoting a person, as here with *tyrannus*.

15. **in aede Bellonae**="in the temple of Bellona" (the goddess of war, sister of Mars). Magistrates frequently convened the senate elsewhere than in the senate house (*curia*; see 14 n. 6A), e.g. on the Capitoline as implied in the 2nd par. of 18.

16. A. **hoc agamus**="let us attend to business"; *agamus* is hortatory (jussive) subj.; see 12 n. 15C.   B. **patres conscripti:** the regular formula of address for the assembled senators. The meaning of the phrase is obscure; it may have referred to all the "registered" senators, or, as Roman tradition asserted, to the original *patres* of Romulus and others added by later kings, thus="(original) Fathers (and) those (later) enrolled."

17. **hoc . . . mentitus**="this was no lie," lit. "he did not lie this." For the use of a neut. pron. as a cognate acc. (of the inner object) see 12 n. 2B.

28

Sulla's settlement did not last long. The decade following his retirement in 79 and death in 78 (see 26 pref.) was filled with violence and change. In Spain, Sertorius (see 26 n. 8B) established an almost independent kingdom and held out against successive Roman generals until 72. In Asia Minor, Mithridates of Pontus (see 24) made a fresh attack on the Roman province and protectorates in 74. In Italy, Lepidus, consul in 78, attempted during his year of office to put aside the Sullan arrangements and in the following year led an open revolt against the senate, but was speedily defeated. Furthermore, a revolt of slaves and gladiators broke out in 73 near Naples under the leadership of Spartacus, and this was suppressed only in 71.

Crassus and Pompey, pacifiers of Italy and Spain respectively, disliked and distrusted each other, but allied to secure the consulship for 70 with a program of freeing the assemblies and tribunes from the restrictions placed on them by Sulla; see 26 pref. Since both had begun their careers as lieutenants of Sulla, this democratic program reflected not idealism, such as had motivated the Gracchi and Drusus, but mere political opportunism. Self-seeking senators who thus sought the support of the tribunes and assemblies not to help the poor, but to promote their own ends, came to be called *populares* and to be regarded as a faction of opposition to the controlling clique of *nobiles* and their supporters the *optimates*; see 18 pref. and n. 13A.

In 70, a corrupt governor of Sicily, Gaius Verres, was tried before a senatorial jury in the *quaestio de rebus repetundis*; see 12 n. 14A and prefs. to 19 and 26. Despite this and strong optimate support, Cicero's opening speech against him (see 67 pref.) was so damning that he went into exile. And shortly thereafter a tribunician *lex Aurelia* divided membership on the juries between senators, equestrians, and a group whose financial status was close to that of the equestrians, called *tribuni aerarii*.

The results, therefore, of this uneasy decade were to abolish the measures by which Sulla had tried to give the optimates permanent control of the state, to prepare the way for further attacks on the constitution by ambitious *populares*, and to bring to the fore Crassus and Pompey.

The following account of the events of this decade, beginning with the young Pompey's adherence to Sulla and ending with his joint consulship with Crassus, is composed from Velleius, Florus, and Aulus Gellius.

Bella post Sullae mortem usque ad consulatum Crassi Pompeiique

Ante adventum in Italiam L. Sullae,[1] Cn. Pompeius[2] (eius Cn. Pompeii filius, quem magnificentissimas res in consulatu gessisse bello

Italico praediximus),[3] tres et viginti annos natus,[4] privatis ut opibus ita consiliis magna ausus magnificeque conata exsecutus,[5] ad vindicandam restituendamque dignitatem patriae firmum ex agro Piceno, qui totus paternis eius clientelis refertus erat, contraxit exercitum.[6]

Post mortem Sullae, M. Aemilius Lepidus consul, cupidus rerum novarum per insolentiam, acta Sullae rescindere parabat.[7] Proximo anno, cum arma et exercitum contra urbem admoveret, a Quinto Catulo Gnaeoque Pompeio retro pulsus est, hostisque a senatu iudicatus,[8] in Sardiniam recessit, ibique morbo et paenitentia interiit. Victores quoque, quod non temere alias in civilibus bellis, pace contenti fuerunt.[9]

Deinde Pompeius, Metello additus, in Sertorium missus est.[10] Quippe Sertorius, vir summae quidem sed calamitosae virtutis, malis suis maria terrasque permiscuit et tandem Hispaniam armavit.[11] Pompeius Metellusque igitur Sertorium per totam Hispaniam persecuti sunt et copias eius attriverunt. Diu et ancipiti semper acie pugnatum est;[12] nec tamen Sertorius prius bello quam suorum scelere et insidiis exstinctus est.[13] Nam M. Perpenna legatus Sertorium inter cenam interemit Romanisque certam victoriam, partibus suis excidium, sibi turpissimam mortem pessimo patravit facinore.[14] Metellus et Pompeius externum id magis quam civile bellum videri voluerunt, ut triumpharent.[15]

Dum Sertorianum bellum in Hispania geritur,[16] quattuor et sexaginta fugitivi e ludo gladiatorio Capua profugientes, duce Spartaco, primo Vesuvium montem petiere,[17] mox, crescente in dies multitudine,[18] gravibus variisque casibus adfecere Italiam. Belli huius patrati gloria penes M. Crassum fuit, mox rei publicae omnium consensu principem.[19]

Tum Gnaeo Pompeio consulatus primus cum M. Crasso designatus est.[20] Eum magistratum Pompeius cum initurus foret,[21] quoniam per militiae tempora senatus habendi consulendique atque rerum expers urbanarum fuit,[22] M. Varronem, familiarem suum, rogavit uti commentarium faceret, ex quo disceret quid facere dicereque deberet cum senatum consuleret.[23]

1. **ante . . . Sullae:** for Sulla's return to Italy see 26.

2. **Cn. Pompeius etc.:** Velleius is fond of separating a subject from its verb by a long succession of phrases modifying the subject—as here *eius . . . exsecutus*—which vary in construction, as well as by the various parts of the predicate—here the gerundive phrase of purpose (see 5 n. 9A) *ad . . . patriae* and the modifiers of the object *exercitum*, namely *firmum* and *ex . . . erat*, for which see nn. 6A and B below. Compare the opening of 24.

3. A. **Cn. Pompeii:** Pompeius Strabo, for whom see 23 n. 10B.   B. **praediximus:** "editorial"; see 23 n. 11 (and 26 n. 8A).

4. **tres . . . natus:** for the acc. of extent of time with *natus* see 10 n. 1A (and 21 n. 23C). Pompey was born in 106; Sulla's return was in 83–82.

5. A. **privatis . . . consiliis** = "both on his own initiative and at his own expense," lit. "as with private resources, so with private plans"; for the correlative use of *ut* and *ita* see 19 n. 11A (and compare 23 n. 7B).   B. **conata:** neut. plur. past part. of *conor* used as a noun (compare *bona* in 26 n. 16B); it may be modified by the preceding *magna* and serve as object of both parts., but it is perhaps more effective to regard *magna* (also used as a noun) as object of *ausus* and *conata* of *exsecutus*, = "having dared great (deeds) and magnificently carried out his attempts (or, undertakings)."

6. A. **firmum:** modifies *exercitum* at the end of the sentence; for the unusual word order (hyperbaton) compare 19 n. 13A. Pompey offered this army and his services to Sulla on his return to Italy; see 26.   B. **ex agro Piceno:** this would normally indicate the source of *contraxit exercitum*, but its position makes it also explanatory of *firmum*: "reliable (because) from etc."   C. **agro** = "territory"; compare 2 n. 2C. Picenum lay on the east (Adriatic) coast of Italy, south of the Po valley. Since Pompeius Strabo had come from this district, he and his son could always count on its inhabitants for support. D. **clientelis:** abl. of means with *refertus*; see 13 n. 7. The abstract is used collectively (compare 8 n. 9A and 20 n. 14A) = "groups of his father's clients." For the obligation of clients to support their patrons by services, including military (as here), compare 7 n. 7 (and 14 n. 6C).

7. A. **M. Aemilius Lepidus:** consul for 78, and father of the Lepidus who was the associate as triumvir of Antony and Octavian; see 43 n. 21A and 44 pref.   B. **rerum novarum:** for the meaning see 24 n. 9B.   C. **per insolentiam:** for *per* + acc. equivalent to an adv. see 5 n. 16A.

8. A. **Quinto Catulo:** this Catulus, a son of the optimate leader of the Marian period (see 22 pref. and 25 n. 10), had been Lepidus' colleague in the consulship of 78. B. **hostis** = "a public enemy" or "an enemy of the nation"; compare 29 n. 2.

9. A. **quod . . . bellis:** *quod* refers to the whole surrounding main clause, *victores . . . fuerunt*, and a verb must be supplied within the rel. clause; = "(a thing) which (has happened) rarely (lit. not readily) at other times in civil wars."   B. **alias:** adv.; see 17 n. 11C.   C. **pace:** abl. (of means or cause, rather than loc.) with *contenti*.

10. **Pompeius . . . missus est:** Metellus Pius (see 23 n. 13A) had been consul with Sulla in 80 and was duly, according to Sulla's constitution, sent to Spain as proconsul in 79. Pompey wanted the command against Sertorius, and, although he was still under the legal age to hold any magistracy, the senate sent him in 77 with a propraetorian *imperium* to join Metellus.

11. A. **Sertorius etc.:** see pref. above and 26 n. 8B.   B. **summae . . . virtutis:** gen. of quality (description); see 6 n. 9.   C. **permiscuit:** figurative; compare *permixtio terrae* in 20 n. 12B.

12. **acie:** for the loc. abl. see 26 n. 6A.

13. A. **prius . . . quam:** *priusquam* (often separated, as here; contrast *ante . . . quam* in 14 n. 12) lit. = "earlier than," but it is often used where the temporal sense is not emphatic. Here, for instance, the means of Sertorius' death is as important as the time, and the sentence might be rendered "Nor, however, was Sertorius killed in (lit. by) war (i.e. by the Romans) before (he was slain) by the criminal treachery (see the next note)

of his own (men)." B. **scelere et insidiis** = "by the crime and treachery," but may be rendered (as above) "by the criminal treachery." For the use of two nouns to express a single thought (hendiadys) see 13 n. 11A; in Eng. one of the nouns is usually best rendered as an adj. (as here) or by a prep. phrase.

14. A. **M. Perpenna legatus etc.**: for the office of *legatus* (here under Sertorius) see 12 n. 13B (and 21 n. 2D). Perpenna (or Perperna) had been Marian governor of Sardinia in 82 and escaped alive after Pompey's defeat of Carbo; see 30 pref. In 78, he joined the revolt of Lepidus (see pref.) and again escaped to join Sertorius in Spain in 77. In 72 he assassinated Sertorius and assumed command of his forces, only to suffer defeat and death at the hands of Pompey in 71.   B. **partibus**: for the meaning see 25 n. 5B.   C. **pessimo** = "by (this) worst (of)"; compare 24 n. 9C.

15.   **externum . . . triumpharent**: technically triumphs were awarded only for victories over foreign enemies; see 9 n. 10C. For this triumph see 30 n. 19.

16.   **dum . . . geritur**: for the pres. with *dum* see 6 n. 8 (and 26 n. 7A).

17. A. **Capua**: a city north of Naples; see 10 n. 12C.   B. **Spartaco**: Spartacus, a Thracian of considerable energy and ability, attempted to lead the runaway slaves to their homes beyond the Alps. But he lost control of them as they increased in numbers and turned to pillaging Italy.   C. **Vesuvium**: the famous volcano just south of Naples, which was at this time dormant but was to erupt some 150 years later in A.D. 79.   D. **petiere** = *petiverunt;* for the omission of -*v*- see 1 n. 4B; for the ending see 15 n. 10 (and 18 n. 14C).

18.   **in dies**: for this idiom see 26 n. 3.

19. A. **belli . . . patrati** = *belli confecti*; see 22 n. 4. The slaves were defeated only after a number of engagements. When the revolt was finally crushed, six thousand slaves were crucified along the *Via Appia*, which led from Capua to Rome.   B. **penes** + acc. + **fuit** = "belonged to."   C. **M. Crassum**: Marcus Licinius Crassus was born in 112, son of a P. Crassus who had committed suicide in the Marian massacres. He, like Pompey, had been one of Sulla's lieutenants; see 26 pref. The credit of defeating the slaves belonged to him, but remnants of the revolt were put down by Pompey on his return from Spain. Pompey then annoyed Crassus by claiming some of the glory.   D. **principem** = "foremost man"; see 1 n. 1G (and 25 n. 9B). Crassus, who had become enormously rich during the Sullan proscriptions, was an important figure in Roman politics until his defeat and death at Carrhae in 53; see 37 pref.

20. A. **tum . . . est**: Crassus, who had been praetor in 72, was eligible for the consulship in 70, but Pompey was only 36 and had held none of the earlier magistracies. Nevertheless, the senate, intimidated by his legions camped just outside Rome, allowed him to stand; compare his appointment to the command in Spain in n. 10 above. B. **designatus est**: this instance, in Aulus Gellius, is the only one cited for the use of *designo* of the office rather than of the person; the verb normally indicates that a person has been elected but has not yet assumed office.

21.   **initurus foret**: for *foret* = *esset* see 21 n. 26C; with the fut. act. part. *initurus* it forms the imperf. subj. of the 1st (act.) periphrastic conj. For the 2nd (pass.) periphrastic see 14 n. 10.

22. A. **per militiae tempora** = "because of long military service," lit. "through the times of service"; for *per* + acc. to connote means or cause see 5 n. 16A.   B. **militiae**: limiting gen., not loc.   C. **senatus habendi consulendique**: partitive gen. with *expers* (see n. E below), as is *rerum urbanarum*; = "in convening and consulting the senate." This phrase is regularly used since a magistrate convened the senate to ask its advice; the senate was never properly legislative; compare 25 n. 3A.   D. **atque rerum . . . urbanarum** = "as in city affairs in general"; *atque* often thus includes what precedes in a more general category.   E. **expers** = "inexperienced (in)"; being a compound of *ex* + *pars*, it takes a partitive gen. and must be carefully distinguished from *expertus*, the past part. of *experior*, which may mean just the opposite of *expers*, i.e. "experienced in," and takes an objective gen., like many adjs. denoting knowledge; compare 13 n. 1C.

23.   A. **M. Varronem:** "the most learned of the Romans," M. Terentius Varro not only was an encyclopedic scholar (compare 4 pref.) and friend of Cicero and Pompey but also participated in politics. His long life (116–27) extended from the aftermath of the Gracchan struggles to the founding of the Augustan principate, for which see 48 n. 11A.   B. **familiarem:** this adj., lit. = "belonging to a *familia*" ("household"; contrast 33 n. 1B), is often used as a noun referring to any member of a household—a servant (as in 44 n. 9A) or, here, a close friend.   C. **rogavit . . . consuleret:** Varro is the subject of *faceret*, Pompey of all the other verbs   D. **uti:** a stronger form of *ut*, to be distinguished from the pres. inf. of *utor*, also spelled *uti*.   E. **commentarium** = "an outline, memorandum," or the like, rather than a finished literary work.   F. **disceret:** subj. not merely by attraction, but in a rel. clause of characteristic expressing purpose; see 8 n. 1B.

29

The years from 70–50 were dominated by the figure of Gnaeus Pompeius (see 28), surnamed *Magnus* as early as 81 (compare 23 n. 10B); for his career until 66 see 30 pref. In the eyes of later ages, he has been overshadowed by Cicero, whose writings have led posterity to think of him as the chief figure of this period, and by Caesar, whose ultimate achievement made his earlier career seem more significant than it must have appeared to his contemporaries.

In 74, when Mithridates (see prefs. to 24 and 28) again threatened the Roman possessions in Asia Minor, the senate had sent out an optimate general, Lucullus, against him. At the same time, encouraged by Mithridates' attack, pirates from the mountainous southern coast of Asia Minor (Cilicia) and from eastern Crete extended their operations into the sea west of Italy and interfered with the transport of grain from Sicily and Africa to Rome. The optimate commanders sent against the pirates were unsuccessful. In 67, therefore, a tribune named Gabinius, later a close henchman of Pompey, passed a bill in the tribal assembly giving Pompey general command over the eastern Mediterranean to suppress piracy. Within three months he had done so.

In the meantime, Lucullus had penetrated into central Armenia, whose king Tigranes was an ally and son-in-law of Mithridates, but there his troops clamored to return. Hence in 66 another tribune, Manilius, introduced a bill to transfer the command against Mithridates from Lucullus to Pompey. The optimates opposed it, but in the preliminary meeting for discussion (called a *contio*) before the voting, Cicero, then praetor, spoke in favor of the bill. He was careful not to alienate the optimates by condemning Lucullus, but he emphasized how much more brilliant a commander Pompey had proved himself. The bill passed, and Pompey, already in the east after his campaign against the pirates, assumed a command which gave him extraordinarily far-reaching authority.

The following passage praising Pompey's military skill and recounting his success against the pirates comes from Cicero's speech in support of Manilius' bill, the *Oratio de Lege Manilia* or *de Imperio Cn. Pompei*.

Pompeius, imperator eximius, praedones superat

Quis igitur hoc homine scientior umquam aut fuit aut esse debuit?[1] Qui saepius cum hoste conflixit quam quisquam cum inimico concertavit,[2] plura bella gessit quam ceteri legerunt,[3] plures provincias confecit quam alii concupiverunt.[4] Cuius adulescentia ad scientiam rei militaris non alienis praeceptis sed suis imperiis, non offensionibus belli sed victoriis, non stipendiis sed triumphis est erudita.[5] Quod denique genus esse belli potest, in quo illum non exercuerit fortuna rei publicae? Civile, Africanum, Transalpinum, Hispaniense, servile, navale bellum,[6] varia et diversa genera et bellorum et hostium non solum gesta ab hoc uno sed etiam confecta nullam rem esse declarant in usu positam militari, quae huius viri scientiam fugere possit.[7]

Testes vero virtutum eius imperatoriarum iam omnes sunt orae atque omnes exterae gentes ac nationes, denique maria omnia, omnes sinus atque portus. Quis enim toto mari locus per hos annos aut tam firmum habuit praesidium ut tutus esset,[8] aut tam fuit abditus ut lateret? Quis navigavit qui non se aut mortis aut servitutis periculo committeret, cum aut hieme aut referto praedonum mari navigaret?[9] Quam provinciam tenuistis a praedonibus liberam per hosce annos?[10] Quod vectigal vobis tutum fuit? Quem socium defendistis? Cui praesidio classibus vestris fuistis?[11]

Tum unius hominis incredibilis ac divina virtus brevi tempore lucem rei publicae attulit.[12] Atque haec qua celeritate gesta sint, quamquam videtis, tamen a me in dicendo praetereunda non sunt.[13] Cn. Pompeius, nondum tempestivo ad navigandum mari, Siciliam adiit,[14] Africam exploravit, in Sardiniam cum classe venit; atque haec tria frumentaria subsidia rei publicae firmissimis praesidiis classibusque munivit.[15] Omnes qui ubique praedones fuerunt partim capti interfectique sunt, partim unius huius se imperio ac potestati dediderunt.[16] Ita tantum bellum, tam diuturnum, tam longe lateque dispersum, quo bello omnes gentes ac nationes premebantur, Cn. Pompeius extrema hieme apparavit, ineunte vere suscepit, media aestate confecit.[17]

1. A. **scientior** = "more knowledgeable," i.e. about military affairs.   B. **esse debuit** = "ought to have been, had reason to be." Lat. regularly uses a pres. inf. with past forms of *debeo*; compare for *possum* 10 n. 12B.

2. **hoste ... inimico** = "a public enemy ... a personal opponent"; compare 28 n. 8B.

3. **legerunt** = "have read (about)"; *lego, -ere* originally meant "pick, choose, select, etc." How it came commonly to mean "read" is not certain, but perhaps it was from the concept of picking out the written letters with the eye. The Romans of Cicero's day may well have thought that there were two similar but distinct verbs, *lego* = "select" and *lego* = "read."

4. **provincias confecit** = "he (subdued and) established provinces" (i.e. after their conquest); compare *bella confecta* = "wars brought to a (successful) conclusion" in n. 7B below. This is a more probable interpretation than to give *provincia* its more general meaning of "a sphere (or, mission) of command" and translate the idiom "to accomplish (successfully) commands (assigned to him)."

5. **stipendiis** = "not (merely) by campaigns"; *stipendium* originally meant "pay," and in the army, "pay for a year of service"; then it came to mean the year of service itself. Rome's early campaigns, waged close to home, usually took place only in the summers, between sowing and harvest, and hence armies were levied anew for each campaign. Pay was first introduced when troops had to remain away all year, traditionally during the siege of Veii, which lasted from 406 to 396; see 8 n. 11. Even when service became in fact continuous for several years, the fiction of yearly levies and yearly pay was maintained.

6. A. **civile etc.**: this and the following adjs. modify *bellum*, which is sing. because each was only one war; the whole phrase is in apposition to *varia . . . hostium*, which generalizes and magnifies Pompey's various campaigns; see 26 and 28.   B. **Transalpinum**: not a major campaign, but Pompey's defeat of some unruly tribes in southern Gaul while en route to join Metellus in Spain in 77; see 26 n. 10.   C. **navale**: Pompey's naval campaign against the pirates in 67; see the 2nd par. below.

7. A. **varia . . . hostium** = "various and diverse kinds of both wars and enemies"; since, however, the past parts. *gesta* and *confecta* = "waged and won" are appropriate only to *bellorum*, not to *hostium*, the phrase might better be rendered: "different kinds of wars against various enemies."   B. **confecta**: compare *bellum . . . confecit* below, in the last sentence of the selection; for the idiom see 22 n. 4 (and compare 28 n. 19A and, for *conficere*, n. 4 above).   C. **in . . . militari** = "lying (lit. having been placed) within (the sphere of) military experience."   D. **quae . . . possit**: a rel. clause of characteristic after the negative antecedent *nullam rem*; the pres. subj. is used to describe an incomplete or potential action in primary sequence; compare 13 n. 6C.

8. A. **quis . . . locus**: for *quis* as an interrog. adj. see 27 n. 14.   B. **toto mari**: the abl. of place where without the preposition (or loc.) is regularly used when a noun is modified by *totus* and frequently when modified by other adjs.   C. **per hos annos** = "during these (recent) years," namely before Pompey's campaign against the pirates; for *per* + acc. to connote the extent of time here and two sentences below see 5 n. 16A. D. **praesidium** = "defense" or "protection"; here used in an abstract sense; compare n. 11A and contrast n. 15B below.

9. A. **qui . . . committeret**: a rel. clause of characteristic, whose antecedent is the interrog. pronoun *quis*; the imperf. subj. is used to describe an incomplete action in secondary sequence; compare n. 7D above.   B. **hieme**: abl. of time when or within which.   C. **praedonum**: gen. after the adj. of fullness *referto*; contrast the abl. in 13 n. 7 (and 28 n. 6D). The ancients ordinarily did not sail in winter, and traders had the choice of facing its bad weather or, in summer, the pirates.   D. **mari**: abl. of place where (as in n. 8B above) or of attendant circumstance.

10. **hosce**: the enclitic -*ce* is emphatic; in some of the forms it became permanently part of the demonstrative; contrast *hic, haec, hoc* with *huius, horum, etc.*

11. A. **cui praesidio**: double dat.; see 17 n. 11A (and 24 n. 20B); *praesidio* is used in an abstract sense as in n. 8D above.   B. **classibus**: abl. of means; = "with your fleets."

12. **lucem** = "safety"; *lux* is often used metaphorically; compare for *lumina* 27 n. 10.

13. A. **atque . . . sunt**: lit. = "and these things, with what swiftness they were accomplished, although you see (this), nevertheless (they) must not be passed over by me in speaking"; since Lat. often uses an indirect question where Eng. uses an abstract noun, and since the pass. (2nd) periphrastic (see 14 n. 10) is usually best made act. in Eng., the sentence might freely be rendered: "And, although you are well aware of it, I would like

to emphasize the swiftness with which these things were accomplished."   B. **haec:** taken before ("proleptically") the indirect question *qua . . . sint*, of which it is subject, because it serves with the indirect question as object of *videtis* and as subject of *praetereunda sint*; = "you see these things, with what speed they have been accomplished etc."   C. **quamquam videtis:** parenthetical but has as objects *haec* and *qua . . . sint*; see the preceding note.   D. **a me:** abl. of agent with the 2nd (pass.) periphrastic (see 14 n. 10) instead of the more usual dat. of reference (agent), for which see 21 n. 15C.   E. **praetereunda non sunt:** strictly should be neut. sing. since the principal subject is the indirect question, but as noted in B above, *haec* is also the subject, and is given emphasis by having the verb agree with it in the neut. plur.

14.   **tempestivo** = "calm (enough)," lit. "timely, seasonable." The whole phrase may be abl. abs. or abl. of attendant circumstance.

15.   A. **frumentaria subsidia** = "sources (lit. aids) of grain."   B. **praesidiis** = "garrisons"; used in a concrete sense; contrast nn. 8D and 11A above.

16.   A. **partim . . . partim:** distributive adv.; see 27 n. 8B.   B. **imperio ac potestati:** the first denotes Pompey's military, the second his civil, authority.

17.   A. **bellum . . . confecit:** as in n. 7B above.   B. **quo bello:** for the repetition of the antecedent within the rel. clause see 8 n. 7A (and 20 n. 6C).   C. **extrema . . . media** = "at the end (of) . . . in the middle (of)"; see 12 n. 7B.   D. **ineunte vere** = "at the beginning of spring," lit. "with spring entering"; *vere* is from *ver, veris*, n.

30

This selection, like the previous one, comes from Cicero's speech in 66, *de Lege Manilia*. The optimates argued that the power which Manilius was proposing for Pompey was too sweeping and unconventional. In the following passage Cicero replies by citing exceptions to custom from recent history and from Pompey's own career, which may be summarized here. Born in 106, he served with his father Pompeius Strabo in the Social War; see 23 pref. and n. 10B. On Sulla's return to Italy in 83, Pompey raised forces on his own initiative (see n. 8 below) and helped in the victory of late 82; see 26 pref. Sulla then sent him with a propraetorian *imperium* to Sicily, where he defeated and slew Carbo and forced Perpenna (see 28 n. 14A) to flee. In 81 he proceeded to Africa and by the end of 80 had eliminated the Marian forces there. On his return to Rome in 79, Sulla unwillingly let him celebrate a triumph; see n. 14 below. In 77, the senate sent him to support Metellus in Spain against Sertorius (see 28 pref. and n. 10) and on the way he helped to defeat the revolt of Lepidus in north Italy; see 28 pref. and n. 7A. After Perpenna had murdered Sertorius in Spain in 72, Pompey found it easy in 71 to defeat their discouraged forces; see 28 n. 14A. As he passed through north Italy on his way back to Rome, he wiped out remnants of the forces of Spartacus, who were fleeing from their defeat by Crassus; see 28 pref. and n. 17B. Pompey celebrated a second triumph late in 71 (see n. 19 below) and assumed the consulship, his first magistracy (see n. 17B below), with Crassus on January 1, 70, at the age of only thirty-six. In 67 he received under the *lex Gabinia* (see 29 pref.) an extensive command against the pirates.

Pompeii extraordinaria imperia

At enim "ne quid novi fiat contra exempla atque instituta maiorum."[1] Non dicam hoc loco maiores nostros semper in pace consuetudini, in bello utilitati paruisse,[2] semper ad novos casus temporum novorum consiliorum rationes accommodasse.[3] Non dicam duo bella maxima, Punicum atque Hispaniense, ab uno imperatore esse confecta duasque urbes potentissimas, quae huic imperio maxime minitabantur, Carthaginem atque Numantiam, ab eodem Scipione esse deletas.[4] Non commemorabo nuper ita vobis patribusque vestris esse visum ut in uno C. Mario spes imperi poneretur, ut idem cum Iugurtha, idem cum Cimbris, idem cum Teutonis bellum administraret.[5] In ipso

Cn. Pompeio, in quo novi constitui nihil vult Q. Catulus,[6] quam multa sint nova, summa Q. Catuli voluntate, constituta recordamini.[7]

Quid tam novum quam adulescentulum privatum exercitum difficili rei publicae tempore conficere?[8] Confecit. Huic praeesse? Praefuit. Rem optime ductu suo gerere?[9] Gessit. Quid tam praeter consuetudinem quam homini peradulescenti, cuius aetas a senatorio gradu longe abesset,[10] imperium atque exercitum dari, Siciliam permitti atque Africam bellumque in ea provincia administrandum?[11] Fuit in his provinciis singulari innocentia, gravitate, virtute;[12] bellum in Africa maximum confecit; victorem exercitum deportavit.[13] Quid vero tam inauditum quam equitem Romanum triumphare?[14] At eam quoque rem populus Romanus non modo vidit, sed omnium etiam studio visendam et concelebrandam putavit.[15] Quid tam inusitatum, quam ut, cum duo consules clarissimi fortissimique essent, eques Romanus ad bellum maximum formidolosissimumque pro consule mitteretur?[16] Missus est. Quid tam singulare, quam ut, ex senatus consulto legibus solutus,[17] consul ante fieret quam ullum alium magistratum per leges capere licuisset?[18] Quid tam incredibile, quam ut iterum eques Romanus ex senatus consulto triumpharet?[19]

1. A. **at enim** = "but then"; supply some such thought as "the optimates argue." *At* is often thus used to introduce an objection which the speaker wishes to answer. B. **ne . . . fiat** = "let nothing new be done"; *quid* is the indefinite pronoun after *ne* (see 4 n. 11B) and *novi* is partitive gen. dependent on it; compare 11 n. 14A.

2. A. **non dicam:** Cicero is fond of a rhetorical figure called *praeteritio* (passing over), i.e. beginning "I shall not say" and then saying it; contrast *praetereunda non sunt* in 29 n. 13E.   B. **hoc loco** = "at this point" (in the argument); when *loco* is in the abl. of place where is modified by an adj., the prep. is regularly omitted; compare 29 n. 8B. C. **consuetudini . . . utilitati:** dats. with *paruisse*, from *pareo* = "obey."

3. A. **semper . . . accommodasse:** Cicero's style, in contrast to Sallust's, is marked by "pleonasm" (Greek; = fullness), i.e. the use of synonyms and repetitions to achieve elaboration and balance. Here the phrases *novos casus temporum* and *novorum consiliorum rationes* mean little more than "emergencies" and "plans" respectively, but the fullness permits rotundity of sound and an elaborate rhetorical arrangement: an acc. adj. and noun + a gen. noun are balanced by a gen. adj. and noun + an acc. noun, producing both chiasmus (acc.-gen.: gen.-acc.; see 17 n. 2) and exact parallelism (adj.-and-noun + noun in both phrases). The clause might be rendered "(and) they have always devised new plans and methods to fit new situations and emergencies."   B. **casus temporum:** both words often have the meaning "critical occasion" or "emergency"; their use together adds emphasis.

4. A. **non dicam . . . esse deletas:** the two wars, Punic and Spanish, in the first indirect statement are balanced by their two capitals in the second; the two clauses

are here joined by -*que*; contrast in the 2nd par. the asyndeton between *imperium atque exercitum dari* and the explanatory *Siciliam permitti atque Africam etc.*; see n. 11 below. For the commands of Scipio Aemilianus in these wars see 16. For the *praeteritio* see n. 2A above.   B. **minitabantur:** not attracted into the subj., because it is an aside by Cicero himself rather than an essential part of the indirect statement, even though he himself is quoting his own statement; compare 15 n. 3D (and 20 n. 4C); *minitor* usually takes the dat. of the person threatened (as here), an acc. or an inf. of what is threatened, and an abl. of means of by which the threat is made.

5.   A. **commemorabo**=*dicam*, as in 15 n. 13C.   B. **nuper ita ... administraret:** the subject of the inf. *esse visum* in indirect statement is the substantive clause *ut ... poneretur*, and such a clause with the pass. of *video*="(it) seems good" (as often) is classified as purpose (i.e. prospective). The *ita* therefore does not anticipate this first *ut* clause but the second, namely *ut ... administraret*, which is thus the result (compare 25 n. 1B) of *ita esse visum* rather than a second purpose clause in explanatory apposition with the first without a connective (compare n. 11A below); = "that the hope of empire (or, of rule) should be placed on C. Marius recently seemed so (desirable) to you and to your fathers that he conducted war alike with Jugurtha and with the Cimbri and with the Teutons"; i.e. the people felt so strongly that Marius alone could save the empire that they put him in command of these wars.   C. **Mario:** for his commands in these wars see 21 and 22.   D. **idem ... idem ... idem:** the repetition is equivalent to Eng. "he successively ..."; compare 13 n. 1A.   E. **bellum:** sing. although three successive wars are meant, since *bellum administrare* conveys a single verbal concept, i.e. *pugnare*; compare *bellum gerere* in 9 n. 1C.

6.   A. **in ... Pompeio:** *in*+a proper name in the abl. is often best rendered by "in the case of."   B. **ipso:** provides an emphatic transition, and may be rendered: "as for Pompey" or "now in Pompey's case."   C. **novi constitui nihil**="nothing new (i.e. no new kind of *imperium*) to be established"; for the gen. compare n. 1B above. Manilius suggested an *imperium aequum infinitum* which would make Pompey equal to all other governors in the whole area and which was to last not for a set term of a year or so, like most *imperia*, but until the war should end.

7.   A. **quam multa ... constituta:** indirect question after *recordamini*; *nova* is used as a noun (compare 26 n. 16B) modified by *multa* and subject of *sint ... constituta*; in Eng. it might be rendered "innovations"; compare 24 n. 9B (and 28 n. 7B).   B. **summa Q. Catuli voluntate**="with the entire (lit. utmost) approval of Q. Catulus." Though the optimates had supported the unusual commands given to Pompey in the 70's (see 28, especially n. 10), they now felt that he had veered toward the *populares* (see 28 pref.) and in addition they were loyal to Lucullus. Under the leadership of Catulus (for whom see 28 n. 8A) they therefore opposed Manilius' bill; see 29 pref.   C. **recordamini:** in the context of this speech it is less clear than it was in 27 n. 7A whether this is pass. plur. imperative or 2nd pers. plur. pres. pass. ind.

8.   A. **quid tam novum ... conficere**="What (was) so novel as for a young man not a magistrate (*privatum*) to levy an army etc."; that the verb to be supplied in the first part of each comparison is *erat* (not *est*) is shown by the secondary sequence of all the subordinate subjs. in the second halves. From *quam exercitum ... conficere* through *quam equitem ... triumphare* the second part of each comparison is an inf. clause; the final three are substantive *ut* clauses, probably "result."   B. **exercitum ... conficere:** for this idiom compare 22 n. 4 (and 29 nn. 4 and 7B).

9.   **praeesse ... gerere:** parallel to *conficere* as further second parts of the comparison after *quid tam novum quam* and with *adulescentulum privatum* continuing as their subject.

10.   **cuius ... abesset:** a relative clause of characteristic expressing concession; = "although his age was far from senatorial rank." At this time, the minimum age for the

quaestorship (see 14 n. 2c), which admitted to the senate, was the completed thirtieth year; Pompey, born in 106, was only 24 when he received his first *imperium* from Sulla late in 82.

11. A. **Siciliam ... administrandum:** an indirect statement in explanatory apposition (and asyndeton; contrast n. 4A above) with the preceding *imperium ... dari*. *Siciliam* and *Africam*, connected by *atque*, are the principal subjects of the inf. *permitti*; *bellum etc.* is closely connected to *Africam* by the *-que* to supplement it as second subject; = "Africa and the war (that had) to be managed in that province." B. **bellum ... administrandum:** for the use of the gerundive in agreement with a noun to indicate purpose or necessity see 4 nn. 1c and 6B.

12. **singulari ... virtute:** abls. of description; see 13 n. 4 (and 14 n. 2A).

13. **victorem exercitum deportavit:** for the adjectival use of *victor* see 21 n. 6B (and compare 21 n. 16). After Pompey's success against the Marians in Africa, Sulla had ordered him to disband his army there, but the young general brought it back to Italy and was granted a triumph in 79 by a very unwilling Sulla. It is curious that Cicero should praise him for such a violation not only of Sulla's orders but of the proscription against bringing troops into Italy under arms, unless he felt that the assembly would be pleased that Pompey had defied the dictator and asserted his claim to what Cicero says was a popular triumph. Perhaps Cicero also meant to imply that Pompey had not used (or left) his victorious troops to plunder the reconquered provinces.

14. **equitem Romanum triumphare:** the last of the inf. clauses in the succession of comparisons; see n. 8A above. In early Rome, the cavalry had consisted of the sons of senators who were rich enough to provide and maintain a horse. They were therefore enrolled on the voting lists as equestrians until they held a magistracy which admitted them to the senate. By the time of the later Republic, young men of senatorial families no longer actually served as cavalry. However, they continued to be enrolled as equestrians until they held the quaestorship (see n. 10 above), even though by then the equestrian order had been greatly enlarged by the enrollment of persons who, though not members of senatorial families, nevertheless had sufficient financial capital to qualify as equestrians; see 17 pref. Pompey, though son of a senator, held his first magistracy as consul in 70 and was until then an *eques*; see nn. 17B and 19 below.

15. A. **rem:** i.e. the triumph; object of *vidit* and subject of the two 2nd (pass.) periphrastic infs. (see 14 n. 10) *visendam et concelebrandam* (with which supply *esse*) in indirect discourse after *putavit*. B. **omnium ... putavit** = "thought that (the triumph) ought to be beheld and celebrated with universal (lit. of all) enthusiasm." C. **studio:** abl. of means, or of manner without *cum*. D. **visendam:** gerundive of *viso, -ere*, a "frequentative" verb derived from *video*; lit. = "see again and again" or "keep seeing."

16. **ut ... mitteretur:** a substantive *ut* clause of result, the first of three such in the second parts of comparisons after *quid ... quam* and replacing, for variation, the inf. clauses used previously; see n. 8A above. Cicero suggests, without so stating, that the consuls of 77 either were unwilling or seemed unsuited for the command against Sertorius. Actually Pompey imposed himself on the senate, which would have been quite content to leave the campaign in charge of Metellus; see 28 n. 10. The consuls for 77 were Decimus Junius Brutus, father of the Decimus Brutus who joined in the assassination of Caesar, and Mamercus Aemilius Lepidus, apparently not a close relative of the revolutionary consul of the previous year, for whom see 28 n. 7A.

17. A. **ex senatus consulto:** the decree of the senate, being advisory to the magistrate, is construed as an abl. of source with *ex* rather than as an abl. of means; see 25 n. 3A (and compare 28 n. 22c). B. **legibus solutus** = "exempted from the (requirements of the) laws," i.e. those governing candidacy for the magistracies. The senate claimed the right of recommending dispensations from the laws, though their grants of such *privilegia* were to be restricted under a tribunician *lex Cornelia* of 67. Presumably in this case they "advised" the consul of 71 to accept Pompey's candidacy for the consulship even though he was six years under the required age of the completed forty-second year;

see 28 n. 20A and, for the age, 12 n. 10B. Pompey had the support both of his troops and of the populace in demanding that the senate admit him to candidacy contrary to the law.

18.   A. **quam ullum . . . licuisset:** subj. because the second half of a comparison in the substantive *ut* clause (of result; see n. 16 above); the pluperf. in secondary sequence indicates time antecedent to that of *fieret*, the verb in the first half of the comparison; no person is expressed, either as dat. after *licuisset* or as acc. subject of *capere*, so that probably not Pompey but anybody is implied; = "before (the age at which) it had (previously) been permitted (for anybody) to hold any other office (at all) by the laws." B. **ante . . . quam:** here a divided conjunction; contrast in 14 n. 12 but compare *prius . . . quam* in 28 n. 13A.   C. **per leges:** equivalent to an abl. of means; see 5 n. 16A.

19.   **ut iterum eques . . . triumpharet:** the senate was also forced by the pressure of soldiers and people to consent that Pompey should triumph a second time for his defeat of Sertorius just before he entered on the consulship with Crassus on Jan. 1, 70 (compare 28 n. 15), that is, while he was still technically not a senator but an *eques*; see n. 14 above.

31

The years from 80–43 are known, particularly in the history of Latin literature, as the Ciceronian Age, and the political history of at least the second half of this period is still seen through Cicero's eyes. His speeches and letters bring us more intimately into touch with events in Rome than is possible for any age until the Renaissance. Especially his letters (864, of which 774 are from Cicero and 90 from his correspondents), preserved as he wrote them on the spur of the moment or for more formal occasions, have the vivacity of on-the-spot evidence.

Yet only for a few years, from his consulship in 63 to about 60, was Cicero really a dominant figure in Roman politics. He was not, indeed, a man who would have been expected to become outstanding in Roman life. He was born on January 3, 106, in Arpinum, birthplace earlier of Marius (see 21 pref.), from a family which was prominent locally and had good Roman connections, but which had never entered into Roman politics. Nevertheless, Cicero resolved to embark on a public career. His father sent him to Rome to study oratory as a preparation for becoming an advocate in the law courts. He gained prominence in several cases in the years from 80–70 (see 28 pref. and 29–30), and rose through the regular sequence of magistracies (*cursus honorum*), being elected, he tells us, to each at the earliest legal age. The circumstances of his consulship are described in 32 pref.

In a speech delivered in 54, Cicero told the following anecdote about his return from his quaestorship in western Sicily in 75. In it he attributed his political success to his assiduous practice of oratory in the courts at Rome.

Cicero fabulam de quaestura sua narrat

Ita multa Romae geruntur ut vix ea quae fiunt in provinciis audiantur.[1] Non vereor ne mihi aliquid, iudices, videar adrogare,[2] si de quaestura mea dixero.[3] Vere me hercule hoc dicam:[4] sic tum existimabam, nihil homines aliud Romae nisi de quaestura mea loqui. Frumenti in summa caritate maximum numerum miseram;[5] negotiatoribus comis, mercatoribus iustus, mancipibus liberalis, sociis abstinens;[6] omnibus eram visus in omni officio diligentissimus; excogitati quidam erant a Siculis honores in me inauditi.[7] Itaque hac spe decedebam, ut mihi populum Romanum ultro omnia delaturum putarem.[8]

At ego, cum decedens e provincia Puteolos forte venissem diebus iis cum plurimi et lautissimi solent esse in iis locis,[9] concidi paene, iudices, cum ex me quidam quaesisset quo die Roma exissem et num quidnam esset novi.[10] Cui cum respondissem me e provincia decedere, "Etiam me hercule," inquit, "ut opinor, ex Africa." Huic ego, iam stomachans, fastidiose, "Immo, ex Sicilia," inquam. Tum quidam quasi qui omnia sciret,[11] "Quid? tu nescis," inquit, "hunc Syracusis quaestorem fuisse?" Quid multa?[12] Destiti stomachari, et me unum ex iis feci, qui ad aquas venissent.[13]

Sed ea res, iudices, haud scio an plus mihi profuerit, quam si mihi tum essent omnes gratulati.[14] Nam destiti quid de me audituri essent homines cogitare; feci ut postea cottidie me praesentem viderent;[15] habitavi in oculis;[16] pressi forum; neminem a congressu meo neque ianitor meus neque somnus absterruit. Ecquid ego dicam de occupatis meis temporibus, cui fuerit ne otium quidem umquam otiosum?[17] Nam quas tu commemoras, Cassi, legere te solere orationes cum otiosus sis, has ego scripsi ludis et feriis, ne omnino umquam essem otiosus.[18] Itaque si quam habeo laudem (quae quanta sit, nescio), parta Romae est, quaesita in foro,[19] meaque privata consilia publici quoque casus comprobaverunt,[20] ut etiam summa res publica mihi domi fuerit gerenda, et urbs in urbe servanda.[21]

1.   A. **ita ... audiantur:** both this sentence and the next are introductory remarks to the anecdote which Cicero is about to tell. He speaks informally and uses no connective, but the train of thought, though elliptical, is easy to fill out: "Nobody at Rome knows what goes on in the provinces. (I can illustrate this from my own experience, and will do so, since) I do not fear etc."   B. **fiunt:** not attracted to the subj. though dependent on *audiantur* (result), because it states a fact.

2.   A. **non vereor ne ... videar adrogare**="I am not afraid that I shall seem presumptuous (lit. claim something for myself)." Expressions suggesting fear take the subj. with *ne* for what it is feared may occur and *ut* (or *ne non*) for what it is feared may not occur; the regular sequence of tenses is followed.   B. **aliquid:** used here, rather than *quid*, because it is separated from *ne* by *mihi*; contrast 4 n. 11B (and 30 n. 1B).   C. **iudices**="members (in Eng., gentlemen) of the jury," as regularly in court speeches; see below in the 2nd par.

3.   **dixero:** fut. perf. in the protasis of a fut. more vivid condition; the fact that it is not attracted into the subj. shows that it is a protasis not for *videar* but for *non vereor*, which is pres. instead of fut. because futurity is connoted by the concept of fearing lest something happen.

4.   **me hercule**="by Hercules"; a common exclamatory interjection (often written as one word), perhaps shortened from some such phrase as *ita me Hercules iuvet*.

5. A. **frumenti . . . inauditi:** in this succession of rapid preliminary narrative statements, Cicero uses no connectives (asyndeton; see 4 n. 5B and 30 n. 11A). B. **in summa caritate** = "at a time of very high prices (lit. in the greatest dearness)." As quaestor (see 14 n. 2C), Cicero was responsible under his governor for the transactions necessary to get grain, either as tithes or by purchase, to send to Rome. He was thus constantly in touch not only with financiers (*negotiatores*) but also with traders (*mercatores*) in grain and contractors (*mancipes*) for taxes paid in kind (i.e. in grain).

6. A. **negotiatoribus . . . abstinens:** as punctuated with a semicolon after *abstinens*, *eram* may be supplied and the four dats. may be regarded as dats. of reference with the four adjs.: "(I was) kindly toward the financiers etc." However, a comma might be substituted for the semicolon and the dats. and adjs. taken with *eram visus* parallel to *omnibus . . . diligentissimus*, in which case, of course, the dats. would be dats. of indirect object. B. **negotiatoribus:** large-scale operators in finance or in trade (as against the small-scale *mercatores*) or in both. C. **abstinens:** here an adj., not a part., so that *sociis* is dat. of reference, not abl. of separation without a prep.; see the preceding note. Cicero means that, unlike many Roman officials, he did not extort money from the Sicilian cities which were allied with Rome and hence not directly under his control for taxation.

7. **excogitati . . . inauditi:** both *quidam* and *inauditi* are masc. nom. plur. modifying *honores*, the subject of *excogitati erant*.

8. A. **hac spe:** abl. of attendant circumstance; the substantive clause (probably consecutive or "result") *ut . . . putarem* is in apposition, explaining what his hope was. In Eng. *putarem* is not strictly necessary, but Lat. regularly uses a verb of thinking or expecting to repeat the idea of *spes*. B. **decedebam:** *decedere* is regularly used for leaving a province after a term of office. C. **omnia delaturum** (*esse*) = "would bestow all (offices)"; *defero*, lit. = "carry (away or to)," has a great variety of meanings depending on its subject and object. When *populus Romanus* is the subject it regularly = "allow" or "confer" (office).

9. A. **Puteolos:** modern Pozzuoli, a city just north of Naples which was a popular resort. It also served as the main port of entry for Rome until Claudius, and later Trajan, developed Ostia at the mouth of the Tiber. For the plur. form compare 5 n. 15A (and 10 n. 10B). B. **solent:** ind., not subj., because the *cum* clause here is not circumstantial, as is *cum . . . venissem*, but merely specifies a time. Cicero arrived at the height of the "season" when Puteoli was filled with the *lautissimi*, the wealthy upper classes.

10. A. **concidi paene** = "I almost fell over" (i.e. from surprise); *concido* is from *cum* + *cado*; compare 27 n. 3B (and contrast 5 n. 12). B. **quidnam . . . novi** = "anything new"; the regular way of expressing "any news?" in Lat.; compare 30 n. 1B.

11. **tum . . . sciret** = "then someone, like a know-it-all," lit. "as if (he were someone) who knew everything"; *sciret* is imperf. subj. in a rel. clause of characteristic after an indefinite antecedent; see 20 n. 12A. This officious bystander made the mistake of saying that Cicero had been quaestor at Syracuse when he was actually stationed at the opposite (west) end of Sicily, at Lilybaeum (modern Marsala).

12. **quid multa** = "in short," lit. "why (say) many things?"; it is a frequent formula in Cicero.

13. **me . . . venissent** = "I made myself one of those who had come for the waters"; *venissent* is pluperf. subj. for a completed action in secondary sequence in a rel. clause of characteristic after the indefinite antecedent *iis*; compare n. 11 above. Cicero means that he gave up expecting people to know that he was on his way back from a province and pretended that he was there simply to bathe in the sulphur springs for which Puteoli was (and still is) famous.

14. A. **haud scio an:** lit. = "I do not know whether." The phrase introduces an indirect question, but it usually implies a positive opinion and is best rendered in Eng. by "I am inclined to think that" + an indirect statement. B. **quam . . . gratulati** =

"than if everybody had congratulated me then"; the pluperf. subj. is used because the clause is the protasis of a past contrary to fact condition; compare 9 n. 6D (and 25 n. 8). The apodosis of *si . . . gratulati* is suppressed, i.e. "I am inclined to think that it profited me more than (it would have) if everybody had then congratulated me."

15. **feci** = "I saw to it that"; the following substantive clause of result, *ut . . . viderent*, is the object.

16. **in oculis**: i.e. in the (public) eye.

17. A. **ecquid ego dicam**: a rhetorical question with, probably, a deliberative subj. (rather than a fut. ind.). Cicero asks why he should speak about his busy periods since he in fact never had any free moments.   B. **cui fuerit**: rel. clause of characteristic expressing cause; = "since I had (lit. to whom there was)"; for this rendering of the dat. of reference with *esse* see 11 n. 9 (and 21 n. 5B).

18. A. **quas . . . has**: a rhetorical arrangement for *has orationes quas tu commemoras te solere legere*. The antecedent is included in the rel. clause, as often (see 12 n. 8B and 15 n. 12B) and then *has* is used to repeat it. For the meaning of *commemoras* see 15 n. 13C (and 30 n. 5A).   B. **Cassi**: voc.; L. Cassius Longinus, brother of C. Cassius Longinus who was a leader in the assassination of Caesar (see 43 n. 2), was one of the prosecutors of Cicero's client in this case, Cn. Plancius, on a charge of illegal canvassing.

19. A. **si quam habeo . . . parta . . . est**: a simple factual condition, mixed pres. and past; for *parta est* (from *pario*) compare 21 n. 9. *Quam* is fem. acc. sing. of the indefinite *quis, qua, quid*, used as an indefinite pronoun after *si*; see 4 n. 11B (and 30 n. 1B).   B. **quae . . . nescio**: Cicero often uses such deprecatory parentheses, so as not to appear boastful.

20. **consilia . . . casus**: *casus*, masc. nom. plur., is subject and *consilia* object.

21. A. **ut . . . fuerit**: the perf. subj. in a result clause after a main verb in a secondary tense stresses the result as an actual or historical fact without reference to the continuance of the action; see 16 n. 13F. Here, therefore, Cicero stresses that the result of the justification of his plans by public events was that the city not only had to be, but in actual fact was, saved by him at home, i.e. in Rome, not in the field.   B. **summa res publica**: a common idiom; lit. = "the highest (affairs of) state," usually rendered "public affairs of the greatest importance," or simply "the general welfare"; compare 19 n. 6B. C. **domi . . . in urbe**: Cicero is contrasting himself with other statesmen, most of whom came to prominence through military exploits (e.g. Pompey). Cicero saved the city, while he was consul in 63, from the conspiracy of Catiline; see 32.

32

Cicero's career, while exceptional for a man of nonsenatorial family (see 31 pref.), would hardly have been enough in itself to induce the *nobiles* to permit him to campaign for their particular prize, the consulship; compare for Marius 21 pref. In these years, however, Rome had been disturbed by the plots of a decadent patrician and former henchman of Sulla, L. Sergius Catilina. Catiline had been twice blocked from the consulship, but he tried again in 64, with the rumored support of Crassus (see 28 nn. 19c and D) and Caesar, who were hoping to weaken the optimates to their own advantage. The optimates put forth one ineffective noble candidate, Gaius Antonius, but to secure the votes of equestrians, Italians, and other *boni* (see 18 nn. 5c and 13A, and 20 n. 5B) permitted Cicero to stand. He was returned head of the list (thus qualifying as a *novus homo*; see prefs. to 13 and 21), with Antonius as his colleague. Catiline then turned to revolutionary plans of assembling a force of malcontents near Florence and seizing Rome by an internal uprising and murder of the magistrates.

The plot and its revelation to the senate and people by Cicero are well known through Cicero's four speeches, *in Catilinam* I–IV, and through the monograph, *Bellum Catilinae*, which Sallust wrote some twenty years later. The plot no doubt constituted a real threat to security and the status quo, but Cicero plumed himself excessively, even by ancient standards, on the discovery of the conspiracy, the execution of those plotters seized in Rome, and the defeat of Catiline and his army early in 62.

The following selections are both drawn from Cicero's *Letters*.

Cicero de consulatu suo

A. M. TVLLIVS M. F. CICERO S. D. CN. POMPEIO CN. F. MAGNO IMPERATORI.[1]

S. T. E. Q. V. B. E.[2] Ex litteris tuis, quas publice misisti, cepi una cum omnibus incredibilem voluptatem;[3] tantam enim spem oti ostendisti, quantam ego semper omnibus, te uno fretus, pollicebar.[4] Ad me autem litteras quas misisti,[5] quamquam exiguam significationem tuae erga me voluntatis habebant, tamen mihi scito iucundas fuisse.[6] Illud enim non dubito quin,[7] si te mea summa erga te studia parum mihi adiunxerint,[8] res publica nos inter nos conciliatura coniuncturaque sit.[9]

Ne ignores quid ego in tuis litteris desiderarim, scribam aperte, sicut et mea natura et nostra amicitia postulat. Res eas gessi, quarum aliquam in tuis litteris et nostrae necessitudinis et rei publicae causa gratulationem exspectavi;[10] quam ego abs te praetermissam esse arbitror, quod vererere ne cuius animum offenderes.[11] Sed scito ea, quae nos pro salute patriae gessimus, orbis terrae iudicio ac testimonio comprobari.[12] Quae, cum veneris, tanto consilio tantaque animi magnitudine a me gesta esse cognosces,[13] ut tibi (multo maiori quam Africanus fuit) me (non multo minorem quam Laelium) facile et in re publica et in amicitia adiunctum esse patiare.[14]

B.   CICERO ATTICO SAL.[15]

Putavi mihi maiores quasdam opes et firmiora praesidia esse quaerenda.[16] Itaque primum eum qui nimium diu de rebus nostris tacuerat, Pompeium, adduxi in eam voluntatem ut in senatu non semel sed saepe multisque verbis huius mihi salutem imperi atque orbis terrarum adiudicarit.[17] Cum hoc ego me tanta familiaritate coniunxi ut uterque nostrum in sua ratione munitior et in re publica firmior hac coniunctione esse possit.[18]

Commentarium consulatus mei Graece compositum misi ad te.[19] Latinum si perfecero, ad te mittam. Tertium poema exspectato,[20] ne quod genus a me ipso laudis meae praetermittatur.

1. A. **M. TVLLIVS . . . IMPERATORI:** this letter was written in April 62, before Pompey had returned from fighting Mithridates. The heading is very formal: Cicero gives both his and Pompey's fathers, *M(arci) F(ilius), Cn(aei) F(ilio)*, and calls Pompey by two titles, *Magno* (which came to serve as a *cognomen*; see 29 pref.) and *Imperatori* (his official position).   B. **S. D.** = *salutem dicit* or *dat*; the phrase is so regular in formal Roman letters that it is ordinarily abbreviated.

2. **S. . . . E.** = *Si tu exercitusque valetis, bene est*; the conventional opening of a formal letter to a commander.

3. A. **litteris:** the plur. is regularly used for a single epistle.   B. **publice:** indicates that Cicero refers to a public dispatch, presumably sent by Pompey to announce his victory over Mithridates, for which see 35 pref.   C. **una** = "together"; it is the fem. abl. sing. of *unus*, used adverbially (compare the advs. *extra, intra,* etc.); it often, as here, reinforces the prep. *cum*.

4. A. **tantam . . . quantam:** for these correlative adjs. see 18 n. 4A.   B. **oti:** gen. sing.; for the spelling see 17 n. 7. *Otium* usually means "(personal) leisure," as in 31 par. 3, but here it may be used instead of *pax* for the peace which Pompey had brought about by his conquest of the pirates and Mithridates; see 29–30 and 35 pref. *Otium* may also mean "freedom from civil strife," so that Cicero may be referring to the fact

that Pompey had no intention of returning to start a civil war, as Sulla had done; see 26.   c. **te uno:** abl. with *fretus*; see 25 n. 4A.   D. **semper ... pollicebar:** for the imperf. see 21 n. 4B (and 23 n. 8B).

5.   **ad me ... misisti:** *ad me* would normally come between *quas* and *misisti* (compare *quas publice misisti* in the opening sentence above); here it is put first because it is emphatic, introducing the real subject of this letter, namely, the fact that Pompey, in a letter to Cicero (personal but not necessarily private), had replied coldly to an earlier letter from Cicero describing the suppression of Catiline.

6.   A. **voluntatis** = "(good) will," as often; compare 30 n. 7B.   B. **scito** = "be sure," i.e. "I assure you"; it is 2nd pers. sing. act. "fut." imperative of *scio*; the so-called fut. imperative is regularly used, especially in legal or religious language, to give a general injunction rather than a specific command, or at most to suggest futurity; Cicero is here using it with formal politeness to Pompey, perhaps having in mind the future moment when Pompey will read the letter rather than the present in which he writes.

7.   A. **illud:** proleptic (anticipatory) in apposition with the object of *dubito*, the *quin ... sit* clause; the phrase might be rendered "for this [emphatic] I do not doubt, (namely) that"; compare *haec* in 29 n. 13B.   B. **non dubito quin ... sit:** *quin* + subj. is usual after *non dubito* = "I do not doubt that," whereas positive *dubito* is usually followed by an indirect question; in either case the regular sequence of tenses is followed. c. **quin** = "that (lit. but that)"; compare for other uses 19 n. 9A, 21 n. 12A, and 27 n. 12A.

8.   A. **mea ... studia** = "my enthusiastic support of you," lit. "my greatest zeals towards you." Cicero had not only endorsed the Gabinian and Manilian laws (see 29 pref.) but also had supported Pompey in the senate on other occasions.   B. **adiunxerint:** perf. subj. by attraction to the subj. in the *quin* clause. If Cicero is referring to Pompey's attitude in the past, it replaces a perf. ind. in a mixed condition: "(even) if my services have not attached you to me closely enough, the Republic will etc." If, however, Cicero is referring to what Pompey's attitude may be after he returns, the perf. subj. replaces a fut. perf. ind. in a future more vivid condition: "(even) if my services do not (lit. shall not have) etc."

9.   A. **res publica:** i.e. the welfare of the Republic, or, more generally, "the political situation"; compare 19 n. 6B (and 31 n. 21B). Cicero thought that during his consulship he had effected a *concordia ordinum* (combination of the moderate men among both senators and *equites*) and he hoped that Pompey would support this ideal.   B. **conciliatura ... sit:** pres. subjs. of 1st (act.) periphrastic conjs. (see 28 n. 21), here used for an action which is not only incomplete but distinctly in the future, i.e. after Pompey's return. The two participles express by hendiadys (see 13 n. 11A and 28 n. 13B) a single idea to make a single compound verb with *sit*.

10.   A. **quarum aliquam ... exspectavi** = "for which I expected some congratulation"; for the unusually long separation between *aliquam* and *gratulationem*, compare 19 n. 13A (and 28 n. 6A).   B. **necessitudinis** = "of our friendship"; *necessitudo* often means a close relationship (of family, friendship, clientship, etc.) rather than "necessity."

11.   A. **vererere:** 2nd pers. sing. imperf. subj. pass.; for the ending -*re* see 14 n. 13E; it is subj. because the *quod* causal clause gives what Cicero assumes to have been Pompey's reason, not his own explanation (see 4 n. 9A and contrast 20 n. 10A), and imperf. in secondary sequence because the sequence is governed by the perf. inf. *praetermissam esse*, not by the introductory pres. *arbitror*. Secondary sequence is regular when the subjs. in an indirect statement represent past tenses in direct discourse; here, in direct discourse, Cicero would have said: "this was neglected by you because you were afraid." B. **offenderes:** for *ne* + the subj. after verbs of fearing see 31 n. 2A; for the secondary sequence see the preceding note.   c. **cuius animum** = "someone's feeling(s)"; for *cuius* = *alicuius* after *ne* see 4 n. 11B (and contrast 31 n. 2B).   D. **animum:** for the meaning here compare 19 n. 3B (and 21 n. 13C).

12.   A. **scito:** see n. 6B above.   B. **nos ... gessimus:** Cicero varies between the 1st pers. sing. and plur. with little difference in meaning; compare *res eas gessi* in the previous sentence.   C. **orbis terrae**=*orbis terrarum*; see 9 n. 6C.

13.   A. **quae:** neut. acc. plur.; the subject of *gesta esse* and used as a connective (see 4 n. 4A and 23 n. 7A); = "but ... these things."   B. **animi magnitudine:** a common phrase, often rendered simply "greatness, heroism"; the Eng. derivative "magnanimity" has acquired a different connotation; for *animi* compare n. 11D above.

14.   A. **ut ... patiare:** the two parentheses are in apposition to *tibi* and *me*, respectively the dat, indirect object and acc. subject of *adiunctum esse*; in the first, *quam* introduces a clause, but in the second simply an acc. noun in apposition. Cicero chose the historical parallel because the friendship of Scipio Aemilianus (Africanus Minor) and Laelius was proverbial; see 16 pref. He then softened what might seem presumptuous to Pompey's touchy vanity by saying that Pompey is much greater than Africanus was, while he himself is somewhat less great than Laelius.   B. **re publica**= "in public life," as opposed to "in (private) friendship"; see 19 n. 14 (and contrast n. 9A above).   C. **amicitia:** though often used for a political association (see 38 n. 17A), here the earlier reference to Scipio and Laelius supports a contrast between public activity and private friendship.   D. **patiare:** for the ending *-re* see n. 11A above.

15.   **CICERO ATTICO SAL.:** the brief names and *SAL.*, a less formal variation on *S. D.* (see n. 1B above), show that this is a private letter to a friend. It was written in 60, on March 15, to Cicero's lifelong close friend T. Pomponius Atticus. Atticus, a Roman knight, never engaged in politics, except indirectly to help Cicero. An adherent of Epicureanism, he lived mostly at Athens (whence his surname), pursuing his literary and business interests. Among his ventures was publishing, that is, he had a number of trained slaves to copy books, including those of Cicero. In spite of his enormous wealth, he escaped all the proscriptions, from Marius' to that of Octavian and Antony (see 44 pref.), and survived until 32.

16.   **opes ... praesidia:** both terms are used in an abstract sense; = "(political) resources ... supports"; for *opes* contrast 1 n. 5B and for *praesidia* compare 29 nn. 8D and 11A (and contrast 29 n. 15B).

17.   A. **eam voluntatem**= "such good will"; *is, ea, id* is often used instead of *talis, -e,* or *tantus, -a, -um*, to introduce a result clause.   B. **voluntatem:** for the meaning here see n. 6A above.   C. **imperi:** the gen. is here written with a single *-i*; compare *oti* in n. 4B above.   D. **orbis terrarum:** contrast *terrae* in n. 12C above.

18.   **in sua ratione ... in re publica**= "in his own policy ... in (his) political position," lit. "in the state"; compare nn. 9A and 14B above.

19.   A. **commentarium**= "an outline"; see 28 n. 23E.   B. **Graece compositum**= "written in Greek." Lat. regularly uses an adv. to indicate in what language something is spoken or written. *Latinum* in the next sentence is an adj. modifying *commentarium* understood.

20.   A. **tertium:** either adj. with *poema* (as *primi* in 5 n. 17A) or neut. acc. sing. used adverbially; in any case render as an adv. in English: "thirdly."   B. **poema:** Greek neut. acc. sing. Cicero actually composed this poem, of which some fragments survive, including the much ridiculed line: *O fortunatam natam, me consule, Romam.* To reproduce the effect of the ugly jingle, this has been rendered: "O happy fate for the Roman state was the date of my great consulate." Another surviving line, *Cedant arma togae, concedat laurea linguae*= "Let war to peace, the wreath to eloquence, give pride of place," expresses one of Cicero's fixed opinions, that statesmen were really more important than military conquerors; compare 31 n. 21A and contrast n. 14A above, where he is self-deprecatory only to flatter Pompey.   C. **exspectato:** fut. imperative used because there is a distinct reference to future time; contrast *scito* in nn. 6B and 12A above.

33

According to the ancient sources, Gaius Julius Caesar was born in 100; if so, he held all magistracies two years before the minimum legal ages as attested by Cicero; see 12 n. 10B and 30 nn. 10 and 17B. Theodor Mommsen, an outstanding German scholar of the nineteenth century, therefore held that he was born in 102; other solutions have been proposed, including the theory that patricians had a two-year advance over plebeians in the *cursus honorum*, the succession of magistracies. The *Iulii* were a patrician *gens* which claimed descent from Venus, through Aeneas' son; see 1 pref. The family of the *Iulii Caesares* had not been prominent, however, until the early part of the first century, when two members, Sextus and Lucius, were consuls; see 23 n. 6A. Apparently Caesar's father died after attaining only the praetorship. His sister Julia, Caesar's aunt, was the wife of Marius. Caesar himself married, in about 85, Cornelia, daughter of Cinna; see 25 and n. 4B below.

Not surprisingly, in view of his family connections, Caesar began his political career as an open supporter of the *populares* (see 28 pref.) against the optimates. Early in 68, when he was quaestor, both his aunt Julia, the widow of Marius, and Cornelia died. Caesar, in pronouncing their funeral eulogies, used these opportunities to win popular favor by open praise of Marius and Cinna. He also displayed images of Marius which had not been seen since Sulla had declared Marius a public enemy.

The rest of his year as quaestor, Caesar served in Further Spain. Returning to Rome, he pursued his political career with the help of loans from Crassus; see 28, especially n. 19D. As aedile in 65 Caesar arranged lavish games which won him popular favor. Both he and Crassus were rumored to have supported Catiline in his early bids for the consulship (see 32 pref.), and Caesar had backed the bills which gave Pompey the commands against the pirates and Mithridates; see 29 and 30. Towards the close of 63 he succeeded, by bribery, in being elected *pontifex maximus*, an office usually reserved for conservative elder statesmen. After his praetorship in 62, Caesar went as governor to Further Spain for a year, during which he tested seriously for the first time his administrative and military talents. On his return in 60, he immediately played a decisive, and for the first time central, role in Roman politics; see 35 pref.

The following passage is composed from Velleius and from Suetonius' life of Caesar in his collection of biographies of "The Twelve Caesars" from Caesar to Domitian, who was murdered in A.D. 96. Suetonius wrote during the early second century A.D.

Gaius Iulius Caesar

C. Caesar, nobilissima Iuliorum genitus familia et ab Anchise ac Venere deducens genus,[1] forma omnium civium excellentissimus, vigore animi acerrimus, munificentia effusissimus,[2] fuit C. Mario sanguine coniunctissimus atque idem Cinnae gener,[3] cuius filiam ut repudiaret nullo metu a Sulla compelli potuit.[4] Magnitudine cogitationum, celeritate bellandi, patientia periculorum Magno illi Alexandro simillimus erat.[5] Quaestor quidem in ulteriore Hispania, animadversa Gadibus apud Herculis templum Magni Alexandri imagine,[6] ingemuit et quasi pertaesus ignaviam suam,[7] quod nihildum a se memorabile actum esset in aetate qua iam Alexander orbem terrarum subegisset, missionem continuo efflagitavit ad captandas quam primum maiorum rerum occasiones in urbe.[8]

Caesar autem fuisse traditur excelsa statura, colore candido, teretibus membris, ore paulo pleniore,[9] nigris vegetisque oculis, valitudine prospera, nisi quod tempore extremo repente animo linqui atque etiam per somnum exterreri solebat.[10] Comitiali quoque morbo bis inter res agendas correptus est.[11] Circa corporis curam morosior; calvitii vero deformitatem iniquissime tulit.[12]

Pronum et sumptuosum in libidines fuisse constans opinio est,[13] plurimasque et illustres feminas corrupisse, in quibus Tertullam Marci Crassi, etiam Gnaei Pompeii Muciam.[14] Sed ante alias dilexit Marci Bruti matrem Serviliam,[15] cui primo suo consulatu sexagiens sestertium margaritam mercatus est.[16] Dilexit et reginas, maxime Cleopatram,[17] cum qua et convivia in primam lucem saepe protraxit et Aethiopiam penetrasset, nisi exercitus sequi recusasset.[18] Quam denique accitam in urbem, non nisi maximis honoribus praemiisque auctam remisit,[19] filiumque natum appellare nomine suo passus est,[20] quem quidem nonnulli Graecorum similem fuisse Caesari et forma et incessu tradiderunt.[21]

Vini parcissimum ne inimici quidem negaverunt.[22] Marci Catonis est:[23] unum ex omnibus Caesarem ad evertendam rem publicam sobrium accessisse. Studium et fides erga clientis ei ne iuveni quidem defuerunt[24] atque amicos magna semper facilitate indulgentiaque tractavit. Iam autem rerum potens quosdam etiam infimi generis ad amplissimos honores provexit,[25] quam ob rem culpatus est. Simultates, contra, nullas tam graves excepit umquam, ut non occasione oblata libens deponeret.[26]

1.   A. **nobilissima . . . familia:** abl. of source (separation) without a preposition after *genitus*; see 5 nn. 2A and B (and contrast with *deducens* in n. C below).   B. **familia:** here=*gens*, not "household" (for which compare 28 n. 23B) or "family" (for which compare 65 n. 8A).   C. **deducens genus**="tracing (lit. leading down) his lineage"; followed by *ab*+abl.; contrast with *genitus* in n. A above.   D. **genus:** often refers to family, birth, etc. For the legend of the descent of the Julian *gens* from Anchises and Venus see 1 pref. and n. 2B. In this introductory sentence, Velleius piles up modifiers of Caesar before coming to the main verb, *fuit*; compare 28 n. 2.

2.   A. **forma . . . vigore . . . munificentia:** abls. of specification with superlative adjs., as in 18 n. 3A. At the opening of the next par., Suetonius uses predicate abls. of description after *fuisse traditur*.   B. **civium:** partitive gen. with the superlative adj., as in 11 n. 11A (compare 16 n. 11B); *ex* or *de*+abl. may also be used, as noted in 9 n. 11.

3.   A. **sanguine**="by family ties," lit. "by blood"; probably also abl. of specification (rather than of means); for the meaning compare 15 n. 15B. Caesar was not, of course, related to Marius by blood but through his aunt Julia, wife of Marius; see pref. B. **idem:** i.e. also; see 11 n. 11B (and compare 13 n. 1A); with it understand *fuit*.

4.   A. **cuius**=*et eius*; see 4 n. 4A (and 32 n. 13A); because of its use as a connective, *cuius* and *filiam*, which it modifies, are placed before the subordinate *ut* clause in which they belong.   B. **ut . . . compelli potuit:** the clause of purpose, *ut repudiaret*, is adverbial with the pres. pass. inf. *compelli*, which, as complementary to *potuit*, has no acc. subject expressed since its subject is the same as that of *potuit*, i.e. Caesar. When Caesar refused to divorce Cornelia (see pref.), he was proscribed, but Sulla was then persuaded by mutual friends to spare the sickly young man's life; according to Suetonius *Iulius* 1.3, Sulla remarked ominously that *Caesari multos Marios inesse*, but this is perhaps a *post eventum* legend.

5.   **Magno illi Alexandro:** *illi* connotes "the well-known"; Alexander the Great was the Macedonian king who between his accession on the death of Philip II in 336 and his untimely death in 323 conquered the Near and Middle East as far as northwest India; his achievements challenged the imagination and rivalry of succeeding rulers and commanders, both Hellenistic and Roman, as suggested, for example, by the title "Great," which was also applied to Antiochus III of Syria (see 10 pref.) and to Pompey; see 29 pref. (and 32 n. 1A). His reputation might well be compared to that of Napoleon in modern Europe.

6.   A. **animadversa . . . imagine:** *animadvertens imaginem* might have been more natural; both Velleius and Suetonius complicate their styles by striving for effect. B. **Gadibus:** plur. place name in the loc.; modern Cadiz in southern Spain; for the plur. form, compare 5 n. 15A (and 31 n. 9A).   C. **apud:** used with acc. instead of *in*+abl. by historians under the Empire.

7.   **pertaesus ignaviam suam**="disgusted at (lit. tired of) his own inactivity." The impersonal *taedet* developed an impersonal perf. pass. in this compound: *pertaesum est*. Under the Empire, *taedere* began to be used personally and the past participle *pertaesus* acquired an active meaning, as if from a semi-deponent verb. In this use it was followed by an acc. (direct object) of the cause of the feeling, though the impersonal is followed by the acc. of the person affected (who becomes the subject in the personal use) and the gen. of the cause of the feeling; compare 22 n. 12B.

8.   A. **missionem . . . ad captandas etc.:** compare Marius in 21, especially n. 14B for *missionem*="discharge" or here perhaps "leave"; in 21 n. 14A it is modified by *gratia*+ a gerund, but here by *ad*+an acc. and a gerundive, to denote the purpose or end.   B. **continuo**="immediately," not "continually," for which the adv. *continue* occurs, but rarely. The adverbial use of the abl. originated from various constructions, such as the loc. abl. or the abl. of time when, means, manner, etc. The abls. of past parts., such as *consulto*, and occasionally of adjs., as probably here *continuo*, seem to have originated as abls. abs. without an expressed substantive.   C. **quam primum**="as soon (lit. first) as possible"; *quam*+a superlative adj. or adv. regularly="as . . . as possible."

9. **ore paulo pleniore** = "(of a) face a little too full"; *ore* is from *os*. Actually, the best surviving portraits show Caesar's face as lean, so that *ore* may here = "mouth," or perhaps *leniore* should be read instead of *pleniore*, = "his face a little too smooth (mild)."

10. A. **tempore extremo** = "at the end (of his) life"; for this idiomatic Lat. construction see 12 n. 7B.   B. **animo linqui** = "to faint," lit. "to be deserted by his spirit"; *animo* is probably abl. of means.

11. A. **comitiali . . . morbo** = "by epilepsy"; probably the cause of the fainting and nightmares just mentioned, and so called because, if a citizen had an attack during a meeting, the *comitia* had to be broken off and begun over again on another day.   B. **inter res agendas** = "when conducting public business"; the phrase might, less probably, mean "when on campaign."

12. **iniquissime tulit:** for the meaning of *fero* + adv. see 3 n. 2A.

13. **pronum . . . in libidines** = "prone to and lavish in (his) love affairs"; for the meaning of *pronus* see 22 n. 3B. Although the inf. clause is presumably indirect statement in predicate apposition with *opinio*, the subject (*eum*) is omitted, as also with *corrupisse*; it is readily understandable from the context.

14. **Tertullam . . . Muciam:** chiasmic order; see 17 n. 2 (and 30 n. 3A). The name of a wife is modified directly by her husband's name in the gen., with no word such as the *f(ilius)* used for a son, as in 32 n. 1A; similarly a slave's name is followed directly by his master's, but a freedman has *l(ibertus)*. This suggests that in the early days the wife was as completely under her husband's *patria potestas* as were his slaves. Crassus and Pompey were, of course, Caesar's partners in the first Triumvirate; see 35 and 36. Pompey divorced Mucia in 61 because of her affair with Caesar.

15. **Marci . . . Serviliam:** Servilia, stepsister of Cato the Younger (for whom see 34), played an influential role in the political life of this period. Marcus Brutus, the assassin of Caesar (see 43), was her son by her second husband, M. Junius Brutus, who supported Lepidus in the revolt crushed by Pompey; see 28 pref. and n. 7A (and 30 pref.). The elder Brutus surrendered on promise of safety, but was executed by Pompey. Servilia's affair with Caesar was so well known that Brutus was reputed to have been their son, but the date of his birth (85, well before the affair) makes this unlikely.

16. A. **primo suo consulatu:** in 59; see 35 pref.   B. **sexagiens sestertium** = "(costing) 6,000,000 sesterces"; in its metallic content this is about $150,000, but comparison with modern prices is hard to make because of the difficulty in comparing the purchasing power of money in antiquity and today. In origin the numeral adv. *sexagiens* went with *centena milia* and *sestertium* was the old 2nd decl. gen. plur. (see 11 n. 14B) dependent on *milia*; hence the phrase = "sixty times a hundred thousands of sesterces." Then *centena milia* came to be commonly omitted, and the Romans themselves were uncertain whether *sexagiens* acted as a quasi noun followed by the gen., or whether *sestertium* was a neut. sing. noun and declinable. Here *sestertium* is gen. plur. dependent either on *centenis milibus* to be supplied as abl. of price or on *sexagiens* to be taken as an indeclinable noun in the abl. of price.

17. **Cleopatram:** Cleopatra was the seventh of that name in the family of the Ptolemies, who descended from the Ptolemy (a Macedonian general) who took over Egypt on Alexander's death in 323. She was the third daughter of the last mature Ptolemy (XII, nicknamed *Auletes* or "Flute Player"). On the death of Auletes in 51, his older son, Ptolemy XIII, succeeded to the throne with, as was customary in Egypt, his by then oldest surviving sister, Cleopatra, as his wife. When Caesar occupied Egypt in 48, Ptolemy XIII was slain in the fighting, and Caesar then installed Cleopatra on the throne with, as her consort, her younger brother Ptolemy XIV, whom she put to death in 44. Some scholars reduce the numbers of these Ptolemies by one; *Auletes* is numbered Ptolemy XI, and so on. See also nn. 19 and 20 below and, for Cleopatra's later career and death, sel. 46.

18. **et convivia ... et Aethiopiam ... recusasset:** Suetonius is especially fond of connecting long clauses by *et ... et,* or other correlatives; compare 8 n. 12 (and 20 n. 10A). In Eng. two clauses so diverse as these would be separate sentences: "with whom ... he also would have etc." For the past contrary to fact condition compare 9 n. 6D (and 31 n. 14B). Caesar and Cleopatra are thought to have planned a journey into Ethiopia to find the source of the Nile.

19. A. **quam ... remisit**="and he invited her to the city (i.e. Rome) and did not send her back until he had honored her with etc."; for *quam=et eam* compare n. 4A above; and for rendering *accitam ... remisit* by two coordinate verbs in Eng. see 4 n. 6A. Actually Cleopatra was still in Rome when Caesar was assassinated in 44; see sel. 43. B. **nisi ... auctam:** lit.="except (her) having been increased by," but *auctam* may be used metaphorically for "honored" or "enriched"; compare 14 n. 7B.

20. **filiumque ... est:** *quam* carries through from the beginning of the sentence as the subject of *appellare,* a complementary inf. with *passus est; natum* is the part.;="who had been born (to her)." Cleopatra named the boy Caesarion and insisted that he was Caesar's son, but there is some doubt about the matter. He was nevertheless recognized as Ptolemy XV and put to death by Augustus in 30 as a possible rival; see 46.

21. **nonnulli Graecorum**="a number of Greeks (i.e. historians)"; a double negative makes a positive and *nonnullus* (sometimes written as two words, as in 37 n. 20B) regularly means "some, several, a considerable number."

22. A. **vini parcissimum ... negaverunt:** supply *eum esse* in indirect statement; compare n. 13 above. *Parcus* is followed by *in* + the abl. or by an abl. of specification in Ciceronian Lat., but in poetry and in Lat. of the Empire it and many other adjs. are followed by a gen. "of specification," denoting that to which the quality given by the adj. refers. B. **inimici:** for the connotation see 29 n. 2.

23. **Marci Catonis est**="there is (a remark) of Marcus Cato"; the remark is given as the indirect statement *unum ... accessisse.* This was the younger Cato, for whom see 34.

24. **clientis:** acc. plur. of an *i*-stem noun; compare 17 n. 14. For the obligations between patron and clients see 7 n. 7 (and 28 n. 6D).

25. A. **rerum potens**="when he was dictator (lit. master of affairs)"; a common idiom. *Potens,* a pres. part. (compare the perf. *potui*) used adjectively, takes an objective gen.; compare 17 n. 12 and the gen. with *potior* in 26 n. 9A. B. **quosdam ... generis**="some (men) of (even) the lowest sort"; *quidam*="one of" (sing.) or "some of" (plur.) is usually followed by *ex* + abl. like a numeral (see 7 n. 5); here the gen. *infimi generis* indicates, almost descriptively, a class or type, rather than a group from which some are selected. Caesar enlarged the senate and increased the number of magistracies; see 42 pref. To both he admitted not only his partisans, some of whom were of low birth, but also sons of freedmen, as well as Gauls, to whom he had only recently extended Roman citizenship. C. **honores:** here probably="honors" generally, as well as specifically "magistracies"; see 8 n. 8C (and 21 n. 12B).

26. **contra:** here an adv., not modifying any verb specifically but used as a connective for the whole sentence;="on the other hand"; compare 20 n. 9 (and 26 n. 15B).

34

Marcus Porcius Cato (95–46) was a great-grandson of Cato the Elder; see chart IV on page 47. Humorless and opinionated, he felt that he must live up to his ancestor's reputation for rectitude, censorship of public morality, and maintenance of the traditional Roman virtues. He also professed a most uncompromising Stoicism. He commanded respect for his personal character, but his idealism and conservatism were somewhat ill-timed, given the problems facing the Roman state during his life. Even Cicero, who stood as staunchly for the old Republic as Cato, confessed that Cato's political actions were too unrealistic to be helpful: *dicit enim sententiam tamquam in Platonis re publica, non tamquam in Romuli faece* (among the dregs of Romulus); *ad Atticum* II 1.8.

The first of the following passages illustrates the mixture of admiration and criticism in Cicero's attitude to Cato. It comes from a speech delivered in 63 in defense of Murena, consul elect for 62, whom Cato, ignoring the dangers of invalidating the consular elections while Catiline was attempting to get elected (see 32 pref.), prosecuted on a charge of illegal canvassing. Cicero was unable to indulge in any ordinary tactics of blackening the prosecution, and his own case was not very strong since Murena was clearly guilty. He therefore had recourse to a polite but effective satire of Cato's Stoic pedantry and severity.

The second passage comes from Sallust's account of the Catilinarian conspiracy. In the debate about the punishment of the conspirators, Caesar spoke in favor of life imprisonment and swayed the timorous senate until Cato argued passionately and successfully that the conspirators deserved death. After reproducing the speeches of Caesar and Cato (or fictitious versions of them), Sallust makes a comparison of the two men's characters. For Cato's lifelong opposition to Caesar see 35–38; for his suicide see 41.

A.   *Catonis stoici mores*

Finxit enim te ipsa natura ad honestatem, gravitatem, temperantiam, magnitudinem animi, iustitiam—ad omnes denique virtutes— magnum hominem et excelsum.[1] Accessit istuc doctrina non moderata nec mitis,[2] sed (ut mihi videtur) paulo asperior et durior quam aut veritas aut natura patitur.[3] Magister enim doctrinae tuae fuit quidam summo ingenio vir, Zeno, cuius inventorum aemuli Stoici nominantur.[4] Huius sententiae sunt et praecepta eius modi:[5] sapientem gratia numquam moveri;[6] numquam cuiusquam delicto ignoscere; neminem misericordem esse nisi stultum et levem. Haec homo ingeniosissimus, M. Cato, auctoribus eruditissimis inductus, adripuit, neque disputandi causa, ut magna pars, sed ita vivendi.[7] Moderatiores ad magistros si qua te fortuna, Cato, cum ista natura detulisset,[8] non tu quidem vir melior esses nec fortior nec temperantior nec iustior—neque enim esse potes—sed paulo ad lenitatem propensior. Ac te ipsum (quantum ego opinione auguror[9]) nunc et animi quodam impetu concitatum et vi naturae atque ingeni elatum et recentibus praeceptorum studiis flagrantem, iam usus flectet, dies leniet, aetas mitigabit.[10]

B.   *Caesaris cum Catone comparatio*

Memoria mea ingenti virtute, diversis moribus fuere viri duo: M. Cato et C. Caesar.[11] Igitur eis genus, aetas, eloquentia prope aequalia fuere, magnitudo animi par, item gloria, sed alia alii.[12] Caesar beneficiis ac munificentia magnus habebatur, integritate vitae Cato. Ille mansuetudine et misericordia clarus factus, huic severitas dignitatem addiderat.[13] Caesar dando, sublevando, ignoscendo, Cato nihil largiendo gloriam adeptus est.[14] In altero miseris perfugium erat, in altero malis pernicies.[15] Illius facilitas, huius constantia laudabatur. Postremo Caesar in animum induxerat laborare, vigilare, negotiis amicorum intentus sua neglegere, nihil denegare quod dono dignum esset.[16] Sibi magnum imperium, exercitum, bellum novum exoptabat, ubi virtus enitescere posset.[17] At Catoni studium modestiae, decoris, sed maxime severitatis erat.[18] Non divitiis cum divite, neque factione cum factioso, sed cum strenuo virtute, cum modesto pudore, cum innocente abstinentia certabat;[19] esse quam videri bonus malebat.[20] Ita, quo minus petebat gloriam, eo magis illum adsequebatur.[21]

1. A. **ad honestatem etc.:** *ad* + acc. is used after adjs. of fitness or use to indicate purpose or end and here *magnum . . . et excelsum* have this connotation; compare the use after *missionem* in 33 n. 8A.   B. **magnitudinem animi:** for the meaning see 32 n. 13B.

2. A. **accessit . . . doctrina** = "there has been added to these (qualities) a (philosophic) doctrine"; *accedo* lit. = "approach," as in Cato's remark quoted in 33 (see n. 23), but it may often be rendered passively in Eng. as "be added."   B. **istuc:** adv., lit. = "thereto" or "thither."   C. **doctrina:** here and in the following sentence probably refers specifically to Stoicism rather than to learning in general; for the latter meaning compare 13 n. 11C.

3. **aut veritas aut natura:** by hendiadys (see 13 n. 11A and 28 n. 13B) may be rendered "the true nature," i.e. of man.

4. A. **Zeno etc.** = "Zeno, the followers of whose doctrines (lit. those emulous of whose discoveries) are called Stoics." Zeno (335–263) came originally from Cyprus and may have been of Phoenician ancestry and familiar with Semitic thought. He studied philosophy at Athens and set up as a teacher in one of the open porticoes in Athens, the *Stoa Poikile* (Painted Stoa); hence the name Stoic for his doctrine and pupils. His doctrine was primarily ethical, to teach the inner self-sufficiency of virtue, but it also included logic, politics, and physics. He emphasized sacrifice of self to duty and service, and his doctrine therefore recommended itself strongly to the Romans. Cicero here speaks as one not familiar with philosophy (note his dubious *quidam . . . vir*), with which he was of course well acquainted, to make the jury regard him as a "simple fellow" compared to the pretentious Cato.   B. **inventorum:** neut. plur. gen. of *inventum*, not of *inventor*; similarly in the last sentence of passage A, *praeceptorum* is gen. plur. of *praeceptum* (compare in the next sentence *sententiae . . . et praecepta*), though there *praeceptor* (parallel to *auctoribus*) would be a more possible alternative.   c. **aemuli:** here (as in 17 nn. 7 and 19D) an adj. used as a noun followed by an objective gen.; here it has the favorable connotation of "emulous" (as against that in 17 of "rival") and may be rendered "followers."

5. **eius modi** = "of this (i.e. the following) sort"; gen. of quality (description); compare 19 n. 5. It is taken up by the following three inf. clauses, which may be regarded as in apposition with *praecepta*.

6. **sapientem** = "a wise man" or "philosopher"; it continues as subject of *ignoscere*. The extreme Stoics had an all-or-nothing attitude; their ideal *sapiens* was the perfect wise man, internally self-sufficient and unswayed by human emotions or external accidents.

7. A. **haec** = "these (doctrines)"; object of *M. Cato . . . adripuit.*   B. **auctoribus:** abl. of means (rather than agent with *a*) because probably they are thought of rather as "books" than as "people"; compare 9 n. 6A.   c. **magna pars** = "the great majority (of people), most people."

8. A. **qua:** fem. nom. sing. of the indefinite adj. *quis*, here after *si*; see 4 n. 11B (and 31 n. 19A).   B. **cum ista natura** = "in view of (lit. along with) your own character" (which was already severe enough); *ista* here has its full force as the "demonstrative of the 2nd pers."

9. **quantum . . . auguror** = "if I may venture a prophecy," lit. "as much as I can foretell from (by) expectation." *Opinio* is often best rendered "expectation" as well as "belief, judgment, etc."

10. A. **quodam:** in Lat., *quidam* or similar words are often used to soften a metaphor. They may usually be rendered "a sort of" or "as it were." Eng. tolerates bolder metaphors, and even in Lat. *impetus*, lit. = "attack," may be used figuratively, without such a qualification as *quidam*, to mean "vehemence, ardor, etc."   B. **iam usus** = "soon experience"; *iam* is often used to denote "soon" with somewhat greater immediacy than *mox*. This last sentence of A is a good illustration of Cicero's skill in using "pleonasm" for rhetorical effect; see 30 n. 3A.

11. **memoria mea:** abl. of specification, = "according to my recollection," or abl. of time within which, = "within my memory."

12. A. **igitur:** for its initial position and meaning in Sallust see 17 n. 1A (and 21 n. 13A).   B. **genus** = "family, (nobility of) birth"; see 33 n. 1D. Both Caesar and Cato were *nobiles* (see 18 pref.), though Caesar was a patrician and Cato a plebeian.   c. **magnitudo animi:** see n. 1B above.   D. **alia alii** = "some (qualities) were to one, others to the other," or "(there were) other (qualities) for each"; i.e. "in other respects they were different"; *alii* is dat. sing. of reference (possession); compare 21 n. 5B.

13. **dignitatem:** for its personal connotation compare 20 n. 3B (and 25 n. 6C).

14. **nihil largiendo** = "by never giving lavishly," i.e. by never resorting to bribery.

15. **miseris . . . erat** = "there was a refuge for the poor"; *miser* and its opposite, *beatus*, are often used to mean "poor" and "rich." Caesar not only spent large sums in bribery during his political career (see 33 pref.) but also passed legislation to relieve the condition of debtors.

16. A. **in animum induxerat** = "had made up his mind," lit. "introduced into his mind"; the four following infs. are the objects.   B. **sua:** supply *negotia*.   C. **quod . . . esset** = "which might be worthy (to be given as) a gift"; *esset* is subj. in a rel. clause of characteristic after a negative antecedent; compare 13 n. 6c (and 29 n. 7D). D. **dono:** abl. with *dignum*; compare 21 n. 12B.

17. **ubi . . . posset:** *ubi* here is equivalent to "in which"; hence the clause modifies *bellum* and is a rel. clause of characteristic implying result.

18. **decŏris:** gen. sing. of *decus*, n., not of *decor*, *decōris*, m.

19. A. **divitiis . . . factione . . . virtute . . . pudore . . . abstinentia:** abls. of specification; the shift in order between the first pair and the second (*divitiis cum divite* and *cum strenuo virtute*) produces chiasmus; compare 17 n. 2 (and 33 n. 14). B. **cum divite . . . factioso . . . strenuo . . . modesto . . . innocente:** abls. of accompaniment, the regular construction with verbs of contention; the adjs. are used as nouns; in Eng. supply "man" with each.   C. **factione** = "party strife"; this is the condemnatory term; favorably the same thought is conveyed by *partes*; see 25 n. 5B (and 28 n. 14B).

20. **esse . . . malebat:** a translation of a famous line (592) in a tragedy entitled "Seven Against Thebes" by the Athenian playwright Aeschylus (525–456).

21. A. **quo minus . . . eo magis** = "the less . . . the more"; these correlative abls. of the rel. and dem. pronouns are abls. of degree of difference, regularly used with adjs. or advs. in the comparative to mean "the more . . ." or "the less . . ." In Eng. "the" is not the definite article, but an old instrumental form of "that," which, of course, is both rel. and dem., so that the Eng. idiom is exactly similar to the Lat.   B. **petebat . . . adsequebatur:** the abrupt change of subject (from *Cato* to *gloria*) is typical of Sallust's style; compare 21 n. 18. *Illum adsequebatur* is printed in most modern editions of Sallust, which must mean "the more it (fame) overtook him," because *adsequor* = "overtake" or "achieve," not "follow." Some manuscripts, however, read *illam adsequebatur* = "the more he achieved it," and St. Augustine quotes the sentence with *illum sequebatur* = "the more it followed him." Either of these last two readings may well be the correct one.

35

Caesar returned in 60 from his propraetorship in Spain (see 33 pref.) to a complicated political situation, which was partly an aftermath of the last Mithridatic war; see 29 pref. Pompey had in the years 66–63 decisively defeated Mithridates, and in 63 had made a general settlement of the East which aimed to create for the Mediterranean world a defensible frontier against the strong Parthian kingdom in Mesopotamia and, also, by increasing the Roman provinces and dependent kingdoms in Asia Minor, to open new fields for Roman governors and investors to enrich themselves. On landing in Italy in 62, Pompey disbanded his army and requested a triumph. This the senate granted, but it persistently refused to confirm his arrangements in the East or to provide land for his veterans; for in spite of Pompey's dismissal of his army, which showed that he had no intention of following Sulla's example (see 32 n. 4B), the conservatives had not forgotten Pompey's alliance with the *populares* in 70–67; see 28 pref. and 29 pref.

Caesar himself likewise met opposition from the senate. He wished to celebrate a triumph for his victories in Spain, which meant that he must stay with his army outside the city limits. Since he wished to stand for the consulship for 59, he asked the senate to waive the usual rule that candidates must be present in person. When the senate refused, Caesar unexpectedly gave up the triumph and entered the city.

Caesar's old creditor and political boss, Crassus, was also having difficulties with the senate. He wanted to secure better terms for the equestrian tax collectors, since he himself had heavy secret investments in their operations. In consequence, these three, Pompey, Crassus, and Caesar, formed the informal partnership later called the First Triumvirate. In the summer of 60, Caesar was elected consul for 59 with an ineffectual optimate named Bibulus as his colleague. Cicero, asked to join the Triumvirs, refused. During his consulship, Caesar overrode the obstructions of Bibulus and the opposition of the optimates, led by Cato (see 34 pref.), to pass the measures desired by Pompey and Crassus. Pompey cemented their alliance by marrying Caesar's daughter, Julia, in 59. Caesar himself secured a command in Gaul for five years, which would afford him the troops, prestige, and resources that he needed to put himself fully on a political par with his two colleagues.

The first of the following passages, from Velleius, describes the formation of the Triumvirate. In the second and third, Cicero recounts to Atticus in extracts from letters of 60 and 58 his reasons for refusing to join the partnership and the ill feeling aroused by the highhanded actions of the Triumvirate, hostility which seems to have been directed mostly against Pompey as its most prominent member.

A.   *Prior Triumviratus initus est*

Inter C. Caesarem et Cn. Pompeium et M. Crassum inita est potentiae societas, quae urbi orbique terrarum nec minus, diverso cuique tempore, ipsis exitiabilis fuit.[1] Hoc consilium sequendi Pompeius causam habuerat,[2] ut tandem acta in transmarinis provinciis, quibus multi obtrectabant,[3] per Caesarem consulem confirmarentur.[4] Caesar autem, quod animadvertebat se, cedendo Pompeii gloriae, aucturum suam, et, invidia communis potentiae in illum relegata,[5] confirmaturum vires suas. Crassus, ut principatum, quem solus adsequi non poterat, auctoritate Pompeii, viribus Caesaris teneret.[6] Adfinitas etiam inter Caesarem Pompeiumque contracta nuptiis; quippe Iuliam, filiam C. Caesaris, Cn. Magnus duxit uxorem.[7]

B.   *Cicero se cum Triumviris coniungere non vult*

Fuit apud me Cornelius, hunc dico Balbum, Caesaris familiarem.[8] Is adfirmabat illum omnibus in rebus meo et Pompei consilio usurum daturumque operam ut cum Pompeio Crassum coniungeret.[9] Hic sunt haec:[10] coniunctio mihi summa cum Pompeio; si placet, etiam cum Caesare; reditus in gratiam cum inimicis;[11] pax cum multitudine; senectutis otium. Sed me hortatio mea illa commovet, quae est in libro tertio:[12]

> Interea cursus, quos prima a parte iuventae
> Quosque adeo consul virtute animoque petisti,[13]
> Hos retine atque auge: famam laudesque bonorum.[14]

C.   *Cicero totam rem publicam perisse queritur*

Tenemur undique neque iam, quo minus serviamus, recusamus,[15] sed mortem et eiectionem timemus. Universa res eo est deducta,[16] spes ut nulla sit aliquando non modo privatos, verum etiam magistratus liberos fore.[17]

Sed de re publica non libet plura scribere. Displiceo mihi, nec sine summo scribo dolore. Me tueor, ut oppressis omnibus, non demisse; ut tantis rebus gestis, parum fortiter.[18] Sed tamen, quod est subinane in nobis, id adficitur quadam delectatione.[19] Solebat enim me pungere, ne Sampsicerami merita in patriam ad annos sescentos maiora viderentur quam nostra.[20] Hac quidem cura certe iam vacuus sum; iacet enim ille sic abiectus.[21] Nam, quondam insolens infamiae, semper in laude versatus, circumfluens gloria,[22] nunc deformatus corpore, fractus animo, quo se conferat nescit;[23] progressum praecipitem, inconstantem reditum videt;[24] bonos inimicos habet, improbos ipsos non amicos.[25]

1.   A. **orbi terrarum:** i.e. the empire; see 9 n. 6c (and 32 n. 17D).   B. **nec . . . ipsis** = "and no less, at a different time for each, to them themselves."

2.   **hoc . . . habuerat** = "Pompey had (as) a reason for following this plan (i.e. of joining the Triumvirate) (the purpose) that"; *sequendi* is the gen. of the gerund dependent on *causam* and taking as direct object *hoc consilium*, instead of the more usual construction of the noun in the gen. with the gerundive modifying it. In the next sentence, a similar main clause should be supplied with *Caesar*, where it is explained not by a second *ut* clause of purpose, but by a clause introduced by *quod* = "(the fact) that"; this use of *quod* seems preferable since, if it were causal, the following imperf. ind. would (as in 20 n. 10A) make Velleius himself authority for a reason which should be more properly attributed (by an imperf. subj.) to Caesar, as in 32 n. 11A. In the following sentence, a similar main clause is again to be supplied for Crassus, and Velleius returns to an *ut* clause to explain it.

3.   **obtrectabant** = "had been obstructing" (i.e. in the senate). For the use in Lat. of the imperf. where Eng. uses the pluperf. see 21 n. 4B (and 32 n. 4D); the ind. subordinated in a subj. clause of purpose indicates that its clause is a parenthetical statement (about the *acta*) inserted as a simple fact by Velleius, and not part of the purpose attributed to Pompey. *Obtrecto*, which may take either the dat., as here, or the acc., is usually translated "disparage, belittle, etc." In a political context, however, it is often best rendered "obstruct, oppose, etc." It is used when the opposition arises from personal ill will and grudges and is accompanied by disparagement.

4.   **per Caesarem:** *per* is used with the acc. (instead of the abl. of agent with *a*) to indicate the persons as instruments rather than as agents; see 5 n. 16A (and compare 34 n. 7B).

5.   **in illum relegata** = "directed toward (or shifted onto) him (i.e. Pompey)."

6.   A. **principatum** = "(a position of) leadership"; compare for *princeps* 19 n. 3c (and 28 n. 19D). For the development of the term "Principate" under Augustus see 48 pref. and n. 11A.   B. **Pompeii, viribus:** for the asyndeton see 4 n. 5B (and 17 n. 2).

7.   **Iuliam:** Julia, Caesar's only legitimate child, was his daughter by his first wife, Cornelia; see 33 pref. She was born in 83 or 82 and married Pompey in 59.

8.   A. **apud me** = "at my house"; a regular idiom; compare 43 n. 21c.   B. **hunc dico Balbum** = "I mean Cornelius Balbus"; the *hunc* saves repetition of *Cornelium* and distinguishes him from the numerous other *Cornelii*. Balbus was a Spaniard from Gades (Cadiz; see 33 n. 6B) who received citizenship in 72 for his services against Sertorius; see 28. He attached himself first to Pompey and then to Caesar, for whom he later served in Gaul as a military engineer or *praefectus fabrum* (= *fabrorum*; see 11 n. 14B).   c. **familiarem** = "close friend"; see 28 n. 23B.

9.   A. **illum:** points more remotely to Caesar, as against the preceding *is* = Balbus. B. **meo et Pompei:** in Lat. a possessive adj. and the gen. of a noun are frequently thus used correlatively. In *Pompēius* the -*ēius* constitutes three syllables (but contrast 77 n.

11B); hence presumably Cicero wrote the gen. sing. with -*ēī*; see 17 n. 7 (and compare 78 n. 31A). For *Pompeii* in n. 6B above (from Velleius) see 17 n. 19C.   C. **consilio**= "advice"; abl. after *usurum* (*esse*); see 14 n. 16B.   D. **usurum** (**esse**)= "would follow," lit. "use"; compare 14 n. 16B.   E. **daturumque operam**: supply *esse*;= "to give attention to" or "to try"; a common idiom regularly followed by an *ut* clause of purpose, as here.   F. **coniungeret**= "reconcile." For the longstanding enmity between Pompey and Crassus, see 28 pref. and n. 19C. More recently Crassus had joined the optimates in blocking ratification of Pompey's eastern settlement.

10.   A. **hic**: the adv. (see 10 n. 18B)= "here, in this matter," i.e. support of the Triumvirs.   B. **haec**= "the following (advantages)."

11.   **reditus in gratiam**= "reconciliation," lit. "a return into favor." *Redeo in gratiam* is a common idiom meaning "reestablish friendly relations," of any kind, depending on the context.

12.   **in libro tertio**: i.e. of his poem on his consulship; see 32 n. 20B.

13.   A. **cursus**: masc. acc. plur.;= "the courses (of action)"; used metaphorically for "objectives," taken up in the 3rd verse by *hos* and specified by *famam laudesque bonorum*.   B. **prima . . . iuventae**= "from your earliest youth," lit. "from the first part of (your) youth." For the position of the prep. see 23 n. 4A.   C. **adeo consul**= "still (when you became) consul."   D. **petisti**: possibly Cicero portrayed Rome as addressing him in a dream, hence the 2nd pers.; for the contracted perf. act. see 1 n. 4B.

14.   A. **famam laudesque bonorum**= "the renown and praises (given by) good (men)"; the two accs. are, as noted in n. 13A above, in explanatory apposition with *cursus . . . hos*.   B. **bonorum**: probably subjective (not objective) gen., i.e. "coming from (not, accorded to) worthy men." Cicero was always concerned for the good opinion of the *boni* (for whom see 18 n. 5C and compare n. 25 below), so that *bonorum* is unlikely to be neut. gen. plur.,= "the renown and praise of (i.e. due to) good (acts)."

15.   **neque . . . recusamus**= "and we no longer refuse to be enslaved." For *quo minus* (lit. "by which the less"; compare 34 n. 21A)+a subj. as the object of a verb of refusing see 27 n. 12A.

16.   **eo est deducta**= "has sunk to this point," lit. "has been led down to there" (compare 33 n. 1C); *eo*, for which see 21 n. 13B, is explained by the following *ut* clause.

17.   A. **spes ut**=*ut spes*; the subject of a dependent clause is often anticipated and the conjunction (*ut*, *ne*, or an interrogative word) placed postpositively; compare 20 n. 4A.   B. **aliquando . . . fore**= "that not only private individuals but even the magistrates will ever be free"; an indirect statement introduced by *nulla spes sit*; for *fore* compare 21 n. 26C (and 28 n. 21).

18.   A. **me . . . fortiter**= "I maintain myself (i.e. my position), considering that everybody is oppressed, without (too much) humiliation; (but) considering such great achievements (as my past ones), with too little courage."   B. **ut**: often used thus to express a restriction.   C. **demisse**: adv. from *demissus*, the past part. of *demitto*.

19.   A. **quod . . . adficitur**= "that which is rather vain in me feels (lit. is affected by)."   B. **subinane**: in compounds *sub*- sometimes means "rather" or "somewhat."   C. **nobis**=*me*; see 32 n. 12B.

20.   A. **solebat**: the subject is the following *ne* clause, which, like similar clauses after verbs of fearing, should be rendered as positive;= "would seem"; see 31 n. 2A (and 32 n. 11B).   B. **me pungere**= "to disturb (lit. prick) me."   C. **Sampsicerami**: Cicero's favorite nickname for Pompey; Sampsiceramus was a Syrian emir of boastful self-conceit whom Pompey had conquered.   D. **ad annos sescentos**: Lat. uses 600 as an indefinitely large number, much as Eng. uses 1000.

21.   **iacet . . . abiectus**= "for he lies so cast down," i.e. "for he has sunk so low."

22.   A. **insolens**= "unaccustomed to," and takes an objective gen.; this meaning is as common as "insolent."   B. **circumfluens**: here intrans.;= "overflowing."   C. **gloria**: abl. of specification, here best rendered in Eng. by "with."

23. A. **deformatus:** either because Pompey had developed an ulcer on his leg or because he was visibly downcast on account of the unpopularity of the Triumvirate; see pref. B. **quo se conferat** = "where to turn," lit. "where he should betake himself"; *se conferre* is a common idiom equivalent to "go." C. **conferat:** pres. subj. in an indirect question after *nescit,* but even the direct question here would be in the deliberative subj.; compare 31 n. 17A.

24. **progressum . . . videt** = "he sees advance as dangerous, withdrawal as inconsistent"; the nouns and adjs. are in chiasmic balance; see 17 n. 2 (and 34 n. 19A).

25. **bonos inimicos habet** = "he has the conservatives as enemies," i.e. they are hostile to him; for *bonos* see n. 14B above, and for *inimicos* see 29 n. 2 (and 33 n. 22B).

36

Caesar took up his governorship of Cisalpine Gaul in 58 and at once began his conquest of Gaul (58–50), which was to have profound effects on the Roman empire and on the history of Europe. This and his two expeditions to Britain (55 and 54), which had no lasting practical results but powerfully impressed the imagination of the Romans, are recounted by him in his *Bellum Gallicum*. The importance of these years for Caesar himself lay in his acquisition of an army devoted to himself and in his experience of administering affairs according to his own ideas and the actual requirements of the situation, unhampered by the multiple obstructions and traditions encountered in Rome.

Crassus and Pompey were left in Rome to watch over the interests of the Triumvirate. These included disposing of some of their opponents, for which they initially supported P. Clodius Pulcher, tribune for 58. He was an unscrupulous young patrician who did not hesitate to use the demagogic tactics of the *populares*—legislation in the assemblies and mob violence—to attack the optimates. In 58 Cato (see 34 pref.) was sent to audit the accounts of King Ptolemy of Cyprus, whose kingdom Rome was about to annex. In November of the same year, Clodius, motivated by a personal grudge (see n. 7B below), but with the acquiescence of the Triumvirs, secured the exile of Cicero on the ground that in executing the Catilinarian conspirators he had put Roman citizens to death without recognizing the ancient right of appeal to the people. The sixteen months of exile, which Cicero passed in western Greece and took very hard, marked the end of his effective leadership in politics.

The first of the following passages is a eulogy of Caesar's conquest of Gaul, taken from a speech delivered by Cicero in 46, when Caesar was dictator. The second and third, on Cicero's exile, are taken respectively from Velleius and from a speech delivered by Cicero in 56.

A. *Caesaris res gestae*

Nullius tantum flumen est ingeni, nullius dicendi aut scribendi tanta vis, tanta copia,[1] quae non dicam exornare, sed enarrare, C. Caesar, res tuas gestas possit.[2] Soleo saepe ante oculos ponere idque libenter crebris usurpare sermonibus,[3] omnis nostrorum imperatorum, omnis exterarum gentium potentissimorumque populorum, omnis clarissimorum regum res gestas cum tuis nec contentionum magnitudine nec numero proeliorum nec varietate regionum nec celeritate conficiendi nec dissimilitudine bellorum posse conferri. Quae quidem ego nisi ita magna esse fatear, ut ea vix cuiusquam mens aut cogitatio capere possit, amens sim.[4] Nam domuisti gentis immanitate barbaras, multitudine innumerabilis, locis infinitas, omni copiarum genere abundantis.[5] Itaque, C. Caesar, bellicae tuae laudes celebrabuntur non solum nostris, sed paene omnium gentium litteris atque linguis, nec ulla umquam aetas de tuis laudibus conticescet.

B.   *Inimicitia Clodii cum Cicerone*

Ante consulatum Caesaris P. Clodius, homo nobilis, disertus, audax, malorum propositorum exsecutor acerrimus, infamis etiam sororis stupro,[6] actus est incesti reus ob initum inter religiosissima populi Romani sacra adulterium.[7] Tum, cum graves inimicitias cum M. Cicerone exerceret et a patribus ad plebem transisset,[8] legem in tribunatu tulit, ut qui civem Romanum indemnatum interemisset, ei aqua et igni interdiceretur.[9] Cuius verbis etsi non nominabatur Cicero, tamen solus petebatur.[10] Ita vir optime meritus de re publica conservatae patriae pretium calamitatem exsilii tulit.[11] Non caruerunt suspicione oppressi Ciceronis Caesar et Pompeius. Sed Cicero intra biennium, sera Cn. Pompeii cura, votisque Italiae ac decretis senatus, virtute atque actione Annii Milonis tribuni plebis, dignitati patriaeque restitutus est.[12] Neque post Numidici exsilium aut reditum quisquam aut expulsus invidiosius aut receptus est laetius.[13]

C.   *Cicero de suo exsilio*

Servavi igitur rem publicam discessu meo, iudices; caedem a vobis liberisque vestris, vastitatem, incendia, rapinas meo dolore luctuque depuli;[14] et unus bis rem publicam servavi, semel gloria, iterum aerumna mea.[15] Nonne, si meam vitam deseruissem, rem publicam prodidissem?[16] In qua quidem nunc, me restituto, vivit mecum simul exemplum fidei publicae.[17] Quod si immortale retinetur,[18] quis non intelligit immortalem hanc civitatem futuram?

1. A. **nullius ... copia:** the first half of this sentence is a rhetorical expansion of "no one's eloquence is great enough" into "of no one is the river of talent so great, of no one is the power of speaking or writing so great, (of no one) is the copiousness (of

speaking or writing) so great." The whole sentence is "pleonastic" (compare 30 n. 3A and 34 n. 10B); in rendering it the fullness should be preserved, e.g. "no flood of eloquence, no power of speaking or writing, is so abundant that it can even relate, much less adorn, your exploits."   B. **nullius**: masc. gen. sing. of the adj. *nullus*, used here twice (as regularly) as the gen. (here possessive) of the pronoun *nemo*, and not as an adj. modifying the following gens.   C. **ingeni** = "(rhetorical) talent," i.e. eloquence. D. **copia** = "a supply," i.e. of words, or "fluency."

2.   **quae ... possit**: a rhetorical expansion of "to describe your exploits" into "that it can, I will not say embellish, but (even) describe your exploits." It is a rel. clause of characteristic expressing result after the demonstrative adjs. *tantum* and *tanta*; *quae* is fem. in agreement with the nearest antecedent *copia* and both it and *possit* are sing. either for that reason or because all three antecedents, *flumen*, *vis*, and *copia*, really constitute a single concept.

3.   A. **ante oculos ponere** = "to describe," lit. "to put before (people's) eyes." B. **id**: object of both *ponere* and *usurpare*: anticipatory, or "proleptic," in apposition with the indirect statement *omnis ... res gestas ... posse conferri*; compare 32 n. 7A. C. **libenter**: adv. with *usurpare*; both it and *crebris* (adj. with *sermonibus*) express the same idea, the frequency of Cicero's praise of Caesar's exploits; for the pleonasm see n. 1A above. Cicero also wrote an epic poem, no longer extant, on Caesar's conquests. D. **usurpare** = "say, talk of," as often.

4.   **fatear ... sim**: pres. subjs. in a fut. less vivid condition; = "(unless) I should admit ... I would be"; compare 15 n. 14B.

5.   **copiarum**: here = "wealth" or "resources"; contrast n. 1D above.

6.   A. **Clodius**: see pref. above. He was a grandson of the Appius Claudius Pulcher who was the father-in-law of Tiberius Gracchus (see 18 n. 8B). Clodius "vulgarized" the spelling of his name from the patrician *Claudius* to curry popular favor, perhaps at the time of his adoption into a plebeian family; see n. 8 below. For his death see 37 pref. B. **nobilis**: here clearly used in the technical political sense of "nobly born" (see 18 pref.), not in a general or moral sense.   C. **propositorum** = "projects"; compare 18 n. 3B.   D. **sororis stupro** = "for seducing his sister," lit. "by the defilement of (his) sister." Cicero, among others, accuses Clodius of committing incest with his sister Clodia, the Lesbia of Catullus' poems; see 74 pref.

7.   A. **actus ... reus** = "was prosecuted on a charge of profanation," lit. "was led (i.e. to court) as a defendant (on a charge) of impurity." *Incesti* is gen. of charge after an expression of accusing; see 12 n. 14A. Clodius was acquitted in May 61, because Crassus lent him money to bribe the jury.   B. **ob initum ... adulterium** = "on account of pursuing an adulterous love affair," lit. "on account of an adultery entered upon." In December 62 the rites of the Bona Dea, an archaic fertility goddess worshiped by women only, were held at Caesar's house. Clodius, disguised as a woman, attended, supposedly because he was carrying on an affair with Pompeia, Caesar's second wife, the granddaughter (not, as Suet. *Inl.* 6.2 says, daughter) of Q. Pompeius Rufus, for whom see 23 n. 16. Caesar refused to join in the prosecution because Clodius was too valuable as a political ally, but he divorced Pompeia, replying to critics of his inconsistency that "Caesar's wife must be above suspicion." Cicero, however, gave evidence against Clodius, and thus incurred the enmity mentioned below.

8.   **a patribus ... transisset**: Clodius, by the authority of Caesar as *pontifex maximus* and with the support of Pompey, had had himself adopted into a plebeian family in order to stand for the tribunate (of 58), for which patricians were ineligible.

9.   A. **legem ... tulit**: for the idiom see 20 n. 7 (and 24 n. 10); the substance of the law is given by the *ut* clause in apposition.   B. **qui ... ei**: for the postponement of the antecedent see 16 n. 9A (and 17 n. 10).   C. **ei ... interdiceretur** = "should be forbidden fire and water," lit. "that it should be forbidden to him from fire and water." To forbid a person the use of fire and water was the regular formula for banishment. *Interdico* takes a dat. (of disadvantage) for the person and an abl. (of separation) for the

thing; here, being pass., it is made impersonal, and both the abl. and the dat. are retained. Verbs which are followed by the dat. of the person become impersonal in the pass., and the person remains in the dat., except that if they take an acc. of the thing or an object clause, this becomes the subject of the pass., while the person remains in the dat. For the tenses compare 30 n. 18A.

10.   A. **cuius** = "and . . . of it" (i.e. the law); for the use of a rel. pronoun as a connective see 4 n. 4A (and 33 n. 4A).   B. **petebatur** = "he was being aimed at." Cicero, when consul in 63, had put some of the Catilinarian conspirators to death without a trial on the ground that as traitors they had forfeited citizen rights.

11.   A. **optime . . . re publica:** a common idiom; = "who had deserved the utmost (reward) from the state," i.e. who had rendered the greatest services to the state.   B. **conservatae . . . tulit** = "in return for having saved the state he received (only) etc.," lit. "as a recompense for the state having been saved." For Cicero's saving of the state by exposing the Catilinarian conspiracy see 32.   C. **conservatae:** Lat. prefers a past part. modifying a noun, i.e. the state having been saved, where Eng. prefers an act. part. with the noun as object: "saving the state"; compare *oppressi Ciceronis* in the next sentence. D. **patriae . . . exsilii:** explanatory (defining or appositional) gens. respectively with *pretium* and *calamitatem*; the force is somewhat different, i.e. "price for" and "calamity of." For the chiasmus compare 17 n. 2 (and 35 n. 24).   E. **pretium . . . tulit:** in this idiom, *fero* = "receive" or "obtain" and *pretium* is acc. in apposition with the object of *fero*, here *calamitatem.*

12.   A. **sera . . . cura** = "through (by) the belated effort(s) of Pompey." Pompey had assured Cicero (falsely) that he had nothing to fear from Clodius and, when Clodius' bill was passed, did nothing to help Cicero. But he did finally aid in securing his recall in 57.   B. **Milonis:** T. Annius Milo, tribune for 57, had been hired by Pompey to form a gang to oppose Clodius and his ruffians, who had got somewhat out of hand during 58–57. Milo's gang protected the voters from Clodius' violence when the consuls presented the bill for Cicero's recall. For Milo's later history see 37 pref. and 38 n. 9A.

13.   **Numidici . . . reditum:** for the exile and return of Metellus Numidicus in 100–99 see 23 n. 13A.

14.   **servavi . . . depuli:** Cicero is assuming that there would have been a civil war if he had attempted to resist Clodius.

15.   A. **unus** = "alone, singlehanded"; in contrast with *bis;* compare 11 n. 2.   B. **semel gloria, iterum aerumna:** i.e. first by suppressing Catiline, then by his exile; the abls. are probably of attendant circumstances (not means).

16.   **nonne:** introduces a question expecting the answer "yes"; = "I would, would I not?"

17.   A. **in qua . . . publicae** = "in which indeed now, since my recall, there lives in (lit. at the same time with) me a pattern of public good faith" (i.e. loyalty of the state to a good citizen, which Rome displayed by recalling Cicero).   B. **exemplum:** may mean a general model or pattern as well as a particular example.

18.   **quod si . . . retinetur** = "and if it (i.e. the *exemplum fidei publicae*) is kept forever." *Retinetur* might be expected to be fut. in the protasis of a fut. more vivid condition, taken up by the fut. inf. in indirect discourse as apodosis; however, Cicero preferred a simple condition with pres. inds. in both protasis and apodosis (*intelligit*).

37

While Caesar was in Gaul, both the extreme optimates, led by Cato, and a more moderate group, with whom Cicero joined after his return from exile, attempted to detach Pompey from Caesar. But in 56 the Triumvirs renewed their pact in a conference at Luca, on the border of Italy and Cisalpine Gaul, a site chosen because Caesar could not leave his province while in active command. There it was agreed that Caesar's command should be extended for a second five years. Pompey and Crassus were to be joint consuls in 55, and both, fearful of Caesar's growing military strength, got commands for themselves. Pompey took Spain with the privilege of governing it *in absentia* so as to represent the Triumvirs in Rome. Crassus took Syria and the command of an expedition against the Parthians, in which he lost his army and his life in a terrible defeat at Carrhae in 53.

But the renewal of the Triumvirate was only temporarily successful. When Julia (see 35 n. 7) died in childbirth in 54, the personal ties between Pompey and Caesar were loosened, and Crassus' death removed a mediator between them. During these years, while Caesar was occupied with revolts in Gaul, affairs at Rome became increasingly chaotic. Bribery and rioting repeatedly prevented the holding of regular elections until in 52 the disorder culminated in the murder of Clodius by Milo and his rival gang (see 36 nn. 6A and 12B). Pompey was drawn closer to the optimates and with their support was elected sole consul (his third consulship) in February 52. By August, order seemed to have been restored, and Metellus Scipio (see 39 n. 16) was then elected as Pompey's colleague for the remaining five months of the year.

After 56, Cicero, who had been forced to acquiesce in the settlement of Luca and to become reconciled with Caesar, took no active part in politics, although he was still preeminent at the bar. He defended, among others, a young friend of his, Caelius Rufus (see 38 pref.), in a suit brought by Clodia (see 36 n. 6D). He also prepared a defense of Milo when he was tried for the murder of Clodius before a special court on public violence (*quaestio de vi*) during Pompey's term as sole consul. The armed guards with whom Pompey surrounded the court to prevent riots so unnerved Cicero that he could not speak effectively and Milo, like Verres (see 28 pref.), went into exile and was condemned in absence. Cicero later published the defense which he had prepared. During these years of enforced leisure Cicero composed many of the rhetorical and philosophical treatises which contributed to his later literary and philosophical influence and reputation.

In his semi-retirement, it was natural that Cicero's thoughts should turn nostalgically to the time when he had played an important role in the Republic. The following passage comes from a letter requesting a friend to write a monograph on his consulship and exile.

M. CICERO S. D. L. LVCCEIO Q. F.[1]

Ardeo cupiditate incredibili (neque, ut ego arbitror, reprehendenda[2]) nomen ut nostrum scriptis inlustretur et celebretur tuis.[3] Genus enim scriptorum tuorum vicit opinionem meam meque ita incendit ut cuperem quam celerrime res nostras monumentis commendari tuis.[4] Quia videbam Italici belli et civilis historiam iam a te paene esse perfectam, dixeras autem mihi te reliquas res ordiri,[5] te admonebam ut civilem coniurationem ab hostilibus externisque bellis seiungeres.[6] Neque tamen ignoro quam impudenter faciam,[7] qui primum tibi tantum oneris imponam, deinde etiam ut ornes mea facta postulem.[8] Quid, si illa tibi non tanto opere videntur ornanda?[9] Sed tamen, qui semel verecundiae finis transierit,[10] eum bene et naviter oportet esse impudentem.[11] Itaque te plane etiam atque etiam rogo,[12] ut et ornes ea vehementius etiam quam fortasse sentis, et in eo leges historiae neglegas, amorique nostro plusculum etiam quam concedet veritas largiare.[13]

Si te adducemus ut hoc suscipias, erit (ut mihi persuadeo) materies digna facultate et copia tua.[14] A principio enim coniurationis usque ad reditum nostrum videtur mihi modicum quoddam corpus confici posse.[15] Multam etiam casus nostri varietatem tibi in scribendo suppeditabunt plenam cuiusdam voluptatis,[16] quae vehementer animos hominum in legendo, te scriptore, tenere possit.[17] Nihil est enim aptius ad delectationem lectoris quam temporum varietates fortunaeque vicissitudines.[18] Quae etsi nobis optabiles in experiendo non fuerunt, in legendo tamen erunt iucundae; habet enim praeteriti doloris secura recordatio delectationem.[19]

Quod si a te non impetro, cogar fortasse facere quod non nulli saepe reprehendunt;[20] scribam ipse de me, multorum tamen exemplo et clarorum virorum.[21] Sed, quod te non fugit, haec sunt in hoc genere vitia:[22] et verecundius ipsi de sese scribant necesse est,[23] si quid est laudandum, et praetereant, si quid reprehendendum est. Accedit etiam ut minor sit fides, minor auctoritas, multi denique reprehendant.[24] Haec nos vitare cupimus et, si recipis causam nostram, vitabimus.[25] Ac ne forte mirere cur a te id nunc tanto opere et tam multis verbis petamus,[26] nos cupiditas incendit ut et ceteri, viventibus nobis, ex libris tuis nos cognoscant et nosmet ipsi vivi gloriola nostra perfruamur.[27]

1. **M. CICERO . . . Q. F.:** this letter was written in June 56 to L. Lucceius, who had been active against Catiline and who, when he failed to secure the consulship in 60, withdrew from politics and devoted himself to historical writing. The heading is semi-formal; see 32 nn. 1 and 15.

2. **neque . . . reprehendenda** = "and not, as I think, reprehensible"; *reprehendenda* is abl. of the gerundive agreeing with *cupiditate*.

3. **nomen ut nostrum:** for *ut* placed postpositively see 35 n. 17A; for *nostrum* instead of *meum* see 32 n. 12B (and 35 n. 19C).

4. A. **genus . . . meam** = "the quality (lit. sort) of your writings has surpassed (even) my expectation"; for *opinionem* compare 34 n. 9.   B. **quam celerrime:** for *quam* + a superlative see 33 n. 8C.   C. **monumentis:** often used in Lat. for anything which served to remind one of the past, whether monuments or writings.

5. A. **videbam . . . dixeras . . . admonebam:** "epistolary tenses"; the imperf. and pluperf. are often used in letters when something, even though present for the writer, is thought of as past when the recipient reads about it; translate as pres. and perf. respectively.   B. **dixeras autem:** still dependent on *quia*; = "and since you have said."   C. **admonebam:** the main verb.   D. **te . . . ordiri** = "that you are beginning (to write about) the other events (of our history)."

6. **seiungeres** = "separate"; i.e. make a special monograph on the Catilinarian conspiracy, as Sallust later did; see 32 pref.

7. **quam . . . faciam** = "how shamelessly I am behaving"; *quam* + an adv. = "how," exclamatory. Indirect exclamations are treated like indirect questions; hence the pres. subj. *faciam.*

8. **qui . . . imponam . . . postulem:** rel. clause of characteristic expressing cause; = "in laying on you (or, because I am laying on you) . . . then also in asking"; compare 31 n. 17B.

9. **tanto opere** = "so greatly"; abl. of manner used adverbially with *ornanda*; compare *magno opere* in 14 n. 17.

10. **qui . . . transierit:** the rel. clause is equivalent to a general condition, that is, "who(ever)" = "if any one." *Transierit* is probably perf. subj. in a rel. clause of characteristic; = "who(ever) has (once) crossed"; compare 9 n. 8D. It might, however, be fut. perf. ind. in a rel. clause equivalent to a fut. more vivid condition; = "who(ever) shall have crossed." In this case the futurity of the apodosis is implied in the concept of obligation in *oportet*. For the postponement of the antecedent of *qui* (namely *eum*) until after the relative clause see 16 n. 9A (and 36 n. 9B).

11. A. **eum . . . impudentem** = "he might as well be completely shameless," lit. "he ought to be well and busily shameless"; *eum* is equivalent to "such a person."   B. **oportet:** may take a simple complementary inf. or, as here, an inf. with subject acc., or a subjunctive clause without *ut*; compare n. 23B below.

12. **etiam atque etiam** = "again and again," i.e. "incessantly" or "insistently."

13. A. **et . . . et . . . -que:** the *et*'s mark the two main correlative parts of the *ut* substantive clause of purpose after *rogo*; the *-que* subdivides the second part, which may be rendered "by granting to our friendship (*amori*) etc."   B. **largiare:** for this 2nd pers. pass. ending see 14 n. 13E (and 32 n. 11A).

14. A. **adducemus . . . persuadeo:** for the variation from the 1st pers. plur. to the sing. compare n. 3 above.   B. **suscipias:** Lucceius agreed, but apparently never finished the work.   C. **facultate . . . copia:** abls. with *dignus*; see 21 n. 12B (and 34 n. 16D); for the meaning of *copia* see 36 n. 1D.

15. A. **a principio . . . nostrum:** for *nostrum* = *meum* see n. 3 above. For the conspiracy see 32 pref.; for Cicero's exile see 36 B and C.   B. **modicum . . . posse** = "a rather modest volume could be composed"; for the meaning of *confici* compare 22 n. 4 (and 29 n. 4).   C. **corpus:** lit. = "body," suggests here that the volume would be a natural unit; in later Lat. and in Eng. it is generally used for a collection, as the *Corpus Inscriptionum Latinarum.*

16. A. **casus nostri:** nom. plur.; = "my misfortunes" (i.e. those attendant on his exile); for *nostri* = *mei* see nn. 3 and 15A above.   B. **cuiusdam voluptatis** = "a kind of pleasure"; gen. with *plenam*; see 13 n. 7.

17. A. **quae . . . possit:** a rel. clause of characteristic after the indefinite antecedent *cuiusdam voluptatis*; compare 20 n. 12A.   B. **te scriptore:** abl. abs. giving attendant circumstance; compare 14 n. 4B.

18. **temporum varietates:** synonymous with *fortunae vicissitudines*; for this meaning of *tempus* and for the rhetorical effect see 30 n. 3.

19. **quae . . . delectationem:** the sentiment that past trials are sweet in recollection is a commonplace in ancient literature. A famous expression of it by Vergil is placed in the mouth of Aeneas, encouraging his shipwrecked comrades; this ends with the line (*Aen.* I 203): *forsan et haec olim meminisse iuvabit,* an echo of two exhortations of Odysseus to his comrades in *Od.* XII 212 and XV 400. Another instance is a line from Euripides, translated by Cicero *de Fin.* 2.105: *suavis laborum est praeteritorum memoria.*

20. A. **quod si . . . non impetro** = "but if I do not gain this" (i.e. my request). From *cogar* in the apodosis, the fut. or fut. perf. would be expected here (compare 36 n. 18), and some editors adopt the emendation *impetraro* (= *impetravero*); compare, however, n. 25B below.   B. **non nulli** = "some"; see 33 n. 21.

21. A. **scribam ipse de me:** Cicero had, of course, already written extensively on his consulship; see 32 nn. 19 and 20B. He had also written a poem *de Temporibus Suis* on his exile, but this was not yet published. Nor had he written any Lat. prose piece which included both his consulship and his exile.   B. **multorum . . . virorum:** Sulla had written his memoirs; Q. Lutatius Catulus (see sel. 22) had written on his consulship in 102; and other eminent Romans had composed autobiographies.

22. A. **quod . . . fugit** = "as I am sure you are aware," lit. "(a thing) which does not escape you"; for the use of *quod* to refer to a whole clause see 28 n. 9A.   B. **fugit:** often has the figurative meaning "be unknown to, escape the notice of."   C. **hoc genere** = "this type (of writing)," i.e. autobiography; *genus* may have a wide variety of Eng. equivalents; compare n. 4A above (and 33 n. 1D).

23. A. **sese:** for the form see 21 n. 20B.   B. **verecundius . . . scribant:** a substantive clause with *ut* or without it (in parataxis, i.e. coordinate; compare 23 n. 1A and 27 n. 13A) may serve as subject of *necesse est* (compare on *oportet* in n. 11B above), as may also an inf. with an acc. subject or an inf. without expressed subject but with the person given in the dat. (of reference) after *necesse est.*

24. **accedit etiam ut** = "moreover," lit. "there is added (approaches) also (the fact) that"; on *accedit* see 34 n. 2A (and compare *adiectum ut* in 26 n. 16A).

25. A. **recipis causam:** a legal idiom meaning "you undertake a case"; Cicero here metaphorically asks Lucceius to be his advocate against public criticism.   B. **recipis:** pres. ind. instead of fut. in the protasis of a fut. more vivid condition; compare n. 20A above.

26. A. **ne . . . mirere** = "so that you may not wonder"; for the ending of *mirere* see n. 13B above. Purpose clauses are often thus used to give the grounds of a statement;

here, something like "I will say plainly" is to be understood before *nos cupiditas etc.*
B. **tanto opere:** i.e. so earnestly; for the adverbial abl. compare n. 9 above.

27.   A. **nosmet ipsi vivi** = "I myself, while alive"; for *nosmet* compare 27 n. 7c.
B. **gloriola:** abl. (of means) with *perfruamur*; a self-deprecatory diminutive which was perhaps coined by Cicero since it appears in Lat. only here and in another letter of his.

38

After Pompey's sole consulship, which was a virtual dictatorship (see 37 pref.), a civil war between Pompey and Caesar became more and more inevitable. The major issue was whether Caesar could be separated from his loyal legions. Pompey and the senate had previously guaranteed that he could retain his command and canvass in absence for a consulship; it is uncertain whether this permission was valid for any future year or specifically for canvassing in 49 for 48. If Caesar were to proceed directly from his command to the consulship he would be immune from attack in courts. The optimates, therefore, led by Cato, sought ways to force him out of his command before the beginning of 49. The legal issues, the actual maneuvers of the optimates, Pompey's waverings, and Caesar's attempts to compromise are too complex for summary here, but finally at the end of 50 it was clear that further negotiation was impossible. According to later historians, though a motion to declare Caesar an enemy of the state failed to pass the senate, the consul Marcellus and the consuls elect, somewhat illegally, offered Pompey a sword representing a commission to defend the Republic, which Pompey accepted. Only in January 49 did the senate formally pass an emergency decree or *senatus consultum ultimum*, for which see 19 pref. (and 18 n. 9).

The following two passages analyze the causes of the war. The first is from a letter to Cicero by a young friend of his, M. Caelius Rufus. One of the laws passed by Pompey in 52 provided that a five-year interval should elapse between tenure of a magistracy in Rome and of a provincial command. To fill the first interval, magistrates who had not previously gone on to provinces were forced to do so. Cicero was one of these and, much against his will, was sent to govern Cilicia in southern Asia Minor for the year 51–50. During his absence Caelius kept him posted on affairs in Rome. The second selection is Caesar's version of his own and Pompey's motives; it is taken from the opening of the *Bellum Civile*. In this passage, as throughout his *Commentaries*, Caesar speaks of himself in the third person, to give an impression of objective impartiality.

De belli civilis secundi causis

A.   CAELIVS CICERONI S.[1]

De summa re publica saepe tibi scripsi me ad annum pacem non videre[2] et, quo propius ea contentio (quam fieri necesse est) accedit, eo clarius id periculum apparet.[3] Propositum hoc est, de quo qui rerum potiuntur sunt dimicaturi,[4] quod Cn. Pompeius constituit non pati C. Caesarem consulem aliter fieri nisi exercitum et provincias tradiderit.[5] Caesari autem persuasum est se salvum esse non posse si ab exercitu recesserit;[6] fert illam tamen condicionem, ut ambo exercitus tradant.[7] Sic illi amores et invidiosa coniunctio non ad occultam recidit obtrectationem,[8] sed ad bellum se erupit. Neque mearum rerum quid consili capiam reperio;[9] quod non dubito quin te quoque haec deliberatio sit perturbatura.[10] Illud te non arbitror fugere quin homines in dissensione domestica debeant, quam diu civiliter sine armis certetur, honestiorem sequi partem;[11] ubi ad bellum et castra ventum sit, firmiorem. In hac discordia video Cn. Pompeium senatum secum habiturum; ad Caesarem omnis qui cum timore aut mala spe vivant accessuros; exercitum conferendum non esse.[12] Si alter uter eorum ad Parthicum bellum non eat,[13] video magnas impendere discordias, quas ferrum et vis iudicabit;[14] uterque et animo et copiis est paratus. Si sine tuo periculo fieri posset, magnum et iucundum tibi Fortuna spectaculum parabat.[15]

B.   Pompeius, ab inimicis Caesaris incitatus et quod neminem dignitate secum exaequari volebat,[16] totum se ab eius amicitia averterat et cum communibus inimicis in gratiam redierat,[17] quorum ipse maximam partem illo affinitatis tempore iniunxerat Caesari;[18] simul infamia duarum legionum permotus, quas ab itinere Asiae Syriaeque ad suam potentiam dominatumque converterat,[19] rem ad arma deduci studebat. Caesar autem non maleficii causa ex provincia egressus est, sed ut se a contumeliis inimicorum defenderet,[20] ut tribunos plebis iniuria ex civitate expulsos in suam dignitatem restitueret,[21] ut se et populum Romanum factione paucorum oppressum in libertatem vindicaret.[22]

1.   S.: probably represents *suo*, very informally, rather than *sal.*; compare 32 nn. 1 and 15 (and 37 n. 1).

2.   A. **summa re publica:** for this idiom see 31 n. 21B.   B. **ad annum** = "for a year" or "in a year's time."

3.   A. **quo ... eo:** for these correlatives see 34 n. 21A.   B. **quam ... est** = "which is inevitable," lit. "which is necessary to happen"; the subject of *est* is the inf. clause *quam fieri*; compare 37 n. 23B.

4.   A. **propositum hoc est** = "the point at issue is as follows"; for *propositum* compare 18 n. 3B (and 36 n. 6C).   B. **qui rerum potiuntur** = "(our) masters," lit. "(those) who are in control of affairs"; see 26 n. 9A (and compare *rerum potens* in 33 n. 25A). C. **sunt dimicaturi:** pres. of the 1st (act.) periphrastic conj.; compare 28 n. 21 (and 32 n. 9B).

5.   A. **quod** = "(namely) that"; the rel. pronoun refers back to *hoc propositum*.
B. **constituit** = "has decided"; *constituo* = "decide" may take as object either a complementary inf. (as here, *non pati*) or an *ut* clause.   C. **nisi ... tradiderit:** perf. subj. because Caelius is giving what Pompey thought. Pompey himself in a direct statement would use the fut. perf. ind. in the protasis of a fut. more vivid condition: "unless he shall have surrendered . . . I will not allow"; compare 32 nn. 8B and 11A.

6.   A. **Caesari ... est** = "Caesar, however, is convinced," lit. "it has been persuaded to Caesar." Caelius here shifts to a main clause, although in fact this statement of Caesar's position balances that about Pompey's given in the *quod* clause of the preceding sentence, and both statements, anticipated by *hoc*, explain the *propositum*; see n. 4A above. When a verb that in the act. takes a dat. of the person and an acc. (often a clause) of the thing is made passive, the thing (here the indirect statement *se . . . posse*) becomes the subject and the person remains in the dat.; see 36 n. 9C. An indirect statement after *persuadeo* gives a fact of which someone persuades (i.e. convinces) someone else, whereas an *ut* clause of purpose (or indirect command) gives an action which someone persuades another to perform.   B. **recesserit:** perf. subj. for the same reason as is *tradiderit* in n. 5C above; Caelius gives this argument as Caesar's.

7.   A. **fert ... condicionem** = "he (i.e. Caesar) offers, however, the following term(s)"; for the meaning of *condicio* see 9 n. 18 (and 26 n. 2).   B. **ut ... tradant:** purpose clause in apposition with *condicionem* and giving the content of the terms; compare 9 n. 17B.

8.   A. **illi ... coniunctio** = "those friendships (compare 37 n. 13A) and hated partnership." This refers especially to the Triumvirate, for the unpopularity of which see 35 C, but also to Pompey's marriage with Julia, for which see 35 n. 7. The verbs are sing. because they agree with the nearest subject, *coniunctio*.   B. **obtrectationem** = "bickering"; compare *obtrecto* in 35 n. 3.

9.   A. **neque ... reperio** = "I do not know (lit. find) what plan I should make about (lit. of) my own affairs"; i.e. Caelius cannot decide whether he should follow Pompey or Caesar. In fact he joined the Caesarians, but in 48, disgusted by Caesar's moderation, he recalled Milo, who had gone into exile after being condemned for Clodius' murder (see 37 pref.), and attempted to stir up a slave revolt. Both were slain in the subsequent disorders.   B. **mearum rerum:** objective gen. depending on *consili*.   C. **capiam:** pres. subj. in an indirect question introduced by *quid* and dependent on *reperio*; but even in direct speech the subj. would have been used, since the question is deliberative; compare 35 n. 23B. *Consilium capere* regularly = "decide" or "make a plan."

10.   A. **quod ... quin** = "and I do not doubt this, (namely) that"; the rel. serves as a connective and a demonstrative, anticipatory (proleptic) of the *quin* clause, as does *illud* in the next sentence; compare 32 n. 7A.   B. **non dubito quin:** followed by the subj.; see 32 nn. 7B and 9B, where the subj. is likewise a 1st (act.) periphrastic, for which compare also n. 4C above.

11.   A. **illud ... quin** = "I am sure that you realize that," lit. "I do not think that the following escapes you, (namely) that"; *quin* reflects a suggestion of doubt in *non arbitror*; compare n. 10A above.   B. **fugere:** for the meaning here see 37 n. 22A.
C. **partem** = "side," in a political sense; see 25 n. 5B (and 28 n. 14B).

12.   A. **mala spe** = "in despair," lit. "with bad hope"; a common idiom in which the abl. is of manner or attendant circumstance rather than loc. (place where).   B.
exercitum ... esse = "(I see) that his army is not to be compared"; i.e. Caesar's is much superior.

13.   A. **si ... eat** = "if one or the other of them should not go"; pres. subj. in the protasis of a fut. less vivid condition (see 36 n. 4); in the apodosis the normal pres. subj. is replaced by the indirect statement *video ... discordias*.   B. **ad Parthicum bellum:** Pompey was supposed to take this command to avenge the defeat and death of Crassus

at Carrhae in 53 (see 37 pref.), but was reluctant to go and lose control of affairs at Rome; nor did he wish Caesar to go, since the campaign offered opportunities for further power and glory. Caesar later, when dictator, planned to carry out this expedition, but was assassinated (see 43) on the eve of his departure.

14.   A. **ferrum et vis:** by hendiadys (see 13 n. 11A and 32 n. 9B) = "force of arms"; hence *iudicabit* is sing.; contrast n. 8A above.   B. **iudicabit:** a subj. might be expected in indirect discourse after *video*, but the ind. shows that Caelius regarded the subordinated clause as giving a fact which was true independently of the subordinated perception; compare 10 n. 10c and 15 n. 3D.

15.   **si ... parabat:** the justification of the moods and tenses depends on what Caelius had in mind; it is simplest to take *parabat* as an epistolary imperf. (see 37 n. 5A) and *posset* as an imperf. subj. in the protasis of a pres. contrary to fact condition of which the apodosis is elided: "the spectacle (which) Fortune is preparing for you (would be) great and pleasant, if it could happen safely (but it can't)."

16.   A. **inimicis Caesaris:** for *inimicis* see 29 n. 2 (and 33 n. 22B). This refers particularly to the extreme optimates, led by Cato, who had always been hostile to Caesar (see 35 pref.) and who had recently been trying to detach Pompey from Caesar; see 37 pref.   B. **quod ... volebat:** with *incitatus*, giving a reason, as *ab inimicis* gave an agent; the reason is Pompey's and properly should be subj., but by using the ind. Caesar gives the allegation the force of a fact; see 4 n. 9A (and 20 n. 10A) and contrast nn. 5c and 6B above.   C. **dignitate** = "in eminence" generally; compare 20 n. 3B (and 34 n. 13). Pompey became increasingly jealous as Caesar's exploits in Gaul (see 36 A) began to rival his own eastern glories; see 29 and 30.

17.   A. **amicitia:** since political alliances in Rome were often reinforced by personal ties, *amicitia* covers both personal and political friendliness; see 32 n. 14c (and contrast n. 16A above). For the effect of Julia's death on the *amicitia* of Caesar and Pompey see 37 pref.   B. **in gratiam redierat:** for the idiom see 35 n. 11.

18.   **quorum ... Caesari** = "of whom he himself (i.e. Pompey) had imposed the greatest part on Caesar in the time of their relationship," i.e. by Pompey's marriage to Julia from 59–54; see 35 n. 7 (and n. 8 above). The exact interpretation of this passage is disputed. If *iniungo* has its ordinary connotation of "lay on as a burden," Caesar is here complaining that his alliance with Pompey imposed on him as enemies a far larger proportion of the optimates than were such before the First Triumvirate; see 35. Some commentators, however, feel that Caesar meant to say that during their relationship Pompey, always eager to remain on good terms with all parties, had at first tried to win over their common enemies, the optimates, to Caesar (who regarded this as an imposition), but had recently given up this attempt and simply joined the optimates himself. Some editors who hold the latter view emend *iniunxerat* to *coniunxerat* or *adiunxerat*.

19.   A. **infamia duarum legionum** = "by the reproach (which he incurred in the matter) of the two legions." Pompey had had the senate recall two of Caesar's legions from Gaul on the excuse of the planned expedition against Parthia (see n. 13B above) and then had held them in Italy; actually on the outbreak of hostilities they remained loyal to Caesar.   B. **ab ... Syriaeque** = "from the expedition to (lit. of) Asia and Syria"; the limiting gens. show the "area" within which *iter* falls and are equivalent to the adjs. *Asiatico Syrioque.*

20.   **ut ... ut ... ut:** the three purpose clauses are coordinate without connectives (in asyndeton), contrasted by *sed* with *non maleficii causa*; they give his real reasons for violating the law by leaving his province and entering Italy with an army; see 39 pref.

21.   A. **ut ... restitueret:** the consul Marcellus authorized Pompey to use military force against Caesar (see pref.) shortly before the close of the tribunician year on Dec. 10, 50. C. Scribonius Curio, who as tribune had watched out for Caesar's interests in Rome, joined Caesar at Ravenna at the end of his tribunate. Two new tribunes for 49, Marcus Antonius and Q. Cassius Longinus (not the later conspirator, C. Cassius,

for whom see 43 n. 2), took up the protection of Caesar. When the consul Lentulus overrode their veto to secure on Jan. 7 a *senatus consultum ultimum* (see pref. above), they also fled to Caesar. He regarded them as "expelled unjustly" (*iniuria* is abl. of manner) and used this as final justification for invading Italy; see 39. For previous incidents involving the forceful expulsion of a magistrate see 18 n. 7D and 25 n. 3A. B. **suam:** refers to the principal topic of this clause, *tribunos* (compare 3 n. 2C), although *se* in the *ut* clauses before and after refers to Caesar; see 18 n. 12B.   C. **dignitatem:** here with a political connotation; compare 19 n. 14C (and 25 n. 2B, and contrast n. 16C above).

22.   A. **factione paucorum:** both political terms; see respectively 34 n. 19C and 20 n. 13C.   B. **in . . . vindicaret:** for the idiom see 20 n. 13B.

39

When all attempts at compromise had failed (see 38), Caesar led his troops across the Rubicon, a small stream on the eastern (Adriatic) coast of Italy between Rimini and Ravenna. The date according to the Roman calendar was the night of January 11/12, 49, but since the Roman civil calendar did not correspond exactly with the solar year and since corrections by "intercalation" had been very erratic during the last years of the Republic, the actual date was about November 25 of the preceding year. The Rubicon marked the frontier between Italy and Caesar's province of Cisalpine Gaul. By a law of Sulla, it was treason (*laesa maiestas*) for a governor to move outside of his province without authority of the senate and even more treasonable to bring troops under arms into Italy except as needed for an authorized triumph. Thus Caesar's action meant an attack on the state and inevitably led to civil war. Caesar quickly defeated the troops posted against him in central Italy, and, as he neared Rome, Pompey and the optimate senators withdrew to south Italy and then crossed to Greece.

The following passage is composed from Velleius and Suetonius.

Belli civilis secundi initia

Intra breve deinde spatium belli civilis exarserunt initia, cum iustissimus quisque et a Caesare et a Pompeio vellet dimitti exercitus.[1] Pompeium senatus auctoritas, Caesarem militum armavit fiducia. Nihil relictum a Caesare, quod servandae pacis causa temptari posset, nihil receptum a Pompeianis.[2] Ad ultimum, saluberrimas condiciones pacis, quas et Caesar iustissimo animo postulabat et Pompeius aequo recipiebat, Curio discussit ac rupit,[3] unice cavente Cicerone concordiae publicae.[4] Deinde Caesar, spretis omnibus quae postulaverat, et adversariis negantibus ullam se de re publica facturos pactionem,[5] transiit in citeriorem Galliam,[6] bello vindicaturus tribunos plebis pro se intercedentis.[7]

Et praetextum quidem illi civilium armorum hoc fuit; causas autem alias fuisse opinantur.[8] Cn. Pompeius enim ita dictitabat Caesarem, quod neque opera consummare quae instituerat, neque populi exspectationem quam de adventu suo fecerat privatis opibus explere posset, turbare omnia ac permiscere voluisse.[9] Alii eum timuisse dicunt ne eorum, quae primo consulatu adversus auspicia legesque et intercessiones gessisset, rationem reddere cogeretur;[10] cum M. Cato identidem, nec sine iure iurando, denuntiaret delaturum se nomen eius, simul ac primum exercitum dimisisset.[11] Quod probabilius facit Asinius Pollio,[12] referens Caesarem, Pharsalica acie caesos profligatosque adversarios prospicientem, haec dixisse:[13] "Hoc voluerunt; tantis rebus gestis, Gaius Caesar condemnatus essem, nisi ab exercitu auxilium petissem."[14] Quidam putant eum imperii consuetudine captum, pensitatisque suis et inimicorum viribus, usum occasione rapiendae dominationis quam ab aetate prima concupisset.[15]

Cum ergo sublatam tribunorum intercessionem ipsosque urbe cessisse nuntiatum esset,[16] progressus est ad Rubiconem flumen, qui provinciae eius finis erat. Ibi paulum constitit, ac reputans quantum moliretur,[17] "Etiam nunc," inquit, "regredi possumus; quod si ponticulum transierimus, omnia armis agenda erunt."[18] Cunctanti ostentum tale factum est.[19] Quidam eximia magnitudine et forma repente apparuit[20] et, rapta ab uno aeneatore tuba, ingenti spiritu classicum exorsus, pertendit ad alteram ripam fluminis.[21] Tunc Caesar "Eatur," inquit, "quo deorum ostenta et inimicorum iniquitas vocat.[22] Iacta alea esto."[23] Atque ita exercitum Rubiconem in Italiam traiecit.[24] Cum autem Caesar Romae appropinquaret, Pompeius consulesque et maior pars senatus, relicta urbe ac deinde Italia, transmisere Dyrrachium.[25]

1. **iustissimus quisque:** for the superlative + *quisque* see 26 n. 4A.

2. **relictum** = "left (undone)"; *relictus* is often thus used elliptically, with "undone," "unsaid, etc." to be understood. With both past parts. supply *est*.

3. A. **postulabat ... recipiebat:** for the conative imperfs. see 19 n. 6A (and 20 n. 7). B. **aequo:** supply *animo* and render here "in a like (spirit)," i.e. Pompey's own attitude (as distinguished from that of "the Pompeians") was as reasonable as Caesar's. *Aequus* itself may also mean "reasonable" and the phrase *aequo animo* is usually idiomatic, = "calmly"; compare the Eng. derivative "equanimity."   c. **Curio:** see 38 n. 21A and n. 7 below. Velleius is somewhat prejudiced against Curio; actually his efforts to reach a compromise on Caesar's behalf were rebuffed by the intransigent optimates.

4. **unice ... publicae:** Cicero was absent in Cilicia during most of the negotiations between Caesar and Pompey (see 38 pref.), but on his return he made efforts to preserve peace.

5. A. **negantibus ... se ... facturos (esse):** for *nego* used in preference to *dico non* see 18 n. 10.   B. **ullam ... pactionem** = "any compromise" (i.e. with Caesar).

6. **citeriorem Galliam** = "Hither (Cisalpine) Gaul." The Po valley had been occupied by Gallic tribes after about 450; see 8 pref. Hence the Romans regarded the area between the Alps and the Apennines as distinct from Italy and treated it as a province until Augustus incorporated it into Italy in 42. The part south of the Po (*Padus*) was called *Gallia Cispadana* and that north of the Po *Transpadana*.

7. **tribunos ... intercedentis:** Curio in 50 and Cassius and Antony after Dec. 10, 50, had vetoed (see 18 n. 7c) senatorial measures against Caesar; for their flight to Caesar when the senate ignored the last veto see 38 n. 21A and n. 16 below.

8. A. **et praetextum ... fuit:** for Caesar's use of this incident as a pretext for civil war see 38 n. 21A.   B. **quidem** = "at least"; it looks forward to the adversative *autem* in the next clause; compare 14 n. 2c.   C. **opinantur:** the subject is indefinite, "people"; Eng. might use the impersonal pass., "it is believed."

9. A. **quod ... posset:** imperf. subj. because the reason is Caesar's, not the speaker's (i.e. Pompey's); see 4 n. 9A, and contrast 38 n. 16B where Caesar uses the ind. even though he is assigning a reason to Pompey. However, the clause would be subj. in any case since it is an integral part of an indirect statement; see 14 n. 2B (and 21 n. 19B). B. **instituerat ... fecerat:** these pluperf. inds., though subordinated to the imperf. subj. *posset*, are in the ind. to emphasize the fact of Caesar's undertaking and of the hopes (expectation) that he had aroused; compare 10 n. 10c.

10. A. **ne ... cogeretur:** for *ne* + subj. after a verb of fearing see 31 n. 2A (and 32 n. 11B).   B. **eorum ... rationem reddere** = "to give an accounting of those things"; for Caesar's legislation during his consulship in 59 and the optimate opposition to it see 35 pref.

11. A. **delaturum ... eius** = "that he would bring his name (before the courts)"; *nomen defero* is the regular term for "indict"; compare 31 n. 8c. If a candidate for office was under indictment he could not run for office, nor, if already designated, could he assume office or a command, since he would be immune from trial during his term. It was to avoid the risk of losing his immunity as a magistrate that Caesar had arranged to continue in his command throughout 49 and to stand in absence for the consulship of 48, which he would then enter directly from his command; see 38 pref. Since the Romans had no state attorney, indictment for "public crime" had to be brought by an individual, in this case Cato.   B. **simul ac primum** = "as soon as."

12. **quod ... Pollio** = "and this (i.e. the second reason) seems more probable because of Asinius Pollio's report that ...," lit. "which Asinius Pollio makes more probable (by) reporting (*referens*)." Pollio had been an adherent of Caesar but later quarreled with Antony and yet never fully supported Octavian. His account of this civil war seems to have been impartial, though perhaps opinionated; since it has not survived, its tone and value cannot be estimated, but there is no reason to doubt that such a quotation as that in the text was heard by him directly or reported by somebody close to Caesar.

13. **Pharsalica acie:** for Caesar's victory over Pompey in the battle of Pharsalus see 40; for the loc. abl. *acie* see 26 n. 6A (and 28 n. 12).

14. A. **hoc voluerunt:** Caesar might have been expected to emphasize the subject by *isti* or *illi*, in order to point the contrast with the second half of his remark, but apparently he was merely reflective: "well, this (is what) they wanted"; "they," of course, refers to his enemies, the optimates.   B. **tantis ... essem** = "(I), Gaius Caesar, in spite of such great achievements, would have been condemned"; for the danger of prosecution which Caesar faced see nn. 10B and 11A above.

15. A. **eum ... captum** = "he, possessed by the habit of (holding) an *imperium*," i.e. "the habit of ruling"; *eum* is subject of the inf. *usum* (*esse*); see n. D below.   B. **pensitatisque ... viribus** = "upon weighing his strength and that of his enemies"; the implication is that he thought his own was greater at this moment. *Pensito* is a "frequentative" (indicating repeated action) verb from *penso*, for which compare 22 n. 12c.   C. **suis et inimicorum:** for the use of a gen. parallel to a possessive adj. see 35 n. 9B.   D. **usum:**

not the noun, but the perf. inf. of *utor* (*esse* to be supplied) in the indirect statement after *putant* and followed by the abl. (of means) *occasione*; see 14 n. 16B (and 35 n. 9C). E. **quam ... concupisset:** the antecedent of *quam* is *dominationis*, not *occasione*.   F. **ab aetate prima** = "from his earliest youth," lit. "from (his) first age"; compare 35 n. 13B.   G. **concupisset:** a strong word; = "desired eagerly" or "greedily"; it is subj. because the clause is an integral part of the thought attributed in indirect discourse to *quidam*; see n. 9A above.

16.   **sublatam (esse):** perf. inf. of *tollo* (not here of *suffero*; compare 16 n. 3B) in the indirect statement after *nuntiatum esset*; = "overridden." On Jan. 2, 49, Metellus Scipio, whose daughter Cornelia Pompey had married in 52 and who had been Pompey's colleague in the consulship for the latter part of that year (see 37 pref.), secured over the veto of Antony and Cassius a senatorial decree recommending that Caesar be treated as a public enemy if he refused to lay down his command before a fixed date. On Jan. 7, the consul Lentulus secured a *senatus consultum ultimum* and Antony and Cassius fled to Caesar; see n. 7 above and 38 pref. and n. 21A. On the night of Jan. 11/12 Caesar crossed the Rubicon.

17.   A. **constitit:** here perf. of *consisto* (not of *consto*, for which see 15 n. 5A); = "halt, pause."   B. **quantum moliretur** = "how great a step he was taking," lit. "how much he was setting in motion."

18.   A. **quod si** = "but if"; it introduces the protasis of a fut. more vivid condition; compare 37 n. 20A.   B. **ponticulum** = "the little bridge," i.e. across the Rubicon.

19.   A. **cunctanti:** agreeing with *ei* to be supplied as dat. of indirect object; for similar parts. compare 7 n. 6B (and 21 nn. 2G and 21A).   B. **ostentum tale** = "the following portent"; *ostentum*, the neut. of the perf. pass. part. of *ostendo* used as a noun, is a technical word of augury for something shown or revealed as an omen; it is generalized as a nom. plur. in Caesar's comment below.   C. **tale:** often thus used to point forward to what is coming.

20.   **quidam** = "a figure" or "being," lit. "someone."

21.   A. **ab uno aeneatore** = "from one (of the) trumpeter(s)," i.e. in Caesar's army. Trumpets were made of bronze, for which the old adj. was *aenus* (or *ahenus*) from *aes, aeris*, n. = "bronze"; this derivative noun of agency is rare.   B. **ingenti ... exorsus** = "sounding (lit. beginning) the trumpet call (for advance) with a mighty blast (lit. breath)."

22.   **vocat:** sing. in agreement with the nearest subject; compare 38 n. 8A.

23.   **iacta alea esto:** the *alea* was a true six-sided die, as against the *talus*, a four-sided "knuckle-bone" (lit. an ankle bone) with rounded ends. The Renaissance scholar Erasmus emended *est*, given by the mss. of Suetonius, to *esto*, the 3rd pers. sing. of the formal "fut." (see 32 n. 6B) imperative, connoting "be the die (as it has been) cast" (i.e. a command implying that the desired action is already completed). Plutarch (*Caes.* 32.6) and Appian (*Bell. Civ.* II 35) state that Caesar used a familiar Greek remark (from dicing): *anerríphthō kúbos*, in which the imperative is 3rd pers. sing. perf. pass. Plutarch adds that this was often said by persons about to embark on hazardous ventures. Such a remark, uttered in Greek (compare 43 n. 14B), suits Caesar's fatalistic willingness to risk all on a bold decision, see 43 pref.

24.   **exercitum ... traiecit:** verbs compound with *trans-* often take not only a direct object (here *exercitum*) but a secondary object (here *Rubiconem*), which was originally governed by the prep.

25.   A. **transmisere:** here intrans.; = "they crossed over"; for the 3rd pers. plur. perf. ending see 15 n. 10 (and 28 n. 17D).   B. **Dyrrachium:** this town, called by the Greeks Epidamnus and in modern times Durazzo, lay on the coast of southern Illyricum close to the northern border of Macedonia; it became important as the main port of debarkation from the ports of southeast Italy, Bari and Brindisi. From it the *Via Egnatia* ran across Macedonia to Thrace and Byzantium (Constantinople).

40

When Pompey left Italy, he was wisely—from a military point of view—falling back on his main resources of men and money in the eastern provinces; from the larger political point of view he surrendered the prizes of victory, Rome and Italy, without a fight, and most of the west rallied at once to Caesar's cause. Republican forces remained in Spain, but Caesar, by a lightning campaign late in 49, defeated them at Ilerda. He then crossed to Epirus during the winter of 48. Though almost defeated while besieging Pompey's camp at Dyrrachium on the eastern shore of the Adriatic (see 39 n. 25B), Caesar succeeded in withdrawing with his forces eastward across Greece. Pompey followed him into Thessaly and there, unwisely induced by his optimate advisers to give battle, suffered a total defeat at Pharsalus on August 9, 48. Pompey's subsequent flight to Egypt and assassination there are recounted in selection 41.

Caesar describes his victory at Pharsalus in the following passage from the *Bellum Civile*, his account of this war; see 38 pref.

Proelium Pharsalicum

Pompeius, ut equitatum suum pulsum vidit atque eam partem, cui maxime confidebat, perterritam animadvertit, aliis quoque diffisus, acie excessit[1] protinusque se in castra equo contulit[2] et iis centurionibus, quos in statione ad praetoriam portam posuerat,[3] clare, ut milites exaudirent, "Tuemini," inquit, "castra et defendite diligenter, si quid durius acciderit.[4] Ego reliquas portas circumeo et castrorum praesidia confirmo."[5] Haec cum dixisset, se in praetorium contulit,[6] summae rei diffidens et tamen eventum exspectans.

Caesar, Pompeianis ex fuga intra vallum compulsis, nullum spatium perterritis dari oportere existimans,[7] milites cohortatus est, ut beneficio fortunae uterentur castraque oppugnarent. Qui, etsi magno aestu fatigati (nam ad meridiem res erat perducta), tamen ad omnem laborem animo parati imperio paruerunt.[8] Castra a cohortibus, quae ibi praesidio erant relictae, industrie defendebantur,[9] multo etiam acrius a Thracibus barbarisque auxiliis.[10] Nam, qui ex acie refugerant milites, et animo perterriti et lassitudine confecti,[11] missis plerique armis signisque militaribus,[12] magis de fuga quam de castrorum defensione cogitabant. Neque vero diutius, qui in vallo constiterant,[13] multitudinem telorum sustinere potuerant, sed confecti vulneribus locum reliquerunt, protinusque omnes, ducibus usi centurionibus tribunisque militum,[14] in altissimos montes, qui ad castra pertinebant, confugerunt.

In castris Pompei videre licuit trichilas structas,[15] magnum argenti pondus expositum, recentibus caespitibus tabernacula constrata, Luci etiam Lentuli et non nullorum tabernacula protecta hedera,[16] multaque praeterea, quae nimiam luxuriem et victoriae fiduciam designarent,[17] ut facile existimari posset, nihil eos de eventu eius diei timuisse, qui non necessarias conquirerent voluptates.[18] At hi miserrimo ac patientissimo exercitui Caesaris luxuriem obiciebant,[19] cui semper omnia ad necessarium usum defuissent. Pompeius, iam cum intra vallum nostri versarentur, equum nactus, detractis insignibus imperatoriis, decumana porta se ex castris eiecit protinusque equo citato Larisam contendit.[20] Neque ibi constitit,[21] sed eadem celeritate, paucos suos ex fuga nactus, nocturno itinere non intermisso, comitatu equitum triginta, ad mare pervenit navemque frumentariam conscendit, saepe, ut dicebatur, querens, tantum se opinionem fefellisse,[22] ut, a quo genere hominum victoriam sperasset, ab eo initio fugae facto,[23] paene proditus videretur.[24]

1.   A. **ut . . . vidit . . . animadvertit:** for *ut* + ind. = "when" see 24 n. 17A.   B. **cui . . . aliis:** *fido* and its compounds take the dat.   C. **diffisus:** this past part. is coordinated by *quoque* with the preceding *ut* temporal clause and gives a further reason for Pompey's withdrawal.   D. **acie:** Caesar uses the abl. of separation with or without a prep. after *excedo*.

2.   **se . . . equo contulit** = "rode," lit. "took himself on (by) a horse"; for *se confero* see 35 n. 23A.

3.   **praetoriam portam:** the Roman camp, ideally a square but often oblong or of a shape determined by the ground, normally had four gates: that toward the enemy was called the *porta praetoria* because the commander's headquarters (*praetorium*; see 59 n. 24B) were close inside it; that on the opposite side, farthest from the enemy, was called the *porta decumana* (mentioned below) because inside it were quartered the tenth cohorts of the legions; on either side were the *portae principales* (*dextra* and *sinistra*) at either end of a broad avenue (*principia*) which ran across behind the *praetorium* and on which were placed the officers' tents.

4.   A. **tuemini:** 2nd pers. plur. pres. pass. imperative; see 27 n. 7A.   B. **si . . . acciderit:** a euphemistic expression for "if we are defeated," lit. "if anything more severe shall have happened."   C. **acciderit:** fut. perf. ind. in the protasis of a fut.

more vivid condition; in the apodosis, the usual fut. ind. is replaced by the imperative *tuemini*, which of course points to fut. time; compare 31 n. 3.

5. **praesidia:** includes both "defenses" in general and "garrisons" in particular; see 29 nn. 8D and 15B (and 32 n. 16).

6. **se in praetorium contulit:** see nn. 2 and 3 above.

7. A. **Pompeianis ... compulsis ... perterritis:** best rendered in Eng. by two clauses: "after the Pompeians had been driven from the rout (i.e. on the field) within the rampart (i.e. of the camp)" and "(to them) while they were (still) badly frightened." Since an abl. abs. is not normally used when the noun can form an integral part of the sentence, *Pompeianis* may be dat. of indirect object with *dari* and the two parts. may be dat. in agreement with it. Here, however, it is more natural to take *Pompeianis ... compulsis* as an abl. abs. and *perterritis* as a part. used as a noun and serving as the indirect object of *dari*; the text above has been so punctuated.   B. **nullum ... oportere:** for the inf. + subject acc. with *oportet* see 37 n. 11B.

8. A. **ad omnem ... parati:** *paro* regularly takes *ad* + acc. for the purpose or goal of the preparation; compare 11 n. 7.   B. **animo:** abl. of specification or, less probably, a loc. abl.   C. **imperio** = "(his) order(s)"; for the dat. with *pareo* see 30 n. 2C.

9. A. **castra:** i.e. Pompey's camp.   B. **praesidio:** dat. of purpose; for the meaning see n. 5 above.

10. **a Thracibus ... auxiliis:** Roman legions were regularly supported by auxiliary troops levied from the provinces or even "barbarian" countries; these auxiliaries sometimes, as here, fought even more desperately than trained troops.

11. A. **milites:** subject of *cogitabant* at the end of the sentence; for its inclusion within the rel. clause see 12 n. 8B (and 15 n. 12B).   B. **confecti** = "worn out"; so *confecti vulneribus* in the next sentence; compare 22 n. 4.

12. **missis:** modifies both *armis* and *signis militaribus* in an abl. abs. which defines *plerique*, a nom. in apposition with *milites*, the subject of the sentence; = "the soldiers ... (when, or since) most (of them) had cast away (their) arms etc."

13. **qui in vallo etc.:** these soldiers, as opposed to those in the previous sentence (see n. 11A above), had not been on the battlefield but were those whom Pompey had posted to defend the camp; see n. 5 above.

14. **ducibus usi** = "taking (lit. using) as leaders"; for the meaning and the abl. see 14 n. 16B (and 39 n. 15D).

15. A. **Pompei:** for this gen. see 35 n. 9B and for *Luci* below see 17 n. 7 (and 20 n. 1A).   B. **videre licuit** = "one could see," lit. "it was permitted to see." In this sense *licet* may take a simple inf. if no person is directly involved, as here; a person appears either in the dat. as indirect object or in the acc. as subject of the inf.; see 30 n. 18A (and compare 38 n. 6A). For *licet* in a concessive sense with the subj. see 23 n. 1A (and 27 n. 13A).   C. **trichilas** = arbors covered with leaves or vines, still common in Mediterranean countries as protection from the sun for persons eating or drinking out of doors. D. **structas:** this and the following past parts. are used adjectivally, not with *esse* understood in indirect discourse after *videre*, which takes the nouns as objects.

16. A. **tabernacula** = "huts"; more substantial structures than the *trichilae*; they were floored (*constrata* is perf. pass. part. of *consterno*) with turfs (*caespitibus*) and in some cases shaded with vines of ivy (*hedera*).   B. **Lentuli:** consul in 49 (see 38 pref.); he is reported to have been a worthless, luxurious, and extravagant optimate.   C. **non nullorum** = "of some (others)"; for *non nulli* see 33 n. 21 (and 37 n. 20B).

17. **quae ... designarent:** a rel. clause of characteristic implying result; = "which (were such that they) indicated"; compare 21 n. 12A. The sequence of tenses throughout this sentence is carefully worked out; see the next note.

18. A. **qui ... conquirerent:** a rel. clause of characteristic expressing cause; compare 31 n. 17B (and 37 n. 8). The imperf. subj. expresses time contemporary with *timuisse*

and this perf. act. inf. is in turn in past time relative to *posset*, which is imperf. subj. in secondary sequence in an *ut* clause of result; = "so that (at the time when Caesar entered the camp) it could easily be concluded that his enemies had not (previously) been afraid concerning the result of that day, since (at that earlier time) they were seeking out unnecessary pleasures."   B. **non:** with *necessarias*, not with *conquirerent*.

19.   A. **at hi:** emphatic; = "and yet these (were the men who)."   B. **obiciebant** = "had been reproaching"; *obicio* takes the acc. of the cause of reproach and the dat. (after *ob-* in composition) of the person or thing reproached. For the use of the imperf. for continued action in past time see 21 n. 4B (and 35 n. 3).   C. **defuissent:** subj. in a concessive (i.e. characteristic; see 30 n. 10) rel. clause; = "although it had lacked," lit. "although to which had been lacking."

20.   A. **decumana porta:** see n. 3 above.   B. **equo citato** = "at a full gallop," lit. "with horse urged on"; a common idiom.   C. **Larisam:** a town in Thessaly.

21.   A. **neque** = "but . . . not," rather than "and . . . not" (as often).   B. **constitit:** from *consisto*; see 39 n. 17A.

22.   **tantum . . . fefellisse** = "that his judgment had so much deceived him"; i.e. that he had been so mistaken in judging the outcome of the battle; *fefellisse* is the perf. inf. of *fallo*.

23.   A. **a . . . facto** = "because the rout had been begun (abl. abs., lit. the beginning of the rout having been made) by that group (lit. sort of men) from whom he had expected victory." The "group" on whom Pompey had relied was his cavalry; see the 1st sentence of this passage.   B. **genere:** the antecedent is, as often (see n. 11A above), incorporated into the rel. clause, and, further, the pronoun *eo* is used to repeat it; compare 31 n. 18A.

24.   **paene:** with *videretur* = "almost seemed betrayed," rather than "seemed almost betrayed."

41

After he fled from the battle of Pharsalus (see 40), Pompey sailed to Egypt, where he expected sanctuary from the young ruler Ptolemy XIII (see 33 n. 17), but instead was treacherously murdered, since Ptolemy and his advisers were afraid of Caesar's wrath. Caesar followed Pompey and occupied Alexandria, where he established Cleopatra and a younger brother Ptolemy XIV as rulers of Egypt (see n. 6 below), after suppressing a short revolt. He then conducted a whirlwind campaign against Pharnaces, a son of Mithridates the Great (see 24 pref. and 29 pref.) and king of the Bosporan kingdom (the Crimea and adjacent territory), who had invaded Asia Minor. Caesar's victory over Pharnaces at Zela (47) was advertised in his later triumph by the famous phrase *veni, vidi, vici* according to Suetonius, *Iulius* 37.2.

Caesar returned briefly to Rome, but in January 46 crossed to Africa, where some of the Republicans, led by Cato, had taken refuge after the defeat and death of Pompey. When Caesar defeated them at Thapsus, Cato committed suicide at Utica (hence his later sobriquet *Uticensis*) rather than live under what he regarded as Caesar's tyranny. He became the pattern of a martyr to tyranny for all those who, under the Empire, opposed arbitrary and wicked emperors. In particular, Lucan, writing under Nero, praised Cato's unyielding opposition to tyranny, even in defeat: *victrix causa deis placuit sed victa Catoni* (*Pharsalia* I 128; see 77 verse 18).

Caesar then returned to Rome to celebrate triumphs for his victories and to arrange other matters there. A final campaign in 45 saw the defeat at Munda in Spain of Pompey's two sons, Gaius and Sextus; Gaius was slain soon thereafter, but Sextus survived to give trouble to the Second Triumvirate after Caesar's death; see 46 pref.

The following description of the deaths of Pompey and Cato is composed from letters of Cicero, and from Velleius, Florus, and Seneca the Younger.

Exitus Pompeii Catonisque

Ciceroni vero in castris Pompeianis nihil boni praeter causam visum est; extra ducem enim paucosque praeterea de principibus, reliqui et in ipso bello rapaces erant,[1] et in oratione ita crudeles, ut ipsam victoriam horreret. Quae cum vidisset, desperans victoriam, primum coepit suadere pacem, cuius fuerat semper auctor; deinde, cum ab ea sententia Pompeius valde abhorreret, suadere instituit ut bellum duceret.[2] Hoc interdum probabat et in ea sententia mansisset

fortasse, nisi quadam ex pugna coepisset suis militibus confidere.[3] Ex
eo tempore, vir ille summus nullus imperator fuit.[4] Signa tirone et
collecticio exercitu cum legionibus robustissimis contulit;[5] victus tur-
pissime, amissis etiam castris, solus fugit.

Aegyptum autem petere proposuit, memor beneficiorum quae in
patrem eius Ptolemaei, qui tum puer regnabat Alexandriae, contulerat.[6] Sed quis in adversis beneficiorum servat memoriam?[7] Aut
quis ullam calamitosis deberi putat gratiam?[8] Aut quando fortuna non
mutat fidem? Consilio itaque Theodoti et Achillae,[9] missi sunt ab rege
qui Pompeium venientem exciperent hortarenturque ut ex oneraria
nave in eam quae obviam processerat transcenderet.[10] Quod cum
fecisset, princeps Romani nominis imperio arbitrioque Aegyptii mancipii iugulatus est.[11] Hic, post tres consulatus et totidem triumphos
domitumque terrarum orbem,[12] sanctissimi atque praestantissimi viri,
duodesexagesimum annum agentis, pridie natalem ipsius vitae, fuit
exitus.[13] Sed certe de Pompeii morte nemini dubium umquam fuit.
Tanta enim desperatio rerum eius omnium regum et populorum
animos occuparat, ut, quocumque venisset, hoc futurum esset.[14]

Pompeio mortuo, reliqui optimates a Caesare Thapsi victi sunt.[15]
Cato vero non interfuit proelio, quod Uticam servabat;[16] sed, accepta
partium clade, nihil cunctatus, ut sapiente dignum erat, mortem sibi
etiam laetus accivit.[17] Nam postquam filium comitesque ab amplexu
dimisit, in noctem lecto ad lucernam Platonis libro qui immortalitatem
animae docet, paulum se quieti dedit.[18] Tunc circa primam vigiliam,
stricto gladio,[19] pectus semel iterumque percussit. Ille autem, virtutum
viva imago, incumbens gladio, simul de se actum esse ac de re publica
palam fecit.[20]

1. A. **principibus:** i.e. the leading optimates who supported Pompey; see 19 n. 3c.
B. **reliqui** = "the rest" (of Pompey's supporters). Cicero was disgusted by the selfish
greed and cruelty of the optimates, who boasted of the vengeance and confiscations
which they would exact when victorious.

2. **duceret** = "prolong," i.e. not seek a decisive battle; the correctness of Cicero's
advice was proved by the outcome at Pharsalus; see 40.

3. A. **quadam ex pugna:** for the place of the prep. compare 23 n. 4. This was presumably one of the defeats suffered by Caesar when he was seeking to invest Dyrrachium;
see 40 pref.   B. **militibus:** for the dat. with *confidere* see 40 n. 1B.

4. **summus:** with the subject *vir ille*, not with the predicate nom. *nullus imperator*.

5.   A.   **signa ... contulit** = "he joined battle," lit. "brought together the standards."
B.   **tirone et collecticio exercitu** = "with an untrained and hastily levied army"; abl. of means, or, as often in military phrases, abl. of accompaniment without *cum*.   C. **tirone**: normally a noun, = "an untrained recruit," but here used as an adj.; compare 21 n. 6B (and 30 n. 13).

6.   **beneficiorum ... contulerat**: in 55, Pompey, in return for a large bribe, had secured the restoration to the Egyptian throne of Ptolemy XII, nicknamed *Auletes*. His son, Ptolemy XIII, the elder of Cleopatra's two brothers, was the ruler at the time of Pharsalus, although he was still a youth of about fifteen. For the Ptolemies see 33 n. 17.

7.   **in adversis**: supply *rebus*; = "in misfortune(s)"; compare 27 n. 5B.

8.   **calamitosis**: an adj. used as a noun; = "to ruined (men)"; compare 34 n. 19B.

9.   **Theodoti et Achillae**: Ptolemy's tutor and his general; the Ptolemies, being Greek (Macedonian) by origin, used Greeks almost exclusively for cultural, administrative, and military posts.

10.   A.   **qui ... hortarentur**: the imperf. subjs. are in a rel. clause of characteristic expressing purpose and serving as the subject of *missi sunt*; see 8 n. 1B (and 28 n. 23F). In translating supply as antecedent "men" or "some persons"; compare 20 n. 12A.
B.   **obviam**: an adv.; see 20 n. 14F.

11.   A.   **princeps Romani nominis** = "a Roman prince," in strong contrast to *Aegyptii mancipii* in n. C below. In this sentence from Velleius the use of *princeps* reflects the change of meaning which took place under the Empire; compare 47 n. 19A (and contrast n. 1A above).   B.   **nominis**: used with an adj. by metonymy (see 49 n. 4) for the people named, as commonly in the phrase *nomen Latinum = Latini*.   C.   **mancipii** = "of a purchased slave"; a derogatory term for Ptolemy XIII, dependent as he was on Roman support. Pompey was actually slain, on Sept. 28, 48, by Septimius, a Roman who had served under him as centurion and who was at this time (disgracefully in Roman eyes) in Egyptian service; see 78.

12.   A.   **hic**: agrees with the last word of the sentence, *exitus*; for the word order compare 19 n. 13A (and 28 n. 6A).   B.   **tres consulatus**: in 70, 55, and 52; see prefs. to 28, 29, 30, and 37.   C.   **totidem triumphos**: in 79 for his victory in Africa (see 30 n. 14); in late 71 for his victory over Sertorius (see 28 n. 15 and 30 n. 19); and in 61 for his victory over Mithridates; see 35 pref.   D.   **domitumque ... orbem**: Lat. uses a past part. with a noun where Eng. would use a noun and a gen., i.e. "the conquest of the world"; compare 36 n. 11C.

13.   A.   **viri**: gen. depending on *exitus*, modified by the two superlatives, for which see 18 n. 1B, and by the participle *agentis*, for the meaning of which see 5 n. 16B (and 14 n. 1).   B.   **pridie ... vitae** = "on the very eve of his birthday," lit. "on the day before the natal day of his very life."

14.   **ut ... esset**: the subjs. not only are in secondary sequence in an *ut* clause, but show potentiality; = "so that wherever he might have arrived, this (i.e. his death) was bound to happen (lit. was going to be)."

15.   **Thapsi**: loc.; a town on the coast southeast of Carthage in Roman Africa; here the Republican forces under Metellus Scipio (see 39 n. 16) were defeated by Caesar in May 46.

16.   **Uticam servabat**: Cato was in command of the reserves at Utica, for which see 21 n. 2A.

17.   A.   **accepta**: for *accipio* = "receive news" or "information" see 11 n. 5C.   B. **partium**: for *partes* in a political sense see 25 n. 5B (and 38 n. 11C).   C.   **sapiente** = "of a philosopher"; abl. after *dignum*; see 21 n. 12B (and 34 n. 16D). For the meaning see 34 n. 6.   D.   **mortem ... accivit** = "he cheerfully summoned death to himself"; i.e. he committed suicide.   E.   **laetus**: the adj., as often, is best rendered adverbially in Eng.; compare 14 n. 18B.

18.   A. **in noctem** = "(far) into the night."   B. **lecto:** past part. of *lego* in an abl. abs. with *libro*; for the meaning see 29 n. 3.   C. **ad lucernam** = "by lamp(-light)"; this use of *ad* is idiomatic, derived from its use to express nearness to; compare 3 n. 6A. D. **Platonis libro:** the *Phaedo*, in which Socrates, before he is put to death, discusses the immortality of the soul with his friends.   E. **paulum . . . dedit** = "he slept a little," lit. "he gave himself to rest for a little while."

19.   **stricto gladio:** for *stringo* with words denoting weapons see 24 n. 4C.

20.   **actum esse . . . palam fecit** = "made (it) clear that all was lost"; "all is lost" is a common idiomatic meaning for impersonal *actum est*; lit. = "it has been completed."

42

Various offices were bestowed on Caesar during these years, including consulships in 48, 46, and 45 and a dictatorship first for a few months, then for ten years, and in 44 for life. His legislative program included a number of useful and urgently needed acts. He reformed the calendar (see 39 pref.); followed the Gracchi (see 18–20) in attempting to solve the problem of Rome's proletariat and of the veterans by such measures as a limited dole of free grain, allotments of land in Italy, and the establishment of colonies overseas; relieved some of the economic problems harassing Rome; and passed a number of laws designed to curb the abuses prevalent in provincial government.

He became, however, increasingly autocratic. He seems to have emphasized a divinity in himself, both through the descent of the Julian *gens* from Venus (see 1 pref. and 33 n. 1D) and in his own person. He treated the senate arrogantly and cavalierly and increased its numbers from 600 to about 1000 by enrolling many foreigners and unworthy persons.

The first of the following passages is Suetonius' account of the quasi-monarchical honors accepted by Caesar, culminating in Antony's offer of a diadem early in 44 on the occasion of a religious ceremony called the *Lupercalia*. The second gives Cicero's criticism of Antony for this act, made after the assassination of Caesar in the second of his "Philippics" (see 44 pref.), a speech written in November of 44 but never delivered.

A.   *Caesaris dictatoris honores immodici*

Caesar vero moderationem clementiamque cum in administratione tum in victoria belli civilis admirabilem exhibuit.[1] Nam cunctis inimicis in Italiam redire permisit magistratusque et imperia capere; et statuas Lucii Sullae atque Pompeii a plebe disiectas reposuit; ac si qua aut cogitarentur gravius adversus se aut dicerentur,[2] inhibere maluit quam vindicare. Praegravant tamen cetera facta dictaque eius,[3] ut et abusus dominatione et iure caesus existimetur.[4] Non enim honores modo nimios recepit:[5] continuum consulatum, perpetuam dictaturam, praefecturamque morum, insuper praenomen Imperatoris, cognomen Patris Patriae, statuam inter reges;[6] sed et ampliora etiam humano fastigio decerni sibi passus est;[7] sedem auream in curia et pro tribunali, templa, aras, simulacra iuxta deos, pulvinar, flaminem, lupercos, appellationem mensis e suo nomine;[8] ac nullos non honores ad libidinem cepit et dedit.[9] Quae omnia praecipuam et exitiabilem ei invidiam moverunt.

Neque infamiam affectati regii nominis discutere valuit,[10] quamquam et plebi regem se salutanti Caesarem se, non regem, esse respondit[11] et Lupercalibus pro rostris[12] a consule Antonio admotum saepius capiti suo diadema reppulit atque in Capitolium Iovi Optimo Maximo misit.[13]

B.   *Ciceronis in Antonium invectio*

Sed nunc ad Lupercalia veniamus.[14] Sedebat in rostris collega tuus, amictus toga purpurea, in sella aurea, coronatus.[15] Escendis, accedis ad sellam, diadema ostendis. Gemitus toto foro.[16] Unde diadema? Non enim abiectum sustuleras, sed attuleras domo meditatum et cogitatum scelus.[17] Tu diadema imponebas cum plangore populi; ille cum plausu reiciebat.[18] Tu ergo unus, scelerate, inventus es qui auctor regni esses eumque quem collegam habebas dominum habere velles.[19] Supplex te ad pedes abiciebas.[20] Quid petens? ut servires?[21] O praeclaram illam eloquentiam tuam, cum es nudus contionatus![22] Ita eras lupercus ut te consulem esse meminisse deberes![23]

Quid hoc turpius?[24] Quid foedius? Quid suppliciis omnibus dignius? Quid indignius quam vivere eum qui imposuerit diadema, cum omnes fateantur iure interfectum esse qui abiecerit?[25] At etiam inscribi iussit in fastis ad Lupercalia:[26] Gaio Caesari dictatori perpetuo Marcum Antonium consulem, populi iussu, regnum detulisse; Caesarem uti noluisse.[27] Ideone Lucius Tarquinius exactus, ut multis post saeculis a Marco Antonio, quod fas non est, rex Romae constitueretur?[28]

1. **cum ... tum** = "not only ... but also"; see 21 n. 24.

2. A. **si ... dicerentur** = "if any (things) against him were either thought or said too seriously"; i.e. if there were any plots or verbal attacks on him. For the euphemism compare 40 n. 4B.   B. **cogitarentur ... dicerentur**: imperf. subjs. in the protasis of a general condition describing a repeated action in past time. In Cicero's time such conditions were usually wholly in the ind., but in later writers the subj. was increasingly used in the protasis. In the apodosis the imperf. ind. is usual, but here the perf. *maluit* is used.

3.   **praegravant**="outweigh"; as object supply "these," i.e. the good qualities just listed.

4.   **iure caesus:** for the thought and the adverbial abl. *iure* compare the phrases used of the Gracchi by Velleius: *iure caesum* (18 n. 17B), and by Cicero: *iure caesorum* (20 n. 2); see also below n. 25C.

5.   A. **non ... modo:** correlative with *sed et* below; for Suetonius' use of remote correlation compare 33 n. 18.   B. **honores:** as the following list shows, this means not only magistracies (as in 8 n. 8C) but "honors" in general, as also probably in n. 9 below; compare 33 n. 25C.

6.   **continuum etc.:** to conservative Romans most of these honors seemed eastern and monarchical; the perpetual dictatorship was derived from Sulla's; see 26 n. 13A. Two, however, had a Roman flavor. Successful generals had been hailed by their troops as *imperator*, though to use this as a first name (*praenomen*) was to assert a claim to be permanently "the" successful general. After the execution of the Catilinarian conspirators towards the end of 63 (see 32 pref.), Cicero had been hailed as *Parens Patriae*. By accepting this title, Caesar presented himself as caring for the Roman people as a father would for his children.

7.   A. **ampliora ... fastigio**="greater (things) than human elevation allows"; i.e. honors too great for a mortal man.   B. **ampliora:** neut. acc. plur.; subject of the complementary inf. *decerni*.   c. **humano fastigio:** abl. of comparison.

8.   A. **pulvinar:** at Roman religious festivals, elaborate couches (*pulvinaria*) were prepared for images of the gods, here for Caesar as a god in person, so that they could participate in the ceremonial feasting.   B. **flaminem:** a special priest attendant on one deity. In allowing himself to be attended by a *flamen* and by *luperci* (see n. 8C) Caesar was, of course, assuming more than mortal honors; see n. 7A above.   c. **lupercos:** priests of the Italic fertility god Faunus, whose shrine was a cave on the Palatine called the *Lupercal*. The cult was evidently connected with Rome's "totem" animal, the wolf (*lupus*); see the story of Romulus and Remus in 4.   D. **appellationem mensis:** the Roman month *Quintilis*, so called because down to the middle of the second century the Roman civil year began with March (see 22 n. 6), was renamed July in honor of Julius Caesar, born on July 12, 100 or 102; see 33 pref. Similarly, the following month, *Sextilis*, was renamed, probably in 27, in honor of Augustus, because various anniversaries of his offices and victories fell in it. Such later autocratic emperors as Domitian and Commodus named months after themselves but these names did not outlast them.

9.   A. **nullos ... dedit**="(there were) no honors (which) he did not receive or award at will"; with *nullos non* equivalent to "all" contrast *non nulli*="some" in 33 n. 21 (and 40 n. 16C).   B. **honores:** here (as against n. 5B above) this might mean simply "magistracies," but in view of the similar remark by Suetonius somewhat earlier (see the last par. of 33 and n. 25C), it probably also means "honors" in general.

10.   A. **affectati regii nominis**="of aspiring to the title of king"; for this rendering of the past part. see 36 n. 11C (and compare 41 n. 12D).   B. **valuit:** equivalent to *potuit*.

11.   A. **et plebi ... et Lupercalibus:** with this remote correlation compare n. 5A above.   B. **plebi ... salutanti:** dat. indirect object of *respondit*; the part. is best rendered as a clause; compare 7 n. 6B (and 39 n. 19A).   c. **Caesarem ... esse**="that he was a Caesar, not a Rex." *Rex* was used as a cognomen in the *gens Marcia*, a prominent family of the later Republic, and Caesar plays on its double meaning; his grandmother was a *Marcia*.

12.   A. **Lupercalibus:** the festival of Faunus (see n. 8C above), which fell on February 15. As passage B shows, Antony, though consul in 44 with Caesar, participated as a priest (*lupercus*) in the ceremony of running naked through the streets and striking women with leather thongs to induce fertility. It was at the conclusion of this ceremony that he offered the diadem to Caesar.   B. **pro rostris:** Cicero states in passage B that

Antony mounted the Rostra (for which see 14 n. 6B and 24 n. 12A) to offer the diadem to Caesar; thus it is difficult to determine whether Suetonius conceived of the whole scene taking place "before the Rostra" or whether the phrase should go closely with *a . . . Antonio* and indicate that Antony came up in front of the Rostra.

13. A. **admotum . . . diadema:** a more normal order would be *diadema a consule* (or *pro rostris;* see above n. 12B) . . . *capiti suo admotum;* Suetonius inverts awkwardly in an effort to be more elegant. B. **saepius:** lit. = "more often," but it may also mean, as here, "several times." Plutarch *Caes.* 61.3–4 says only twice; Cicero, in passage B, suggests an offer and an entreaty. C. **diadema:** Greek neut. acc. sing. A diadem was not, as today, a circlet of gold, but a ribbon worn by rulers around their hair and often decorated with jewels. D. **in Capitolium:** for this hill, on which stood the temple of Jupiter *O.M.,* see 12 n. 4. E. **Iovi:** dat. of reference (advantage); = "(as a gift) for Jupiter."

14. **veniamus:** Cicero means in his speech. In the second *Philippic* Cicero sometimes addresses Antony in the 2nd pers., as in this par., and sometimes refers to him in the 3rd pers., as in the next par.

15. **sedebat . . . coronatus:** Caesar, as consul with Antony in 44, was presiding over the *Lupercalia* on the Rostra in the Forum while Antony participated in the ceremony; see n. 12B above. Everything about Caesar's appearance would have suggested royalty to a Roman audience. A wholly purple toga instead of the normal magisterial one, simply bordered with purple (*praetexta;* see 8 n. 8C and 15 n. 12A), was worn only by generals for a triumph. The grant to Caesar of the permanent title *Imperator* (see n. 6 above) carried with it the right to wear the purple toga on all official occasions. For the golden curule chair see the 1st par. above, and compare 8 n. 8B for the normal ivory one. The laurel wreath with which Caesar was crowned had been voted to him by the senate and was, according to Suetonius *Iul.* 45.2, much appreciated by Caesar because it concealed his baldness.

16. A. **gemitus:** a noun; supply *erat.* B. **toto foro:** for the omission of the prep. with *totus* see 29 n. 8B.

17. A. **abiectum** = "thrown down," i.e. just lying handy on the ground. B. **scelus:** Cicero substitutes the act for the object.

18. **imponebas . . . reiciebat:** for the conative imperfs. compare 19 n. 6A.

19. **habebas:** ind. because it states a fact not closely dependent on *velles,* which, like *esses,* is subj. in a rel. clause of characteristic; compare 20 n. 4C.

20. **supplex:** for a consul to fall as a suppliant at Caesar's feet was both undignified for his office and an acknowledgment of Caesar's "majesty." Other authorities do not mention this action.

21. **ut servires** = "that you might be a slave"; the clause is the object of *petens,* in apposition with *quid.*

22. A. **O . . . eloquentiam:** acc. of exclamation; compare 13 n. 2A. B. **es . . . contionatus:** Cicero claims that Antony not only entreated Caesar but made a formal harangue (*contio;* see 29 pref.) to the people; other authorities say nothing either of the entreaty (see n. 12B above) or of such an oration.

23. **ita . . . deberes** = "you were a *lupercus* (see n. 8C above) in such a fashion (or, on condition) that you should remember that you were (also) consul," i.e. "although you were . . . you should have remembered." Cicero felt that Antony had demeaned the consulship.

24. **hoc:** abl. of comparison; it refers to the whole episode just described.

25. A. **vivere eum:** the inf. clause is the second term of the comparison, balancing *quid;* compare 30 n. 8A. Cicero elsewhere blames the conspirators for not having assassinated Antony as well as Caesar. B. **imposuerit . . . abiecerit:** perf. subjs. in

subordinate clauses closely dependent on infs.; contrast n. 19 above.   c. **iure inter-fectum esse**: the unexpressed subject acc. is the readily understood antecedent of the following rel. clause. For the thought and for the adverbial abl. *iure* compare n. 4 above.

26.   A. **fastis**: the *fasti* were annual lists of the magistrates and important events; the word also means "calendar."   B. **ad Lupercalia** = "next (i.e. under the heading of) the Lupercalia"; for this use of *ad* compare 3 n. 6A (and 41 n. 18c).

27.   A. **populi iussu**: Antony presumably claimed that popular applause of his *contio* (see above n. 22B) meant public authority for his offer of a crown to Caesar. But since there was clearly no formal action by an assembly, Cicero implies that the popular reaction was one of disapproval.   B. **detulisse**: for this use of *defero* compare 31 n. 8c.   c. **uti**: inf. of *utor*; contrast *uti* = *ut* in 28 n. 23D. As the abl. with it supply *regno* from *regnum* in the preceding clause.

28.   A. **Tarquinius**: for the expulsion of the last Tarquin see sel. 5.   B. **quod . . . est**: the antecedent of *quod* is the clause *rex . . . constitueretur*; compare 28 n. 9A. c. **fas**: an indeclinable noun, wider in meaning than *ius* ("law"), and connoting all that is right in the eyes of men and of gods; compare 8 n. 7B. After the expulsion of the Tar-quins, the Romans took an oath never to have another king, thus aligning the gods, as well as their own legislation, against monarchy.

43

As the preceding selection showed, Caesar's autocratic behavior in the final year of his life aroused widespread hostility among the senators. In consequence, a conspiracy was formed against him which included many of his close associates. Although Caesar probably had warning of the existence of the plot, his self-confidence (or sense of fatality; see 39 n. 23) led him to attend a meeting of the senate on the Ides (15th; see 8 n. 6) of March, 44. There the conspirators, as they had already planned, assassinated him. Cicero, not included in the conspiracy, rejoiced at the death of one whom he had come to regard as a tyrant. He soon became spokesman for the "liberators" and, even after events proved that the assassination had been in vain (see 44 pref.), he never regretted the deed itself; see the second paragraph of 42 B.

The account of the conspiracy and assassination in A below comes from Suetonius; Shakespeare used the parallel version in Plutarch, which he read in North's translation. No full letter of Cicero from the moment survives, but the brief and excited note to Basilus, one of the conspirators, given first in B, was perhaps written on the very eve of the Ides. A series of letters to Atticus during April, a part of one of which is given second in B, shows Cicero's increasing concern over the failure of the "liberation" but his continuing admiration for the assassination itself.

A. *Caesaris caedes*

Conspiratum est in Caesarem a sexaginta amplius,[1] Gaio Cassio Marcoque et Decimo Bruto principibus conspirationis.[2] Qui, postquam senatus Idibus Martiis in Pompeii curiam edictus est,[3] tempus et locum ut maxime idoneum praetulerunt. Caesarem curiam introeuntem et adsidentem conspirati specie officii circumsteterunt;[4] ilicoque Cimber Tillius, qui primas partes susceperat, quasi aliquid rogaturus propius accessit;[5] renuentique et gestu in aliud tempus differenti ab utroque umero togam apprehendit;[6] deinde clamantem "Ista quidem vis est!"[7] alter e Cascis aversum vulnerat paulum infra iugulum.[8] Caesar Cascae bracchium adreptum graphio traiecit[9] conatusque prosilire alio vulnere tardatus est; utque animadvertit undique se strictis pugionibus peti,[10] toga caput obvolvit, simul sinistra manu sinum ad ima crura deduxit,[11] quo honestius caderet etiam inferiore corporis parte velata.[12] Atque ita tribus et viginti plagis confossus est, uno modo ad primum ictum gemitu sine voce edito,[13] etsi tradiderunt quidam Marco Bruto inruenti dixisse: *"kaì sù, téknon?"*[14] Exanimis, diffugientibus cunctis, aliquamdiu iacuit,[15] donec lecticae impositum, dependente bracchio, tres servoli domum rettulerunt.[16] Nec in tot vulneribus, ut Antistius medicus existimabat, letale ullum repertum est, nisi quod secundo loco in pectore acceperat.[17]

Illud plane inter omnes fere constitit, talem ei mortem paene ex sententia obtigisse.[18] Nam et quondam, cum apud Xenophontem legisset Cyrum ultima valetudine mandasse quaedam de funere suo,[19] aspernatus tam lentum mortis genus, subitam sibi celeremque optaverat; et pridie quam occideretur,[20] in sermone nato super cenam apud Marcum Lepidum, quisnam esset finis vitae commodissimus,[21] repentinum inopinatumque praetulerat.

B.   *Ciceronis de Caesaris caede duae sententiae*

CICERO BASILO SAL.[22]

Tibi gratulor, mihi gaudeo;[23] te amo, tua tueor;[24] a te amari et quid agas quidque agatur certior fieri volo.[25]

CICERO ATTICO SAL.

Equidem doleo, quod numquam in ulla civitate accidit, non una cum libertate rem publicam recuperatam.[26] Horribile est quae loquantur, quae minitentur.[27] Ac vereor Gallica etiam bella, ipse Sextus quo evadat.[28] Sed omnia licet concurrant,[29] Idus Martiae consolantur. Nostri autem heroes quod per ipsos confici potuit gloriosissime et magnificentissime confecerunt;[30] reliquae res opes et copias desiderant, quas nullas habemus.

1.   A. **conspiratum est** = "a conspiracy was made." This is a true impersonal pass., in which in Lat. the subject is implied in the verb (see 10 n. 10D) but should be expressed in Eng.; it emphasizes the act rather than the agents, who are indicated by *a* with the abl.   B. **sexaginta amplius** = "more (than) sixty (senators)"; for the omission of *quam* see 22 n. 11 (and 23 n. 9).

2.   **Gaio Cassio . . . Decimo Bruto**: in this series, *-que* serves as the principal connective of a "pair" of which the second element consists of the two *Bruti*, connected by *et*; contrast 23 n. 16. C. Cassius Longinus was perhaps a cousin of Q. Cassius, the

Caesarian tribune of 49, for whom see 38 n. 21A; for Gaius' brother Lucius see 31 n. 18B. Gaius had served as quaestor for Crassus and led the survivors of Carrhae (see 37 pref.) back to Syria, which as proquaestor he defended against the Parthians until 51. He became, along with Quintus, tribune for 49, but was opposed to Caesar. For M. Junius Brutus see 33 n. 15; his relationship to the more prominent family to which the other Brutus, Decimus, belonged is uncertain. Both M. Brutus and C. Cassius fought with Pompey in the civil war but were generously pardoned by Caesar after Pharsalus; see sel. 40. In 44 they were respectively urban and peregrine praetor; for their deaths at Philippi in 43 see sel. 45. Decimus Junius Brutus had served with Caesar in the Gallic and civil wars and was already designated for the consulship of 42. Hence his participation in the conspiracy, more than that of Cassius and Brutus, indicates how far Caesar had alienated even his loyal supporters. After the assassination, Decimus took up the province of Cisalpine Gaul, which Caesar had assigned to him for 43 and whence Antony presently tried to dislodge him; see 44 pref. When later he tried to block the return of Antony and Lepidus into Italy, his army deserted him and he was executed on Antony's orders.

3.   A. senatus . . . edictus est: with this idiom compare 28 n. 22c.   B. Idibus Martiis: for the divisions of the Roman month see 8 n. 6.   c. in Pompeii curiam: *in* + acc. because the proclamation told the senate to come to the curia. Since Caesar had an *imperium* for the planned Parthian campaign (see 38 n. 13B), the senate had to meet outside the sacred limits of the city (the *pomerium*); compare 27 n. 15. Caesar had summoned it to a hall attached to the colonnade behind the theater which Pompey had built in the Campus Martius during his consulship in 55. This was Rome's first permanent stone theater and always its largest and most magnificent. Plutarch *Caesar* 66.7 says that in the hall there was a statue of Pompey before which Caesar fell dead.

4.   specie officii = "with the appearance of duty," i.e. under the guise of paying their respects; *specie* is abl. of manner, with *cum* omitted because of the limiting gen.

5.   A. Cimber Tillius: Tillius Cimber had earlier been a strong supporter of Caesar; for the inverted order of his name compare 22 n. 13B (and 23 n. 14B).   B. primas partes = "the opening role"; he detained Caesar with a petition for the recall of his exiled brother.

6.   renuenti . . . differenti: the participles agree with *ei* (or *Caesari*) to be understood; it would be a dat. of reference either taken closely with *umero* and *togam* as what is miscalled "possession" or going more generally with the whole clause as "disadvantage"; for similar omission of a pronoun compare 39 n. 19A. As usual in such clauses, the participles should be rendered by clauses in Eng.; compare 7 n. 6B (and 42 n. 11B); = "as (Caesar) was refusing and putting him off to another time with a gesture, he grasped his toga by both shoulders (lit. from each shoulder)."

7.   deinde . . . est = "then as (Caesar) cried 'This then is violence!'"; *clamantem* agrees with *eum* to be supplied as the object of *vulnerat* below; compare the preceding note.

8.   A. alter e Cascis = "one of the (two brothers) Casca"; both were in the conspiracy, and this one, who aimed the first blow, was tribune at the time.   B. aversum = "from behind (lit. turned away)"; it is masc. acc. sing. of the past part. of *averto* and, like *clamantem*, modifies *eum* to be understood; see n. 7 above.

9.   A. Caesar . . . traiecit = "Caesar grasped Casca's arm and stabbed it with (his) stylus," lit. "Caesar pierced with a stylus the arm for Casca, (it) having been seized." B. Cascae: dat. of reference (possession or disadvantage) with a part of the body (see n. 6 above), rather than gen. of possession.   c. adreptum: as frequently (see 4 n. 6A), a subordinate but earlier action is given by a past part. modifying the object but placed before the main verb.   D. graphio: from the Greek verb *grapho* = "write"; a less common term than *stilus* (or *stylus*; also Greek) for the pointed metal instrument used for writing (by incising the wax) on the wax tablets used for notes, short letters, drafts of

documents, accounts, etc.   E. **traiecit:** the meaning "stabbed" or "pierced" derives from the basic meaning of "throw (or, shoot) across."

10.   **strictis pugionibus** = "with drawn daggers"; compare 23 n. 4C (and 41 n. 19).

11.   **toga . . . deduxit** = "he covered his head with his toga and at the same time with his left hand drew the fold (of his toga) down to his ankles," lit. "to the lowest legs." The toga was so wrapped around the body that it passed under the right arm from behind to leave it free, across the chest, and over the left shoulder. The fold across the chest was the *sinus* which Caesar pulled down to cover himself.

12.   **quo . . . caderet:** a rel. clause of characteristic expressing purpose (see 8 n. 1B and 41 n. 10A); = "so that he might fall more decorously," lit. "by which the more decorously." When a purpose clause includes a comparative adj. or adv., *ut* is regularly replaced by *quo* (see 34 n. 21A) as abl. of degree of difference.

13.   **uno . . . edito** = "only groaning once at the first blow, but not speaking," lit. "with one groan only issued without voice," i.e. without articulate speech. *Ad* + acc. here = "in response to" as against an abl. of time when; compare 42 n. 26B.

14.   A. **Marco . . . inruenti dixisse:** for this use of the participle, see n. 6 above (and 21 n. 2G). The subject of *dixisse* is *Caesarem* understood.   B. **kai su, teknon:** Greek; = "you too, child?" *Et tu, Brute?* is the Lat. equivalent usually given. Romans of the later Republic spoke Greek as readily as Lat. and particularly in moments of emotion. Since *teknon* was a term of affection for a younger person, this remark does not support the apparently baseless gossip that Brutus was Caesar's illegitimate son by Servilia; see 33 n. 15.

15.   A. **exanimis:** masc. nom. sing.; = "lifeless."   B. **cunctis:** i.e. all the senators and bystanders.

16.   A. **lecticae** = "on a litter"; dat. after *impositum*; see 6 n. 13.   B. **dependente bracchio** = "with his arm hanging down," i.e. over the side of the litter.   C. **servoli:** the diminutive suggests their unimportance and emphasizes to what a degree everybody significant had fled. After consonantal *v*, an original short *o* (ordinarily reduced to *u*) is often retained.

17.   A. **ut . . . existimabat** = "as Antistius the physician judged" (after examination), not simply "thought." Antistius is otherwise unknown.   B. **secundo loco** = "at the second blow (lit. place)"; the loc. abl. *loco* (see 30 n. 2B) is here almost abl. of "time when" since the emphasis is on the order of the stabs, not the location, which is given by *in pectore*.

18.   A. **illud . . . constitit** = "the following (point) has been clearly agreed upon among almost all (authorities)"; *illud* anticipates the indirect statement *talem . . . obtigisse* as subject; compare 32 n. 7A.   B. **constitit:** from *consto*; see 15 n. 5A and contrast *consisto* in 39 n. 17A (and 40 n. 21B).   C. **paene ex sententia** = "almost according to (his) wish (lit. feeling)."

19.   A. **et quondam:** in remote correlation with *et pridie* below; compare 33 n. 18 (and 42 n. 11A).   B. **apud:** with the name of an author regularly = "in the works of"; contrast n. 21C below.   C. **Xenophontem . . . Cyrum:** Xenophon, the Greek historian of the fourth century, wrote a fictional account, called *Cyropaedia*, of the education, personality, and death of Cyrus the Great, founder of the Persian Empire in the 6th century.   D. **legisset:** for the derivation see 29 n. 3 (and compare 41 n. 18B).   E. **ultima . . . funere suo** = "in (his) last illness gave certain orders (lit. ordered certain things) about his funeral"; *valetudo* means "health," either good or, as here, bad. The context shows that *suo* is reflexive to the subject of the indirect statement, *Cyrum*, not to that of the main verb, i.e. Caesar; compare 18 n. 14E.

20.   **pridie:** *pri-* was an original adverb which survived only as a prefix (as here, or in *pridem*) and in the comparative and superlative *prior, primus*. Thus *pridie quam* is here construed like *priusquam* with an anticipatory imperf. subj. of an event not yet actual; compare 2 n. 3B.

21.   A. **in sermone ... Lepidum** = "in a conversation which arose during (lit. over) dinner at the house of Marcus Lepidus." Lepidus, son of the revolutionary consul of 78 (see 28 pref. and n. 7A), was consul in 46 and served as *magister militum* (second in command) under Caesar when the latter was dictator in 45 and 44. Lepidus later became a member of the Second Triumvirate with Antony and Octavian; see 44 pref.   B. **nato:** *nascor* is used = *orior* and vice versa.   c. **apud:** with the name of a person = "at the house of"; see 35 n. 8A (and contrast n. 19B above).   D. **quisnam** = "(as to) which"; it introduces an indirect question dependent on the idea of question and answer implied in *sermone*.

22.   **SAL.** = *sal(utem dat);* see 32 n. 15.

23.   **tibi ... mihi:** dats. of reference, the first "of the person" as usually with *gratulor*, which is intrans., and the second with *gaudeo*, either of advantage (= "for myself") or of a type called "ethical" indicating simply that a person is indirectly concerned about the action of the verb (i.e. "for my part").

24.   **tua tueor** = "I am looking out for your (interests)"; compare *easque tueor* in the 3rd par. of 14. Cicero means by the sing. possessive adj. *tua* the interests of Basilus himself, though he may by implication include those of the liberators generally.

25.   **quid agas ... certior fieri:** *certiorem facere aliquem* may be followed by *de* + an abl., by an indirect statement, or, as here, by an indirect question; in the pass., with *fio*, the object (modified by *certiorem*) becomes subject (here not repeated because the inf. is complementary and hence "I" carries through) and the indirect questions remain in the predicate.

26.   **doleo ... recuperatam:** the object of *doleo* is the inf. clause *non ... recuperatam* (*esse*), the regular construction with *doleo*. The inf. clause is modified by the *quod* rel. clause; = "a (thing) which has never happened"; compare 28 n. 9A (and 42 n. 28B).

27.   **horribile ... minitentur:** this colloquial expression perhaps originated in a paratactic (coordinate; compare 23 n. 1A and 37 n. 23B) construction of *horribile est* followed, without connective, by a question in the deliberative subj.: "it is horrible; what may they be saying?"; hence the *est* remains singular and the *quae* clauses are indirect questions (rather than rel. clauses of characteristic with omitted antecedents); compare Eng. "it is horrible what they are saying."

28.   A. **vereor:** has two objects without connective: *bella* and the subjunctive clause *ipse ... evadat;* = "what course Sextus himself will take," lit. "whither he may break out." For the postponement of *quo* compare 35 n. 17A.   B. **Gallica etiam bella:** the *etiam* goes with *vereor*. Disturbances in Gaul might have resulted either from the natives' discontent at their recent subjection (see 36 pref.) or because commanders there, such as Lepidus, were loyal to Caesar's memory.   c. **Sextus:** the second son of Pompey the Great, who, having escaped from the battle of Munda (see 41 pref.), was now at large as a semi-pirate in the Mediterranean; see 46 pref.

29.   **omnia ... concurrant** = "let (i.e. although) everything combine (against us)"; for *licet* + the subj. without *ut* see 23 n. 1A (and contrast 40 n. 15A).

30.   A. **heroes:** a Greek nom. plur., i.e. the "liberators."   B. **per ipsos** = "through their own efforts (lit. themselves)"; for *per* + the acc. of person see 35 n. 4; for *ipsos* without *se* see 15 n. 14c.

44

At Caesar's funeral, his henchman Mark Antony began to arouse the sympathies of the mob against the assassins, and their leaders were shortly forced to withdraw from Rome: Brutus and Cassius to Greece and the other Brutus, Decimus, to Cisalpine Gaul; see 43 n. 2. For a time, Antony pretended to work with the senate, but soon became more and more Caesarian. During 44–43 Cicero delivered a series of speeches against him, called the "Philippics" (see 42 pref.) from their resemblance to those delivered against Philip of Macedon by Demosthenes in Athens in the mid-fourth century.

Caesar in his will had adopted and designated as his principal heir his great-nephew Gaius Octavius, who, born in 63, was not yet nineteen at the time of the assassination. Octavius was across the Adriatic at Apollonia in southern Illyria with the forces which Caesar had assembled for his planned expedition against Parthia; see 38 n. 13B (and 43 n. 3C). He returned to Italy to claim his inheritance and, in virtue of the adoption, called himself Gaius Julius Caesar Octavianus. Since Antony refused to release Caesar's funds and belittled him, and the senate was suspicious of him, he went to Campania and secured the armed support of two Caesarian legions and of veterans whom Caesar had settled there. In the meantime, Antony had marched north to dislodge Decimus Brutus from Cisalpine Gaul. Octavian, backed by his troops, forced the senate to grant him a propraetorian *imperium* and associate him with the consuls of 43, Hirtius and Pansa, in the pursuit of Antony. In two battles at Mutina, near Bologna, both consuls lost their lives. Antony was, however, forced to raise the siege of Decimus Brutus but escaped to Narbonese Gaul. There he was received by the then governor, Marcus Lepidus, for whom see 43 n. 21A.

Octavian returned to Rome in command of all the senatorial forces and compelled the senate to permit his election as consul, despite his youth, for the remainder of 43. He then marched north and, instead of fighting Antony, joined with him and Lepidus. Late in 43 they were created by law *tresviri rei publicae constituendae*, a title recalling that of Sulla's dictatorship; see 26 pref. This Second Triumvirate therefore had a legal status such as the First never had had; see 35 pref. For Octavian's own summary of these stages in his rise to power see the opening of 47.

One of the first acts of the Triumvirs was to order wholesale proscriptions of their enemies (see 83), in part to avenge themselves and in part to acquire money for their projects and land to distribute to their veterans; see 84. Antony demanded Cicero's life and, though Cicero had supported Octavian, the latter sacrificed him.

The following account of Cicero's execution on December 7, 43, comes from one of the later books of Livy. These are lost, but this passage was fortunately preserved by the Elder Seneca (father of the philosopher), often called Seneca Rhetor, who wrote in the early first century A.D.

Ciceronis proscripti mors

Marcus Cicero sub adventum triumvirorum urbe cesserat,[1] pro certo habens id quod erat, non magis se Antonio eripi quam Caesari Octaviano Cassium et Brutum posse.[2] Primo in Tusculanum fugerat;[3] inde transversis itineribus in Formianum,[4] ut ab Caieta navem conscensurus, proficiscitur.[5] Unde aliquoties in altum provectum,[6] cum modo venti adversi retulissent, modo ipse iactationem navis, caeco volvente fluctu, pati non posset,[7] taedium tandem eum et fugae et vitae cepit. Regressusque ad superiorem villam, quae paulo plus mille passibus a mari abest, "Moriar," inquit, "in patria saepe servata."[8]

Postero die autem a familiaribus ei persuasum est ut iterum fugam experiretur,[9] sed descendentem ad mare milites Antonii adsecuti sunt. Satis constat servos fortiter fideliterque paratos fuisse ad dimicandum;[10] ipsum deponi lecticam et quietos pati quod sors iniqua cogeret iussisse.[11] Prominenti ex lectica praebentique immotam cervicem, caput praecisum est.[12] Nec satis stolidae crudelitati militum fuit;[13] manus quoque scripsisse aliquid in Antonium exprobrantes praeciderunt.[14] Ita relatum caput ad Antonium iussuque eius inter duas manus in rostris positum,[15] ubi ille consul, ubi saepe consularis, ubi eo ipso anno adversus Antonium, quanta nulla umquam humana vox cum admiratione eloquentiae, auditus fuerat.[16] Vix attollentes prae lacrimis oculos, homines intueri trucidati membra civis poterant.[17]

Vixit tres et sexaginta annos, ut, si vis afuisset, ne immatura quidem mors videri possit.[18] Ingenium et operibus et praemiis operum felix; ipse fortunae diu prosperae;[19] et in longo tenore felicitatis magnis interdum ictus vulneribus[20]—exsilio, ruina partium pro quibus steterat, filiae morte, exitu tam tristi atque acerbo[21]—omnium adversorum nihil ut viro dignum erat tulit praeter mortem;[22] quae vere aestimanti minus indigna videri potuit,[23] quod a victore inimico nil crudelius passurus erat, quam quod eiusdem fortunae compos ipse fecisset.[24] Si quis tamen virtutibus vitia pensaret, vir magnus ac memorabilis fuit,[25] et in cuius laudes exsequendas Cicerone laudatore opus fuerit.[26]

1. **sub adventum triumvirorum** = "just before the arrival of the Triumvirs"; *sub*, from the connotation "close under," may be used of time to connote "just before" (as here), "along with" or "during," or "just after," according to the context. Octavian, Antony, and Lepidus returned to Rome from the north in Oct. or Nov. 43.

2. A. **non . . . posse:** an indirect statement introduced by *pro certo habens*, which is equivalent to a verb of knowing; it is in apposition with the proleptic phrase *id quod erat* = "that which was," i.e. "was in fact true." B. **Antonio . . . Caesari Octaviano:** dats. of reference (separation) with *eripi*; compare 18 n. 7A (and 25 n. 3B). Cicero rightly felt that Octavian would relentlessly pursue the assassins of his adoptive father; see 45 n. 1A.

3. **Tusculanum:** a favorite villa of Cicero's in Tusculum, above modern Frascati in the Alban Hills just south of Rome; there Cato the Elder (see sels. 13 and 14) had been born. Romans of the upper classes usually owned several country estates which are regularly designated by the adjectival form of the nearest town (as here, *Tusculanum*) with *praedium* (= "farm, estate") understood.

4. A. **transversis itineribus** = "by cross-country roads"; abl. of means ("way by which"); compare 18 n. 14D. B. **Formianum:** for this adj. compare n. 3 above. This villa of Cicero was near Formiae, on the coast between Rome and Naples.

5. A. **ut . . . conscensurus** = "with the intention of (lit. as if about to) taking ship from Caieta"; *conscendo* is regularly used of embarking on (lit. "mounting") a ship and is here treated as if it meant "to depart" and construed with an abl. of place from which, in which *a* used with the name of a town means "from the vicinity of"; see 1 n. 5C. In Lat. of the Empire, the fut. act. part. often expresses intention or purpose; compare the connotation of the gerundive, which some grammarians regard as a fut. pass. part. B. **Caieta:** modern Gaeta, a peninsula running out from Formiae with a harbor so well sheltered that until recently it was an Italian naval base. C. **proficiscitur:** since this is pres. ind., it cannot form a purpose clause with *ut* (which is therefore rendered "as if" in the preceding note) but is the main verb with *inde . . . Formianum*; it would be tempting to construe the latter with *fugerat* and emend to *profisceretur* = "in order to embark and depart from near Caieta," although in that case, Livy would probably have used *conscendens* rather than *conscensurus* and *ut* + the fut. act. part. is regularly used to indicate a purpose, as stated in the preceding note. The pres. ind. is historical, for vividness in beginning the main topic of Cicero's death; the preceding pluperfs. *cesserat* and *fugerat* describe antecedent preliminary actions.

6. **in altum provectum** = "although he sailed out to sea," lit. "(him) having been carried into the deep"; for thus rendering the part. compare 43 n. 6; it is acc. in agreement either with an understood *eum* as object of *retulissent* or with the *eum* which is object of the main clause at the end of the sentence; the latter is perhaps more likely since *unde . . . provectum* seems to modify the whole sentence and not to belong (by anticipation) only within the *cum* clause.

7. A. **modo . . . modo** = "first . . . then"; compare 17 n. 24. There is an abrupt change of subject between the two clauses, as often in this sel., a variation which suggests the style of Sallust; see 21 n. 18. B. **caeco volvente fluctu:** abl. abs.; = "since a directionless (lit. blind) swell was making (the ship) roll."

8. A. **superiorem villam:** i.e. the villa at Formiae. The phrase may mean "the aforementioned villa" or "the villa where he had been before going to sea," or, taken literally, "the higher villa," i.e. above the seashore. B. **paulo . . . abest** = "which lay a little more than a mile from the sea," lit. "which was away from the sea by a little more than a thousand paces." *Mille passibus* (i.e. "by a mile") is abl. of comparison after *plus*; *paulo* is abl. of degree of difference, which is regularly used with expressions of distance as well as of time; compare 14 n. 3. C. **moriar:** more effective if taken as a fut. ind. expressing resolution; it may, however, be hortatory subj.

9. A. **a familiaribus** = "by (his) servants"; contrast 28 n. 23B (and 35 n. 8C). B. **ei persuasum est:** as regularly with verbs which in the act. take a dat. of the person and

an acc. of the thing, in the pass. the acc. (here the clause of purpose *ut . . . experiretur*) becomes subject and the person remains in the dat.; see 36 n. 9c (and compare 38 n. 6A).

10.   A. **satis constat** = "it is generally agreed"; see 15 n. 5A (and 43 n. 18A). The subject is the combined indirect statements *servos . . . fuisse* and *ipsum . . . iussisse*. B. **paratos fuisse:** for the use of the perf. system of *sum* with the past part. see 3 n. 1; it is especially frequent with *paratus*.

11.   A. **ipsum:** used pronominally for *eum ipsum* (i.e. Cicero); compare 15 n. 14c (and 43 n. 30B). It is the subject acc. of *iussisse*.   B. **deponi . . . pati:** both infs. are objective with *iussisse*, but their subjects differ (compare n. 7A above), namely *lecticam* for *deponi* and *quietos* for *pati*.   C. **quietos:** the adj. is here used alone, since a demonstrative pronoun can readily be understood (compare 19 n. 15B); it may best be rendered in Eng. by a pronoun and an adv. (compare 11 n. 12A and 14 n. 18B), i.e. "he ordered (them, namely, the slaves) to suffer quietly etc."   D. **quod . . . cogeret:** as often (compare 21 n. 20c), an antecedent *id* is understood to serve as the object of *pati*; the imperf. subj. may be by attraction in a subordinate clause in the indirect statement *ipsum . . . iussisse*, or it may represent a pres. subj. in direct statement, in a general or characteristic rel. clause, depending on whether Livy imagined Cicero to have said: "endure quietly (that) which unjust fortune compels" or "(that) which . . . may compel."

12.   **prominenti . . . praebentique:** in agreement with *ei* to be understood as dat. of reference (either possession with *caput* or disadvantage); see 43 n. 6.

13.   A. **nec . . . fuit:** understand "this" (i.e. the severing of his head) as the subject of *fuit*.   B. **stolidae crudelitati** = "unfeeling cruelty"; dat. of reference with *satis*.

14.   A. **scripsisse:** inf. in indirect discourse after *exprobrantes; manus* is both its subject and the object of *praeciderunt*.   B. **aliquid in Antonium** = "something against Antony"; a euphemistic expression for the bitter invective of the *Philippics* (see pref.); for similar euphemisms compare 40 n. 4B and 42 n. 2A.

15.   **rostris:** see 14 n. 6B (and 42 n. 12B), and for the custom of displaying heads 24 n. 12A. Dio Cassius XLVII 8.4 (early 3rd cent. A.D.) reports that Antony's wife Fulvia stuck pins through the tongue which had pronounced the *Philippics*. Fulvia's first husband had been Clodius, for whose enmity with Cicero see sel. 36 B.

16.   A. **quanta . . . eloquentiae** = "with admiration of eloquence as great (as that with which) no human voice ever (had been heard)"; i.e. Cicero's eloquence when he delivered the Philippics had been more admired than any speeches had been ever before. B. **quanta . . . cum admiratione:** condensed for *tanta cum admiratione quanta* (compare 16 n. 4); it encloses the subject of the *quanta* clause, *nulla . . . vox*.   C. **auditus fuerat:** for the tense see n. 10B above.

17.   **prae lacrimis** = "for (because of) their tears"; *prae* is often thus used of a hindrance.

18.   **ut . . . possit** = "so that, if violence had been absent, his death can seem not even untimely." In spite of the perf. *vixit*, which is a secondary tense, the result is envisaged as present to the speaker (see 13 n. 6A and compare 16 n. 13F); hence *possit* is equivalent to a *potest* in a direct statement. The contrary to fact protasis, however, is envisaged as in the past, at the time of Cicero's death; hence *afuisset*.

19.   **fortunae diu prosperae:** gen. of description (see 6 n. 9); supply "he was a man of"; compare 13 n. 4.

20.   A. **ictus:** past part. of the rare verb *ico* = "strike" or "hit"; it modifies the subject of *tulit* with a connotation of "when" or "although smitten."   B. **vulneribus:** here, as often, metaphorical for "misfortunes," specified by *exsilio . . . acerbo*.

21.   A. **exsilio:** for Cicero's exile see sels. 36 B and C.   B. **ruina partium:** compare the similar phrase *partium clade* in the 3rd par. of sel. 41.   C. **filiae:** Tullia (born ca.

78) was thirteen years older than Cicero's son Marcus (65–ca. 25) and her father's favorite; his grief for her death in 45 was as unbounded as his self-pity in exile.   D. **tam ... atque:** although *atque* may be used to introduce the second half of a comparison after expressions of likeness or equality and under the Empire after comparative adjs. and advs., it does not seem to be used instead of *quam* correlatively with *tam*; the latter therefore goes here with both adjs. connected by *atque*; = "so sad and bitter."

22.   **omnium ... tulit** = "he bore none (lit. nothing) of all his misfortunes."

23.   A. **quae vere aestimanti** = "and (even) this, to (one who) judges truly"; for *quae* = *et ea* (i.e. *mors*, as subject of *videri potuit*) compare 4 n. 4A (and 33 n. 4A).   B. **aestimanti:** dat. of reference (or indirect object) with *videri*; with this use of the part. alone compare 3 n. 4 (and n. 12 above).

24.   A. **passurus erat:** the speaker places himself in the position of one observing the scene and uses the 1st act. periphrastic (see 28 n. 21 and 32 n. 9B) imperf. of something which was about to take place, rather than the simple perf. which would be appropriate to one looking back at the event.   B. **quam ... fecisset** = "than (that) which he himself would have inflicted (if) possessed of the same good fortune"; i.e. if Cicero had defeated Antony. For this kind of contrary to fact condition, in which the protasis is replaced by an expression equivalent to a verb, compare 9 n. 6D.   C. **eiusdem fortunae:** objective gen. with the adj. *compos.*

25.   A. **pensaret ... fuit:** the pres. (potential) subj. might have been expected in the protasis, i.e. "if anybody should compare," but the perf. ind. statement of fact in the apodosis has attracted the protasis into the past general (or potential) tense; compare 42 n. 2B.   B. **pensaret:** for this verb compare 22 n. 12C (and 39 n. 15B); it takes the acc. of what is weighed, here *vitia*, and the abl. of means of whatever is weighed against it, here *virtutibus.*

26.   A. **in ... fuerit** = "to set forth his praises (lit. for the setting forth of whose praises) there would have been need of a (second) Cicero as *laudator*"; for the abl. with *opus est* see 25 n. 5A.   B. **fuerit:** perf. subj. because the rel. clause is characteristic.

45

In 42, after the Triumvirs had temporarily arranged matters at Rome, Antony and Octavian crossed to Greece to fight Brutus and Cassius, who had levied a strong army from the eastern provinces after they fled from Italy in 43; see 44 pref. In two successive engagements at Philippi, in eastern Macedonia, first Cassius and then Brutus were defeated. Each committed suicide.

The following description of the battle of Philippi is mostly Velleius'; there are a few insertions from Suetonius' life of Augustus.

Pugna Philippica

Caesar Octavianus nihil convenientius duxit quam necem avunculi vindicare tuerique acta.[1] Itaque lege Pedia, quam consul Pedius collega eius tulerat,[2] omnibus qui Caesarem patrem interfecerant aqua ignique interdictum erat.[3] Cum igitur Cassius et Brutus in Macedoniam ab Asia exercitus traiecissent, Caesar quoque et Antonius in Macedoniam profecti sunt et apud urbem Philippos cum Bruto Cassioque acie concurrerunt.[4] Primo pugnae die cornu cui Brutus praeerat, repulsis hostibus, castra Caesaris cepit; id autem in quo Cassius fuerat fugatum ac male mulcatum in altiora se receperat loca.[5]

Tum Cassius, ex sua fortuna eventum collegae aestimans, dimisit evocatum[6] iussitque nuntiare sibi quae esset multitudo hominum quae ad se tenderet.[7] Tardius eo nuntiante, cum in vicino esset agmen cursu ad eum tendentium,[8] neque pulvere aut facies aut signa denotari possent,[9] existimans hostes esse qui inruerent, lacerna caput circumdedit extentamque cervicem interritus liberto praebuit.[10] Deciderat Cassii caput, cum evocatus advenit nuntians Brutum esse victorem. Qui cum imperatorem prostratum videret, "Sequar," inquit, "eum quem mea occidit tarditas,"[11] et ita in gladium incubuit.

Post paucos deinde dies Brutus iterum conflixit cum hostibus et, victus acie, cum in tumulum nocte ex fuga se recepisset,[12] impetravit a Stratone, familiari suo, ut manum morituro commodaret sibi[13] impel-

lensque se in mucronem gladii eius, uno ictu transfixus, expiravit
protinus. Hunc exitum M. Bruti septimum et tricesimum annum
agentis Fortuna esse voluit, incorrupto animo eius in diem quae illi
omnes virtutes unius temeritate facti abstulit.[14] Fuit autem dux Cassius
melior quanto vir Brutus;[15] e quibus Brutum amicum habere malles,
inimicum magis timeres Cassium;[16] in altero maior vis, in altero virtus.
Qui si vicissent, quantum rei publicae interfuit Caesarem Octavianum
potius habere quam Antonium principem, tantum retulisset habere
Brutum quam Cassium.[17]

Fractis Bruti Cassiique partibus, Antonius, transmarinas obiturus
provincias, ad Orientem ordinandum substitit.[18] Caesar autem in
Italiam ad veteranos municipalibus agris collocandos regressus est.[19]
Nec successum victoriae moderatus est, sed, capite Bruti Romam
misso ut statuae Caesaris subiceretur,[20] in alios splendidissimos
captivos non sine verborum contumelia saeviit.[21]

1. A. **Caesar . . . acta:** Octavian justified his attack on the "liberators" as vengeance for the assassination of his great-uncle and adoptive father Caesar; see the
selection from his *Res Gestae* in 47, especially nn. 5 and 6. B. **avunculi:** used loosely
for maternal great-uncle.

2. A. **lege Pedia:** for the naming of Roman laws see 24 n. 6B. B. **quam . . .
tulerat:** for this idiom see 20 n. 7 (and 24 n. 10). C. **consul Pedius:** Q. Pedius was a
nephew, or less probably a great-nephew, of Julius Caesar. Octavian had him elected
consul with himself for the last months of 43.

3. A. **Caesarem patrem:** for (Julius) Caesar's adoption of Octavius see 44 pref.
B. **aqua . . . interdictum erat:** for this formula of exile see 36 n. 9C. Velleius uses an
impersonal passive (compare 22 n. 2c) with *lege* as abl. of means rather than making
lex subject of a perf. act.

4. A. **Philippos:** in apposition with *urbem*; for the plur. form compare 5 n. 15A (and
33 n. 6B). Philippi lay in eastern Macedonia. B. **acie:** for this loc. abl. see 26 n. 6A
(and 39 n. 13).

5. **se receperat:** for this idiom see 3 n. 6B and compare *se conferat* in 35 n. 23.

6. **evocatum:** a past part. used as a noun (compare *proeliantes* in 3 n. 4); = a soldier
who had re-enlisted (lit. "having been recalled") after completing his required twenty
years' service.

7. A. **nuntiare sibi** = "to report (back) to himself"; as subject carry over *evocatum*
from the previous clause and render "him." B. **tenderet** = "was marching"; for the
intransitive meaning compare 3 n. 3.

8. A. **agmen . . . tendentium** = "the band of (those) marching towards him at full
speed"; for the part. alone compare 44 n. 23B (and n. 6 above). B. **cursu:** abl. of
manner without *cum*; the regular term for an army marching "on the double"; compare
17 n. 20B.

9. **aut facies aut signa** = "either (their) appearance or (their) military) standards."

10.   A. **lacerna . . . circumdedit:** compare Caesar's gesture in 43 n. 11; Cassius, being on a battlefield, was wearing a *lacerna* (military cloak), not a toga.   B. **extentam . . . praebuit:** for the similar suicides of Gaius Gracchus and of Brutus see 19 n. 10 and n. 13c below. Cato the Younger apparently committed suicide unaided; see 41.

11.   **sequar:** more effective as fut. than subj.; compare Cicero's *moriar* in 44 n. 8c.

12.   A. **acie:** see n. 4B above.   B. **se recepisset:** see n. 5 above.

13.   A. **Stratone:** a Greek name.   B. **familiari suo:** presumably one of Brutus' slaves or freedmen; see 44 n. 9A.   C. **ut . . . sibi** = "that he (Strato) should lend a hand to him (Brutus) being about to die"; i.e. help him to commit suicide; compare Cassius' suicide in n. 10B above.   D. **morituro:** fut. part. indicating intention; see 44 n. 5A.   E. **sibi:** reflexive to the subject of the main verb, as usually in an indirect command; see 18 n. 12B.

14.   A. **incorrupto animo:** abl. abs. in the sense of attendant circumstance.   B. **in diem** = "until (that) day"; here fem. of a specific day, as is shown by the following *quae*; see 12 n. 8B.   C. **illi:** dat. of reference (separation) with *abstulit*; compare 18 n. 7A (and 44 n. 2B).   D. **unius temeritate facti** = "by a single rash act," lit. "by the rashness of a single act." For the use of an abstract noun with a gen. instead of a concrete noun modified by an adj. see 15 n. 4 (and 18 n. 18B). Velleius means the assassination of Caesar. In this estimate of Brutus he is torn between admiration for him as superior in character to Cassius and condemnation of his participation in the murder of Octavian's adoptive father, Julius Caesar.

15.   A. **fuit . . . Brutus:** such correlative expressions are often condensed; compare 16 n. 4 (and 44 n. 16A). Here *tanto* is to be supplied with *dux*, and *melior fuit* to be repeated with *vir*; = "(as much) better a leader as Brutus (was a better) man."   B. **quanto:** abl. of degree of difference; lit. "by so much."

16.   A. **e quibus** = "and of (the two of) them"; compare 43 n. 8A.   B. **malles . . . timeres:** past potential subjs.; see 11 n. 8A (and 26 n. 1A).

17.   A. **quantum . . . tantum:** these correlative clauses would be reversed in Eng.; = "it would have profited (the Republic) as much . . . as it did (i.e. profit the Republic)"; compare n. 15A above.   B. **interfuit . . . retulisset:** synonymous in meaning.

18.   **obiturus** = "(since he was) about to visit"; compare n. 13D above.

19.   **ad veteranos . . . collocandos:** though Velleius says that the fields on which Octavian settled the veterans belonged to cities, the ancient lives of the poet Vergil state that his family's farm near Mantua was among those scheduled for confiscation but that his friends interceded with Octavian to spare it; see 55 pref. and 84.

20.   **statuae** = "(at the foot of) the statue," lit. "to the statue"; dat. with *subiceretur*, a verb compounded with *sub-*. Compare the treatment of Cicero's corpse in 44 n. 15.

21.   A. **in . . . saeviit:** Octavian's cruelty here and his participation in the proscription (see 44 pref.) contrast with his later reputation for clemency and kindness; see 47. Opinion is divided as to whether his later conduct was a hypocritical facade assumed to win popularity or whether with age he learned the wisdom of following Julius Caesar's example, rather than that of Marius and Sulla. Perhaps also such stories are remnants of hostile propaganda spread by Antony's supporters when the conflict between him and Octavian developed in the thirties (see 46), and each tried to make the other responsible for the early excesses of the Second Triumvirate.   B. **verborum contumelia** = *verbis contumeliosis*; compare n. 14D above.

46

In 41, the year following the battle of Philippi (see 45), Antony's brother Lucius, consul in that year, and his wife Fulvia (for whom see 44 n. 15) joined in a revolt against Octavian centered on Perugia in north central Italy. They were soon suppressed and both died in 40. During the same year, Antony and Octavian met at Brundisium, a port on the southeast coast of Italy, and agreed that Octavian should control Italy and the west and Antony the east. Antony also married Octavian's beloved sister Octavia. This agreement and marriage recall the cementing of the First Triumvirate by the union of Pompey with Julia (see 35 pref.) and the conference at Luca, for which see 37 pref.

From 38–36, Octavian was engaged in operations to eliminate Sextus Pompey, Pompey's surviving son (see 43 n. 28c), who had set himself up as a piratical freebooter based on Sicily. When Lepidus, who had crossed to Sicily ostensibly to assist in the final defeat of Sextus in 36, attempted to assert himself, Octavian won his troops from him and forced him into retirement. In 37, Antony suffered a severe defeat at the hands of the Parthians and returned to Egypt. There during the succeeding years he behaved as a Hellenistic monarch with Cleopatra for his consort. His treatment of Rome's eastern provinces as if he were an absolute ruler and his desertion of Octavia for the Egyptian queen alienated Roman and Italian sentiment.

As consul for the third time in 31, Octavian shed his triumviral powers and presented himself as champion of western *Romanitas* against the Hellenistic and oriental ambitions of Antony and Cleopatra. In a decisive naval battle off the promontory of Actium in northwest Greece, on Sept. 2, 31, Octavian routed the fleet of Antony and Cleopatra; when they fled back to Egypt, their land forces surrendered without a fight. Octavian pursued the pair to Alexandria, where, in August 30, Antony committed suicide and Cleopatra, after perhaps trying without success to ingratiate herself with the new Roman conqueror, followed suit.

The following account of the defeat and deaths of Antony and Cleopatra is composed from Velleius, Florus, and Suetonius' life of Augustus.

Bellum Actiacum

Antonius, cum contra Parthos profectus esset, fame et pestilentia laborans pro victo recessit.[1] Expeditione repulsa, captus amore Cleopatrae in regio se sinu reficiebat.[2] Ita mulier Aegyptia ab ebrio

imperatore pretium libidinum Romanum imperium petiit;[3] et promisit
Antonius. Hic igitur coepit non sibi dominationem parare sed Cleopatrae; nec tacite, sed patriae, nominis, togae oblitus,[4] totus in monstrum illud ut mente ita victu quoque cultuque desciverat:[5] aureum in
manu baculum, in latere acinaces, purpurea vestis ingentibus obstricta
gemmis;[6] diadema tantum deerat ut regina rex et ipse frueretur.[7]
Crescente deinde amentia, bellum patriae inferre constituit. Regina
igitur comitante, milites suos regiasque naves ad Actium, Ambracii
sinus promunturium, contraxit.[8]

Ad primam horum novorum motuum famam Caesar Octavianus a
Brundisio traiecerat, ut venienti bello occurreret.[9] Advenit deinde
maximi discriminis dies, quo Caesar Antoniusque, productis classibus,
pro salute alter, in ruinam alter terrarum orbis apud Actium navali
proelio dimicavere. In serum dimicatione protracta,[10] prima occupavit
fugam Cleopatra. Antonius fugientis reginae quam pugnantis militis
sui comes esse maluit, et imperator, qui in desertores saevire debuerat,[11]
desertor exercitus sui factus est.

Proximo deinde anno Caesar Aegyptum petiit, obsessaque Alexandria, quo Antonius cum Cleopatra confugerat, brevi potitus est.[12]
Antonius quidem seras condiciones pacis frustra temptans, se ipse non
segniter interemit, adeo ut multa desidiae crimina morte redimeret.[13]
At Cleopatra ad pedes Caesaris provoluta temptavit oculos ducis; sed
nequiquam, nam pulchritudo eius infra pudicitiam principis fuit. Nec
illa de vita, quae offerebatur, sed de parte regni laborabat.[14] Quod ubi
desperavit et Caesarem se triumpho servare magno opere cupere vidit,[15]
incautiorem nancta custodiam, in mausoleum (sepulchra regum sic
vocant) se recepit.[16] Ibi ornatissimos, ut solebat, induta cultus in
referto odoribus sarcophago iuxta suum se collocavit Antonium[17] et,
inlata aspide, morsu eius, expers muliebris metus, spiritum reddidit.[18]
Caesar ambobus communem sepulturae honorem tribuit[19] ac tumulum
ab ipsis incohatum perfici iussit. Sic ultimam bellis civilibus imposuit
manum. Fuitque et fortuna et clementia Caesaris dignum, quod nemo
ex eis qui contra eum arma tulerant ab eo iussuve eius interemptus
est.[20]

1.   A. **contra Parthos:** for Crassus' ill-fated expedition against the Parthians, see 37 pref.; for Caesar's projected invasion see 38 n. 13B. Antony retreated from his expedition with heavy losses in 36.   B. **fame ... recessit** = "overcome (lit. laboring) by famine and disease, he withdrew as if defeated."

2.   **captus amore Cleopatrae:** for Cleopatra and her connection with Caesar see 33 nn. 16B–20. Antony had already met Cleopatra at Tarsus, in Cilicia, in 41 (as described in Shakespeare's play) and had spent the following winter in Egypt. However, his serious infatuation with Cleopatra and his plans to make himself joint ruler of the east with her seem to have matured only in 35 when he returned from Parthia to Egypt.

3.   **ebrio:** Antony was charged by his enemies with drunkenness; contrast Cato's remark about Caesar in 33 n. 23.

4.   A. **patriae ... oblitus:** verbs of forgetting take the gen. (as here) or the acc. B. **togae:** here symbolizes Roman culture, supplementing *patria* and *nomen*; contrast *toga* used as a symbol for peace in 27 n. 13B.

5.   A. **monstrum:** i.e. Cleopatra, whom the Romans ranked with the Gauls and Hannibal (see 8 pref. and 11 pref.) as one of the worst threats to their empire.   B. **ut ... ita** = "both ... and," lit. "as ... so"; see 19 n. 11A (and 28 n. 5A)   C. **victu ... cultuque** = "in way of life and attire." When Antony adopted Greek behavior and dress he was regarded by the Romans with suspicious distaste, rather as the British would have regarded a governor of India who "went native."   D. **desciverat:** for the connotations of *descisco* see 17 n. 20C (and 20 n. 4C).

6.   A. **baculum ... diadema:** a gold scepter, Persian scimitar, heavily jeweled garments, and a diadem (a jewel-studded ribbon; see 42 n. 13C) were all parts of the costume of Hellenistic monarchs.   B. **in latere** = "at (his) side"; from *latus, -eris,* n.   C. **acinaces:** masc. nom. sing.

7.   A. **tantum ... ut ... frueretur** = "only a crown was lacking so that he might enjoy the queen as a king himself." The exact connotation of this *ut* clause is hard to determine; the Eng. rendering "might" suggests that it is purpose, but since the basic meaning of *tantum* remains "so much" even when it is rendered "only," the *ut* clause may have had in Lat. a connotation of result (consecutive), which is the normal construction after such words as *tantus, ita,* and *sic.*   B. **tantum:** for the meaning "only" compare 21 n. 6C.   C. **regina:** abl. (of means) after *fruor;* compare 37 n. 27B.

8.   **Ambracii sinus** = "on the bay of Ambracia," lit. "of the Ambracian bay"; Ambracia was a town on a bay in southern Epirus, in northwestern Greece. The promontory of Actium was on the south side of the entrance to the bay.

9.   **a Brundisio:** for the use of the prep. instead of the simple abl. of place from which see 1 n. 5C. Brundisium, on the Adriatic in southeast Italy, was the main port of embarkation for Greece; see 39 n. 25B.

10.   **in serum** = "until late" (in the day).

11.   **debuerat:** for the use of the pluperf. instead of the perf., compare *potuerat* in 18 n. 15C.

12.   A. **obsessaque Alexandria:** abl. (of means) after *potitus est* (contrast the gen. in 26 n. 9A) rather than abl. abs.; render in Eng. "he besieged ... and got possession of." Alexandria, capital and chief port of Egypt, was, after Rome, the largest city in the Roman empire and a famous center of Hellenistic culture.   B. **brevi:** understand *tempore*; see 9 n. 6B.

13.   **crimina** = "charges," not "crimes."

14.   **nec ... laborabat** = "nor was she striving for (her) life ... but for some measure (lit. a part) of sovereignty." Octavian would have spared her life, but she was unwilling to live except as queen.

15.   A. **triumpho:** dat. of purpose; compare 40 n. 9B.   B. **magno opere:** for this adverbial abl. see 14 n. 17.

16. A. **mausoleum:** the term derives from the elaborate tomb which Mausolus, a 4th-cent. king of Halicarnassus in Asia Minor, built for himself and his wife Artemisia. B. **se recepit:** for this idiom see 3 n. 6B (and 45 n. 5).

17. A. **cultus:** masc. acc. plur.; verbs meaning "to clothe" take two accs., of the person and of the clothes. Hence in the pass., when the person becomes the subject, the clothes remain in the acc.   B. **in ... sarcophago** = "in the sarcophagus filled with perfumes"; for the abl. with *refertus* see 13 n. 7 (and 28 n. 6D).   C. **iuxta suum ... Antonium** = "beside her (husband) Antony." Cleopatra had had his body brought into the royal mausoleum after his suicide.

18. **expers muliebris metus** = "free from a woman's (natural) fear"; for the gen. with *expers* see 28 n. 22E. Cleopatra's courage in committing suicide impressed even the hostile Romans.

19. **communem ... honorem:** by "hypallage" (Greek; = transference, i.e. of epithet) = "the honor of burial together," lit. "the shared honor of a burial."

20. A. **ultimam ... manum:** i.e. put an end to; the construction is the same as in *dextram ... flammis imposuit* in 6 n. 13 (and compare 43 n. 16A) but the meaning here is figurative; compare Eng. "put the finishing touch to."   B. **nemo ... est:** Velleius goes on in the lines following this passage to show that the deaths of Octavian's enemies were either due to suicide or caused by others.   C. **iussuve:** for the enclitic -*ve* = "or" see 2 n. 4B.

47

Octavian returned from the east and in 29 celebrated triumphs for his various victories. In 28 and 27, his sixth and seventh consulships, he canceled all the illegal acts of the Triumvirate and re-established the senate as the representative and supreme authority of the Roman state. He also tried to make the magistrates exercise their republican functions, and the popular assemblies their responsibility for legislation and election. For this "restoration of the Republic" the grateful senate voted him the title *Augustus* on January 16, 27, and restored to him enough of the powers which he had laid down so that he continued to be, in fact, the ruler of the Roman state. In addition to being "ordinary" consul annually until 23, he had two specific powers of great importance. The *tribunicia potestas* permitted him to initiate legislation or decrees in the senate and presented him as the champion of the *plebs*. And the *imperium proconsulare* gave him direct control over those provinces (about half) in which there were legions and which he governed by appointing senatorial *legati propraetore*. The senate continued to send proconsuls to the peaceful provinces, but Augustus kept an eye on these and on Rome and Italy in virtue of his *auctoritas*, not a specific or legal power but that quality in him which commanded respect and obedience. Moreover, the personality of Augustus, and his success in restoring peace and prosperity to the whole Mediterranean world, inspired feelings of admiration and gratitude which often took the form of worship of him as a "divine" ruler.

The first of the following passages comprises selections from Augustus' own account of his achievements, his *Res Gestae*, which, Suetonius *Aug.* 101 says, was found among his papers at his death in A.D. 14 and inscribed on two tablets in front of his mausoleum in Rome. An almost complete copy of the Latin text and a Greek translation have survived on the walls of a temple dedicated to Augustus in Ancyra (modern Ankara, the capital of Turkey), whence the document is often called the *Monumentum Ancyranum*. Fragments of two further copies, one Greek and one Latin, have been discovered elsewhere in Asia Minor, suggesting that it was widely used to commemorate him. The record was first composed about 2 and then added to. Final corrections, such as his age at death, were presumably made by order of his successor Tiberius. It emphasizes first his services to the Roman state and people, secondly his avoidance of monarchical offices, the justice of his conduct towards his enemies, and his restoration of the Republic.

The second passage, from Velleius, reflects the grateful devotion to Augustus which figures also in the poets of the "Augustan Age," especially in Vergil and Horace.

A. *Rerum gestarum divi Augusti capita selecta*

Annos undeviginti natus exercitum privato consilio et privata impensa comparavi,[1] per quem rem publicam a dominatione factionis oppressam in libertatem vindicavi.[2] Res publica ne quid detrimenti caperet, senatus me pro praetore simul cum consulibus providere iussit.[3] Populus autem eodem anno me consulem, cum consul uterque in bello cecidisset, et triumvirum rei publicae constituendae creavit.[4] Qui parentem meum trucidaverunt, eos in exsilium expuli, iudiciis legitimis ultus eorum facinus,[5] et postea bellum inferentis rei publicae vici bis acie.[6] Bella terra et mari civilia externaque toto in orbe terrarum saepe gessi victorque omnibus veniam petentibus civibus peperci.[7] Externas gentes quibus tuto ignosci potuit conservare quam excidere malui.[8] Senatu populoque Romano consentientibus ut curator legum et morum summa potestate solus crearer,[9] nullum magistratum contra morem maiorum delatum recepi.[10] Quae tum per me geri senatus voluit, per tribuniciam potestatem perfeci.

In consulatu sexto et septimo,[11] postquam bella civilia exstinxeram, per consensum universorum potitus rerum omnium, rem publicam ex mea potestate in senatus populique Romani arbitrium transtuli. Quo pro merito meo senatus consulto Augustus appellatus sum et clupeus aureus in curia Iulia positus est,[12] quem mihi senatum populumque Romanum dare virtutis clementiaeque iustitiae et pietatis causa testatum est per eius clupei inscriptionem.[13] Post id tempus auctoritate omnibus praestiti;[14] potestatis autem nihilo amplius habui quam ceteri qui mihi quoque in magistratu conlegae fuerunt.[15] Tertium decimum consulatum cum gerebam, senatus et equester ordo populusque Romanus universus appellavit me Patrem Patriae.[16] Cum scripsi haec, annum agebam septuagesimum sextum.

B.   *Pax Augusta*

Nihil deinde optare a dis homines, nihil dii hominibus praestare possunt, nihil voto concipi, nihil felicitate consummari, quod non Augustus post reditum in urbem rei publicae populoque Romano terrarumque orbi repraesentaverit. Finita vicesimo anno bella civilia,[17] sepulta externa, revocata pax, sopitus ubique armorum furor; restituta vis legibus, iudiciis auctoritas, senatui maiestas; imperium magistratuum ad pristinum redactum modum, prisca illa et antiqua rei publicae forma revocata. Rediit cultus agris, sacris honos, securitas hominibus, certa cuique rerum suarum possessio; leges emendatae utiliter, latae salubriter; senatus sine asperitate nec sine severitate lectus.[18] Principes viri triumphis et amplissimis honoribus functi hortatu principis ad ornandam urbem inlecti sunt.[19] Consulatus usque ad undecimum continuavit Augustus, dictaturam, quam pertinaciter ei deferebat populus, constanter repulit.[20]

1. **exercitum:** i.e. the troops which Octavian raised in 43 among Caesar's veterans in Campania; see 44 pref. and compare Pompey's raising of troops among his father's followers in Picenum in 28 nn. 5A and 6A.

2. **a dominatione . . . vindicavi:** for Caesar's description of his mission in almost identical terms see 38 n. 22 (and compare 20 nn. 13B and C). Augustus presumably used *a dominatione*, an abl. of agent rather than of means, because he had in mind the members of the "faction"; for *factio* see 34 n. 19C (and 38 n. 22A). Editors previous to the discovery of one of the fragmentary copies preserving this phrase read the abl. of means without *a* and the Greek translator apparently regarded it as abl. of separation, since his version would translate as "I freed the commonwealth from the slavery of those sworn together (i.e. the conspirators)." It might also be observed that Augustus uses *per*+acc. twice for instrument (see 5 n. 16A): *per quem* here and *per inscriptionem* below, and once for agent (see 35 n. 4): *per me geri* below.

3. A. **res . . . caperet**="that the Republic should not suffer any harm"; object of *providere*. This was the phrasing of a *senatus consultum ultimum*, for which see 19 pref. B. **pro praetore**="with the rank of (lit. in place of) a praetor."

4. A. **me consulem . . . et triumvirum:** after the deaths of Hirtius and Pansa (*consul uterque*) in the previous April (see 44 pref.), Octavian came to terms with Antony and Lepidus, marched on Rome, and enforced his own election on Aug. 19, 43, as consul with his cousin Q. Pedius as his colleague (see 45 n. 2C); Velleius II 65.2 says that they entered office on Oct. 1. Octavian was elected one of the *tresviri rei publicae constituendae* (see 44 pref.) by virtue of a *lex Titia* of Nov. 27. B. **creavit**=elected; see 5 n. 17B (and 7 n. 2B).

5. **iudiciis legitimis:** the Triumvirs conducted trials of the absent "liberators" for the murder of Caesar. These trials were much criticized and are therefore justified by Augustus as "legitimate"; compare the beginning of 45.

6. A. **inferentis:** agrees with *eos* above, specifically Brutus and Cassius. B. **vici bis acie:** for the two engagements at Philippi see 45; for the loc. abl. *acie* see 26 n. 6A (and 45 n. 4B).

7. **peperci:** from *parco*, which takes the dat; *parco* should be carefully distinguished from *pareo*, which also takes the dat. (see 30 n. 2C), and from *pario, -ere* (see 21 n. 9), which does not.

8. A. **quibus . . . potuit:** for verbs which take the dat. used impersonally in the pass. see 36 n. 9C (and 44 n. 9B). B. **tuto**="safely"; *tuto* is regularly used instead of *tute*; compare 33 n. 8B.

9. **curator legum et morum:** such an office would have been a sole censorship and would have empowered Augustus to enquire widely into the conduct of individuals and to make rules himself which would have had the validity of law. He therefore refused this (and other) "unconstitutional" offices or powers; contrast for Caesar 42, especially nn. 6-9. Augustus initiated his important series of social and moral reforms by laws

which he himself introduced in virtue of his tribunician power or which he had the regular magistrates introduce for him.

10. **magistratum . . . delatum:** for this use of *defero* see 31 n. 8c (and 42 n. 27b).

11. **in . . . septimo:** in 28 and 27; see n. 20a below.

12. A. **clupeus:** Greek; see 61 n. 26b; =a round gold shield, which was inscribed with the four virtues listed below.   B. **curia Iulia:** the senate house in the Forum begun by Caesar and completed by Augustus to replace an older one, for which see 14 n. 6a.

13. A. **quem . . . inscriptionem** = "and that the senate . . . gave me this (shield) was stated (lit. witnessed) by (its) inscription"; the rel. makes the whole clause modify *clupeus* and is itself the object of the inf. *dare* in an indirect statement which serves as the subject of *testatum est* and gives the content of the inscription on the shield. In Eng. *quem* may be rendered, as above, by a connective and a demonstrative; compare 4 n. 4a.   B. **senatum . . . Romanum:** subject of the inf. *dare*; presumably the shield was voted by the assembly on the initiative of a decree of the senate.   C. **virtutis . . . pietatis:** there is little difference in force between *-que* and *et* as connectives for the two pairs of virtues and there is no connective between the two pairs; the Greek translation of the inscription simply links the four by three "ands." The four virtues listed derive from Stoicism, for which see 34 n. 4a.   D. **testatum est:** here with a pass. meaning, though the deponent verb *testor* normally has an act. meaning; the subject is, as indicated above, the indirect statement *quem . . . causa.*   E. **per . . . inscriptionem:** instead of an abl. of means; see n. 2 above.

14. **auctoritate:** this word is lacking in the Latin text from Ancyra and Mommsen (see 33 pref.) restored (from the Greek) *dignitate.* A fragment of one of the other copies shows *auctoritate* to be the right word. This discovery has led modern scholars to place great (perhaps too much) emphasis on Augustus' *auctoritas* as the prime basis of his power.

15. A. **nihilo amplius** = "no more," lit. "more by nothing"; *nihilo* is abl. of degree of difference; compare *paulo* in 44 n. 8b.   B. **quoque:** abl. of *quisque*, with *magistratu*, not the adv. = "also"; for the placing of the prep. between, see 23 n. 4a.   C. **conlegae:** the inscription reads *-nl-*; elsewhere in these selections the assimilated *-ll-* has been printed.

16. **Patrem Patriae:** though such extravagant terms smacked of flattery appropriate to Hellenistic monarchs, Augustus at least had Cicero's and Caesar's precedents for this title (see 42 n. 6), which he valued. Some modern scholars emphasize it as symbolizing his protective care or "patronage" of the whole *populus Romanus*, the three elements of which apparently (from the wording here) participated as separate entities in its bestowal.

17. A. **nihil . . . consummari:** the pass. infs. depend on *potest* to be supplied from *possunt*, and *nihil* is here subject.   B. **voto concipi:** a religious phrase, i.e. "be conceived of (or: wished for) by prayer."   C. **finita:** with this and the following past parts. supply *sunt* or *est.*   D. **vicesimo:** calculated from 49 through 30.

18. **senatus . . . lectus** = "the (roll of the) senate was revised"; *lego* was the technical term used of the censors reading the roll of qualified senators; compare 29 n. 3. In addition to those whom Caesar had admitted (see 42 pref.), many unworthy men had crept into the senate during the Second Triumvirate. Augustus gradually reduced its size to Sulla's 600 (see 26 pref.) and ensured that senators had the proper financial, moral, and political qualifications.

19. A. **principes . . . principis:** though Augustus was the *princeps* par excellence (see 41 n. 11a and 48 n. 6), he tried to encourage other "leading citizens" (see 1 n. 1g and 28 n. 19d) to contribute public buildings etc.   B. **triumphis . . . functi** = "who had enjoyed (lit. performed) triumphs and the highest magistracies"; for the abl. of means after *fungor* see 23 n. 12b.   C. **honoribus:** here probably = "magistracies" (see 8 n. 8c), rather than more generally "honors" (as in 42 n. 5b) as *amplissimis* might suggest.

20.   A. **consulatus . . . undecimum:** after his first consulship in 43, on the deaths of Hirtius and Pansa (see 44 pref. and n. 4A above), Augustus did not hold another until 33, when he took the office to signify his return to a "constitutional" position and abandonment of the extraordinary powers of the Triumvirate. He held the consulship for the third time in 31 and then every year (hence *continuavit*, inexactly), though often not for a full year, until his eleventh in 23, the one referred to here. Thereafter he held it only twice, briefly, in 5 and 2, for the coming of age (assumption of the *toga virilis*) of his grandsons Gaius and Lucius Caesar.   B. **dictaturam . . . repulit:** contrast Caesar's acceptance of a perpetual dictatorship, for which see 42 pref.

48

For forty-four years, from September 31 until his death at age 76 in August, A.D. 14, Augustus was the outstanding man, the *princeps* as he called himself (see n. 6 below), in the Roman state. However sincere he may have been in his "restoration of the Republic," his long dominance accustomed men to a single ruler and convinced them that only thus could the dissensions which had brought the Republic to an end be prevented. At Augustus' death the "Principate" (see n. 11A below) passed to Tiberius, his stepson, whom he had adopted and clearly indicated as his successor. The senate gave him the same powers which Augustus had held, and many scholars would see in this act the real beginning of a monarchical form of government for the Roman Empire.

The historian Tacitus, however, writing early in the second century, attributes the actual end of the Republic to Augustus. The following selection consists of passages from the opening chapters of his *Annales*, a history which covered the years from the death of Augustus either to that of Nero in June 68 or to the following January 1, 69, where his *Historiae*, which he composed first, began. The *Historiae* continued to the assassination of Domitian in A.D. 96. Neither of these works survives in its entirety.

Praefatio Annalium Cornelii Taciti

Urbem Romam a principio reges habuere; libertatem et consulatum L. Brutus instituit.[1] Dictaturae ad tempus sumebantur;[2] neque decemviralis potestas ultra biennium, neque tribunorum militum consulare ius diu valuit.[3] Non Cinnae, non Sullae longa dominatio;[4] et Pompeii Crassique potentia cito in Caesarem, Lepidi atque Antonii arma in Augustum cessere,[5] qui cuncta discordiis civilibus fessa, nomine principis, sub imperium accepit.[6]

Sed veteris populi Romani prospera vel adversa claris scriptoribus memorata sunt;[7] temporibusque Augusti dicendis non defuere decora ingenia, donec gliscente adulatione deterrerentur.[8] Tiberii Gaiique et Claudii ac Neronis res, florentibus ipsis, ob metum falsae, postquam occiderant, recentibus odiis compositae sunt.[9] Inde consilium mihi pauca de Augusto et extrema tradere,[10] mox Tiberii principatum et cetera,[11] sine ira et studio, quorum causas procul habeo.[12]

Postquam, Bruto et Cassio caesis, nulla iam publica arma, Pompeius apud Siciliam oppressus,[13] exutoque Lepido, interfecto Antonio, ne Iulianis quidem partibus nisi Caesar dux reliquus;[14] posito triumviri nomine, consulem se ferens et ad tuendam plebem tribunicio iure contentum,[15] ubi militem donis, populum annona, cunctos dulcedine otii pellexit,[16] insurgere paulatim, munia senatus, magistratuum, legum, in se trahere,[17] nullo adversante, cum ferocissimi per acies aut proscriptione cecidissent,[18] ceteri nobilium, quanto quis servitio promptior, opibus et honoribus extollerentur[19] ac, novis ex rebus aucti, tuta et praesentia quam vetera et periculosa mallent.[20] Neque provinciae illum rerum statum abnuebant, suspecto senatus populique imperio, ob certamina potentium et avaritiam magistratuum, invalido legum auxilio, quae vi, ambitu, postremo pecunia turbabantur.[21]

Bellum ea tempestate nullum nisi adversus Germanos supererat,[22] abolendae magis infamiae ob amissum cum Quintilio Varo exercitum quam cupidine proferendi imperii aut dignum ob praemium.[23] Domi res tranquillae, eadem magistratuum vocabula; iuniores post Actiacam victoriam, etiam senes plerique inter bella civium nati; quotus quisque reliquus qui rem publicam vidisset?[24]

1. A. **urbem ... habuere:** this opening sentence of the *Annales* forms a dactylic hexameter verse; similarly, the opening phrase of Livy's *History* comprises the first four feet of a hexameter: *facturusn(e) operae pretium sim.* Cicero *de Or.* III 182 says that the use of full verses in prose constituted a stylistic fault, and Quintilian IX 4.75 specifically cites Livy's dactylic opening. It is possible, however, that the two historians wished to suggest their descent from the earliest Roman historical works written in Latin, the *Bellum Punicum* of Naevius (d. about 201) which was written in an early Italic meter called Saturnian, and the much longer *Annales* of Ennius (d. 169), which set forth the history of Rome from the beginning to his own times and which was the first Latin epic to be written in the dactylic hexameter, borrowed from the Greek epic.   B. **libertatem ... instituit:** i.e. by the expulsion of the kings in 509; see sel. 5.

2. **ad tempus** = "on occasion"; i.e. to meet specific crises, as when Fabius Maximus was appointed dictator against Hannibal; see 10 n. 13A. Others interpret as "for a limited time," since Tacitus is showing that "monarchical" power had been limited in time until the Principate of Augustus.

3. A. **decemviralis potestas:** for the decemvirate in 451–450 see sel. 7.   B. **tribunorum ... ius:** i.e. military tribunes with the authority of consuls. This device was frequently used in the period 444–368, traditionally in order to open the highest power to plebeians without letting them become consuls; see 56 n. 6B.

4. **Cinnae ... dominatio:** for the period 87–78 see sels. 25–28.

5. A. **Pompeii ... Caesarem:** for the period from the First Triumvirate to Caesar's victory over Pompey see sels. 35–40.   B. **Lepidi ... cessere:** for Octavian's suppression of his colleagues in the Second Triumvirate see 46 pref.

6. **nomine . . . accepit** = "assumed control over everything (*cuncta*) under the name (or title) of *princeps*," lit. "took under his *imperium*"; *nomine* is an extended use of the abl. of means. Augustus took the term *princeps*, used under the Republic for "chief men of the state," and used it specifically (but not uniquely, see 47 n. 19A) for himself; compare n. 11A below. Tacitus' phrase therefore contrasts Augustus' presentation of himself as a civilian leader and the real basis of his power in his military *imperium*, the supreme power of command which went back through the consuls to the kings. The whole paragraph is a summary, not of Roman history, but of the extraordinary powers exercised from time to time in the Republic until Augustus made them permanent.

7. **sed etc.**: in this paragraph Tacitus explains that he has chosen to begin his history with the end of Augustus' reign because both the glories and defeats (*prospera vel adversa*) of early Roman history had been satisfactorily treated, notably by Livy, while the history of the succeeding emperors, being written by contemporaries, was distorted by flattery, fear, or hatred.

8. A. **temporibus . . . dicendis** = "for describing the times"; *dico* may take *tempora* as an object in poetry and in early prose, many stylistic features of which Tacitus uses, but not in Ciceronian prose.   B. **decōra**: neut. nom. plur. of the adj. *decŏrus*, from *decŏr, -ōris*; contrast 34 n. 18.

9. A. **Tiberii . . . Neronis**: the "Julio-Claudian" successors of Augustus were: Tiberius (A.D. 14–37), Gaius "Caligula" (A.D. 37–41), Claudius (A.D. 41–54), and Nero (A.D. 54–68).   B. **res**: not merely the "deeds" of these four emperors but the (history of) affairs generally during their reigns.

10. **consilium . . . tradere**: supply *est* as the main verb; = "(it is) my plan to relate (only) a few (things) concerning Augustus and (those) the last."

11. A. **principatum**: the term originally meant simply "a chief rank or position," in either political or military life; see 35 n. 6A. But later it acquired the meaning "reign, empire, etc." because of Augustus' long tenure as *princeps* (see n. 7 above) and because of the fact that at his death his powers and functions were transferred en bloc by the senate and Roman people to an heir designated by him; see pref. above.   B. **cetera** = "the remaining (events)," i.e. between the accession of Tiberius and the death of Nero.

12. **quorum . . . habeo** = "the causes of which I hold far from me"; i.e. he can put away favorable or unfavorable bias. Others interpret *habeo* as = "I have"; i.e. his remoteness in time means that he is remote from bias. Nevertheless, Tacitus' account shows much bias, especially against Augustus (contrast sel. 47 B) and Tiberius.

13. A. **Bruto et Cassio caesis**: for the suicides of Brutus and Cassius see sel. 45.   B. **Pompeius**: i.e. Sextus, Pompey's son; see 46 pref. (and 43 n. 28c).

14. A. **exutoque Lepido**: Lepidus was "stripped" of his power (see 46 pref.), but since he was *pontifex maximus* he was allowed to live in retirement until his death in 13. B. **interfecto Antonio**: for Antony's suicide see sel. 46.   c. **Iulianis . . . partibus**: Julius Caesar's party was still so called even after his death; for the meaning of *partes* see 25 n. 5B (and 41 n. 17B).

15. A. **posito** = "laid aside." For Augustus' position after the settlement of 28–27, see 46 pref.   B. **se ferens** = "presenting himself as"; for Augustus' consulships see 47 n. 20A.   c. **contentum**: agrees with *se* as object of *ferens* and is correlated with *consulem* by *et*; if *contentum* agreed with *Caesar*, which carries on as nom. subject of the historical infs. (see n. 17 below), it would, of course, be nom. itself.

16. A. **donis**: it was customary for a Roman general to make gifts of money to his troops after victories or on other significant occasions. In addition, Augustus substituted a money bonus on discharge for the previous practice of making grants of land to veterans.   B. **annona**: Augustus continued the distribution of grain to the poor as instituted by Gaius Gracchus (see 19 n. 7), made free by Clodius (see 20 n. 11c), and restricted by Caesar; see 42 pref. Under Augustus there were about 200,000 recipients.

In addition he undertook the general oversight of the provisioning of Rome with grain (the *cura annonae*, first undertaken by Pompey in 57) in order to prevent shortages and speculation.

17. **insurgere . . . trahere:** historical infs.; see 17 n. 16A (and 21 n. 17A).

18. A. **ferocissimi** = "the most spirited (men)," lit. "the fiercest."   B. **per acies:** parallel to *proscriptione*, which is abl. of means; the use of *per* + acc. instead of an abl. (see 5 n. 16A and 47 n. 2) grew increasingly frequent in Lat. of the Silver Age. Tacitus, even more than Sallust, avoids the balance and exact parallelism of Cicero's style; see 17 n. 4A (and 30 n. 3A).

19. A. **ceteri:** supply "and since" before this second part of the *cum* clause; Tacitus, like Sallust (see 17 nn. 2 and 6A), often omits connectives and the verb "to be."   B. **quanto quis** = "according as each," lit. "by as much as anyone"; *quis* is here used as an indefinite pronoun; compare 4 n. 11B.

20. **aucti:** for the metaphoric use of the pass. of *augeo* see 14 n. 7B (and 33 n. 19B).

21. A. **potentium** = "of powerful men"; i.e. Marius, Sulla, Pompey, and Caesar, from whose conflicts the provinces suffered severely, since much of the fighting and much of the raising of troops, supplies, and funds took place in them.   B. **ambitu:** originally *ambitus* meant the soliciting of votes for election; then it came to mean improper or illegal solicitation, especially bribery. Here, however, it means improper solicitation in general, since it is used in contrast to *pecunia* (= "open bribery"). For the chaotic period 58–52 see 37 pref.

22. **ea tempestate** = *eo tempore*; compare 22 n. 7. The time meant is the death of Augustus.

23. A. **abolendae magis infamiae** = "more for the sake of wiping out the disgrace"; a gen. of a noun modified by a gerundive is often used by Tacitus to qualify (or limit) a whole sentence. Here the gen. might also be regarded as gen. of quality (see 6 n. 9) with *bellum*.   B. **ob . . . exercitum:** explaining the cause of the *infamia*; = "on account of the loss of the army with Varus." Quintilius Varus was defeated in A.D. 9 by the Germans north of the Rhine in the Teutoburg Forest. He lost his life and three legions. This disaster may have determined Augustus to abandon hope of conquering Germany; if so this decision fixed the Rhine as the historical boundary between *Romanitas* and *Germanitas*.   C. **aut . . . praemium** = "or for any worthy reward"; i.e. the German war was not being waged even to acquire glory, booty, or slaves.

24. **quotus quisque reliquus** = "how rare (was) anyone left?"; *quotus* = "how many" regularly implies a small number. The phrase, like most phrases containing *quisque*, is best rendered as plur.; = "how few were left"; compare 26 n. 4B.

PART II

Selections 49 – 90

Prose and Verse

49

Publius Ovidius Naso (43 B.C.–?A.D. 17) was the first important Roman author born after the end of the Republic. His youth was passed at Sulmo in central Italy during the years of the Second Triumvirate (see 44–46), and as a young man he went to Rome in the early years of Augustus' Principate (see 47–48) with means enough to devote himself to poetry. His reputation is twofold. As the last of the elegiac poets of love, successors to Catullus (see 74), his emotion, though not as unreal as that of Horace (see 87), was physical, witty, and fickle. His attitude was deeply alien to Augustus' efforts to restore traditional Roman morality and patriotism. Thus when Ovid became indirectly involved, probably, in the adultery of Augustus' granddaughter Julia, the *princeps* exiled the poet in A.D. 8 to the bleak frontier town of Tomi on the Black Sea. There Ovid spent the last decade of his life in unhappy longing for all that Rome had meant to him, most urbane of poets.

His second claim to fame is as the poet of mythology in his *Metamorphoses* and *Fasti*. The fifteen books of the first work traced "transformations" of gods and humans into other shapes from creation to the deification of Caesar (see 80), with love as the usual leitmotiv. They are written in continuous dactylic hexameters, rather than in the elegiac distich used by Ovid in his other works, and were probably published just before his exile and revised later. In the following verses selected from book XIV, Ovid describes the arrival of Aeneas in Latium and his war with Turnus, occasioned by their rivalry for Lavinia; see 1–3.

Aeneas, in Latium advectus, Latinos bello superat

Tunc lucos petit Aeneas,[1] ubi nubilus umbra
in mare cum flava prorumpit Thybris harena;[2]
Faunigenaeque domo potitur nataque Latini,[3]
non sine Marte tamen.[4] Bellum cum gente feroci
suscipitur, pactaque furit pro coniuge Turnus.[5]
Concurrit Latio Tyrrhenia tota,[6] diuque
ardua sollicitis victoria quaeritur armis.[7]
Auget uterque suas externo robore vires;
et multi Rutulos, multi Troiana tuentur
moenia.[8] Habetque deos pars utraque, quodque deorum est
instar, habent animos.[9] Nec iam dotalia regna

nec sceptrum soceri nec te, Lavinia virgo,

sed vicisse petunt;[10] deponendique pudore

bella gerunt.[11] Tandemque Venus victricia nati

arma videt,[12] Turnusque cadit; cadit Ardea, Turno

sospite dicta potens.[13]

1.   **Aenēās:** in Greek a vowel may be long before a following vowel, and the Romans retained such quantities in borrowed names and words, as here *-ēā-*; *-ās* is a Greek nom. ending of the 1st decl.; compare 1 n. 2B.

2.   A. **nubilus umbra** = "darkened (lit. clouded over) with shade" (i.e. of trees along the banks); the adj. modifies *Thybris* in the next verse.   B. **cum flava . . . harena:** the Tiber breaks out into the Mediterranean with quantities of silt; hence its original name was *Albula* (= "whitish") according to Pliny the Elder (*Nat. Hist.* III 5–9); he also cites as an early name for the river the Greek spelling of *Tīberis: Tybris*, which appears here as *Thȳbrĭs*, in which the first syllable is scanned long before the mute and liquid.

3.   A. **Faunigenae:** an adj. having only fem. terminations, here in agreement with the masc. gen. *Latīni*. Latinus, king of the Latins, was son of the mythical king Faunus (see 42 n. 8c), later worshiped as a rustic god (= Greek Pan) or gods (= Greek *Satyri*). A verse such as this, with the verb in the middle enclosed by balanced nouns and adjs., is called "golden."   B. **domo . . . nata:** abls. with *potior*, which is an intrans. verb meaning "I become powerful" and thus regularly takes an instrumental abl. (of means) in classical Lat.; see 46 n. 12A and compare *utor* in 14 n. 16B.

4.   **Marte:** the name of the god is used for his sphere, i.e. war, by "metonymy" (Greek; = a change of name, i.e. one name used for another).

5.   **pacta** = "betrothed"; with *coniuge*, i.e. Lavinia. For her, Turnus, and the *Rutuli* see 3 pref.

6.   A. **Latio:** dat., not loc. abl. In poetry the dat. is often used to indicate a place to which rather than *ad* with the acc. Some scholars regard the dat. as originally directional in meaning, but more probably the concept of limit of motion developed from the concept of the indirect object of an action, particularly in connection with the use of the dat. after verbs compounded with preps., many of which convey an idea of motion, as here.   B. **Tyrrhēnia** = Etruria; used by metonymy (see n. 4 above) for its people, variously called *Tyrrheni, Tusci,* and *Etrusci*. Vergil *Aen.* X says that they came to the aid of Aeneas.

7.   **ardua . . . armis:** in this interlocking order, the nom. adj. is followed by the abl. adj. and the nom. noun by the abl. noun. This verse is not quite "golden" (see n. 3A above) since the verb is not in the middle.

8.   **Trōiāna . . . moenia:** *moenia*, properly "city walls," is here substituted for Ovid's *castra* to preserve the meter where two passages are run together.

9.   A. **quodque . . . instar** = "and, what is as good as divine help," lit. "equal to gods." The indeclinable *instar* is a noun taking the gen.; it is here a predicate nom. referring to the subject of the clause, the rel. pronoun *quod*. In direct apposition, *instar* comes to resemble an indeclinable adj. The whole rel. clause modifies the following main clause *habent animos*; compare 28 n. 9A (and 42 n. 28B).   B. **habent:** the plur., implied in *pars utraque*, shifts attention from the whole armies to their individual warriors.

10.   A. **nec iam** = "and now no longer"; the contrasting correlative is *sed*.   B. **dotalia regna:** i.e. the rule would go as the dowry (Lat. *dos*) of *Lāvīnia*; in poetry, the neut. plur. is often used collectively, equivalent to the sing.   c. **vicisse:** perf. act. inf. as an object of *petunt*, parallel to *regna, sceptrum, te,* and equivalent to *victoriam*.

11. **deponendi:** gen. of a gerund depending on *pudore*; *bella* serves as its object as well as that of *gerunt*.

12. **victricia ... arma:** *victrix*, originally a fem. noun of agency, became an adj. of one termination, plur. *victrices, victricia*; compare the adjectival use of *victor* in 21 n. 6B (and 30 n. 13). Vergil *Aen.* VIII describes the invincible arms which Venus had Vulcan make for Aeneas; see 55.

13. A. **Ardea:** capital of the Rutuli, about 20 miles southwest of Rome.   B. **Turno ... potens** = "reputed powerful while Turnus was alive," lit. "safe." In Ovid's day, Ardea was an almost abandoned site.

50

Rome lies in the center of the western coastal plain of Italy, about fifteen miles in from the coast. The river Tiber, flowing down from central Italy, emerges from the rugged limestone Apennines into a volcanic coastal plain, which it divides into Etruria to its north and west and Latium to its east and south. This plain was created in prehistoric times by various long since inactive volcanoes, of which the Alban Hills, just south of Rome, are the most prominent. Into the plain, the Tiber has cut a deep and winding channel, leaving in places isolated hills and elsewhere steep bluffs running out from the higher land. Where Rome now stands, the Tiber makes a large S curve. On the east bank, this curve encloses an open field on which the early Romans assembled their troops and which therefore was called the Campus Martius. South of this field, three hills stretch along the Tiber. Between two of these, the Capitoline and the Palatine, and two of the spurs of high land to the east, the Quirinal and the Esquiline, lies a depression which was early drained to form a market place, or Forum, with a place for public meetings, or Comitium, adjacent to it.

The traditional total of seven "hills" were variously named and identified, but the following passage, composed from lists in several guidebooks of the Later Empire, gives the usual list.

Septem montes urbis Romae

Haec sunt nomina septem montium urbis Romae: Capitolinus (vel Tarpeius), Esquilinus, Palatinus, Caelius, Aventinus, Quirinalis, Viminalis. Capitolinus mons ita appellatus est quod Romulus ibi Capitolium constituit,[1] vel Tarpeius quod ibi Tarpeia virgo obruta est clipeis Sabinorum.[2] Esquilinus mons duos colles habet, Oppium Cispiumque.[3] In Palatino monte sepultus est Pallas, filius Evandri qui ab Arcadia Romam migratus est.[4] Caelius mons a Caele quodam dictus est qui Romulo auxilium ex Etruria adversus Sabinos praebuit. Aventinus mons nomen habet ex rege Albanorum Aventino, qui, bello extinctus, ibi sepultus est.[5] Quirinalis mons a templo Quirini, id est Romuli, appellatus est, sive quod ibi Quirites, id est Sabini, habitabant.[6] Viminalis mons autem ita dictus est a silva viminum.

Duo alii montes trans Tiberim iacent, Ianiculus et Vaticanus. In

Ianiculo monte Ianus deus aedem aut lucum olim habuit.[7] Vaticanus mons ita appellari dicitur quod, expulsis Etruscis, Romanus populus eo vatum responso potitus sit.[8]

1.   A. **quod:** followed by the ind. throughout the 1st par. because the explanations are asserted by the writer; in the 2nd par., *dicitur* suggests that the writer is uncertain, so that *quod* is followed by the subj. *sit*; see 4 n. 9A.   B. **Capitolium:** the Capitoline hill originally had two summits, separated by a depression in which Romulus established the "asylum" for refugees from other towns when he needed men for his new community. The western summit was the seat of the fortified citadel, where later the great temple of Jupiter Capitolinus stood; see 8 n. 9C (and 18 n. 14D). The eastern summit was crowned by the temple of Juno Moneta, the "Warner," because she once advised about sacrifices to be made after an earthquake. Here the Romans later started their mint, and this word, as well as "money," derives from Juno's epithet.

2.   **Tarpeia:** a maiden said to have betrayed the Capitoline citadel to the Sabines on the promise of "what they carried on their left arms," expecting their gold arm-bracelets. Instead they crushed her with their shields. This legend was dated to the reign of Romulus. Since *Tarpeius* also occurs as an adj. (see 55 n. 12B), the girl's name (and legend) may have been invented from the adj.

3.   **Esquilinus:** this adj. (with *collis* understood) becomes common as a name for the hill only under the Empire and no legend of its meaning occurs; it is apparently opposed to *inquilinus* = "a dweller within" (from the verb *colo*); that is, the hill lay outside the earliest community.

4.   **Evandri:** Vergil *Aen.* VIII describes a visit by Aeneas to this Greek settler on the site of Rome. Evander's son Pallas fought and died bravely for Aeneas (*Aen.* X), who returned his body to Evander with high honors (*Aen.* XI). Actually *Palatinus* may be related to *Pales*, an Italic divinity; see 51 n. 12B.

5.   **Caele . . . Aventino:** obscure figures of legend scarcely attested in other sources. For the Aventine hill see 7 n. 14A; the *Albani* were inhabitants of Alba Longa; see 4 pref.

6.   A. **Quirini . . . Quirites:** these words, the second a common term for the Roman citizens, were traced by Roman antiquarians to the Sabine town of *Cures* and were regarded as a memorial of the union between Latins and Sabines in Rome under Romulus. They probably derive in fact from a Sabine word for spear, *quiris*, and indicated the Romans as "People of the Spear," i.e. warriors; see 27 n. 7B. The spear was a regular symbol of sovereignty and ownership in Rome.   B. **id est** = Eng. "i.e."; of the two occurrences, the first introduces *Romuli* as a parenthetical explanation; the divinity Quirinus was identified with Romulus after his deification, for which see sel. 60 A.

7.   **Ianus:** the god with two faces, looking forward and back; his worship on the Janiculum is not attested in historical times, but his shrine in the Forum was open in times of war and closed in peace. Augustus claimed that it had been closed only twice between the reign of Romulus and his own Principate, during which it was closed three times. The first of the two earlier occasions was under Romulus' peaceful successor, Numa Pompilius, and the second after the conclusion of the First Punic War in 241.

8.   A. **eo . . . potitus sit** = "got possession of it (i.e. the Vatican hill) through a response of seers" (probably augurs; see 4 n. 8); *eo* does not modify *responso* but is the 3rd pers. pronoun in the abl. (of means) after *potior* (see 49 n. 3B), while *responso* is a second abl. of means (or cause) showing how (or why) the Roman people occupied the hill.   B. **vatum:** gen. plur. of *vates*, which, though an *i*-stem noun, usually has *-um*, not *-ium*, in this case. A *vates* was anybody who spoke from divine inspiration, whether prophet or, as regularly in Lat., poet.

51

After completing the *Metamorphoses* and during his exile (see 49 pref.), Ovid composed in elegiac distichs (Greek; = couplets) six books of *Fasti* in which he described the religious festivals of the first six months of the year. Under April 21, the festival of the *Parilia* and the traditional anniversary of the founding of Rome, he relates in the following two selections the story of Romulus and Remus; see 4. The first describes the omen which indicated Romulus as founder of Rome and the ceremony of founding.

Romulus, augurio victor, Romam condit

Iam luerat poenas frater Numitoris,[1] et omne
    pastorum gemino sub duce vulgus erat.[2]
Contrahere agrestes et moenia ponere utrique
    convenit;[3] ambigitur, moenia ponat uter.[4]
"Nil opus est" dixit "certamine" Romulus "ullo.[5]
    Magna fides avium est; experiamur aves."[6]
Res placet. Alter adit nemorosi saxa Palati;[7]
    alter Aventinum mane cacumen init.[8]
Sex Remus, hic volucres bis sex videt ordine.[9] Pacto
    statur,[10] et arbitrium Romulus urbis habet.
Apta dies legitur qua moenia signet aratro.[11]
    Sacra Palis suberant.[12] Inde movetur opus.
Fossa fit ad solidum;[13] fruges iaciuntur in ima
    et de vicino terra petita solo.
Fossa repletur humo, plenaeque imponitur ara,[14]
    et novus accenso fungitur igne focus.[15]
Inde premens stivam designat moenia sulco;[16]
    alba iugum niveo cum bove vacca tulit.[17]

1. **frater Numitōris:** i.e. the usurper Amulius; see 4.
2. **gemino sub duce:** i.e. under the leadership of twins, *Rōmulus* and *Remus*.
3. **contrahere . . . ponere:** the two inf. clauses serve as a single subject to the historical pres. *convenit* = "is agreeable to" (i.e. is agreed on by).

4. **moenia . . . uter:** this indirect question is subject of *ambigitur*.

5. **certamine:** abl. (of means) with *opus est*; see 25 n. 5A.

6. **fides:** here = "trustworthiness (or reliability)" of someone rather than someone's confidence in someone else.

7. A. **alter . . . alter:** Livy I 6.4 says that Romulus chose the Palatine and Remus the Aventine; Ennius, quoted by Cicero *de Div.* I 107 ff., says just the opposite. Ovid does not commit himself.   B. **Palāti:** the *Palatium* (Palatine hill) overlooks the Forum across from the Capitoline and was the traditional site of Romulus' settlement; the steeper Capitoline served as a citadel and religious center; see 50 pref. and nn. 1B and 4. Under the Empire, imperial buildings spread over the whole top of the Palatium, which therefore came to mean "palace."

8. **Aventīnum:** here an adj. with *cacumen* (= "summit"); when used as a noun, it is either masc. or neut. The Aventine hill rises south of the Palatine, close to the Tiber; see 7 n. 14A (and 50 n. 5).

9. A. **hic** = Romulus.   B. **volucres** = "birds," traditionally vultures; see 4 n. 8. *Volucer* is in origin an adj. = "winged," but the fem. *volucris* in agreement with *avis* understood came to be used as a noun.   C. **ordine** = "in a line"; adverbial abl. (of manner); compare 5 n. 3A (and 18 n. 17B).

10. **pacto statur** = "they abide (lit. it is stood) by the agreement"; compare 7 n. 4. *Pacto* is loc. abl. (place where) without the prep.

11. A. **qua:** abl. of time when; *dies* is usually fem. when meaning a fixed day; see 12 n. 8B (and 45 n. 14B).   B. **aratro:** the Romans marked out a new settlement by ploughing counterclockwise around the line of the walls, turning the ridge inward to represent the mound (*vallum* or *agger*) and letting the furrow (*sulcus*) represent the ditch (*fossa*) in front of it; the plough was lifted over the spaces where gates would be, so that the magic of the line would not be defiled by anything which in the future passed through the gates.

12. A. **sacra . . . suberant** = "the festival (lit. things sacred) of Pales was (lit. were) at hand." The imperf. interrupts a succession of historical pres. to indicate the inclusive time of the action.   B. **Palis:** the ceremonies described are those of the founding of a Roman colony rather than of the worship of Pales, who, however, seems to have given the name *Palatium* (see n. 7B above) to the site (see 50 n. 4) as well as that of *Parilia* to the festival. In *Parilia*, the *-r-* is changed from an original *-l-* to differentiate the sound from the following *-l-*. Pales was a goddess of flocks, suggesting that the original Roman community was more pastoral than agricultural.

13. A. **fossa:** here not the ditch in front of the wall, which would not yet have been dug along the line of the *sulcus* (see n. 11B above), but a short trench for the burial of consecrated materials as described in this and the following lines, which indicate how informative the *Fasti* are about details of Roman ceremonies and beliefs.   B. **ad solidum** = "down to bedrock."

14. **plenae:** agreeing with *fossae*, easily understood from the preceding *fossa*; dat. after a verb compounded with *in-*; see 6 n. 13 (and 46 n. 20A).

15. A. **novus . . . focus** = "and a new hearth (first) fulfills its function by means of a fire lit (upon it)." The hearth may have been the top of the altar but was more probably separate and consecrated to Vesta, whose sacred fire was kept burning continuously in a temple in the Forum.   B. **accenso . . . igne:** either (as translated above) an abl. (of means) with *fungitur* (see 23 n. 12B) or an abl. abs., = "when a fire was (first) lit."   C. **fungitur:** though this reading has weak support in the manuscripts, the thought seems to be that lighting the sacred fire gave the sacred hearth its permanent function. This verse is almost "golden" since only *et* disturbs the balance; see 49 n. 7.

16. A. **stivam** = "plough handle"; see n. 11B above.   B. **designat:** the subject

becomes Romulus, sufficiently present to the thought throughout to be introduced here without specific designation.

17.   **alba . . . vacca:** a white cow with a snow-white bull would be of good omen and would be sacrificed at the end of the ceremony; *vacca* is always fem., i.e. "a cow"; *bos* may be either masc. or fem., and hence may indicate either a bull, as here, or a cow.

52

This selection, in elegiac couplets (distichs), follows directly on the preceding one in the *Fasti* of Ovid; see 51 pref. It relates Romulus' prayer of dedication at the founding of Rome and how his brother Remus, scorning the first low wall, leapt across it and was put to death, presumably as much for impiety toward a dedicated site as for insult to his brother; see the conclusion of 4.

Caedes Remi

Vox fuit haec regis: "Condenti, Iuppiter, urbem,
    et genitor Mavors Vestaque mater, ades;[1]
quosque pium est adhibere deos, advertite cuncti.[2]
    Auspicibus vobis hoc mihi surgat opus.[3]
Longa sit huic aetas dominaeque potentia terrae,[4]
    sitque sub hac oriens occiduusque dies."
Ille precabatur; tonitru dedit omina laevo
    Iuppiter et laevo fulmina missa polo.[5]
Augurio laeti iaciunt fundamina cives,[6]
    et novus exiguo tempore murus erat.
Hoc Celer urget opus, quem Romulus ipse vocarat,[7]
    "Sint"que, "Celer, curae" dixerat "ista tuae;[8]
neve quis aut muros aut factam vomere fossam
    transeat;[9] audentem talia dede neci."[10]
Quod Remus ignorans humiles contemnere muros
    coepit, et "his populus" dicere "tutus erit?"[11]
Nec mora; transiluit. Rutro Celer occupat ausum.[12]
    Ille premit duram sanguinolentus humum.[13]
Haec ubi rex didicit, lacrimas introrsus obortas
    devorat et clausum pectore vulnus habet.[14]
Flere palam non vult exemplaque fortia servat;[15]
    "Sic"que "meos muros transeat hostis" ait.[16]

1. A. **condenti . . . urbem:** supply *mihi* as dat. of reference (advantage) after *ades*, a verb compounded with *ad-*. The speaker is Romulus.   B. **Iuppiter:** this form was originally a voc. (as here) with *p* doubled for emphasis; it came to be used also as a nom. in place of an original nom. *Diespiter. Dies* = "day" was also used as the name of the god of the bright day or of the sky and was combined in the nom. and voc. with *pater*; in the oblique cases it yielded *Diovis, etc.*, later reduced to *Iovis, etc.*   C. **Māvors:** an old alternate form for *Mars*, who was in origin an agricultural god and as such appropriately invoked at the founding of a new settlement with the over-all sky god Jupiter, and with the goddess of the hearth, *Vesta*. By Rhea Silvia (see sel. 4), Mars was parent (*genitor*) of Romulus and Remus and hence symbolically of the Roman people. When the Romans came in contact with Greek religion, Mars was identified with the Greek *Ares*, god of war; see 49 n. 4.   D. **ades:** pres. sing. imperative; each god is invited individually.

2. **quos . . . deos** = "Ye gods whom it is pious to invoke" (lit. "make available," i.e. summon). The antecedent (*deos*) of the rel. pronoun is drawn into the clause; see 8 n. 7A. It represents a voc. *Di* in apposition with the subject of *advertite*. The inf. clause *quos adhibere* is subject of *est*, with *pium* in predicate agreement.

3. **auspicibus vobis:** either abl. of attendant circumstance or abl. abs. An *auspex* (from *aves spicere*) was one who in the old Italic fashion observed omens given by the flight of birds. Originally the right of *auspicium* pertained to the *imperium*, the supreme power held by the *rex, consul, praetor*, or *dictator*. However, the interpretation of omens came to be undertaken for the magistrate by an *augur*, one of a board of specialists in the understanding of omens or prodigies of all sorts; *augur* and *augurium* (see 4 n. 8 and 14 n. 15) come from the root of *augeo* and signify the increase or success which the gods may give to an enterprise. Another science of taking omens, the observation of the entrails of sacrificed animals, was imported from Etruria and remained the province of specialists called *haruspices* (compare 21 n. 3B); *haru-* is an old root meaning "entrails." Here *auspicibus vobis* is equivalent to "under your auspices" since in fact the gods would give, not observe, the favorable omens. And, indeed, the omen (*augurium*) which Jupiter gives is not by birds but by thunder and lightning on the left.

4. A. **dominaeque:** the *-que* connects *aetas* and *potentia*, which by hendiadys (see 13 n. 11A and 34 n. 3) constitute a single subject for *sit*.   B. **dominae:** a noun in apposition with *huic . . . terrae* and either equivalent to an adj. or may be rendered "to this land as mistress." Augustan literature is permeated by the sense of Rome's divinely given "manifest destiny" to rule the then known world.

5. A. **tonitru . . . laevo:** thunder on the left was a good sign because in Roman religion a person faced south to take the auspices and regarded as good omens those which occurred on the left, the side on which the sun rose. Since, however, the Greeks faced north to take omens, for them the right was favorable, and Latin poets, when not regarding strict Roman usage (as is Ovid here), frequently regard the right as favorable and the left as unfavorable. The Celts, like the Greeks, felt the right to be favorable and the left unfavorable, but apparently for a different reason, because the right hand was more dextrous and hence things occurring on the left were more sinister, from Lat. *sinistra* = "left (hand)."   B. **fulmina missa:** perhaps better taken as object of *dedit* in the preceding verse, correlated by *et*; however, *missa* might be taken as = *missa sunt* and the *et* as correlating this with *dedit*, i.e. "Jupiter gave . . . and lightnings were sent." In either case, the poet makes the lightning follow the thunder, contrary to the usually perceived sequence.   C. **polo** = "from (or, in) the sky." *Polus*, lit. = "pole," is here generalized for "sky"; it is either abl. of place from which without the prep. in poetry, or abl. of place where, depending on whether the lightning is thought of as flashing down out of the sky or in it.

6. **augurio:** for the meaning see n. 3 above; it is probably abl. of cause with *laeti cives*, = "the citizens joyful on account of (this favorable) augury," rather than abl. of

attendant circumstance with *iaciunt*, = "under (this favorable) augury"; but very common is *bonis auspiciis* = "under favorable auspices."

7.   A. **Celer:** Ovid, followed by the author of the *Liber* (see sel. 4), used a version which shifted responsibility for the murder of Remus from Romulus to this subordinate. Livy I 7.2 has Remus slain either in a general fight or in anger by his brother.   B. **vocarat** = *vocaverat*; see 1 n. 4B.

8.   A. **curae . . . tuae:** not fem. nom. plural in predicate apposition with *ista* but dat. sing. of purpose; *tuae* is equivalent to *tibi*, dat. of reference (to constitute a double dat.; see 17 n. 11A); = "let these be for thy care," i.e. for a care to you.   B. **ista** = "those (tasks)," i.e. the work of construction.

9.   A. **neve . . . transeat:** since the regular connective between a negative command and a preceding clause is *neve* (compare 12 n. 15c), this prohibitive injunction is probably correlative with *sint . . . tuae* and means "and let no one etc." However, the *neve* clause might be taken as a negative clause of purpose parallel to *ista* as a further subject of *sint . . . curae*, i.e. "and (let it be your care) that no one shall etc."   B. **quis:** indefinite after *neve*; see 4 n. 11B (and 34 n. 8A).   C. **vomere:** by the ploughshare. For this ceremony see 51 n. 11B; since it antedated the introduction of iron into Italy, the share was of bronze.   C. **fossam:** here the wall-ditch; contrast 51 n. 13A.

10.   A. **audentem:** agrees with an indefinite object to be supplied for *dede* from the previous *quis*, for which see n. 9B above. For similar omission of nouns or pronouns implied in parts., see 21 n. 21A (and 43 n. 6).   B. **dēdĕ:** 2nd pers. sing. of the pres. imperative act. of *dēdō*; the compounds of *dō*, *dare* derive from a parallel root *dĕ-*. *Dedo* (or *do*) *neci* (dat. of *nex* = "death") is a common idiom = "I kill."

11.   A. **quod Remus ignorans** = "and Remus, not knowing this (command)." The meaning "ignoring" for *ignorans* would be appropriate here; compare *quod Remus inridens* in sel. 4, where, however, the *quod* probably refers specifically to the *vallum* (see 4 n. 12) rather than, as here, to the whole prohibition. However, *ignorare* = "to ignore" occurs rarely and mostly in late Lat.; Ovid meant, perhaps, somewhat to excuse Remus by making his action the result of ignorance of a rule, though still a flouting of his brother's project.   B. **quod** = *et id*; compare 4 n. 4A (and 36 n. 10A).   C. **his:** supply *muris*; it is abl. of means.

12.   A. **rutro . . . occupat** = "Celer attacks with a spade him (who had thus) dared." In sel. 4, Celer uses a *rastrum* (or, *raster*) = "rake, mattock"; Livy (see n. 7A above) mentions no weapon.   B. **ausum:** agrees with *eum* understood as object; compare n. 10A above.

13.   **duram . . . humum:** Ovid uses an almost similar phrase of the death of Servius in sel. 54, where see n. 11.

14.   **lacrimas . . . devorat** = "he smothers (lit. devours) the sorrow (lit. tears) which arose within (him)."

15.   **exemplaque fortia:** a Roman was expected not to display emotion in public.

16.   **sic . . . hostis** = "thus may (any) enemy cross my walls," i.e. may the same happen to any enemy who does so hereafter.

53

The first of the last three kings of Rome (see 5 pref.), the Etruscan Tarquinius Priscus, is said to have selected as his son-in-law a boy of Latin parentage named Servius Tullius. When Tarquin was murdered by the jealous sons of his predecessor, Ancus Marcius, the queen Tanaquil ensured the succession of Servius. To Servius, Roman tradition ascribed the first major fortification of the city and the division of the people by two systems on which were based two popular assemblies. He created four local "tribes," later expanded to thirty-five, which (perhaps later) became the basis for the *comitia tributa*; and for military service he classified the people by their landed property and organized them into companies or "centuries," which served as the basis for the *comitia centuriata*. Servius was in his turn murdered by his son-in-law, who ruled so harshly that he was cast out by the Romans and thereafter known as Tarquinius Superbus; see 5. Whether or not the bloody tradition concerning the Tarquins has any foundation in fact, the account in Livy seems influenced by the concept of Greek tragedy, namely, that overweening pride induces a mad extravagance of behavior, and this in turn incites divine vengeance and bloodshed.

The following summary of Livy's account of Servius is adapted from the *Liber de Viris Illustribus*; see 4 pref.

Servii Tullii omen, regnum, caedes

Cum Servius Tullius in domo Tarquinii Prisci educaretur, flammae species caput eius amplexa est.[1] Hoc visu Tanaquil regina summam dignitatem puero portendi intellexit.[2] Servius igitur gener a Tarquinio adsumptus est. Cum autem rex occisus esset, Tanaquil, mortem coniugis dissimulans, populum Servio Tullio dicto audientem esse iussit.[3] Servius recte imperium administravit; urbem muro cinxit; populum in quattuor tribus atque in classes centuriasque distribuit.[4]

Filiam autem alteram ferocem, mitem alteram habens,[5] cum Tarquinii filios pari animo videret,[6] ut omnium mentes morum diversitate leniret,[7] ferocem miti, mitem feroci in matrimonium dedit. Sed mites seu forte seu fraude perierunt;[8] feroces morum similitudo coniunxit. Statim Tarquinius Superbus a Tullia uxore incitatus, advocato senatu, regnum patrium repetere coepit.[9] Qua re audita, Servius, dum ad curiam properat,[10] iussu Tarquinii de gradibus deiectus et, domum refugiens, interfectus est. Tullia interea in Forum properavit et prima coniugem regem salutavit,[11] a quo iussa ex turba decedere,[12] cum domum rediret, viso patris corpore, mulionem evitantem super ipsum corpus carpentum agere praecepit.[13] Unde vicus ille Sceleratus dictus est.[14]

1.   A.   **in domo:** used rather than the loc. since it means "in the household."   B. **flammae species:** the omen had only a likeness of a flame; a real flame either would not have burned on the head or would have harmed it. Such childhood signs of future greatness are common in popular legend; compare 12 n. 2A.

2.   A.   **hoc visu:** abl. of means; equally acceptable would be an abl. abs. with *viso*. B. **Tanaquil:** an Etruscan name, less Latinized than Tarquinius (from *Tarchon*); Tarquin was supposed to have been the son of a Greek who migrated from Corinth to Tarquinii in Etruria and married an Etruscan girl. Although Tarquin in turn married Tanaquil, a woman of high rank, as half foreign he was excluded from public office at Tarquinii and therefore migrated to Rome. There he got into the good graces both of Ancus Marcius, the fourth king, and of the Roman people, who chose him to succeed as king to the exclusion of the sons of Ancus, who therefore later assassinated him.   C. **portendi:** pres. pass. inf. in indirect discourse after *intellexit*; compare 21 n. 3A.

3.   A.   **dissimulans:** basically = "making something unlike its real nature," hence here = "concealing."   B.   **dicto audientem** = "obedient," lit. "heeding the word." Originally *audio* in the meaning "I obey" took the dat. regular with verbs of this meaning; then the phrase *dicto audio* came to mean "I obey" and took a second dat., here *Servio Tullio*, rather than a gen. dependent on *dicto*.

4.   **in quattuor ... centurias:** there is not room here to enlarge on the vexed questions connected with the origins, organization, and functions of the *comitia tributa* and the *comitia centuriata* and other Roman assemblies; compare 21 n. 11A (and 25 n. 1B).

5.   **alteram ferocem, mitem alteram:** when four words fall in the order a–b:b–a, whether as to character, construction, or meaning, such an order is called by the Greek term "chiasmus"; see 17 n. 2.

6.   A.   **filios:** Livy I 46.4 says that tradition differed as to whether they were sons or grandsons of Tarquin the First.   B.   **pari animo:** abl. of description, = "like-minded," i.e. one was fierce and one mild, like the girls.

7.   **omnium:** possessive with *mentes* and not modifying *morum*, which depends on *diversitate*. Naturally only the fierce Tullia and Tarquin would be softened by the opposite natures of their respective spouses.

8.   **seu forte seu fraude:** Livy definitely states that the fierce ones slew their mild spouses in order to marry one another.

9.   A.   **Tullia:** Roman girls regularly had as names merely a fem. form of their fathers' gentile name—an indication of their unimportant and almost servile condition in the early family; compare the 1st n. on genealogical chart II after sel. 15.   B. **patrium:** adj. with *regnum*, equivalent to the gen. *patris*; compare 5 nn. 2c and 6.

10.   A.   **curiam** = "the senate house"; the *curia* now standing in the Forum is a restoration by Diocletian (*ca.* A.D. 300) of one begun by Caesar and completed by Augustus in 29 (see 47 n. 12B) probably on a different site from the original *curia* (see 14 n. 6A) attributed to Tullius Hostilius, the third king of Rome. The senate might meet elsewhere, as on the Capitol (as implied in the 2nd par. of 18), in the temple of Bellona

(see 27 n. 15), or in the hall attached to Pompey's theater; see 43 n. 3c.   B. **properat:** *dum* = "while" takes the pres. ind. of "inclusive action"; see 6 n. 8 (and 28 n. 16).

11.   A. **prima:** equivalent to "was the first to"; see 5 n. 17A.   B. **coniugem regem:** a verb meaning to "name" takes an acc. of the direct object, here *coniugem*, and a predicate acc. (not an acc. in apposition), here *regem*. In Eng. "called him king" is exactly parallel, but "saluted" would require "him as king."

12.   A. **a quo** = *et ab eo*; compare 4 n. 4A (and 52 n. 11B).   B. **decedere:** *iubere* is followed regularly by an object inf. with an acc. subject; possibly in origin the acc. was direct object and the inf. was a verbal noun expressing purpose (end of motion). *Praecipere* below takes the same construction here but usually has the regular construction for verbs of commanding (e.g. *imperare*), namely, a dat. of the person and a substantive *ut* (or, *ne*) clause of purpose.

13.   A. **mulionem evitantem** = "the muleteer, hesitating," lit. "avoiding"; *super* . . . *agere* depends on *praecepit* (see preceding note), not on *evitantem*.   B. **carpentum:** a two-wheeled covered wagon used by women; the word is of Gallic (Celtic) origin, as is *carrus* = "a four-wheeled carriage." This suggests that the early Romans did not use the horse for draft but only for riding, and borrowed terms for horse-drawn vehicles from Gaul, where horses were more widely used.

14.   **vicus . . . Sceleratus** = "Crime Alley"; the story of Tullia's act may well be an "aetiological" legend, invented to explain a name whose true origin had been forgotten. A *vicus* was a lesser city street (here), a quarter of a city, or a country village; from it are derived *vicinus, etc.*   B. **Sceleratus:** perhaps an adj. formed from *scelus, -eris*, rather than the past part. of a rare verb, *scelero*; compare 6 n. 12B (and 15 n. 12A).

54

In his *Fasti* (see 51 pref.) under June 11, Ovid tells the legend of the murder of Servius (see 53) to explain why in the temple of Fortune a statue purported to be of that king was veiled. His account resembles that given by Livy I 47–48, who may have published the early books of his history in the twenties B.C., while Ovid probably worked on the *Fasti* before and after his exile in A.D. 8. Ovid may therefore either have known Livy's account or have used a similar earlier version.

The following elegiac couplets (distichs) show his power of evoking a ruthless and ambitious woman and of making poetically vivid the scene so prosaically condensed from Livy by the *Liber* in selection 53.

Tullia virum exstimulat

Tullia, coniugio sceleris mercede parato,[1]
  his solita est dictis exstimulare virum:
"Quid iuvat esse pares—te nostrae caede sororis
  meque tui fratris—si pia vita placet?[2]
Vivere debuerant et vir meus et tua coniunx,[3]
  si nullum ausuri maius eramus opus.[4]
Regia res scelus est; socero cape regna necato,[5]
  et nostras patrio sanguine tingue manus."[6]
Talibus instinctus, solio privatus in alto
  sederat. Attonitum vulgus ad arma ruit.[7]
Hinc cruor et caedes, infirmaque vincitur aetas.[8]
  Sceptra gener socero rapta Superbus habet.[9]
Ipse, sub Esquiliis (ubi erat sua regia) caesus,[10]
  concidit in dura sanguinolentus humo.[11]
Filia carpento, patrios initura penates,
  ibat per medias alta feroxque vias.[12]
Corpus ut aspexit, lacrimis auriga profusis
  restitit. Hunc tali corripit illa sono:[13]
"Vadis? An expectas pretium pietatis amarum?[14]

Duc, inquam, invitas ipsa per ora rotas." 15

Certa fides facti: dictus Sceleratus ab illa

vicus, et aeterna res ea pressa nota.16

1. **Tullia, coniugio . . . parato** = "Tullia, having purchased marriage at the price of crime"; taking *mercede* as abl. of means (price); if, however, *mercede* is in apposition with *coniugio*, the phrase means "(when her) marriage had been won as the reward of crime."

2. A. **quid . . . pares** = "what boots it to be equal," i.e. to one another in crime; the subjects of *esse* are *te . . . meque*, and the inf. clause is subject of *iuvat*, with which *quid* is cognate acc.   B. **iuvat:** here = "helps" or "benefits."   C. **nostrae:** in Lat. the 1st pers. plur. is sometimes used for the sing.; compare 32 n. 12B (and 37 n. 3). The 2nd pers. plur. is not; hence *tui fratris*.

3. A. **vivere:** the pres. inf. shows time contemporary with that of the main verb; in Eng. the inf. would be past of past time; see 10 n. 12B.   B. **debuerant . . . si nullum ausuri . . . eramus** = "they ought to have lived (or, remained alive) if we were going to dare no etc."; i.e. not going to dare any. In this past contrary to fact condition, the pluperf. subj. might be expected; see 19 n. 14A. However, in contrary to fact conditions *possum, debeo,* and *oportet* may be in the imperf. or, as here, pluperf. ind. when the possibility or obligation is not itself contrary to fact; that is, here it was actually fitting for their spouses to survive if they themselves were not (at the time of the murder) about to dare some (further) greater deed; compare 10 n. 12A (and 18 n. 15C). Furthermore, the imperf. ind. of the 1st (act.) periphrastic conjugation (see 28 n. 21 and 44 n. 24A) is sometimes used in the protasis ("if" clause; see 9 n. 6D) of a contrary to fact condition, since this conjugation in itself suggests the uncertainty of immediate futurity. The forms therefore simply put into past time a condition which, at the moment of murder, Tullia might have expressed with pres. inds., e.g. *vivere debent nisi ausuri sumus.*

4. **nullum . . . opus:** the two elements of the 1st periphrastic verb (see preceding note) are interlocked between the three elements of its object.

5. A. **regia . . . est** = "crime is a deed (fit) for kings"; a remark worthy of Lady Macbeth.   B. **socero . . . necato:** the abl. abs. is best rendered in Eng. coordinately with *cape*; = "slay (your) father-in-law and seize the rule"; see 3 n. 2B.   C. **socero:** probably not dat. "of separation," as perhaps in n. 9A below, because *cape* does not strongly connote "take away."   D. **regna:** poetic plur. for *regnum* = "rule"; see 49 n. 10B.

6. A. **nostras . . . manus:** Tullia, though inciting her husband to the actual murder of her father (*patrio = patris*; see 53 n. 9B), joins herself in it; *nostras* may mean "my" (see n. 2C above) or "our." Undoubtedly she did not dream afterward, as did Lady Macbeth, of bloody hands that might "the multitudinous seas incarnadine."   B. **tingue** = *tinge*; since the perf. *tinxi* resembled the perf. *unxi* of *unguo*, a pres. *tinguo* developed by analogy.

7. A. **solio privatus:** the throne and the private (citizen) are placed in contrasting juxtaposition; for *privatus* compare 30 n. 8A. Livy says: *in regia sede pro curia* (= "senate house") *sedens, patres in curiam per praeconem* (= "herald") *ad regem Tarquinium citari* (= "to be summoned") *iussit*; the *Liber* omits the braggadocio of sitting on the throne.   B. **attonitum . . . ruit:** so Livy: *concursus populi fiebat in curiam*; the *Liber* omits the street fighting.

8. **aetas** = "(old) age," by metonymy (see 49 n. 4) for the old man, i.e. Servius.

9. A. **gener socero:** contrasting juxtaposition; *socero* may be dat. of reference (separation) after a verb meaning "to take away from" (see 18 n. 7A and 44 n. 2B) or abl. of separation without *a* in poetry.   B. **sceptra:** perhaps poet. plur. for "the scepter" (see n. 5D above), but often used as a collective plur. meaning "rule."

c. **rapta Superbus habet:** best translated coordinately (compare n. 5B above); = "Superbus snatches from his father-in-law and holds." Livy does not mention the scepter.

10.   A. **ipse:** i.e. Servius.   B. **Esquiliis:** a plur. name for the hill called in 50 n. 3 by the adj. *Esquilinus* (*collis*); it rose to the northeast of the Forum, and presumably the street mentioned below (see n. 16B) lay on its slope so that Servius' palace was localized there.   C. **regia** = "palace"; fem. nom. sing. of the adj. (for which see n. 5A above) used as a noun, probably because *domus* is to be supplied.

11.   **in dura . . . humo:** Ovid uses an almost similar phrase of the death of Remus in sel. 52, where see n. 13.

12.   A. **carpento:** abl. of means; for the word see 53 n. 13B.   B. **penates:** the household gods (see 1 n. 2A) are used by metonymy (see n. 8 above) for the house. c. **per medias . . . vias** = "through the middle of the streets" (see 12 n. 7B) rather than "through the mid streets," i.e. those in the middle of the city. Ovid means that Tullia drove boldly through the streets after her terrible deed, rather than stealing home through byways.   D. **alta feroxque:** Livy says: *amens agitantibus furiis sororis ac viri.* The *Liber* does not characterize Tullia at this point, though earlier it calls her *ferocem.*

13.   A. **lacrimis . . . restitit:** compare Livy's *restitit pavidus.* The *Liber* simplifies to *mulionem evitantem.*   B. **tali . . . sono** = *talibus verbis.*

14.   **vadis . . . amarum** = "are you going on? or are you waiting for a severe (lit. bitter) reward for your respect (toward the dead king)?"

15.   **invitas . . . rotas:** the unwillingness to drive not merely over the body but over its very features is vividly transferred from the driver to the wheels by hypallage; see 46 n. 19. *Ora* is poetic plur. for *os*; compare n. 5D above. Livy restricts himself to *patris corpus*, which the *Liber* copies.

16.   A. **certa fides facti:** supply *est*; = "(there is) sure proof of the deed"; for *fides* compare 51 n. 6.   B. **dictus Sceleratus . . . vicus:** so Livy: *Sceleratum vicum vocant*; compare 53, especially n. 14. It is hard to know whether in this and the following phrase *est* is to be supplied, as in the preceding, or whether *dictus* and *pressa* are simply parts. modifying *vicus* and *res* respectively and these nouns are in apposition with *certa fides* (compare 52 n. 5B), i.e. "sure proof . . . (namely) the street called . . . and the event stamped." However, Livy's statement suggests the former interpretation, i.e. "the street (was) called . . . and the event (was) stamped."   C. **ab illa:** generally taken to refer to Tullia rather than to *fides*; one manuscript and some editors read *ab illo*, i.e. *facto.* D. **aeterna . . . nota** = "and that event (was) stamped with an eternal note (of infamy)." Because the censors might put a *censoria nota* on the citizen rolls against the name of a person of ill repute, *nota* may have a pejorative implication.

55

Publius Vergilius Maro (70–19) was born, as were Catullus (see 73 pref.) and Livy (see 56 pref.), in Cisalpine Gaul; Vergil, near Mantua. Virgil, the common English form, represents a medieval misspelling of his gentile name. Ancient *Lives* say that his father, a farmer, lost his property in the proscriptions of 42 and that Vergil's powerful friends restored it; see 44 pref. and 45 n. 19. Though the *Lives* say that later in life he received financial help from friends, the property sufficed to support Vergil as a young man in the study of philosophy in Campania, near Naples. There, probably between 42 and either 40 or 37, he composed his pastoral *Eclogues*; see 84 pref. These brought him to the attention of Augustus' associate Maecenas but, though the *Lives* say that Maecenas "patronized" him, there is no evidence for anything like the direct subvention which Maecenas gave to Horace; see 86 pref. Vergil says, however, that at Maecenas' suggestion he composed four books on Italian agriculture, the *Georgics* (37–30), to give literary support to Augustus' program for the revival of Italian agriculture and the morale of the Romans. During the last decade of his life, Vergil, probably at the instigation of Augustus himself, worked on a major epic. For it he chose as subject not the deeds of Augustus but those of Aeneas, who traveled from Troy to Italy, established himself by war, and became the ancestor of Romulus; see 1–3 and 49. Since the *Aeneid* had not received his final polish when he died, he wished it destroyed, and many critics have found higher technical perfection in the *Georgics*. However, the *Aeneid*, published by order of Augustus, at once established itself in the place which it has held ever since, as one of the great literary achievements of Western humanism.

Vergil's works are in dactylic hexameter, except for some minor poems dubiously attributed to him. The *Aeneid* constantly looks forward prophetically to Rome's coming heroes and achievements, culminating in Augustus, notably in books VI (see 88) and VIII. In the latter, Vergil describes the arms which Venus asked Vulcan, her divine husband, to make for Aeneas, her son by her human lover Anchises. The shield, which Vergil modeled on Homer's description in *Iliad* XVIII of the Shield of Achilles, was decorated with scenes from Roman history, beginning with the Wolf and the Twins (see 4) and reaching to the Battle of Actium and the triple triumph of Augustus; see 46 and 47 pref. The following verses extracted from this description deal with events covered in selections 4, 6, and 8.

Aeneae clipei non enarrabile textum[1]

Illic res Italas Romanorumque triumphos[2]

haud vatum ignarus venturique inscius aevi

fecerat Ignipotens,[3] illic genus omne futurae

stirpis ab Ascanio pugnataque in ordine bella.[4]

Fecerat et viridi fetam Mavortis in antro

procubuisse lupam,[5] geminos huic ubera circum

ludere pendentis pueros[6] et lambere matrem

impavidos,[7] illam tereti cervice reflexa

mulcere alternos et corpora fingere lingua.[8]

Nec non Tarquinium eiectum Porsenna iubebat

accipere[9] ingentique urbem obsidione premebat.

Aeneadae in ferrum pro libertate ruebant.[10]

Illum indignanti similem similemque minanti

aspiceres, pontem auderet quia vellere Cocles.[11]

In summo custos Tarpeiae Manlius arcis[12]

stabat pro templo et Capitolia celsa tenebat.[13]

Atque hic auratis volitans argenteus anser

porticibus Gallos in limine adesse canebat;[14]

Galli per dumos aderant arcemque tenebant,[15]

defensi tenebris et dono noctis opacae.[16]

Aurea caesaries illis atque aurea vestis;[17]

virgatis lucent sagulis;[18] tum lactea colla

auro innectuntur;[19] duo quisque Alpina coruscant

gaesa manu, scutis protecti corpora longis.[20]

---

1. **non enarrabile textum** = "the fabric beyond description"; *textum* is a neut. sing. past part. used as a noun (compare 18 n. 3B), here nom., though in Vergil, where the phrase is used in the verse immediately preceding this text, it is acc. The Eng. "text" comes from the derivative 4th decl. noun *textus*, which has a more abstract connotation —of the action rather than, as here, the product of "weaving together" or "making."

2. A. **illic** = "there," i.e. on the shield; with this adv. compare *hīc* in 10 n. 18B. B. **Italas:** the initial *i-* is here short, as in 88 n. 1C, but is long in 59 n. 16B and elsewhere. C. **Rōmānorumque:** a gen. is frequently thus correlated with an adj. (see 35 n. 9B); the choice here instead of *Romanos* may be purely to fit the meter, but more probably contrasts "Italian history" with "triumphs of Roman (heroes)."

3. A. **vatum** = "of seers"; for the meaning and the gen. plur. ending see 50 n. 8B; the persons are used here by metonymy (see 49 n. 4 and 54 n. 8) for their function, "prophecies." Adjs. of knowledge, ignorance, etc. take the gen.; compare 13 n. 1C.   B. **Ignipotens:** i.e. Vulcan; a rare compound adj. (here used as a noun), apparently first used by Vergil; compare Lucretius' *Mavors armipotens* in 69 n. 25.

4. **genus . . . Ascanio:** Ascanius, also called Iulus, was the son of Aeneas, the mythical ancestor of the Romans and particularly of the Julian *gens*; see prefs. to 1 and 33.

5. A. **fetam ... lupam** = "a she-wolf who has just given birth"; she would therefore have milk for the twins. For this story see sel. 4.   B. **viridi ... Māvortis in antro** = "in a green cave of (i.e. sacred to) Mars"; for *Mavortis* = *Martis* see 52 n. 1C. Since the traditional cave, called *Lupercal* (see 42 n. 8C), was actually sacred to Faunus (see 49 n. 3A), it would be tempting to take *Mavortis* with *lupam*, and indeed the wolf was sacred to him as a sort of "totem" of the Roman people. However, the order of words throws *Mavortis* closely with *in antro* and separates it from *lupam*.   C. **procubuisse:** this and the following inf. clauses are in indirect discourse after *fecerat*, which is treated as if it were a verb of "saying." Three main pictures are presented: of the wolf, of the twins, and again of the wolf. These are not connected, i.e. are in asyndeton; see 4 n. 5B. The second and third main pictures each contain two infs. connected by *et*. The perf. inf. *procubuisse* may indicate time antecedent to *fecerat* or action completed in the past resulting in a state contemporary with *fecerat*, that is, he had represented the she-wolf either having lain down or lying down.

6. A. **geminos ... pueros** = "the twin boys playing as they hung about her teats." B. **huic:** dat. of reference, often used instead of a possessive pronoun in connection with parts of the body; see 43 n. 6 (and 44 n. 12).   C. **circum:** here, as often, follows its acc., *ubera*.   D. **pendentis:** the acc. plur. ending *-is* (for *-ēs*) is found not only in *i*-stem nouns and 3rd decl. adjs. (see 15 n. 14A) but also commonly in pres. act. parts.; see 16 n. 13C. It is frequently a matter of editorial choice whether *-is* or *-ēs* should be written; compare 17 n. 14 (and 63 n. 15B).

7. **lambere matrem impavidos:** either acc. might be subject or object; compare 9 n. 2A. Some older editors took *matrem* as subject, both because it seems more natural for her to lick the cubs than vice versa and because of similar phrases in other descriptions of this or similar scenes; e.g. Livy I 4.6 says of the wolf: *lingua lambentem pueros*. However, the *et* connects *lambere* closely to *ludere ... pueros*, while the *illam* marks a strong shift of attention to the wolf; compare 35 n. 9A. Hence modern translators feel that Vergil envisaged the twins, like cubs, licking about the wolf's teats and confine her licking to the clause *illam ... lingua*. As often, the Lat. adj. (*impavidos*) may be rendered in Eng. by an adv.; compare 11 n. 12A (and 14 n. 18B).

8. A. **tereti cervice reflexa:** abl. abs.; the she-wolf is so represented in the pictures of this scene on coins and reliefs. Since the famous bronze she-wolf (probably Etruscan of the 6th cent.) now in the Conservatori Museum in Rome looks straight ahead, she was probably not meant to be the Roman wolf, and the 15th-cent. sculptor Pollaiolo was therefore mistaken to add the twins under her.   B. **mulcere ... lingua** = "with her tongue was caressing first one, then the other, and shaping (their) bodies." The ancients believed that the mother's constant licking of cubs served to shape their bodies; Aulus Gellius XVII 10.3 reports that Vergil said that he "licked his poems into shape" by constant reworking as a bear might her young.

9. A. **nec non:** this double negative (often written as one word) makes a strong positive, equivalent here to "and also"; compare *nonnulli* in 33 n. 21.   B. **accipere:** *Romanos* is easily understood as subject; *Tarquinium eiectum* is object. This and the following verse end in a rhyme of *-ebat* as do the 6th and 8th below; Lat. poets do not use rhyme to mark verse, as does much Eng. poetry, but occasional rhymes appear, and the author must have been conscious of the repetition of sound; compare 77 n. 6A.

10. A. **Aenĕădae** = "the descendants of Aeneas"; for the patronymic compare 9 n. 2B; in it the two middle vowels are short, in contrast to *Aenēās*, for which see 49 n. 1. Such patronymics extend their meaning from "son of" to "descendants of," as here, or even "followers of."   B. **in ... ruebant** = "were throwing themselves (lit. rushing) on the steel (of the enemy) for the sake of freedom." This interpretation is preferable to "were rushing to (their own) steel," i.e. to regarding *in ferrum* as = *ad arma*. Since Vergil goes on to describe (Horatius) Cocles as tearing down the bridge (see n. 11C below), he might seem to have reversed the usual account (see sel. 6) in which Horatius defended the

Pons Sublicius until the Romans had time to chop it down. However, he was a careful antiquarian and may, therefore, have envisaged the opening scene of Porsenna's attack, when the Romans met the Etruscans across the bridge and, as they were driven back, Horatius urged that the bridge be destroyed and volunteered to check the Etruscans with the help of two others in its narrow approaches.

11. A. **illum**: i.e. Porsenna. For the contrasting effect of this demonstrative pronoun, compare *illam* in n. 7 above. B. **aspiceres**: to address the reader, Vergil shifts from the imperf. ind. to the potential imperf. subj. which Lat. uses for possible action in past time where Eng. uses a compound tense with "have." Therefore render here: "you might have seen it (if you had been there)"; compare 11 n. 8A (and 26 n. 1A). C. **pontem...Cocles** = "because (Horatius) Cocles dared to tear down the bridge"; see n. 10B above and for *Cocles*, 6 n. 1B. D. **auderet**: imperf. subj. to express Porsenna's reason for being angry and threatening. E. **vellere**: lit. = "to pluck out"; a vivid verb to use here.

12. A. **in summo**: Servius, a commentator on Vergil of the 4th cent. A.D., explains this as "at the top (of the shield)," i.e. not "on the top (of the Capitol)," which would be *in summa Tarpeia arce* (see 12 n. 7B and 54 n. 12C), which would also fit the meter. B. **Tarpeiae**: here an adj., but in 50 n. 2 a noun. It was said that Tarpeia, besides being crushed by the Sabines beneath their shields, was thrown over a cliff on the Capitoline, which was therefore used for executions; here the epithet is extended from the cliff to the whole citadel. C. **Manlius**: for this defender of the citadel see 8 n. 9B. D. **arcis**: objective gen. with *custos*. In this verse, every foot except the 5th is a spondee, which creates a slow and solemn movement; see 60 n. 5B.

13. A. **pro templo** = "in front of (i.e. to defend) the temple," i.e. of Jupiter; see 12 n. 4. This stood on the *Capitolium* proper, the southern of the two summits of the Capitoline. *Templum* meant originally an open area consecrated for taking the auspices (see 52 n. 3), then a sacred area containing a shrine; in Republican Lat. the actual building is almost always called *aedes* (sing.). B. **Capitōlia**: poetic plur. for sing.; see 49 n. 10B (and 54 nn. 5D and 9B).

14. **auratis...porticibus**: i.e. the porticoes were worked in gold and the geese in silver. *Porticibus* is an instrumental abl. called "of the way by which" (see 18 n. 14D), = "through the porticoes," rather than abl. of place where, = "in the porticoes"; the reference is probably to covered colonnades surrounding the open area in which the temple stood, rather than to the porch and side columns of the temple itself. For the adj. *auratus* from *aurum* = "gold" compare 6 n. 12B (and 53 n. 14B).

15. A. **Galli per dumos**: Vergil imagines that in the early days there were thickets under the cover of which the Gauls could approach and scale the Capitoline. B. **tenebant** = "were on the point of seizing"; for the imperf. ind. used to indicate action attempted or about to occur ("conative" imperf.) see 19 n. 6A (and 20 n. 7).

16. **dono noctis opacae** = either "the gift (of protection made by) dark night" (subjective gen.) or "the gift (of the gods which consisted) of dark night" (appositional or explanatory gen.).

17. A. **aurea**: refers both to the material and the color of the hair and clothing. B. **illis**: dat. of reference (possession; see 11 n. 9) with *est* to be supplied (rather than *erat*) in view of the following historical pres. The manuscripts read *ollis*, an archaic form apparently used occasionally by Vergil.

18. **virgatis lucent sagulis** = "(the Gauls) shine with (their) striped cloaks." The subject is easily understood from the preceding *illis*; *sagulis* is an instrumental abl., probably of means rather than specification. For the adj. *virgatus* from *virga* = "rod" compare *auratis* in n. 14 above.

19. **lactea...innectuntur** = "(their) milk-white necks are entwined with gold." The Gauls commonly wore neckbands and armbands of twisted gold, called torques, as on

the statue of the Dying Gaul, actually a Galatian of Asia Minor, in the Capitoline Museum in Rome.

20.   A. **duo ... manu** = "they brandish each in his hand two Alpine javelins"; the *quisque* individualizes the members of the group, who are understood as the plur. subject of the verb; see 26 n. 4B.   B. **manu:** instrumental abl. (of means), not loc. (place where).   C. **gaesa:** plur. of *gaesum*, a weapon of the Gauls, who lived both in Cisalpine Gaul (the Po Valley) and in Transalpine Gaul (modern France); see prefs. to 8 and 22.   D. **corpora:** a "Greek" acc. of specification, = "protected (as to their) bodies"; less probably *protecti* is used with a "middle" meaning (of a subject acting on itself), = "protecting (their own) bodies."

56

During the century following the dramatic victory of the *plebs* over the decemvirs (see 7 pref.), their leaders sought to break the patrician monopoly of civil and religious office. First they obtained the frequent substitution for consuls of boards of military tribunes with consular power (see n. 6B below), an office to which plebeians were eligible. But they were not satisfied with this, and two tribunes, Lucius Sextius Lateranus and Gaius Licinius Stolo, were re-elected annually, according to tradition for ten years from 376–367, on a program of opening the consulship to the plebeians and of relieving the poor. In 367 they finally secured passage of the "Licinio-Sextian Rogations"; see n. 11B below. These provided that one consul should be a plebeian and compensated the patricians by establishing the praetorship and two new aedileships for them, reduced interest on loans, and perhaps limited the holding of public land, unless the report of this last measure reflects the agitation about public land in the Gracchan period; see 18 pref. During the following half century, all civil and religious offices became accessible to the plebeians, though Roman conservatism is demonstrated by the fact that the first pair of plebeian consuls occurs only in 172 and the first pair of censors in 131. However, a distinguished plebeian jurist named Tiberius Coruncianus became *pontifex maximus* in 253, less than fifty years after all the religious offices were opened to plebeians by the *lex Ogulnia* of 300. The "conflict of the orders" (see n. 16 below) was finally ended when in 287 the *lex Hortensia* provided that the senate must give advance approval of whatever measure might be presented to the assemblies; see n. 13B below.

The admission to office of the plebeians meant the emergence during the following centuries of a new aristocracy of patrician and plebeian families which tended to monopolize the consulship, that is, the *nobiles*; see 18 pref. On the other side, the ability of the Romans to suspend or resolve internal conflicts in time of external danger enabled them to recover from the Gallic sack (see 8) and extend their power in central Italy during the struggle, and created the sense of political unity which carried them through the much greater wars of the third and second centuries; see 9–16.

In the early books of his history *ab Urbe Condita* (see 11 pref.), Titus Livius enlarged on the struggle of the plebeians against the patricians, as an illustration of the way in which Roman patriotism, rising above class interest, would always reach a fair solution of internal struggles, particularly in the face of external threats. Livy, from Padua in Cisalpine Gaul (see 55 pref.), lived probably from 59 B.C. to A.D. 17. Though he began his history with a strong Republican tone, he apparently became reconciled to Augustus and the Principate. Unfortunately, since only thirty-five of the early books survive (see 11 pref.), the tone of his contemporary history cannot be judged. In the following passage adapted from book VI, he describes how Sextius and Licinius first secured admission of plebeians to one of the religious colleges and then, after the repulse of a raid of Gauls, won one consulship for the plebeians.

Alter consul tandem de plebe creatus

Refecti decumum tribuni,[1] Sextius et Licinius de decemviris sacrorum ex parte de plebe creandis legem pertulere.[2] Creatis quinque patrum, quinque plebis,[3] gradu eo iam via facta ad consulatum videbatur.[4] Hac igitur victoria contenta,[5] plebs cessit patribus ut, in praesentia consulum mentione omissa, tribuni militum consulari cum potestate rursus crearentur.[6]

Eodem anno fama repens belli Gallici perpulit civitatem ut Marcus Furius dictator quintum diceretur.[7] Signis cum Gallis conlatis,[8] nec dubia nec difficilis Romanis, quamquam ingentem Galli terrorem memoria pristinae cladis attulerant, victoria fuit.[9] Sed vixdum perfunctum Furium bello atrocior domi seditio excepit.[10] Et per ingentia certamina dictator senatusque victi sunt, ut rogationes tribuniciae acciperentur.[11] Cum igitur comitia consulum adversa nobilitate habita essent, Lucius Sextius primus de plebe consul factus est.[12] Sed ne is quidem finis certaminum fuit. Quia patricii se auctores futuros esse negabant, prope secessionem plebis res veniebat,[13] cum tandem, condicionibus a dictatore propositis, sedatae discordiae sunt.[14] Concessum est ab nobilitate plebi de consule plebeio; a plebe nobilitati de praetore, qui ius in urbe diceret, ex patribus creando.[15] Ita ab diutina ira tandem in concordiam redactis ordinibus,[16] dignam eam rem senatus censuit esse ut gratiae deis immortalibus merito agerentur.[17]

1.   A. **refecti:** here simply a part., not a perf. pass. with *sunt* omitted; the main verb is *pertulere*; see n. 2B below. In this passage, both *facere* (and *reficere*) and *creare* (for which see 5 n. 17B and 47 n. 4B) mean "to elect."   B. **decumum** = "for the tenth time"; adverbial neut. sing. of the ordinal (numeral adj.); compare *quintum* below and *primum, iterum, tertium* (in 32 n. 20A), *etc.* Lat. had a short vowel sound which appears in writing either as *u* or *i*, e.g. in *decu/imus* and the superlative ending *-u/imus.*   C. **tribuni:** when a verb of naming, etc., which takes a double acc. (see 53 n. 11B), is made pass., the person becomes subject nom. and the title or office becomes predicate nom. in apposition.

2.   A. **de decemviris . . . creandis:** the topic of a book, law, agreement, etc. (here the election of decemvirs), is regularly expressed by *de* + the abl.; compare 9 n. 1B. The board here mentioned, usually called *Xviri sacris faciundis* (for the dat. of purpose see 7 n. 2A; and for the gerundive ending *-undus* see 12 n. 14A), was at this time raised from 2 to 10 members and later to 15. Election to the four major civil boards (*collegia*) in charge of religion was by co-optation by the members until the *lex Domitia* of 104 provided for election by 17 of the 25 tribes. This law, repealed by Sulla, was revived by Caesar in 63 to enable him to secure the post of *pontifex maximus*; see 33 pref. Besides these *Xviri* there were two old colleges, of augurs (see 52 n. 3) and of pontiffs, both of which

were opened to the plebeians in 300 (see pref.) and raised from 4 members to 9 and 8, respectively. Sulla raised both to 15, and Caesar to 16. In 196 a fourth college, the *IIIviri* (later *VIIviri*) *epulonum*, was created to offer formal feasts to the images of the gods; compare 42 n. 8A.   B. **legem pertulere**= *legem pertulerunt*; for the ending see 15 n. 10 (and 39 n. 25A), and for the phrase compare *legem ferre* in 20 n. 7.   C. **ex parte**= "partly" (i.e. one half); the simple abl. is also used. In law, *ex parte* meant "on the side of," hence an *ex parte* argument is not "partial" but "one-sided."

3.   **patrum ... plebis:** partitive gens. instead of *ex* or *de* with the abl. (for which see 7 n. 5); they might better have been abls. with the numerals modifying them. In this passage, *patres* means both patricians (see n. 13A below) and senators, since until this time these were identical.

4.   A. **gradu eo**= "by this step (forward)"; for the meaning compare 17 n. 20A. B. **facta:** i.e. opened; supply *esse*.

5.   **victoria:** abl. (instrumental or causal rather than loc.) after *contentus* (see 28 n. 9C), one of five adjs. followed by the abl.

6.   A. **ut ... crearentur:** since *cedo* is rarely used transitively in classical Lat. and then with a noun or inf. as object, rather than with a substantive *ut* clause, the *ut* clause here is probably an adverbial result clause, = "the plebs gave in to the patricians with the result that" rather than "the plebs granted that."   B. **tribuni ... potestate:** military tribunes, though lesser officers of the legion, were often men of experience (see 14 n. 4A) and could be plebeians. When, therefore, after the expulsion of the decemvirs (see 7), the plebeians had pressed for admission to the consulship, the patricians had yielded as an alternative the substitution for consuls on occasion of a board of military tribunes with consular powers (see 48 n. 3B), of which plebeians could be members. Tradition gave, for the period 444–367, 51 boards of varying numbers of consular military tribunes as against only 22 pairs of consuls and also listed plebeian consular military tribunes only after 400. Hence some scholars hold that the consular military tribunate was actually only an increase in the number of commanders in times of emergency and that under the pressure of the siege of Veii (406–396) and the sack by the Gauls (390; see n. 9B below), able plebeians were elected. Later tradition then elevated this into a plebeian victory.   C. **rursus**= "once again," i.e. instead of continuing to press for plebeian consuls.

7.   A. **civitatem:** abstract, for the whole *populus*; see 19 n. 6B.   B. **Marcus Furius:** the now elderly Camillus, for whom see 8 n. 10A.   C. **diceretur:** during the early Republic the consuls might for emergencies appoint (*dicere*) a single dictator to exercise their joint command (*imperium*); see 8 n. 10B.

8.   **signis ... conlatis:** a regular idiom for joining battle; see 41 n. 5A.

9.   A. **ingentem Galli terrorem:** *Galli* is subject and *ingentem ... terrorem* object of *attulerant*; Livy is fond of such rhetorical interlocking of words.   B. **memoria:** abl. of means; the dependent gen. *pristinae cladis* refers to the sack of Rome by the Gauls in 390; see 8.

10.   A. **Furium ... excepit:** Livy often makes an event, as here *seditio*, or some abstract word the subject of a sentence and the person, as here *Furium*, the object. B. **bello:** abl. (of means) with a compound of *fungor*; see 23 n. 12B (and 51 n. 15B).

11.   A. **ut ... acciperentur:** the result clause gives the consequence of the defeat of the dictator and the senate; *accipio* is regularly used of the passage, i.e. the acceptance, of a law by an assembly.   B. **rogationes:** for this technical equivalent for *leges* see 18 n. 7B; the verb *rogo*, from which it derives, was used of the magistrate who proposed a law or presented a candidate for office; it takes either a double acc., of *populum* or *plebem* and of the measure or magistrate (*consulem etc.*, not of the candidate), or, in place of the second, an *ut* clause containing the content of the proposal; these are the regular constructions with verbs of asking. In 18 nn. 7A and D, *abrogavit* took for the person a dat. of reference (disadvantage), *Octavio*, and an acc. of the office, *tribunatum*.

12. A. **adversa nobilitate:** abl. of attendant circumstance (see 9 n. 4) or abl. abs.; in either case with a concessive connotation. For *nobilitas* = "the nobility" see 20 n. 14A (and 21 n. 11B).   B. **primus . . . factus est:** *primus* may be taken closely with the subject, where Eng. might use an adv. (compare 11 n. 12A); = "was first elected consul from the *plebs*." Or it may be taken in the predicate (see 5 n. 17A and 53 n. 11A); = "was the first (man) to be elected consul from the *plebs*." The meaning in either case is the same.

13. A. **patricii:** equivalent to *patres* (see n. 3 above) but probably emphasizing them as patricians rather than as senators.   B. **auctores:** until 287 (see pref.), the patricians claimed the right to confirm (*auctores esse*) legislation by the *plebs* (and probably by the *populus* as well) before it could be valid. The *lex Hortensia* of 287, with typical Roman conservatism, did not abolish this *patrum auctoritas* but required that it be given as blanket approval before any measure was proposed.   C. **prope . . . res veniebat** = "the incident was coming close to"; the imperf. ind. shows time contemporary with the "*cum inversum*" clause; see following note.

14. A. **cum . . . sedatae . . . sunt:** a *cum* temporal clause of past time may have the perf. or historical pres. ind. (instead of the imperf. or pluperf. subj.) when it expresses the main thought; for this so-called "*cum inversum*" see 26 n. 12.   B. **condicionibus:** the regular word for terms of an agreement; compare 9 n. 18 (and 38 n. 7A).

15. **praetore:** this new junior colleague of the consuls "pronounced law" (*ius dixit*), i.e. administered justice, between Roman citizens and was later called the *praetor urbanus* because in 242 a second praetor, called *peregrinus*, was instituted to handle cases involving foreigners, who were entitled to trial in accordance with their different legal systems. Further praetors were created in 207 and 197 to govern the provinces then established; see prefs. to 10 and 15. By Cicero's day, however, they presided over the standing courts (*quaestiones perpetuae*; see prefs. to 19 and 28) in Rome and, like consuls, went to govern provinces after their year of office, as propraetors.

16. **ordinibus:** here means the patricians and plebeians (see 7 pref.); hence the traditional phrase "conflict of the orders." By Cicero's day the *ordines* were the senators and the equestrians; see 32 n. 9A.

17. **ut . . . agerentur:** after *dignus* and *indignus*, Livy sometimes uses an adverbial *ut* clause of result rather than the normal rel. clause of characteristic or result (see 25 n. 16A), in order to gain more flexibility of construction.

57

Appius Claudius, known as "the Censor" or "the Blind," was a descendant of the decemvir (see 7) and a member of a patrician *gens* traditionally proud, stubborn, and conservative; see n. 5B below. Yet he seems to have worked against the patricians and for the poorer plebeians. As censor in 312, he initiated two of Rome's first great public works, both called after him: the *Via Appia* and the *Aqua Appia*; see nn. 2A and B below. He also enrolled in the senate men not merely plebeians but of low birth; see n. 3 below. As consul in 307 and 298, he held commands in the wars against the Etruscans, Sabines, and Samnites which consolidated Rome's power in central Italy and opened the road to the south, eventually bringing on the conflict with Tarentum and Pyrrhus; see 9 pref. and 9A. As an old man and blind, he was led into the senate to deliver a powerful appeal not to accept the peace proposals offered by Pyrrhus after his victory at Heraclea in 280; see n. 7 below. Cicero says that a speech purporting to be this was extant in his day; see n. 14B below.

The following account of Appius' character and career is composed of passages from Livy's book IX (see 56 pref.) and from Cicero's treatise on old age, the *de Senectute*; see 14 pref.

Appii Claudii Caeci mores

Memoriae felicis ad posteros nomen Appi[1] quod viam munivit et aquam in urbem duxit.[2] Eaque unus perfecit, quia, ob infamem atque invidiosam senatus lectionem verecundia victus,[3] collega Gaius Plautius magistratu se abdicaverat.[4] Appius iam inde antiquitus insitam pertinaciam familiae, gerendo solus censuram, obtinuit.[5]

Ad Appi Claudi senectutem accedebat etiam, ut caecus esset;[6] tamen is, cum sententia senatus inclinaret ad pacem cum Pyrrho foedusque faciendum,[7] non dubitavit dicere illa quae versibus persecutus est Ennius:[8]

Quo vobis mentes,[9] rectae quae stare solebant

antehac,[10] dementes sese flexere viai?[11]

Ceteraque gravissime;[12] notum enim vobis carmen est;[13] et tamen ipsius Appi exstat oratio.[14] Atque haec ille egit septimo decimo anno

post alterum consulatum, cum inter duos consulatus anni decem inter-
fuissent censorque ante superiorem consulatum fuisset.[15] Ex quo
intellegitur Pyrrhi bello eum grandem sane fuisse; et tamen sic a
patribus accepimus.[16]

Quattuor robustos filios, quinque filias, tantam domum, tantas
clientelas Appius regebat et caecus et senex.[17] Intentum enim animum
tamquam arcum habebat,[18] nec languescens succumbebat senectuti.
Tenebat non modo auctoritatem, sed etiam imperium in suos;[19]
metuebant servi, verebantur liberi, carum omnes habebant.[20] Vigebat
enim in illa domo mos patrius et disciplina.[21]

1. A. **memoriae felicis:** predicate gen. of description (see 6 n. 9) with *nomen* (*est*).
B. **ad posteros:** the construction of place to which (rather than place where) is used
even though no verb of motion is expressed because "memory" implies survival into
the future.   C. **Appi:** at the time Livy wrote, the spelling of the 2nd decl. gen. sing.
of nouns in *-ius* or *-ium* was just changing from *-i* to *-ii*; see 17 n. 7. The text printed
here conforms to the Republican usage, but the title above, like all the titles in this
book, follows the custom of the Empire.

2. A. **viam:** the *Via Appia*, which Appius as censor in 312 constructed south from
Rome across the Pontine Marshes through Terracina to Capua. It was originally meant
to facilitate the movement of Roman troops into Campania, which had recently been
conquered. But it became the highway by which commerce, especially grain, and
travelers, like St. Paul later, moved from the ports on the Bay of Naples to Rome. It
was later extended across the Apennines to Brindisi, the port on the Adriatic which gave
access to Greece and the East; see 39 n. 25B (and 46 n. 9).   B. **aquam ... duxit:** i.e.
Rome's first "aqueduct," named the *Aqua Appia*, also built in his censorship to bring
water into the city from the Alban Hills to the south, for which see 50 pref.

3. **ob ... lectionem:** the censors were instituted, in 443, to make up the list of
citizens qualified for military service and to vote; compare 53 n. 4. Between 318 and 312,
a tribune Ovinius secured the passage of a law which transferred the right of revising
the roll of the senate (*senatus lectio*; compare 47 n. 18) from the consuls to the censors.
Appius was therefore probably a member of the first pair of censors to exercise this
power. His revision was considered *infamis* and *invidiosa* by the patricians because he
admitted to the senate men of low birth, not merely plebeians since theoretically
plebeians could become consuls (since 366) and thus secure admission; see 56.

4. A. **Gaius Plautius:** Appius' colleague in the censorship, otherwise unknown.
B. **magistratu se abdicaverat:** for this technical phrase for giving up an office see 7
nn. 15A and B. In the later Republic, if the censors disagreed they could not accomplish
anything. Hence scholars have thought that perhaps Appius continued to function
alone after the expiry of their term in order to finish the business which they had undertaken. The censors were elected for a term of 18 months, originally every 4th year and
later every 5th, though in Cicero's day the periods, called *lustra*, were very irregular
and only one pair of censors (in 55) completed its term between the revival of the
censorship in 70, after Sulla had abolished it (compare 26 pref.), and the founding of the
Principate by Augustus in 27; see 47 pref.

5. A. **iam inde antiquitus** = "long since (and) of old"; emphatic adverbial phrase
with *insitam*.   B. **insitam ... familiae** = "the stubbornness implanted in the family";

for the figurative meaning of *insitam* compare 17 n. 21A.   c. **familiae:** dat. after a verb compounded with a prep. The Claudian *gens* was supposed to be characterized by the stubborn conservatism exemplified by the decemvir (see 7), yet later members were often liberals, like the father-in-law of Tiberius Gracchus (see 18 n. 8B), or even demagogues, like Cicero's enemy Clodius, for whom see 36 pref.   D. **gerendo . . . censuram:** the gerund (here abl. of means) and a direct object are occasionally used instead of the usual noun modified by a gerundive; see 35 n. 2.   E. **obtinuit:** i.e. "got a reputation for."

6.   **accedebat etiam, ut** = "there was also added (the fact) that"; for this idiomatic meaning of *accedo* see 34 n. 2A. The substantive *ut* clause of result is subject of *accedebat*, as in 26 n. 16A (and 37 n. 24).

7.   **ad . . . faciendum:** for this way of expressing purpose see 5 n. 9A; the gerundive agrees in gender and number with the nearest noun, *foedus*, but is also to be taken with *pacem*. Pyrrhus, after he had defeated the Romans at Heraclea in 280 (see 9 n. 3), is said to have tried to frighten them by a raid toward Rome and to have received a Roman embassy to negotiate the ransom of prisoners and himself to have offered terms of peace, which the senate was about to accept when Appius dissuaded them.

8.   A. **dubitavit dicere:** *dubito* + an inf., = "I hesitate"; contrast the construction when with *non* it means "I do not doubt" and is followed by a *quin* clause in the subj., for which see 32 n. 7B.   B. **Ennius:** author of an epic history of Rome called *Annales* into which he clearly inserted many speeches either entirely invented or based on scanty report of what had actually been said; see 60 pref. (and 9 n. 2A).

9.   A. **quo** = "whither"; adv. with *flexere* in the next verse and modified by the gen. *viai*, for which see n. 11B below.   B. **vobis:** dat. of reference, often used instead of the possessive gen. or adj. when parts of the body are involved; see 43 n. 6 (and 55 n. 6B).   c. **mentes:** subject of *flexere* (= *flexerunt*; see 15 n. 10 and 56 n. 2B) and modified both by *rectae* (see following note) and by *dementes*. The collocation *mentes . . . dementes* is a rhetorical figure called "oxymoron" (Greek; = sharp foolishness), i.e. a contrast of meaning or paradox.

10.   A. **rectae . . . stare** = "to stand upright," i.e. be sound. In Eng. "upright," though defined as an adv. as well as an adj., may in this phrase be a predicate adj. like Lat. *rectae*; contrast n. 11A below.   B. **antehac:** scanned, and presumably pronounced, as only two syllables by internal elision, which suggests that Ennius regarded it as two words.

11.   A. **dementes:** Eng. would here use the adv. "senselessly"; see 14 n. 18B (and 44 n. 11C, and compare 56 n. 12B).   B. **viāī:** partitive gen. with *quo* (see n. 9A above), = "whither of the way," i.e. in what direction. The original ending of the fem. sing. gen. of the 1st decl. was *-āī*, pronounced as two long syllables. Although later Lat. regularly reduced it to the diphthong *-ae*, it was kept to give a solemn archaic tone in formulas and by such poets as Cicero's contemporary Lucretius, for whom see 69 pref.

12.   **ceteraque gravissime:** *scripsit Ennius* or *dixit Appius* is readily supplied from the context. *Gravitas* connotes qualities of seriousness and weightiness and impressiveness which were much admired by the Romans both in oratory and in personal character.

13.   A. **notum . . . est:** the *Annales* of Ennius (see n. 8B above) were widely read both in school and elsewhere until displaced by Vergil's *Aeneid*. Cicero quotes frequently from Ennius, as here through the "mask" of Cato.   B. **vobis:** i.e. Scipio Aemilianus and Laelius, whom Cicero makes an audience to Cato in the *de Senectute*; see prefs. to 14 and 16.   c. **carmen:** often = "poem" or "passage of poetry," as well as "song."

14.   A. **et tamen** = "and in any case," i.e. apart from Ennius' poetic version; so also at the end of the last sentence of the paragraph.   B. **ipsius . . . oratio:** Cicero speaks through the mouth of Cato in the mid-2nd cent., but in his *Brutus* 55 and 61, he implies that Appius' speech could be read in his own day, in the mid-1st cent.

15. **atque etc.**: for the dates of Appius' censorship and two consulships see pref. In the late 3rd cent., the censorship might still be held before the consulship and this might be held in the middle thirties; see 12 n. 10B. Later consuls were usually in their forties (see 21 n. 23C), and the censorship was held by distinguished former consuls. If Appius was in his sixties in 280, he would have been regarded as old; but since Cato, born in 234 (see 13 pref.), was 84 in 150, the dramatic date of the *de Sen.* (see 14 n. 1), Cicero probably thought of Appius as about the same age.

16. A. **eum ... fuisse**: indirect statement as subject of *intellegitur*.   B. **grandem sane** = "old indeed," i.e. very old; it is predicate adj. with *eum*, i.e. Appius.   C. **accepimus**: often used of historical tradition; compare 11 n. 5C (and 41 n. 17A).

17. A. **tantam ... tantas**: used colloquially with the connotation of "as is well known" and equivalent to simple *magnam ... multas*.   B. **clientelas**: the abstract is used for the concrete *clientes*; see 28 n. 6D.

18. **arcum**: i.e. a strung (taut) bow.

19. **auctoritatem ... imperium**: for the first, = "influence," see especially 47 pref.; for the second, = "actual power or command," see 52 n. 3. Both words are here applied to an individual to elevate his position in the household to that of a magistrate in the state; *patria potestas* was the usual term for the "authority," both legal and customary, of a father over his entire household, whether members of the family or slaves.

20. **metuebant ... liberi**: the early Romans made little distinction between the relation of slaves and of children under the *patria potestas*, for which see the preceding note. Beginning in Cato's day, and certainly by Cicero's, the increase in the number of slaves and the loosening of a father's control over his children meant that slaves were likely, unless pampered household slaves, to be treated with harshness and terror, leading to *metus* on their part, while children would be treated with strictness but affection, leading to reverence (implied here in *vereor*) on their part.

21. **mos patrius** = *mos maiorum*, for which see 15 n. 13B; for *patrius* = *patrum* compare 53 n. 9B.

58

Historical writing among the Greeks and Romans was traditionally adorned by speeches delivered by various historical personages; compare 57 n. 8B. These were often largely fictitious, composed by the historian with all the rhetorical skill at his command, and designed to illuminate character and interpret events. When Livy in his history describes Hannibal directly he emphasizes his perfidy, cruelty, etc. (see 11 pref. and B), but through the speeches which he puts into Hannibal's mouth, the Carthaginian general emerges as a character of some fascination and psychological complexity.

In the following selection from book XXX, Livy (see 56 pref.) represents Africanus the Elder (see 12) as meeting Hannibal on the eve of the battle of Zama (see 10 pref.) in an unsuccessful attempt to negotiate a peace. There is no historical evidence for this meeting, nor for the dialogue between the two generals, but it is probable that Hannibal, being aware of the weakness of his position, especially his lack of cavalry (compare 12 n. 11), did attempt to avoid the battle. For the sake of dramatic impact, and perhaps influenced by the meeting between Priam and Achilles as described by Homer in book XXIV of the *Iliad*, Hannibal is represented as an older man, still proud, but exhausted by long warfare and aware of the bitter fruits of military success; he still hates the Romans, but can admire their valor as exemplified by their young general Scipio.

Colloquium inter Hannibalem et Scipionem fictum

Submotis pari spatio armatis,[1] cum singulis interpretibus Hannibal et Scipio congressi sunt, non suae modo aetatis maximi duces, sed omnis ante se memoriae.[2] Paulisper alter alterius conspectu, admiratione mutua prope attoniti, conticuere.[3] Tum Hannibal prior:[4] "Quoniam hoc ita fato datum erat,[5] ut qui primus bellum intuli populo Romano, quique totiens prope in manibus victoriam habui, is ultro ad pacem petendam venirem,[6] laetor te mihi sorte potissimum datum, a quo peterem.[7] Quod ad me attinet,[8] iam aetas, senem in patriam revertentem unde puer profectus sum, iam secundae, iam adversae res ita erudierunt,[9] ut rationem sequi quam fortunam malim;[10] tuam et adulescentiam et perpetuam felicitatem metuo. Non temere incerta casuum reputat, quem fortuna numquam decepit.[11]

Quod ego fui ad Trasumennum, ad Cannas, id tu hodie es.[12] Potest victoriam malle quam pacem animus. Novi spiritus magnos magis quam utiles;[13] et mihi talis aliquando fortuna adfulsit.[14] Quod si in secundis rebus bonam quoque mentem darent di,[15] non ea solum quae evenissent, sed etiam ea quae evenire possent, reputaremus.[16] Melior tutiorque est certa pax quam sperata victoria; haec in tua, illa in deorum manu est."[17]

1. A. **pari spatio:** abl. of degree of difference (compare 14 n. 3); = "(separated) by an equal distance," i.e. from the line of battle. B. **armatis** = "the armed (men)," i.e. the soldiers; the past part. is used as a noun; compare 3 n. 4 (and 45 n. 6).

2. **non ... modo ... sed** = "not only ... but"; *suae*, which modifies *aetatis*, is inserted between *non* and *modo* to make it more emphatic and bring out the contrast with *omnis*; compare 56 n. 9A.

3. A. **alter alterius conspectu** = "each at (lit. by) the sight of the other." Since both are involved, the following verb is plur. *Alter* when used twice regularly means "the one ... the other (of two)." B. **conticuere** = *conticuerunt*; see 15 n. 10 (and 57 n. 9C).

4. **tum Hannibal prior** = "then Hannibal (spoke) first"; *dixit* is easily supplied from the context. The comparative adj. *prior* is used in Lat. where Eng. idiom prefers an adv.; see 11 n. 12A (and compare 57 n. 11A). *Prior* is properly used here instead of the superlative *primus* because only two persons are in question.

5. A. **quoniam ... datum erat** = "since it had to happen"; lit. "since this had been given thus by fate." B. **hoc:** neut. nom. sing.; proleptic, anticipating the real subject of *datum erat*, the substantive clause of result *ut ... venirem*; compare 32 n. 7A (and 43 n. 18A). *Hoc* is reinforced by *ita*, which seems redundant in Eng. but is often thus used in Lat. C. **datum erat:** pluperf. because the action of fate is thought of as preceding the action of arranging the conference, which is already past from the viewpoint of the immediate pres. *laetor.* The result clause *ut ... venirem* then follows the regular sequence of tenses, using an imperf. subj. to stress the causal connection between circumstances (i.e. *fatum*) and Hannibal's coming; contrast 16 n. 13F (and 31 n. 21A).

6. A. **qui ... quique ... is** = "I, that (man) who was the first to wage war ... and who have had." *Is* is the antecedent to the rels. and in apposition to the subject of *venirem*; it is often thus used to emphasize the 1st and 2nd pers.; for its postponed position compare 16 n. 9A (and 37 n. 10). B. **primus:** Hannibal means that he, rather than the Romans, started the war; Eng. would similarly use "first" but in Lat. *prior* might be expected, as in n. 4 above. C. **intuli ... habui:** inds. even though subordinate to the subj. *venirem* because they are an assertion of fact by Hannibal; compare 10 n. 10C (and 20 n. 4C).

7. A. **te ... datum (esse):** for an inf. clause with verbs of emotion, as here *laetor*, see 43 n. 26. B. **te ... potissimum** = "you particularly," i.e. rather than anyone else. *Potissimum*, which may be either acc. masc. sing. in agreement with *te* or acc. neut. sing. used adverbially, is a subtle compliment because it skillfully suggests that Hannibal views Scipio as a worthy opponent; he develops this thought more explicitly in the following sentences. C. **a quo peterem:** a rel. clause of characteristic expressing the purpose (see 8 n. 1B and 41 n. 10A) for which Scipio was "given" to Hannibal, = "from whom I was to seek (peace)." *Peterem* is imperf. subj. because in indirect discourse, which the inf. after *laetor* resembles, a perf. inf. may have secondary sequence in subordinate clauses even when the main verb is primary.

8. **quod ... attinet** = "as far as concerns me"; lit. "as to (that) which." For this use of a *quod* clause to modify the whole main clause compare 28 n. 9A.

9. A. **iam ... iam ... iam:** repetition for emphasis; translate by a single "long since" or by "first ... then ... then."   B. **aetas ... secundae (res) ... adversae res:** all subjects of *erudierunt*; its object is *senem ... revertentem,* which modifies *me,* to be supplied from the preceding *ad me.*   C. **secundae** = "favorable"; see 27 n. 5B.   D. **(me) senem ... (ego) puer:** in Eng. use "as" to express the apposition; compare 9 n. 10A.

10. **malim:** pres. subj. of *malo;* for the use of a pres. subj. in a result clause in secondary sequence see 13 n. 6A.

11. **quem ... decepit** = "one whom etc."; the rel. clause modifies the subject of *reputat;* compare n. 6A above. Hannibal politely uses a general statement to indicate that Scipio is too inexperienced to estimate the risk of defeat.

12. **ad ... Cannas:** for *ad* = "in the vicinity of" see 3 n. 6A; here by extension the phrases mean "at the time of the battles," for which see 10 pref.

13. A. **novi:** perf. act. ind. 1st pers. sing. of *nosco* denoting a completed action in past time resulting in a present state; = "I have learned," i.e. "I (now) know." The perf. system of "inchoative" verbs in *-sco* is often used to denote a state in the pres. resulting from action completed in the past.   B. **spiritus ... utiles** = "(instances of) courage (which have been) splendid rather than useful (to one's country)." The plur. *spiritus* may connote, like Eng. "spirits," "courage" or "pride"; compare 9 n. 19B.

14. **talis** = "such (as you now enjoy)," i.e. good fortune.

15. A. **quod si** = "but if"; compare 37 n. 20A.   B. **si ... darent ... reputaremus** = "if they gave ... we would take into consideration"; in Lat., pres. contrary to fact conditions regularly have the imperf. subj. in both the *si* clause and the conclusion, i.e. in the protasis and the apodosis; compare 9 n. 6D.   C. **bonam quoque mentem** = "good sense also," i.e. as well as good luck. The theme of "keeping your head" both in success and in failure was common in ancient philosophy.   D. **di** = *dei;* see 13 n. 2B.

16. **quae evenissent ... possent:** the verbs in the rel. clauses are attracted into the subj. by the subj. in the contrary to fact condition; *evenissent* denotes actions prior to *reputaremus, possent* actions contemporary with it; translate: "not only those (things) which have happened, but also those (things) which could happen."

17. A. **haec ... illa:** these do not refer here, as they often do, to the nearer and further in the sentence, but to the nearer and further in the speaker's mind; i.e. *haec* = *pax, illa* = *victoria.*   B. **tua:** supply *manu;* for the use of a possessive adj. parallel to a possessive gen., as here *deorum,* compare 35 n. 9B (and 55 n. 2c).

59

The first of the following passages is Livy's description of Hannibal's death; see the end of 10. In this, as in selection 58, the speech which he attributes to Hannibal, though brief, is evocative of an extraordinary character.

The second passage is part of the famous *Tenth Satire* of Juvenal (?50–after A.D. 127), "On the Vanity of Human Wishes." In this satire Juvenal asks: "What do men pray for?" and then proceeds to lavish scorn on the folly or futility of each of the answers, wealth, power, and so on. Hannibal is used as an example of those who desire military glory above all else. The meter is dactylic hexameter, as regularly in Roman satire.

A. *Hannibalis exitus*

Hannibal, postquam est nuntiatum milites regios in vestibulo esse [1] et sensit se fugere non posse, venenum, quod multo ante praeparatum ad tales habebat casus, poposcit.[2] "Liberemus," inquit, "diuturna cura populum Romanum,[3] quando mortem senis exspectare longum censent.[4] Nec magnam nec memorabilem ex inermi proditoque Flamininus victoriam feret."[5] Hospitales deinde deos violatae a rege Prusia fidei testes invocans, poculum exhausit.[6] Hic vitae exitus fuit Hannibalis.[7]

B. *Hannibalis exemplum gloriae vanitatem declarat*

Expende Hannibalem; quot libras in duce summo
invenies?[8] Hic est, quem non capit Africa Mauro
percussa oceano[9] Niloque admota tepenti,[10]
rursus ad Aethiopum populos aliosque elephantos.[11]
Additur imperiis Hispania;[12] Pyrenaeum
transilit.[13] Opposuit natura Alpemque nivemque;[14]
diducit scopulos et montem rumpit aceto.[15]
Iam tenet Italiam,[16] tamen ultra pergere tendit.
"Acti," inquit, "nihil est,[17] nisi Poeno milite portas

frangimus[18] et media vexillum ponŏ Subura."[19]

O qualis facies et quali digna tabella,[20]

cum Gaetula ducem portaret belua luscum![21]

Exitus ergo quis est?[22] O gloria! Vincitur idem

nempe[23] et in exsilium praeceps fugit atque ibi magnus

mirandusque cliens sedet ad praetoria regis[24]

donec Bithyno libeat vigilare tyranno.[25]

Finem animae, quae res humanas miscuit olim,

non gladii, non saxa dabunt,[26] nec tela, sed ille

Cannarum vindex et tanti sanguinis ultor

anulus.[27] I demens, et saevas curre per Alpes,[28]

ut pueris placeas et declamatiŏ fias.[29]

---

1. A. **est nuntiatum ... esse:** for the inf. clause as subject of *nuntiatum est* see 2 n. 2B.   B. **milites regios** = "the soldiers of the king"; for the use of the adj. see 5 n. 6 (and compare 57 n. 21). The king here is Prusias of Bithynia; see 10 pref.

2. **multo ante:** for this use of the abl. of degree of difference + an adv. see 14 nn. 3 and 11c.

3. **liberemus:** hortatory (jussive) subj.; see 12 n. 15c (and 52 n. 9A). Like verbs of deprivation, verbs of setting free take an abl. of separation, here *diuturna cura*; see 4 n. 2B.

4. A. **quando ... censent:** the clause is causal rather than temporal, as often with *quando*. The subject of *censent* is "the Romans," easily supplied from *populum Romanum*. B. **longum:** i.e. "(a) long (affair), tedious"; it is a predicate adj. modifying the inf. clause *mortem exspectare*; to connect them understand *esse* in an indirect statement.

5. A. **ex inermi proditoque** = "from (a man) unarmed and betrayed"; masc. sing. adjs. used as nouns; see 6 n. 16A (and compare 58 n. 1B).   B. **Flamininus:** at this time (184/3), Roman ambassador to Bithynia. When he reported to the senate that Hannibal was at the court of King Prusias, he was ordered by the senate, and allowed by the King, to try to seize Hannibal. For his earlier career see 15 pref.

6. **hospitales ... invocans** = "calling on the gods (who guarantee) hospitality (as) witnesses of the pledge violated by King Prusias." The *fides* (compare 51 n. 6 and 54 n. 16A) that Prusias violated was the pledge of protection which he gave Hannibal when he offered him sanctuary after the defeat of Antiochus; see 10 pref. The ties of hospitality were especially sacred in antiquity, and Prusias' betrayal of Hannibal, however expedient politically, would have been regarded as a grave sin.

7. **hic ... Hannibalis:** for *vitae exitus* compare 19 nn. 13A and D. Livy uses a possessive gen., here *Hannibalis*, in the predicate after *esse* where other Lat. authors would use a dat. of reference (possession).

8. **expende Hannibalem etc.:** the 1st sentence literally refers to the ashes of the dead Hannibal, which will weigh only a few pounds at most; the implied answer to *quot libras* is "not many." Figuratively, they mean "how much does all his greatness as a general really amount to?"

9. A. **capit** = "contains," i.e. satisfies his ambition; "historical" pres. for dramatic vividness.   B. **Africa:** subject of *capit* and modified by the following phrases, which

give the boundaries of Carthaginian territory with mock epic grandeur.   c. **Mauro**
... oceano: instrumental abl.; the "Moorish ocean" means the Atlantic off Mauretania;
Carthaginian rule did not in fact extend so far west.   D. **percussa** = "beaten," i.e.
washed by the ocean.

10.   **Nīloque ... tepenti** = "extended (lit. moved up to) the warm Nile"; *Nilo* is dat.
because *admota* does not really involve motion (contrast the dat. *Latio* in 49 n. 6A) but
connotes "bordering on." Equally, Carthaginian rule did not extend across Cyrenaica
(modern Tripoli) to Egypt.

11.   A. **rursus ... elephantos:** supply *admota*, which here is followed by *ad* + the acc.;
the change is for rhetorical variety and perhaps metrical convenience. Render in Eng.:
"and on the south toward the people of the Ethiopians and other elephants," i.e. those
of Central Africa rather than those from Mauretania, already used by the Carthaginians; see 13 n. 13. Carthage traded across the Sahara with Central Africa but never
controlled the desert tribes.   B. **rursus:** lit. "backward," (contrast 56 n. 6C), i.e.
south from the Mediterranean.   c. **Aethiopum:** gen. plur. of *Aethiops*. The impression
of geographical vastness rhetorically and exaggeratedly points up the magnitude of
Hannibal's ambition, which, not content with all this, went on to Europe; it also
contrasts with the small dimensions of the funerary urn implied in the first verses (see
n. 8 above) as his eventual resting place. The following verses trace Hannibal's career of
conquest, defeat, exile, and death; see 10.

12.   **additur ... transilit** = "(when) Spain (*Hispānĭa*) is placed under his command
(lit. added to his orders), he rushes (lit. leaps) across the Pyrenees." Such an abrupt
change of subject, from Spain to Hannibal, the lack of a connective (asyndeton), and
the use of the vivid (rather than historical) pres., are characteristic of Juvenal's rhetorical
style, as of Sallust's, for whom see 21 n. 18 (and 34 n. 21B). Although the two clauses
are coordinate (in parataxis; compare 23 n. 1A), the first is implicitly subordinate to the
second. The next sentence is similarly constructed.

13.   **Pȳrēnaeum:** a dactylic hexameter with a spondee in the 5th foot instead of the
normal dactyl is called "spondaic" and often affords a tone of solemnity; see 60 n. 14B.

14.   A. **opposuit ... nivemque** = "nature put in (his) way both the Alp(s) and snow,"
i.e. (by hendiadys; see 13 n. 11A) the snowy Alps; for a like use of *-que ... -que* instead
of *et ... et*, see 17 n. 4B.   B. **Alpem:** may be sing. for the usual plur. *Alpes* or may
refer to the single mountain on which, because of a landslide, Hannibal's advance was
blocked; see the following note.

15.   **aceto:** the story that Hannibal opened a path through a landslide by heating
the rocks and pouring on vinegar to splinter them is told by Livy XXI 37.2 but not by
his predecessor Polybius, for whom see 16 pref. Though repeated by later ancient
historians, the story has always been doubted because there seems to be no reason why
vinegar should have been more effective than plain water or snow in suddenly cooling
and thus splintering the heated rocks, and also because it seems unlikely that Hannibal
would have carried with him enough vinegar to accomplish any substantial result.

16.   A. **iam tenet:** the shift to the pres. with *iam* creates vividness.   B. **Ītaliam:** the
initial *i*- is long here, in 86 n. 24A, and in 87 n. 41D, but short in 55 n. 2B and 88 n. 1C.

17.   **acti:** partitive gen. with *nihil* (see 11 n. 14A), i.e. "no accomplishment" or "no
success." Many manuscripts and editors read *actum* with *est* = "nothing has been
accomplished, achieved"; a common idiomatic meaning, as against that of "finished,
done with," for which see 41 n. 20.

18.   A. **Poeno** = "Punic"; see 11 n. 14C.   B. **milite:** the sing. may be used collectively = "soldiery" or "troops" (compare *iuventus* in 8 n. 9A), and for this reason
is here construed as an abl. of means rather than as an abl. of agent with the prep. *a*;
compare 9 n. 6A (and 41 n. 5B).

19.   A. **media** = "in the middle of"; see 12 n. 7B (and 55 n. 12A).   B. **pōnŏ:** from
the time of Ovid, final *-ō* in the 1st pers. sing. of the pres. act. ind. might be scanned as

short; compare n. 29B below.   C. **Subūra**: abl. of place where, without the prep. because of *media*; compare 29 n. 8B. This district, lying in a valley east of the Forum, was the most heavily populated and busiest district in Rome and therefore regarded as the heart of the city.

20.   A. **qualis facies**: nom. of sarcastic exclamation, as is *gloria* 2 verses below; the acc. is perhaps more usual in exclamations; see 13 n. 2A. *Qualis* has here a derogatory connotation, and the verse may be rendered in Eng.: "What a sight! How fit for caricature!"   B. **quali . . . tabella**: abl. (of specification) with *digna*; see 21 n. 12B; lit.= "worthy of what a little picture."

21.   A. **Gaetūla . . . belua**: "Gaetulian (by metonymy for African; see 49 n. 4) beast," i.e. elephant. Livy XXII 2 says that from the Po Valley, Hannibal moved south during the winter of 218/7 and, to avoid the Roman forces in the eastern Apennines, made a difficult crossing further west and came down into marshes, presumably in the lower Arno Valley, across which he rode on the one surviving elephant.   B. **luscum**: during this march Hannibal lost one eye from cold and fatigue.

22.   **exitus**: here= "outcome" rather than, as in n. 7 above, "exit," i.e. death; compare 19 n. 13D.

23.   A. **O gloria**: see n. 20A above; it might be paraphrased: "What price glory?" B. **vincitur idem**= "the same man (who had been so successful) is (finally) defeated," i.e. by Scipio at Zama in 202; see prefs. to 10 and 58. In 11 n. 11B, *idem* is similarly used of Hannibal, where Eng. might employ an adv. such as "likewise" or "also"; compare 33 n. 3B.

24.   A. **magnus . . . cliens**: in these verses, Hannibal is anachronistically pictured as waiting humbly, great and worthy of admiration though he was, from early dawn for an audience with King Prusias of Bithynia, for whom see 10 pref. In Juvenal's day, clients (see 7 n. 7) were expected to attend their patrons' morning levees and receive a dole of food or money.   B. **praetoria**= "headquarters," i.e. palace. This word, in either the sing. or the plur., was used for the quarters of the commander of an army in camp (see 40 n. 3); it derives from the early use of *praetor* for the supreme Roman magistrate and commander, for which *consul* was a later substitute, and lends support to the derivation of *praetor=prae-itor* from the function of "going ahead of," i.e. leading, the army. After *consul* had replaced *praetor* for the supreme magistrate, the latter term was revived in 367 for the then instituted junior judicial colleague of the consuls; see 56 n. 15.

25   A. **donec Bīthȳno etc.**= "until it should please the Bithynian tyrant (see n. 24A above) to awake." In poetry and imperial Lat., *donec*= "until" takes the pres. or imperf. subj. in temporal clauses connoting expectancy; in classical Lat. it is used with the perf. ind. for actions which have actually occurred; see 6 n. 3.   B. **vigilare**: inf. as subject of *libeat*; the person to whom the action of the inf. is pleasing is the dat. *tyranno*; compare 5 n. 4.

26.   A. **finem animae . . . dabunt**= "will make an end of the soul which etc.," i.e. of Hannibal; *finem dare* (or *facere*) regularly= "put an end to, make an end of."   B. **animae**: gen. depending on *finem*, not dat. as the Eng. idiom might suggest.   C. **miscuit**= "threw into confusion"; see 17 n. 9 (and 18 n. 6B, and contrast 23 n. 2A).

27.   A. **ille . . . anulus**= "that little ring . . . (will put an end to his life)," *dabit* being implied from *non dabunt*. In one version Hannibal is supposed to have carried the poison with which he committed suicide in a ring; contrast A above.   B. **vindex . . . ultor**: in apposition with *anulus* and each modified by a dependent gen.; they should be translated after *anulus*.   C. **Cannarum**: for Hannibal's defeat of the Romans at Cannae see 10 pref. and nn. 9–11.

28.   **i**: 2nd pers. sing. pres. imperative of *eo, ire*. It and *curre* are addressed by Juvenal either to Hannibal or to any "mad" reader who prays for military glory. In Eng. the commands might be expressed: "So go, madman, run etc."

29.   A. **ut . . . fias:** under the Empire, when rhetorical schools flourished, Hannibal became a favorite theme for declamations. The *ut* clauses should logically be ones of result, since Hannibal did not invade Italy in order to become a *declamatio*, but Juvenal ironically implies that the purpose for which he or anybody else undertakes military exploits can only be to become a topic for rhetorical practice.   B. **dēclāmātiŏ** = "(a subject for) declamation." The final -*iŏ* was probably pronounced as two short syllables by a phenomenon apparently common in spoken Lat. and occurring often in early poetry, namely that in iambic units, i.e. those scanned ⏑ _, the long syllable tended to be pronounced as short when immediately preceded or followed by the word accent, i.e. ⏑́ _ ⏑́ yielded ⏑́ ⏑ ⏑́. It may have been the frequency of this "iambic shortening" in the 1st pers. sing. of verbs that led to the general shortening in them of final -*ŏ*, for which see n. 19B above. Since the 5th foot of the dactylic hexameter is regularly a dactyl and rarely a spondee (see n. 13 above), it is preferable to see here iambic shortening rather than "synizesis" (Greek; = a falling together), another phenomenon common in spoken Lat. and in early poetry, by which two adjacent vowels not forming a regular

diphthong were slurred together, which would here produce a single long syllable: -*iō*.

60

Quintus Ennius (239–169) was born in Calabria, the southeastern "heel" of Italy, and grew up in the area of Greek culture that centered at Tarentum. He saw military service with the Romans during the Second Punic War (see 10 pref.) and was brought to Rome in 204 by Cato the Elder; see 13 pref. He soon attached himself to the liberal "philhellene" Scipio Africanus; see 12 pref. Though not Rome's earliest poet, he remained until Vergil her outstanding writer, for he not only expressed Rome's sense of greatness in her "heroic age" but also developed the first sonorous and elevated poetic style in Latin. His genius ranged widely over tragedy, comedy, miscellaneous comment, and sceptical philosophy. But his fame rested chiefly on his eighteen books of *Annales* (see 9 n. 2A and 57 n. 8B), an epic account of Roman history down to his own times. In this he first adapted the dactylic hexameter to Latin and gave noble expression to the Roman character and achievements, without disparaging her enemies. None of his works survives, unfortunately, but many passages are quoted by grammarians and by commentators on Vergil, who, as the next selection will show, was much influenced by him. Cicero, who admired him greatly, has preserved some of the finest passages.

Among Cicero's quotations are the moving verses on the grief felt by the Romans for Romulus (A), Pyrrhus' generous offer to free Roman captives without ransom (B), the noble single verse characterizing Rome (E), and the description of Pyrrhus' family which illustrates Ennius' fondness for forming compounds (F). Cicero's contemporary, the scholar Varro (see 28 n. 23A), quotes Ennius' invocation to the Muses (G), which has fine assonance of the sounds *ae*, *m*, and *p*. Aulus Gellius (see 16 pref.), a scholar of the second century A.D., preserves Antiochus' criticism of Hannibal (D) and, supplemented by Horace (see 86 pref.), the verses on how war corrupts the arts of peace (C). The last two verses (H and I), cited by grammarians of the Empire, show Ennius' addiction to excessive alliteration.

Versus ex Ennii Annalibus

A.   Pectora dulce tenet desiderium,[1] simul inter

sese sic memorant: "O Romule, Romule dīe,[2]

qualem te patriae custodem di genuerunt![3]

O pater, O genitōr, O sanguen dis oriundum,[4]

tu produxisti nos intra luminis oras!"[5]

B.   Nec mi aurum posco nec mi pretium dederītis;[6]

nec cauponantes bellum sed belligerantes,[7]

ferro non auro vitam cernamus utrique.[8]

Vosne velit an me regnare era, quidve ferat, Fors,[9]

virtute experiamur.[10] Et hoc simul accipe dictum:[11]

quorum virtuti belli fortuna pepercit,[12]

eorundem libertati me parcere certum est.[13]

Dono—ducite—doque, volentibŭs cum magnis dis.[14]

C.   Postquam Discordia taetra[15]

belli ferratos postes portasque refregit,[16]

pellitur e medio sapientia, vi geritur res,

spernitur orator bonus, horridŭs miles amatur.[17]

Haud doctis dictis certantes, sed maledictis,[18]

miscent inter sese, inimicitias agitantes.[19]

Non ex iure manum consertum;[20] sed magĭs ferro

rem repetunt regnumque petunt; vadunt solida vi.[21]

D.   Hannibal audaci dum pectore de me hortatur[22]

ne bellum faciam, quem credidit esse meum cor

suasorem summum[23] et studiosum robore belli.[24]

E.   Moribus antiquis res stat Romana virisque.[25]

F.   stolidum genus Aeacidarum

bellipotentes sunt magĭs quam sapientipotentes.[26]

G.   Musae quae pedibus magnum pulsatis Olympum.[27]

H.   O Tite tute Tati tibi tanta tyranne tulisti![28]

I.   Africa terribili tremit horrida terra tumultu.[29]

---

1. A. **pĕctŏră dūlcĕ tĕnĕt dēsīdĕrĭūm**: as he does in the last verse, Cicero *de Rep.* I 61 breaks this phrase off from the rest and gives *dĭū*, for which *dulce* is an emendation to preserve the dactylic meter; perhaps he paraphrased and the original cannot be recovered.   B. **tenet**: a historical pres., as is *memorant* in the next verse; if Ennius wrote *diu*, they represent continued or repeated action; compare 21 n. 4B for the parallel use of the imperf.

2. **dĭĕ** = "divine"; voc. sing. masc. of the adj. *dĭus*, related to *dĭes*, but showing a long *i* before a following vowel. It originally meant "bright," then "connected with the (bright) sky" (compare 52 n. 1B), and finally, perhaps with some assimilation to *deus*, "divine." It is rare, archaic, and religious; classical Lat. used *dīvus*, from *dĕus*, as an adj. or noun meaning one who, like *Rōmulus*, was translated to a state of divinity just beneath the gods; compare 80 pref.

3.   A. **qualem ... genuerunt** = "how (fine) a guardian of (our) country the gods brought you to birth (to be)."   B. **te ... custodem:** an extended use of the double acc.   C. **patriae:** objective gen.; see 55 n. 12D.   D. **genuerunt:** perf. of *gigno*; compare 5 n. 2B.

4.   A. **genitor:** the *-or*, shortened in classical Latin, here retains the quantity of the original ending *-ōs*, perhaps because it precedes the caesura.   B. **sanguen** = *sanguis*: an archaic neut., here voc. sing. and scanned as two long syllables because *gu* occasionally, as *qu* regularly and *su* sometimes, represents a single consonantal sound; compare *anguis* and *suavis*.   C. **dis** = *deis*; see 12 n. 15D (and compare 58 n. 15D). Verbs meaning "to be born from" take an abl. of separation (source) without a prep.; see 5 n. 2A (and 33 n. 1A).   D. **oriundum** = "sprung from"; this gerundive has the meaning of the past part.; like *eundus* and *secundus* (= *sequuundus*), it always has this archaic ending (see 12 n. 14A and 56 n. 2A) for the classical *-endus*; some other verbs show both, as *capiendus* or *capiundus*.

5.   A. **tu ... oras:** by founding Rome (see 4 and 51–52), Romulus brought, so to speak, the Roman people to birth.   B. **intra luminis oras** = "within the shores of light"; a fine poetical metaphor for "into life," used at least nine times by Lucretius, for whom see 69 pref. Presumably the thought is metaphorical; that is, "brought into life" means not "produced" but brought together into a civilized community. In this verse every foot except the 5th is a spondee, which gives it a slow tone of elevation; see 55 n. 12D, and compare verses B 2, 3, 6, 7; C 2, 5. Such verses are not, however, technically called "spondaic"; see n. 14B below.

6.   A. **mi** = *mihi*. After the Battle of Heraclea in 280 (see 9 n. 3 and 57 n. 7), the Romans apparently sent an embassy to Pyrrhus to offer ransom for his prisoners. Ennius presumably invented this noble reply by Pyrrhus; compare 57 n. 8B and 58 pref. Later Roman tradition, represented by the story of Regulus (see 9 B), felt that it was disgraceful and bad for morale to ransom soldiers who had preferred capture to death in battle.   B. **dederitis:** the *-ĭ-*, required by the meter, indicates that this is probably perf. subj. in a prohibition (i.e. jussive or hortatory) rather than fut. perf. ind. (for fut.), in which *-ĭ-* is regular and *-ī-* very rare; compare 74 n. 5A.

7.   A. **cauponantes** = "bartering"; the dep. verb comes from *caupo* = "a petty trader" or "huckster."   B. **ferro non auro:** the first balances *belligerantes* and the second, *cauponantes* in chiasmus; compare 17 n. 2 (and 53 n. 5).

8.   **vitam cernamus utrique** = "let us on each side (lit. both) make trial of (lit. decide) life," i.e. settle the issue of life and death; *utrique* is probably nom. masc. plur. modifying the subject, rather than dat. sing. = "for each other," which would presumably have been *utrisque*. The use of *cernere* with an acc. of what is settled seems to be old legal Lat.

9.   A. **velit:** the vowels of the pres. subj. endings were originally long and frequently so appear in early Lat. The double indir. question introduced by *-ne . . . an* depends on the hort. subj. *experiamur* in the next verse.   B. **era . . . Fors** = "Mistress Chance"; *era* is a noun, = "mistress (of a house)."   C. **quidve ferat:** is intruded as a parenthetical afterthought to the preceding double question; = "or whatever she may bring." This verse, as do several later verses, ends with a forceful monosyllable; Vergil avoided such monosyllabic endings except when consciously archaizing; see n. 14B below.

10.   **virtute:** abl. of means. The concept is Stoic (see 34 n. 4A and 47 n. 13C), namely that one should confront challenges like a man, even though Fortune, the expression of a divine order inscrutable to humans, will finally determine the issue.

11.   **accipe:** apparently addressed to the chief Roman envoy, whereas *ducite* in the last verse is addressed to them all.

12.   **virtuti ... libertati:** dats. after a verb meaning "to spare"; see 47 n. 7. Pyrrhus offers to free without ransom those whose courage the fortune of war has spared.

13.   A. **eōrūndēm:** *eo-* is scanned as one long syllable by synizesis; see in 59 n. 29B.

B. **cert(um) est:** probably = "it is determined that (i.e. I am resolved to)" rather than "it is certain that." Because this phrase resembles a compound verb with elision it probably should not be regarded as a monosyllabic verse ending; contrast n. 9c above. Manuscripts of Plautus, a writer of Latin comedies contemporary with Ennius, frequently show such spellings as *certus* for *certus es* (compare n. 14B below) and *certumst*, which indicate that in these cases the initial *e-* was "prodelided" rather than the preceding final syllable elided.

14. A. **dono ... doque:** such repetition is regular in legal formulas; the prisoners are readily understood as object. *Ducite*, meaning "take (them with you)," is parenthetical; see n. 11 above. B. **vŏlēntĭbŭs cūm māgnis dīs:** abl. of attendant circumstance with *cum* where an abl. abs., like the common *deo volente*, might be expected. In early Lat. verse, final *-s* before an initial consonant often does not make a preceding short syllable, as here *-bŭs*, long "by position," probably because it was only lightly pronounced. Before *es* or *est* it might be absorbed into the following *s* by "prodelision"; see n. 13B above. Since the 5th foot of this verse is a spondee, it is "spondaic"; see 59 n. 13, and contrast n. 5B above. Despite his avoidance of monosyllabic verse endings (see n. 9c above), Vergil twice ends a verse with *pĕnātĭbŭs ēt māgnis dīs* (*Aen.* III 12 and VIII 679), probably echoing Ennius and perhaps using a religious formula.

15. **Discordia:** it is hard to tell whether this should be personified or not. The opening half verse and following full one are quoted by Horace *Sat.* I 4. 60–62 to illustrate his famous statement that if you should tear such lines to pieces, their parts would still be poetic: *invenias etiam disiecti membra poetae*. Though they do not necessarily lead directly to the following verses quoted by Gellius (see n. 20 below), if so arranged they yield both grammar and sense; see n. 16B below. Both fragments are believed to come from Ennius' introduction to the Second Punic War (see 10 pref.); if so, they indicate his preference for the orderly ways of peace, anticipating Cicero's famous verse on arms yielding to the toga, quoted in 32 n. 20B. Cicero in fact quotes some of the verses in this extract both in his speech in defense of Murena sec. 30 (delivered in 63; see 34 pref.) and in a letter of 53, *ad Fam.* VII 13.2.

16. A. **belli ... portasque** = "the ironclad doorposts and doors of war"; probably with reference to the opening of the doors of the temple of Janus in time of war; see 50 n. 7. This verse and the one three lines below are effectively heavy with spondees; see n. 5B above. For the adj. *ferratus* from *ferrum* = "iron," compare 6 n. 12B (and 55 nn. 14, 18). B. **refregit:** since the following verses are not in fact preserved as directly continuous on the first two (see n. 15 above), it is not certain what tense was used in the main clause following the *postquam* clause. *Pellitur* and the following verbs may be either pres. in a general statement or historical pres. of some specific occasion. *Postquam* takes the perf. or historical pres. ind. whether the main verb is pres. or past, i.e. the tense of the subordinate ind. is, like that of a subj., relative to the time of the main verb and not absolute as relates to the speaker or writer. Eng. idiom ordinarily uses the perf. with a pres. main verb, but a pluperf. with a past main verb.

17. A. **orator bonus:** Cato the Elder, who first brought Ennius to Rome (see pref.), is said to have defined an orator as *vir bonus, dicendi peritus*, and undoubtedly here also the force of *bonus* is more moral than technical. B. **hŏrrĭdŭs mīlĕs ămātŭr:** for *-ŭs* before *m-* see n. 14B above.

18. **doctis ... maledictis:** the contrast would suggest *benedictis*, not *doctis*, but Ennius sets the studied and measured oratory of peace against the inflammatory rhetoric of war.

19. **inimicitias agitantes** = "stirring up hostilities," i.e. not only against the enemy but within the body politic; compare 29 n. 2 (and 38 n. 17A). Ennius may also have in mind the legal meaning of *agitare* = "to press accusations of (personal) enmity."

20. **non ... consertum** = "(there is) no shaking hands legally"; lit. "from law." Gellius (2nd cent. A.D.) cites these verses to illustrate this archaic legal formula for

confirming a contract. In the full formula, *consertum* is supine of purpose (acc. of "end of motion") after *vocare* and takes *manum* as its object, = "to summon (some one) to clasp hand." Here it is easier to supply *est* (as rendered above) rather than *vocant* or, from the following verse, *vadunt*.

21. A. **măgĭs fērrō:** i.e. by violence. For *-is* before *f-* see nn. 14B and 17B above. B. **regnum:** used in Cicero's day as a slang term for political control, i.e. "being a boss," and applied e.g. to Caesar; the same connotation is probably present here; contrast its literal use for Caesar's final ambitions at the end of sel. 42 B.   C. **vadunt solida vi** = "(people) proceed by outright (lit. complete) violence"; *vi* is abl. of manner; compare 5 n. 3A.

22. A. **Hannibal:** in 196/5 he had fled from Carthage to Antiochus in Syria and urged the king to declare war on Rome; see 10 pref. Livy XXXV 14 ff. says that Antiochus later became suspicious of Hannibal; perhaps in this fragment Antiochus gives his reason, namely, because Hannibal had begun to dissuade him from war. Hannibal may very well have felt that Antiochus' plan for an invasion of Greece by land was over-ambitious, as it indeed proved to be; see prefs. to 12 and 15.   B. **audaci ... pectore:** abl. either of source ("from") or of attendant circumstance ("with") rather than of means ("by"). The breast or heart (see n. 23C below) was often regarded as the seat of emotion or intelligence; Antiochus refers to Hannibal's bold "change of heart."   C. **de ... hortatur:** Ennius occasionally thus separates prefixes from verbs, a practice known by the Greek term "tmesis" = cutting. In early Lat., such prefixes as *circum* and *trans* may have been looked upon as almost separate advs., but *de* could hardly stand alone except as a prep. with a noun in the abl.; *me* is of course the acc. object of *de ... hortatur* (= "dissuade"), which is pres. after *dum* = "while" (inclusively); see 6 n. 8. Since *me* is elided, this is a spondaic verse; see n. 14B above.

23. A. **quem:** i.e. Hannibal; subject of *esse* in indirect discourse after *credidit*. B. **esse:** Lat. uses a pres. inf. (time contemporary with the main verb) in indirect discourse after a past verb, where Eng. uses a past tense; compare 10 n. 12B (and 54 n. 3A).   C. **meum cor:** subject of *credidit*. For the heart as the seat of intelligence see n. 22B above. Gellius (see n. 20 above) quotes this passage to refute a friend who used the first two verses only to prove that *cor* could be masc. because he thought that *quem* modified it! D. **suasorem:** in predicate agreement with *quem* after *esse*.

24. A. **studiosum:** either a predicate modifier of *quem*, correlative with *suasorem*, or a modifier of *suasorem*, correlative with *summum*. In either case, Ennius has used an abl. of specification modified by a gen. to define it, rather than the more usual simple gen. The sense is clear; = "a leading advocate and zealous in violent war."   B. **robore belli:** for the Lat. use of an abstract noun and a gen. where Eng. would use an adj. and a noun, see 15 n. 4 (and 18 n. 18B).

25. A. **moribus ... virisque:** these abls. may be either instrumental (means) or loc. (place where), depending on whether *stat* means "stands (firm) by," i.e. is maintained by, or "stands (firmly) on," i.e. is firmly based on; for *stare* compare 57 n. 10A. In either case, the men are treated as things, like the customs. This verse so admirably epitomizes the Roman reliance on *mos maiorum* (see 15 n. 13B and 57 n. 21) and *vir-tus* (compare n. 10 above) that Cicero commented: *vel brevitate vel veritate tamquam ex oraculo quodam mihi esse effatus videtur*.   B. **res ... Romana:** primarily the *res publica* (see in 19 n. 6B, and 38 n. 2A), but also generally Roman welfare and affairs.

26. A. **genus Aeacidarum:** i.e. the descendants of Aeacus, grandfather of Achilles, whom Pyrrhus claimed as an ancestor; see 9 n. 2B. *Genus* as a collective noun may take a plur. verb. Cicero cites these verses in his argument that Ennius invented the famous prophecy said to have been given to Pyrrhus at Delphi (see 9 n. 2A) for four reasons: the oracle then spoke in prose, not in verse; the Greeks had no record of this prophecy; the oracle would not have used Lat.; and Pyrrhus, however stupid, could hardly have missed the double meaning of the prophecy.   B. **bellipotentes ... sapientipotentes:** compare *belligerantes* in B verse 2 above. The short *-ĭ-* is part of the stem in all three,

not the ending of a gen. with *potens*, for which see 33 n. 25A. *Bellipotens* appears in Vergil and later poets as a compound noun to indicate Mars or Minerva; compare *Ignipotens* in 55 n. 3B. This is the one occurrence of *sapientipotens* in extant Lat. literature.   C. **măgĭs quam:** for *-ĭs* before *qu-* see nn. 14B, 17B, and 21A above.

27.   A. **Musae:** Ennius invokes the Muses, presumably at the opening of his poem; he uses their Greek name (the Roman equivalent was *Camenae*) and recalls Homer *Il.* II 484: "Tell me now, O Muses, who have your homes on Olympus."   B. **pedibus ... pulsatis** = "you beat with your feet"; a common poetic phrase = "you dance (on)." Such references to Roman dancing suggest that, like many primitive (or, folk) dances, it was marked by vigorous stamping rather than by gliding.

28.   A. **O ... tulisti:** in this excessively alliterative verse (compare 14 n. 20), the vocs. *Tite ... Tati ... tyranne* interlock with the main statement: "thou broughtest to (i.e. upon) thyself (these) so great (disasters? woes?)." Titus Tatius, legendary king of the Sabines, led out his forces against Romulus to recover the girls seized by the Romans in the "Rape of the Sabine Women"; the girls intervened to make peace, and Romulus shared his rule with Tatius.   B. **tute** = *tu* + an intensive suffix *-te*; the verse is cited by a late grammarian to illustrate this pronoun.   C. **tyranne:** here probably merely = "monarch" (as originally in Greek) rather than "tyrant," as in 59 n. 25A.

29.   **Africa ... tumultu:** an equally alliterative and interlocking verse, in which *terribili* modifies *tumultu* and *horrida terra*, = "rough (lit. bristling) land," is in apposition with Africa. It is uncertain to what occasion of Roman intervention in Africa the verse refers; perhaps to the "revolt of the mercenaries" at Carthage after the First Punic War (see 9 pref.), or to Scipio's landing in Africa at the end of the Second Punic War (see 10 pref.), but possibly to some other event.

61

Macrobius wrote in the early fifth century a lengthy discussion of Vergil's *Aeneid*. This he entitled *Saturnalia* because it purported to represent conversations between noble and learned Romans during the holidays which had come to extend for nearly a week beyond the actual festival of Saturn on December 17. In the sixth book, Macrobius quotes extensively from older Latin poets, notably Ennius, to show Vergil's use of them. In many instances, the Latin poets drew on Homer. Thus the first of the following pairs of passages from the *Annales* of Ennius (see 60 pref.) and the *Aeneid* depends on Homer's description in *Il*. XXIII 114–122 of how the Greeks cut wood for the funeral of Patroclus. Ennius probably described the disposal of the dead after the battle with Pyrrhus at Heraclea in 280 (see 9 n. 3), while Vergil was writing about the cremation of Aeneas' trumpeter Misenus, who drowned just after the Trojans landed in Italy; see n. 9A below. Similarly, for the last pair, Homer *Il*. XVI 102–111 described Ajax hard-pressed in the fighting at the Greek ships; Ennius, the bravery of a legionary officer against the Istrians in 178; and Vergil, how Turnus let himself get trapped in the Trojan camp. The three verses which so notably describe Fabius Maximus in the early years of the Second Punic War (see 10 n. 13A) are given by Cicero; Macrobius cites only the first, which Vergil used. In this case there was no Homeric model.

These passages not only illustrate the development of the dactylic hexameter in the century and a half or so between Ennius and Vergil and the respective poetic talents of the two; they also suggest the high literary value that the ancients placed on successful *imitatio*, which did not mean simply plagiarizing some earlier work, but reshaping it and improving it for one's own use.

Vergilius Ennii imitator

A.   Incedunt arbusta per alta,[1] securibŭs caedunt;[2]

          percellunt magnas quercus.[3] Exciditur ilex;[4]

          fraxinŭs frangitur atque abies consternitur alta.[5]

          Pinus proceras pervortunt.[6] Omne sonabat

          arbustum fremitu silvai frondosai.[7]

Quos versus imitatus est Vergilius in sexto Aeneidos:[8]

          Itur in antiquam silvam, stabula alta ferarum.[9]

          Procumbunt piceae; sonat icta securibus ilex

          fraxineaeque trabes cuneis;[10] et fissile robur

          scinditur;[11] advolvunt ingentes montibus ornos.[12]

B.   Unus homo nobis cunctando restituit rem.[13]

Noenum rumores ponebāt ante salutem.[14]

Ergo postque magisque viri nunc gloria claret.[15]

Quos versus imitatus est Vergilius etiam in sexto Aeneidos:

Tu Maximus ille es,

unus qui nobis cunctando restituis rem.[16]

C.   Undique conveniunt velut imber tela tribuno;[17]

configunt parmam.[18] Tinnīt hastilibus umbo;[19]

aerato sonitu galeae.[20] Sed nec pote quisquam

undique nitendo corpus discerpere ferro.[21]

Semper adundantes hastas frangitque quatitque.[22]

Totum sudor habet corpus; multumque laborat;[23]

nec respirandi fit copia. Praepete ferro

Histri tela manu iacientes sollicitabant.[24]

Quos versus Vergilius de incluso Turno in nono Aeneidos gratia elegantiore imitatus est:[25]

Ergo nec clipeo iuvenis subsistere tantum

nec dextra valet,[26] iniectis sic undique telis

obruitur.[27] Strepit adsiduo cava tempora circum

tinnitu galea,[28] et saxis solida aera fatiscunt,[29]

discussaeque iubae capiti,[30] nec sufficit umbo

ictibus.[31] Ingeminant hastis et Troes et ipse

fulmineus Mnestheus.[32] Tum toto corpore sudor

liquitur[33] et piceum (nec respirare potestas)

flumen agit;[34] fessos quatit aeger anhelitus artus.[35]

---

1. A. **incedunt:** the subject of the plur. verbs is presumably the Roman soldiers, preparing to burn their dead; see pref. above. In this and other passages, Ennius freely changes the subject from sentence to sentence. In this verse the caesura apparently falls after *āltă*, i.e. it is "feminine" (after the first short syllable of the dactyl) in the 4th foot; such a caesura was avoided by later poets.   B. **arbusta** = "grove," whether planted or natural; this neut. plur. of an adj. from *arbor* is more commonly used as a noun than the sing. appearing in the last verse of this passage; see n. 7 below.

2. **sĕcūrĭbŭs caedūnt** = "they fell with axes"; *sĕcūris, -is,* comes from *sĕcare* = "to cut," not from *sēcūrus* = *sē + cūra,* i.e. "without care, secure." For final *-s* failing to make *-bus* long before an initial consonant see 60 n. 14B. Vergil, in adapting this passage, placed *securibus* before a vowel (*ilex*) since by his time *-s* was strongly enough pronounced to "make position."

3. **quercus etc.**: Italy's richness in trees is suggested by the names given by Ennius and by Vergil's variations on them: for *quercus* = "oak," Vergil uses *robur*; he retains *ilex* = "holm oak" and, in adjectival form, *fraxinus* = "ash," but adds *ornus* = "mountain ash"; he omits *abies* = "fir tree"; and for *pinus* = "pine," he substitutes *picea* = "pitch pine." Names of trees are regularly fem., and often 4th decl.

4. **exciditur**: as the -*ĭ*- shows, this is from *caedere*, not *cadere*; compare 5 n. 12 (and 8 n. 5B). The preponderance of spondees in this verse, as in the 4th, suggests heavily falling trees; compare 60 n. 5B.

5. **fr̄axĭn̆us fr̄angĭt̆ur**: alliteration, as there is of *p* in the next verse and again of *fr* in the last; *arbusta . . . alta* and *abiēs . . . alta* probably also constitute deliberate echoes of sound. Vergil avoids alliteration in his imitation, except perhaps in *procumbunt piceae*; the echoes of *a* in his 1st verse and of *f* in his 3rd are too far separated to be effective. The final -*s* in *fraxinus* does not "make position"; see n. 2 above.

6. **pervortunt** = later *pervertunt*. Early Lat. -*ŏ*- was often weakened later to -*ĕ*-, as in *bĕne* from *bŏnus*.

7. **sīlvāī frŏndōsāī**: this gen. goes either with *arbustum* (compare n. 1B above) or with *fremitu*; = "the crashing of the leafy wood." For the ending -*āī* see 57 n. 11B. This verse is spondaic; see 59 n. 13 (and contrast 60 n. 5B).

8. **sexto Aeneidos**: supply *libro*; *Aeneidos* is the Greek gen. sing. from the nom. fem. *Aeneis*.

9. A. **itur etc.**: when Aeneas (see 1 and 49) made his first landing in Italy, at Cumae just north of the Bay of Naples, his trumpeter Misenus aroused the jealousy of the sea god Triton by his playing, and Triton drowned him. In these verses, Vergil adapted Ennius to describe preparations for the cremation of the body. *Itur* is a true (and common) impersonal; = "there is a going," i.e. people go (see 12 n. 9B); it is a vivid "historical" pres. In these verses, Vergil, like Ennius (see n. 1A above), changes the subject of the verbs without indication.   B. **stabula** = "lairs"; usually this noun, formed on the root of *stare* with the instrumental suffix -*bulum*, means "a man-made enclosure for animals."

10. **sonat . . . cuneis**: *sonat* is sing. in agreement with the nearest subject; = "the ilex, cut down with axes, and the ashen beams, split with wedges, resound." Since splitting the ashen beams seems more akin to splitting oak (which follows), some editors punctuate after *ilex* and regard -*que* as the main connective, with *et* joining two parts of the second element (see 43 n. 2); in this case *scinditur* would be sing. in agreement with the nearest subject.

11. **fissile robur** = "oak easy to split"; oak must be very straight grained to split easily.

12. **montibus**: probably abl. of place where, or possibly from which, in either case without a prep., as often in poetry; it can hardly be dat., although *advolvere* may take the dat. (after *ad*- in composition; compare 59 n. 10) to indicate place toward which.

13. A. **unus homo**: Fabius Maximus Cunctator; see pref. above.   B. **cunctando**: abl. (of means) of the gerund (verbal noun).   C. **rem** = *rem publicam*, in the general sense of common welfare; compare 60 n. 25B.

14. A. **noenum**: archaic for *non*, as derived from *ne* + *oinum* (= *unum*).   B. **rumores**: presumably the gossip critical of his delaying tactics; gossip which Livy XXII 34 says occasioned the election of the rash consul Varro, who committed the Roman forces to the catastrophic defeat of Cannae in 216; see 10 pref. and n. 13A.   C. **pōnēbāt**: the -*a*- of the imperf. ind. ending was originally long; compare 60 n. 9A.

15. **pōstqŭe mă̄gĭsqŭe** = "both since (then) and more (and more)"; advs. with *claret*, which is pres. of Ennius' own day (*nunc*); i.e. Fabius' fame grew even brighter from his own time to Ennius'. With the long -*īsque*, contrast 60 nn. 21A and 26C.

16.   A. **tu Maximus:** Anchises, showing Aeneas the spirits of future Roman heroes, addresses that of Fabius directly; see *Aen.* VI 845–846, given in sel. 88. Hence Vergil's change in the next verse to *restituis*.   B. **ūnūs quī:** since in Vergil's day final *-s* made position (see n. 2 above), he can substitute this for Ennius' *ūnŭs hŏmō*. The slight *variatio* in Vergil's *imitatio* (see pref. above) marks high art.

17.   A. **conveniunt** = "come together"; the subject is *tela*.   B. **tribuno:** dat. of reference, relating the tribune to the whole thought rather than specifically to *conveniunt*, which in this literal use would probably have been followed by *in*+ the acc.; only in the derivative meaning of "to be agreeable, to fit, etc." does it take the dat. A military tribune, as against a *tribunus plebis* (for whom see 7 pref.), was a junior officer in a legion; see 14 n. 4A (and 21 n. 7A). Macrobius identifies this tribune as Gaius Aelius.

18.   **parmam:** normally a small shield used by cavalry and light infantry; either the officers used such shields, or Ennius employed the word loosely for the heavy oblong legionary *scutum*.

19.   A. **tĭnnĭt hāstĭlĭbŭs** = "jangles with the javelins" (i.e. striking it). The vowel in the ending of the 3rd pers. sing. pres. act. ind. might in early Lat. be long; for the pres. subj. compare 60 n. 9A and for the imperf. ind. n. 14c above.   B. **hastilibus:** this neut. plur., derivative from *hasta*, here means "thrown javelins"; the term is perhaps used because the Istrian javelin differed from the Roman legionary *pilum*.   C. **umbo:** the round central metal boss is perhaps used here and in the passage below from Vergil by metonymy (see 49 n. 4 and in 59 n. 21A) for the whole shield, the rest of which was probably made of leather on a wicker framework.

20.   A. **aerato sonitu galeae:** supply *tinniunt;* = "his helmet jangles with brassy clang"; *sonitu* is abl. of manner.   B. **galeae:** nom. plur. apparently used for the sing., which Vergil has below.

21.   A. **nec:** redundant with *sed*; = *non*.   B. **pote:** supply *est*; the masc. *potis* might be expected but both forms are used for all genders. *Possum* is not a direct contraction from *potis sum* but developed under the influence of such "prodelided" (see 60 n. 13B) forms as *potis'st* and *pot' est*.   C. **quisquam** = "any one," i.e. of the enemy. *Quisquam* is the indefinite pronoun (rather than *aliquis* or *quidam*) regularly used after a universal negative.   D. **undique nitendo** = "by pressing (on him) from every side"; the gerund *nitendo* is abl. of means (compare n. 13B above) with the whole phrase. Though *quisquam* is sing., Ennius thinks of individuals pushing in from all sides on the tribune; compare 55 n. 20A.   E. **ferro:** a second abl. of means but going closely with *discerpere*. It may mean here, as in verse 7 (see n. 24A below), a javelin, or perhaps a sword used at close quarters.

22.   A. **adundantes:** an emendation for *abundantes* given by Macrobius; though the word is only dubiously attested elsewhere, the picture of waves of javelins rolling in on the tribune seems more vivid than that of javelins in excessive numbers.   B. **frangitque quatitque** = "(the tribune) either breaks off or shakes (from his shield)"; the correlatives *-que . . . -que* may be rendered here "either . . . or." For the unkeyed changes of subject here and in the following verses, compare nn. 1A and 9A above.

23.   **sudor:** subject of *habet*; but the tribune becomes subject again of *laborat*.

24.   A. **praepete ferro** = "with flying weapon"; i.e. with javelins (compare n. 21E above); possibly each Istrian has one javelin or perhaps *ferro* is collective sing.; compare 59 n. 18B).   B. **praepete:** an adj. of uncertain derivation; it usually modifies *avis*, to mean a bird whose flight is of good omen.   C. **Histri:** the inhabitants of the peninsula at the northeast top of the Adriatic, still called Istria.   D. **sollicitabant:** as the passage stops here in Macrobius, the tribune must be supplied as object; but perhaps he was mentioned in the lost following verse.

25.   A. **incluso:** i.e. in the Trojan camp; see pref. Turnus had broken in during an attack, and the Trojans had closed the gate on his followers, leaving him to defend

himself alone.   B. **gratia elegantiore:** abl. of manner; the phrase is Macrobius' literary judgment.

26.   A. **clipeo ... dextra:** abls. of means with *subsistere*.   B. **clipeo:** a round Greek shield; compare 47 n. 12A.   C. **iuvenis:** i.e. Turnus; subject of *valet*.   D. **subsistere tantum** = "to bear up sufficiently." Servius, the 4th-cent. commentator on Vergil, explains *subsistere* as = *resistere*, which would take a dat.; hence *tantum* is an adv., implying *quantum opus erat* or the like; i.e. "as much as was necessary."   E. **dextra:** supply *manu*.

27.   **iniectis:** the reading of the manuscripts of Vergil; Macrobius gives *obiectis*.

28.   A. **cava tempora circum** = "around (his) hollow temples"; *circum* here follows its acc., as in 55 n. 6C.   B. **tempora** = "temple (of the head)"; usually, as here, in the plur. and a different word from *tempus* = "time."   C. **cava:** if neut. acc. plur. with *tempora*, as the word order suggests, it is a "transferred epithet" since "hollow" would more naturally be used of the helmet around the temple than of the temple itself; it may, however, be fem. nom. sing. modifying *galea* grammatically as well as going with it in sense.

29.   A. **solida aera fatiscunt** = "the solid brass (plates?) gape open"; *aera*, neut. nom. plur. of *aes* = "bronze," may refer to parts of the helmet, which alone seems to be in question here rather than all his armor; or it may be used for the sing. in imitation of Ennius' *galeae*; see n. 20B above.   B. **fatiscunt:** an act. or dep. verb related to a rare noun *fatis* = "a crack"; the meaning for it and related words of "to grow weary" is derivative; compare American slang "to crack up."

30.   A. **discussae ... capiti** = "the crests are struck from (his) head"; supply *sunt*. Early Italic helmets often had several plumes, hence probably the plur. *iubae*.   B. **capiti:** apparently an extended use of the dat. of reference (separation), which is usually used of persons after verbs meaning "to take away from"; compare 18 n. 7A (and 54 n. 9A).

31.   **nec ... ictibus** = "nor did the boss (see n. 19C above) suffice for (i.e. to bear) the blows."

32.   A. **hastis:** Vergil *Aen.* I 747 also uses an abl. of means (rather than an acc.) with *ingeminare* = "to redouble."   B. **Trŏĕs:** Greek nom. plur. of *Trōs*, a mythical ancestor of Priam and Aeneas; here used for the people of Troy.   C. **fŭlmĭnĕūs Mnēstheūs:** Aeneas, going to seek aid from Evander (see 50 n. 4) and the Etruscans (see 49 n. 6B), had left this hero and Serestus in charge of the Trojan camp. Here Mnestheus throws javelins "like lightning." The first -*eus* is a Lat. adjectival dissyllabic ending; the second a Greek nom. monosyllabic (diphthong) ending.

33.   A. **toto corpore:** abl. of place where; = "on (over) his whole body."   B. **liquitur** = "runs liquid," from the dep. verb *liquor*.

34.   A. **piceum ... flumen** = "a pitch-black stream," i.e. of sweat, dirt, and gore.   B. **nec respirare potestas:** supply *est*; the inf. is used with *potestas* by Vergil and later poets, but in prose the gen. of the gerund (cf. *respirandi fit copia* in verse 7 of C above) or of a noun modified by a gerundive is more usual. The inf. is probably used because (*est) potestas* has the verbal connotation of "it is possible" rather than constituting a parallel to the use of the inf. with some adjs., and in early Lat. with some nouns, as "explanatory" (also called "Greek" or "of purpose"), or being treated as an indeclinable noun in the gen. dependent on *potestas* (like the more usual gerund); = "power of breathing." The whole clause is a parenthetical interruption of the sentence *piceum ... agit*.   C. **agit:** *sudor* is subject, *flumen* object.

35.   **aeger anhelitus** = "a labored panting." Vergil uses almost the same half verse in *Aen.* V 432. Book IX concludes with Turnus' escape by jumping into the Tiber, on the bank of which Aeneas had built his camp.

62

In spite of the difference in their political outlook, the Gracchi (see 18 and 19) shared in the cultural atmosphere that surrounded the Scipios (see 16 pref.), partly because of the close family connections between them; see the genealogical charts following 15. Their mother Cornelia, daughter of Scipio Africanus the Elder (see 18 n. 2), was famous both for her own learning and for the care with which she educated her twelve children, especially the three who survived to adulthood, namely the tribunes Tiberius and Gaius, and Sempronia, the wife of Scipio Aemilianus; see 18 n. 16A. The Gracchi were among the first notable orators at Rome, and Cornelia maintained, even after the deaths of her sons, a salon attended by Greeks and cultivated Romans.

The following passage, composed from Quintilian (see 13 pref.) and Cicero, shows that the speeches of the Gracchi and the letters of Cornelia, though neither are extant now, were read and admired at Rome for many years; it acknowledges also the contribution which Cornelia made to the eloquence of the Gracchi. The tone of the passage, that the great talents of the Gracchi were devoted to wrongful ends, may be compared with Cicero's judgment on them given in 20 A.

Eloquentia Gracchorum

Gracchorum eloquentiae multum contulisse accepimus Corneliam matrem, cuius doctissimus sermo in posteros quoque est epistulis traditus.[1] Ex eis enim apparet filios non tam in gremio educatos quam in sermone matris.[2] Utinam in Tiberio Graccho talis mens ad rem publicam bene gerendam fuisset, quale ingenium ad bene dicendum fuit;[3] profecto nemo huic viro gloria praestitisset.[4] Sed propter turbulentissimum tribunatum ab ipsa re publica est interfectus.[5] Fuit tamen summus orator. Atque hoc memoria patrum teste dicimus;[6] nam Gracchi habemus orationes nondum satis splendidas verbis, sed acutas prudentiaeque plenissimas. Fuit Gracchus diligentia Corneliae matris a puero doctus et Graecis litteris eruditus. Nam semper habuit exquisitos e Graecia magistros, in eis Diophanem Mytilenaeum, Graeciae temporibus illis disertissimum.[7] Sed ei breve tempus ingeni augendi et declarandi fuit.[8]

Fuit autem vir et praestantissimo ingenio et flagranti studio et doctus a puero C. Gracchus. Noli enim putare quemquam pleniorem aut uberiorem ad dicendum fuisse.[9] Damnum vero illius immaturo interitu res Romanae Latinaeque litterae fecerunt.[10] Utinam non tam fratri pietatem quam patriae praestare voluisset![11] Quam ille facile tali ingenio, diutius si vixisset, vel paternam esset vel avitam gloriam consecutus![12] Eloquentia quidem nescio an habuisset parem neminem.[13] Grandis est verbis, sapiens sententiis, genere toto gravis.[14] Manus extrema non accessit operibus eius;[15] praeclare incohata multa, perfecta non plane. Legendus autem est hic orator, si quisquam alius, iuventuti;[16] non enim solum acuere sed etiam alere ingenium potest.

1. **doctissimus sermo**="well-educated discourse"; *sermo* may connote various forms of talk, e.g. formal discourse, informal discussion or conversation (as in 43 n. 21A), and style or diction.

2. **in gremio . . . in sermone:** i.e. "in the physical care . . . in conversation with"; see preceding note.

3. A. **utinam . . . fuisset:** for the pluperf. subj. used in a past unaccomplished ("unreal") wish see 26 n. 14B.   B. **talis mens ad . . . quale ingenium ad:** the construction *ad*+gerundive or gerund to denote purpose (see 5 n. 9A) may be used, as here, after adjs., as well as after verbs or nouns; compare *uberiorem ad dicendum* in the 2nd par. below. With this sentence may be compared the last of the 1st par. of 20 A: *ut dolerent . . . esse conversa.*

4. **huic . . . praestitisset:** for *praesto*="I surpass" with an abl. of specification, here *gloria*, see 16 nn. 9C and D, and contrast n. 11B below. Since *praestare* is a compound verb, the person or thing surpassed goes in the dat., here *huic viro.*

5. **ab ipsa re publica:** the use of the prep. with the abl. of agent (instead of means with no prep.) shows that the Republic is personified; compare 19 n. 14A (and contrast 61 n. 13C). Cicero here completely identifies the interests of the Republic with those of the optimates; compare 20 pref. and 76.

6. **teste:** in apposition with *memoria* to form an abl. abs.="our fathers' memory (being) evidence"; contrast 34 n. 11. Cicero means that Tiberius' reputation as an orator depended on the oral tradition of his actual delivery, since, as he goes on to say, Tiberius' surviving speeches showed a keen intelligence but not an elegant style.

7. **Graeciae:** probably partitive gen. equivalent to *Graecorum* (compare 49 n. 6B); ="most learned at that time of the Greeks"; for this gen. with a superlative compare 11 n. 11A. If *disertissimum*="the most learned (man)," *Graeciae* might be possessive gen.,="of Greece," or loc.,="in Greece."

8. A. **sed ei . . . fuit:** for the common idiom of the dat. of reference (possession)+ *esse*="to have," see 11 n. 9 (and 55 n. 17B).   B. **ingeni:** the objective gen. of the noun+the gerundives *augendi et declarandi* is used here to express the notion of "purpose" instead of the common construction of *ad*+acc., for which see n. 3B above. The connotation of *tempus fuit*="there was time (for)" is different here from that of the common idiom *tempus est*="it is time (to do something)," which is regularly followed by the inf., as in 86 n. 17B.

9. A. **noli . . . putare:** one of the regular ways of expressing a prohibition (negative command) in Lat. is the imperative of *nolo*, either sing. (as here) or plur.,+the inf.

Other ways are *cave*+the pres. subj. or *ne*+the perf. subj. (hortatory).   B. **quem-quam**: for the use of *quisquam* after a universal negative see 61 n. 21c (and compare n. 16A below).

10. **damnum . . . fecerunt**="suffered (lit. made) a loss"; a regular idiom.

11. A. **utinam . . . voluisset**: see n. 3A above. For the sentiment compare the end of 20 B.   B. **non . . . praestare**="to fulfill his duty (lit. show loyalty) not to his brother but to his country." For *praestare* contrast n. 4 above. For the importance of *pietas* among the Romans see in 23 n. 13A.

12. **quam . . . consecutus**: for the past contrary to fact condition see 19 n. 14A. The same general idea, that the Gracchi should have lived up to their family traditions, is expressed throughout sels. 18–20; compare especially the sentence *nihil . . . deflexisset* in the middle of the 1st par. of 20 A. For Gaius' father see especially 18 n. 1A; for his maternal grandfather (Scipio Africanus) see 18 n. 2.

13. **nescio an . . . neminem**: *nescio an* lit.="I do not know whether" and introduces an indirect question; hence the pluperf. subj. *habuisset*, the subject of which is still Gaius. But the phrase, like *haud scio an* (see 31 n. 14A), regularly connotes a positive opinion, as is here shown by the use of *neminem*; it is therefore best rendered: "I am inclined to think that . . . no one."

14. A. **grandis . . . sapiens . . . gravis**: adjs. common in various contexts. Here they pertain to rhetoric and may be rendered: "noble in his diction (or, more specifically, varied in his choice of words, i.e. using a large vocabulary), penetrating in his ideas, impressive in his whole style." The terms cover the three main aspects of oratory as recognized by ancient rhetorical theory: language, content, and style; contrast the appraisal of Tiberius in the 1st par., where only the first two (*verbis* and *prudentiae*) are covered.   B. **gravis**: for the meaning compare 57 n. 12.

15. A. **manus . . . accessit**="the last hand was not applied to," i.e. "he had not put the finishing touches to."   B. **manus**: often used in this and similar figurative senses, as *in manibus*="in process" in the 1st sentence of the 3rd par. of 14, or *manu*="in hand-to-hand fighting" in 24 n. 2A. Here compare *ultimam . . . manum* in 46 n. 20A.   C. **accessit**: for the meaning see 34 n. 2A (and 57 n. 6); it is here followed by the dat. as a verb compounded with a prep., rather than by *ad*+the acc., because the idea of motion is absent; compare 59 n. 10.

16. A. **quisquam**: used in conditions after *si* instead of *quis*=*aliquis* (see 4 n. 11B and 52 n. 9B) when there is a universal rather than a particular connotation; compare n. 9B above. Eng. often gives this connotation by saying "anyone else."   B. **iuventuti**: dat. of reference (agent) with the 2nd (pass.) periphrastic *legendus . . . est*; see 21 n. 15c. For the abstract sing. used for the concrete plur. see 8 n. 9A (and 59 n. 18B).

63

After the Gracchi (see 18–20), the next severe threat to the optimate control of the Republic came from Gaius Marius; see 21–25. Though Marius is condemned by conservative writers, even by Cicero, his fellow-townsman (see 27 pref. and 64 A), Sallust gives a more favorable picture in his *Jugurthine War*. Gaius Sallustius Crispus (86–*ca.* 34) was born of an equestrian family at Amiternum in central Italy. Thus, like Marius and Cicero, he was the first of his family to enter the senate but, since he did not attain the consulship, should not be called a *novus homo*; see prefs. to 13, 21, 31, and 32. As tribune in 52, he supported the *populares* and opposed Cicero in the trial of Milo; see 37 pref. The optimate censors of 50 removed him from the senate, ostensibly for immorality but perhaps actually as a Caesarian; see 38 pref. Caesar restored him to the senate in 49 by making him quaestor for a second time and in 46 appointed him as quaestor to govern the newly conquered province of Numidia; see 41 pref. There Sallust seems to have enriched himself and, after the assassination of Caesar in 44 (see 43), to have given up public life for writing; see 17 pref. He composed at least three historical monographs: on the Catilinarian Conspiracy (see 17 A, 34 B), on the Jugurthine War (see 20 B, 21, 22, 65), and on the period from 78 to 67; see 65 nn. 5 and 6. In these he pretends to high standards of private and public morality which accord ill with what is said of his own career. Throughout his writings, he criticizes the violence and corruption which had increasingly characterized Roman political life since the Gracchi; see 23–25 and 62. Nor does he underestimate Marius' contribution thereto by his conduct in the First Civil War; see 24, 25, and 64. But Sallust also views the nobility as lazy, incompetent, irresponsible, and arrogant; see 17 A. By contrast, he presents Marius as able and energetic, and even as possessing the old Roman virtues of hardihood and frugality.

In his *Bellum Iugurthinum*, Sallust, following a regular practice of ancient historiography (see 58 pref.), places in Marius' mouth a speech to the Roman people, probably of his own composition, in which the newly elected consul replies to his senatorial critics and seeks to arouse popular enthusiasm for service. The following selection is composed of portions of this speech; in it, as against the selections from Sallust in Part I, archaic spellings found in the manuscripts of his works and in modern editions have been retained.

Marii apud populum contio

Marius, cupientissuma plebe consul factus,[1] postquam ei provinciam Numidiam populus iussit,[2] antea iam infestus nobilitati, tum vero multus atque ferox instare.[3] Neque illi senatus, quamquam advorsus erat, de ullo negotio abnuere audebat.[4] Tum Marius et plebem hortandi causa et nobilitatem uti consueverat exagitandi contionem populi advocavit.[5] Deinde hoc modo disseruit:

"Bellum me gerere cum Iugurtha iussistis, quam rem nobilitas aegerrume tulit.[6] Comparate nunc, Quirites, cum illorum superbia me hominem novom.[7] Quae illi audire et legere solent, eorum partem vidi, alia egomet gessi; quae illi litteris, ea ego militando didici.[8] Nunc vos existumate facta an dicta pluris sint.[9] Contemnunt novitatem meam, ego illorum ignaviam.

"Quod si iure me despiciunt, faciant idem maioribus suis, quibus uti mihi ex virtute nobilitas coepit.[10] Invident honori meo; ergo invideant labori, innocentiae, periculis etiam meis, quoniam per haec illum cepi.[11] Sed quoniam vostra consilia accusantur, qui mihi summum honorem et maxumum negotium imposuistis, etiam atque etiam reputate num eorum paenitendum sit.[12] Non possum fidei causa imagines neque triumphos aut consulatus maiorum meorum ostentare, at hastas, vexillum, phaleras, alia militaria dona, praeterea cicatrices advorso corpore.[13] Hae sunt meae imagines, haec nobilitas, non hereditate relicta, ut illa illis, sed quae ego meis plurumis laboribus et periculis quaesivi."[14]

Huiuscemodi oratione habita, Marius, postquam plebis animos adrectos videt, propere omnibus utilibus navis onerat.[15] Interea milites scribere, non more maiorum ex classibus sed capite censos plerosque.[16] Igitur cum aliquanto maiore numero quam decretum erat in Africam profectus est.[17]

---

1.   A. **cupientissuma plebe:** either abl. abs. or abl. of attendant circumstance.   B. **cupientissuma:** archaic ending for -*imus*; see 56 n. 1B. Sallust seems to have preferred archaic forms; compare nn. 4A, 7B, and 9A below.   C. **plebe:** Sallust used *plebs* inexactly for the urban mob; see 21 n. 11A. In fact consuls were elected in the *comitia centuriata* by the whole *populus*.   D. **consul factus:** in 108 for 107; see sel. 21. For the use of *facere* = "to elect" see 56 n. 1A.

2.   **populus iussit:** *iubere* is a technical verb for the enactment of a law and takes a direct object of what the law ordered or, here, entrusted to Marius (the dat. *ei*). Though the details of the measure are lost, Sallust earlier (chap. 73.7) attributes it to a tribune so that it was probably passed by the *populus* in the *comitia tributa*, not by the *plebs* in the *concilium plebis*; compare 21 n. 11A. In the Ciceronian era, tribunes often induced the *populus* to usurp the senate's traditional function of conferring provincial commands by assigning commands through a *lex tribunicia*; compare, for example, the command

against Mithridates given to Marius in 88 (24 pref.); those given to Pompey against the pirates in 67 and against Mithridates in 66 (29 pref.); that to Caesar in Gaul in 59 (35 pref.).

3. A. **nobilitati** = "the nobles"; see 20 n. 14A (and 56 n. 12A; contrast n. 14C below). B. **multus atque ferox:** i.e. "continually and fiercely"; Lat. often uses an adj. where Eng. idiom requires an adv.; see 14 n. 18B (and 57 n. 11A). C. **instare:** historical inf., as is *scribere* in the final paragraph; Sallust is fond of the historical inf.; see 17 n. 16A (and 21 n. 17A).

4. A. **advorsus:** archaic -*o*- for later -*e*-, as in *advorso* below; compare n. 7B below (and 61 n. 6). B. **illi ... de ... abnuere** = "to refuse him anything"; *abnuere* usually takes the simple acc. of the thing denied, rather than, as here, *de* + abl., but regularly the dat. of the person to whom it is denied, as *illi* here.

5. A. **plebem ... exagitandi:** the gen. gerunds depend on the abl. *causa* to express purpose; see 19 n. 4A. The gen. of the gerund with an object is occasionally used instead of a noun modified by the gerundive; compare 35 n. 2 (and 57 n. 5D). In this sentence, as in n. 1A above, a contrast is drawn between *plebs* = "mob" and the *populus* = "all citizens" gathered formally to be addressed by a magistrate in a *contio*, for which see 29 pref. (and 42 n. 22B). B. **uti consueverat** = "as he had been accustomed," i.e. as was his custom; *uti* is a stronger form of *ut*; see 28 n. 23D. For the use of the pluperf. of verbs in -*sco* as equivalent to the imperf., compare 58 n. 13A. In retrojecting Marius' hostility to the nobility Sallust exaggerates, since Marius seems in his early career to have steered a middle course between the optimates and the demagogues.

6. **aegerrume tulit** = "bore illy"; i.e. the nobility were angry at the popular vote of the command to Marius; for the idiom compare 3 n. 2A (and 33 n. 12). For the form of the superlative see n. 1B above.

7. A. **Quirites:** for this term of address for Roman citizens when assembled see 27 n. 7B (and 50 n. 6A). B. **novom:** the original endings of the 2nd decl. nom. and acc. masc. and neut. sing. were -*os* and -*om*, later reduced to -*us* and -*um* but frequently used until the mid-1st cent. A.D. after consonantal -*u*- (printed in these selections -*v*-); modern editions generally print -*us* and -*um* except in early authors, e.g. Plautus and Terence, and in authors like Sallust known to have preferred archaic forms; compare 43 n. 16C. A *novus homo* was a man who was the first in his family not only to get elected to a lesser magistracy (i.e. to enter the senate) but to attain the consulship; see pref.

8. A. **quae ... didici:** with this rhetorical contrast between the "doer" and the "talker," compare Cicero on Pompey at the opening of sel. 29. B. **vidi, alia:** the lack of connective (asyndeton; see 4 n. 5B and 17 n. 2) here is also suited to the Eng. idiom. C. **egomet:** for the intensive ending -*met* added to personal pronouns see 27 n. 7C (and 37 n. 27A).

9. A. **existumate:** for archaic -*u*- for later -*i*- compare n. 1B above. B. **facta ... sint:** *utrum ... an* introduce a double or alternative question (here indirect), as in the 2nd sentence of 11 B, but the *utrum* is frequently omitted, as here. C. **pluris:** gen. of indefinite value; see 11 n. 1A.

10. A. **faciant ... suis** = "let them do the same (thing) to their (own) ancestors," i.e. look down on them as they do on me. B. **quibus ... mihi:** dats. of reference (advantage) with *coepit*, which is here used absolutely (without a complementary inf.) in the meaning "started, originated." C. **uti** = *ut;* see n. 5B above.

11. A. **honori** = "(my) consulship" (see 8 n. 8C and compare 33 n. 25C) rather than abstractly "(my) honor." B. **illum** = *honorem.*

12. A. **etiam ... reputate:** i.e. consider carefully; for this connotation of *etiam atque etiam* compare 37 n. 12. B. **eorum:** i.e. the popular decisions (*consilia*); gen. after *paenitendum sit*; see 22 n. 12B (and contrast 33 n. 7).

13. A. **fidei causa** = "for the sake of (creating) confidence (in me)"; for the gen. see n. 5A above. *Fides* here means the confidence which he would inspire in the voters; contrast 51 n. 6 (and 59 n. 6). B. **imagines:** in the funerals of distinguished Romans, attendants wore the masks and insignia (see 8 n. 8D) of ancestors who had held high office. The masks, with appropriate inscriptions, are said to have been kept in niches on the wall of the central hall (*atrium*) of their houses and to have been connected by lines (*stemmata*) showing descent. C. **hastas, vexillum, phaleras:** a spear without an iron point (*pura*), a small standard hung from a crossbar on a pole, and plaques to be worn on armor were all regular military decorations in the Roman army. D. **cica-trices advorso corpore:** wounds on the part of the body turned toward the enemy (i.e. the front) were a sign of courage; compare 9 n. 4 (and contrast 43 n. 8B); *advorso* (see n. 4A above) *corpore* is abl. of place where.

14. A. **hae ... haec:** though both refer to all the items just listed, these nom. fem. pronouns agree with their respective predicate noms, one plur. and one sing. B. **nobilitas:** i.e. descent from a "consular" family; compare 18 pref. (and 36 n. 6B, and contrast n. 3A above). C. **relicta:** probably not nom. fem. sing. under the influence of the *haec nobilitas*, but rather, like *illa*, nom. neut. plur. past part. used as a noun in apposition with *imagines* and *nobilitas*; = "(things) left (or, bequeathed) by inheritance." This is indicated by the following acc. neut. plur. rel. pronoun *quae* (not *quam*).

15. A. **huiuscemodi:** often written as two words; for this gen. of quality (description) compare *eius modi* in 34 n. 5; for the intensive suffix -*ce* on forms of *hic* see 29 n. 10. B. **navīs:** Sallust seems to have used -*īs* as the acc. plur. ending of *i*-stem nouns; see 17 n. 14 (and compare 55 n. 6D).

16. **ex classibus ... capite censos:** in early Rome, citizen soldiers provided their own armor, so that only those with sufficient property to buy full armor served in the legions; the poor served as light-armed skirmishers (*velites*) or as camp servants, etc. Eventually those rich enough to serve in the legions were divided into five "classes" according to their wealth, perhaps only for political and not for military purposes; see 53 pref. Those poorer than the lowest class were called *infra classem* or, as here, *capite censi* = "listed (on the census rolls) by head only," since all that they had to offer for service was their persons; *caput* is often used in Lat. to connote "person" or "individual." Marius' recognition that service in the legions should no longer be regarded as an obligation on property owners to defend home and fatherland, but rather as affording a profitable career to poorer citizens, confirmed what had been going on for more than a century. Whereas the early Roman army had been a citizen militia, foreign wars had made service increasingly long-term and professional. The legionaries looked no longer to the state but to their commanders for rewards during service and for care after retirement. Though Marius' innovation was realistic in terms of recruitment, it accentuated the problem of satisfying the veterans, a problem which continued to vex the Republic to the end.

17. A. **igitur:** usually placed by Sallust at the opening of the sentence instead of postpositively; see 17 n. 1A (and 34 n. 12A). B. **aliquanto ... erat:** this phrase suggests what Sallust earlier (chap. 84.3) had said explicitly, that though the senate had opposed Marius' command, it did not deny him the customary levy but that he supplemented this by accepting poor volunteers. C. **decretum erat:** probably impersonal, since "than (the number) which had been decreed" would have been expressed as *quam qui* (*numerus*) *decretus erat*. *Cernere* and *decernere* are regularly used of the voting of a *senatus consultum*; see 18 n. 9. The senate had the responsibility of assigning forces to magistrates who would command in the field; contrast n. 2 above.

64

Cicero occasionally shows admiration for Marius, the *novus homo* from his own small town of Arpinum who became a successful Roman general and seven times consul; see prefs. to 27 and 63. Generally, however, he shares the standard optimate disapproval for the hero who allied himself with demagogues (see 63), as he does in the first of the following passages, taken from his essay on obligations, the *de Officiis*, which he wrote in 44, after the assassination of Caesar.

The second passage, in dactylic hexameters, is a poetic version of Marius' dramatic escape from Sulla in the First Civil War. It is taken from Lucan's epic poem on the civil war between Pompey and Caesar (see 38–41 and 77), which is called either *Bellum Civile* or, more commonly, *Pharsalia*, from their decisive battle in 49 (see 40), and which was probably based principally on Livy's now lost account.

Marcus Annaeus Lucanus (A.D. 39–65), nephew of the philosopher Seneca the Younger, began as a member of Nero's literary circle, and the opening of his epic flatters the Emperor excessively, though the passage is sometimes taken as satirical. Later he became estranged from Nero, either because of poetical jealousy or through discontent with the Emperor's increasingly absolute regime, and the general tone of the epic is strongly "republican," for example, in his praise of Cato, for whom see 41 pref. In 65 Lucan joined a senatorial conspiracy against Nero whose figurehead was a certain Piso and, when the plot was discovered, committed enforced suicide.

A. *Ciceronis de Mario sententia*

Gaius Marius, cum a spe consulatus longe abesset et iam septimum annum post praeturam iaceret,[1] neque petiturus umquam consulatum videretur,[2] Quintum Metellum cuius legatus erat, summum virum et civem, cum ab eo, imperatore suo, Romam missus esset, apud populum Romanum criminatus est bellum illum ducere;[3] si se consulem fecissent, brevi tempore aut vivum aut mortuum Iugurtham se in potestatem populi Romani redacturum.[4] Itaque factus est ille quidem consul,[5] sed a fide iustitiaque discessit, qui optimum et gravissimum civem, cuius legatus et a quo missus esset, in invidiam falso crimine adduxerit.[6]

B.   *Marii fortuna*

Et post Teutonicos victor Libycosque triumphos

exul limosa Marius caput abdidit ulva.[7]

Stagna avidi texere soli laxaeque paludes

depositum, Fortuna, tuum;[8] mox vincula ferri

exedere senem longusque in carcere paedor.

Consul et eversa felix moriturus in urbe,

poenas ante dabat scelerum.[9] Mors ipsa refugit

saepe virum. Servus nam primo caedis in actu

deriguit,[10] ferrumque manu torpente remisit.

Viderat immensam tenebroso in carcere lucem

terribilesque deos scelerum Mariumque futurum,[11]

audieratque pavens: "Fas haec contingere non est

colla tibi;[12] debet multas hic legibus aevi

ante suam mortes.[13] Vanum depone furorem."

Deinde ferus vir per pelagum delatus iniquum

hostilem in terram, vacuisque mapalibus actus[14]

nuda triumphati iacuit per regna Iugurthae[15]

et Poenos pressit cineres.[16] Solacia fati

Carthago Mariusque tulit.[17]

---

1. A. **cum ... abesset:** for the reasons why Marius was far from any hope of the consulship, see especially the end of the 1st par. of 21.   B. **septimum annum:** the acc. sing. of a noun and an ordinal numeral is often used instead of the acc. plur. of extent of time (see 10 n. 1A) to express time during which or within which; the abl. of time when may also be used, e.g. here *septimo anno.*   C. **iaceret** = "had remained in obscurity," lit. "was lying (idle)"; contrast its literal meaning in n. 14A below. For the translation of the Lat. imperf. by the Eng. pluperf. see 21 n. 4B. *Iacere* was regularly used of one who was not elected to the next office in the *cursus honorum* (see 31 pref. and compare 12 n. 10B) within the usual interval. At least three years had to elapse between the praetorship and the consulship, but Marius had been praetor in 115 and was not consul till 107.

2. **petiturus** = "(likely to) run for (lit. seek)"; for the use of *peto* with an office see 21 n. 14A. For the tone of likelihood or intention in the fut. act. part. compare 44 n. 5A (and 45 n. 13D).

3. A. **Metellum:** object of *criminatus est.* For Metellus' career and character see 21, especially n. 2E. Cicero here implies that he helped Marius in his quest for the consulship; for Sallust's account of his reluctance see the 2nd par. of 21.   B. **ab eo:** i.e. by Metellus.   C. **bellum ... ducere** = "that he (Metellus) was prolonging the war (against Jugurtha)." This meaning of *ducere* is common; compare 41 n. 2. The inf. is due to the indirect discourse implied, as regularly, in *criminatus est:* "He denounced

Metellus (charging that) etc." The wrongfulness of accusing one's general is brought out later; see n. 6B below.

4. A. **si ... redacturum (esse):** the implied indirect discourse continues, with "claiming that" understood. The direct statement would have had a fut. more vivid condition: *si fecerint ... redigam.* In quotation the fut. ind. of the apodosis becomes a fut. inf., and the fut. perf. ind. of the protasis becomes a pluperf. subj.   B. **fecissent**= "should elect," lit. "should have elected"; see 56 n. 1A (and 63 n. 1D); its subject is "the voters," easily supplied from *populum Romanum.*

5. **quidem ... sed:** for this contrast compare 14 n. 2C.

6. A. **qui ... adduxerit**="in that he brought"; the rel. clause of characteristic expresses cause. The pluperf. subj. would be normal here since the sequence is secondary, but the perf. subj. is used to stress the actual fact; compare its use in secondary sequence result clauses, for which see 16 n. 13F (and 31 n. 21A).   B. **cuius legatus (esset) et a quo missus esset:** these clauses are closely parallel to the similar clauses above, *cuius legatus erat* and *cum ... missus esset,* which are merely descriptive, and the ind. would normally be used here also; *missus esset* above is due to the *cum* temporal. The subj. is used, however, either by attraction, because the clauses are subordinate to the subj. in the rel. clause *qui ... adduxerit,* or to express concession, for which see 30 n. 10 (and 40 n. 19C). In the latter case, translate: "although he was his legate and although he had been sent by him (to Rome)." A legate was supposed to be loyal to his commander, as was a quaestor to his consul; this loyalty was a form of *pietas,* for which see 23 n. 13A (and 62 n. 11B), and compare in the 3rd par. of 28 the condemnation of Perpenna for killing his commander Sertorius. The fact, as Cicero claims in contrast to Sallust (see n. 3A above), that Metellus had sent Marius to Rome added to Marius' disloyalty.

7. A. **post Teutonicos ... Libycosque triumphos:** for Marius' victories over the Teutons and Cimbri and his triumph over Jugurtha, see 22.   B. **limosa ... ulva:** probably abl. of place where without a prep., as frequently in poetry, rather than abl. of means, although *abdo* may take an instrumental abl. for that by which one conceals, as well as an acc. of place to which, as in 24 n. 14C.   C. **Marius:** for a detailed account of his capture in the swamps near Minturnae and his subsequent escape to Carthage see 24.

8. A. **stagna ... paludes**="quicksand and spongy swamps covered etc."; lit. "pools of greedy soil and loose swamps."   B. **texere:** the ending *-ēre* (see 15 n. 10 and 57 n. 9C) shows that this is 3rd pers. plur. of the perf. act. ind. of *tego,* not the pres. act. inf. of *texo, texĕre;* compare *exēdēre* 2 verses below.   C. **depositum:** a technical term for any deposit or surety, as of money deposited either in a bank or for bail. Marius is here called Fortune's "deposit" against the civil war which she had in store for Rome.   D. **Fortuna:** Lucan frequently apostrophizes Fortune as the guiding and malevolent, or at least callous, force in human life.

9. A. **consul ... urbe:** *consul* and *felix* are predicate noms. after the fut. part. *moriturus,* which modifies the subject of *dabat.* For Marius' return to power and his death at the beginning of his 7th consulship see 25.   B. **ante:** adv.;="beforehand"; i.e. Marius was paying through exile for the crimes which he would commit after his return, though he would in the end die *felix.*

10. A. **servus nam:** *nam* is occasionally placed postpositively in poetry. For the episode of the slave refusing to kill Marius see the 3rd par. of 24, where a moralistic explanation is offered instead of Lucan's more dramatic portent of the supernatural light and warning voice.   B. **primo ... deriguit**="in the first gesture of slaying grew rigid"; i.e. as he made his first move toward Marius he stiffened with fright.   C. **deriguit:** probably perf. of a frequentative of which the present in *-esco* is not found; nor is the base pres. *derigeo;* simple *rigeo* exists only in the pres. system.

11. **terribilesque deos scelerum:** i.e. the Furies, Greek "chthonic" (=earth) deities who were believed to avenge certain crimes by haunting the perpetrator and driving him mad, as Marius was to become on his return to Rome; see 25.

12.   A. **fas:** for the connotations of *fas* and *nefas* see 8 n. 7B (and 42 n. 28C).   B. **colla:** i.e. of Marius; poetic plur. for sing.; compare *sceptra* in 54 n. 9B.   C. **tibi:** i.e. for the slave; dat. of reference after *fas est*, of which the subject is the inf. clause *haec contingere . . . colla* = "to touch this neck."

13.   A. **debet . . . mortes** = "he (Marius) owes many deaths to the laws of (i.e. that govern) time before (he owes) his own (death)."   B. **aevi:** probably = "of time" (in general); the phrase is roughly equivalent to "the fates." The reference is especially to the Marian massacres, for which see 25.

14.   A. **per . . . actus:** as punctuated, supply *est* with *delatus* to make it a main verb correlated by *-que* with *iacuit*. If so, in the second member *mapalibus* must be taken as abl. of place where with *iacuit*, and *actus* must carry over to the *per regna*; = "and he lay in empty huts, driven through the devastated (lit. naked) kingdom of defeated (lit. triumphed over) Jugurtha." It would be possible to punctuate with a comma after *vir*, omit that after *terram*, and place one after *actus*, and thus to regard *delatus* and *actus* as past parts. correlated by *-que*, modifying *vir* as subject of *iacuit*. It is, however, more awkward to take the abl. *mapabilibus* with *actus*, i.e. driven among huts, and the *per regna* with *iacuit*, i.e. he lay (here and there) through the kingdom.   B. **mapalibus:** possibly a Punic word, applied especially to African huts.

15.   A. **nuda . . . Iugurthae:** as suggested in n. 14A above, all except *iacuit* goes with *actus.* There is a doubly interlocking arrangement, of *mapalibus . . . iacuit* with *actus . . . per regna* and, in this verse, of the accs. and gens. The balance around a central verb makes this a "golden verse"; see 49 n. 3A.   B. **nuda:** the very Marius who now had to take refuge in huts had earlier stripped Jugurtha's kingdom bare.   C. **regna:** here = "kingdom"; contrast 49 n. 10B (and 54 n. 5D); with the poetic plur. compare n. 12B above.

16.   **Poenos pressit cineres:** Marius lay upon the ashes either of Carthage itself (see next verse, and, for the destruction of the city by Scipio Aemilianus, 16 n. 4) or of dead and cremated Carthaginians in general. Lucan's rhetorical exaggeration leads him to have Marius settle both on the ruins of Carthage and amid the huts of the adjacent kingdom, Numidia. For *Poenos* = "Punic" see 11 n. 14C (and 59 n. 18A).

17.   A. **solacia fati:** *solacia* is poetic plur.; compare nn. 12B and 15C above. With it *fati* may be subjective, appositional, or objective gen., and the phrase may accordingly be rendered in several ways: (a) "consolation given by fate," (b) "consolation of a (similar) fate," or (c) "consolation for fate" (i.e. for misfortune); of these the objective gen. (c) is perhaps the most probable, but the others cannot be entirely ruled out. B. **Carthago . . . tulit:** i.e. Carthage and Marius (each) offer (to the other); compare the end of 24. *Tulit* (= *obtulit*) is sing. because of the concept of each subject acting separately.

65

Lucius Cornelius Sulla first appears in Sallust's account of the war against Jugurtha (see 63) when he reported as quaestor to Marius as consul in 107. Sallust then pauses to assess the character of one who was the chief figure during the generation immediately preceding his own; see n. 5 below.

The following selection gives Sallust's appraisal of Sulla. Archaic spellings have again been kept; see 63 pref. and nn. 1B, 4A, 7B, and 9A.

De Sullae natura cultuque

Ceterum dum ea res geritur,[1] L. Sulla quaestor cum magno equitatu in castra Romanorum venit.[2] Sed quoniam nos tanti viri res admonuit,[3] idoneum visum est de natura cultuque eius paucis dicere.[4] Neque enim alio loco de Sullae rebus dicturi sumus[5] et L. Sisenna, optume et diligentissume omnium qui eas res dixere persecutus, parum mihi libero ore locutus videtur.[6]

Igitur Sulla gentis patriciae nobilis fuit,[7] familia prope iam extincta maiorum ignavia;[8] litteris Graecis et Latinis iuxta atque doctissume eruditus; animo ingenti; cupidus voluptatum sed gloriae cupidior;[9] otio luxurioso esse;[10] tamen ab negotiis numquam voluptas remorata, nisi quod de uxore potuit honestius consuli;[11] facundus, callidus, et amicitia facilis; ad simulanda negotia altitudo ingeni incredibilis;[12] multarum rerum ac maxume pecuniae largitor. Atque illi, felicissumo omnium ante civilem victoriam,[13] numquam super industriam fortuna fuit, multique dubitavere fortior an felicior esset.[14] Nam postea quae fecerit,[15] incertum habeo an pigeat magis disserere.[16]

Igitur Sulla, uti supra dictum est, postquam in Africam atque in castra Mari cum equitatu venit, rudis antea et ignarus belli, sollertissumus omnium in paucis tempestatibus factus est.[17] Ad hoc milites benigne appellare;[18] multis rogantibus, aliis per se ipse dare beneficia;[19] invitus accipere, sed ea properantius quam aes mutuum reddere;[20] ipse ab nullo repetere, magis id laborare ut illi quam plurumi deberent;[21] ioca atque seria cum humillumis agere;[22] in operibus, in agmine, atque ad vigilias multus adesse;[23] neque interim, quod prava ambitio solet, consulis aut cuiusquam boni famam laedere;[24] tantum modo neque consilio neque manu priorem alium pati,[25] plerosque antevenire. Quibus rebus et artibus brevi Mario militibusque carissumus factus est.[26]

    1. A. **ceterum:** often used by Sallust to mark a transition to a new thought and sometimes best rendered simply "now," sometimes adversatively "but." He may have been influenced in its use by one of his chief historical models, the *Origines* of Cato the Elder, for which see 13 pref.   B. **ea res:** i.e. the capture by the Romans of a Numidian fort on a hill, which Sallust has just described in detail.

    2. A. **geritur . . . vēnit:** since *dum* = "while" takes the pres. ind. (here *geritur*) even when the main verb is past (see 6 n. 8 and 53 n. 10B), *venit* is probably perf. rather than historical pres.   B. **magno equitatu** = "with a great force of cavalry"; the use of the abstract for the concrete, "many cavalrymen," is somewhat "ornate" and poetic; see 8 n. 9A (and 62 n. 16B).

    3. **tanti viri:** verbs of reminding take the acc. of the person reminded (here *nos*) and the gen. of that of which one is reminded; compare the gen. with verbs of forgetting in 46 n. 4A.

    4. A. **natura cultuque:** *natura* is that which is "inborn," here equivalent to *ingenium*; *cultus* is that which is acquired by "cultivation"; it is wider than Eng. "culture" and may include also clothing, self-adornment, general way of life, etc.; here perhaps "character and manner" would do.   B. **paucis:** i.e. *paucis verbis* (instrumental abl.), but often thus used alone adverbially, = "briefly." It is equivalent to *pauca dicere*.

    5. **neque . . . sumus:** Sallust composed a historical monograph, the *Historiae*, which began where Sisenna (see following note) left off, after the death of Sulla in 78, and ran apparently to 67. He probably wrote the *Historiae* after the monographs on Catiline and the Jugurthine War, so that the statement in the latter that he would not elsewhere discuss Sulla may indicate that he did not yet have the *Historiae* in mind. However, if he began these only with 78, he presumably included little or nothing on Sulla so that this statement would be reasonably true even if he were planning them already. The *Historiae* survive only in fragmentary citations and in collections of letters and speeches excerpted from all of Sallust in the later Empire as examples for rhetorical studies.

    6. A. **Sisenna:** a younger contemporary and supporter of Sulla who wrote, from the optimate point of view (see 18 n. 13A), a history of the period from the outbreak of the Social War in 90 (see 23) to the death of Sulla in 78; see prefs. to 26 and 28. An ancient historian who wished to deal with only a portion of history often began where some predecessor had left off; Sisenna may have continued a history by a certain Sempronius Asellio, and Sallust continued Sisenna's.   B. **parum . . . ore:** abl. of manner; = "with mouth too little free"; i.e. too guardedly. Sallust, like other liberal advocates of "free speech," regarded a conservative position as really dictated by fear, in this case perhaps of Sulla himself, though presumably Sisenna wrote after the dictator's death; hence Sallust possibly felt that Sisenna feared to offend the *nobiles*; see 18 pref. Tacitus probably had more reason for his criticism of those who wrote under the Julio–Claudian emperors; see 48 n. 7.

    7. A. **igitur:** for its opening position usually in Sallust see 17 n. 1A (and 63 n. 17A). Throughout the following description Sallust characteristically varies his construction, often abruptly; compare 17 n. 4A (and 21 n. 5B).   B. **gentis patriciae:** gen. of origin or

source, used with *fuit* instead of the more usual abl. of source with some such verb as *natus* or *genitus est*, for which see 5 n. 2A (and 33 n. 1A).   C. **nobilis:** Suetonius describes Caesar in the 1st sentence of 33 as *nobilissima Iuliorum genitus familia* and Velleius II 17 says of Sulla *natus familia nobili*. These phrases suggest that *nobilis* is gen. with *gentis*; if so, since the *Cornelii Sullae* were, as Sallust goes on to say, far from being "consular" (i.e. noble; see 18 pref. and 36 n. 6B), the *nobilis gens* would be that of the *Cornelii* in general, other branches of which, like the *Cornelii Scipiones* (see the genealogical charts following 15), had long had consuls in successive generations and were thoroughly "noble." However, two gen. sing. adjs., *patriciae* and *nobilis*, seem heavy, if not redundant, with *gentis* and, if so, *nobilis* may be nom. sing. with Sulla and used loosely, since, as just noted, his family was not technically "noble."

8. A. **familia:** if *gens* means, as suggested in the preceding note, all the *Cornelii*, *familia* is here distinguished as the Sullan branch thereof; if, on the contrary, *gens* means only the *Sullae*, then *familia* is simply used for variety; in either case it means the branch as against the *gens*, contrary to Suetonius' use in 33 n. 1B. It is abl. of source, for variation from the gen. just before; see n. 7B above. The difference might be rendered: "Sulla was (a member) of ... from a branch ..."   B. **extincta:** i.e. "reduced to obscurity" rather than "wiped out."   C. **ignavia:** here = "slothfulness," rather than "cowardice"; for the charge compare Marius' remarks about the *nobiles* in the 2nd par. of 63 and Cicero's remarks in the 1st par. of 67.

9. A. **litteris ... cupidior:** Sallust throws out the elements of his description without connectives (in asyndeton; see 4 n. 5B and 63 n. 8B) and with abrupt shifts of construction (see n. 7A above); here a part. used adjectivally, an abl. of description, and two forms of the adj. *cupidus.*   B. **iuxta:** here = "equally"; an adv. often used after a pair of items.

10. **otio luxurioso esse** = "(he) was (a man of) extravagant leisure"; i.e. in his leisure he devoted himself to expensive and luxurious living. Sallust shifts abruptly to a historical inf. (see 17 n. 16A and 21 n. 25) without an expressed subject and with an abl. of description in the predicate.

11. A. **tamen ... remorata:** another abrupt shift; *eum*, i.e. Sulla, must be understood as object of *remorata* (*est*); compare 21 n. 18.   B. **nisi ... consuli** = "except that he might have behaved more properly about his wife." The construction shifts to an impersonal pres. pass. inf. *consuli* after *potest* with *ab eo* understood; lit. "it could have been thought about more honorably (by him)."   C. **consuli:** this verb often connotes "decide on a line of action." Sallust probably refers to Sulla's conduct toward his fourth wife Caecilia Metella, a niece of Metellus Numidicus (see 21 n. 2E and 64 n. 3A), and therefore representing a strong political connection with the optimate nobles. Sulla married her in 88, only a few days after divorcing his third wife. Though she appears to have commanded his affection and respect, when she fell sick at the time of his triumph over Mithridates in 81, he divorced her so as not to have the ceremonies polluted by her death. Nevertheless he gave her a magnificent funeral. Shortly thereafter he married his fifth, and last, wife Valeria, sister of Cicero's rival, the orator Hortensius.

12. **altitudo ingeni incredibilis** = "an unbelievable depth of ingenuity"; i.e. he was very secretive.

13. **felicissumo ... victoriam:** for the partitive gen. with the superlative compare 11 n. 11A (and 33 n. 2B) and *sollertissumus omnium* below. Sulla set great store by his luck as well as by his industry and intelligence, as shown by his adoption of the title *Felix*, for which see the 1st sentence of the last par. of 26. With the thought that his conduct after his victory sullied his felicity compare the end of 66.

14. **dubitavere:** i.e. "have hesitated to decide"; for *dubito* + an inf. expressed or (as here) implied see 57 n. 8A. Here the idea of deciding is followed by a double indirect question depending on some such inf. as *statuere*; the 1st interrogative conjunction *utrum* is, as often, omitted; see 63 n. 9B (and compare n. 16A below).

15. **postea quae fecerit:** as often (see 21 n. 20c and 44 n. 11d), the antecedent of this rel. clause (*ea*) is not expressed; here also the adv. is placed outside the clause; the clause itself is object of *disserere* at the end of the sentence. The reference is to Sulla's proscriptions, for which see 26, 27 B, and 66.

16. A. **incertum habeo:** a regular idiom for "I regard it as uncertain" and followed by an indirect question which in this case implies through *magis* an alternative (compare n. 14 above); i.e. "whether it is more shameful to discuss what he did thereafter (than to keep silent about it)." B. **disserere:** the inf. is used absolutely; the Eng. idiom requires some such subject as "for one." The inf. is often regarded as complementary after an impersonal, since if the cause of the feeling is a noun, it is in the gen. and the person affected in the acc.; see 22 n. 12b (and 63 n. 12b). However, the inf., or a clause, may really be the subject, here of *pigeat*, since these verbs may have a neuter pronoun or even a noun as subject.

17. **in paucis tempestatibus** = *brevi tempore*; compare n. 26c below. For *tempestas* = *tempus* see 48 n. 22 (and compare 22 n. 7).

18. A. **ad hoc** = "in addition to this," "besides"; contrast the common Eng. use, e.g. "an *ad hoc* committee" = a committee for this (specific purpose only). B. **appellare:** this and the following infs. are historical, as often in Sallust; see n. 10 above.

19. A. **multis rogantibus:** dat. after *dare*, as is *aliis*, placed after it without connective (in asyndeton; see 4 n. 5b and 63 n. 8b). B. **per se ipse** = "on his own initiative"; i.e. without being asked.

20. A. **sed ea . . . reddere** = "but (if he did accept benefits) he gave them back even more quickly (than he repaid) a loan." B. **mutuum:** from *mutare*; = "exchanged, mutual, reciprocal"; hence "borrowed."

21. A. **ipse . . . deberent** = "he himself asked (loans) back from nobody (but) rather worked (on) this, that as many (persons) as possible should owe (money) to him"; *id* is often thus used to anticipate an objective clause, here of purposes; compare *illud* anticipating a *quin* clause in 32 n. 7a. B. **laborare:** since this verb is intrans., the *id* taken up by the *ut* clause is an acc. of the inner object or cognate acc. C. **quam:** with superlative = "as . . . as possible"; see 33 n. 8c.

22. **ioca . . . agere** = "he exchanged jokes and serious remarks with (even) the humblest (soldiers)."

23. A. **ad vigilias** = "for sentry duties"; contrast 9 n. 19b. The change from the preceding *in* + abl. may be simply by variation but suggests "in volunteering for" or "in going on guard." B. **multus adesse:** i.e. "he was always present" or, in American slang, "on the job"; for this meaning of *multus* compare 63 n. 3b.

24. **neque . . . laedere:** intended as a contrast to Marius' belittlement of the consul Metellus under whom he served as legate; see the end of 21 and 64 A, especially n. 6b. Here, perhaps, Sallust has succumbed to the Ciceronian implication of *bonus*; see 18 n. 5c (and 20 n. 5b).

25. **neque consilio neque manu** = "neither in planning nor in doing"; *consilio* means "in giving advice," i.e. on the commander's staff; *manu* means "in action"; see 62 n. 15b. The abls. are probably of specification, as regularly with expressions of superiority; compare 18 n. 3a.

26. A. **quibus rebus et artibus** = "and by these actions and practices"; for the rel. pronoun used as a connective see 4 n. 4a (and 47 n. 13a). B. **artibus:** pejorative, = "tricks" or, simply, "qualities," as in 16 n. 11a. C. **brevi:** i.e. *brevi tempore* (abl. of time within which), but used alone adverbially; see 9 n. 6b, and compare n. 17 above. For the use of the adj. alone, compare n. 4b above.

66

The following verses are selected from a long and vivid description by Lucan of the proscriptions of Sulla, which left a deep impression of horror on the minds of succeeding generations of Romans; see especially 27 pref. The subject offered great scope to Lucan's considerable powers of lurid rhetorical description, by which his poem on the Civil War (see 64 pref.) is often characterized.

Proscriptio Sullana

Sulla quoque immensis accessit cladibus ultor.[1]
Ille quod exiguum restabat sanguinis urbi
hausit;[2] dumque nimis iam putria membra recidit,
excessit medicina modum.[3] Periere nocentes,
sed cum iam soli possent superesse nocentes.[4]
Tunc data libertas odiis, resolutaque legum
frenis ira ruit.[5] Non uni cuncta dabantur,[6]
sed fecit sibi quisque nefas;[7] semel omnia victor
iusserat. Infandum domini per viscera ferrum
exegit famulus;[8] nati maduere paterno
sanguine; certatum est, cui cervix caesa parentis
cederet;[9] in fratrum ceciderunt praemia fratres.[10]
Colla ducum pilo trepidam gestata per urbem
et medio congesta Foro;[11] cognoscitur illic
quidquid ubique iacet.[12] Densi vix agmina volgi
inter et exsangues immissa morte catervas
victores movere manus.[13] Vix caede peracta
procumbunt, dubiaque labant cervice.[14] Sed illos
magna premit strages,[15] peraguntque cadavera partem
caedis;[16] viva graves elidunt corpora trunci.
Intrepidus tanti sedit securus ab alto
spectator sceleris;[17] miseri tot milia volgi
non timuit iussisse mori. Congesta recepit

omnia Tyrrhenus Sullana cadavera gurges;[18]

in fluvium primi cecidere, in corpora summi.[19]

Praecipites haesere rates;[20] et strage cruenta

interruptus aquae fluxit prior amnis in aequor,

ad molem stetit unda sequens.[21] Iam sanguinis alti

vis sibi fecit iter, campumque effusa per omnem

praecipitique ruens Tiberina in flumina rivo

haerentes adiuvit aquas.[22] Nec iam alveus amnem

nec retinent ripae; redditque cadavera campo.[23]

Tandem Tyrrhenas vix eluctatus in undas

sanguine caeruleum torrenti dividit aequor.[24]

Hisne salus rerum, felix his Sulla vocari,

his meruit tumulum medio sibi tollere Campo?[25]

1. A. **Sulla quoque etc.**: in the immediately preceding verses, Lucan has described the many lives lost in the Marian massacres and the battles after Sulla's return from Asia; see 25–26. B. **immensis ... cladibus:** from its position, dat. after *accessit* but also to be taken with *ultor*; = "avenger for (i.e. of) the (previous) immense slaughters." C. **accessit:** for meaning see 34 n. 2A and for the dat. see 62 n. 15C.

2. A. **quod exiguum ... sanguinis:** as often, the antecedent, *exiguum sanguinis*, is placed within the rel. clause; see 12 n. 8B. B. **sanguinis:** partitive gen. in an extension of the common use with indefinite neut. pronouns or adjs.; see 6 n. 6 (and 11 n. 14A).

3. A. **dumque ... recidit:** for the pres. ind. with *dum* see 6 n. 8 (and 65 n. 2A). Sulla is compared to a surgeon who cuts away gangrenous flesh too extensively (*nimis*). B. **mĕdĭcĭnă:** the scansion shows that this is nom. rather than abl., i.e. "(his) remedy exceeds measure," not "Sulla by his medicine exceeds measure"; such abrupt changes of subject are common in rhetorical Lat., as in that of Sallust; see especially 65 nn. 7A and 9A–11B.

4. **sed cum ... nocentes** = "but (at a time) when only the guilty could still be surviving"; i.e. all those still alive must have been guilty, because not only the guilty opponents (Marians) mentioned in the preceding verse but also the innocent had already perished or become involved in the guilt of others.

5. A. **resolutaque ... ruit:** "and hatred (lit. anger), freed from the restraints (lit. bridle) of the laws, rushed (headlong)." B. **frenis:** abl. of separation (not means) after a verb meaning "to free from"; *frena* is usually plur. and includes the bit, bridle, and reins. C. **ruit:** presumably perf. since the other verbs nearby are in past tenses. Lucan means that those who indulged personal hatreds by getting their enemies proscribed did so with legal impunity.

6. **non ... dabantur** = "not all (crimes) were given to (only) one (person)"; Lucan means that not all crimes were committed for the benefit only of Sulla, since he goes on to say that each person did evil for his own sake but sheltered his act under the excuse that the victor had once and for all ordered everything, no matter who committed it.

7. **nefas ... infandum** (= *nefandum*): these words have a strongly religious connotation of impiety; see 8 n. 7B and compare *fas* in 42 n. 28C (and 64 n. 12A).

8. **famulus** = "a member of the household" (*familia*; compare 44 n. 9A and contrast 65 n. 8A), usually either a servant or a slave, as here with *domini*. The murder of a master by slaves was regarded as a particularly heinous and impious crime, like parricide and fratricide in the following verses.

9. **certatum ... cederet:** i.e. "children disputed which of them should commit parricide and receive the reward," lit. "it was disputed to whom the severed neck of a parent should fall"; the rel. clause is the subject of *certatum est*, and *cederet* is intrans.

10. A. **in ... fratres** = "brothers fell for the profit of brothers"; for *in* + the acc. to express purpose see 5 n. 13c (and 7 n. 8B).   B. **fratrum:** possessive gen. with *praemia*, and the phrase probably means that if a man committed fratricide, he got a reward from Sulla, not that the murder of a brother would profit him by securing an inheritance or the like.

11. A. **colla ... Foro:** during the bitterness of the proscriptions the heads of notable men were sometimes paraded through the city on spears and then displayed in the Forum; see 24 n. 12A (and 44 n. 15).   B. **ducum:** here = "of leading men" rather than "of generals."   C. **pilo:** technically a javelin of the legionary, but about half of a *pilum* was soft iron so that when it pierced an enemy it would bend and could not be extracted and thrown back; therefore the word is probably used loosely here instead of *hasta*, a regular spear with a solid shaft.

12. A. **quidquid ... iacet:** indefinite rel. clause as subject of *cognoscitur*; Lucan means that whatever (body) lay anywhere else was recognizable only from the head shown in the Forum.   B. **illic:** adv.; = "there," see 55 n. 2A.

13. A. **densi ... catervas:** the prepositional phrase is unusually broken in its word order; = *inter agmina densi volgi et exsangues ... catervas. Volgi = vulgi*; the manuscripts and modern editions of Lucan give the older spelling *vo-* for words in *vu-*; compare 63 n. 7B.   B. **vix:** placed after *densi*, which gives the reason for the difficulty; it goes with *movere* 2 verses below.   C. **immisa morte:** abl. of cause giving the reason for *exsangues* = "lifeless," i.e. crowds lifeless because death had been let loose (among them). With this metaphor from hunting compare Shakespeare *Julius Caesar* III 1: "Cry havoc, and let slip the dogs of war!"   D. **vix ... victores movere manus** = "the victors could scarcely move their hands"; i.e. wield their weapons for further slaughter amid the piles of those already dead.

14. A. **vix ... procumbunt** = "when the slaughter is finished, they (i.e. people, or their corpses) scarcely fall down"; i.e. they are kept standing by the piles of previous corpses.   B. **dubiaque labant cervice** = "and they (still referring to the dying) totter with unsteady necks." *Dubius* and *labare* are here literal, though both are often used figuratively; *labare* is from the same root as the dep. *labor, labi, lapsus*.

15. **illos** = "those (others)," i.e. the still living; it is not clear whether this refers to people unwounded or people who fell from a wound but might have survived had they not been crushed beneath further corpses.

16. **peragunt ... caedis** = "and corpses perform a share of the slaughter"; explained by the next statement that heavy trunks (i.e. corpses) crush living bodies. In these 2 verses, the same statement is made in three different forms, a characteristic rhetorical overelaboration.

17. A. **intrepidus etc.:** Sulla is the callous spectator of the deaths he had ordered; compare the similar episode in 27 C.   B. **ab alto spectator** = "an onlooker from (his) lofty (seat)."

18. **Tyrrhēnus Sullāna ... gurges:** the Tiber, which divided Etruria and Latium and is often modified by some adj. meaning "Etruscan," as here by *Tyrrhenus*, for which see 49 n. 6B. Bodies of criminals were often thrown into the Tiber to deprive them of proper burial and hence their souls of admission to the lower world; compare the 2nd par. of 19 for this disposition of the corpses of the Gracchi.

19. **primi ... summi** = "the first ... the last"; though the reference is to *cadavera*, the masc. adjs. must stand for the people themselves.

20. **praecipites ... rates:** i.e. boats normally carried swiftly by the current become grounded on the corpses. This and the following 7 verses afford an example of Lucan's rhetorical exaggeration in describing how the piles of bodies blocked the river's flow.

21. A. **et strage ... unda sequens:** i.e. "the stream is broken in two by the pile of bloody corpses, and the water below (*prior amnis*) continues to the sea while that above (*unda sequens*) is stopped at the dam (*molem*) formed by the corpses."   B. **aequor:** originally = "a flat surface," from *aequus*; later, as here, specialized for the flat surface of the sea.

22. A. **iam ... aquas** = "then the force of the deep (stream of) blood made a course for itself, and, (first) spread through all the plain and (then) rushing with swift flood into the Tiber's river, it helped the blocked waters."   B. **iam:** indicates the next stage; i.e. "already" in the sense of "then."   C. **-que ... -que:** as translated above, these are not correlative; the first connects the main verbs *fecit* and *adiuvit* while the second joins the two parts. *effusa* and *ruens*, which modify the subject (still *vis*) of *adiuvit*. D. **campum:** probably the Campus Martius; see 50 pref.   E. **Tiberina ... flumina:** poetic plur.; compare 54 n. 9B (and 64 n. 17A). For the short first *-i-* in *Tiberina* compare 49 n. 2B.   F. **haerentes:** lit. = "hesitating," i.e. because blocked by bodies; see n. 21A above. The added force of the stream of blood helped the Tiber break through this obstruction; see following notes.

23. A. **nec iam ... campo:** i.e. "its bed and banks no longer keep in the Tiber, which, raised to flood level by the blood, washes the corpses back onto the plain."   B. **amnem:** becomes subject of *reddit*, and of *dividit* 2 verses below; compare n. 3B above.

24. A. **tandem ... aequor:** i.e. "the river, finally and with difficulty breaking through the dam of corpses to the sea, flows out into its clear surface (*caeruleum ... dividit aequor*) with a torrent of blood."   B. **sanguine ... aequor:** the nouns and adjs. are arranged in interlocking and chiasmic (see 17 n. 2 and 53 n. 5) order.   C. **caeruleum** = "sky-blue"; an adj. from *caelum*. For the change from *-l-* to *-r-* before a following *-l-* compare *Parilia* in 51 n. 12B.

25. A. **hisne ... meruit** = "(was it) by (or, because of) these (actions that) Sulla deserved"; the abl. of means (cause) *his* is repeated for emphasis. With the thought compare 65 n. 13.   B. **salus rerum, felix:** there is no evidence that Sulla was called the "safety (i.e. savior) of the state" except in popular parlance; for *rerum* = *rerum publicarum* compare 61 n. 13C. *Felix*, however, did become an official epithet; see the last par. of 26 (and 65 n. 13).   C. **medio ... Campo:** On his death in 78 (see 26 pref.), Sulla was given a splendid funeral at public expense and the honor, reserved for distinguished persons, of a tomb in the Campus Martius, for which see 50 pref. This verse suggests that Sulla erected his own tomb before his death, as did many Romans including Augustus, for whom see 47 pref.

67

In 70 Cicero was retained by the Sicilians to prosecute before the *quaestio de rebus repetundis* (see 12 n. 14A) Gaius Verres (see 28 pref.), who had been their governor as propraetor from 73–71 with unusual harshness and corruption. Verres enjoyed full support from the optimates, and his defense was undertaken by the then leader of the Roman bar, Q. Hortensius. Cicero, who had been a popular quaestor in western Sicily in 75 (see 31), was already known as a rising pleader with sympathy for the equestrians (see 17 pref.), whose financial interests in Sicily had been interfered with by Verres. Though Cicero risked loss of his case before a senatorial jury and opposition from the optimates for his political future (he was campaigning at the time for the aedileship), he delivered as an opening speech so devastating a review of Verres' iniquities that Verres availed himself of the opportunity to go into exile lest he be utterly ruined and he was condemned to a heavy fine in absence. Cicero was elected aedile for 69, and the senate lost control of the courts by the *lex Aurelia*; see 28 pref.

After his successful prosecution of Verres, Cicero displaced Hortensius as leader of the Roman bar and became a prominent "liberal." He was not, however, a *popularis*, aiming to gain personal power by the support of the urban mob; see prefs. to 28–30. Rather, from background and inclination (see 31 pref.), he was a liberal, favorable to the equestrians and sympathetic toward the Italians and provincials; see 32 pref. Though he is often charged with having become more conservative after his consulship in 63 admitted him to the highest group in the senate (see 32 pref.), this is somewhat unfair. The situation in Rome changed rapidly between 70 and 63, and while Cicero continued to condemn the extreme and selfish optimate position (compare 41 n. 1B), by 63 he felt that the only hope of resisting what he regarded as the demagogic, subversive, and tyrannical programs of such *populares* as Catiline, Clodius, and later Caesar lay in uniting men of property and good sense in a *concordia ordinum* of senators and equestrians (see 32 n. 9A) supported by all men of sound opinion, the *boni* (see 18 n. 5C and 35 n. 14B), and directed by the *auctoritas* of the senate which, in turn, would be guided by its outstanding members or *principes*; see 19 n. 3C and selection 76.

The following selection shows why in 70 Cicero had felt that the only way for him to achieve political success was to oppose the optimate monopoly of high office. It comes from the last of five speeches which Cicero had prepared against Verres but which, in consequence of the success of his first summary of the evidence and Verres' departure into exile, he did not deliver but simply published later. These five, together known as the second pleading or *actio secunda in Verrem*, present by categories the detailed evidence against Verres from the beginning of his public career. The last, *de Suppliciis*, exposes the illegal punishments that he inflicted while governor of Sicily in 73–71. Near the end of the speech, Cicero writes as if addressing Verres' optimate supporters in court and explains why he undertook a case which involved him in enmity with so many powerful men. He speaks with bitterness of the obstacles which confronted a politically ambitious *novus homo* like himself.

Cicero Verrem accusans inimicitias optimatium suscipit

Quaeret aliquis fortasse: "Tantumne igitur laborem, tantas inimicitias tot hominum suscepturus es?"[1] Non studio quidem hercule ullo neque voluntate;[2] sed non idem licet mihi quod iis qui nobili genere nati sunt,[3] quibus omnia populi Romani beneficia dormientibus deferuntur;[4] longe alia mihi lege in hac civitate et condicione vivendum est.[5] Venit mihi in mentem M. Catonis, hominis sapientissimi et vigilantissimi;[6] qui cum se virtute, non genere, populo Romano commendari putaret, cum ipse sui generis initium ac nominis ab se gigni et propagari vellet,[7] hominum potentissimorum suscepit inimicitias,[8] et maximis laboribus suis usque ad summam senectutem summa cum gloria vixit. Postea Q. Pompeius, humili atque obscuro loco natus,[9] nonne plurimis inimicitiis maximisque suis periculis ac laboribus amplissimos honores est adeptus? Modo C. Fimbriam, C. Marium, C. Coelium vidimus non mediocribus inimicitiis ac laboribus contendere,[10] ut ad istos honores pervenirent ad quos vos per ludum et per neglegentiam pervenistis.[11] Haec eadem est nostrae rationis regio et via;[12] horum nos hominum sectam atque instituta persequimur.[13]

Videmus[14] quanta sit in invidia quantoque in odio apud quosdam nobiles homines novorum hominum virtus et industria;[15] si tantulum oculos deiecerimus, praesto esse insidias; si ullum locum aperuerimus suspicioni aut crimini, accipiendum statim vulnus esse.[16] Semper nobis vigilandum, semper laborandum videmus. Inimicitiae sunt, subeantur;[17] labor, suscipiatur. Etenim tacitae magis et occultae inimicitiae timendae sunt quam indictae atque apertae.[18] Hominum nobilium non fere quisquam nostrae industriae favet;[19] nullis nostris officiis benivolentiam illorum adlicere possumus;[20] quasi natura et genere diiuncti sint, ita dissident a nobis animo ac voluntate.[21] Quare quid habent eorum inimicitiae periculi,[22] quorum animos iam ante habueris inimicos et invidos quam ullas inimicitias susceperis?[23]

1.   A. **quaeret aliquis fortasse** = "perhaps someone will ask"; the fut. is used rather than a deliberative (or potential) subj.   B. **inimicitias:** connotes political hostility, as below in connection with Cato; see 60 n. 19 (and compare 29 n. 2). The passage contains many paired words or phrases of similar import; for such "pleonasm" (fullness of expression) in Cicero see 30 n. 3A (and 36 nn. 1A and 3C).

2.   **hercule:** a common ejaculation, often preceded by *me*; compare 31 n. 4.

3.   **nobili genere:** abl. of source; see 5 n. 2A (and 65 n. 8A).

4.   A. **quibus ... deferuntur:** for a similar criticism of the way in which the nobility was elected almost automatically, see Sallust in connection with Marius in sel. 21, especially n. 11B; Cicero repeats the theme below in the clause *quos ... pervenistis*. B. **omnia ... beneficia:** refers particularly to public office, as often.   C. **deferuntur:** *defero* is often used of conferring a public office; as in Cicero's hope that the Roman people would elect him to further office after his successful quaestorship (31 n. 8C), and in Antony's attempt to bestow *regnum* on Caesar at the *Lupercalia*; see 42 n. 27B.

5.   **longe alia ... condicione:** *condicio* may denote either a clause (or provision), particularly of a will but also of any contractual document (compare 9 n. 18 and 38 n. 7A), or a person's legal or social standing. Most editors take it here in the first sense and connect it with *lege* = "by a far different law and provision" or, taking *lex* as = "contract" and regarding the two as a hendiadys (see 13 n. 11A and 52 n. 4A), "by a far different contractual provision." If this is what Cicero meant, he has placed *in hac civitate* within the first member of the pair rather than before or after the whole. If, however, *condicio* here denotes "status," Cicero may have said: "by a far different law (or, contract) in this state and (in my) status," as if he were a member of a community in which his status was defined on different terms from those applying to the *nobiles*.

6.   **venit ... Catonis:** *venit in mentem* is used impersonally as a verb of remembering followed by a gen. (compare 65 n. 3) instead of having *Cato* as subj. This is Cato the Elder, for whom see 13 and 14.

7.   A. **qui** = *et is*; see 4 n. 4A (and 65 n. 26A). It serves both as subject of the later main ind. verbs *suscepit* and *vixit* and also as subject of the verbs in the two *cum* clauses, *putaret* and *vellet*.   B. **cum ... putaret, cum ... vellet:** of these two clauses, the first seems to be temporal, "when he thought," and the second causal dependent on it, "because he wishes"; both, however, may be causal: "since he thought," "because he wished." But to convey the latter meaning Cicero, unlike Sallust, would probably have connected them with a coordinating "and" rather than subordinating the second to the first or having them coordinate without a connective. Though the manuscripts show no variants here, it is possible that an original *et* was dropped in copying before the second *cum*, under the influence of the immediately preceding verbal ending *-et*.

8.   **hominum potentissimorum:** refers especially to the Scipios; see prefs. to 12 and 13.

9.   A. **Pompeius:** a *novus homo* who became consul in 141 and censor in 131; he was a friend of Scipio Aemilianus and opposed Tiberius Gracchus. He was either father or grandfather of the Q. Pompeius Rufus who was the optimate colleague of Sulla in the consulship of 88 (see 23 n. 16) and father of Caesar's second wife Pompeia, for whom see 36 n. 7B.   B. **loco:** abl. of place where without a prep.; contrast n. 3 above and compare 43 n. 17B.

10.   A. **Fimbriam:** consul in 104 with Marius (see 22 pref.) and father of the notorious Fimbria, a violent Marian who, serving as legate under Flaccus, consul of 87, against Mithridates, murdered his commander in 86 and then on Sulla's arrival was deserted by his troops and committed suicide in 85.   B. **Marium:** the outstanding *novus homo* between Cato the Elder and Cicero; see 21, 63, 64.   C. **Coelium:** though the manuscripts read *Caelium*, this is undoubtedly C. Coelius Caldus, consul in 94, whom Cicero mentions elsewhere (*de Or.* I 117) as a successful *novus homo*.

11.   **ad quos ... pervenistis** = "which you have reached (lit. to which you have come) as if in carefree sport"; with the hendiadys of "through sport and through negligence"

compare 34 n. 3; for the almost instrumental use of *per* see 5 n. 16A (and 47 n. 13E); for the thought compare n. 4A above. Though Cicero did not deliver this speech, he composed it as if he were addressing in court Verres' optimate supporters, and perhaps also the senatorial members of the jury; see pref.

12. **haec . . . via** = "this same (course) is the area and route of my plan"; i.e. I have directed my life on the pattern of the men just enumerated. *Haec eadem* is fem. sing. looking forward to agree with its nearest predicate appositive (*regio*), but it refers back to the actions just described; compare 63 n. 14A. Cicero apparently had a deliberate program for achieving his political ambitions quite early; compare the last par. of 31 and the verses at the end of 35 B.

13. A. **sectam atque instituta** = "school and principles" or "precedents"; a philosophical (or legal) phrase used here of politics.   B. **secta**: originally = "path" or "way of life," and therefore suggests the immediately preceding *regio et via*. Cicero does not mean that he followed the men mentioned as demagogues, since at least Cato the Elder and Rufus had been conservatives, but as "new men" who had discovered the road to high office and political success.

14. **videmus etc.**: as punctuated in the text with a period after *vulnus esse*, the opening *videmus* is followed first by an indirect question, *quanta . . . industria*, and then by two conditions in indirect statement. The protases of the two conditions are fut. more vivid, in which the fut. perfs. representing completed action in fut. time are attracted (without change of spelling) into the perf. subjs. *deiecerimus* and *aperuerimus*; compare 64 n. 4. The first apodosis, *praesto esse*, is pres. inf. representing in direct discourse a vivid pres. ind. in place of a fut.; compare 31 n. 3. The second apodosis, *accipiendum . . . vulnus esse*, is a 2nd (pass.) periphrastic inf. with an acc. subject; the idea of necessity connotes futurity. In the next sentence, the second *videmus* takes in indirect statement two impersonal 2nd (pass.) periphrastic infs. with which *esse* is understood with the gerundives and *nobis* is dat. of reference (agent); see 21 n. 15C (and 62 n. 16B). However, it would be equally possible to stop the 1st sentence after *industria* and connect the following clauses with the final *videmus*. In this case, the conditions may still be in indirect statement, or the *si* clauses may be fut. perf. ind. protases in mixed conditions for which the second pres. ind. *videmus* provides the apodosis in conjunction with the first two inf. clauses, and then is independent with the last two infs. It is probable that Cicero conceived of all the intervening clauses as in indirect discourse dependent on *videmus*, which he simply repeated at the end to emphasize this.

15. **sit**: the subject is postponed to the end of the clause and doubled: *virtus et industria*; the sing. verb may be justified by regarding the subjects as a hendiadys (see nn. 5 and 11 above) for one idea or by assuming that Cicero "forgot" his sing. verb by the time that he reached them.

16. A. **si . . . deiecerimus** = "if we shall have turned our eyes ever so little aside (from our path)." Cicero means that he must keep a sharp watch for pitfalls and not give any opening for the "wounds" of suspicion or accusation. For *crimen* compare 46 n. 13 and for the figurative use of *vulnus* compare 44 n. 20B.   B. **tantulum**: Cicero is fond of such emotional diminutives; compare *gloriola* in 37 n. 27B.

17. **inimicitiae sunt**: as in n. 1B above. The direct statement in the ind. followed directly without connective by the hortatory subj. is much more vivid than would be a condition; as is the following *labor* without even *est* expressed.

18. **etenim . . . apertae**: i.e. it is better to act boldly and incur open hostility than to try to please those who will in any case be secretly hostile. The thought is developed in the following sentences.

19. **non fere quisquam** = "almost no one," i.e. scarcely anyone; for *quisquam* in universally negative statements see 61 n. 21C (and 62 n. 9B). Lat., unlike Eng., frequently separates the negative from the indefinite, as here by *fere*.

20.   **officiis:** a word of wide connotation, covering social, political, and other obligations; see 43 n. 4. Cicero later wrote a treatise *de Officiis*; see 64 pref.

21.   **quasi . . . sint:** in Lat. comparative protases take the pres. or perf. subj. (but contrast 82 n. 22) as if they were part of a fut. less vivid condition in which the apodosis is implied in the comparative particle or phrase, as here in *quasi* (=*quam si*); i.e. Lat. understood: "as (they would) if they should be distinct from us . . . so do they differ" where Eng. uses a contrary to fact protasis: "as if they were distinct . . . they differ." The abls. of specification (or means) followed by the verb in this protasis are balanced in chiasmus (see 17 n. 2 and 66 n. 24B) by the verb and abls. of specification (or loc.) in the main statement.

22.   **quid . . . periculi** = "what (of) danger"; the neut. sing. of the interrog. pronoun, like other neut. pronouns and adjs. (see 6 n. 6 and 66 n. 2B), may take a partitive gen.

23.   A. **animos:** for the meaning see 32 n. 11C (and compare 19 n. 3B).   B. **habueris . . . susceperis:** both are perf. subjs.; *habueris* is in a rel. clause of characteristic which means "the (open) hostility of the sort of people whose feelings you have (found to be) already hostile."   C. **susceperis:** "anticipatory" subj. with *ante . . . quam*; see 12 n. 1.

68

In the crowded years after Sulla's death (see 28 pref.), Rome's dominant foreign problem was a renewed attack by Mithridates; see 24 pref. After his defeat by Sulla in 84 (see 26 pref.), Mithridates easily repelled a Roman attack in 81 so that his second onslaught, launched in 74 when Rome annexed Bithynia (see n. 15A below), is known as the Third Mithridatic War. Rome's first major commander was the optimate Lucius Licinius Lucullus, born *ca.* 117 into a noble plebeian family, able quaestor in charge of Sulla's fleet in Asia in 87, praetor in 78, and consul in 74. The command against Mithridates was assigned to him by the senate late in 74 (see n. 2c below) and was made "extraordinary" both in the number of provinces subjected to him and in being limited in time only by the prospective defeat of the enemy. Initially he secured marked successes and drove Mithridates to take refuge with his son-in-law Tigranes, king of Armenia. Lucullus led his troops in pursuit, but in 67 was forced by a mutiny to withdraw and was recalled to Rome; see n. 22B below. Lucullus was opposed in part by the *populares* but mainly by the *equites*, whose rapacity in Asia he had restricted. He was not granted a triumph until 63 and after his return withdrew entirely from public affairs to devote himself to a life of ease in gardens outside of Rome later famous for their elegance, where he reputedly gave dinners so rich that they became proverbial as "Lucullan feasts."

In the following year, 66, the tribune Manilius passed a law in the *comitia tributa* assigning the command against Mithridates to Pompey, who had just finished off the pirates in a swift campaign; see 29. Pompey's ultimate success (64/63) in defeating Mithridates and vastly increasing the Roman dominions in Asia Minor and Syria (see 35 pref.) was built, though he would never have admitted it, on the initial campaigning of Lucullus.

In the first of the following passages, Velleius describes the rivalry between Lucullus and Pompey, which he places after the transfer of the command but which in fact applied to their whole careers. In the second, Cicero, though supporting the *lex Manilia* (see 29–30), pays tribute to the successes of Lucullus; he is thus already paving the way for the policy of his consulship in 63, of uniting the senate and *equites* in a *concordia ordinum*; see 67 pref.

A. *Iurgia Luculli atque Pompeii*

Cum esset in fine bellum piraticum[1] et L. Lucullus, qui ante septem annos ex consulatu sortitus Asiam Mithridati oppositus erat[2] magnasque et memorabiles res ibi gesserat,[3] idem bellum adhuc administraret, Manilius, tribunus plebis, legem tulit ut bellum Mithridaticum

per Cn. Pompeium administraretur.[4] Accepta ea, magnis certatum est
inter imperatores iurgiis,[5] cum Pompeius Lucullo infamiam pecuniae,
Lucullus Pompeio interminatam cupiditatem obiceret imperii.[6] Nam
neque Pompeius, ut primum ad rem publicam adgressus est,[7] quemquam omnino parem tulit, et in quibus rebus primus esse debebat,
solus esse cupiebat.[8] Neque eo viro quisquam aut alia omnia minus aut
gloriam magis concupiit; in appetendis honoribus immodicus, in
gerendis verecundissimus.[9] Et Lucullus, summus alioqui vir, profusae
huius in aedificiis convictibusque et apparatibus luxuriae primus
auctor fuit,[10] quem, ob iniectas moles mari et receptum suffossis
montibus in terras mare,[11] haud infacete Magnus Pompeius Xerxen
togatum vocare adsueverat.[12]

B.   *Luculli res gestae*

Atque,[13] ut omnes intellegant me Lucio Lucullo tantum impertire
laudis, quantum forti viro et sapienti homini et magno imperatori
debeatur, dico[14] eius adventu maximas Mithridati copias omnibus
rebus ornatas atque instructas fuisse,[15] urbemque Asiae clarissimam
nobisque amicissimam Cyzicenorum obsessam esse ab ipso rege
maxima multitudine et oppugnatam vehementissime;[16] quam L.
Lucullus virtute, adsiduitate, consilio summis obsidionis periculis
liberavit.[17] Ab eodem imperatore classem magnam et ornatam, quae
ducibus Sertorianis ad Italiam studio atque odio inflammata raperetur,
superatam esse atque depressam;[18] magnas hostium praeterea copias
multis proeliis esse deletas patefactumque nostris legionibus esse
Pontum, qui antea populo Romano ex omni aditu clausus fuisset;[19]
Sinopen atque Amisum, quibus in oppidis erant domicilia regis,
omnibus rebus ornatas ac refertas,[20] ceterasque urbes Ponti et Cappadociae permultas uno aditu adventuque esse captas;[21] regem spoliatum
regno patrio atque avito ad alios se reges atque ad alias gentes supplicem contulisse;[22] atque haec omnia salvis populi Romani sociis
atque integris vectigalibus esse gesta.[23]

1. **bellum piraticum:** for Pompey's rapid success against the pirates in 67 see 29.

2. A. **ante septem annos:** in such expressions of time, *ante* or *post* may be used either as preps. with the acc. sing. or plur., as here, or as advs. with the noun in the abl. of degree of difference; see 14 n. 3.   B. **ex consulatu** = "after (his) consulship," i.e. in 73; to be taken with *sortitus*. This meaning of *ex* with the abl. of a magistracy presumably arose from the concept of leaving it, and is found in Cicero. It was extended in imperial Lat. and gave rise in late Lat. to the use of *ex* with the abl. of the title of an officer to denote a former holder of an office, as *ex consule*; from this derives the modern use, as in "ex-president."   C. **sortitus Asiam:** originally the use of the lot in assigning public office was supposed to make the choice an expression of the will of the gods; later it simply removed the choice from bargaining and intrigue and was therefore introduced for the assignment of provinces by a law of Gaius Gracchus, for whom see 19. The drawing took place before actual individuals were elected to the magistracies which would entitle the holder to a province in the following year. It is clear, however, that even in the later Republic the senate could manipulate the allotment and in this case did so to give the command to the best optimate general, Lucullus.

3. A. **erat . . . gesserat:** inds. because the rel. clause is a parenthetical statement of fact by Velleius, not subordinated to the imperf. subj. *administraret* in the *cum* temporal clause in past time; compare 10 n. 10C (and 58 n. 6C).   B. **magnasque . . . res:** for Lucullus' achievements see B below.

4. A. **Manilius:** as tribune in 66, he passed the law through the *comitia tributa* (see 21 n. 11A) which transferred the Mithridatic command from Lucullus to Pompey; see 29 pref. For similar instances in which the assembly interfered with the senate's traditional prerogative of assigning provinces and commands, see 63 n. 2.   B. **legem tulit:** for this idiom see 20 n. 7 (and 56 n. 2B).   C. **per Cn. Pompeium:** for *per* + an acc. to denote the agent see 35 n. 4.

5. A. **accepta ea** = "when it (the law) was passed"; *accipio* is used for the acceptance by the assembly of a law; see 56 n. 11A.   B. **certatum est:** a true impersonal, without expressed subject; see 10 n. 10D (and contrast 66 n. 9).

6. A. **Lucullo . . . imperii:** in both balanced clauses, the verb *obicio* = "I reproach" takes the acc. of the cause of blame and the dat. (after *ob* in composition) of the person blamed; see 40 n. 19B. Throughout the rest of this par. Velleius' rhetorical balancing of clauses and phrases is marked; compare, for Cicero, n. 14 below.   B. **infamiam pecuniae** = "a bad reputation for (coveting) money"; compare 38 n. 19A.   C. **interminatam:** since the verb *termino, -are* is common in Cicero, this is probably the negative prefix *in-* + its past part., rather than an adj. from *terminus*; contrast *illaborata* in 79 n. 14D.

7. A. **nam neque Pompeius:** *neque* is correlative with the *neque* which introduces the next sentence, but in the second case, Pompey ceases to be subject and is represented by *eo viro* as abl. of comparison after *minus . . . magis*; i.e. "for Pompey did not . . . and no one (else) . . . less . . . or . . . more than that man (i.e. Pompey)."   B. **ad rem . . . est** = "he entered public life"; a common idiom. For *res publica* see 19 n. 6B (and 60 n. 25B).

8. **quemquam . . . cupiebat:** Caesar also charged Pompey with being unable to tolerate an equal (see the beginning of 38 B), and Lucan echoes this; see 77 n. 11A.

9. **in . . . verecundissimus:** for Pompey's offices and commands, see especially 28–29 and 37. His moderation in the use of his position and powers is illustrated by his disbanding his army on returning from Asia in 62; see 35 pref.

10. A. **profusae . . . luxuriae** = "of this (contemporary) luxury"; i.e. that with which Velleius and his audience were familiar.   B. **apparatibus:** lit. may = "furnishings, decorations, etc." or, figuratively, "splendor, pomp." For Lucullus' reputation for luxury see pref. above.

11. A. **ob . . . mare** = "on account of the masses (of masonry which he) cast into the sea and the sea (which he) received into the lands by digging away mountains." The huge

masses of masonry pushed out into the sea for foundations of seaside villas are rhetorically balanced by the excavations of seaside cliffs to provide harbors. Such complaints of extravagant building in resorts like Baiae on the Bay of Naples are common in Augustan and later writers.   B. **mari:** dat. after a part. compounded with a prep.

12.   A. **haud infacete** = "rather wittily"; lit. "not unwittily." This rhetorical figure is called "litotes" (Greek; = simplicity, understatement).   B. **Magnus Pompeius:** the honorific title (see 29 pref.) has become so much part of the name that the order may be inverted, as often with Roman names; see 22 n. 13B (and 43 n. 5A).   c. **Xerxen togatum:** i.e. a Roman Xerxes, in the characteristic Roman garb; *-en* is a Greek 1st decl. acc. sing. ending; contrast 1 n. 2B (and 15 n. 9). When Xerxes, king of Persia, invaded Greece in 480, to move his great army and fleet he first built a bridge of boats across the Hellespont and then cut a canal across the isthmus of Mt. Athos to avoid its stormy promontory. He thus became a prototype of an extravagant and grandiose builder. D. **adsueverat** = "had become accustomed to," i.e. was used to; for the pluperf. see 63 n. 5B.

13.   **atque, ut etc.:** as indicated in the pref., Cicero did not wish to alienate optimate opinion by condemning Lucullus while he sought to win the favor of the *equites* and people by promoting Pompey for the command.

14.   **dico etc.:** the remainder of the par. is in indirect discourse. In this sentence the infs. describe the situation on Lucullus' arrival; the perf. infs. *obsessam esse . . . oppugnatam (esse)* indicate a condition contemporary with his arrival resulting from a previous action, i.e. they are true perfs. so that the "pluperf." infs. *ornatas atque instructas fuisse* (see n. 15B below) are created to indicate action completed before his arrival. For Cicero's fondness for pairing words or phrases of similar meaning see 67 n. 1B, and for Velleius compare n. 6A above.

15.   A. **eius adventu etc.:** In 74 Nicomedes of Bithynia died and, following a practice which became common among late Hellenistic monarchs, left his kingdom to Rome. Bithynia extended along the north coast of Asia Minor from the Sea of Marmara (the ancient Propontis) eastward along the Black Sea. Mithridates, whose kingdom of Pontus adjoined Bithynia to the east, at once invaded, so the senate sent Lucullus' colleague in the consulship of 74, M. Aurelius Cotta, to secure the new province. When Lucullus reached the Hellespont (modern Dardanelles) late in 74, Mithridates was besieging Cotta in Chalcedon, across the Bosporus from Byzantium (modern Constantinople), but he then moved westward to Cyzicus, an important city on the south shore of the Propontis.   B. **Mithridati:** this dat. of reference indicates the difficulty of assigning a more specific connotation to such a dat. If, as suggested in n. 14 above, *fuisse* is used instead of *esse* (compare 44 n. 10B) with the past parts. to form perf. pass. infs., representing pluperfs. in direct discourse, then *M.* might be called a dat. of agent (see 21 n. 15C) and translated "very great forces had been prepared and equipped with everything as far as M. was concerned" (i.e. by M.). However, the placing of *M.* within *maximas . . . copias,* parallel to a possessive gen., suggests advantage, = "had been prepared and equipped for M." Or *ornatas atque instructas* might be taken as predicate adjectival parts. after *fuisse* and *M.* as dat. of reference (possession; see 11 n. 9 and 21 n. 5B); = "there were for M. forces prepared and equipped," i.e. "M. had forces etc." The Roman hearer probably did not bother about such distinctions but simply understood what was meant.

16.   A. **Cyzicenorum** = "(that of) the Cyzicenes"; the name of the people is used in the possessive gen. instead of the name of the city (*Cyzicum*) in apposition with *urbem.* B. **ab ipso rege** = "by the king himself"; the abl. of agent is in immediate juxtaposition to the abl. of means, as in the next clause the abls. of means *virtute . . . consilio* are to the abl. of separation (without a prep.) *summis . . . periculis.* Such juxtapositions of the same case with very different connotations indicate how much of the understanding of Lat. depends on its being heard, with proper pauses, phrasing, and emphasis.

17. A. **periculis:** abl. of separation; compare 66 n. 5B.   B. **liberavit:** this and *erant*
5 lines below are ind. since the rel. clauses contain emphatic statements of fact by
Cicero; compare n. 3A above. However, *raperetur* and *fuisset* are subjs. because they are
subordinated in the whole indirect statement; compare 14 n. 2B. Lucullus cut off
Mithridates' supplies, and in 73 the King withdrew from Bithynia back into Pontus,
suffering heavy losses but escaping personally.

18. A. **classem . . . ornatam:** Sertorius in Spain (see 28 pref. and nn. 11–14) and
Mithridates seem to have allied in an effort to squeeze Rome by a "pincers" attack.
In 73 Mithridates started his fleet toward Italy, but Lucullus intercepted and sank it.
B. **ducibus Sertorianis:** probably an abl. of accompaniment without *cum*, = "with (i.e.
under) Sertorian commanders," rather than an abl. abs. (like *Glabrione consule* in 14
n. 4B), = "the commanders being Sertorians." Other sources state that a single Sertorian
officer reached Asia Minor from Spain and was put in charge of the fleet by Mithridates;
the plur. is therefore rhetorical.   C. **studio:** often = "(partisan) zeal"; i.e. for one
side against the other.   D. **inflammata:** grammatically agrees with *quae*, but the zeal
and hate were really felt by Mithridates, the Sertorians, and the others in the fleet.
E. **raperetur:** the pass. of *rapere* is often used vividly for "hasten."

19. A. **Pontum:** Mithridates' kingdom, on the south shore of the Black Sea, east of
Bithynia; see 24 pref. In 63 Pompey formed it and Bithynia into a single province.
B. **ex omni aditu:** the Eng. idiom is "on (from) every side"; the Lat. seems to envisage
the impression of the blocking off as being received from every direction. *Aditu* is as
ambivalent as Eng. "approach"; here, perhaps, a way of approach but in the next
sentence the act of approaching; see n. 21B below.

20. **Sinopen atque Amisum:** the capital and another principal city of Pontus; for the
Greek acc. ending -*en* see n. 12C above.

21. A. **Cappadociae:** a state south of Pontus in east central Asia Minor.   B. **uno
. . . adventuque** = "at the mere (lit. single) approach and arrival" (hendiadys; see 13
n. 11A and 67 n. 15), i.e. of the Roman legions. *Permultas* and *uno* are immediately
juxtaposed in rhetorical contrast, and the whole statement is exaggerated since, though
the inland cities of Pontus fell easily, the conquest of Pontus took from 73–70 and
Sinope and Amisus were captured only after long sieges.

22. A. **regno:** verbs meaning "to despoil" take an abl. of separation (without a
prep.) of the thing of which somebody is despoiled; see 4 n. 2B and compare n. 17A
above.   B. **ad alios . . . contulisse:** upon his withdrawal from Bithynia in 73, Mithridates sent for help to his son Machares, king of Bosporus (modern Crimea), to his son-
in-law Tigranes, king of Armenia, and even to the kings of Scythia and Parthia. They
failed to respond, and Lucullus' advance into Pontus forced Mithridates in 72 to flee
to Tigranes. Lucullus pursued him in 69 with considerable success, but in 67 his troops,
discouraged by the hardships of the march and perhaps conscious that opposition at
Rome was mounting, mutinied. Lucullus was forced to withdraw and was recalled to
Rome by the senate. Mithridates reoccupied Pontus, and Lucullus, after briefly trying
to maintain some position against Pompey (see A), who had advanced from Cilicia in
66, went home. Pompey quickly dislodged Mithridates, who this time found no welcome
from Tigranes. In 65 the King seized the Bosporan kingdom from his own son Machares.
There in 63 he committed suicide when another son, Pharnaces, revolted against him.
C. **supplicem:** since this is usually adjectival, it may be used here where Eng. would use
an adv., i.e. "suppliantly"; see 11 n. 12A (and 63 n. 3B). However, it may be equivalent
to a predicate noun, i.e. "as a suppliant."

23. **salvis . . . vectigalibus:** i.e. without exactions from the provincial allies or impair-
ment of Rome's revenues, because Lucullus paid for the campaign out of the booty.
The remark is not addressed so much to the *equites*, despite their concern for their
profit from collecting taxes (see pref.), as to the people, who were fully conscious that
much of their well-being and amusement was paid for by provincial taxation.

69

The *de Rerum Natura*, a noble epic poem on philosophy and physics, was written by a contemporary of Cicero called in the manuscripts of his work Titus Lucretius Carus. Lucretius' life is almost unknown except that St. Jerome, the Church Father of the fourth century A.D., says that he was born in 94, driven mad by a love potion, wrote several books in the intervals between periods of insanity, books which Cicero afterwards edited (or corrected), and finally committed suicide at the age of forty-four. This confused and lurid note may represent mere conjecture based on statements in the poem itself and may also represent Christian antipathy to Epicurean materialism. A casual and enigmatic reference in one of Cicero's letters to his brother (*ad Q. fr.* II 9.3) and a comment on Lucretius' style in Quintilian X 1.87 do nothing to clear up the confusion about either Lucretius' life or Cicero's role in regard to his poem.

Lucretius' didactic poem in six books, written in dactylic hexameters, expounds a scientific theory used by Epicurus, a Greek philosopher of the fourth century, to justify his materialistic rationalism. This scientific theory went back to two fifth-century physical speculators, Democritus and Leucippus. They took from their predecessors the view that the material universe was composed of small, indivisible particles of matter, called "atoms" (Greek *a-tomos* = "uncuttable"). According to Democritus, these did not differ in quality but only in size and shape so that the differences in material objects were due solely to the various ways in which atoms combined, and material change reflected simply the formation or dissolution of atomic complexes. Even human souls were merely complexes of very fine atoms which were dissolved by death.

Epicurus, followed by Lucretius, used this mechanical explanation of the nature of the universe to prove that current beliefs about divine intervention in human affairs, about fortune and fate, about immaterial and immortal souls, and about a hereafter of rewards and punishments were false superstitions. Freed from the terrors engendered by religion, men could live pleasantly, undisturbed by excessive commitment to any activity, belief, or superstition. Since a life of "pleasure" might readily degenerate into self-indulgent hedonism (Greek *hēdonē* = "pleasure"), Epicureanism fell into disrepute among Romans, who became increasingly devoted to Stoicism (see 34 pref. and n. 4A), and later among Christians. But as advocated by Epicurus and Lucretius, the life of "pleasure," though selfish, was almost ascetic.

Although Lucretius was professedly a materialistic rationalist, his poem shows both high poetic imagery and frequent passages of strong emotional content. Indeed, though he denied the intervention of the gods in human affairs, he did not dispute their existence and opened his poem with the following impassioned invocation of Venus and of Mars, both important Roman deities; see nn. 1B and 25 below. This invocation is suffused with Roman patriotism and with a desire for peace which reflects the searing memories left by the civil wars of the Sullan period; see 25–28, and 66.

Venus omnium animantium genetrix

Aeneadum genetrix,[1] hominum divomque voluptas,[2]
alma Venus,[3] caeli subter labentia signa[4]
quae mare navigerum, quae terras frugiferentis
concelebras,[5] per te quoniam genus omne animantum
concipitur visitque exortum lumina solis—[6]
te, dea, te fugiunt venti, te nubila caeli
adventumque tuum;[7] tibi suavis daedala tellus
submittit flores,[8] tibi rident aequora ponti,[9]
placatumque nitet diffuso lumine caelum.
Nam simul ac species patefactast verna diei[10]
et reserata viget genitabilis aura Favoni,[11]
aeriae primum volucres te, diva, tuumque
significant initum perculsae corda tua vi.[12]
Inde ferae, pecudes persultant pabula laeta
et rapidos tranant amnis;[13] ita capta lepore
te sequitur cupide quo quamque inducere pergis.[14]
Denique per maria ac montis fluviosque rapacis[15]
frondiferasque domos avium camposque virentis
omnibus incutiens blandum per pectora amorem,[16]
efficis ut cupide generatim saecla propagent.[17]
Quae quoniam rerum naturam sola gubernas,[18]
nec sine te quicquam dias in luminis oras
exoritur, neque fit laetum neque amabile quicquam,[19]
te sociam studeo scribendis versibus esse[20]
quos ego de rerum natura pangere conor
Memmiadae nostro,[21] quem tu, dea, tempore in omni
omnibus ornatum voluisti excellere rebus.[22]
Quo magis aeternum da dictis, diva, leporem.[23]
Effice ut interea fera moenera militiai
per maria ac terras omnis sopita quiescant.[24]

Nam tu sola potes tranquilla pace iuvare

mortalis, quoniam belli fera moenera Mavors

armipotens regit,[25] in gremium qui saepe tuum se

reicit, aeterno devictus vulnere amoris.[26]

Hunc tu, diva, tuo recubantem corpore sancto

circumfusa super,[27] suavis ex ore loquellas

funde, petens placidam Romanis, incluta, pacem.[28]

Nam neque nos agere hoc patriai tempore iniquo

possumus aequo animo,[29] nec Memmi clara propago

talibus in rebus communi desse saluti.[30]

1. A. **Aenĕădum:** gen. plur.; for the quantities see 55 n. 10A.   B. **genetrix:** the Romans regarded Venus as their ancestress through Aeneas and his son Iulus (or Ascanius) and later Romulus (see 1 pref.), through whom they also traced descent from Mars; see 4 n. 4B (and 55 n. 5B) and n. 25 below. Lucretius perhaps wrote too early to be influenced by Caesar's promotion of *Venus Genetrix* as the particular ancestress of the Julian *gens* (see 33 pref. and opening), though the resemblance of epithet is striking. The emotion-charged invocation of Venus in these verses appears inconsistent with the Epicurean belief that the gods took no part in the world or in human affairs. Without enlarging upon this much-discussed question, it may be noted that an invocation of a deity was conventional in ancient poetry (compare 60 n. 27A), and also that Venus is here not so much the traditional anthropomorphic goddess as a poetic personification of the creative power of nature and of the joys of procreation, perhaps standing for Epicurean "pleasure" as felt by the "nature of things." Yet the tone is too intense to permit regarding the passage as pure allegory; noteworthy are the 5 direct appeals to Venus as *dea* or *diva*, and a 6th as *incluta*; in 4 of the 5 the voc. is preceded or enclosed by *tu, te, tuum,* or *tuo,* and there is marked emphasis throughout on the 2nd pers. sing. pronoun.

2. A. **divomque:** for the old 2nd decl. gen. plur. ending *-um* compare *deum* = *deorum* in 11 n. 14B (and *sestertium* in 33 n. 16B); for the spelling *-vom* = *-vum* see 63 n. 7B.   B. **voluptas:** voc., in apposition with *genetrix.* The word recalls the Greek *hēdonē* = "pleasure" (see pref.) and suggests that Venus is pleasurable love, the creative force in life.

3. **alma:** a traditional epithet of Venus, here appropriate because related to *alere* = "to nourish."

4. A. **caeli . . . signa:** this prepositional phrase belongs in the following rel. clause, with *concelebras.*   B. **subter:** a rare equivalent of *sub* and generally followed by the acc., as here.   C. **labentia:** frequently used by Lucretius of heavenly bodies or constellations (*signa*) and perhaps suggesting that their motion is a gliding down toward the horizon; contrast Vergil's *surgentia sidera* in 88 n. 31C.

5. A. **navigerum . . . frugiferentis:** Lucretius is fond of such compound adjs., many first used by him, especially those formed on the roots *-fer-* and *-ger-*; compare *frondiferas* 15 verses below. In this and such other poetical devices as alliteration (frequent in these verses; see n. 20 below) and monosyllabic verse endings (see n. 12F below), he follows the precedents set by Ennius, for whom compare 60 and 61, especially 60 n. 9C for monosyllabic endings, 60 n. 26B for compounds, and 60 nn. 28 and 29 for alliteration. B. **frugiferentis:** for the *i*-stem acc. plur. ending *-is* see 15 n. 14A (and, in pres. parts., 55 n. 6D).   C. **quae . . . concelebras** = "(you) who fill (with offspring)"; this literal

meaning fits the description of Venus as the inspirer of procreation better than the more figurative "fill (with your presence)."

6. A. **quoniam . . . solis:** at first sight, this clause seems to look forward to some conclusion abruptly cut off but in fact it looks back to and explains *concelebras*.   B. **animantum** = "of living things"; Lucretius prefers the ending *-um* for the gen. plur. of pres. parts. to the regular *-ium*, used in the title above.   C. **exortum:** with the subject (*genus*), = "and, when born etc."   D. **lumina solis:** *lumina* is poetic plur.; see 49 n. 10B. Ennius *Ann.* frag. 278 (Loeb) uses the phrase *lumine solis* literally, as does Lucretius here. *Lumen* may also mean "life" (see 70 n. 24A and compare n. 19B below), "famous men" (see 27 n. 10), or "eyes"; see 77 n. 34B.

7. A. **te, dea, te:** the opening voc. (see n. 1B above) is thus resumed after the lengthy intervening qualifications of Venus.   B. **adventumque:** correlative with the preceding *te* as objects of *fugiunt*, which frequently is trans. with the meaning "flee from (or at)."

8. A. **suavis:** better taken as acc. plur. with *flores* than as nom. sing. with *tellus*, to give a balanced order; for the ending *-is* compare n. 5B above.   B. **daedala** = "variegated," from the Greek *daidălos* = "cunningly worked," often of embroidery or metal inlay. It became the name of the mythological archetype of the skillful workman, Daedalus, who wrought several marvels for King Minos of Crete and was credited with the invention of various tools.   C. **submittit:** lit. = "sends up from below"; a favorite verb with Lucretius to describe the productive action of the earth.

9. **aequora:** here has its original meaning of "flat surfaces" (see 66 n. 21B) so that *ponti* is not tautological.

10. A. **simul ac . . . dĭēī** = "as soon as the vernal appearance of the day is revealed"; i.e. when days begin to be springlike. *Ac* or *atque* after words of comparison = "as" or "than"; for *simul ac* compare 39 n. 11B.   B. **verna:** epithet transferred from *diei* to *species* by hypallage, for which see 46 n. 19 (and 54 n. 15).   C. **dĭēī:** usually pronounced as a trisyllable, though *reī* was monosyllabic; compare on *-āī* in n. 24D below. D. **pătĕfāctāst:** for prodelision of *est* (and *es*) in early Lat. verse see 60 n. 13B; *pătĕfăcĕrĕ*, from the root of *pătēre*, should have *-ē-* in the stem but it is often short, probably through "iambic shortening," for which see 59 n. 29B.

11. A. **reserata . . . Favōni** = "the procreative breeze of the West Wind (is) released (and) freshens." *Favonius* (compare 73 n. 12c) is "unlocked and becomes strong" either because spring releases the icy fetters imposed by winter or perhaps because during the winter it had been shut up by Aeolus, god of the winds.   B. **genitabilis:** here act. in meaning, although adjs. in *-bilis* are usually pass.; it is probably nom. with *aura* rather than gen. with *Favoni*.

12. A. **ăĕriae:** in Lat. the Greek *āēr* = "air" retains the *ā-* before a following vowel; compare 49 n. 1. In the oblique cases and the derivative adj. (here), the *-ĕ-* becomes short. The adj. should be distinguished from *aereus* (from *aes* = "bronze"); compare 61 n. 29A. The birds here and the animals in the following verses are female.   B. **te etc.:** the birds of the air herald (by their song) the coming of love into the spring world; for the personification and the address to Venus compare nn. 1B, 2B, and 7A above.   C. **initum:** correlated with *te* as is *adventum* in n. 7B above. *Initus* is more literal than *initium*; compare *exitus* and *exitium* in 19 n. 13D.   D. **perculsae . . . vi** = "smitten (in their) hearts by your power (or, violence)"; for the metaphorical use of *percello* see 15 n. 3A (and compare 20 n. 14C).   E. **corda:** Greek acc. of specification (or respect); compare *corpora* in 55 n. 20D. For the head and the breast as seats both of emotion and of intelligence, compare n. 16B below and 60 nn. 22B and 23C.   F. **vi:** Lucretius, like Ennius (see 60 n. 9C), occasionally ends a verse with a monosyllable; compare *tuum se* 20 verses below and *aetherius sol* 6 verses before the end of 70 B.

13. A. **inde** = "next," taking up *primum* 2 verses above; *denique* 3 verses below may be equivalent to "furthermore" or may simply resume the whole previous picture of

love's effects by a "then" or "indeed." B. **ferae, pecudes:** probably to be taken separately with no connective as = "wild beasts (and) cattle" rather than "flocks, (made) wild (by love)." The first interpretation might be supported by regarding the two following verbs as applying, in chiasmic (see 17 n. 2) order, the leaping to the flocks and the swimming to the wild beasts; if the swimming goes with the flocks, the unnaturalness of the action might justify taking *ferae* with *pecudes* as = "made wild (by love)," since in Vergil *Georg.* III 264–270 love maddens mares so that they swim streams: *flumina tranant.* C. **laeta:** Lucretius uses *laetus* in its original meaning of "fruitful," "rich," rather than in the derived sense of "joyful," for which compare 52 n. 6.

14. A. **capta lepore:** *capta* agrees with a subject *quaeque* (*fera* or *pecus*) to be understood from the following *quamque*; Lucretius easily moves from the plur. to the sing. and back to the plur. in *omnibus* 4 verses below. B. **lepore:** here connotes more than external charm (compare n. 23B below); it suggests the delight in love-making inspired by Venus, as indicated by the adv. *cupide* in the next verse. C. **quo ... pergis =** "whither you proceed to lead each"; *pergo* may be followed by an inf. in prose as well as in verse, probably because its connotation of "continue" (and in later Lat. "undertake") suggested a complementary inf., but perhaps because verbs of motion in early and poetic Lat. may be followed by an inf. called of "purpose" but really representing the use of the inf. as a noun indicating place to which (goal or end of motion), corresponding to the acc. supine.

15. **fluviosque rapacis:** rivers are commonly conceived in poetry as hurrying objects away in their rapid flow. This verse covers the wilder seas, mountains, and torrents; the next, the more peaceful woods and fields.

16. A. **omnibus:** probably dat. of reference (possession) with a part of the body (compare 43 n. 6 and 55 n. 6B), i.e. instilling (lit. "driving, pounding") through the breasts of all (lit. "for all through their breasts"), rather than dat. after a verb compounded with a prep., i.e. "instilling in all through their breasts." B. **pectora:** for the breast as the seat of emotion see n. 12E above.

17. A. **efficis ut ... propagent:** the substantive clause of result is object of *efficis*, a verb of striving or accomplishment; compare 31 n. 15. B. **generatim saecla =** "the (various) species, each after its own kind"; Lucretius is fond of advs. in *-atim.* C. **saecla:** object of *propagent*, of which the subject is supplied from *omnibus*. Lucretius prefers the early Lat. *saecla*; in Ciceronian Lat. *-cl-* (and *-pl-*) came to be separated by a light *-u-* for greater ease of pronunciation. Lucretius often uses this word as a plur. for *genus* as well as in its temporal sense of "ages" or "generations."

18. **quae quoniam etc.:** the rel. is here equivalent to *et ... tu* (see 4 n. 4A and 65 n. 26A), and the *quoniam* belongs not only with (*tu*) *gubernas* but with the two following clauses *nec ... exoritur* and *neque ... quicquam*; i.e. "and since you alone govern ... and since neither does anything arise ... nor does anything become (i.e. is anything created)."

19. A. **quicquam ... exoritur ... fit ... quicquam:** chiasmic order; compare n. 13B above. B. **dias in luminis oras:** for the old adj. *dius = divus* see 60 n. 2, and for the remainder of the phrase as used by Ennius see 60 n. 5B. "Divine shores of light" connotes life; compare n. 6D above.

20. **scribendis versibus:** Lucretius expresses purpose by the dat. of a noun and a gerundive more widely than did Ciceronian Lat., which generally confined it to stereotyped descriptions of the functions of magistrates; see 7 n. 2A (and 56 n. 2A). This verse is strongly alliterative with *s*.

21. A. **de rerum natura:** whether or not Lucretius so intended, this early occurrence of this phrase gave his poem its title. B. **pangere =** "to compose" (a poem); a traditional poetic verb, perhaps derived from building. C. **Memmiadae nostro:** dat. of reference (advantage); = "for my (friend) Memmius." Since the simple *Memmio* could not be fitted into a dactylic hexameter, Lucretius invents a patronymic (see 9

n. 2B and 55 n. 10A) or at the end of this passage uses an equivalent *Memmi clara propago*. This friend, or patron, whom Lucretius addresses with apparent warmth and respect in books I, II, and V, is usually identified with Gaius Memmius, a plebeian senator of dubious reputation and husband of Fausta, the daughter of Sulla; for Sulla see 24–27 and 65–66. Memmius was praetor in 58 and went out in 57 as propraetorian governor of Bithynia (see 68 n. 15A), where the poet Catullus (see 73 pref.) served on his staff. D. **nostro** = *meo*; compare 32 n. 12B (and 54 n. 2C).

22. **omnibus ornatum ... rebus:** this may refer to Memmius' wealth and public distinctions or to his personality, including sufficient knowledge of philosophy to appreciate this poem; or it may be a conventionally vague laudatory phrase.

23. A. **quo magis:** *quo* is abl. (of degree of difference; compare 34 n. 21A) of the rel. used as a main connective (compare n. 18 above); it may be rendered "wherefore" or "and therefore." Lucretius means that since Memmius will gain credit from the success of the poem dedicated to him, Venus, who has already endowed him with so much, should all the more add to (the poet's) utterances (and to his philosophy) the same eternal charm that she engenders in living creatures. Lucretius habitually uses similar terms for physical creation and literary production. B. **leporem** = "charm" or "attraction"; compare n. 14B above.

24. A. **effice ut ... quiescant:** for the use of the substantive *ut* clause of result as object of *effice* see n. 17A above. B. **interea:** with an imperative = "for the time being"; i.e. (here) while I compose my poem. It may also denote that a previous train of thought has been abandoned. C. **fera moenera militiai** = "the fierce activities of war"; lit. "burdens (tasks) of soldiering." The early Lat. diphthong -*oe*- was reduced in classical Lat. to -*ū*-, hence *moenera* = *mūnera*. D. **militiāi:** for the early Lat. fem. gen. sing. ending -*āi* (pronounced as two syllables) see 57 n. 11B (and 61 n. 7, and compare on *diēi* in n. 10C above), and note *pătriāi* below in the 3rd verse from the end.

25. **Māvors armipotens:** for *Māvors* = "Mars" see 52 n. 1C; for the compound adj. compare *ignipotens* in 55 n. 3B and *bellipotens* in 60 n. 26B. With the introduction of Mars, in Greek mythology the lover of Venus, the poet seems to speak more directly of his own world, since Mars is regarded purely as the god of war, whom the force of love can soften, and not in his early Italic guise as a god of agriculture. Nor does the poet explicitly suggest his parentage, through Romulus (see 4, and n. 1B above), of the Romans, as Venus is called *Aeneadum genetrix* (see n. 1B above), though his Roman readers must have been aware of both these aspects of his divinity.

26. A. **in ... reicit** = *qui saepe in gremium tuum se reicit*; for the word order compare 66 n. 13A. B. **aeterno ... vulnere:** the wound may be eternal because they are immortal gods, or the adj. may simply be conventional, as in *aeternum ... leporem* 6 verses above. C. **devictus:** emphatic, = "completely subdued."

27. A. **hunc ... super** = "bending over him as he lies (on your lap) with your divine body"; *circumfusa* may have the "middle" meaning of "pouring yourself around" and therefore takes *hunc ... recubantem* as a direct object, or, if it is pass., = "being poured around," the acc. may depend on the prep. *circum* in composition with the verb. B. **super:** adv.; = "from above." C. **corpore:** abl. of means.

28. A. **loquellas** = "words," probably in the sense of "words of love" since such diminutives are affectionate or familiar. B. **petens placidam ... pacem:** this alliterative phrase suggests the Epicurean ideal of *ataraxia* = "absence of disturbance," "peace of mind," as well as the peace from war overtly meant here; compare *aequo animo* in n. 29D below. C. **incluta** = "glorious (one)," an archaic and poetic adj. not found in Ciceronian prose, here used alone as a voc.

29. A. **nos ... possumus** = *ego ... possum*; compare n. 21D above. B. **agere hoc:** i.e. to preach Epicurean "salvation" in his poem. C. **patriai ... iniquo:** for the fem. gen. sing. in -*āi* see n. 24D above. *Iniquo* here connotes "dangerous," but is contrasted

in its basic meaning of "uneven" or "unstable" with *aequo* in the next verse.   D.

aequo animo: a common phrase (see 39 n. 3B) which here has an Epicurean implication; see n. 28B above. The reference to "troubled time for our country" may be general or may refer to the uncertainties of the years 59–55 (see 35–37 prefs.) during which Lucretius may have been writing; see pref. above.

30.   A. **communi . . . saluti:** Lucretius means, apparently, that in such troubled times Memmius cannot fail the common safety of the state, that is, he cannot practice the Epicurean withdrawal from public life and devote himself wholly to philosophy. Cicero's friend Atticus (see 32 n. 15) and, in his later life, Horace's friend Maecenas, as well as Horace himself (see prefs. to 86 and 87), did so; other Roman Epicureans, like Caesar, followed the Roman ideal of service to the state, as Memmius is supposed to do here. B. **desse:** a poetic contraction for *deesse*; with it supply *potest* from *possumus* in the preceding verse. For similar internal elision compare *antehac* in 57 n. 10B.

70

In the third book of his *de Rerum Natura* (see 69 pref.), Lucretius tries to dispel one of the greatest obstacles to Epicurean peace of mind, the fear of death. To do so, he argues that the soul is composed of very light atoms which disperse when death supervenes. There survives no personal entity to feel pain, to be affected by affairs on earth, or to suffer punishment in any hereafter.

The following two passages come from the later part of the book, which offers less scientific and more emotional arguments against the fear of death. In the first, Lucretius uses a technique common in Roman satire, that of the fictitious dialogue. He quotes two lamentations which mourners might make for the deceased and replies to them. Survivors may lament the family affection of which the dead are deprived; but, replies the poet, the dead, being nonexistent, have no sense of deprivation. The mourners may go on to bewail their own loss; but they should rather realize that the dead are free from disturbance and not to be mourned. In the second passage, Lucretius again uses a device common to satire and to ethical exhortation, the direct address to the reader, envisaged as a "pupil" listening to the arguments of a master. Lucretius asks his pupil why he, an ordinary mortal, should be indignant at death when all the greatest figures of the past have alike come to it and when so much of ordinary life is in any case passed in sleep or in distracting worry.

A.   *Mors neque miseranda neque deflenda est*

"Iam iam non domus accipiet te laeta,[1] neque uxor
optima nec dulces occurrent oscula nati
praeripere[2] et tacita pectus dulcedine tangent.[3]
Non poteris factis florentibus esse, tuisque
praesidium.[4] Misero misere", aiunt, "omnia ademit
una dies infesta tibi tot praemia vitae."[5]
Illud in his rebus non addunt:[6] "Nec tibi earum
iam desiderium rerum super insidet una."[7]
Quod bene si videant animo dictisque sequantur,[8]
dissoluant animi magno se angore metuque.[9]
"Tu quidem ut es leto sopitus,[10] sic eris aevi
quod superest, cunctis privatŭs doloribus aegris.[11]
At nos horrifico cinefactum te prope busto

insatiabiliter deflevimus,[12] aeternumque
nulla dies nobis maerorem e pectore demet."[13]
Illud ab hoc igitur quaerendum est,[14] quid sit amari
tantopere, ad somnum si res redit atque quietem,
cur quisquam aeterno possit tabescere luctu.[15]

B. *Mors omnibus aeque stabilita timenda non est*

Hoc etiam tibi tute interdum dicere possis:[16]
"Lumina suis oculis etiam bonus Ancŭs reliquit[17]
qui melior multis quam tu fuit, improbe, rebus.[18]
Inde alii multi reges rerumque potentes
occidĕrunt, magnis qui gentibus imperitarunt.[19]
Ille quoque ipse,[20] viam qui quondam per mare magnum
stravit iterque dedit legionibus ire per altum[21]
ac pedibus salsas docuit super ire lacunas[22]
et contempsit equis insultans murmura ponti,[23]
lumine adempto animam moribundo corpore fudit.[24]
Scipiadas, belli fulmen, Carthaginis horror,[25]
ossa dedit terrae proinde ac famul infimus esset.[26]
Ipse Epicurus obīt decurso lumine vitae,[27]
qui genus humanum ingenio superavit et omnis[28]
restinxit, stellas exortus ut aetherius sol.[29]
Tu vero dubitabis et indignabere obire?[30]
Mortua cui vita est prope iam vivo atque videnti,[31]
qui somno partem maiorem conteris aevi
et vigilans stertis nec somnia cernere cessas
sollicitamque geris cassa formidine mentem."[32]

---

1. A. **iam iam non:** i.e. now no longer; compare 34 n. 10B. Lucretius introduces abruptly the remarks of mourners; *aiunt* comes 4 verses below. B. **laeta ... optima ... dulces:** these adjs., descriptive of home, wife, and children, heighten the pathos. C. **laeta:** apparently used here in its ordinary meaning of "happy"; contrast 69 n. 13c.

2. **occurrent ... praeripere** = "will run (to meet you and) to snatch kisses"; *praeripere* is an inf. used in poetry to express purpose after a verb of motion; see 69 n. 14c.

3. A. **tacita:** i.e. too deep for words. B. **pectus:** i.e. the father's heart; compare 60 n. 22B (and 69 n. 16B).

4. **factis . . . esse** = "to be prosperous in your affairs," lit. "of prosperous doings"; the abl. is probably a predicate abl. of description (quality) modifying "you" as subject of *poteris*, rather than an abl. abs.

5. A. **misero misere:** the first is the adj. with *tibi* in the following verse (see n. C below); the second is the adv. with *ademit*. The collocation of similar words, or of words of a similar sound, is common in early Lat.; compare 60 C verse 5 and 61 A verses 3 and 4.   B. **aiunt:** i.e. the surviving mourners say; see n. 1A above.   C. **tibi:** dat. of reference (separation) with *ademit* (compare 18 n. 7A and 54 n. 9A), but its position after *infesta* also suggests "hostile (i.e. bitter) to thee."   D. **praemia:** equivalent to *gaudia*, as elsewhere in Lucretius.

6. **illud . . . rebus** = "the following in this connection"; a common formula in Lucretius, in which *illud* calls attention to the statement about to be made; compare 43 n. 18A.

7. A. **super:** here an adv. (see 69 n. 27B); either equivalent to *insuper* = "besides" or making *insidet* equivalent to *superest* = "remains."   B. **una:** also an adv., emphasizing *tibi . . . insidet*, and = "withal" or "as well."

8. A. **quod . . . sequantur** = "but if the mourners should realize this," lit. "see this well with their mind and follow out (their insight) in their words," i.e. by refraining from lamentations.   B. **quod . . . si:** refers back, as often, to the argument just given, as well as being adversative; compare 37 n. 20A.

9. **dīssŏlŭānt:** editors scan thus, although *dīssōlvānt* would fit the meter, since consonantal -*u*- following -*l*- is occasionally scanned as a short vowel even in Vergil; compare the regular pronunciation *bēlŭă* in 59 n. 21A, and contrast the dissyllabic scansion of *sanguen* in 60 n. 4A.

10. **tu quidem:** contrasted with *at nos* 2 verses below. Here Lucretius passes to the second lamentation, in which the mourners think more of their own sorrow than of the suffering of the dead.

11. A. **aevi quod superest:** i.e. for all eternity; the rel. clause is equivalent to an acc. of extent of time. For the partitive gen. with the neut. sing. rel. pronoun see 66 n. 2B (and compare n. 15A below).   B. **prīvātŭs** = "freed from" rather than "deprived of." In early Lat. final -*s* after a short vowel did not necessarily "make position" before a following initial consonant; see 60 n. 14B. Editors of Lucretius frequently indicate this by printing, e.g. here, *privatu'*.

12. A. **horrifico . . . busto:** probably abl. of means with *cinefactum*, which occurs only here and is explained by a late lexicographer as = *in cinerem dissolutum*. But *busto* may be abl. of place where without a prep. (compare 64 n. 7B), modified by the adv. *prope* = "nearby." In either case the mourners are envisioned as standing beside the funeral pyre.   B. **insatiabiliter etc.:** this verse consists of only three words and is "spondaic" (see 59 n. 13); both features give it a tone of appropriate solemnity. Furthermore, it lacks the usual caesura (Lat.; = "a cutting"), i.e. a break in sense coinciding with the ending of a word within a foot. Instead, there is a diaeresis (Greek; = "a tearing apart") after *deflevimus*, i.e. a break in sense coinciding with the ending of a word at the end of a foot.

13. A. **dies:** i.e. lapse of time; compare the last sentence of 34 A.   B. **nobis:** this dat. of reference indicates the difficulty of finding too specific connotations in such dats.; compare 68 n. 15B. Within the general meaning of "as far as we are concerned" it may suggest both "separation" after *demet* (compare n. 5C above) and advantage ("possession") with a part of the body, i.e. "for us from (our) bodies"; compare 43 n. 6 (and 69 n. 16A).

14. A. **illud** = "the following," referring to the indirect question *quid . . . luctu*; compare n. 6 above.   B. **ab hoc:** i.e. from the mourner. The second speech was apparently

attributed to a single speaker, unlike the first; see n. 1A above. For the shift between sing. and plur. compare 69 n. 14A.

15.   A. **quid . . . amari** = "what is so very bitter"; lit. "what of bitterness is there so greatly." For the partitive gen. used with the neut. sing. interrog. pronoun see 67 n. 22 (and compare n. 11A above).   B. **tantopere:** adv. from abl.; see 37 n. 9.   It may go closely with *amari* or generally with the whole clause.   C. **ad somnum . . . quietem** = "if it returns (at last) to sleep and quiet." *Res* is almost as colorless as Eng. "it" but might be rendered "everything."   D. **cur** = "on account of which" or, simply, "that"; it is here not interrog. but rel., going closely with *quid . . . amari*.

16.   A. **hoc etiam:** the more usual phrase for "the following also"; contrast nn. 6 and 14A above. Lucretius has already given various arguments against the fear of death.   B. **tute:** for intensive *-te* see 60 n. 28B. Lucretius probably addresses his "pupil" or reader (see pref. above) rather than Memmius, for whom see 69 n. 21c.

17.   A. **suis oculis:** *suis* is here pronounced as a monosyllable by synizesis; see 59 n. 29B. The manuscripts and editors here read *sis*. In this verse Lucretius echoes Ennius *Ann.* frag. 154 (Loeb): *postquam lumina sis oculis bonus Ancus reliquit.*   B. **oculis:** Festus, a grammarian of the 2nd cent. A.D., regarded this as dat., presumably of reference, i.e. "left light as far as his eyes were concerned"; it might, however, be abl. of separation without a prep., i.e. "gave up vision from his eyes."   C. **bonus Ancŭs:** Ancus Marcius, fourth king of Rome (see 5 pref.), is regularly called *bonus*. For *-ŭs* before an initial consonant see n. 11B above.

18.   A. **multis . . . rebus** = *multo*; abl. of degree of difference rather than of specification, since Homer *Il.* XXI 107, here imitated, says: "Patroclus also died, who was much better than thou."   B. **improbe:** rather harshly addressed to the reader-pupil, who is regarded as "not good" or unworthy, both vis-à-vis Ancus and because he protests against what his betters have accepted, i.e. death.

19.   A. **rerumque potentes:** i.e. rulers; for the gen. with *potens* see 33 n. 25A, where this idiom is used of Caesar.   B. **occĭdĕrunt:** from *occĭdere* = "to fall down," i.e. die (compare 27 n. 3B); not from *occīdere* = "to kill" (see 5 n. 12). Lucretius here and often uses the original *-ĕ-* in the ending of the 3rd pers. plur. of the perf. act. ind., though by his time it had become long.   C. **imperitarunt:** contracted 3rd pers. plur. perf. act. ind.; see 1 n. 4B (and 7 n. 14B). *Imperito*, a frequentative (or intensive; compare 39 n. 15B) of *impero*, occurs regularly in dactylic hexameters, into which many forms of the simple verb did not fit metrically.

20.   **ille etc.:** Xerxes, king of Persia who invaded Greece in 470; for his bridge across the Hellespont see 68 n. 12c.

21.   A. **iterque dedit . . . ire:** in Lat. the inf. may occasionally be used instead of a subj. clause after *habere, dare,* or *ministrare,* a use classified as "purpose" (compare n. 2 above), but in fact simply an inf. used as a verbal noun denoting the action. If this is the construction here, *iter* is a cognate (internal) acc. with *ire*; = "he gave to (i.e. enabled) his troops to go a passage over the deep." However, *iter* may be the object of *dedit* and *ire* a Greek use of the inf. to expand it, called "epexegetic," i.e. explanatory, and in Lat. also classified as "purpose"; = "he gave to his troops a passage to go across the deep."   B. **legionibus:** used loosely for "armies," since Xerxes would not have had regular legions.   C. **altum:** lit. = "the deep"; this adj. used as a noun often means "sea, ocean"; compare 44 n. 6.

22.   A. **docuit:** understand *eas* (from *legionibus*) to form a double acc. with the inf. *ire* after a verb meaning "to teach."   B. **super:** here a prep. governing *salsas lacunas* = "over salt(-water) pools"; contrast n. 7A above.   C. **lacunas:** diminutive of *lacus* = "hole" or "lake"; also used figuratively to mean "gap," "void," hence the Eng. use.

23.   A. **insultans:** here the literal meaning "prancing upon" is primary, but the figurative meaning "scorning" or "scoffing at" is also present, since Xerxes' bridging

of the Hellespont became a stock rhetorical example of man arrogantly setting himself above nature.   B. **murmura**: object of both *contempsit* and *insultans*.

24.   A. **lumine adempto** = "once life was taken away"; compare n. 17B above and 69 nn. 6D and 19B. Vergil and Ovid also use *lumen* metaphorically for "life"; for Ennius compare 60 n. 5B.   B. **animam . . . fudit**: a fairly common idiom for "he died," but here carrying an overtone of the Epicurean theory that at death the tiny atoms of the soul are poured forth and dispersed; see pref.   C. **corpore**: abl. of separation without a prep.; compare n. 17B above.

25.   **Scīpiadās**: nom. sing. (see 49 n. 1) of a poetic patronymic; compare the dat. sing. *Memmiadae* in 69 n. 21C. The reference might be to either Scipio (see 12 and 16) but is probably to the older Africanus, because of the two he was perhaps the chief *Carthaginis horror* and because in this passage Lucretius imitates Ennius; see n. 26B below. For Vergil's imitation of this phrase see 88 n. 25B.

26.   A. **proinde ac** = "like, just as"; for *atque* (*ac*) = "as" or "than" after words of comparison see 69 n. 10A. For the pronunciation of -*oi*- as a diphthong by synizesis compare n. 17A above; in *deinde* (= *de* + *inde*) this synizesis became established as the ordinary pronunciation.   B. **famul** = *famulus*, for which see 66 n. 8; an archaic use of the stem without the nom. ending, which became regular in such words as *puer* (= *puerus*) or *vir* (= *virus*). Lucretius here imitates Ennius *Ann.* frag. 313/314 (Loeb): *mortalem summum Fortuna repente | reddidit e summo regno ut famul ultimus esset.*

27.   A. **ipse Epicūrus**: see 69 pref. *Ipse* marks him as the supreme example and recalls the extreme devotion of Epicureans to the exact words of the master, so that they cited him with the phrase (which has become proverbial) *ipse dixit*. This is the only mention of Epicurus by name in the poem; elsewhere he is addressed as *deus* or by other honorific titles, and, although he is also called *homo* and *vir*, perhaps Lucretius was influenced in avoiding his name by the common religious feeling that the name of a god is too sacred to be mentioned publicly.   B. **obĭt**: perf., for *obiit*; in verse, perfs. in -*ivi* occasionally contract fully, like those in -*avi*, *etc.*; compare 1 n. 4B.   C. **decurso lumine vitae** = "when the light of (his) life had been run through"; an unusual variant on the usual *decurso vitae* (or *aetatis*) *spatio*; but compare n. 24A above.

28.   **omnīs** = "all (others)"; *i*-stem acc. plur.; compare 15 n. 14A (and 69 nn. 5B and 8A).

29.   A. **ut** = "just as"; used postpositively to introduce a comparison common in poetry, namely that Epicurus "extinguished" all (other philosophers or men) just as the risen ethereal sun does the stars.   B. **aethĕrius**: the *aethēr* was the upper "ether" in which the sun and planets moved, as distinct from the *āēr* = "air" (see 69 n. 12A) enveloping the earth.   C. **sōl**: for the monosyllabic verse ending compare 69 n. 12F.

30.   A. **tu . . . obire** = "will you, forsooth, be angry and think yourself undeserving to die?" Lucretius still addresses the reader-pupil; see pref. and n. 16B above.   B. **obire**: goes not only with *dubitabis*, which may take an inf. (57 n. 8A and 65 n. 14), but also with *indignabere*, which may take an inf. or a clause introduced by *quod* or *si*. For -*re* as an ending of the 2nd pers. sing. pass. see 14 n. 13E (and 32 n. 11A).

31.   A. **mortua**: predicate adj. after *est*, agreeing with *vita*; the collocation of two contrasting words forms an "oxymoron"; see 57 n. 9C.   B. **prope iam**: probably not to be taken together with *mortua*, i.e. as = "almost already dead," but *prope* with *mortua* and *iam* with *vivo etc.*; = "is almost dead while you are still alive etc."

32.   **geris**: more vivid than *habes*, suggesting the burden which a mind troubled with empty fear imposes on those unenlightened by Epicurean rationalism.

71

Cicero, as consul in 63, had to resist a succession of moves by the *populares* either to win favor with the urban mob or to intimidate the government. How far prominent *populares* like Crassus and Caesar had previously lent secret support to Catiline, or did so in 63 when he stood for consul for the third time, cannot now be ascertained. When, however, having been defeated again, he turned to conspiracy in Rome and armed revolt in Etruria (see 32 pref.), the *populares* must have withdrawn from any direct involvement. Even so, Cicero, though informed fully of the plot, did not dare arrest Catiline outright for fear that this would arouse popular sympathy for him. Instead, on November 7 or 8 he summoned the senate to meet in the temple of Jupiter Stator; see n. 17 below. When Catiline brazenly attended, Cicero loosed upon him the full power of his invective and made it clear that he was cognizant of the conspiracy. Catiline, as Cicero urged, withdrew to join his forces in Etruria. On the following day Cicero exposed the plot to the people in a second oration and a month later, on December 3, he informed them in a third oration that he had secured ample evidence to justify the arrest of the agents whom Catiline had left in Rome. Though he felt that these traitors had forfeited citizen rights, he still did not dare to put them to death on his own authority, in virtue of a *senatus consultum ultimum* (see n. 12 below), for fear that he might be accused of executing Roman citizens without recognizing the traditional right of appeal to the people; see 36 pref. In a fourth oration, therefore, he asked the advice of the senate as to what he should do. Caesar almost carried the vote for imprisonment, but Cato the Younger swung it back to death; see 34 pref. Cicero had the prisoners executed immediately, in an ancient underground chamber near the Forum called the *Tullianum*.

The first two paragraphs of the following selection open, and the last two close, Cicero's *First Oration against Catiline*. The famous opening sentences are justly admired for their rapid, rapierlike thrusts. They differ greatly in their ejaculatory brevity and lack of transition or subordination from Cicero's more formal and complex "periodic" style, to which he works up in his solemn concluding invocation of the state and of Jupiter.

Cicero in Catilinam invehit

Quo usque tandem abutere, Catilina, patientia nostra?[1] Quam diu etiam furor iste tuus nos eludet? Quem ad finem sese effrenata iactabit audacia?[2] Nihilne te nocturnum praesidium Palati, nihil urbis vigiliae, nihil timor populi, nihil concursus bonorum omnium, nihil hic munitissimus habendi senatus locus, nihil horum ora voltusque moverunt?[3] Patere tua consilia non sentis? Constrictam iam horum omnium scientia teneri coniurationem tuam non vides?[4] Quid proxima, quid superiore nocte egeris, ubi fueris, quos convocaveris, quid consili ceperis, quem nostrum ignorare arbitraris?[5]

O tempora! O mores![6] Senatus haec intellegit, consul videt; hic tamen vivit. Vivit? Immo vero etiam in senatum venit, fit publici consili particeps, notat et designat oculis ad caedem unum quemque nostrum.[7] Nos autem, fortes viri, satis facere rei publicae videmur, si istius furorem ac tela vitemus.[8] Ad mortem te, Catilina, duci iussu consulis iam pridem oportebat;[9] in te conferri pestem quam tu in nos omnes iam diu machinaris.[10] An vero vir amplissimus Publius Scipio, pontifex maximus, Tiberium Gracchum mediocriter labefactantem statum rei publicae privatus interfecit—Catilinam, orbem terrae caede atque incendiis vastare cupientem, nos consules perferemus?[11] Habemus senatus consultum in te, Catilina, vehemens et grave.[12] Non deest rei publicae consilium neque auctoritas huius ordinis; nos, nos, dico aperte, consules desumus.[13]

Sed polliceor hoc vobis, patres conscripti, tantam in nobis fore diligentiam, tantam in vobis auctoritatem, tantam in equitibus Romanis virtutem, tantam in omnibus bonis consensionem, ut Catilinae profectione omnia patefacta, illustrata, oppressa, vindicata esse videatis.[14] Hisce ominibus Catilina, cum summa rei publicae salute, cum tua peste ac pernicie, cumque eorum exitio qui se tecum omni scelere parricidioque iunxerunt, proficiscere ad impium bellum ac nefarium.[15]

Tu, Iuppiter, qui isdem quibus haec urbs auspiciis a Romulo es constitutus,[16] quem Statorem huius urbis atque imperi vere nominamus,[17] hunc et huius socios a tuis ceterisque templis, a tectis urbis ac moenibus, a vita fortunisque civium omnium arcebis;[18] et homines bonorum inimicos, hostes patriae, latrones Italiae, scelerum foedere inter se ac nefaria societate coniunctos, aeternis suppliciis vivos mortuosque mactabis.[19]

1. A. **quo usque tandem** = "how far, then," implying "how long"; *tandem*, lit. = "finally," often thus strengthens a question or command.   B. **abutēre:** Cicero regularly uses the 2nd sing. pass. ending -*ris* in the pres. ind., as *arbitraris* and *machinaris* below, but -*re* (see 14 n. 13E and 70 n. 30B) in other tenses of the ind. (here fut.) and

subj.   c. **patientia**: abl. (of means) after a compound of *utor*; see 14 n. 16B and compare *abusus dominatione* in the 3rd sentence of the 1st par. of 42A.

2.   A. **furor ... tuus**: for the connotations of *furor* see 19 n. 1c (and 22 n. 13c). *Iste* is here pejorative (or derogatory) as well as "of the 2nd pers." (as in 34 n. 8B); in the second connotation it is supplemented for emphasis by *tuus*.   B. **eludet** = "will make sport of," i.e. frustrate; Eng. "elude" has acquired the connotation of "escape the notice of."   c. **effrenata**: perhaps an adj. from the adj. *effrenus*, rather than the past part. of a rare verb *effreno*; compare 6 n. 12B (and 60 n. 16A).

3.   A. **nihilne**: this and the following *nihil*'s are adverbial (or "inner") accs., as in 20 n. 4A, and more emphatic than simple *non*.   B. **nocturnum ... Palati**: Cicero and other prominent Romans lived on the slopes of the Palatine (see 50 n. 4 and 51 n. 7B) above the Forum, so that the guards may have been to protect them. Indeed some of Catiline's associates had visited Cicero's house for his morning reception in hopes of murdering him in his bed. The guards may also have been to ensure that the senators could get safely to the temple of Jupiter Stator.   c. **bonorum omnium** = "of all right-minded (citizens)"; compare nn. 14B and 19B below (and 18 n. 5c).   D. **ora voltusque**: a common hendiadys (see 13 n. 11A and 68 n. 21B) for "the looks on the faces."

4.   **non sentis ... non vides**: omission of the interrog. -*ne* indicates abrupt astonishment, blame, or the like; the interrog. force was given by the tone of voice.

5.   A. **quid proxima ... ceperis**: a series of indirect questions dependent on *ignorare*, for which see n. c below.   B. **proxima ... superiore nocte** = "last (night) ... the night before."   c. **quem nostrum** = "who of us"; the interrog. pronoun followed by the partitive gen. is made subject of the inf. *ignorare* in indirect statement after *arbitraris*.

6.   **O tempora! O mores!**: probably accs. of exclamation (see 13 n. 2A); not vocs. or noms., as in 59 n. 20A.

7.   A. **immo vero etiam** = "not only that, but he even etc."; *immo*, with or without *vero*, traditionally rendered "nay rather," restates a previous assertion either correcting, denying, strengthening, or removing a doubt.   B. **oculis** = "by (his) glances."

8.   A. **fortes viri**: sarcastic.   B. **si ... vitemus**: protasis not of *videmur* but of *satis facere*, hence subj. in indirect discourse.

9.   **te ... oportebat** = "you ought to have been led." But in Lat. *oportet* is a true impersonal, so that the person (*te*) is acc. subject of the complementary pass. inf. *duci*, which is pres. because the past time is expressed by *oportebat*; compare 10 n. 12B (and 54 n. 3A). The imperf., especially with *iam pridem* (as here), is often used for an action which has been true for some time, but has just become clear at the time of speaking.

10.   A. **conferri pestem**: dependent on *oportebat*.   B. **quam ... machinaris**: this clause, though subordinated to the complementary inf. *conferri* (*oportebat*), is not changed to the subj. because it represents an assertion by the speaker himself, not an indirect quotation of another's statement; contrast n. 8B above.   c. **iam diu**: indicates an action in the pres. which has been going on for a long time, hence the pres. pass. ind. *machinaris*, for which Eng. can use a progressive perf. "you have been plotting," to convey both ideas. Contrast *iam pridem* with the imperf. in n. 9 above, but compare the use of the imperf. where Eng. would use progressive pluperf. for an action continuing into some moment in the past, for which see 21 n. 4B.

11.   A. **an ... perferemus**: *an* (compare 63 n. 9B) sometimes introduces a single question, to connote indignation or surprise; this rhetorical question comprises two main clauses without a connective and might be rendered in Eng.: "then indeed did Scipio kill ... (and) shall we endure?" Or in Eng. the first clause may be subordinated: "then indeed, although Scipio killed ... shall we endure?"   B. **Publius Scipio etc.**: for the assassination of Tiberius Gracchus by a mob led by his cousin Scipio Nasica, see 18, especially n. 11.   c. **mediocriter ... rei publicae**: Cicero implies that Tiberius Gracchus was less harmful than Catiline threatened to be, and indeed Cicero felt that

Tiberius did less harm than Gaius; see 20 A.   D. **privatus:** the *pontifex maximus* had no legal authority to exercise police powers, so Scipio acted in this case merely as an ordinary citizen (compare 30 n. 8 and 54 n. 7A), here contrasted with the *consules* who are doing nothing.

12.   **senatus consultum:** the senate had passed a *s.c. ultimum* (see 18 n. 9) ordering the consuls, in view of rumors about Catiline's plot, "to take care that the state should suffer no harm," a form of declaration of emergency first used against Gaius Gracchus in 121; see 19 pref.

13.   A. **consilium . . . auctoritas:** as punctuated in the text, these are both defined by the possessive gen. *huius ordinis* (i.e. the senate) since *rei publicae* is dat. after *deest.* Some editors put a comma after *consilium* and regard it as general.   B. **consilium:** has in this selection all three of its most common connotations: in the 1st par. *tua consilia* = "your (concrete) plans" (i.e. plots), then *publici consili particeps* = "sharer in (lit. of) public deliberation" (i.e. in a deliberative body), and here *consilium* = either "a general program" or "wisdom," "foresight."

14.   A. **patres conscripti:** for this regular formula of address to the senate see 27 n. 16B.   B. **tantam . . . consensionem:** this drawing together of the magistrates (= *principes*), the *senatus auctoritas*, the loyalty of the knights, and the *consensus omnium bonorum* (compare n. 3C above) is perhaps the first specific expression of the *concordia ordinum* which was for the next decade Cicero's political program against the disintegration of the Republic; see 67 pref.   C. **profectione:** probably abl. of means, = "by," not of time when, = "at." During his speech, Cicero had repeatedly urged Catiline to leave Rome, ostensibly to relieve the city of his dangerous presence but actually because Cicero was not sure of public support if Catiline should be arrested; see pref. above.

15.   A. **hisce ominibus:** abl. of attendant circumstance; compare *auspicibus vobis* in 52 n. 3. Cicero probably means that that unity of all elements in the state against Catiline was an omen of his ultimate failure. For the demonstrative suffix -*ce* see 29 n. 10 (and 63 n. 15A).   B. **cum . . . cum . . . cumque:** since these *cum* phrases of accompaniment express what the omens predict, they are best rendered in Eng. by "to" or "for." In Lat. a series of three or more regularly has either a connective with each unit or none at all; for the latter see toward the end of 34 B. Here the use of -*que* only with the last item indicates that the last two phrases are to be taken as a unit balanced against the first.   C. **scelere parricidioque:** possibly abls. of means rather than loc. abls. in view of *foedere . . . ac . . . societate coniunctos* below; Eng. idiom might use "for" rather than "by" or "in."   D. **proficiscere:** pres. pass. (dep.) imperative sing. In the plur. the imperative pass. is identical with the 2nd pers. plur. ind. (see 27 n. 7A), but in the sing. -*re* is always used, not -*ris*; compare n. 1B above.

16.   A. **Iuppiter:** for the form and origin of this voc. see 52 n. 1B.   B. **qui . . . es constitutus:** i.e. whose temple was founded; the reference is to Romulus' foundation of a temple to Jupiter on the Capitoline; see 50 n. 1B (and 51–52) and contrast n. 17 below. C. **isdem quibus . . . auspiciis** = "under the same auspices as"; for the case see n. 15A above; for the inclusion of the antecedent within the rel. clause see 12 n. 8B (and 66 n. 2A). For the *auspicia* by which the gods showed their favor (or disfavor) toward a public enterprise see 52 n. 3.

17.   **Statorem:** the senate was meeting on this occasion in a temple dedicated to Jupiter "The Stayer"; for this meaning of *sto* and its derivatives compare 60 n. 25A, and for meetings of the senate in places other than the *curia* see 27 n. 15 (and 80 n. 13B). The epithet derived from the fact that Jupiter had "stayed" the flight of the Romans in a battle against the Sabines, and Romulus had vowed a temple to him. However, the temple seems not to have been built (on the brow of the Palatine overlooking the Forum) until Jupiter intervened similarly in a battle between Romans and Samnites in 294; hence the reference in n. 16B above to a temple dedicated by Romulus to Jupiter must be to the Capitoline temple.

18. **arcebis . . . mactabis:** the futs. indicate confident certainty, as against hortatory subjs. or even imperatives; compare 44 n. 8c (and 45 n. 11) and contrast 52 n. 1d.

19. A. **et homines etc.:** though this continues as an address to Jupiter, it is in fact a solemn cursing of Catiline, living and dead, such as was occasionally pronounced officially against someone leaving Rome on an unauthorized adventure or one contrary to the omens.   B. **bonorum inimicos:** i.e. personal enemies (in politics; compare 60 n. 19 and 67 n. 1b) of right-minded citizens (see n. 3c above and 35 n. 25), balanced with *hostes patriae* = "(public) foes of the fatherland"; compare 29 n. 2. Since *inimicos* is here a noun, not an adj., it governs an objective gen., not a dat.   C. **mactabis:** *macto* originally meant "extol" or "honor" and then "honor a god by sacrifice"; hence it came to mean "sacrifice an animal" and, since the execution of criminals was regarded as a sort of sacrifice, "punish," usually by death as here. The word thus had in classical Lat. two opposite meanings, occasionally "honor" and often "punish," in both cases usually with the connotation of a solemn act.

72

Lucius Sergius Catilina, degenerate scion of a patrician *gens*, had been an unscrupulous agent of Sulla in his proscriptions (see 26 pref. and 66) and, in 67, a corrupt propraetor of Africa. His three futile attempts to secure the consulship and the defeat of his final conspiracy by Cicero in 63 have already been described; see 32 and 71. Seven years later, in 56, Cicero defended a protégé, Caelius (see 38 pref.), on five charges, including those of poisoning and of disturbing the peace. One of the incidental accusations made against Caelius, an able but hotheaded young man, was that of friendship and complicity with Catiline. Cicero, unable to deny this association wholly, sought to excuse Caelius by the following description of Catiline's complex and deceptive personality.

Catilinae ingenium

Studuit Catilinae Caelius—sed et multi hoc idem ex omni ordine atque ex omni aetate fecerunt.[1] Habuit enim ille permulta maximarum non expressa signa sed adumbrata lineamenta virtutum.[2] Utebatur hominibus improbis multis;[3] et quidem optimis se viris deditum esse simulabat. Erant apud illum inlecebrae libidinum multae;[4] erant etiam industriae quidam stimuli ac laboris.[5] Flagrabant vitia libidinis apud illum; vigebant etiam studia rei militaris. Neque ego umquam fuisse tale monstrum in terris ullum puto,[6] tam ex contrariis diversisque et inter se pugnantibus naturae studiis cupiditatibusque conflatum.[7] Quis clarioribus viris quodam tempore iucundior,[8] quis turpioribus coniunc-tior? quis civis meliorum partium aliquando,[9] quis taetrior hostis huic civitati? quis in voluptatibus inquinatior, quis in laboribus patientior? quis in rapacitate avarior? quis in largitione effusior?

Illa vero, iudices, in illo homine admirabilia fuerunt:[10] compre-hendere multos amicitia,[11] tueri obsequio, cum omnibus communicare quod habebat; servire temporibus suorum omnium pecunia,[12] gratia, labore corporis, scelere etiam si opus esset, et audacia; versare suam naturam et regere ad tempus atque huc et illuc torquere ac flectere;[13] cum tristibus severe, cum remissis iucunde, cum senibus graviter, cum iuventute comiter, cum facinerosis audacter, cum libidinosis luxuriose vivere.[14]

Hac ille tam varia multiplicique natura cum omnes omnibus ex terris homines improbos audacesque collegerat,[15] tum etiam multos fortes viros et bonos specie quadam virtutis adsimulatae tenebat. Neque umquam ex illo delendi huius imperi tam consceleratus impetus exstitisset nisi tot vitiorum tanta immanitas quibusdam facultatis et patientiae radicibus niteretur.[16] Me ipsum, me inquam, quondam paene ille decepit, cum et civis mihi bonus et optimi cuiusque cupidus et firmus amicus ac fidelis videretur.[17] Cuius ego facinora oculis prius quam opinione, manibus ante quam suspicione deprehendi.[18] Cuius in magnis catervis amicorum si fuit Caelius, magis est ut ipse moleste ferat errasse se[19] (sicuti non numquam in eodem homine me quoque erroris mei paenitet)[20] quam ut istius amicitiae crimen reformidet.[21]

1. **studuit** = "was a supporter of," lit. "was zealous for"; compare *studium* in 68 n. 18c. It is followed by the dat.

2. **non expressa . . . lineamenta** = "not express evidence but (at least) foreshadowed outlines," i.e. Catiline (*ille*) gave indications of good qualities which in fact he never actually displayed. The metaphor perhaps comes from painting.

3. **utebatur:** i.e. "he used to associate with." Throughout the following description, Cicero makes effective use of contrast, balance, and culmination; compare the 1st par. of 29.

4. **apud illum** = "in him," i.e. in his character or way of life; contrast *apud* = "in the house of" in 35 n. 8A (and compare 43 nn. 19B and 21c).

5. **quidam stimuli:** nom. plur. modified by the gens. (probably "defining" or "limiting") *industriae . . . ac laboris.*

6. **tale monstrum** = "such a portent"; for the meaning of *monstrum* = "something extraordinary" see 86 n. 26B where, as in 46 n. 5A, it is similarly used of Cleopatra.

7. A. **tam . . . conflatum** = "so fused together from contrary and diverse and contradictory urgent impulses of character"; the first two adjs. are connected closely by -*que* and balanced by *et* against the participial phrase; compare 23 n. 16 (and contrast 43 n. 2). B. **inter se pugnantibus:** a common idiom for "contradictory," perhaps to be rendered "at odds with one another." C. **naturae** = "character"; compare 65 n. 4A. D. **studiis cupiditatibusque:** may by hendiadys (see 13 n. 11A and 71 n. 3D) be rendered as an adj. and noun. E. **conflatum:** lit. used of "melting" (by heating and "blowing") metals together to form an alloy.

8. **quis . . . effusior:** for the device of a series of rhetorical questions compare the 2nd par. of 30. For the conventional elements in this kind of description of character (e.g. endurance combined with a devotion to pleasure, adaptability, politic friendliness, etc.), compare the descriptions of Hannibal in 11 B, of Caesar and Cato in 34 B, and of Sulla in 65.

9. **meliorum partium:** for *partes* = "political party" see 25 n. 5B. Cicero here regards Catiline's adherence to Sulla as support of the senatorial party, and therefore commendable.

10. A. **illa ... fuerunt** = "the following (characteristics) ... were paradoxical" or "there were the following paradoxical (characteristics)." *Ille* may refer to what follows, as in 70 nn. 6 and 14A, as may also *hic*, as in 70 n. 16A; when used together they refer to the further (*ille*) and the nearer (*hic*), as in 58 n. 17A.   B. **admirabilia:** the manuscripts uniformly give *mirabilia*, but this ordinarily connotes "admirable" and only a few of the qualities mentioned are admirable; it has therefore been proposed to emend to *admirabilia*, which connotes "worthy of wonder" for any reason, and hence "paradoxical."

11. A. **comprehendere etc.:** this and the following infs. through *vivere* at the end of the par. are not historical but substantive in predicate apposition to *admirabilia*, and define the paradoxical characteristics.   B. **amicitia:** for the political connotations of this word see 38 n. 17A (and contrast 60 n. 19 and 71 n. 19B).

12. **temporibus suorum omnium** = "the times (of need) of all his (followers)"; for this meaning of *tempus* compare 30 n. 3B; for *suorum* = "of his (men)" see 3 n. 6C.

13. **versare ... ad tempus** = "to direct and control his nature toward the time," i.e. according to the needs of the moment; compare the preceding note (and 48 n. 2).

14. **iuventute:** collective abstract for *iuvenibus*; see 8 n. 9A (and 62 n. 16B); *senectute* does not appear to have been similarly used for *senibus* (just before).

15. A. **natura:** abl. of description with *ille*.   B. **cum ... tum:** correlatives (see 21 n. 24 and 42 n. 1), since *collegerat* would be pluperf. subj. if *cum* were temporal; compare 2 n. 2B.

16. A. **consceleratus:** probably an adj., like *sceleratus* in 53 n. 14B (compare 71 n. 2C), rather than past part. of the rare verb *conscelero*, though this is used by Catullus once. B. **exstitisset ... niteretur:** a mixed contrary to fact condition, in which the pluperf. subj. of the apodosis represents a single past action, while the imperf. subj. of the protasis indicates a state continuing in the past and giving rise to the single action. For the continuing past state Eng. would use a compound tense to express both the continuity and the past time, as here "had been based"; compare 71 n. 10C.   C. **exstitisset:** from *exsisto* = "I step forth" rather than from *exsto* = "I stand out"; compare 39 n. 17A.   D. **quibusdam ... radicibus** = "on some elements," lit. "roots"; abl. after *nitor* and either loc. = "on" or instrumental = "by."

17. A. **cum ... videretur:** *cum* may here be temporal (contrast n. 15 above) or causal, depending on whether Cicero meant that Catiline deceived him "when" or "because."   B. **optimi cuiusque cupidus** = "eager for (the acquaintance of) each best (citizen)" or "a supporter of etc."; *quisque* with the superlative implies a plur. "all"; see 26 n. 4B.   C. **cupidus:** with a gen. (compare 17 n. 12) of the person may be equivalent to *studiosus*.

18. A. **cuius ... deprehendi:** Cicero claims that only proof of Catiline's crimes (*facinora* is neut. acc. plur. of *facinus*), found by the unmasking of the conspiracy, convinced him that Catiline was not the *civis bonus* that he had pretended to be.   B. **opinione:** here = "by (mental) understanding"; contrast 34 n. 9 (and 37 n. 4A).   C. **manibus:** here connotes "by (holding the evidence in my own) hands"; contrast 62 n. 15B (and 65 n. 25).

19. A. **cuius ... Caelius:** Cicero naturally minimizes Caelius' intimacy with Catiline. B. **magis ... ferat** = "it is preferable (lit. rather) that he should take it badly (i.e. be sorry)"; resumed by *quam ut* after the parenthesis. For this meaning of *fero* and an adv. see 3 n. 2A (and 63 n. 6).

20. A. **sicuti** = *sicut*; compare *uti* in 28 n. 23D (and 63 n. 5B).   B. **non numquam:** i.e. often; compare 33 n. 21 (and 55 n. 9A).   C. **in eodem homine** = "in (the case of

this) same man"; compare 30 n. 6A.   D. **me . . . paenitet:** for the acc. of the person and the gen. of the cause with impersonal verbs of feeling see 22 n. 12B (and 63 n. 12B).

21. **istius:** probably gen. of the demonstrative adj. modifying *amicitiae*, rather than objective gen. of the demonstrative pronoun depending on *amicitiae*; the connotation "friendship with him" would be the same in either case.

73

Gaius Valerius Catullus (*ca.* 84–*ca.* 54) was born in Cisalpine Gaul, as were, slightly later, Vergil (see 55 pref.) and Livy; see 56 pref. Like them also, he went as a young man from his native Verona to Rome with sufficient means to move in good society. Though wellborn and well-to-do young Romans were expected to undertake a public career leading to the magistracies and membership in the senate, Catullus did not do so, except that, perhaps to forget frustration in love (see 74 pref.), he spent the year 57 in Bithynia on the staff of the propraetor Gaius Memmius; for whom see 69 n. 21c. He belonged to a group of "new poets" who introduced into Latin poetry a directly personal lyricism, based in part on the Greek lyric of the seventh and sixth centuries and in part on Alexandrian models. Of this group, Catullus' verse alone survives. He wrote both with a vigorous and sensitive feeling for language, style, and meter and with a strongly emotional content; witness his affection for his deceased brother (A) and for his friend the poet Calvus in his bereavement (D), his tone, whether sarcastic or humorous (see nn. 36A and B below), toward Cicero (E), his bitter aversion to Caesar (F), and his appreciation of his villa at Sirmio (C). But his strongest passions were expended on a woman whom he called Lesbia, as the following selection (74) will indicate.

One hundred and sixteen poems survived the Middle Ages in a single manuscript, found at Verona in the Renaissance, copied, and since lost. In this collection, the poems are arranged neither chronologically nor by topic but by meter; first short poems in various meters, principally two: the hendecasyllabic or Phalaecian (B and E), a verse of five feet (eleven syllables), of which the second is a dactyl and the remainder trochees or spondees; and the choliambic or scazon (C), a verse of six feet, of which the first five are iambs or spondees and the last a trochee or spondee, which gives a "limping" (= the Greek adj. *cholos* or pres. part. *skazon*) effect to the conclusion. For these two meters see the metrical schemes immediately following the selections. There follow several longer poems in varied meters, notably a short epic (or "epyllion") in dactylic hexameter on the marriage of the parents of Achilles, Peleus and Thetis, in which there is a long inserted "episode" about Theseus and Ariadne. The last third of the collection comprises poems in elegiac distichs (A, D, F); it is noteworthy that these do not differ in themes or attitudes from the other lyrics.

Catulli carmina varia

A.   Multas per gentes et multa per aequora vectus[1]
   advenio has miseras, frater, ad inferias,[2]
   ut te postremo donarem munere mortis[3]

et mutam nequiquam adloquerer cinerem.[4]
  Quandoquidem fortuna mihi tete abstulit ipsum,[5]
    heu miser indigne frater adempte mihi,[6]
  nunc tamen interea haec,[7] prisco quae more parentum
    tradita sunt tristi munere ad inferias,[8]
  accipe fraterno multum manantia fletu;[9]
    atque in perpetuum, frater, ave atque vale.[10]

B.   Iam ver egelidos refert tepores;[11]
     iam caeli furor aequinoctialis
     iucundis Zephyri silescit auris.[12]
     Linquantur Phrygii, Catulle, campi[13]
     Nicaeaeque ager uber aestuosae;[14]
     ad claras Asiae volemus urbes.
     Iam mens praetrepidans avet vagari,[15]
     iam laeti studio pedes vigescunt.[16]
     O dulces comitum valete coetus,[17]
     longe quos simul a domo profectos
     diversae varie viae reportant.[18]

C.   Paene insularum, Sirmio, insularumque
     ocelle,[19] quascumque in liquentibus stagnis
     marique vasto fert uterque Neptunus,[20]
     quam te libenter quamque laetus inviso,[21]
     vix mi ipse credens Thyniam atque Bithynos
     liquisse campos et videre te in tuto.[22]
     O quid solutis est beatius curis,[23]
     cum mens onus reponit, ac peregrino
     labore fessi venimus larem ad nostrum,[24]
     desideratoque adquiescimus lecto?
     Hoc est quod unum est pro laboribus tantis.[25]
     Salve, o venusta Sirmio, atque ero gaude;[26]
     gaudete vosque, O Lydiae lacus undae;[27]
     ridete quidquid est domi cachinnorum.[28]

D.   Si quicquam mutis gratum acceptumve sepulcris

        accidere a nostro, Calve, dolore potest,[29]

      quo desiderio veteres renovamus amores[30]

        atque olim missas flemus amicitias,[31]

    certe non tanto mors immatura dolori est

        Quintiliae, quantum gaudet amore tuo.[32]

E.   Disertissime Romuli nepotum,[33]

      quot sunt quotque fuere, Marce Tulli,[34]

      quotque post aliis erunt in annis,[35]

      gratias tibi maximas Catullus

      agit pessimus omnium poeta;[36]

      tanto pessimus omnium poeta,

      quanto tu optimus omnium patronus.[37]

F.   Nil nimium studeo, Caesar, tibi velle placere,[38]

      nec scire utrum sis albus an ater homo.[39]

    1. **multas etc.**: Catullus' brother had died in the East sometime previous to Catullus' own trip thither; the poet says elsewhere that the grave was near Troy, in the northwest corner of Asia Minor, and therefore on his route to Bithynia, for which see 68 n. 15A. Catullus envisages himself as fulfilling tardily at the grave the rites which should have been performed at his brother's burial. The preponderance of spondees in this and the 3rd and 4th verses gives a solemn tone; see 60 n. 5B.

    2. A. **advenio**: not only "I do come" but "I am (or, have) come," as suggested by *vectus*, and therefore followed, like a historical pres., by secondary sequence. The perf. *ādvēn(i)* would fit the meter equally well, but the pres. gives the immediacy of direct address.   B. **has . . . ad inferias** = "to (or, for) these sad funeral rites"; *ad* may here be directional, repeating *ad-* in *advenio*, or it may connote purpose (compare 5 n. 9A), as in the 6th verse below.

    3. A. **te . . . donarem**: *dono* may take either the acc. of the thing given or, as here, the acc. of the person with the abl. of means of the thing with which he is "presented."   B. **munere mortis** = "with an offering for the dead"; the possessive gen. indicates that the gift is suitable to death.

    4. **mutam . . . cinerem** = "I may address (your) mute ash(es, though) to no purpose"; *cinis*, usually m., is f. in Catullus here and in poem 68 v. 90. Here, in D below, and in 74A, Catullus has little faith in a real afterlife, though he suggests that living persons' concern can reach the consciousness of the dead; contrast Lucretius in 70.

    5. **tete**: intensive for *te*; see 60 n. 28B (and 70 n. 16B).

    6. **indignē**: adv. with the voc. past part. *ademptĕ*, which agrees with *frater*; the interlocking order is effective.

    7. **interea** = "for the time being," i.e. until I can do something more suitable; for this use of *interea* with the imperative compare 69 n. 24B.

    8. A. **prisco . . . more parentum** = "by the ancient custom of our parents," i.e. by the *mos maiorum*; compare 15 n. 13B (and 60 n. 25A). The abl. is "instrumental"

(manner or circumstance).   B. **tristi munere:** abl. of means, = "by (this) sad rite"; *munere* is here the act (or duty) of giving rather than the actual gift as in the 3rd verse; see n. 3B above. Some editors read *tristis* with *inferias* (see n. 2B above), and *munera* in predicate apposition with *quae*, meaning "as gifts."

9.   **fraterno . . . fletu** = "bedewed (lit. dripping) with a brother's (i.e. Catullus') tears"; *manantia* agrees with *haec* 2 verses above, which is object of *accipe.*

10.   **in . . . vale** = "hail and farewell forever, (my) brother." This was a ritualistic formula at burials. Tennyson's verses, composed at Sirmio and entitled *Frater, Ave atque Vale,* have reminiscences of this poem and of C below.

11.   A. **iam vēr etc.:** Catullus here rejoices at leaving Bithynia simply because he was homesick; in other poems he indicates that Memmius was not generous to his staff. B. **ēgelidos . . . tepores** = "balmy warmth"; the prefix *ē-* (= "away from") is here almost equivalent to a negative, i.e. "not cool"; it is, however, sometimes intensive, so that this word may also mean "chilly."

12.   A. **furor** = "storms"; contrast the meaning "radicalism, violence" in a political context, as in 19 n. 1C (and 71 n. 2A). Storms are frequent at the spring (as here, in March) and autumn equinoxes.   B. **aequinoctialis:** either nom. with *furor* or gen. with *caeli*; the latter seems to be preferred by critics. In this poem, only this verse ends with a trochee rather than a spondee; in E below only two (the 2nd and 3rd) out of seven end in spondees. Moreover, in this poem all the verses open with spondees, whereas in E the 3rd and 4th verses begin with trochees and the 5th with a rare iamb. Possibly E was an earlier poem; or perhaps the more trochaic rhythm gave it a lighter tone.   C. **iucundis Zephyri silescit auris** = "grows calm (lit. silent) at (lit. by) the pleasing (i.e. mild spring) breezes of Zephyr"; the last is the Greek name for the mild west wind which the Romans called *Favonius,* as in 69 n. 11A.

13.   A. **linquantur:** hortatory subj., as is *volemus* (from *volo, -are,* not from *volo, velle*) 2 verses below; *linquo* is common in poetry for the prose compound *relinquo.* B. **Phrygii:** Phrygia was actually south of Bithynia, in western Asia Minor behind coastal Ionia; however, at an early period the Phrygians seem to have extended north to the Black Sea.

14.   **Nicaeae . . . aestuosae** = "the fertile plain of hot (and therefore unhealthy) Nicaea." Nicaea, in Asia Minor at the southeast corner of the Sea of Marmara, shared with Nicomedia, at the entrance to the Bosporus opposite Constantinople (Byzantium), the distinction of being the chief city of western Bithynia and retained its importance into the late Roman Empire, when it was the seat of the first Christian "ecumenical" (of the whole church) council in A.D. 325. Since Nicaea was never an important trading port, the source which suggested Poe's phrase in *To Helen,* "those Nicaean barks of yore," remains obscure.

15.   **praetrepidans** = "trembling in advance," i.e. eagerly anticipating.

16.   **laeti:** perhaps best rendered in Eng. as an adv. with *vigescunt* = "joyfully grow eager" (compare 14 n. 18B and 63 n. 3B); then *studio* = "with desire (to leave)" is abl. of means (or cause) modifying the whole phrase, though its position also joins it closely with *laeti.*

17.   **dulces . . . coetus:** in other poems also, Catullus speaks warmly of his fellows on Memmius' staff.

18.   A. **longe . . . profectos** = "whom, after having journeyed together far from home."   B. **varie:** adv. with *reportant*; but some manuscripts and most editors read *variae,* i.e. "routes diverse (in course and) varied (in character)."

19.   A. **paene:** adv. used as adj. with *insularum* to form a new noun; = "of peninsulas"; *paeninsula* appears also in Lat. as one word.   B. **Sirmiō:** a peninsula at the southern end of Lake Garda (Lat., *Benacus lacus*), the easternmost of the lakes in North Italy (Cisalpine Gaul), close to Verona.   C. **insularumque ocelle** = "and darling of

islands (as well as of peninsulas)"; *ocellus*, a diminutive of *oculus* (= "eye"), is used of persons or things highly valued.

20. A. **liquentibus stagnis** = "lakes," as opposed to the *mari vasto*, which probably also follows *in*, though it might be construed as a simple abl. of place where, like *toto mari* in 29 n. 8B.   B. **liquentibus** = *liquidis*; the forms of *liqueo* and *liquor* (see 61 n. 33B), both = "flow" or "be liquid," should be carefully distinguished from those of *linquo*, for which see n. 13A above.   c. **vasto**: connotes not only size but empty desolation.   D. **uterque Neptūnus**: he is doubled to represent by metonymy both types of water; compare *Marte* = "war" in 49 n. 4. Pagan gods, like Christian saints, frequently assumed almost distinct individualities appropriate to different functions or different places of worship.   E. **uterque** = "each of two," i.e. both; compare in 47 n. 4A.

21. A. **quam . . . inviso**: *quam* is here the exclamatory adv. = "how," not a rel. The adv. *libenter* and the adj. *laetus* are used coordinately where Eng. would use two advs. and Lat. might have used two adjs.; compare n. 16 above, and contrast the use of *laetus* as a true adj. in 69 n. 13c.   B. **inviso**: seems here simply equivalent to *video* = "see" and not to have the frequentative connotation of "keep seeing" (as does *visendam* in 30 n. 15D) or "visit."

22. A. **mi** = *mihi*, as in 60 n. 6A, and is dat. after *credens*; metrically *me* could have been used as acc. subject of *liquisse*.   B. **Thȳniam** = *Bithȳnia*; of which *Bithȳnos* is the masc. acc. plur. adj.   c. **liquisse** = *reliquisse*: see n. 13A (and contrast n. 20B) above.   D. **in tuto**: adverbial, almost equivalent to the adv. *tute* (compare 47 n. 8B), i.e. he has returned in safety to see his home.

23. **solutis . . . curis** = "than cares done away with"; the abl. is after the comparative *beatius* (in predicate agreement with *quid*), and the phrase is explained by the *cum* temporal clause.

24. A. **vēnimus**: the meter requires the perf. here; however, the other pres. verbs in the sentence suggest that this is a pres. perf., i.e. "we are arrived," and indeed the perf. of *venio* is often used in this sense; contrast *advenio* in n. 2A above.   B. **larem**: used by metonymy for his home; compare 54 n. 12B. The *lares* (usually plur.), originally ancient Italic spirits (*numina*) either of the dead or of the fields, became protectors of crossroads or households. In household shrines, usually in the kitchen near the hearth, two *lares* are shown flanking some of the recognized Olympian gods, who may therefore have been identified with the originally nonanthropomorphic (*di*) *penates* or "pantry spirits" of that house, for whom see 1 n. 2A.

25. **hoc . . . tantis**: lit. = "this is which alone is in exchange for such labors," i.e. this of itself recompenses me for all the effort of traveling.

26. **ero**: abl. of *erus*, for which compare *era* in 60 n. 9B. The abl. after *gaudere* and similar verbs is either loc. ("in") or instrumental ("because of").

27. A. **gaudete vosque etc.** = "and rejoice, O you waves" (see following note); in this text, which is the reading of the manuscripts, the *-que* is irregularly attached to the second word of the clause which it connects.   B. **O Lȳdiae lacus undae** = "O Lydian waves of the lake"; for the transfer of the epithet from the masc. gen. sing. *lacūs* to the fem. nom. plur. *undae* by hypallage, see 46 n. 19 (and 69 n. 10B).   c. **Lȳdiae**: *Benacus lacus* (see n. 19B above) is called "Lydian" because the Etruscans, who were supposed to have emigrated to Italy from Lydia or thereabouts in Asia Minor, had expanded into the eastern Po Valley before its occupation by the Gauls; see 8 pref. Some manuscripts and editors read for *Lydiae* either *limpidae* or *liquidae*, in which the *-i-* is occasionally long; contrast n. 20B above.

28. **quidquid . . . cachinnorum**: voc. with *ridete*; = "whatever (of) laughter(s)"; for the partitive gen. compare 6 n. 6 (and 66 n. 2B).

29. A. **mutis**: dat. with *sepulcris*; compare *mutam . . . cinerem* in n. 4 above. In view of the interlocked word order, the dat. depends most closely on *gratum* and *acceptum*,

though it should also be extended to *accidere*.   B. **Calve:** Gaius Licinius Macer Calvus (82–47) was an orator and "new" poet (see pref. above) and a close friend of Catullus. His elegiac poems are said to have included a lament for his wife Quintilia, for whose recent death Catullus here seeks to console him. For the solemn effect of the spondees in this and the 5th verse compare n. 1 above.

30.   A. **quo desiderio:** the rel. clause modifies *dolore*, and *desiderio* is inserted in apposition to enlarge the concept from mere grief to a sense of loss and longing; compare its use in the 1st verse of 60 A.   B. **renovamus:** though a subj. might be expected in a rel. clause of purpose, the ind. is both given here by the manuscripts and required in the next verse where *fleamus* would not fit the meter; the ind. is poetically more effective as "by which longing we do renew," not "we may renew."

31.   A. **olim:** usually = "long since" or "formerly"; but, since Quintilia's death was presumably recent, it probably has here a more general connotation of "at any time" or "ever."   B. **missas:** i.e. "let go involuntarily," equivalent to *amissas*; compare 40 n. 12.   C. **amicitias:** normally less passionate than *amores* (but compare *amori* in 37 n. 13A) and perhaps used here as appropriate to the settled love of marriage. Both words were also used in a political context; for *amor* see 38 n. 8A and for *amicitia* 38 n. 17A (and 72 n. 11B).

32.   A. **tanto . . . dolori:** dat. of purpose, forming a double dat. with *Quintiliae*; see 17 n. 11A (and 52 n. 8A).   B. **tanto:** adj. correlative with the adv. *quantum*; = "is not for so great grief to Q. as she greatly rejoices in your love," i.e. does not grieve her as much as she rejoices etc.   C. **amore:** abl. after *gaudet*; see n. 26 above.

33.   A. **disertissime:** an epithet of praise of which Cicero was fond; Catullus uses it here ostensibly to flatter him; whether sincerely or not depends on his attitude in this poem; see n. 36 below.   B. **Rōmuli nepotum:** i.e. of the Romans; for Romulus as progenitor of the Romans see 60 A, especially n. 5A.

34.   **Marce Tulli:** i.e. Cicero (see 31 pref. etc.); this use of the *praenomen* and gentile name was formal.

35.   A. **post:** adv.; = "afterward."   B. **aliis:** i.e. future; in agreement with *annis*, which is abl. after *in*.

36.   A. **gratias etc.:** the occasion for which Catullus thanked Cicero is unknown, and critics differ as to whether he was sincere or poking fun at the vain orator (compare 37) by exaggerating both his flattery and his self-depreciation. The flattery, though extravagantly phrased for modern taste, would not have seemed so to Cicero's contemporaries (or, indeed, in modern Italy), particularly as coming from a younger and less prominent man to one of the outstanding figures of the time.   B **ăgĭt pēssĭmŭs etc.:** an infrequent substitution of an iamb for the first trochee (or spondee) of the hendecasyllabic verse; compare n. 12B above. Catullus' humorous self-depreciation is made effective by the repetition and interlocking of the last three lines. Cicero was a well-known wit and would have savored this, particularly when the wit flattered him. Again, critics differ as to whether Catullus was sincerely playing up to Cicero or being ironically sarcastic; see the preceding note.

37.   **patronus:** the Romans expressed the relation between an advocate and the one for whom he pleaded in the same terms that they used for the relation between a person of position and wealth and those after whom he looked; see 7 n. 7 (and 59 n. 24A). Eng. has kept "patron" and "client" for the social relationship but only "client" for the legal.

38.   **nil nimium** = "not too much," i.e. not at all; compare 33 n. 21 (and 72 n. 20B). Catullus' attacks on Caesar and on his henchman and engineer Mamurra are generally too frank for modern ears; this is one of the mildest, and simply expresses complete disregard for Caesar.

39.   **albus an ater** = "light or dark" rather than "white or black"; a proverbial

expression. Unconcern for such an obvious characteristic as a person's complexion implies complete unconcern for him. According to Suetonius *Iul.* 73, Catullus' father reconciled his son to Caesar just before Catullus' death. Thornton Wilder, in his *Ides of March*, incorrectly prolonging Catullus' life into 45, explores both the hostility and the eventual reconciliation between the two men.

74

The poems in which Catullus (see 73 pref.) expressed the stormy course of his love for Lesbia have won him an outstanding rank among personal lyricists. He refers to Lesbia as a married woman of high social position, and not as a professional courtesan of freedman status, such as were the girls celebrated by the Augustan love poets Gallus (whose works have not survived), Tibullus, Propertius, and Ovid, or by Horace in his lyric *Odes*, for which see 87. As was customary, Catullus disguised the real name of his girl by a term that recalls the Greek lyric love poetry of Sappho, who wrote in Lesbos about 600. Such disguised names were supposed to be metrically equivalent to the real name, and Apuleius (second century A.D.) states that Catullus *Lesbiam pro Clodia nominavit.*

Clodia, sister of Cicero's enemy Clodius (see 36 pref. and B), belonged to the patrician *gens Claudia* though, like her brother, she gave this name a popular "demagogic" spelling; see 36 n. 6A. She was married to Quintus Caecilius Metellus Celer, a member of the leading plebeian *gens* of the Caecilii Metelli, though of a different branch from those with the *agnomina* Numidicus and Pius of the period of the Civil War, for whom see 21 n. 2E, 23 n. 13A, and 28 n. 10. Metellus was consul in 60 and died in 59, so that Catullus' affair with Clodia presumably began in the late sixties, soon after his arrival in Rome. Clodia became so notorious for her affairs, particularly after Metellus' death, that she earned the epithet *quadrantaria,* i.e. a girl who sold her favors for a farthing; compare n. 2B below. By 58 Caelius, Cicero's young friend (see 38 pref.), had replaced Catullus in her affections, which may have led the poet to accept a post on the staff of Memmius in Bithynia; see 73 pref. By 56 Clodia had broken with Caelius and instigated a prosecution against him. Cicero, defending Caelius, not only excused his association with Catiline (see 72 pref.) but excoriated Clodia for her loose behavior and even accused her of incest with her brother; see 36 n. 6D. Her further fortunes are not known.

It seems plausible to interpret the course of the love affair somewhat as follows, though some scholars object to any attempt at biographical interpretation. Catullus' love started with the happy intensity of youth, illustrated in A (hendecasyllabics). Soon he began to suspect that Clodia's devotion to him was not wholehearted, as he humorously says in B (elegiacs). There seems to have been a first breach, followed by a reconciliation. Eventually, however, Catullus came unwillingly to realize her complete faithlessness, though he could not rid himself of his passion, as in C and D (elegiacs). Finally he made a decisive break, yet in E (choliambics) he still realized that "a sorrow's crown of sorrows is remembering happier things."

Lesbia

A.   Vivamus, mea Lesbia, atque amemus,[1]

rumoresque senum severiorum

omnes unius aestimemus assis![2]
Soles occidere et redire possunt;
nobis cum semel occidit brevis lux,
nox est perpetua una dormienda.[3]
Da mi basia mille, deinde centum,
dein mille altera, dein secunda centum,
deinde usque altera mille, deinde centum;[4]
dein, cum milia multa fecerimus,
conturbabimus illa, ne sciamus,[5]
aut ne quis malus invidere possit,
cum tantum sciat esse basiorum.[6]

B.   Nulli se dicit mulier mea nubere malle
          quam mihi, non si se Iuppiter ipse petat.[7]
      Dicit—sed mulier cupido quod dicit amanti,
          in vento et rapida scribere oportet aqua.[8]

C.   Odi et amo—quare id faciam, fortasse requiris.
          Nescio̅—sed fieri sentio et excrucior.[9]

D.   Dicebas quondam solum te nosse Catullum,
          Lesbia, nec prae me velle tenere Iovem.[10]
      Dilexi tum te non tantum ut vulgus amicam,
          sed pater ut gnatos diligit et generos.[11]
      Nunc te cognovi;[12] quare etsi impensius uror,
          multo mi tamen es vilior et levior.
      "Qui potis est?" inquis?[13] Quod amantem iniuria talis
          cogit amare magis, sed bene velle minus.[14]

E.   Miser Catulle, desinas ineptire;[15]
      et quod vides perisse, perditum ducas.[16]
      Fulsere quondam candidi tibi soles,[17]
      cum ventitabas quo puella ducebat
      amata nobis quantum amabitur nulla.[18]
      Ibi illa multa cum iocosa fiebant,
      quae tu volebas nec puella nolebat,

fulsere vere candidi tibi soles.[19]

Nunc iam illa non vult. Tu quoque impotens noli;[20]

nec quae fugit sectare; nec miser vive;[21]

sed obstinata mente perfer, obdura.

Vale, puella. Iam Catullus obdurat;

nec te requiret nec rogabit invitam.[22]

At tu dolebis, cum rogaberis nulla.[23]

Scelesta, vae te—quae tibi manet vita?[24]

Quis nunc te adibit? Cui videberis bella?[25]

Quem nunc amabis? Cuius esse diceris?[26]

Quem basiabis? Cui labella mordebis?[27]

At tu, Catulle, destinatus obdura.[28]

1. **vivamus, mea Lēsbĭa etc.**: Catullus, in the full flush of youthful passion, urges Lesbia to live and love despite criticism, since dark death waits.

2. A. **rumoresque senum severiorum** = "the (critical) gossip (see 61 n. 14B) of over-censorious elders"; *senum* (see 8 n. 8A) covers men and women; compare n. 11E below. B. **unius ... assis**: gen. of price; the pronominal gen. ending -*ius* often becomes -*ĭus* in poetry. The bronze *as*, though not coined during the Ciceronian age, remained the common unit of small value, like a penny; its subdivisions were of even less value, as the quarter *as* or *quadrans*, from which was formed the adj. *quadrantaria* applied to Clodia; see pref. above.

3. A. **nobis**: dat. of reference, both of "disadvantage" with *occĭdit* (see 70 n. 19B) and of "agent" with the pass. periphrastic *est ... dormienda* (for which see 21 n. 15C); compare 68 n. 15B (and 70 n. 13B). B. **brevis lux**: an almost unique monosyllabic ending for a hendecasyllabic verse; *lux* = "light" (i.e. day) is brought into sharp contrast with the immediately following *nox*. With these metaphors for life and death compare 60 n. 5B (and 70 n. 24A). C. **perpetua una** = "one unbroken." Catullus shows little confidence in an afterlife; see 73 nn. 4 and 29A.

4. A. **mī** = *mihi*, as in D verse 6 below; see 60 n. 6A (and 73 n. 22A). B. **basia**: *basium* first occurs in this verse of Catullus and is thereafter used rarely in Lat. compared with *osculum* or *suavium*; yet it alone descended to the Romance languages. It is thought possibly to have been a Celtic or Germanic word, perhaps brought from Cisalpine Gaul by Catullus himself, but not generally accepted into literature because it was felt to be colloquial or vulgar. C. **deinde** = *de* + *inde* (compare *dehinc*); the -*ei*- was pronounced as a diphthong; compare 70 n. 26A. Cicero says that *dein* was a shortened form (compare *exin* from *exinde*). *Dein* occurs only in literature and only before a consonant; *deinde* alone is attested in inscriptions. The alternation of the two forms here is effective. D. **altera etc.**: these neut. plurs. agree with *basia* understood, since *centum* and *mille* are adjs.; contrast *multa milia* below. The rapid buildup of sums prepares for the confusion envisaged in the last verse.

5. A. **fēcĕrĭmŭs**: cited as the only instance of -*ĭ*- in this form of the fut. perf. act. ind.; contrast 60 n. 6B. The perf. subj. would be very irregular in a *cum* fut. temporal clause. B. **conturbabimus ... sciamus**: popular superstition among many peoples regards "counting one's blessings" as likely to cause the envy not merely of other humans but of the divine powers (*numina*) or of God.

6. **invidere** = "to cast the evil eye upon"; even in prose, *invideo* and *invidia* often connote "ill will" rather than "envy." To cause harm effectively with his evil look, the *malus* would need to know the exact number of kisses; see the preceding note.

7. A. **nulli ... malle**: *se* is probably the subject of *malle* in indirect discourse, rather than reflexive object (see n. c below) of *nubere*, since the subject of an inf. in indirect discourse is only occasionally omitted, even when it is the same as that of the main verb, whereas *nubere* is often used absolutely, without an object.   B. **mulier**: occasionally used in love poetry for a mistress, rather than the usual *puella*, found in the 4th and 7th verses of E below, or *amica*, for which see n. 11c below.   C. **nubere** (**se**) = "to veil (oneself)," i.e. in preparation for marriage; it takes a dat. of advantage of the man for whom the bride did so, here *nulli* = *nemini*; compare 36 n. 1B. Only in later Lat. is it ever used of a man marrying, for which the regular term was *duco uxorem*, as at the end of 35 A.   D. **non si ... petat** = "not (even) if Jupiter himself should woo her"; the protasis of a fut. less vivid condition with the pres. subj. (see 36 n. 4) and not simply subj. by attraction in indirect discourse, though the apodosis is represented by *se malle*, for which Lesbia would have said *malim* in direct discourse. E. **se**: refers not to the subject (*Iuppiter*) of *petat* but to that (*mulier*) of the main verb. F. **Iuppiter**: nom.; see 52 n. 1B (and 71 n. 16A).

8. A. **cŭpĭdō**: dat. of the adj. with *amanti*, not the fem. nom. noun *cŭpĭdō, -ĭnĭs*. Both it and *mulier* precede the rel. clause in which they belong.   B. **scribere oportet**: the inf. is used absolutely (without subject) with the impersonal (see 37 n. 11B and compare 65 n. 16B) and is here best rendered in Eng. by a pass. "ought to be written," since the Eng. indefinite "one" suggests some other subject, whereas in the Lat. the woman is the center of thought throughout. The object of *scribere* is the preceding *quod* clause with its subject, *mulier*, anticipated and no antecedent expressed; compare 21 n. 20c (and 65 n. 15). The impermanence of anything written in water is a commonplace of literature; compare Keats's epitaph for himself: "Here lies one whose name was writ in water."

9. A. **odi et amo**: the coexistence of love and hate is a commonplace both of literature and of psychology; this sentiment is paraphrased by Ovid *Am.* II 4.5 and by Martial I 32, among others.   B. **nĕscĭō**: the final *-o* should probably be scanned as short by iambic shortening, as commonly in early comedy, rather than the *-ĭo* as a single long syllable by synizesis; compare *declamatĭŏ* in 59 n. 29B.   C. **fieri** = "that (this) happens"; the understood subject is the combination of loving and hating.   D. **excrucior**: the *ex-* is here separative in an intensive rather than in a negative sense; contrast 73 n. 11B.

10. A. **solum ... Catullum**: the fem. *te* (i.e. Lesbia) is subject, and *solum Catullum* object, of *nosse* = *novisse*; for the contraction see 1 n. 4B. In this poem Catullus refers to himself in both the 1st and 3rd pers.; contrast A, B, and C above, where he uses only the 1st pers., and compare n. 15A below.   B. **velle**: *te* continues as subject; *Iovem* is object of *tenere*. For her remark see B above.

11. A. **non tantum ut** = "not so much as," i.e. not merely as.   B. **vulgus** = "ordinary men"; an abstract sing. for a concrete plur.; compare 8 n. 9A (and 72 n. 14). Colloquial Eng. might say "the crowd."   C. **amicam**: more commonly implies "mistress" than simply "a female friend"; compare n. 7B above.   D. **pater ut**: for *ut* used postpositively to introduce a comparison see 70 n. 29A.   E. **gnatos ... generos** = "children and children-in-law"; *gnatos* is archaic for *natos*. The females are included in the collective masc. plur.; compare n. 2A above.

12. **cognovi**: pres. perf., as regularly; = "I have learned," i.e. "I now know"; compare 58 n. 13A.

13. A. **qui ... inquis**: as punctuated in the text, Catullus asks: "Do you say: 'How can it be'?" and the *qui* clause is, as regularly with *inquam*, the direct (not indirect) quotation of Lesbia's question to him. Many editors, however, punctuate *inquis* with a

period, as a simple statement: "You say: 'How can it be?'" Since *inquam* is generally used with a direct quotation it is less likely that there are two independent questions: "How can it be? Do you ask?"   B. **quī:** an old *i*-stem abl. used as an interrog. adv. C. **potis:** neut. (where *pote* might be expected; see 61 n. 21B) in agreement with the unexpressed subject of *est*, namely the whole idea of hating and loving at the same time.

14.   **bene velle:** lit. = "to wish well," here = "to feel affection (or respect) for"; as against *amare*, which would mean "to love with passion."

15.   A. **miser Cătulle etc.:** in this poem Catullus exhorts himself to forget Lesbia in a moving expression of firmness and regret; he begins with the 2nd and changes to the 3rd pers. form of referring to himself; compare n. 10A above.   B. **desinas . . . ducas:** these hortatory subjs. are more effective than direct imperatives would be since they have an overtone of wish; not only "cease" but "may you cease."   C. **ineptire:** this verb, from the adj. *ineptus*, occurs only rarely in early Lat. and not after Catullus.

16.   A. **quod . . . perisse:** rel. clause without antecedent (*id* may be understood; compare n. 8B above) serving probably as subject in indirect discourse rather than as object of *ducas*; see n. C below.   B. **perisse:** in classical Lat. the perf. forms of *eo* are contracted from *-ivi-* before *-s-* to *-i-*, not to *-ii-*; compare 1 n. 4B. Hence the form here as against Plautus' *periisse* in the next note.   C. **perditum:** since *duco* in the sense of "regard something as something" commonly takes *pro* or *in*+an abl., or a simple dat., and only rarely an acc. with an adj. modifying it appositionally, *perditum* should probably be taken as inf. in indirect discourse with *esse* understood, rather than as an adj. modifying the *quod* clause; see n. A above. With this verse compare Plautus *Trinummus* 1026: *quin tu quod periit periisse ducis?*

17.   A. **fulsēre:** 3rd pers. plur. perf. ind. act. of *fulgeo*, not of *fulcio*; for the ending compare 15 n. 10 (and 64 n. 8B).   B. **candidi . . . soles** = "bright suns," i.e. days; compare A verse 4 above; *candidus* is more intensive than *albus*.

18.   A. **ventitabas:** the frequentative meaning is intensified both by the use of the imperf. and by the repetition of the suffix *-(i)to*, with which compare *pensito* in 39 n. 15B (and *imperito* in 70 n. 19C).   B. **nobis:** dat. of reference (agent) with the perf. pass. part. *amata*; see 21 n. 15C (and compare n. 3A above).

19.   A. **ibi . . . cum** = "then when"; *ibi* may be thus used to intensify temporal words. Since the imperf. ind. is rare in classical Lat. after *cum* temporal to denote a specific past time, some manuscripts and many editors read *ibi . . . tum* = "then" and punctuate with a full stop after *nolebat* at the end of the following verse.   B. **illa multa . . . iocosa** = "those many merriments," i.e. great fun.   C. **quae . . . volebas:** this positive statement is effectively balanced against the following double negative *nec . . . nolebat.*   D. **nec** = *et non;* here used in place of the usual *neve*.   E. **fulsere vere:** an effective echo (with variation) of the 3rd verse; compare n. 17A above.

20.   **impotens noli:** an emendation; if correct, it may mean either "(though) powerless, (nevertheless) say no" or "being powerful, say no," since *impotens* is ambiguous. Modern scholars derive the second meaning, "overpowerful," from the first, "powerless," on the view that lack of self-control may lead to excessive display of power. However, a late Roman grammarian took the two meanings to show that the prefix *in-* might in this word be either negative or intensive; compare *e-* in 73 n. 11B and n. 9D above. If *impotens* is taken in the second sense, the clause might well be rendered in Eng. by two correlative imperatives: "master yourself and refuse."

21.   **sectare:** pres. pass. (dep.) imperative sing.; compare 71 n. 15D.

22.   **rogabit** = "will he ask for"; i.e. seek out, court.

23.   **nulla:** the negative adj. is used colloquially for an emphatic *non*; compare the use of *nihil* = *non* in 71 n. 3A.

24.   **vae te:** *vae* = "alas" or, as here, "woe"; the acc. is less common after it than the dat., as in *vae victis.*

25. **bella**: fem. nom. sing. in predicate agreement with the subject of *videberis*; from *bellus*, a contracted diminutive from *bonus*; i.e. *bonulus* > *benulus* > *bellus*; compare *oculus* > *ocellus* in 73 n. 19c. *Bellus* is used colloquially of women and children and of men often disparagingly or ironically, like Eng. "pretty"; in popular language (as possibly here) it became equivalent to *pulcher* and descended in this sense to the Romance languages.

26. **cuius esse dicēris** = "whose will you be said to be"; for the gen. compare 59 n. 7.

27. **cui**: dat. of reference (possession) with a part of the body; see 43 n. 6 (and 70 n. 13B). Biting the loved one's lips in kisses is frequently mentioned by the Lat. love poets.

28. **destinatus** = *obstinatus*; this verse effectively echoes (with variation) verse 11 above; compare n. 19E above. The part. and imperative are best rendered in Eng. by two imperatives; compare n. 20 above.

75

The conquest of Gaul by Caesar in the years of his proconsulship (58–50) are best known from his *Bellum Gallicum*; see 36 pref. This gives a detailed account of the military operations which he undertook and of the country itself, but no general statement of the importance and difficulty of the task of adding this territory to the Roman Empire. This is provided by the following selection, adapted from a speech of Cicero's on the "consular provinces" delivered in June or July 56, after the renewal of the Triumvirate at Luca, in which Cicero was forced to acquiesce; see 37 pref.

Caesar's enemies naturally objected to the extension of his command in Gaul which had been agreed upon at Luca and were making efforts to have him relieved; compare 38 pref. Cicero, however, as part of his submission to the Triumvirs, undertook to persuade the senate that Caesar should be left to complete not only the conquest but the pacification of Gaul. He succeeded, and the wisdom of this decision was demonstrated by the fact that in the following years (55–50) Caesar made his demonstrations across the Rhine (55) and into Britain (55–54) and had to suppress several revolts, culminating in the great uprising under Vercingetorix and the siege of Alesia (52). Gaul was not fully subdued until the end of 50, just before Caesar crossed the Rubicon.

Bellum Gallicum Caesare imperatore gestum

Bellum Gallicum, patres conscripti, Gaio Caesare imperatore gestum est, antea tantum modo repulsum.[1] Semper illas nationes nostri imperatores refutandas potius bello quam lacessendas putaverunt. Gai Caesaris longe aliam video fuisse rationem. Non enim sibi solum cum iis, quos iam armatos contra populum Romanum videbat, bellandum esse duxit, sed totam Galliam in nostram dicionem esse redigendam.[2] Itaque cum acerrimis nationibus et maximis Germanorum et Helvetiorum proeliis felicissime decertavit;[3] ceteras conterruit, compulit, domuit, imperio populi Romani parere adsuefecit. Et, quas regiones quasque gentes nullae nobis antea litterae, nulla vox, nulla fama notas fecerat, has noster imperator nosterque exercitus et populi Romani arma peragrarunt.[4]

Semitam tantum Galliae tenebamus antea, patres conscripti;[5]

ceterae partes a gentibus aut inimicis huic imperio aut infidis aut incognitis aut certe immanibus et barbaris et bellicosis tenebantur; quas nationes nemo umquam fuit quin frangi domarique cuperet.[6] Nemo sapienter de re publica nostra cogitavit iam inde a principio huius imperi, quin Galliam maxime timendam huic imperio putaret;[7] sed propter vim ac multitudinem gentium illarum numquam est antea cum omnibus dimicatum; restitimus semper lacessiti.[8] Nunc denique est perfectum ut imperi nostri terrarumque illarum idem esset extremum.[9]

Alpibus Italiam munierat antea natura, non sine aliquo divino numine. Nam, si ille aditus Gallorum immanitati multitudinique patuisset, numquam haec urbs summo imperio domicilium ac sedem praebuisset.[10] Quae iam licet considant.[11] Nihil est enim ultra illam altitudinem montium usque ad Oceanum, quod sit Italiae perti-mescendum.[12]

Bellum igitur in Gallia maximum gestum est; domitae sunt a Caesare maximae nationes. Sed nondum legibus, nondum iure certo, nondum satis firma pace devinctae. Una tamen atque altera aestas vel metu vel spe vel poena vel praemiis vel armis vel legibus potest totam Galliam sempiternis vinculis astringere.[13] Impolitae vero res et acerbae si erunt relictae, quamquam sunt accisae, tamen efferent se aliquando et ad renovandum bellum revirescent.[14] Quare sit in eius tutela Gallia, cuius fidei, virtuti, felicitati commendata est.[15]

1. A. **patres conscripti:** for this formula of address to the senate see 27 n. 16B (and 71 n. 14A). B. **Gaio Caesare imperatore** = "under Caesar as general"; Cicero, instead of using *a* with an abl. of agent, employs an abl. abs. defining the time or cir-cumstance of the main verb; compare *Glabrione consule* in 14 n. 4B (or *te scriptore* in 37 n. 17B).

2. A. **sibi . . . bellandum esse:** here the pass. periphrastic with dat. of reference (agent; see 21 n. 15C and 74 n. 3A) is a true impersonal without a subject other than the action contained in the neut. acc. sing. gerundive itself; compare 22 n. 2C (and 43 n. 1A) and *est . . dimicatum* in the 2nd sentence of the 2nd par. below; contrast the other gerundives in this selection. B. **armatos** = "having been armed," i.e. in arms; con-trast 58 n. 1B.

3. **proeliis:** abl. of means with *decertavit*: not modified by *maximis*, which, like *acerrimis*, modifies *nationibus*.

4. A. **fecerat:** sing. either in agreement with the nearest subject or because the three subjects (*litterae, vox, fama*) really constitute one concept, all being ways of con-veying information; compare 36 n. 1A. B. **peragrarunt** = *peragraverunt*; see 1 n. 4B (and 70 n. 19C).

5. **semitam:** Narbonese Gaul had been annexed in 121 (see 22 pref.) to provide a "path" for safe communication by land with Spain, for which see 16 pref.

6. A. **quas nationes:** anticipated subject of the objective pass. infs. *frangi domarique* which depend on *cuperet* in the following subordinate *quin* clause.   B. **quas** = *et has*; see 4 n. 4A (and 65 n. 26A).   C. **quin ... cuperet** = "who did not desire"; adversative *quin* after a general negative is equivalent to *qui non* and is followed by the subj. as in a rel. clause of characteristic implying result, i.e. "no one was such as not to desire" or "such that he did not desire"; see 21 n. 12A.

7. A. **nemo ... quin ... putaret:** see the preceding note.   B. **Galliam ... timendam:** ever since the Gauls sacked Rome in 390 (see 8), they had been a feared enemy, as in the 3rd sentence of the 1st par. of 22.

8. **restitimus ... lacessiti:** i.e. the Romans merely resisted any particular Gallic tribe which harassed them.

9. A. **nunc ... perfectum** = "now at last it has been brought to pass"; although pres. perf. connotation is suggested by *nunc*, in the substantive clause of result which serves as subject (see 26 n. 16A and 57 n. 6) *esset* is used in secondary sequence as if *est perfectum* connoted simple past time. Normally a subj. dependent on a pres. perf. is in primary sequence.   B. **idem esset extremum** = "there is the same boundary"; i.e. the Gauls no longer make incursions into Roman territory.

10. A. **aditus** = "way of approach" (i.e. of attack); compare 68 nn. 19B and 21B. B. **immanitati multitudinique:** by hendiadys = *immani multitudini*; compare 13 n. 11A (and 72 n. 7D).

11. **quae ... considant** = "but now these (Alps) may subside" (i.e. vanish); for the connective rel. see n. 6A above; for *licet* used with the subj. without *ut* see 23 n. 1A (and 43 n. 29).

12. A. **illam altitudinem montium** = *illos altos montes*; for the use of an abstract noun and a gen. instead of an adj. and a noun see 15 n. 4.   B. **Oceanum:** i.e. the Atlantic Ocean (compare 59 n. 9C), as opposed to the Mediterranean, which was called *mare*.

13. **una ... aestas:** summer is personified as subject of *potest*, as in Eng. Cicero was overoptimistic; see pref. above.

14. **efferent se** = "they will revive," lit. "carry themselves up again." The metaphor may be that of vines which, if pruned (*accisae* = "cut back") while still not fully grown and ripe (*impolitae et acerbae*, lit. = "unfinished and crude"), will revive and become green again.

15. **eius:** i.e. Caesar's.

76

After his return from exile in 57 (see 36 and 37), Cicero became involved in negotiations to recover his property, which Clodius had confiscated for the state, and in the defense of his supporters whom Clodius attacked. One of these, Sestius, who had as tribune worked with Milo for Cicero's recall, was charged in February 56 both with illegal canvassing (*ambitus*) for his office and with violence in his agitation for Cicero's recall. Not only Cicero but Hortensius and other leaders rallied to his defense. Cicero used the occasion to describe and defend his own political position (for which see 67 pref.), and his speech is, in effect, a prelude to his treatise *de Republica*, published in 51.

In the following passage, he defines the optimates as the *optimi* or "best citizens."

Cicero optimates definit

Duo genera semper in hac civitate fuerunt eorum qui versari in re publica atque in ea se excellentius gerere studuerunt;[1] quibus ex generibus alteri se populares, alteri optimates, et haberi et esse voluerunt.[2] Qui ea quae faciebant quaeque dicebant multitudini iucunda volebant esse, populares; qui autem ita se gerebant ut sua consilia optimo cuique probarent, optimates habebantur.[3] Quis ergo iste optimus quisque?[4] Numero, si quaeris, innumerabiles (neque enim aliter stare possemus):[5] sunt principes consili publici;[6] sunt qui eorum sectam sequuntur;[7] sunt maximorum ordinum homines, quibus patet curia;[8] sunt municipales rusticique Romani;[9] sunt negoti gerentes;[10] sunt etiam libertini optimates.[11] Numerus, ut dixi, huius generis late et varie diffusus est; sed genus universum, ut tollatur error, brevi circumscribi et definiri potest.[12] Omnes optimates sunt qui neque nocentes sunt nec natura improbi nec furiosi nec malis domesticis impediti.[13] Est igitur ut ii sint qui et integri sunt et sani et bene de rebus domesticis constituti.[14] Horum qui voluntati, commodis, opinionibus in gubernanda re publica serviunt, defensores optimatium;[15] ipsique optimates gravissimi et clarissimi cives numerantur et principes civitatis.[16]

Quid est igitur propositum his rei publicae gubernatoribus, quod intueri et quo cursum suum derigere debeant?¹⁷ Id quod est praestantissimum maximeque optabile omnibus sanis et bonis et beatis: cum dignitate otium.¹⁸ Hoc qui volunt, omnes optimates; qui efficiunt, summi viri et conservatores civitatis putantur.¹⁹ Neque enim rerum gerendarum dignitate homines efferri ita convenit ut otio non prospiciant, neque ullum amplexari otium quod abhorreat a dignitate.²⁰ Huius autem otiosae dignitatis haec fundamenta sunt, haec membra, quae tuenda principibus et vel capitis periculo defendenda sunt:²¹ religiones, auspicia, potestates magistratuum, senatus auctoritas, leges, mos maiorum, iudicia, iuris dictio, fides, provinciae, socii, imperi laus, res militaris, aerarium.²²

1. **se ... gerere** = "to conduct themselves rather prominently," i.e. to become more prominent than others.

2. A. **alteri ... alteri** = "the one (group) ... the other (group)"; when *alter* refers to two groups (as here) it is sometimes plur.; it may also be in the plur. when it means "second" or "further," as in 74 n. 4D.   B. **populares ... optimates:** for the first see 28 pref., and for the second see 18 n. 13A.   C. **se ... haberi:** the *se* is not repeated with the second *alteri*, and a reflexive pronoun would not normally be expected as the subject of infs. not in indirect discourse (they are here complementary); if the text has been correctly transmitted, *se* must be used here for emphasis and should be understood also with the second *alteri*, i.e. "they have wished themselves both to be regarded as and to be" rather than simply "they wished to be"; for the contrast between "being" and "seeming" compare 34 n. 20.

3. **optimo cuique:** i.e. to all best citizens; see 26 n. 4B (and 72 n. 17B).

4. **quis ... quisque** = "who, then, is that 'best citizen'?" Cicero puts this rhetorical question in the mouth of his opponent, as the use of *iste* shows; see 34 n. 8B (and 71 n. 2A). The plur. implied by *quisque* and the superlative (see n. 3 above) is made explicit in the following plurs.

5. A. **numero** = "in number"; abl. of specification, with which supply *sunt* from the preceding question.   B. **stare** = "to stand," i.e. to survive; compare 60 n. 25A (and 71 n. 17). Cicero regards the great number of good men as a guarantee of public security.

6. **consili publici:** probably = "the senate," which served as an advisory body to the magistrates and hence is often called a *consilium* in the concrete sense; however, Cicero may mean "public policy," using *consilium* in the abstract sense; compare 71 n. 13B. *Consilium* = "advisory body" should be distinguished from *concilium* = "an assembly" (e.g. *concilium plebis* in 21 n. 11A), which derives from *con-calare* = "to call together."

7. **sectam** = "school," hence "party" (Eng. "sect"); see 67 n. 13B.

8. A. **maximorum ordinum:** i.e. the equestrian and senatorial classes, which were called *ordines* in Cicero's day; compare 56 n. 16. For Cicero's view that the *concordia ordinum* was fundamental to the Republic see 71 n. 14B.   B. **curia:** basically the senate house (see 14 n. 6A and 53 n. 10A) but used by metonymy for the senate. Actually, apart from sons of senators who were enrolled among the *equites* until they themselves became

senators (see 30 n. 14), relatively few equestrians become senators and very few rose, like Cicero, as *novi homines* to the consulship; see prefs. to 21, 31, and 32.

9. **municipales . . . Romani:** those who entered the senate from equestrian status during the Ciceronian period came mostly from the municipalities in Italy, as Cicero himself came from Arpinum (see 31 pref.), especially after citizenship had been extended to all Italians in 90/89 (see 23 pref.). Cicero here distinguishes from these well-to-do equestrians the bulk of ordinary Roman citizens in the towns (*municipales* includes residents of *municipia* and *coloniae*) and countryside; Cicero had great faith in the loyal conservatism of these "upstate voters," from among whom he himself had come, as against the selfish radicalism of the "city gangs."

10. **negoti gerentes** = "businessmen"; compare 31 n. 6B. *Gerentes* is here used as a noun with a dependent gen. rather than as a part. with an acc.

11. **libertini** = "freedmen." In Cicero's time a freed slave was called a *libertus* vis-à-vis his former master (now patron) but a *libertinus* vis-à-vis freeborn citizens or *ingenui*. Though freedmen of Roman citizens became full citizens in law, by Cicero's time they could not hold public office. Their children (called *libertini* in the early Republic) were fully recognized politically as *ingenui*, but even they still retained a social stigma of servile origin. Since freedmen normally followed the political line of their former masters, *libertini* whose patrons were optimates would themselves count as *optimi*, i.e. as Cicero explains below (see n. 16), as supporters of the optimates.

12. **ut tollatur error:** i.e. that there may be no misunderstanding.

13. A. **omnes etc.:** in this sentence, Cicero first defines the optimates negatively and implies that those who had the bad features denied to these were *populares*, e.g. Catiline or Clodius; in the next, he defines the optimates positively.   B. **malis . . . impediti** = "involved in troubles at home," probably with the connotation of "heavily in debt," as were so many of the more extravagant young "nobles" like Catiline (see 71 and 72) and Caesar; see 33 pref.

14. A. **est igitur** = "(the fact), therefore, is"; the subject is the substantive *ut* clause of result; see 26 n. 16A (and 75 n. 9A).   B. **sunt:** ind., though subordinated in the *ut* clause of result, because the rel. clause defines or limits (rather than characterizes) the *ii* and also states what Cicero himself regarded as a fact about them; compare 10 n. 10C (and 68 nn. 3A and 17B).

15. A. **horum:** i.e. of the optimates; possessive gen. with *voluntati etc.*, which are dats. after *serviunt*.   B. **qui . . . serviunt:** this rel. clause, or its implied antecedent *ei* (compare 21 n. 20C and 74 n. 8B), provides the subject (with *sunt* understood; see n. 16 below) with which *defensores optimatium* is in predicate apposition.   C. **opinionibus:** the manuscripts and some editors read *opibus*, which may be correct since Cicero regarded wealth as an important element of conservatism; if *opinionibus* is a correct emendation, *in gubernanda re publica* may go closely with it rather than also with *voluntati* and *commodis*, i.e. "who follow their desires and interests and their opinions on government."

16. **defensores . . . optimates:** as punctuated with a semicolon, *sunt* (or *numerantur* from the second clause) should be supplied with *defensores* (see n. 15B above), and Cicero divides the general group of optimates as already defined into two halves: the supporters of the optimate leaders and the *ipsi optimates*. The latter are to be reckoned weighty and notable citizens and leaders of the state. Without the semicolon, the *ipsi* continues the previous clause and defines the party of the *integri et sani* as both defenders of the optimates and themselves weighty optimates (taking in this case *gravissimi* with *optimates*) and notable citizens and leaders of the state. In either case, Cicero first calls all conservative citizens *optimates* and then, somewhat inconsistently, calls some followers and some leaders; compare the sentence *hoc . . . putantur* in the next paragraph. However, the text may be corrupt.

17. A. **propositum:** perhaps the noun, = "aim" or "objective"; compare 18 n. 3B

(and 36 n. 6c). If so, it is in predicate agreement with *quid* and modified by the rel. clauses *quod . . . debeant*. If it is perf. part. with *est*, denoting a present state, the rel. clauses are predicate modifiers of *quid*.   B. **quod . . . quo**: the rel. is repeated because a different case is required with each of the two infs.; *quo* is probably the adv. = "whither" (see 21 n. 13b) rather than abl. of means.

18.   A. **omnibus . . . beatis**: dats. of reference, best rendered as dats. of agent since *optabile* = *optanda*; compare 17 n. 11b (and 21 nn. 15b and c).   B. **beatis**: probably used here in its idiomatic sense of "wealthy"; compare 34 n. 15. However, it was also used by the Stoics to mean the person who is truly happy and right-minded, and Cicero probably intended to suggest this as well.   c. **cum dignitate otium**: this famous and much discussed political ideal for the individual involves two concepts difficult to render in Eng. *Dignitas*, like such other abstract qualities as *gravitas* and *auctoritas*, was important to the Roman; it included his standing in his own and others' eyes, and its loss (like "loss of face" for an Oriental) was serious; compare 19 n. 14c and n. 20a below. *Otium* might mean simply "leisure" (as in the 3rd sentence of the 3rd par. of 31), but it also, like the Greek *scholē*, connoted that freedom from mundane chores and concerns which was equally necessary for the man of culture and for the statesman; it also connoted personal and public calm, or peace, from disturbance (see 32 n. 4b)— the sort of inner self-possession advocated by both Stoics and Epicureans; see 69 pref. and n. 30a. As applied to the state, the phrase suggests the Eng. "peace with honor."

19.   **putantur**: goes with both clauses in the sentence; compare *numerantur* in n. 16 above.

20.   A. **neque etc.**: when, at the Rubicon in 49 (see 39 pref.), Caesar appealed to his troops *ut eius existimationem dignitatemque defendant* (*Bell. Civ.* I 8.7; compare 38 B), to Cicero he might well have seemed so carried away by the "dignity" resulting from his achievements that he no longer considered either his own or the country's peace or *otium*; to which he might himself have replied that to "lie down" under the indignities placed upon him by the senate and Pompey would be to accept a personal "peace without honor," apart from the specific setbacks to his career that would result.   B. **efferri**: here = "to be carried away"; contrast 75 n. 14.

21.   A. **vel**: here not the conjunction = "or" (see 27 n. 1), but the intensifying adv. = "even."   B. **capitis periculo** = "at the risk of their lives"; abl. of means or of manner without *cum*. For this meaning of *caput* see 63 n. 16. It is regularly sing. (as here) in this usage because each has only one life.

22.   A. **religiones etc.**: these political foundations of the state are discussed fully in Cicero's two political essays, *de Republica* and *de Legibus*.   B. **auspicia**: the omens and the magistrate's right of taking them, both of which guaranteed divine favor to the state; see 52 n. 3 (and 71 n. 16c).   c. **mos maiorum**: for the importance of tradition in Roman thought and life, particularly in the political and moral sphere, see 15 n. 13b (and 73 n. 8a).   D. **iudicia, iuris dictio** = "courts and jurisdiction (of the magistrates)"; compare 56 n. 15.   E. **fides** = "(financial) trustworthiness," i.e. credit; compare 51 n. 6 (and 63 n. 13a).   F. **imperi laus** = "the reputation of (our) rule."

77

In the first book of his *Pharsalia* (see 64 pref.), Lucan finds the cause of the civil war between Pompey and Caesar (see 38–41) in their rivalry. The following verses in dactylic hexameter summarize the break between them, characterize them, and compare them respectively to a magnificent but decaying oak and a vigorous flash of lightning.

Pompeii Caesarisque ingenia a Lucano descripta

Ubi Crassus

Assyrias Latio maculavit sanguine Carrhas,[1]
non cepit Fortuna duos.[2] Nam pignora iuncti
sanguinis et diro ferales omine taedas[3]
abstulit ad manes Parcarum Iulia saeva
intercepta manu.[4] Quod si tibi fata dedissent
maiores in luce moras,[5] tu sola furentem
inde virum poteras atque hinc retinere parentem.[6]
Morte tua discussa fides, bellumque movere
permissum ducibus.[7] Stimulos dedit aemula virtus:
tu, nova ne veteres obscurent acta triumphos[8]
et victis cedat piratica laurea Gallis,
Magne, times;[9] te iam series ususque laborum
erigit impatiensque loci fortuna secundi;[10]
nec quemquam iam ferre potest Caesarve priorem
Pompeiusve parem.[11] Quis iustius induit arma,
scire nefas;[12] magno se iudice quisque tuetur:[13]
victrix causa deis placuit, sed victa Catoni.[14]
Nec coiere pares.[15] Alter vergentibus annis
in senium longoque togae tranquillior usu
dedidicit iam pace ducem;[16] famaeque petitor
multa dare in volgus,[17] totus popularibus auris
impelli,[18] plausuque sui gaudere theatri,[19]

nec reparare novas vires, multumque priori

credere fortunae.[20] Stat magni nominis umbra;[21]

qualis frugifero quercus sublimis in agro,

exuvias veteres populi sacrataque gestans

dona ducum;[22] nec iam validis radicibus haerens

pondere fixa suo est;[23] nudosque per aera ramos

effundens,[24] trunco, non frondibus, efficit umbram.

Usque tamen colitur.[25] Sed non in Caesare tantum

nomen erat nec fama ducis, sed nescia virtus

stare loco,[26] solusque pudor non vincere bello.[27]

Acer et indomitus, quo spes quoque ira vocasset,

ferre manum[28] et numquam temerando parcere ferro,[29]

successus urgere suos, instare favori

numinis,[30] impellens quidquid sibi summa petenti

obstaret,[31] gaudensque viam fecisse ruina;[32]

qualiter expressum ventis per nubila fulmen

emicuit, rupitque diem,[33] populosque paventes

terruit, obliqua praestringens lumina flamma.[34]

1. A. **Assyrias:** here adj.; Assyria, properly the region east of the Tigris, was extended by classical writers to all of northern Mesopotamia.   B. **Latio . . . Carrhas:** Crassus and an army of perhaps as many as seven legions were annihilated by the Parthians in 53 at Carrhae, a site in northern Mesopotamia about 60 miles east of the Euphrates. This verse is balanced around the verb, or "golden"; see 49 n. 3A (and 64 n. 15A).

2. **non . . . duos:** i.e. with the elimination of the third of the Triumvirs, Fortune did not find room at Rome for two powerful rivals; for this meaning of *cepit* see 59 n. 9A; for Fortune in Lucan see 64 n. 8D.

3. A. **pignora . . . sanguinis** = "the pledge (consisting) of united blood" (i.e. by marriage); compare 33 n. 3A. For the marriage of Julia, Caesar's daughter, and Pompey to cement the First Triumvirate see 35 pref. and n. 7; for Julia's death in childbirth (the child died too) see 37 pref. Lucan throughout the poem stresses the former family ties between Pompey and Caesar in order to accentuate the horror of the war between them. B. **diro . . . taedas** = "marriage torches (made) funereal by dread omen." There is no contemporary indication of ill-omen at the wedding of Julia and Pompey, so that Lucan may be indulging here in rhetorical exaggeration.

4. A. **ad manes:** i.e. to the underworld. *Manes* were in origin the collective spirits of the undifferentiated dead; later the word was used (still in the plur.) for the soul of a deceased person or (as here) for spirits, whether ancestral or of the lower world in general, who watched over the lower world.   B. **Parcarum:** possessive gen. with the abl. of means *saeva . . . manu*. Parcae was the Lat. name for the Greek *Moirai* = goddesses of destiny or Fates; usually three in number.

5. A. **quod si** = "but if"; compare 37 n. 20A (and 58 n. 15A).   B. **tibi . . . tu:**

Lucan addresses *Iūlia* directly; for a similar apostrophe compare Juvenal in 59 n. 28.
C. **luce** = *vita;* compare 74 n. 3B.

6. A. **furentem ... parentem:** the sing. part. agrees with *virum* but probably also
extends to *parentem* through the force of *inde ... hinc* = "on the one (lit. that) side ...
on the other (lit. this)." Some editors propose reading *furentes* both because of the agreement and to avoid the rhyme with *parentem*, but this seems unnecessary; for occasional
rhyme in Lat. poetry see 55 n. 9B; in sel. 66, also from Lucan, the 29th and 31st verses
end in *omnem ... amnem.*   B. **poteras:** the imperf. or pluperf. ind. of this and other
verbs in which the meaning itself suggests doubts may be used for the imperf. or pluperf.
subj. in the apodosis of a contrary to fact condition; see 10 n. 12A (and 54 n. 3B). Here
the imperf. is used to emphasize the fact in past time; = "you were (then) able (had you
lived)."

7. **discussa ... permissum:** the subject of *discussa* (*est*) is *fides* (compare 51 n. 6 and
76 n. 22E), i.e. the loyalty which Pompey and Caesar owed each other. That of *permissum*
(*est*) is the inf. clause *bellum movere*, meaning "to start war."

8. A. **tu:** i.e. Pompey, taken up two lines below by the voc. *Magne* (see n. 9B
below) and by the verb *times*, upon which depend the clauses *ne ... obscurent ... cedat*;
for the direct address compare n. 5B above.   B. **nova ... acta:** i.e. Caesar's recent
achievements in Gaul in 58–50, for which see 36 pref. and 75.   C. **veteres ... triumphos:** i.e. Pompey's victories in the East in 66–63, for which see 35 pref.

9. A. **piratica laurea:** i.e. Pompey's defeat of the pirates in 67/66, for which see 29
pref. With *laurea* understand *corona*; a laurel wreath was awarded to a victorious general
for his triumph; compare in 32 n. 20B. This verse approximates the "golden" balance;
see n. 1B above (and 51 n. 15C).   B. **Magne:** Lucan frequently uses Pompey's epithet
Magnus (see 29 pref.) in preference to his cognomen *Pompeius*; compare 68 n. 12B.

10. A. **te:** i.e. Caesar; compare nn. 5B and 8A above.   B. **series ususque:** express
a single idea by hendiadys (see 13 n. 11A and 75 n. 10B), hence the sing. verb *erigit* =
"aroused" or "stirred up"; compare 75 n. 4A.   C. **fortuna:** added as something of
an afterthought; it here means Caesar's personal fate or luck, rather than the personified
general goddess, for whom see n. 2 above.   D. **loci ... secundi** = "second rank" (contrast 43 n. 17B); gen. with *impatiens*, which modifies *fortuna*. The word order is interlocking; compare 64 n. 15A.

11. A. **quemquam ... priorem ... parem** = "anyone as a superior ... (any one) as an
equal"; the relative status of the two rivals is aptly expressed; compare 68 n. 8.   B.
Pompēiusve: in this name the -*ei*- is not a diphthong; the -*e*- is long and the -*i*- is pronounced as a separate sound, either vowel (see 35 n. 9B) or here consonantal so that
-*ēius* represents two, not three, syllables; compare 78 n. 31A.

12. A. **quis ... induit:** an indirect question may have the ind. in early Lat. and in
poetry. This represents an original independent (paratactic; compare 23 n. 1A) statement
of the question clause as fact; the subj. came to be used when the speaker quoted the
question dependently as if on someone else's authority. In imperial Lat. poetry, *quis*
may be used instead of *uter* = "one of two."   B. **scire nefas:** the indeclinable noun
nefas (compare 8 n. 7B and 66 n. 7) is here a predicate nom. with *est* understood; in the
Eng. "it is wrong to know," "wrong" is a predicate adj. The subject of *est* is the inf.
scire plus its object, the indirect question *quis ... arma*; see the preceding note.   C.
scire: used absolutely, without an expressed acc. subject; compare 65 n. 16B (and 74
n. 8B). It is not "divinely permitted" for anyone to know whether Pompey or Caesar
took up arms more justly because both sides were under the protection of a divinity
(see following note), and it would be presumptuous for a man to decide that one side
and its divinity were more worthy than the other.

13. **magno ... tuetur** = "each (i.e. Caesar and Pompey) is defended by (i.e. invokes
in his own defense) a powerful arbiter"; *iudice* is probably abl. of means, not of agent
without a prep., since Lucan actually means "by the judgment of a powerful authority";
compare 59 n. 18B.

14. **victrix . . . Catōni:** for the adjectival use of the fem. noun of agency see 49 n. 12 (and compare 21 n. 6B). The meaning is that the gods gave Caesar the victory, but Cato supported Pompey; this verse, perhaps the best known in the whole poem, specifies the *iudex* (see the preceding note) invoked by each. The Stoics of the Empire, in opposition to such tyrannical emperors as Nero (see 64 pref.), made Cato into a hero or "saint" of the cause of liberty, which was identified with that of the senate and Pompey as against the tyranny of Caesar; see prefs. to 34 and 41.

15. **cŏiērĕ:** 3rd pers. plur. perf. act. ind. of *cŏĕō, cŏīrĕ*; for the ending see 15 n. 10 (and 74 n. 17A).

16. A. **vergentibus . . . senium** = "because (his) years were declining into old age"; *annis* is abl. of cause with *tranquillior*, parallel with *longo . . . usu.*   B. **senium** = "old age"; the neut. acc. sing. of the noun *senium*, not the gen. plur. of *senex*, which is usually *senum*; see 8 n. 8A (and 74 n. 2A). Actually, Pompey had been born in 106, only shortly before Caesar, born in 102 or 100; see 33 pref. For the similar rhetorical contrast made by Livy between Hannibal and Scipio see 58 pref.   C. **togae** = *pacis*; see 27 n. 13B (and compare in 32 n. 20B).   D. **dedidicit:** the perf. is vivid for the pluperf.; the prefix *de-* (= "down from") has a negative force, i.e. "unlearn."   E. **ducem** = "leadership," by metonymy; see 49 n. 4 (and 73 n. 20D).

17. A. **multa . . . volgus** = "he distributed much among the common people" (see 74 n. 11B); *dare*, like the infs. in the following 3 verses, is historical (compare 17 n. 16A and 65 n. 18B), as is shown by the nom. *petitor*, which is in apposition with the understood subject "he." It is less likely that a positive *didicit* is to be understood from the preceding *dedidicit*. Lucan probably refers to Pompey's lavish games and distributions of grain and money to the Roman common people, not generally to Pompey as yielding to popular pressure, since this is stated in the next phrases.   B. **volgus** = *vulgus*; see 66 n. 13A.

18. **popularibus auris** = "by favor" or "by popularity"; lit. "by breezes of the people."

19. **plausu . . . theatri:** i.e. by the applause for himself in his theater; for the abl. with *gaudeo* see 73 n. 26. Pompey used the booty of his eastern conquest to build during his consulship in 55 the first permanent stone theater in Rome; see 43 n. 3C.

20. A. **nec . . . vires** = "and he did not build up new (sources of political) strength."   B. **multumque . . . credere** = "but he trusted (too) much"; *-que* may have an adversative as well as a merely additive connotation.

21. A. **stat . . . umbra** = "he stands as a shadow of a great name," i.e. of a great reputation; compare *tantum nomen* of Caesar in the 6th and 7th verses below.   B. **stat:** though often used as an intensive synonym for *est*, its connotation is here literal, anticipating the following simile of the lofty oak which still stands though rotten at its roots; compare 60 n. 25A (and 76 n. 5B).   C. **umbra** is predicate nom., not abl. as in 49 n. 2A.

22. **exuvias . . . ducum:** it was customary to hang offerings on trees to pacify the spirits of a locality (*numina*; compare n. 30B below and in 73 n. 24B), and to use trunks of trees as supports for trophies of arms of defeated enemies, here appropriate to Pompey.

23. **pondere . . . suo** = "(only) by its own weight"; i.e. because its roots have rotted away.

24. **āĕră:** for the stem quantities see 69 n. 12A; the final *-ă* is an ending of the acc. sing. in Greek. This form should be distinguished from the Lat. neut. nom. and acc. plur. *aera*, from *aes* = "bronze," for which see 61 n. 29A.

25. A. **usque . . . colitur** = "yet it still is venerated," i.e. by the local inhabitants, meaning here that the Romans venerated Pompey despite his loss of power.   B. **usque:** usually joined with an adv. (as in 71 n. 1A) or prep., but may stand alone as an adv., = "continuously" or "still."   C. **colitur** = "is tended," i.e. in any way: by cultivation

(farming: *agricola*, *incola*), by worship, as here (compare *cultus*, which also means "adornment" or the like; see 65 n. 4A), by filial care, etc.

26. A. **erat:** sing. because *nomen . . . nec fama* express a single concept by hendiadys; compare n. 10B above.   B. **virtus:** understand *erat*.   C. **stare loco** = "to stand still," lit. "in (one) place"; compare n. 21B above. The inf. is not historical but depends on the force of a part. in *nescia* = "(which did) not know how to."

27. A. **solusque . . . bello** = "and (his) only (feeling of) shame was not to conquer by war"; Lucan probably means that Caesar would have been ashamed to have negotiated with Pompey rather than to defeat him in war, but he could also mean in a general sense that Caesar's only fear was that he might sometime lose a battle.   B. **vincere:** in predicate apposition with *pudor*, with *erat* understood.

28. A. **quo . . . vocasset** = "wherever hope and wherever (*quoque* = *et quo*) wrath might have summoned (him)." The pluperf. subj. is used because the adverbial rel. clause is general or potential and antecedent in time to its main verb, the historical inf. *ferre* (see following note); compare 41 n. 14.   B. **ferre manum:** it is better to take this and the following infs. as historical (compare n. 17 above) and regard *acer et indomitus* as modifying their subject nom. "he," rather than to make the infs. dependent on the adjs., with which *erat* would then have to be supplied.

29. A. **et . . . ferro** = "and he never spared (from using his) sword (so as to) desecrate (it)"; *ferro* is dat. after *parcere* (see 47 n. 7) and is modified by the gerundive.   B. **temerando:** *temerare* is derived from the adv. *temere* = "hastily" or "impetuously"; but the verb came to have the specialized meaning of treating religious things carelessly, and hence of defiling or desecrating. Although the rendering "never spared using his sword impetuously" would fit here, Lucan probably intended the specialized connotation that Caesar would defile his sword with the blood of fellow citizens; compare *temeritas* used of Caesar's assassination in 45 n. 14D.

30. A. **successus . . . numinis** = "he pressed hard upon (i.e. he advanced, got the most out of) his successes and followed up the favor (shown by) the divinity."   B. **numinis:** originally a local "divine force" (compare n. 22 above), *numen* came to mean the divine power of a god, just as *imperium* became abstract when it was separated from the magistrate who exercised it. Hence in Stoic thought *numen* was used of the impersonal divine power which directed the universe.

31. A. **summa** = "supremacy"; object of *petenti* and a neut. plur. used collectively to express an abstract concept; compare *sceptra* in 54 n. 9B.   B. **obstaret:** subj. in a general or potential indefinite substantive rel. clause (see n. 28A above) and imperf. because contemporary with *impellens*; the secondary sequence goes back to the historical infs.

32. **ruina** = "by destruction"; i.e. by destroying anything that stood in his way, including the constitution. This leads to the following comparison of Caesar to a forceful and destructive bolt of lightning, which balances the comparison above of Pompey to a magnificent but decayed oak.

33. A. **qualiter** = "just as"; this adv. introduces the second comparison dynamically, in contrast to the adj. *qualis* 13 verses above, which introduced the comparison of Pompey statically.   B. **expressum . . . fulmen:** one ancient explanation of thunder and lightning was that they were squeezed out of clouds when these were driven together by winds.   C. **diem:** *dies* meant both the day and its source, the bright sky; compare in 52 n. 1B (and in 60 n. 2).

34. A. **obliqua . . . flamma** = "dazzling (people's) eyes with (its) slanting flash"; *praestringo*, a poetic and imperial verb, lit. = "bind fast," but also "touch lightly" or "blunt."   B. **lumina:** often = "eyes," among its various metaphorical meanings, for which see 69 n. 6D.

78

Pompey fled from his defeat by Caesar at Pharsalus in 48 (see 40) to Egypt. There he was put to death by order of the young ruler, Ptolemy XIII, at the instigation of his ministers Pothinus, Theodotus, and Achillas; see 41. A principal participant in the deed was a Roman, Septimius, who, after having served under Pompey, had joined the Egyptian army. His turncoat and ungrateful act profoundly shocked Roman sentiment; see 41 n. 11c.

The following selection is composed of dactylic hexameter verses from the lengthy and rhetorical description of Pompey's death in book VIII of Lucan's *Pharsalia*; see prefs. to 64 and 77.

Magni caedes infamis

Adsensere omnes sceleri.[1] Laetatur honore
rex puer insueto,[2] quod iam sibi tanta iubere
permittant famuli.[3] Cecidit civilibus armis
qui tibi regna dedit;[4] tanti, Ptolemaee, ruinam
nominis haud metuis?[5] Sceleri delectus Achillas
exiguam sociis monstri gladiisque carinam
instruit.[6] Et Magnus remis infanda petebat
litora.[7] Quem contra non longa vecta biremi
appulerat scelerata manus.[8] Magnoque patere
fingens regna Phari, celsae de puppe carinae
in parvam iubet ire ratem;[9] litusque malignum
incusat bimaremque vadis frangentibus aestum,
qui vetet externas terris appellere classes.[10]
Non ulli comitum sceleris praesagia derant:[11]
quippe, fides si pura foret, si regia Magno,
sceptrorum auctori, vera pietate pateret,[12]
venturum tota Pharium cum classe tyrannum.[13]
Sed cedit fatis;[14] classemque relinquere iussus,
obsequitur, letumque iuvat praeferre timori.[15]
Ibat in hostilem praeceps Cornelia puppem,[16]

hoc magis impatiens egresso desse marito,[17]
quod metuit clades. "Remane, temeraria coniunx,
et tu, nate, precor;[18] longeque a litore casus
expectate meos" dixit. Transire parantem
Romanus Pharia miles de puppe salutat
Septimius,[19] qui (pro superum pudor!) arma satelles
regia gestabat posito deformia pilo;[20]
immanis, violentus, atrox, nullaque ferarum
mitior in caedes.[21] Magno iam venerat horae
terminus extremae;[22] Phariamque ablatus in alnum
perdiderat iam iura sui.[23] Tum stringere ferrum
regia monstra parant.[24] Ut vidit comminus enses,[25]
involvit voltus atque, indignatus apertum
fortunae praebere, caput;[26] tum lumina pressit
continuitque animam,[27] ne quas effundere voces
vellet et aeternam fletu corrumpere famam.[28]
Sed postquam mucrone latus funestus Achillas
perfodit, nullo gemitu consensit ad ictum.[29]
Degener atque operae, miles Romane, secundae[30]
Pompei diro sacrum caput ense recidis.[31]
Fortuna hac Magnum summo de culmine rerum
morte petit.[32]

1. A. **omnes:** Ptolemy's advisers, whom Lucan has just described as discussing the news of Pompey's approach.   B. **sceleri:** dat. after a verb compounded with *ad* and not connoting actual motion toward (compare 59 n. 10 and 62 n. 15c); i.e. to the murder of Pompey, proposed, according to Lucan, by Ptolemy's eunuch Pothinus; Velleius attributes the idea to his tutor Theodotus; see 41 n. 9.

2. **laetatur honore:** for the abl. (instrumental or loc.) with such verbs as *laetor*, compare 73 n. 26 (and 77 n. 19). The elder of Cleopatra's two brothers, both named Ptolemy, was about fifteen, hence *rex puer*; see 33 n. 17 (and 41 pref. and n. 6). Lucan underlines the tradition that he was a mere puppet by making him take childish pleasure in the unaccustomed honor of being allowed to give the order agreed upon by his household.

3. A. **quod ... famuli:** the subj. *permittant* makes *quod* causal rather than simply explanatory, i.e. "namely the fact that." Verbs of permitting may take either a sub-stantive clause of purpose or, as here, an objective inf.; compare 27 n. 12A. The person involved may be dat. of indirect object, as here *sibi* (referring back to the subject of the main clause), or either acc. subject of the inf. or nom. subject of the *ut* clause, depending on whether the emphasis is on permitting to a person that he act or on allowing a person

to act.   B. **famuli:** i.e. his advisers, lit. "servants," as in 66 n. 8 (and 70 n. 26B); compare Eng. "ministers" of a king.

4.   A. **cĕcĭdit ... dedit:** Pompey, who had given Ptolemy the kingdom by restoring his father to the Egyptian throne, had (now) fallen (*cădo*; see 27 n. 3B) by civil war and should have been helped by the young King, not slain like a defeated enemy.   B. **tibi ... Ptolemaee:** for Lucan's use of apostrophe see 77 nn. 5B, 8A, and 10A.   C. **regna:** collective plur. (compare 77 n. 31A); see 49 n. 10B (and 64 n. 15C).

5.   **tanti ... nominis:** i.e. of a person of such a reputation as Pompey had; compare 77 n. 21A.

6.   A. **Achillās:** Greek nom. sing.; see 49 n. 1 (and 70 n. 25). In Velleius, this Greek general of the Egyptians helps both to plan and to execute the assassination; see 41 n. 9.   B. **monstri:** probably a sort of objective gen. with both *sociis* and *gladiis*, = "for the monstrous (crime)"; it is less likely to be possessive gen. referring either to Achillas himself or to Septimius, who has not yet been mentioned. *Monstrum* may, however, connote a person, as in 46 n. 5A (and 72 n. 6); compare n. 24B below.

7.   A. **Magnus:** for Lucan's use of Pompey's epithet see 77 n. 9B.   B. **infanda ... litora:** the (Egyptian) shore was "unspeakable" because of the crime of ingratitude about to be committed; for *infandus* = "impious" see 66 n. 7.

8.   A. **quem contra:** i.e. to meet him, but with the implication of hostility, "against him."   B. **non longa ... biremi** = "carried in (lit. by) a not long (i.e. small) boat." A bireme was usually a warship with only two banks of oars, but here it is a dispatch boat contrasted with a *navis longa* = "warship," for which see 9 n. 12B.   C. **appulerat** = "had come alongside," from *appello, -ere* (not *appello, -are* = "to name" or "call"); it usually means "to put into shore," as it does 4 verses below.   D. **scelerata manus** = "the criminal band"; a frequent meaning of *manus*; it continues as subject of *fingens*, *iubet*, and *incusat* in the next 3 verses.   E. **scelerata:** perhaps an adj., not a past part.; see 53 n. 14B.

9.   A. **Magnoque ... Phari** = "and, pretending that the kingdom of Egypt (lit. of Pharus) lay open for Magnus"; *regna* is a poetic plur.; see n. 4C above.   B. **Phari:** an island off the harbor of Alexandria on which the Ptolemies had erected a lighthouse so famous that the name Pharos was used for others, and is still so used in French "phare." Lucan regularly uses it by metonymy (see 49 n. 4 and 77 n. 16E) for Egypt.   C. **carinae:** lit. = "of the keel," but used (as in Eng.) by metonymy for the ship.

10.   A. **litusque ... classes:** under this specious excuse of dangerous shoal water, the Egyptians cloaked their real purpose of getting Pompey alone into the small boat.   B. **bimaremque ... aestum** = "a two-sea surf on the breaking shoals," i.e. the surf breaking on shoals where two currents meet.   C. **vadis frangentibus:** abl. of place where, or abl. of attendant circumstance, or abl. abs.   D. **vetet:** probably subj. in a subordinate clause in indirect discourse implied in *incusat*, rather than in a rel. clause of characteristic, giving the reason for their "accusation" of the shoals.

11.   **dĕrant** = *dĕĕrant*, by internal elision; compare *desse* = *dĕĕsse* in 69 n. 30B and 7 verses below. It is followed by the dat. of reference (disadvantage) *ulli* modified by the partitive gen. *comitum*; = "to any of (Pompey's) companions."

12.   A. **quippe** = "for indeed," adding the explanation of the evidences of treachery suspected by Pompey's companions.   B. **fides ... foret** = "if there had been sincere trustworthiness"; *fides* is here the trustworthiness of the Egyptians toward Pompey, not his confidence in them; compare 51 n. 6 (and 76 n. 22E).   C. **regia:** supply *domus* = "palace"; see 54 n. 10C.   D. **sceptrorum:** poetic plur. (compare nn. 4C and 9A above) connoting by metonymy (see n. 9B above) "rule"; see 54 n. 9B. For the reference to Pompey see n. 4A above.

13.   A. **venturum:** supply *fuisse*, = "would have come." This "perf." form of the fut. inf. (compare in 68 n. 15B) is regularly used for the apodosis of a contrary to fact

condition in indirect discourse, here implied in *quippe* (see n. 12A above); the protases (*si . . . foret, si . . . pateret*) remain in the imperf. (or pluperf.) subj. of direct discourse. B. **Pharium . . . tyrannum** = "the Egyptian king"; for the adj. *Pharius* compare n. 9B above. C. **tyrannum:** may mean simply "ruler" (see 60 n. 28C) but considering Lucan's bitterness against Ptolemy and hatred of absolute rule, it is probably here pejorative, as in 59 n. 25A.

14. **cedit fatis** = "he (Pompey) yields to the fates." Though this might mean simply a recognition of inevitability (compare 41 n. 14), Lucan's poem is pervaded by a sense that the personified Fates, or Fortune, governed the destiny of Rome during the Second Civil War; compare 64 nn. 8D and 13B (and 77 n. 2).

15. **letumque . . . timori** = "and it pleases (him) to prefer (the risk of) death to (showing) fear"; the inf. clause is subject of *iuvat*; see 54 n. 2A.

16. A. **ibat** = "was trying to go"; for the conative use of the imperf. see 19 n. 6A. B. **hostilem . . . puppem:** i.e. the Egyptian bireme; see n. 8B above. C. **Cornēlia:** Pompey had married her in 52, after the death of Julia; see in 39 n. 16.

17. A. **hoc magis . . . quod** = "especially . . . because," lit. "by this the more . . . because"; compare 69 n. 23A. B. **impatiens . . . marito** = "not enduring to fail (i.e. not to accompany) her husband as he left (her)"; for *desse* = *dēesse* see n. 11 above.

18. A. **temeraria** = "rash"; compare 77 n. 29B. The fem. with *coniunx* shows that though Cornelia has been the subject, this remark is addressed to her by Pompey; such abrupt shifts are common in rhetorical prose and verse. B. **nate:** Pompey's second son Sextus, for whom see 43 n. 28C (and 46 pref.).

19. A. **Rōmānus . . . miles . . . Septimius:** see pref. above. B. **Pharia . . . puppe:** for the adj. *Pharius* here and 5 verses below see n. 13B above; for the interlocking order of nouns and adjs. compare 64 n. 15A (and 77 n. 10D).

20. A. **pro . . . pudor:** the interjection *pro* is here followed by the nom. *pudor*; contrast the acc. in 26 n. 8C (and compare 59 n. 20A). B. **superum** = "of (those) above," i.e. the gods; for the old ending -*um* in the gen. plur. see 11 n. 14B (and 69 n. 2A). C. **arma . . . regia . . . deformia** = "the disgracing royal arms"; i.e. military service under a king was disgraceful for a Roman; compare 41 n. 11C. D. **satelles:** in apposition with *qui*, = "as a bodyguard." This word is generally used of attendants on kings and has a pejorative connotation. E. **posito . . . pilo** = "after he had abandoned his (Roman) javelin"; for this meaning of *posito* see 48 n. 15A; for *pilum* see 66 n. 11C.

21. **nullāque . . . mitior** = "and gentler than no one of wild beasts," i.e. more savage than any wild beast. For the "litotes" (negative understatement) compare 68 n. 12A.

22. **horae . . . extremae:** defining gen.; = "the end (that was) his last hour."

23. A. **alnum:** the material, alder-wood, is used by metonymy (see n. 9B above) for the boat made from it; compare n. 9C above. This 2nd decl. word is fem., as are most names of trees; see 61 n. 3. B. **iura sui** = "rights of (i.e. over) himself," i.e. the right to control his own movements. The sing. *ius* is more common in this phrase, and *sui* is objective gen. rather than possessive, for which the possessive adj. *sua* would be used.

24. A. **stringere:** here = "to unsheathe," as in 24 n. 4C (and 43 n. 10). B. **regia monstra:** probably = "the monstrous (agents) of the king" (compare n. 6B above), i.e. all the Egyptians in the boat, rather than Septimius alone by a poetic plur. like those in nn. 4C, 9A, and 12D above.

25. **vidit:** Pompey becomes subject of this and the verbs in the following verses through *consensit*, except for *perfodit*.

26. A. **involvit . . . caput:** compare the similar gestures of modesty in the face of death made by Caesar in 43 n. 11 and by Cassius in 45 n. 10A. B. **voltus** = *vultus*; see 66 n. 13A (and 77 n. 17B). C. **apertum:** with *caput*, which is object both of *involvit* and of *praebere*.

27.   A. **lumina pressit** = "he closed his eyes"; for *lumina* = "eyes" see 77 n. 34B; for *pressit* contrast 64 n. 16.   B. **animam**: here = "(his) breath"; contrast 70 n. 24B.

28.   **ne quas . . . famam**: for *quas* as the indefinite adj. after *ne* see 4 n. 11B (and 52 n. 9B). Lucan perhaps intends Pompey's dignified death to match that of Caesar, for which see 43, especially nn. 11–13. If so, he ruins the effect by a long description of the thoughts which passed through Pompey's mind, a long lament by Cornelia, and an elaborate description of the murder; the first two are omitted here and the last reduced to the following 4 verses.

29.   A. **lătus**: the neut. noun = "side" (of his body; see 46 n. 6B), not the adj. *lātus* = "wide."   B. **consensit ad ictum** = "did he admit (to feeling) the blow." Lucan attributes to Pompey greater Stoic endurance than Caesar had shown, since the latter uttered a single groan; see 43 n. 13.

30.   **operae . . . secundae** = "of a second task," i.e. playing a subordinate role. As punctuated in the text, this gen. is descriptive, parallel to the adj. *degener* and modifying the subject of *recidis*, "thou." The comma might be placed after *miles*, leaving *Rōmāne* alone as voc. and making the adj. and gen. modify *miles* in apposition with "thou"; = "thou, O Roman, a degenerate soldier in a subordinate role." For the direct address to a character see n. 4B above; for the scorn that Septimius should not only take part in the murder but a subordinate part to an Egyptian Greek, see pref. and n. 20C above.

31.   A. **Pompēī**: here (as against in 77 n. 11B) Lucan treats the -*i*- in -*ēius* as a vowel (see 35 n. 9B) and, for the sake of the meter, contracts the gen. sing. to a single long -*i*- even though he wrote after Augustus; compare 17 nn. 7 and 19C.   B. **diro . . . ense**: there is effective contrast (oxymoron; see 57 n. 9C) in the collocation *diro sacrum*, and the abl. *diro . . . ense* embraces the acc. *sacrum caput*. Pompey's head should have been sacred to Septimius as that of his former commander as well as of a guest of his master (compare 59 n. 6) and of a noble Roman hero.

32.   A. **Fortuna**: compare n. 14 above.   B. **petit**: i.e. sought him out and tore him down; the form is perf. (not pres.) for *petiit* (see 1 n. 4B), since in the original the following verbs are perf.; compare 70 n. 27B.

79

Caesar was, in the judgment of ancient critics, almost a rival to Cicero in oratory and the ablest exponent of the simple and direct style called "Attic" because modeled on the fourth-century Athenian orator Lysias. This style was opposed to the ornate and complex style known as "Asiatic," of which Cicero's rival Hortensius (see 67 pref.) was the principal practitioner. Cicero himself preferred a "mean" style modeled on that of Demosthenes.

Caesar was also author of now lost works on a variety of topics as well as of the surviving *Commentarii* on the Gallic and Civil Wars, for which see n. 6 below. Both he and Cicero wrote poetry; from Caesar's only a few verses survive (see n. 5A below) but from Cicero's verses considerable quotations, some in his own works, have been preserved, as from the poem on his consulship; see nn. 5B, 21A, and 23A below. Cicero's poetry covered a wide variety of topics besides his consulship (for which see 32 n. 20B): Caesar's conquest in Gaul (see 36 n. 3C), Marius, translations from Greek drama, from Greek astronomical works, and from other Greek verse, etc.

In selection A below, the first paragraph combines estimates of Caesar's oratory from Quintilian (see 13 pref.) and from a *Dialogue on Oratory* attributed to Tacitus, for whom see 48 pref. The second paragraph gives Cicero's praise of Caesar's *Commentaries on the Gallic War* with the inclusion of a sentence from the preface to book VIII of these *Commentaries*, which was added by Caesar's lieutenant Aulus Hirtius, for whom see 44 pref. In B, the prose passage gives Quintilian's evaluation of Cicero's achievement in oratory, and the verses in dactylic hexameter are from Juvenal's *Tenth Satire*, for which see 59 pref.

A. De Caesaris eloquentia commentariisque

Gaius Caesar si Foro tantum vacasset, non alius ex nostris contra Ciceronem nominaretur.[1] Tanta in eo vis est, id acumen, ea concitatio, ut illum eodem animo dixisse quo bellavit appareat.[2] Exornat tamen omnia mira sermonis, cuius proprie studiosus fuit, elegantia.[3] Concedamus igitur ei ut propter magnitudinem cogitationum et occupationes rerum minus in eloquentia effecerit quam divinum eius ingenium postulabat.[4] Fecit quoque carmina, non melius quam Cicero, sed felicius, quia illum fecisse pauciores sciunt.[5]

Sed commentarii quos scripsit rerum suarum valde probandi sunt.[6] Nudi enim sunt, recti et venusti, omni ornatu orationis tamquam veste detracta.[7] Constat autem inter omnes nihil tam operose ab aliis esse perfectum quod non horum elegantia commentariorum superetur.[8] Nihil est enim in historia pura et illustri brevitate dulcius.[9] Ita dum voluit alios habere parata unde sumerent qui vellent scribere tantarum rerum historiam,[10] ineptis gratum fortasse fecit qui illa volent calamistris inurere;[11] sanos quidem homines a scribendo adeo deterruit ut omnium iudicio praerepta, non praebita, facultas scriptoribus videatur.[12]

B.   *De Ciceronis eloquentia*

Quis Cicerone docere diligentius, movere vehementius potest? Cui tanta umquam iucunditas adfuit? Iam in omnibus quae dicit tanta auctoritas inest ut dissentire pudeat;[13] cum interim haec omnia, quae vix singula quisquam intentissima cura consequi posset, fluunt illaborata,[14] et illa, qua nihil pulchrius auditum est, oratio prae se fert tamen felicissimam facilitatem.[15] Quare non immerito ab hominibus aetatis suae regnare in iudiciis dictus est;[16] apud posteros vero id consecutus, ut "Cicero" iam non hominis nomen sed eloquentiae habeatur.[17] Sed haec tam beata eloquentia tandem ei exitiabilis fuit, ut Iuvenalis poeta his verbis testatur:[18]

> Eloquio Cicero ille perīt orator, eumque
> largus et exundans leto dedit ingenii fons.[19]
> Ingenio manus est et cervix caesa; nec umquam
> sanguine causidici maduerunt rostra pusilli.[20]
> "O fortunatam natam me consule Romam"—[21]
> Antoni gladios potuit contemnere, si sic
> omnia dixisset.[22] Ridenda poemata malo
> quam te, conspicuae divina Philippica famae.[23]

1. A. **Gaius ... vacasset** = "if only Caesar had had leisure for the Forum," i.e. for the practice of oratory; *Foro* is dat. of purpose.   B. **ex nostris:** i.e. from Lat. orators. *Alius* is here construed like a numeral with *ex*+abl.; see 7 n. 5.   C. **contra Ciceronem:** i.e. as a rival to Cicero.

2. A. **id ... ea:** equivalent to *tantum ... tanta*; compare 32 n. 17A.   B. **bellavit:** not attracted into the subj. because it represents the author's own statement of fact; compare 71 n. 10B.   C. **appareat:** the subject is the inf. clause *illum ... dixisse*; render in Eng.: "it appears ... that he spoke"; compare 2 n. 2B (and 59 n. 1A).

3.   A. **tamen** = "and yet," i.e. despite his vigorous speed, which might have led him to neglect elegance of style.   B. **mira . . . elegantia** = "an extraordinary elegance of diction (style)"; probably nom., subject of *exornat*, not abl. of means.   C. **sermonis:** may simply = "conversation" (as in 43 n. 21A), but it often has a more technical connotation of "diction, style," as it does here; see 62 nn. 1 and 2. Caesar is said to have been especially careful and conservative in his choice of words both in speaking and writing.

4.   A. **propter . . . postulabat:** for the thought that Caesar's (military) ambitions and political activities (particularly as dictator) prevented him from making full use of his literary and rhetorical abilities, compare n. 1A above.   B. **divinum eius ingenium:** that outstanding talent partook of the divine was a regular doctrine of Stoicism as well as a normal compliment, particularly in court literature of the Hellenistic world. When Quintilian wrote this, Caesar had long since been deified (see 80), but there is probably no conscious reference to him as a god.   C. **postulabat:** not attracted into the subj.; see n. 2B above.

5.   A. **carmina** = "poems"; see 57 n. 13C. Suetonius *Iul.* 56. 5 and 7 says that Caesar wrote a *poema quod inscribitur Iter*, a *Laudes Herculis*, and a *tragoedia Oedipus*, poems which Augustus suppressed; hence they were generally unknown when Tacitus wrote this sentence.   B. **Cicero:** for his poetry see pref. above and nn. 21A and 23A below; see also 32 n. 20B, 35 nn. 12–14, and 37 n. 21A.

6.   **commentarii . . . rerum suarum:** for the meaning of *commentarius* see 28 n. 23E (and 32 n. 19A); it is often followed by the gen., as here and in the 1st sentence of the 2nd par. of 32B (*commentarium consulatus mei*), as well as by *de*+abl. For Caesar's *Commentarii de Bello Gallico* see prefs. to 36 and 75; for those *de Bello Civili* see 38 pref. The latter may not have been available as early as 46, the date of Cicero's *Brutus* (see 57 n. 14B), a discussion of Roman orators in which occur his comments on Caesar.

7.   A. **nudi . . . recti et venusti** = "stark (i.e. unadorned) . . . correct (i.e. accurate) and pleasing"; *nudi*, used metaphorically of style, suggests the literal simile following.   B. **omni . . . detracta** = "with all elaboration of style stripped off like a garment"; *detracto* in agreement with *ornatu* would be more correct in this abl. abs., but the manuscripts read *-a*, which was probably due to the nearness of *veste*.   C. **orationis** = "eloquence" (in general); not here any specific speech.

8.   A. **constat . . . inter omnes** = "it is agreed among everybody," i.e. everyone agrees; the subject is the indirect statement *nihil . . . esse perfectum*; see 15 n. 5A (and 44 n. 10A), and for the thought compare *omnium iudicio* below in the last sentence of A.   B. **superetur:** pres. subj. of *superare* in a rel. clause of result, as indicated by the preceding *tam*.

9.   A. **pura et illustri:** with *brevitate*, not with *historia*, and by hendiadys (see 13 n. 11A and 77 n. 10B) = "clear."   B. **pura** = "clear" or "straightforward"; not here "pure" from foreign words or rhetorical ornament.   C. **illustri** = "well-lit"; its basic meaning; compare *illustrata* in the 1st sentence of the 3rd par. of 71; i.e. it means "distinct" rather than derivatively "illustrious." Quintilian V 14.33 speaks of arguments presented *sermone puro et dilucido et distincto . . . minime elato ornatoque*.

10.   A. **dum voluit:** the perf. ind. is used with *dum* to make a time emphatic by contrast; here Caesar's original intention of writing his *Commentarii* as source material is contrasted with the later result that they were considered too good to be adapted. For *dum* with the pres. for an action inclusive of that of the main verb see 6 n. 8 (and 65 n. 2A).   B. **parata unde sumerent** = "(source material) prepared on which they might draw." *Unde* is used instead of the rel. *ex quibus* modifying *parata*; *sumerent* is subj. in a rel. clause of characteristic expressing purpose (see 7 n. 8A and 58 n. 7C); compare *commentarium . . . ex quo disceret* in 28 nn. 23E and F.   C. **qui vellent** = "(those) who wished"; another rel. clause of characteristic, this one with an indefinite (omitted) antecedent; compare 20 n. 12A (and 65 n. 15). The rel. clause *qui . . . historiam* both modifies *alios* and provides a subject for *sumerent*.

11. **ineptis ... inurere** = "he perhaps did a favor (lit. something pleasing) to fools, who might want to embellish these (accounts)." The comparison of overadorned style to overcurled hair, singed with curling irons (*calamistris inurere*), occurs elsewhere in Lat.

12. A. **sanos ... homines** = "but wise men at least"; adversative asyndeton; see 13 n. 11B (and 15 n. 8C). B. **facultas**: i.e. the opportunity to improve on the *Commentaries*. C. **scriptoribus**: dat. of reference (separation) after *praerepta* = "taken from" (compare 18 n. 7A and 70 n. 5C), and also dat. of indirect object after *praebita* = "provided to." For a noun in a given case (usually dat.) used in two constructions compare 14 n. 7A (and 70 n. 13B). D. **videatur**: the pres. subj. is rare after secondary tenses in result clauses but is occasionally used to represent a present result of a completed action.

13. **dissentire pudeat**: the inf., used absolutely, is probably subject of *pudeat*, not complementary (see 65 n. 16B); it may be rendered "one is ashamed to disagree."

14. A. **cum interim** = "when in the meanwhile," i.e. while at the same time. B. **quae ... singula** = "which one by one" or "which individually"; object of *consequi*. C. **posset**: the imperf. subj. after the primary tense *fluunt* is read by the manuscripts and editors. It technically gives the rel. clause an "unreal" connotation, with some such protasis as *si vellet* implied; however, it seems here to have little more force than would the potential pres. subj. *possit*. D. **illaborata** = "not worked on," i.e. without effort or abundantly. The form is an adj., not a past part. (contrast *interminatam* in 68 n. 6C), and is post-Augustan; compare 6 n. 12B (and 71 n. 2C) Eng. idiom would here use a prepositional phrase or an adv.

15. A. **illa ... oratio** = "that eloquence (of his) than which nothing finer has (ever) been heard"; for *oratio* see n. 7C above; for the separation of *illa* from *oratio* by the rel. clause compare *mira ... elegantia* in n. 3B above. For the sentiment compare that of Livy in his description of Cicero's death in 44 n. 16A. B. **prae se fert**: lit. = "bears before itself," i.e. displays; compare 48 n. 15B. C. **felicissimam facilitatem**: Quintilian means that despite the unparalleled beauty of Cicero's oratorical style, it seems both effortless and most successful. For *felix* with the connotation of success given by fortune compare Sulla's title in 65 n. 13.

16. **regnare**: in Lat. slang this meant "to be pre-eminent in"; compare *regnum* in 60 n. 21B. After his success against Verres (see 67 pref.), Cicero was acknowledged the most effective pleader in the Roman courts.

17. **id**: object of *consecutus*, anticipating the substantive result clause; compare 32 n. 7A (and 65 n. 21A). For the result clause as object compare 31 n. 15 (and 69 nn. 17A and 24A).

18. **Iuvenalis**: see 59 pref. Quintilian, from whom the prose passage is drawn, published his *Institutio oratoria* in the 90's A.D. and hence would not have known the work of Juvenal, who probably published his *Satires* during the first quarter of the 2nd cent. A.D. This sentence has been added to make the transition to the verses from Juvenal's *Tenth Satire*.

19. A. **eloquio**: instrumental abl. (cause or means), as is *ingenio* 2 verses below. Antony insisted on Cicero's death because of anger at the speeches, called *Philippics*, in which Cicero had assailed him during 43; see prefs. to 42 and 44. B. **Cicero ille** = "that (famous) Cicero." C. **perit** = *periit*; compare 70 n. 27B (and 78 n. 32B).

20. A. **manus ... caesa**: Antony had Cicero's hands and head cut off and displayed on the rostra; see 44, especially n. 15. B. **nec umquam** = *et numquam*. Juvenal generalizes from the specific example of Cicero to say that the platform never drips with the blood of a poor and insignificant pleader, that is, only with that of a distinguished one.

21. A. **O ... Rōmam**: for this much ridiculed verse from Cicero's poem on his consulship see 32 n. 20B. The acc. is exclamatory (see 13 n. 2A and 71 n. 6), and the verse is

here without syntactical construction but is taken up by *si sic omnia dixisset*, i.e. if everything that he had said had been as insipid as this verse, he would never have perished.   B. **fortunatam:** adj. from *fortuna*, rather than past part. of the rare verb *fortuno*; compare n. 14D above.

22.   A. **Antōnī:** since the *-o-* is long, the gen. in *-ī* rather than *-ī* is required by the meter although Juvenal wrote much later than Augustus; see 17 n. 7 (and compare 78 n. 31A) and contrast *ingenii* 4 verses above.   B. **potuit ... dixisset:** in the apodosis of a contrary to fact condition (here past), the ind. of *possum* and similar verbs may be used because the unreality is implied in the verb itself; see 10 n. 12A (and 77 n. 6B).

23.   A. **poemata:** Greek acc. plur. (compare 32 n. 20B); the *-ŏē-* are pronounced as separate vowels, a short and a long, as in *poeta* or *poesis*; for Cicero's ridiculous (or, laughable) poems see n. 21 above.   B. **malo quam:** since *malo = magis volo* it is followed regularly by *quam* in Lat.; Eng. idiom would say: "I prefer ridiculous poems to you."   C. **conspicuae ... famae:** gen. of quality (description); see 6 n. 9 (and 63 n. 15A).   D. **divina Philippica:** fem. voc. sing., defining *te*; the reference is specifically to the bitter *Second Philippic* (see 42 B) rather than a collective sing. used for all the *Philippics*, for which see n. 19A above. For *divina* compare n. 4B above. Juvenal frequently apostrophizes directly a person or, as here, a thing: see 59 n. 28 (and for Lucan compare 78 n. 4B).

80

After the assassination of Caesar (see 43), the populace, aroused by Antony, forced the senate to give him a magnificent public funeral, burned his body in the Forum, and claimed that a comet which appeared four months later represented his soul ascending to the gods; see n. 20A below. The senate refused to recognize the divinity of Caesar until forced to do so by the Second Triumvirate (see 44 pref.), as of January 1, 43. Thereafter Octavian (later named Augustus), who had been adopted in Caesar's will, called himself no longer *Gai filius* but *Divi filius*; a *divus* was not a *deus* but closely akin, like a Greek "hero" or a Christian "saint"; compare 60 n. 2. Thus Octavian endowed himself with an immediate divine parentage rather than the remote descent from Venus claimed by Caesar; see the opening of 33. After the death of Augustus in A.D. 14, the senate recognized him also as a *divus* (compare the title of 47 A), as it did those later emperors whom it admired.

Ovid devoted the last two books of his *Metamorphoses* (see 49 pref.) to Roman transformations and concluded with the deification of Caesar. The following selected and slightly adapted dactylic hexameters describe the natural and supernatural portents which heralded his assassination, the intervention of Venus to translate his soul to the sky as a comet or new star, and the even superior role of Augustus, who is made an earthly Jupiter. The portents are very similarly described by Vergil at the end of his first poem on agriculture, *Georgic* I 466–514, which was probably written in the mid-thirties, quite close to the event. Shakespeare made vivid use of Plutarch's description of the same portents in the third scene of the first act of *Julius Caesar*. Ovid's flattery of Augustus can be paralleled in earlier poems by Horace and Vergil; see n. 24B below.

Caesar post caedem signis diris portentam deus fit

Aeneae genetrix, vidit cum triste parari
pontifici letum et coniurata arma moveri,[1]
palluit et superos adiit, qui, rumpere quamquam
ferrea non possunt veterum decreta sororum,
signa tamen luctus dant haud incerta futuri.[2]
Arma ferunt inter nigras crepitantia nubes
terribilesque tubas auditaque cornua caelo
praemonuisse nefas.[3] Solis quoque tristis imago
lurida sollicitis praebebat lumina terris.
Saepe faces visae mediis ardere sub astris;[4]

saepe inter nimbos guttae cecidere cruentae;[5]
caerulus et vultum ferrugine Lucifer atra
sparsus erat, sparsi lunares sanguine currus.[6]
Tristia mille locis Stygius dedit omina bubo;[7]
mille locis lacrimavit ebur;[8] cantusque feruntur
auditi sanctis et verba minantia lucis.[9]
Victima nulla litat; magnosque instare tumultus
fibra monet; caesumque caput reperitur in extis.[10]
Inque Foro circumque domos et templa deorum
nocturnos ululasse canes umbrasque silentum
erravisse ferunt motamque tremoribus urbem.[11]
Non tamen insidias venturaque vincere fata
praemonitus potuere deum;[12] strictique feruntur
in templum gladii.[13] Neque enim locus ullus in urbe
ad facinus diramque placet nisi curia caedem.[14]

Vix occisus erat, media cum sede senatus
constitit alma Venus, nulli cernenda,[15] suique
Caesaris eripuit membris, nec in aera solvi
passa, recentem animam caelestibus intulit astris.[16]

Caesar in urbe sua deus est;[17] quem, Marte togaque
praecipuum,[18] non bella magis finita triumphis
resque domi gestae properataque gloria rerum[19]
in sidus vertere novum stellamque comantem[20]
quam sua progenies.[21] Neque enim de Caesaris actis
ullum maius opus quam quod pater exstitit huius.[22]
Ne foret hic igitur mortali semine cretus,
ille deus faciendus erat.[23] Nunc Iuppiter arces
temperat aetherias et mundi regna triformis;[24]
terra sub Augusto est. Pater est et rector uterque.

1.   A. **Aenēae genetrix:** i.e. Venus, the subject of *vidit, palluit,* and *adiit.* The phrase indicates how well known Vergil's *Aeneid* had made the story of Aeneas (see 1 pref.) on its publication after his death in 19; it also recalls Caesar's cult of Venus Genetrix (see 33 pref.) and the opening of Lucretius' poem; see 69 n. 1B.   B. **vĭdit:** perf. act. ind. after *cum* temporal, defining a precise time; compare 31 n. 9B.   C. **pontifici:** Caesar had been *pontifex maximus* since 63; see 33 pref. (and compare in 56 n. 2A). Here and at the end of this first section, Ovid heightens the enormity of the assassination by making it a sacrilege.

2. A. **superos** = "the (other) gods" (see 78 n. 20B); direct object of *adiit* = "approached"; see 2 n. 6.   B. **ferrea ... veterum decreta sororum:** the decrees of the three sister Fates (see 77 n. 4B) were as immovable as iron.   C. **luctus ... futuri:** i.e. of grief to be for the whole Roman world rather than for the gods only.

3. A. **arma ... tubas ... cornua:** all acc. subjects of *praemonuisse*, the inf. in indirect discourse after *ferunt*. The *-que ... -que* connect each item with the next; contrast 71 n. 15B. For the nature of the portents, compare the vision which appeared to Caesar on the banks of the Rubicon (39 nn. 19–21).   B. **ferunt** = "(people) say"; compare 4 n. 13 (and 21 n. 21B). By placing *ferunt* at the beginning and end (see n. 11A below) and *feruntur* in the middle (see n. 9A below) of his description of the portents, Ovid probably meant to suggest that the whole account was merely report, though the intervening sentences are made statements of fact in the ind.   C. **nefas:** an indeclinable noun; compare 8 n. 7B (and 77 n. 12B). It is here object of *praemonuisse*. For Caesar's murder as sacrilege see n. 1C above, and for Pompey's compare 78 n. 31B.

4. **visae:** supply *sunt*; upon it depends the pres. act. inf. *ardere*.

5. **cĕcĭdēre:** 3rd pers. plur. perf. act. ind. of *cădo*; compare 27 n. 3B (and 78 n. 4A), and for the ending see 15 n. 10 (and 77 n. 15).

6. A. **caerulus ... Lūcifer:** the "Day-bringer" usually means the morning star, the planet Venus (or Mercury), and probably does so here, since the sun has already been mentioned 4 verses above and also since these verses deal mainly with nocturnal portents, except perhaps for the *guttae ... cruentae*. However, although the morning star might change its color from bright to dark-blue (*caerulus* = *caeruleus*; see 66 n. 24C), it is rather extreme to imagine that its face would show large enough to be sprinkled with dark, rust-colored spots (*ferrugine ... atra*). Moreover, Vergil *Georg.* I 467 applies to the sun the words *caput obscura nitidum ferrugine texit*. Thus it is possible that Ovid here returns to the sun in order to balance the following "chariots of the moon." In the notes hereafter, Vergil's parallel passage in *Georg.* I 466–514 will be cited by verse number only.   B. **vultum:** Greek acc. of specification; see 55 n. 20D (and 69 n. 12E).

7. A. **mille locis:** abl. of place where without a prep., as regularly when *locus* is modified by an adj.; see 30 n. 2B (and 43 n. 17B).   B. **Stygius** = adj. derived from the river Styx, which the souls of the dead had to cross in Charon's skiff to reach Hades. Vergil 470 speaks of *importunae volucres*.   C. **bubo:** a variety of horned owl, whose mournful call was regarded as an omen of calamity and death, as is here connoted by its modifier.

8. **lacrimavit ebur:** in sudden rises of temperature, the still cool surface of ivory will condense moisture and seem to weep. Ivory is perhaps mentioned here rather than bronze or marble to make the portent more precious and hence more marvelous. Vergil 480 says: *et maestum inlacrimat templis ebur aeraque sudant*. The portent may have been an imaginative development of the tradition taken by Shakespeare from Plutarch *Caesar* 66.7 that the murdered Caesar fell "at the base of Pompey's statue, which all the time ran blood."

9. A. **feruntur** = "are said"; see n. 3B above. When a verb of saying is put in the pass., nouns which after the act. would be acc. subject of the inf. become nom. subject of the verb of saying, and modifiers become nom. in agreement; so here *auditi* (*esse*) agrees with the nearer of the two subjects, *cantus ... verba*.   B. **lūcīs:** abl. (of place where; compare n. 7A above) of *lucus* (compare the 1st verse of 49), not the gen. sing. of *lux, lūcĭs*.

10. A. **litat** = "gives favorable omens"; *lito* is a technical religious term used either of the sacrificer or (as here) of the victim who provides a favorable auspice.   B. **fibra:** fem. nom. sing.; lit. = "a fiber, vein"; but used also for a division of or the whole liver, whose appearance was interpreted by a *haruspex*; see in 52 n. 3. Vergil 484 refers to *fibrae ... minaces*.   C. **caesumque caput** = "and the severed lobe (of the liver)."

If this was accidentally cut off as the *haruspex* opened up the entrails (*exta*), the auspice was very bad.

11.   A. **inque ... urbem:** for these final portents, Ovid returns to report (*ferunt*, see nn. 3B and 9A above).   B. **nocturnos ... canes:** *ululasse* connotes abnormal howling, not normal barking; Vergil 470 speaks of *obscenae canes* (fem., hence specifically bitches). Contrast the 3rd sentence of 12, where the unusual silence of the dogs at night suggests something supernatural or divine about Scipio the Elder.   C. **umbrasque silentum:** i.e. ghosts; compare Vergil's *simulacra ... pallentia* (477). In poetry, pres. parts. (in *-ns*) may have the gen. plur. in *-um* instead of in *-ium*; compare 69 n. 6B.   D. **motamque ... urbem:** Vergil 475 more miraculously locates the earthquakes (*insolitis ... motibus*) in the Alps rather than in Rome. The Alps and Apennines represent the basic limestone formation of Italy, which is firm, but the west coast (from Etna in Sicily to the island of Elba) is broken by a volcanic fault, on which both Vesuvius and Rome lie and along which earthquakes are common.

12.   **praemonitus:** nom. plur., subject of *potuere* and modified by the possessive gen. plur. *deum*, for which see 11 n. 14B (and compare 78 n. 20B). For the thought compare n. 2B above.

13.   A. **stricti ... gladii** = "drawn daggers are carried," i.e. by the conspirators. For the drawn daggers see 43 n. 10 (and compare 78 n. 24A). Contrast the literal meaning of *feruntur* here with that of "are said" in n. 9A above.   B. **templum:** a sacrosanct open space with or without a temple in it; see 55 n. 13A. Ovid may use it here for the meeting place of the senate because the senate often met in temples (see 14 n. 6A), as in the temple of Fides (according to Valerius Maximus III 2. 17, for whom see 83 pref.) on the Capitoline at the time of the assassination of Tiberius Gracchus (compare 18 n. 14D), or in the temple of Bellona under Sulla (see 27 n. 15), or in that of Jupiter Stator when Cicero gave the First Oration against Catiline; see 71 n. 17. But the senate's meeting would endow any place with sacrosanctity, and Ovid may use *templum* here in its general sense to stress this; compare nn. 1C and 3C above (and the following note).

14.   **curia:** not the senate's regular *curia* in the Forum (see 14 n. 6A and 53 n. 10A) but a hall attached to the portico of Pompey's theater; see 43 n. 3C (and 77 n. 19). Here again Ovid implies that Caesar's assassination was sacrilege, since by using *curia* alone he endows Pompey's hall with the sacrosanctity which attached to the regular *curia*; see preceding note.

15.   A. **media ... sede:** abl. of place where without a prep. because of *media*; see 59 n. 19C (and compare n. 7A above).   B. **cum:** temporal conjunction, here followed by the perf. ind. as in n. 1B above.   C. **constitit:** probably perf. ind. of *consisto* = "place oneself" (as in 39 n. 17A), not from *consto* = "stand"; compare *exstitisset* in 72 n. 16C. D. **alma Venus:** for the epithet see 69 n. 3.   E. **nulli** = *nemini;* see in 74 n. 7C (and compare 36 n. 1B). It is dat. of reference (agent) with the adjectival gerundive *cernenda*; see 21 n. 15C (and 74 n. 3A).

16.   A. **suique Caesaris** = "of her (descendant) Caesar"; gen. with both *membris* and *animam*; here used instead of the normal dat. of reference (possession) with parts of the body (for which see 43 n. 6 and 74 n. 27), perhaps to avoid a possible misconstruction as a dat. of reference (separation; see 18 n. 7A and 79 n. 12C) with *eripuit*.   B. **membris:** abl. of separation without a prep. (but see the *e-* prefixed to the verb), not dat. of "separation," which is used only of persons; contrast 61 n. 30B.   C. **nec ... passa** = "and, not allowing"; *nec* = *et non*, with the *et* connecting the two main clauses (of which *eripuit* and *intulit* are the verbs) while the negative goes only with *passa*.   D. **āĕrä:** For the quantities and form see 77 n. 24 and contrast *aera* (= "bronze statues") in the quotation from Vergil in n. 8 above.   E. **recentem animam:** object of the two main verbs *eripuit* and *intulit* and also acc. subject of the pass. inf. *solvi*, which is complementary with *passa*. For *anima* = "soul" and the theory that it is ordinarily dispersed at death, see 70 n. 24B; it is described as "recent" here because it is just separated from

the body.   F. **astris:** dat. either after a verb compounded with *in-* (see 6 n. 13), or indicating place to which, as often in poetry, e.g. in 49 n. 6A.

17.   **Caesar ... deus est:** see pref. above and compare Suetonius *Iul.* 88: *in deorum numerum relatus est, non ore modo decernentium* (i.e. the senate) *sed et persuasione vulgi.*

18.   A. **Marte togaque:** abls. of specification with *praecipuum*; = "outstanding in peace and war." Compare the common prose phrase in the loc. *domi militiaeque*, as in 13 n. 5A, and Cicero's contrast of *togae* and *laurea* in 32 n. 20B.   B. **Marte:** the god is used by metonymy for his sphere, as in 49 n. 4; compare *Neptunus* in 73 n. 20D.   C. **toga:** by metonymy for peace, as in 27 n. 13B (and 77 n. 16C).

19.   **properataque gloria rerum** = "and the swift (i.e. swiftly won) glory of Caesar's military achievements" in Gaul (see prefs. to 36 and 75) and in the Civil War, for which see 41 pref.

20.   A. **sidus ... novum stellamque comantem:** lit. = "changed (him) into a new star (and) a comet"; see n. C below. Pliny the Elder *Nat. Hist.* II 93–94 quotes Augustus' own statement that, at the time when he celebrated games in honor of Venus Genetrix shortly after Caesar's murder (actually on July 14, 44), a comet appeared for seven days, and the crowd believed that it represented Caesar's soul received among the immortal gods. Augustus, then called Octavian (see 44 pref.), therefore mounted a star on the forehead of a statue of Caesar which he dedicated in the temple of Venus Genetrix in Caesar's Forum. Suetonius *Iul.* 88 repeats this in closely similar terms, and the star is shown on posthumous coinage commemorating Caesar in 43. Ovid may have identified the *sidus* and *stella* by hendiadys (see 13 n. 11A and 79 n. 9A), or conceived of the comet as a temporary phenomenon of Caesar's soul going to heaven, which then became a star as its fixed abode.   B. **vertēre:** the length of the second *-e-* shows that this is not pres. act. inf. but 3rd pers. plur. perf. act. ind.; compare n. 5 above. Its subjects are *bella, res,* and *gloria,* and its object is *quem* 3 verses above.   C. **comantem:** the adjs. *comans* and *comatus* were formed, on the analogy of parts., from the noun *coma*; compare 6 n. 12B (and 79 n. 14D). This is almost the only instance of the use of either adj. with *stella* to translate the Greek *komētēs*, Eng. "comet." Augustus, as quoted by Pliny, called it a *sidus crinitum* and Suetonius, a *stella crinita,* terms which suggest that Ovid meant to identify his *sidus* and *stella;* see n. A above. Lat. also regularly used the Greek *comētēs.*

21.   A. **quam** = "than," taking up from *non ... magis* 3 verses above.   B. **sua progenies:** i.e. Octavian, Caesar's adopted son, later the Emperor Augustus; see 44 pref. and n. 20A above. Ovid flatters him, as was customary (see pref.), by suggesting here that he, rather than Caesar's civil and military achievements (see nn. 18A and 19 above), was the chief justification for Caesar's deification.

22.   A. **neque ... ullum maius opus** = "nor was there any greater achievement." B. **quam ... huius** = "than (the fact) that he (Caesar) was the father of him (Octavian)," i.e. that Caesar when deified afforded Augustus divine parentage; see pref. The idea is repeated in the next 2 verses.

23.   A. **hic ... ille:** i.e. Augustus ... Caesar.   B. **foret ... cretus** = *esset* (see 21 n. 26C) *natus* and therefore is followed by the abl. of source (separation without a prep.); see 5 n. 2A (and in 65 n. 8A).

24.   A. **Iuppiter:** for the spelling see 52 n. 1B (and 74 n. 7F).   B. **mundi ... triformis:** i.e. the sky (Jupiter himself), the sea (Neptune; see 73 n. 20D), and the lower world (Pluto or Hades). The earliest meaning of *mundus* is debated but, assuming it to be the word also used for female adornment, it would have been applied, like the Greek *kosmos,* to the starry adornment of heaven and, hence, either to the vault of heaven or to the universe (as here). The earth is left to Augustus as a fourth equal part of the world, making him comparable to the greatest gods. Horace also compares Augustus to Jupiter in *Odes* I 12.49 ff. and II 5.1 ff., while Vergil several times speaks of him as a *deus;* see 84 n. 4.

81

In August 44, Cicero wrote to an old friend, Gaius Matius, who was being criticized by the optimates because he had expressed sorrow for Caesar's death. Cicero's letter and Matius' reply are preserved in the collection of Cicero's correspondence (see 31 pref.) known as the *ad Familiares* = "To his Friends." Cicero, who naturally approved of the assassination (see 43 pref. and B), told Matius that despite this difference of opinion, his personal regard and affection were unchanged and that he had been defending Matius against criticism rather than adding thereto.

In the following selection from his reply, Matius justifies with dignity his loyalty to Caesar's memory as that of a personal friend, despite his disapproval of the course of action on Caesar's part which led to the Second Civil War; see 38 and 39. He criticizes the "liberators" for trying to stifle any views contrary to their own and concludes that his honorable record will defend his reputation against false criticism. Matius, a cultivated man, wrote with an elegance comparable to Cicero's own, and his letter records a sincere personal feeling honestly expressed in a time of tension when such utterance required courage as well as loyalty.

Matius mortem Caesaris amici dolet

Nota vero mihi sunt quae in me post Caesaris mortem contulerint.[1] Vitio mihi dant quod mortem hominis necessari graviter fero atque eum, quem dilexi, perisse indignor;[2] aiunt enim patriam amicitiae praeponendam esse, proinde ac si iam vicerint obitum eius rei publicae fuisse utilem.[3] Sed non agam astute;[4] fateor me ad istum gradum sapientiae non pervenisse; neque enim Caesarem in dissensione civili sum secutus sed amicum;[5] quamquam re offendebar,[6] tamen non deserui, neque bellum umquam civile aut etiam causam dissensionis probavi, quam etiam nascentem exstingui summe studui.[7] Itaque in victoria hominis necessari neque honoris neque pecuniae dulcedine sum captus, quibus praemiis reliqui, minus apud eum quam ego cum possent, immoderate sunt abusi.[8] Atque etiam res familiaris mea lege Caesaris deminuta est,[9] cuius beneficio plerique, qui Caesaris morte laetantur, remanserunt in civitate.[10] Civibus victis ut parceretur aeque ac pro mea salute laboravi.[11]

Possum igitur—qui omnes voluerim incolumes—eum, a quo id impetratum est, perisse non indignari?[12] cum praesertim iidem homines illi et invidiae et exitio fuerint.[13] "Plecteris ergo," inquiunt, "quoniam factum nostrum improbare audes." O superbiam inauditam, alios in facinore gloriari, aliis ne dolere quidem impunite licere![14] At haec etiam servis semper libera fuerunt, ut timerent, gauderent, dolerent suo potius quam alterius arbitrio;[15] quae nunc isti, ut quidem ipsi dictitant, "libertatis auctores" metu nobis extorquere conantur.[16] Sed nihil agunt.[17] Nullius umquam periculi terroribus ab officio aut ab humanitate desciscam;[18] numquam enim honestam mortem fugiendam, saepe etiam oppetendam putavi. Sed quid mihi suscensent, si id opto ut paeniteat eos sui facti?[19] Cupio enim Caesaris mortem omnibus esse acerbam.

Hominis mihi coniunctissimi ac viri amplissimi doleo gravem casum. Sed non vereor ne aut meae vitae modestia parum valitura sit in posterum contra falsos rumores[20] aut ne etiam ii, qui me non amant propter meam in Caesarem constantiam, non malint mei quam sui similes amicos habere.[21]

1. **quae ... contulerint** = "(the sort of criticisms) which they have brought"; this rel. clause of characteristic with omitted antecedent (compare 20 n, 12A and 79 n, 10c) is subject of *nota sunt*; the subject of *contulerint* is general, including both Caesar's murderers and those who approved of the assassination.

2. A. **vitio mihi dant** = "they criticize me," lit. "give it to me as a fault"; double dat.; compare 17 n, 11A (and 73 n, 32A). B. **necessari** = "(who was) a close friend"; with the adj. *necessarius* compare the noun *necessitudo* in 32 n, 10B. C. **graviter fero** = "I am grieved at," lit. "I bear heavily"; compare 3 n, 2A (and 63 n, 6).

3. A. **proinde ac ... vicerint** = "just as if they had proved"; for *proinde ac* see 70 n, 26A; for the perf. subj. where Eng. uses a contrary to fact pluperf., see 67 n, 21. B. **vicerint:** this meaning of *vinco* arises from its use for "I win (a case in court)," for which see 7 n, 9; it takes an objective inf. clause. C. **obitum ... utilem:** for Cicero's own admission that the "liberation" was a failure, even from the optimate position, see 43 B.

4. A. **non agam astute** = "I will not discuss cunningly"; Matius means he will not indulge in philosophical quibbling on the claims of patriotism *vs.* friendship or on what was really good (i.e. *utile*) for the Republic. B. **agam:** with the meaning here, contrast n. 17 below.

5. **Caesarem ... amicum:** *Caesarem* becomes almost a political term, i.e. Matius was not a Caesarian in politics but only a personal friend.

6. **re** = "by (Caesar's) action," i.e. in taking the steps which led to the Civil War; see prefs. to 38 and 39.

7. A. **quam ... studui** = "which, even (lit. also) when it began (lit. was being born), I was most (lit. very highly) eager to have stopped (lit. to be extinguished)." B.

quam: rel. pronoun referring back to *dissensionis* (rather than to *causam*) and subject of the inf. *exstingui*; the inf. clause is object of *studui*.

8. A. **quibus praemiis:** abl. with *sunt abusi*; see 71 n. 1c.   B. **reliqui . . . possent** = "the rest (of Caesar's supporters), although they had less influence with him than I etc."   c. **reliqui:** for the meaning here, compare 41 n. 1b.   D. **possent:** this verb when not followed by a complementary inf. regularly means "have power, influence, ability," or the like.   E. **apud eum:** with the meaning here, compare 72 n. 4.

9. A. **res familiaris mea** = "my property" or "money," lit. "household thing"; compare 44 n. 9a.   B. **lege Caesaris:** probably the *lex Iulia de pecuniis mutuis* (= "on loans"; compare 65 n. 20b) passed in 49. Matius, as a wealthy equestrian and investor, suffered from Caesar's measures designed to relieve pressure on debtors; compare 42 pref.

10. A. **cuius . . . civitate:** people who were in debt might have had to go into exile if they had not been aided by Caesar's financial measures; see preceding note.   B. **morte:** for the abl. with verbs of rejoicing see 73 n. 26 (and 78 n. 2).

11. A. **ut parceretur** = "that mercy should be shown," lit. "that it should be spared"; *parceretur* is a true impersonal pass. (compare 10 n. 10d and 75 n. 2a) followed by the dat. (see 47 n. 7 and 77 n. 29a) and the substantive clause of purpose is the object of *laboravi*; see 65 n. 21b.   B. **aeque ac** = "just as much as, no less than"; compare 69 n. 10a (and 3a above).

12. A. **possum etc.:** for the omission of the interrog. *-ne* in an indignant question see 71 n. 4.   B. **perisse:** for this contracted perf. act. inf. see 74 n. 16b.   c. **indignari:** may take an acc. object or an objective inf. clause, as here *eum . . . perisse*.

13. **illi . . . exitio** = "to him (a cause of) both unpopularity and death"; a double dat. construction; compare n. 2a above. Matius means that the pardon of opponents such as Brutus and Cassius had made Caesar unpopular with his more loyal followers, and that the very men whom he had pardoned assassinated him; see 43, especially n. 2.

14. A. **O superbiam:** acc. of exclamation; see 13 n. 2a (and 79 n. 21); the two following inf. clauses, *alios . . . gloriari* and *aliis . . . licere*, are in explanatory apposition with it.   B. **alios . . . licere** = "that some should boast in (i.e. of their) crime, (while) to others it is permitted not even to grieve with impunity." Eng. idiom would place "not even" with "permitted" but the Lat. is perhaps more effective. The two inf. clauses are without connective (in asyndeton; see 4 n. 5b).   c. **alios:** though it would be tempting to emend this to *aliis* and thus to make both infs., *gloriari* and *dolere*, depend on *licere* as the only inf. directly in apposition with *superbiam* (i.e. "that it be permitted to some to boast, to others not even to grieve"), the manuscripts show no variant reading, and the accepted text is probably more forceful.

15. A. **at haec . . . fuerunt** = "but these (actions) have always been open (lit. free) even to (or, for) slaves"; *haec* looks forward to the following *ut* clauses (see 79 n. 17) while also recalling the preceding *dolere*.   B. **suo (arbitrio) . . . alterius arbitrio:** for the parallel use of a possessive adj. and a possessive gen. see 35 n. 9b.   c. **alterius:** strictly = "of the other (of two)," is regularly used for the gen. of *alius* = "of another," since the gen. of this latter would resemble the nom. masc.

16. A. **isti . . . auctores** = "those 'authors of liberty,' as at least they themselves keep saying," i.e. calling themselves; perhaps something like *se esse* should be understood with *dictitant*. Both *isti* and *quidem* make *libertatis auctores* sarcastic.   B. **dictitant:** a double frequentative; compare *ventitabas* in 74 n. 18a.

17. **agunt** = "they accomplish"; compare 59 n. 17 (and contrast n. 4b above).

18. A. **nullius:** adj. with *periculi*; contrast in 36 n. 1b. In Eng. the negative in it goes better with the verb, i.e. "I will not desert."   B. **desciscam:** for the connotations see 17 n. 20c (and 20 n. 4c).

19.   A. **quid** = "why," as often; compare 31 n. 12.   B. **opto:** here, as often, takes a substantive clause of purpose *ut paeniteat* (see following note); it may also, like *cupio*, take an objective inf. clause; compare the next sentence. In either case a neut. demonstrative pronoun, as here *id*, is often used proleptically in apposition; see in 65 n. 21A (and n. 15A above).   C. **paeniteat . . . facti:** for the acc. of person and gen. of cause with verbs of feeling like *paenitet*, see 22 n. 12B (and 72 n. 20D).

20.   **vereor:** for the construction with verbs of fearing see 31 n. 2A. Upon *non vereor* depend two coordinate clauses connected by *aut . . . aut*. The first, introduced by *ne*, is positive; the second, introduced by *ne . . . non* (=*ut*), is negative; = "I do not fear that the modesty of my life will prevail too little . . . or that also they . . . will not prefer etc." The effect of the negation is to give a strong positive connotation, i.e. "I am confident that the modesty will prevail . . . and that even they will prefer." The variation in order of *ne aut . . . aut ne* suggests that Matius first meant to introduce the alternatives with a single *ne* but then put a second *ne* after the second *aut* to go with the following *non*.

21.   **mei . . . similes** = "like me (rather) than (like) themselves." In classical Lat., *similis* is regularly followed by the dat. (see 19 n. 2) but in early Lat. it took the gen., which continued to be used (as here) for personal pronouns. Matius contrasts his own loyalty with the treachery of the assassins, most of whom had been supporters of, or benefited by, Caesar; see 43 nn. 2 and 5A.

82

Under the Empire, when the political passions that had attended the death of the Republic lost their significance, the stature of Cicero grew as compared with that of Pompey and Caesar who had been more exclusively involved in political life. For Cicero's writings—not only his orations but also his treatises on rhetoric and the dialogues on q estions of wider philosophical interest—continued to be read and admired both for their style and for their grasp of Greek and Roman humanistic culture.

The following passages are tributes from several ages to the enduring fame of Cicero. The first is excerpted from Velleius, who, when he narrates Cicero's death, pauses to praise him as an orator and philosopher.

The second passage, adapted from a letter of the Christian Church Father St. Jerome (Hieronymus, *ca.* A.D. 340–420), describes the struggle which he underwent before he could free himself from his addiction to classical, and therefore pagan, authors in order to devote himself to commenting on and translating the Bible; see 89 pref.

The third passage is from one of the *Epistulares ad Familiares* which the Renaissance humanist Petrarch (1304–1374) composed in imitation of Cicero's collection (see 81 pref.), the manuscript of which he found. In it he portrays an old man of Vicenza as defending Cicero against all criticism, including that of himself. Petrarch, although he inspired the Renaissance admiration for Ciceronian style, became somewhat disillusioned about Cicero as a man after his discovery of the letters in which Cicero sometimes appears as vain, self-pitying, and vacillating; see, for example, 32 B, 35 B and C, and 37.

Ciceronis laudes

A. Nihil tam indignum illo tempore fuit quam quod aut Caesar Octavianus aliquem proscribere coactus est aut ab ullo Cicero proscriptus est.[1] Itaque abscisa scelere Antonii vox publica est, cum eius salutem nemo defendisset qui per tot annos et publicam civitatis et privatam civium salutem defenderat.[2] Nihil tamen egisti, Marce Antoni.[3] Rapuisti tu Ciceroni lucem sollicitam et aetatem senilem et vitam miseram;[4] famam vero gloriamque factorum atque dictorum eius non abstulisti. Vivit vivetque per omnem saeculorum memoriam,[5] dum hoc vel forte vel providentia vel utcumque constitutum rerum naturae corpus, quod ille paene solus Romanorum animo vidit, ingenio complexus est, eloquentia illuminavit, manebit incolume.[6] Omnisque posteritas illius in te scripta mirabitur, tuam in eum crudelitatem exsecrabitur;[7] citiusque e mundo genus hominum quam Ciceronis nomen cedet.

B. Cum ante annos plurimos domo, parentibus, sorore, cognatis propter caelorum me regna castrassem et Hierosolymam militaturus pergerem,[8] bibliotheca, quam mihi Romae summo studio ac labore confeceram, carere non poteram. Itaque miser ego lecturus Tullium ieiunabam.[9] Sed postquam febris corpus invasit exhaustum, subito raptus in spiritu ad tribunal Iudicis pertrahor, ubi tantum luminis erat ut proiectus in terram sursum aspicere non auderem. Interrogatus condicionem, Christianum me esse respondi;[10] et ille qui residebat,[11] "Mentiris," ait, "Ciceronianus es, non Christianus; ubi thesaurus tuus, ibi et cor tuum."[12] Tum clamare coepi et eiulans dicere: "Miserere mei, domine, miserere mei.[13] Si umquam habuero codices saeculares, si legero, te negavi."[14] Et post hoc somnum tanto dehinc studio divina legere incepi quanto mortalia ante non legeram.[15]

C. Senex ille nihil aliud vel mihi vel aliis quod responderet habebat,[16] nisi ut adversus omne quod diceretur splendorem nominis obiectaret, et rationis locum teneret auctoritas.[17] Succlamabat identidem, protenta manu: "Parcius, oro, parcius de Cicerone meo."[18] Cumque ab eo quaereretur, an errasse umquam ulla in re Ciceronem opinari posset,[19] claudebat oculos et, quasi verbo percussus, avertebat frontem ingeminans:[20] "Heu! mihi ergo Cicero meus arguitur?"[21] quasi non de homine sed de deo quodam ageretur.[22] Quaesivi igitur, an deum fuisse Tullium opinaretur an hominem. Incunctanter "deum," ille respondit;[23] et tum, quid dixisset intelligens, "deum," inquit, "eloquii."

1. A. **illo tempore:** the period between the death of Caesar and Philippi; see 44 and 45. For the abl. with *indignum* see 21 n. 12B.   B. **quod ... est** = "(the fact) that Caesar etc."; *quod* (= "that" or "the fact that") often introduces an ind. clause which is used substantively, without an antecedent, as the subject, or in apposition with the subject (as here with *nihil*), of a sentence.   C. **Caesar ... coactus est:** the official (and perhaps sincere) propaganda of Octavian after Actium in 30 (see 46) was that he had been forced by Antony to acquiesce in the proscriptions; see 45 n. 21A. Plutarch *Cicero* 49.3–4 reports that Octavian made Cicero's son Marcus his colleague in the consulship

for the last four months of 30 so that he might preside over the removal of the statues and other honors of Antony, and that later, when he himself found a grandson surreptitiously reading a book by Cicero, he reassured him, remarking: "A learned man, my boy, and a lover of his country."

2. **eius . . . qui:** i.e. "Cicero's . . . who."

3. **egisti:** "you accomplished"; compare 81 n. 17. Velleius, in his indignation, rhetorically apostrophizes Antony directly.

4. **Ciceroni:** dat. of reference (separation) with *rapuisti*; see 18 n. 7A (and contrast 80 n. 16B). For the thought that Cicero's death at this time was really a blessing in disguise, compare the last par. of 44.

5. **saeculorum** = "of the ages"; for the meaning contrast n. 14A below.

6. A. **dum . . . manebit:** for *dum* with the fut. = "as long as" see 20 n. 1B; contrast *dum* with the pres. ind. = "while" in 6 n. 8 (and 65 n. 2A), and with the perf. ind. in 79 n. 10A.   B. **hoc . . . corpus:** i.e. the universe, however it was created, whether by chance or providence.   C. **rerum naturae:** with this phrase (modifying *corpus*) compare 69 n. 21A.   D. **quod . . . illuminavit:** the three verbs are without connectives (in asyndeton; see 4 n. 5B and 81 n. 14B). Velleius exaggerates here; Cicero's philosophical writings are primarily ethical and only incidentally deal with the physical universe. But he may have in mind the ethical framework of the universe as a facet of its general constitution.

7. **illius . . . scripta:** Cicero's *Orationes Philippicae* against Antony, for which see prefs. to 42 and 44, and 79 nn. 19A and 23D.

8. A. **ante annos plurimos** = "many years ago"; see 68 n. 2A.   B. **me . . . castrassem** = "I had cut myself off from," i.e. from the things expressed by the preceding abls. of separation without a prep. Jerome echoes *Matthew* 19 vv. 29 and 12, the latter of which speaks literally of eunuchs *qui seipsos castraverunt propter regnum caelorum*; a metaphorical use of the verb, as here, occurs as early as Cicero.   C. **militaturus** = "to serve as a soldier" (i.e. of God); for *milito* compare 7 n. 6B, and for the connotation of purpose in the fut. act. part. see 44 n. 5A (and 45 n. 13D).

9. A. **lecturus . . . ieiunabam** = "(even though) about to read Tully, I used to fast"; i.e. when he read the pagan Cicero, he used to fast in repentance, only to read him anew.   B. **Tullium:** the gentile name is used instead of the more usual cognomen *Ciceronem*; compare 73 n. 34. In the 17th and 18th cents. Eng. authors commonly called Cicero "Tully."

10. A. **interrogatus condicionem:** in Ciceronian Lat. *interrogo* takes the acc. of the person questioned and *de* + the abl. of that about which he is questioned but in imperial Lat. it may take a double acc. like other verbs of asking. When a verb taking a double acc. is made pass., the person becomes subject (nom.) and the acc. of the thing remains. B. **condicionem** = "status"; a legal term, for which compare 67 n. 5.

11. **qui residebat** = "who was sitting," i.e. in judgment.

12. **ubi . . . tuum:** from Matthew 6.21.

13. **mei:** for the gen. with verbs of pitying see 24 n. 18A.

14. A. **saeculares:** though *saeculum* could suggest a very long time, as in n. 5 above and in the common Christian formula *in saecula saeculorum* (i.e. forever), it also connoted a fixed period, a human generation or lifetime, as in 69 n. 17B. In this sense the Christians contrasted it with the eternity of God, and hence used the adj. to mean "human, temporal, or secular," in contrast to "divine, eternal, or spiritual."   B. **negavi:** the use of the perf. instead of the fut. perf. ind. probably echoes the use of *negavit* for the first and second of Peter's three denials of Christ in both the accounts, Matthew 26.70 and 72, and Mark 14.68 and 70, in the Lat. Vulgate, for which see 89 pref.

15. **divina . . . mortalia:** i.e. the Scriptures . . . classical literature; compare n. 14A above.

16.   A. **responderet:** subj. in a rel. clause of characteristic (modifying *nihil*; compare 13 n. 6c) and here expressing purpose; compare 7 n. 8A (and 79 n. 10B). The subject throughout is the old man about whom Petrarch is writing; see pref.   B. **habebat:** this imperf. may be justified as indicating continued action, but *succlamabat, claudebat,* and *avertebat* are used to describe a state as actually observed. In contrast, the perfs. *quaesivit* and *respondit* at the end are used simply to state what happened.

17.   **splendorem . . . auctoritas** = "he would (only) put up the splendor of (Cicero's) name (i.e. his splendid reputation; compare 77 n. 21A) and authority took the place of reason." As in a legal or theological argument, the mere citation of an authority was substituted for real argument.

18.   **parcius** = "(speak) more mercifully," i.e. less critically; understand some such imperative as *loquere. Parcius* has here the sense of *parco* = "be merciful to" (as in 81 n. 11A) rather than = "be sparing (i.e. economical) of," as in 77 n. 29A.

19.   **quaereretur:** the subject is the following indirect question *an . . . posset.*

20.   **verbo:** perhaps used (instead of *dicto* = "remark") with specific reference to the word *errasse.*

21.   **mihi:** dat. of reference (ethical; see in 43 n. 23), indicating that the old man was indirectly concerned about the action of the verb *arguitur*; render: "is accused before me." Eng. might express this by a possessive: "my Cicero." *Mihi* does not go with the immediately preceding *heu* as the Eng. idiom "alas for me" might suggest, since this interjection is followed by the nom. or acc. of exclamation.

22.   **quasi . . . ageretur** = "as if the discussion was," lit. "as if it was being treated"; *ageretur* is a true impersonal, in which the subject is implied in the verbal action; compare 10 n. 10D (and 81 n. 11A). It is imperf. subj. instead of the pres. or perf. subj. usual in a conditional clause of comparison (see 67 n. 21) to connote potentiality in past time, contemporary with *avertebat* in the preceding sentence; it is not in a pres. contrary to fact protasis.

23.   **incunctanter** = "unhesitatingly"; this adv. and its adj. *incunctans* do not appear until the late Empire.

83

The proscriptions of the Second Triumvirate in 42 (see 44 pref.), like those of Sulla in 82 (see 26 and 66), meant the death or exile of many prominent Romans. In addition many were proscribed who were not distinguished in politics but who had property which could be confiscated, for the Triumvirs were in urgent need of funds.

The first of the following passages (from Velleius) is a general statement of the effect of these proscriptions on family relationships. The second illustrates this concretely with extracts adapted from a long inscription in which a bereaved husband commemorated his wife, who had not only exemplified all that a Roman expected of a wife but who had also saved his life and fortune during the proscriptions of 42. The wife is commonly, but probably wrongly, identified with a certain Turia whose similar noble deeds are commemorated by Valerius Maximus (early first century A.D.) and by Appian (mid-second century A.D.). The author of the inscription, although presumably of the upper classes, was not a polished writer, but the occasional clumsiness of the Latin only renders more appealing his sincerity.

A.   *Proscriptio secunda*

Huius totius temporis fortunam ne deflere quidem quisquam satis digne potuit, adeo nemo exprimere verbis potest.[1] Id tamen notandum est, fuisse in proscriptos uxorum fidem summam, libertorum mediam, servorum aliquam, filiorum nullam; adeo difficilis est hominibus utcumque conceptae spei mora.[2]

B.   *Laudatio matronae Romanae ignotae*

Rara sunt tam diuturna matrimonia finita morte, non divortio interrupta;[3] nam contigit nobis ut ad annum XXXXI sine offensa perduceretur.[4] Domestica bona pudicitiae, obsequi, comitatis, facilitatis, lanificiis tuis adsiduitatis, religionis sine superstitione, ornatus non conspiciendi, cultus modici cur memorem?[5] Cur dicam de tuorum caritate, familiae pietate, cum aeque matrem meam ac tuos parentes colueris?[6] Amplissima subsidia fugae meae praestitisti ornamentis;[7]

ut ea ferrem mecum, omne aurum margaritaque corpori tuo detracta tradidisti.[8] Et subinde, callide deceptis adversariorum custodibus, absentiam meam locupletasti.[9] Vitam tutata absentis, quod ut conarere virtus tua te hortabatur,[10] pietas tua me muniebat clementia eorum contra quos ea parabas;[11] semper tamen vox tua est firmitate animi emissa. Absente Caesare Augusto, cum per te de restitutione mea M. Lepidus conlega praesens interpellaretur,[12] et ad eius pedes prostrata humi non modo non adlevata sed tracta esses et servilem in modum rapsata, livoribus corporis repleta,[13] firmissimo animo eum admonuisti edicti Caesaris, cum gratulatione restitutionis meae.[14] Quid hac virtute efficacius, praebere Caesari clementiae locum?[15] Iure Caesar dixit tibi esse referendum exstare adhuc me patriae redditum a se;[16] nam nisi parasses quod servaret, cavens saluti meae, inaniter opes suas polliceretur.[17] Ita non minus pietati tuae quam Caesari me debeo.

Pacato orbe terrarum, restituta re publica, quieta deinde nobis et felicia tempora contigerunt. Nunc praecucurristi fato.[18] Delegasti mihi luctum desiderio tui, nec liberos habentem solum virum reliquisti.[19] Sed fructus vitae tuae non deerunt mihi. Occurrente fama tua,[20] firmatus animo et doctus actis tuis resistam fortunae, quae mihi non omnia eripuit, cum laudibus crescere tui memoriam passa sit. Te di manes tui ut quietam patiantur atque ita tueantur opto.[21]

1. A. **huius totius temporis:** i.e. of the period of proscriptions in 42. B. **ne ... quidem quisquam ... potuit, adeo nemo ... potest** = "not even could anyone ... much less can anyone."

2. **adeo ... mora** = "to such a degree is delay of a hope, however (it may have been) conceived, difficult for men." This remark applies particularly to the last group in the preceding sentence, the sons whose hopes of inheritance would not brook the delays which protecting their parents might have imposed; compare 66 n. 9.

3. **divortio interrupta:** this statement confirms the impression gained from the literature, that among the upper classes of the later Republic divorce was frequent and that such marital devotion as this inscription evidences was not common.

4. **ut ... perduceretur** = "that (our marriage) should be prolonged to (its) forty-first year without (any) quarrel"; this result clause is subject of *contigit*.

5. A. **pudicitiae ... cultus:** the gens. are defining or limiting with the neut. acc. plur. adj. *bona* used as a noun. They illustrate the virtues expected of a Roman wife. B. **lanificiis tuis adsiduitatis** = "of assiduousness at your woolworking"; *lanificiis* is abl. of specification. Equally, Livia, wife of Augustus, with the help of her slaves, is said to have spun and woven all the woolen cloth used in his household. Compare also Lucretia in 5 n. 8. C. **ornatus ... modici** = "of inconspicuous jewelry, of modest clothing." D. **cur memorem ... dicam** = "why should I mention ... why should I speak"; the

questions are deliberative or dubitative, so the pres. subj. is used; compare 31 n. 17A (and 35 n. 23B).

6. A. **tuorum . . . pietate** = "love for your (family) . . . devotion toward your household"; the gens. are objective.   B. **cum . . . colueris:** the perf. subj. shows *cum* to be causal; for the connotations of *colo* see 77 n. 25c.   C. **aeque . . . ac** = "just as much as"; compare 69 n. 10A (and 81 n. 11B).

7. A. **fugae:** probably dat. of purpose, as commonly with *subsidium*, with which a gen. would usually be defining; i.e. aid that consists in something.   B. **ornamentis** = "by your ornaments" (i.e. jewelry); abl. of means.

8. A. **ea:** looks forward to the gold and pearls; the whole sentence *ut . . . tradidisti* explains the preceding *amplissima . . . ornamentis.*   B. **corpori:** here equivalent to herself, as the use of the dat. of reference (separation) rather than the abl. shows; compare 61 n. 30B (and contrast 80 n. 16B).

9. **absentiam meam:** i.e. me in my absence. For the use of the abstract see n. 11 below and contrast (*mei*) *absentis* in the next sentence.

10. A. **tutata:** perf. pass. part. of *tutor*, frequentative of *tueor*; it is act. in meaning (contrast *emenso* in 1 n. 6B) and agrees with *pietas* later in the sentence; see n. 11 below. B. **quod . . . hortabatur:** the whole rel. clause modifies the idea *vitam . . . absentis*, but *quod* itself is object of *conarere* in the subordinate clause of purpose which serves as object of *hortabatur*. Since in Eng. "which that you should attempt" is awkward, it would be better to render *tutata* as a main verb coordinate with *muniebat* and the *quod* clause as a parenthesis: "(and your virtue [or, courage] urged you to attempt this)."   C. **cona-rēre:** 2nd pers. sing. imperf. pass. subj. of the dep. *conor*; for the ending compare 14 n. 13E (and 71 n. 1B).

11. **pietas . . . parabas** = "your loyalty defended me by (winning) the clemency of those (very persons) against whom you were preparing those (deceits; i.e. the assistance to him just mentioned)." For the connotations of *pietas* see 23 n. 13A (and compare 62 n. 11B). The author often uses abstract qualities for persons, instead of adjs. agreeing with a pronoun; compare in Eng. "Your Majesty" or "Your Excellency," forms of polite address which derived from the great extension of this practice in late Lat. Here *virtus* may stand as subject of *hortabatur*, but *pietas tua* would better be rendered "you loyally."

12. A. **cum etc.:** this clumsy temporal clause is subordinate to the main verb *admonuisti*. It contains two parts: the first is in the imperf. subj. of time contemporary to that of the main verb, namely *interpellaretur*; and the second is in the pluperf. subj. of time before that of the main verb, namely the compound passives *adlevata . . . tracta . . . rapsata*, all to be taken with *esses*. The past part. *prostrata* is subordinate to *non adlevata* (*esses*), and *repleta* to *rapsata* (*esses*).   B. **Caesare Augusto:** this designation shows that the inscription was composed after the grant to Octavian of the title "Augustus" in 27; see 47 pref.   C. **per te:** for *per*+acc. to indicate agency see 5 n. 16A (and in 47 n. 2).   D. **Lepidus:** remained in charge of Italy in 42 when Antony and Octavian crossed to Greece to fight Brutus and Cassius; see prefs. to 44 and 45. E. **conlegae:** thus in the inscription for *coll*-; see 47 n. 15c.

13. A. **tracta . . . rapsata** = "you were (lit. had been) pulled and dragged about like a slave"; *rapso, rapsare* is an alternate form of *rapto*, an intensive derivative from *rapio*. B. **in modum:** often used instead of the abl. of manner *modo.*   C. **livoribus . . . repleta** = "covered (lit. filled) with bruises on (lit. of) your body."

14. A. **eum . . . Caesaris:** verbs of reminding take the acc. of the person (*eum* = Lepidus) and the gen. of the thing of which one is reminded (*edicti*); compare 65 n. 3 (and 67 n. 6). The edict in question can hardly have been a general amnesty issued jointly by all three Triumvirs. Octavian had apparently issued one which removed the author individually from the list of proscribed and, since he was away from Italy, Lepidus may at first have been unwilling to recognize its validity.   B. **cum . . . meae**

= "with gratitude for my return," i.e. she said that she would be grateful if her husband (who is speaking) were recalled from exile.

15.   **praebere:** this inf. is clear in meaning but not in syntax; it may be in apposition with *virtute*, = "what more efficacious than this (act of) virtue (namely) to afford"; or it may express purpose (as in poetry; compare in 69 n. 14c), = "so as to afford."

16.   A. **tibi ... referendum** = "that it was due to you," lit. "must be referred to you"; the subject of *esse referendum* is the inf. clause *exstare adhuc me*; *me*, in turn, is modified by the participial phrase *patriae ... se*; see following note.   B. **exstare ... a se:** the subject of *exstare* is *me* with which the part. *redditum* agrees, but the order of inf. and part. is that of the successive facts. To express the thought that it was due to his wife that he survived until he could be restored to his country by Octavian, the author might have used the gerundive *reddendum*; compare the use of both part. and gerundive in 4 n. 6.

17.   **quod servaret** = "that which he might save," i.e. her husband; the rel. clause of characteristic without expressed antecedent (see 20 n. 12A and 81 n. 1) connotes purpose; see 7 n. 8A (and 82 n. 16A).

18.   A. **orbe terrarum:** the writer conceives of the Roman peace as embracing the whole earth; for the phrase see 9 n. 6c (and 35 n. 1A).   B. **praecucurristi fato** = "you have gone (lit. run) on ahead by fate," i.e. she died first.

19.   A. **desiderio tui** = "by (my) longing for you" (compare 73 n. 30A).   B. **tui:** objective gen., as also with *memoriam* below.   C. **nec** = *et non*, of which the *et* would connect the two main clauses and the *non* would go only with *habentem*; compare 80 n. 16c.

20.   **occurrente** = "before my eyes," lit. "meeting (me)."

21.   A. **te ... quietam:** supply *esse* as objective inf. after *patiantur*.   B. **di manes tui** = "your (benevolent ancestral) spirits"; subject of *patiantur*. Here *manes* is used in its original sense ("good, benevolent") as an adj. referring to the ancestral spirits which were supposed to await each individual in the underworld; compare 77 n. 4A.   C. **ut ... patiantur ... tueantur:** for the substantive purpose clauses used as objects of *opto* see 81 n. 19B.   D. **ita** = *quietam*, i.e. in peace.

84

In 42 the Second Triumvirate confiscated for distribution to their veterans (see 44 pref.) many estates in Cisalpine Gaul (the Po Valley), including that of Vergil's family; see 45 n. 19. Through the intervention of friends with Octavian (later Augustus; see 47 pref.), the estate was returned and Vergil was able to devote himself to study and writing; see 55 pref. During the years 42–37 (probably), he published ten pastoral poems, called *Eclogae* (Greek; = selected poems) or *Bucolica* (Greek; = poems on herding cattle), imitated from those of the Greek poet Theocritus, who wrote in the third century. In these Vergil disguised under pastoral themes, landscapes, and figures references to contemporary events, places, and persons.

In the following dactylic hexameter verses selected from the *First Eclogue*, Meliboeus, who has lost his fields to a veteran and is driving his herds to some foreign land, voices the widespread despair and dislocation which the confiscations created in North Italy. Tityrus, an older man (*senex* in verse 26 below) who has recovered his property by a visit to Rome, expresses Vergil's gratitude to Octavian.

Meliboeus et Tityrus[1]

M. Tityre, tu patulae recubans sub tegmine fagi
silvestrem tenui musam meditaris avena;[2]
nos patriae finis et dulcia linquimus arva.
Nos patriam fugimus; tu, Tityre, lentus in umbra
formosam resonare doces Amaryllida silvas.[3]

T. O Meliboee, deus nobis haec otia fecit.[4]
Namque erit ille mihi semper deus; illius aram
saepe tener nostris ab ovilibus imbuet agnus.[5]
Ille meas errare boves, ut cernis, et ipsum
ludere quae vellem calamo permisit agresti.[6]

M. Non equidem invideo; miror magis; undique totis
usque adeo turbatur agris.[7] En, ipse capellas
protinus aeger ago; hanc etiam vix, Tityre, duco.[8]
Sed tamen iste deus qui sit, da, Tityre, nobis.[9]

T. Urbem quam dicunt Romam, Meliboee, putavi,
    stultus ego, huic nostrae similem, quo saepe solemus
    pastores ovium teneros depellere fetus.
    Sic canibus catulos similes, sic matribus haedos
    noram;[10] sic parvis componere magna solebam.
    Verum haec tantum alias inter caput extulit urbes[11]
    quantum lenta solent inter viburna cupressi.[12]
    Hic illum vidi iuvenem, Meliboee, quotannis
    bis senos cui nostra dies altaria fumant.[13]
    Hic mihi responsum primus dedit ille petenti:
    "Pascite, ut ante, boves, pueri; submittite tauros."[14]

M. Fortunate senex, ergo tua rura manebunt.
    At nos hinc alii sitientis ibimus Afros,[15]
    pars Scythiam et toto divisos orbe Britannos.[16]
    Impius haec tam culta novalia miles habebit,[17]
    barbarus has segetes.[18] En, quo discordia civis
    produxit miseros! His nos consevimus agros![19]
    Insere nunc, Meliboee, piros, pone ordine vitis![20]
    Ite meae, quondam felix pecus, ite capellae.
    Non ego vos posthac viridi proiectus in antro
    dumosa pendere procul de rupe videbo;[21]
    carmina nulla canam;[22] non, me pascente, capellae,
    florentem cytisum et salices carpetis amaras.[23]

T. Hic tamen hanc mecum poteras requiescere noctem
    fronde super viridi.[24] Sunt nobis mitia poma,
    castaneae molles et pressi copia lactis.[25]
    Et iam summa procul villarum culmina fumant
    maioresque cadunt altis de montibus umbrae.[26]

---

1. A. **Meliboeus**: this name does not occur elsewhere and its meaning is uncertain.
Servius (see 55 n. 12A) thought that it meant "cowherd," from Greek *bous* = cow.
There is a rare Greek adj. *meliboas* = sweet-singing. Both Vergil and Lucretius apply to
the color purple the adj. *meliboeus*, which apparently derives from a town in Thessaly
called Meliboea, but the connection is unknown, if correct.   B. **Tityrus**: the name of
a shepherd in Theocritus III; the meaning is uncertain, but it may be connected with a rare
word for a reed pipe (see n. 2D below), or with a Doric form of "satyr."

2.   A. **patulae** agrees in the gen. sing. with the 2nd decl. fem. *fagi* = "of a beech tree"; for the gender compare 61 n. 3 (and 78 n. 23A).   B. **silvestrem ... musam meditaris** = "you meditate (on) the sylvan muse," i.e. compose pastoral songs (or poetry); *meditor* may take a direct object, like *cogito*.   C. **musam**: used by metonymy (see 49 n. 4 and 80 n. 18B) for her function; compare Eng. "woo the muse."   D. **avena**: lit. = "on an oaten straw," but equivalent here to *calamo* = "on a reed," 8 verses below. The shepherd's pipe (Greek *syrinx*) might be a single reed with holes which could be stopped with the fingers for the notes and blown through a mouthpiece at the top like a modern flageolet, rather than across a hole like a fife or flute; or, more commonly, it had the form of Pan's *syrinx*, different lengths of reeds bound together and blown across the top to give the notes. The more formal *tibia* (Greek *aulos*) was a single pipe with a "reed" in the mouthpiece and holes to be stopped, like a modern clarinet or oboe; it should not be translated as a "flute."

3.   A. **lentus** = "at ease," lit. "slow, pliant"; compare n. 12 below.   B. **formosam ... silvas** = "you teach the woods to resound (with the name of) fair Amaryllis."   C. **Amaryllida**: a Greek acc. sing. (compare *āĕră* in 77 n. 24) used as a cognate acc. with *resonare*, which more usually takes an abl. of means for the sound.

4.   **deus**: as early as 42, Vergil regards the political achievement of Octavian as superhuman; compare 80 pref. and n. 24B. The degree to which the identification of Augustus with gods by poets represents sincere belief or simply flattery borrowed from Hellenistic literature or a deliberate effort on Augustus' part to present himself as superhuman is much disputed.

5.   A. **illĭŭs**: for *-ĭŭs*, as often in poetry; see 74 n. 2B.   B. **imbuet** = "will stain," i.e. with its blood when sacrificed.

6.   A. **errare ... ludere**: for the objective inf. after verbs of permitting, see 78 n. 3A; the persons involved, *boves* and (*me*) *ipsum* (see following notes), are here made subject of the infs. rather than dats. after *permisit*; i.e. "allowed that ..." rather than "permitted to ... that ..."   B. **boves**: this *Eclogue* shows that the figures of Vergil's pastoral were not only young shepherds but sometimes older men (*senex*, of Tityrus, below) and also kept cattle and goats (*capellas* below) as well as sheep (*ovium* below), and had fields, orchards, and vineyards (*agros, piros, vitis, castaneae* below).   C. **ipsum**: understand *me* as subject of *ludere* (see n. A above); for the use of the intensive rather than the reflexive pronoun see 15 n. 14C.   D. **ludere**: the use of this verb for music is parallel to, and perhaps the source of, the use of the Eng. "play" in the same context.   E. **quae vellem**: this rel. clause without expressed antecedent serves as object of *ludere*; see 21 n. 20C (and compare 83 n. 17). Since the inf. is not in indirect discourse but objective after *permisit*, *vellem* is subj. not in indirect discourse but because the clause denotes a general or indefinite possibility rather than a specific fact.   F. **calamo**: abl. of means with *ludere*; for the instrument see n. 2D above.

7.   **undique ... agris** = "on every side there is such disturbance in all the fields"; construed correlatively with, rather than subordinate to, *miror magis*. The use of *turbatur* as a true impersonal (see 10 n. 10D and 82 n. 22) bothered even Roman scholars, and both Quintilian I 4.28 (see 13 pref.) and Servius (see n. 1A above) mention a variant *turbamur*, though they prefer *turbatur*.

8.   A. **en ... duco**: Meliboeus turns from the general disaster to his own trouble at the moment; sick though he is (*aeger*), he has to drive (*ago*) his she-goats along, and even has to drag (*duco*) a weak one behind him.   B. **capellas**: fem. throughout since the bulk of the herd would be she-goats, to give milk for cheese (see n. 25 below) and to produce kids; however the fem. also heightens the pathos of his enforced departure.

9.   **dă**: equivalent to *dic* and followed by an indirect question. Though the *-a-* in the pres. system of *dăre* is short, corresponding to *-ĕ-* in verbs of the 3rd conj., it is lengthened in *dās* and *dā* because of a tendency in Lat. to lengthen meaningful monosyllables (*dat* was also lengthened in early Lat.); contrast the compound *dēdĕ* in 52 n. 10B.

10. **noram** = *noveram* (see 1 n. 4B and compare in 74 n. 10A) and is equivalent to an imperf.; compare 58 n. 13A.

11. **alias:** not the adv. (for which see 17 n. 11C and 28 n. 9B), but acc. with *urbes* after *inter*.

12. **lenta ... cupressi:** cypresses stand up conspicuously straight among the more pliant (*lenta*; see n. 3A above) shrubs and trees of the Italian landscape; the shrub *viburnum* keeps its Lat. name in the United States.

13. A. **hīc:** adv. here and 2 verses below; see 10 n. 18B (and compare *illic* in 55 n. 2A). B. **quotannis:** though commonly written as one word equivalent to an adv., this really combines the indeclinable plur. adj. *quot* + *annis*, abl. plur. of time when.   C. **bis senos ... dies:** with *quotannis*; the whole phrase belongs in the rel. clause introduced by *cui*. The acc. of extent of time apparently does not mean that he will sacrifice for twelve days continuously in every year, but rather on twelve separate days (probably the first of each month) during every year, i.e. "during (each of) twice six (whole) days in every year." The acc. of extent of time indicates that each sacrifice will last throughout a whole day. To express figures by multiplication, the numeral adv., here *bis*, is used with the distributive numeral adj., here *senos*, rather than with the simple cardinal, which would here be *sex*.

14. A. **pueri:** Vergil may have in mind the usual age of "shepherd lads," though in the next verse Tityrus is called *senex*; however, *puer* might be used of superiors to inferiors (especially slaves) of any age, as Eng. "boy" in the colonies or French "garçon" for waiters.   B. **submittite:** a common meaning of this verb is "raise, rear," of animals or plants (compare 69 n. 8C); hence it probably means only this here, not "put under (the yoke)" or "put to (a cow)."

15. A. **alii ... pars** = "some ... others"; *pars* is equivalent to a plur. correlative with *alii* in partitive apposition with *nos*.   B. **Āfros ... Scythiam ... Britannos:** the acc. of place to which is used freely without a prep. in verse, as are the abls. of place where and from which. These represent distant, frontier wilds; and for the first and last, the people are used instead of place names.

16. **toto divisos orbe** = "sundered from the whole (rest of the) world"; *dividere* is usually followed in prose by *a* + abl. but in verse by a simple abl. of separation (here not means). For the Romans of Vergil's day, Britain was a remote island, only slightly known from Caesar's two visits and from its relations with northern Gaul.

17. **tam culta novalia** = "so (well) cultivated fields"; *novalia* properly means "newly cultivated land" but here seems to mean simply any "tilled field."

18. **barbarus:** recruits for the Roman legions were supposed to be citizens, but citizenship seems occasionally to have been granted to likely provincial or barbarian recruits; also, barbarians served as auxiliary units in the Roman army; compare 40 n. 10.

19. A. **hīs** = "for these (new possessors)."   B. **consevimus:** from *consero* = "sow (seeds), plant"; whereas *insere* in the next verse is a compound = "graft," from *sero* = "join, tie together, sew."

20. A. **insere nunc, Meliboee:** Meliboeus apostrophizes himself with sad bitterness in a vivid pres., = "now graft your pears," with the innuendo "you fool, you did so only for others to enjoy them." In the next verse he comes back to reality and tells his once happy flock to move on into exile.   B. **ordine** = "in order," i.e. in rows; abl. of manner; compare 51 n. 9C.

21. A. **viridi ... in antro:** the noonday rest of shepherds in a cool, green cave is a common theme in pastoral poetry.   B. **dumosa ... de rupe:** the sure-footed goats seem to hang on the edge of the cliff as they nibble the brambles.   C. **dumosa:** adj. from *dumus* = "bramble," as in 55 n. 15A.

22. **carmina nulla:** song was the characteristic "outlet" of a happy shepherd; compare nn. 2B and 3B above.

23. **florentem cytisum ... salices ... amaras** = "blossoming clover and bitter willow branches (osiers)"; the adjs. show that Meliboeus' she-goats enjoyed a healthy "mixed diet."

24. A. **hīc**: adv.; see n. 13A above. Tityrus' invitation to Meliboeus to rest the night with him before finally departing illustrates Vergil's ability to cast a romantic half-light over harsh reality and to conclude deep emotion in quiet repose. The *Eclogues* throughout represent the actualities of contemporary Italy through a veil of pastoral Arcadia; see pref. above.   B. **poteras**: the imperf. is used of something which was true all along although just now recognized or mentioned; see in 71 n. 9.

25. **pressi lactis**: i.e. "cottage cheese." The Greeks and Romans seldom drank milk but used it for cheese. Moreover, they used chiefly milk from goats or sheep; cattle were kept for work, for sacrifice, and for eating, but not for milk.

26. **maiores**: i.e. longer, because of the setting sun.

85

In 40, probably on the occasion of the reconciliation at Brundisium between Octavian and Antony (see 46 pref.), Vergil saluted the birth (or the expected birth) of a child under whose guidance he envisaged the return of the Golden Age. The child has never been securely identified: perhaps a son of the then consul, Asinius Pollio, to whom the poem is addressed; perhaps a child which Octavian's then wife, Scribonia, was expecting (and who turned out to be a girl); perhaps a hoped-for son of the marriage between Antony and Octavian's sister Octavia, which formed part of the reconciliation; perhaps no actual child but a symbol of the new era.

This *Fourth Eclogue*, of which a third is here omitted, is, like the others (see 84 pref.), in dactylic hexameter. Its imagery so closely resembles that of Isaiah's prophecy of the coming of the Hebrew Messiah (see 89) that Christians later saw Vergil as a pagan prophet of Christ; this meant that his works were not merely accepted by the Church but were recognized by it, as by the pagans, as the highest achievement of Latin literature. The Middle Ages, indeed, regarded Vergil not only as a prophet but as a magician, and Dante found in him a guide through Hell and Purgatory to the threshold of Paradise.

Novus ordo saeculorum[1]

Sicelides Musae, paulo maiora canamus.[2]

Non omnis arbusta iuvant humilesque myricae;[3]

si canimus silvas, silvae sint consule dignae.

    Ultima Cumaei venit iam carminis aetas;[4]

magnus ab integro saeclorum nascitur ordo.[5]

Iam redit et Virgo;[6] redeunt Saturnia regna;[7]

iam nova progenies caelo demittitur alto.[8]

Tu modo nascenti puero, quo ferrea primum

desinet ac toto surget gens aurea mundo,[9]

casta fave Lucina; tuus iam regnat Apollo.[10]

Teque adeo decus hoc aevi, te consule, inibit,[11]

Pollio, et incipient magni procedere menses.[12]

    At tibi prima, puer, nullo munuscula cultu[13]

errantis hederas passim cum baccare tellus

mixtaque ridenti colocasia fundet acantho;
ipsa tibi blandos fundet cunabula flores.[14]
Ipsae lacte domum referent distenta capellae
ubera, nec magnos metuent armenta leones.
Occidet et serpens, et fallax herba veneni
occidet; Assyrium volgo nascetur amomum.[15]

    At simul heroum laudes et facta parentis
iam legere et quae sit poteris cognoscere virtus,[16]
molli paulatim flavescet campus arista,[17]
incultisque rubens pendebit sentibus uva,
et durae quercus sudabunt roscida mella.[18]
Pauca tamen suberunt priscae vestigia fraudis,[19]
quae temptare Thetim ratibus, quae cingere muris
oppida, quae iubeant telluri infindere sulcos.[20]
Alter erit tum Tiphys, et altera quae vehat Argo
delectos heroas;[21] erunt etiam altera bella
atque iterum ad Troiam magnus mittetur Achilles.[22]

    Hinc, ubi iam firmata virum te fecerit aetas,[23]
cedet et ipse mari vector,[24] nec nautica pinus
mutabit merces; omnis feret omnia tellus.[25]
Non rastros patietur humus, non vinea falcem;
robustus quoque iam tauris iuga solvet arator;[26]
nec varios discet mentiri lana colores,[27]
ipse sed in pratis aries iam suave rubenti
murice, iam croceo mutabit vellera luto;[28]
sponte sua sandyx pascentis vestiet agnos.[29]

    "Talia saecla," suis dixerunt, "currite," fusis[30]
concordes stabili fatorum numine Parcae.[31]

---

    1. **Novus ordo saeculorum:** this title is from the reverse of the Great Seal of the United States, both faces of which appear on the reverse of dollar bills. The form there is the medieval *seclorum*, imitating *saeclorum* here in the 5th verse below, which is the earlier spelling, expanded in Cicero's day to *saeculum*; see 69 n. 17c. For the meaning here of *saecula* see 82 n. 5.

    2. A. **Sīcelides Mūsae:** i.e. pastoral Muses, because Theocritus (see 84 pref.) was born in Sicily, though most of his writing was done on the Aegean island of Cos, then under the rule of the Ptolemies of Egypt, for whom see 33 n. 17. It was common to

address the Muses (see 60 n. 27A and compare 69 n. 1B) by a patronymic appropriate to the type of poetry being written.   B. **paulo maiora:** i.e. themes somewhat loftier than usual for pastoral; *paulo* is abl. of degree of difference and *maiora* a neut. acc. plur. comparative adj. used as a noun (compare *bona* in 83 n. 5A) in the cognate acc. with the hortatory subj. *canamus*; compare 84 n. 3C. Two verses below, *canimus* is followed, as often, by the acc. of the topic (*silvas*) of song, which is usually regarded as a direct object, parallel to similar accs. after *dico* (as in 87 n. 31A); however, it might be regarded as an extension of the cognate acc. as used in this 1st verse; compare the similar accs. in nn. 18A and 27 below.

3.   A.   **omnis:** *i*-stem acc. plur. as object of *iuvant*; for the ending compare 15 n. 14A (and 70 n. 28). The same ending is used on pres. parts., as *errantis* in the 2nd verse of the 3rd par. and *pascentis* in the last verse of the 5th par.; compare 55 n. 6D (and 69 n. 5B). B. **arbusta:** neut. nom. plur. adj. used as a noun; see 61 n. 1B.   c. **iuvant** = "please"; contrast 54 n. 2B.

4.   **Cūmaei:** the Cumaean Sibyl was a prophetic priestess (or succession of priestesses) who gave responses in a cave tunneled under the acropolis of Cumae, on the coast just north of the Bay of Naples. In book VI of the *Aeneid*, Aeneas visits her and is guided by her to the lower world; see 88 pref. She was supposed to have sold a collection of her utterances (in Greek) to King Numa, and these were consulted by the Roman state on occasions of emergency; they were not prophecies but instructions for appropriate religious ceremonies. The collection of "Sibylline Oracles" in Greek which have come down from antiquity are quite different; they are attacks on Roman rule, cast in prophetic form, which originated in the Near East, largely under Jewish inspiration.

5.   **magnus . . . ordo:** the ancients held that in a long period of time, called a "great year," the "precession of the equinoxes" would bring all the heavenly bodies back to the position they had occupied at the beginning of the universe. The "Golden Age" would then return to replace the last of the degenerations therefrom, sometimes calculated as the four ages of gold, silver, bronze, and iron, and sometimes as a succession of ten ages, over the last of which Apollo had control. The old, degenerate race of men would be wiped out, and the Virgin Justice (*Astraea*; see n. 6B below), exiled to heaven because of their wickedness, would return with a new race sent down from heaven. Then the cycle of ages would start anew (*ab integro*).

6.   A.   **et:** here perhaps = *etiam*, but Vergil often uses *et* as if a second correlative *et* were to follow and instead repeats the verb, as here *redit . . . redeunt*; contrast the 7th and 8th verses of the 3rd par., where *occidet et* is repeated as *et . . . occidet*.   B. **Virgō:** Astraea, daughter of Zeus and Themis (Greek; = Justice). She lived among mortals during the Golden Age but, as mankind degenerated, she withdrew to heaven and became the constellation *Virgo*; see n. 5 above. Vergil here pictures her as returning to earth at the inception of the new Golden Age.

7.   A.   **Sāturnia:** adj. from *Saturnus*, an early Italic deity whom the Romans identified with the Greek *Kronos*, the father of Zeus and in one myth the ruler of gods and men during the Golden Age.   B. **regna:** collective plur., here used more abstractly for "rule" (as in 49 n. 10B), rather than more concretely for "kingdom," as in 64 n. 15C.

8.   **caelo . . . alto:** abl. of place from which without a prep., as often in poetry; compare 52 n. 5C (and 61 n. 12).

9.   A.   **tu:** voc. with *casta . . . Lucina* 2 verses below.   B. **modo nascenti puero** = "boy (see n. 16A below) just being born," i.e. about to be born; dat. after *fave* 2 verses below.   c. **quo** = "under whom"; probably not abl. of agent without a prep. but abl. of attendant circumstance or time when, on the analogy of such phrases as *te consule*; see n. 11A below (and compare 75 n. 1B).   D. **ferrea:** supply *gens* from the next verse. E. **toto . . . mundo:** abl. of place where without a prep., as regularly even in prose when a noun is modified by *totus*; see 29 n. 8B (and compare 80 n. 15A).

10.   A.   **Lūcīna:** properly an epithet of Juno as the goddess of childbirth, who brings

the child "into the light," but here applied to Diana, sister of Apollo (see following note), because the goddess of childbirth for the Greeks was Artemis, with whom the Romans equated Diana.   B. **tuus ... Apollō** = "your (brother) Apollo." He was the special patron of Octavian and the presiding deity of the last of the ten ages (see n. 5 above); both connotations would justify *regnat*.

11.   A. **teque:** i.e. *Pollio* (see pref.); abl. anticipating the abl. abs. *te consule*, for which see 14 n. 4B.   B. **adeo:** Vergil is fond of placing this second in a sentence to emphasize the first word, as here *te.*   C. **decus hoc aevi** = "this glory of an age"; i.e. this glorious age, taking *aevi* as an appositional gen.; compare 15 n. 4 (and 75 n. 12A). Others refer *decus hoc* to the child, = "this glory of (our) age."   D. **inibit** = "will commence" or, if *decus* refers to the child, "will come to birth." The first meaning is supported by the common use of *ineo* to denote the beginning of a period of time; compare *ineunte vere* in 29 n. 17D and the common phrases *anno ineunte* and *ineunte aetate*.

12.   **menses:** the "great year" was divided into "great months" and, since the Roman year primitively had only ten months, these may have corresponded to the ten periods; see n. 5 above. Vergil, however, uses elements of various cyclical theories without trying to be "scientifically" exact.

13.   A. **prima ... cultu** = "first (and) uncultivated gifts (lit. gifts with no cultivation)"; most translators take *nullo cultu* (here lit.; contrast 65 n. 4A) with *tellus* to show that the earth of its own accord, without being cultivated, sent forth the gifts, but the interlocking order ties this phrase closely to *prima munuscula.*   B. **munuscula:** the diminutive connotes affectionate gifts, suited to a child; it is object of *tellus ... fundet* below and is expanded by the appositional phrases "ivy wandering all about with foxglove and marsh lilies mixed with smiling acanthus."

14.   A. **ipsa ... flores:** the manuscripts give this verse after the following two and with *fundent* for *fundet*; their text means "your cradle of its own accord (*ipsa cunabula*) will pour forth kindly flowers for you." The objection to the manuscript text that the image of a cradle sprouting flowers is forced is not serious if the cradle be thought of as a soft piece of turf. But the manuscript order of verses interrupts the sequence of scenes from animal life, while the order in the text above places this verse logically among those describing flowers; see following note.   B. **ipsa:** the emendation *fundet* for *fundent* makes this fem. nom. sing., with *tellus* to be supplied as subject from 2 verses above, instead of neut. nom. plur. with *cunabula* (see preceding note), i.e. the earth of her own accord (and quite naturally) will pour forth flowers, instead of the cradle doing so unnaturally. *Ipse* here, in the next verse, and in the 2nd and 7th verses of the 5th par. (see nn. 24B and 28B below) is equivalent to "spontaneously" or "of its own accord." The reordering of the verses adopted here makes an effective echoing of *ipsa-ipsae* at the openings of this and the following verse, just as *occǐdet* (for which compare 70 n. 19B) is repeated at the beginnings of the 3rd and 4th verses below.   C. **cunabula:** neut. plur. with a sing. meaning; compare *arbusta* in n. 3B above.

15.   A. **veneni:** probably a defining or limiting gen. rather than possessive, = "the herb (that is) poison" rather than "the herb of a poisonous plant"; compare n. 11C above.   B. **Assyrium:** i.e. eastern; see 77 n. 1A.   C. **amomum:** an eastern plant, unidentified by moderns, used for making perfume; such rare plants will grow commonly in the new Golden Age.

16.   A. **at simul etc.:** *simul* is used alone for *simul ac* (see 69 n. 10A) and subordinates the fut. ind. *poteris* in the next verse to the main fut. ind. *flavescet* in the verse following. The fulfillment of the new Golden Age keeps pace with the growth of the child, who has begun as a *puer*, i.e. up to about his 14th year; see n. 9B above. He here becomes an *adulescens*, from about 14 to about 25, and apt for the study and performance of noble actions; compare n. 23 below. At the same time, the earth passes from the spontaneous production of childish flowers and perfumes to that of useful crops: fields yellow with waving grain, brambles bearing grapes, and oaks dripping honey like dew drops.   B.

hērōum: this Greek word (see 43 n. 30A) retains the *-ō-* before a following vowel; compare 49 n. 1 (and 69 n. 12A).

17. **molli** = "soft, tender, flexible"; it may mean here simply young grain or tender grain waving in the breeze.

18. A. **sudabunt:** though *sudo* = "sweat" is intrans. in republican prose, it may be trans. in verse (as here) and in imperial prose, possibly by an extension of the cognate acc.; compare n. 2B above and n. 27 below.   B. **roscida mella** = "dewy honey"; i.e. drops of honey; *mel* is commonly used in a collective plur.; compare nn. 3B and 14C above.

19. **pauca ... vestigia fraudis:** i.e. a few traces of man's depraved nature before the new Golden Age. Active youth still requires the challenge offered by some survivals of artificial society: seafaring, wars and sieges, and cleaving furrows in the earth to increase the already abundant natural yield.

20. A. **temptare ... cingere ... infindere:** infs. used absolutely, without expressed subject (supply "men"), as objects of *iubeant*.   B. **temptare ... ratibus** = "to attempt the sea with ships." The Romans, following Plato, rationalized their instinctive distrust of the sea by regarding commerce and economic rivalry as the cause of war and of the fortification of cities.   C. **Thetim:** the sea-nymph mother of Achilles is mentioned as a familiar and typical sea deity and means by metonymy her province, the sea; compare *musam* in 84 n. 2C (and *Neptunus* in 73 n. 20D).   D. **ratibus ... muris:** abls. of means. E. **iubeant:** subj. in a rel. clause of characteristic with connotation of either purpose or potentiality.   F. **telluri:** dat. after a verb compounded with *in-*; see 6 n. 13 (and 80 n. 16F).

21. A. **Tiphys:** the helmsman of the ship *Argō*, in which Jason with a band of chosen heroes went to seize the Golden Fleece from Colchis, at the east end of the Black Sea. Tiphys may be mentioned rather than the leader, Jason, because the latter diminished his heroic stature by falling in love with the daughter of the king of Colchis, Medea, by using her magical help to overcome the tests set for him, and by carrying her off, only to desert her later. Or Tiphys may represent better than Jason the skill and daring used in navigation.   B. **hērōăs:** see n. 16B above; here the verse *ictus* ("stress") falls on the *-ō-* rather than on the *-ē-*; *-ăs* is a Greek acc. plur. ending of the 3rd decl.

22. A. **ad Troiam etc.:** the Trojan War, as described in Homer's *Iliad*, was the foremost saga of valiant conflict by land, as the Argonautic voyage was of daring adventure by sea.   B. **Achilles:** Lat. rendered the ending of Greek names in *-eus* by *-es* (as *Perses* in 15 n. 6) and in early Lat. the *-e-* was probably short; however, the ending must easily have been confused with the regular Greek ending *-ēs* of patronymics (see 88 n. 8A) and other personal names (see 88 n. 1B) and is frequently found to be long (compare 88 n. 22C); since it is here the final syllable of the verse, its quantity is uncertain (*syllaba anceps*). Homer made Achilles the central figure of the Trojan War, not the Greek leader Agamemnon or any other hero like Ajax or Odysseus; moderns admire Hector but he is not the central personage, even though the poem ends with his death and funeral.

23. **hinc** = "thereafter, next"; i.e. in young manhood, from about 25 to about 40, here represented by *te virum* but usually called *iuventus*; compare n. 16A above. This maturity (*firmata ... aetas*) witnesses the consummation of the Golden Age when sailing and commerce and agricultural labor and wool-dyeing all become unnecessary.

24. A. **et:** probably correlative with the following *nec*, rather than = *etiam*; compare n. 6A above.   B. **ipse** = " of his own accord"; see n. 14B above.   C. **mari:** best taken as abl. of separation without a prep. (compare n. 8 above) after *cedet* = "will withdraw from" rather than as dat. after *cedet* = "will yield to." The hope is that the merchant will give up his voyaging, not that he will give in to the sea. The placing of *mari* between *ipse ... vector* also suggests a loc. abl., = "the merchant on the sea."

D. **vector**: lit. = "the carrier (of goods)"; as against the ship captain, though naturally the two were often the same man.

25.   A. **nautica pinus**: the "nautical pine" is used by metonymy for the ship constructed from it; compare *alnum* in 78 n. 23A.   B. **mutabit** = "will move from place to place"; contrast n. 28G below. Horace *Sat.* I 4.29 similarly says of the merchant: *mutat merces a . . . ad*. The meaning is that in the Golden Age trading ships will no longer carry merchandise from port to port. In ancient commerce a trader would normally sell part of his cargo and pick up some new goods at every port.   C. **merces**: acc. plur. of *merx, mercis* = "goods," not the nom. sing. of *merces, mercedis* = "price."
D. **omnis**: fem. nom. sing. with *tellus*; contrast n. 3A above; the final -*is* is short by nature though long by position.

26.   A. **tauris**: dat. of reference (separation) rather than abl. of separation; = "will loose the yoke from (lit. for) his bulls"; see 18 n. 7A (and compare 83 n. 8B).   B. **iuga**: the use of the sing. in the last verse of 51 suggests that here the plur. is literal, not collective (for which see nn. 7B, 14C, and 18B above), i.e. that the (single) ploughman used several yoked pairs of bulls (or, oxen) to draw his plough, as was often true on large farms in modern Italy, before tractors became common.

27.   **mentiri**: here = "to counterfeit"; this dep. verb may take a cognate acc. (compare 27 n. 17), which may be the construction here of *colores*, rather than direct object: compare nn. 2B and 18A above.

28.   A. **ipse . . . luto**: depending on the meaning of *mutabit* (see n. G below), this may be translated either "the ram of his own accord will alter (the color of his) fleece (by dyeing it) now with softly blushing purple, now with saffron yellow," or "will exchange (his white) fleece now for (one of) . . . purple, now (for one of) . . . yellow."   B. **ipse** = "of his own accord," as in nn. 14B and 24B above.   C. **aries**: subject of *mutabit* in the next verse.   D. **iam . . . iam**: correlate the abls. of means *murice* and *luto* with *mutabit*.   E. **suave**: neut. acc. sing. adj. used as an adv.   F. **murice**: the *murex* was a shellfish boiled to obtain a dye which ranged from crimson to purple; it and *luto* are used by metonymy (compare n. 25A above) for the colors which they produced.   G. **mutabit** = "will alter" or "will exchange" (for which compare 65 n. 20B); contrast the meaning "will move" in n. 25B above, and see the translation in n. A above.   H. **vellera**: neut. plur. commonly with a sing. meaning; compare nn. 3B, 14C, and 18B above (and *frena* in 66 n. 5B).   I. **lūto**: the saffron plant, from which a yellow dye was derived and used here by metonymy for the dye; it should be distinguished by the long -*ū*- from *lŭtum* = "mud."

29.   **sandyx**: Vergil varies his image by making scarlet clothe the pasturing lambs; it is uncertain whether *sandyx* was a mineral (so Pliny the Elder) or a plant (so Servius); it is used, like *murex* and *lutum* (see n. 28F above), by metonymy for the scarlet color produced from it.

30.   A. **talia saecla . . . currite** = "(O) such (wonderful) ages run (on and on)"; this rendering takes *saecla* (for the spelling see n. 1 above) as voc. and assumes that although the Fates address their spindles, they apostrophize the new and happy centuries which are being spun by them. Some editors, more harshly, take *saecla* as object (or cognate acc.) with *currite*, i.e. "run (off) centuries such (as I am describing)" or "make such centuries run on."   B. **fusis** = "to their spindles." Before the invention of the spinning wheel, thread was made by starting to twist between the fingers of the right hand fibers drawn from a bunch tied on the distaff held in the left. When enough thread had been formed, it was tied to a short stick weighted at the lower end, the spindle. As the fingers continued to twist the fibers into the thread, the spin of the weighted spindle gave it an even tighter twist. As the thread lengthened it was wound on the shaft of the spindle. Traditionally, only one of the three Fates (see following note), Clotho, spun the thread of destiny; the second, Lachesis, measured off the length allotted to each person, event, etc.; and the third, Atropos, fixed destiny inevitably by cutting the thread. Here Vergil makes all three spin.

31.   A. **concordes . . . Parcae** = "the Fates (see 77 n. 4B) harmonious with respect to (or, by means of; or, because of) the fixed power (i.e. the inevitability) of destiny (lit. of things fated)."   B. **numine:** for the meaning see 77 n. 30B; it is (as translated in the preceding note) abl. either of specification, or of means or cause, depending on whether the three Fates are conceived of as by their agreement fixing the power of destiny, or in agreement through (or because of) that power.

86

Quintus Horatius Flaccus (65–8), born in southeast Italy, rose from humble beginnings (his father was a freedman) to be a member of the highest social and literary circles. He served on the Republican side at Philippi (see 45) and on his return to Rome was forced, perhaps because his property had been confiscated, to work as a treasury clerk. But in the late thirties his poetry brought him to the favorable attention of Maecenas, a wealthy equestrian friend of Octavian and a patron of literary figures, including Vergil. Maecenas assured Horace of a modest income and provided him with a house in Rome and a small country estate.

Horace's substantial poetic production is varied in kind. From 35 to 30 his output was mainly satirical: a book of *Epodes* in iambic meters modeled on the bitter Greek poet Archilochus of about 700, and two books of *Sermones* ("talks"; see 62 n. 1) or *Satires* in dactylic hexameters following Lucilius, a member of the second-century Scipionic circle (see 16 pref.) who was supposed to have originated the native Roman genre of satire (*satura*). In the next two decades he composed four books of *Carmina* or *Odes* in various Greek lyric meters and on a wide range of topics, from fictitious love poems to serious patriotic ones. In addition he wrote a hymn, the *Carmen Saeculare*, to be sung at a great religious festival, the "Secular Games," organized by Augustus in 17. Finally, he continued his conversational satires in three books of letters, *Epistulae*, in dactylic hexameters. The third epistle of the third book is usually separated off under the special title *Ars Poetica*.

Horace achieved an immediate and enduring reputation, not so much for deep emotion, like Catullus (see 73 and 74), nor for profound philosophy, like Lucretius (see 69 and 70), nor for elevated poetic concept and expression, like Vergil (see 55, 84, 85, and 88), but for subtle skill in the choice and arrangement of words and masterly adaptation of Latin to the intricacies of Greek meters.

As did other writers, for example Catullus (compare 73 pref.), Horace arranged his poems not chronologically but so as to secure variety of subject or meter. Hence though the first of the following poems is the first of the *Epodes*, it was probably one of the latest composed. In it Horace expresses what must have been a widespread feeling of anxiety at Rome, as he bids farewell to Maecenas accompanying Octavian in 31 against Antony. The meter is one which gives its name to this collection, the epodic distich (also called iambic strophe); the couplet consists of an iambic trimeter (three dipodies or six feet) followed by an iambic dimeter (two dipodies or four feet).

The second poem comes from near the end of book I of the *Odes*, published in 23, but it may well be early and reflect the intense relief felt at Rome at the news of the victory of Actium on September 2, 31; see 46. The poem is in a four-verse strophe or stanza called "Alcaic" after the Greek lyric poet Alcaeus, who lived in Lesbos around 600. It is uncertain whether the basic rhythm is iambic with free substitution of spondees and anapaests, or trochaic with free substitution of spondees and dactyls. For the metrical schemes of both these strophes, iambic and Alcaic, see the pages immediately following the selections.

It is noteworthy that in neither poem, and particularly not in the second, does Horace suggest that the war was between Romans. Octavian is portrayed, as he wished to be, as the defender of Rome against a foreign queen, Cleopatra.

Horatii carmina Actiaca

A. Ibis Liburnis inter alta navium,
         amice, propugnacula,[1]
     paratus omne Caesaris periculum
         subire, Maecenas, tuo.[2]
     Quid nos, quibus te vita si superstite
         iucunda; si contra, gravis?[3]
     Utrumne iussi persequemur otium
         non dulce ni tecum simul?[4]
     An hunc laborem mente laturi, decet
         qua ferre non molles viros?[5]
     Feremus, et te vel per Alpium iuga
         inhospitalem et Caucasum
     vel Occidentis usque ad ultimum sinum
         forti sequemur pectore.[6]
     Roges, tuum labore quid iuvem meo,
         imbellis ac firmus parum?[7]
     Comes minore sum futurus in metu,
         qui maior absentes habet[8]—
     ut adsidens implumibus pullis avis
         serpentium adlapsus timet
     magis relictis,[9] non ut adsit auxili
         latura plus praesentibus.[10]
     Libenter hoc et omne militabitur
         bellum in tuae spem gratiae,[11]
     non ut iuvencis inligata pluribus
         aratra nitantur meis,[12]

　　　pecusve Calabris ante sidus fervidum
　　　　　Lucana mutet pascuis,[13]
　　neque ut superni villa candens Tusculi
　　　　　Circaea tangat moenia.[14]
　　Satis superque me benignitas tua
　　　　　ditavit; haud paravero
　　quod aut avarus ut Chremes terra premam,
　　　　　discinctus aut perdam nepos.[15]

B.　　　Nunc est bibendum, nunc pede libero
　　pulsanda tellus,[16] nunc Saliaribus
　　　　　ornare pulvinar deorum
　　　　　　　tempus erat dapibus, sodales.[17]
　　Antehac nefas depromere Caecubum
　　cellis avitis,[18] dum Capitolio
　　　　　regina dementes ruinas,
　　　　　　　funus et imperio parabat,[19]
　　contaminato cum grege turpium
　　morbo virorum;[20] quidlibet impotens
　　　　　sperare fortunaque dulci
　　　　　　　ebria.[21] Sed minuit furorem
　　vix una sospes navis ab ignibus;[22]
　　mentemque lymphatam Mareotico
　　　　　redegit in veros timores
　　　　　　　Caesar,[23] ab Italia volantem
　　remis adurgens,[24] accipiter velut
　　molles columbas aut leporem citus
　　　　　venator in campis nivalis
　　　　　　　Haemoniae,[25] daret ut catenis
　　fatale monstrum.[26] Quae generosius
　　perire quaerens nec muliebriter
　　　　　expavit ensem nec latentes
　　　　　　　classe cita reparavit oras.[27]

Ausa et iacentem visere regiam

vultu sereno,[28] fortis et asperas

tractare serpentes, ut atrum

corpore combiberet venenum,[29]

deliberata morte ferocior;[30]

saevis Liburnis scilicet invidens

privata deduci superbo,[31]

non humilis mulier, triumpho.[32]

1. A. **ibis:** the fut. indicates certainty; see 71 n. 18 (and compare 67 n. 1A). Its position makes it emphatic.   B. **Liburnīs** = "in Liburnian (galleys)"; the abl. is probably instrumental rather than loc. *Liburnae* (*naves*) were light, fast ships with only one bank of oars, copied from those used by the piratical tribe of the *Liburni* on the Dalmatian coast. In the Battle of Actium, they outmaneuvered the heavy but slow five-bank ships (*quinqueremes*) of Cleopatra, with their lofty "castles" at bow and stern. C. **propugnacula:** defensive bulwarks; see preceding note.

2. A. **Caesaris:** i.e. of Octavian; see 44 pref. (and 47 pref., and contrast 83 n. 12B). B. **Maecēnās:** see pref.   C. **tuo:** understand *periculo* from *periculum* above; = "at your own (risk)"; abl. of attendant circumstance or of manner without *cum*; compare 76 n. 21B.

3. A. **nos** = *ego*; see 32 n. 12B (and 54 n. 2C); supply some such verb as *agemus*. B. **quibus . . . gravis:** Horace is especially fond of elaborately interlocked word order; these 2 verses = *quibus vita iucunda* (*sit*) *si te superstite; si contra, gravis* (*sit*). The first *si* is redundant since the abl. abs. alone would express the protasis of a condition.   C. **superstīte:** here = "remaining alive" rather than, as usually, "surviving (somebody else)."   D. **si contra:** an elliptical euphemism for some phrase which might sound ill-omened, such as "if you die"; compare 40 n. 4B.

4. A. **utrumne:** Horace is the first Lat. author to combine these two interrog. particles, and he does so only three times in all; in imperial Lat. the combination is more common.   B. **iussi:** masc. nom. plur. past part.; = "ordered," i.e. to do so by you. C. **otium** = "a life of ease"; compare 76 n. 18C.

5. A. **an . . . viros** = "are we to bear this labor with the (strength of) mind with which it becomes tough (lit. not soft) men to bear (it)?" With the punctuation in the text and this rendering, *sumus* is to be understood with *laturi*; some editors make *laborem* a second object of *persequemur*, balancing *otium*, and *mente laturi* modify the subject, i.e. = "or will we pursue this labor, to bear it with the (sort of) mind with which etc."   B. **non molles:** i.e. unlike the normal Horace, who both by inclination and as a lyric poet was a lover of peace and ease; see n. 7C below, and for *mollis* compare 85 n. 17. For the "litotes" compare 68 n. 12A.

6. A. **feremus . . . sequemur:** futs. instead of hortatory subjs. to denote resolve—the first is emphatic in position; compare n. 1A above.   B. **inhospital(em) et Caucasum:** joined with *Alpium iuga* (see 59 n. 14B) as examples of rugged mountains in west and east; compare 84 n. 15B.   C. **et:** may occasionally be placed second in its phrase: compare -*que* in 73 n. 27A.   D. **Occidentis . . . sinum:** the physical hardships which Horace is willing to face while accompanying Maecenas are completed by a voyage to the furthest bay of the West, either the Bay of Biscay or the Atlantic itself, outside the Straits of Gibraltar.

7. A. **roges:** subj. in a deliberative question, equivalent to "perhaps you may ask"; compare 31 n. 17A (and 83 n. 5D).   B. **tuum:** supply *laborem* as object of *iuvem*, here = "help" as in 54 n. 2B (contrast 85 n. 3C); usually the *laborem* would be expressed and

labore supplied with *meo*, as in *omne . . . periculum . . . tuo* in n. 2c above.   c.
imbellis . . . parum: Horace regularly portrays himself as unwarlike (compare n. 5B
above), and his health was apparently poor.   D. **firmus:** here used literally of bodily
strength, not in its equally frequent sense of "steadfast, loyal."

8.   A. **comes . . . metu:** "as your comrade, I will be in less fear"; the positive answer
to the question *roges etc.*   B. **qui . . . habet:** the fear, modified by *maior*, is made
subject and (*nos*) *absentes* object of *habet*; compare 56 n. 10A.

9.   A. **ut etc.:** Horace is fond of similes from nature; this one was earlier used by,
among others, the 5th-cent. Greek tragedian Aeschylus.   B. **adsidens . . . avis** = "a
nesting (mother) bird"; to be taken generally since the nestlings (*implumibus pullis*) are
immediately described as having been left alone (*relictis*) by the mother.   C. **pullis:**
dat., both with *adsidens*, and either with *timet* = "she fears for the chicks" or perhaps
with *adlapsus* (acc. plur.) = "she fears the approach of serpents toward the chicks."

10.   A. **non . . . praesentibus:** i.e. "though not likely to bring more help (to them)
present, even if she were at hand."   B. **ut:** the connotation of "purpose" may express
an assumption or concession; i.e. "not so that she would be there" becomes "even if
she were there."   C. **adsit . . . praesentibus:** i.e. mother and young are, so to speak,
present each to the other; such redundancy is common in Horace.   D. **latura:** the
fut. part. with a concessive implication may indicate possibility or likelihood; compare
44 n. 5A (and 82 n. 8c).

11.   A. **hoc et omne . . . bellum:** subject of *militabitur*, with which understand *a me*
or *mihi*; for the inversion of what might be the expected order compare n. 8B above.
B. **gratiae:** Maecenas' simple approval is contrasted with the more material rewards
which some might have expected from his favor and which Horace denies desiring by
non and an *ut* clause of purpose mentioning rich farms, extensive flocks, or a fine villa.
Maecenas had already (in 32) given Horace an estate beyond Tivoli (see pref.) which
the poet presumably did not consider sufficiently impressive to contradict his profession
now (in 31) of pure motives in his loyalty to his patron.

12.   **ut iuvencis . . . meis:** in this interlocking phrase, the toiling is transferred by
hypallage (see 46 n. 19 and 69 n. 10B) from the heifers to the ploughs. Some manuscripts
and editors read *mea* with *aratra*. In modern Italy ploughs drawn by several pairs of
oxen were until recently still a common sight; compare in 85 n. 26B.

13.   A. **pecusve . . . pascuis** = "or that (my) flock should before the (rising of the)
blazing (dog)star exchange Calabrian pastures for Lucanian (ones)."   B. **pecusvĕ
Cǎlǎbris:** the only instance in this poem of the substitution of a tribrach (three short
syllables)—or indeed of any foot of three syllables—for a dissyllabic iamb or spondee.
C. **sidus fervidum:** Sirius, called (*stella*) *Canicula* in 87 n. 29A, is the brightest star in the
constellation of Orion's dog. When the sun, in its annual course through the zodiacal
constellations, had passed so far along that Sirius rose before it, the ancients regarded
this as a harbinger of full summer heat; in Horace's time this occurred in early August.
D. **Lūcāna:** adj.; with it supply *pascua* from the abl. *pascuis*; compare nn. 2c and
7B above.   E. **mutet** = "should exchange" (see 85 n. 28G) and takes an acc. and
abl.; only the context tells which is being exchanged for which. In this case, at the
approach of summer heat, the sheep are being driven from the low coastal meadows of
Calabria in the very dry "heel" of Italy to better-watered meadows in mountainous
Lucania in the "instep."

14.   A. **superni . . . Tusculi:** usually taken as gen. with *moenia*, but its position joins
it closely with *villa candens*, = "a gleaming villa of lofty Tusculum," i.e. white with
marble. Some manuscripts read *superne* = "on high," which would let *Tusculi* be
loc. = "In Tusculum." Rich Romans, both in antiquity and later, have had summer villas
on the cool heights of Tusculum in the Alban Hills south of Rome; see 44 n. 3.
B. **Circaea tangat moenia** = "may touch (i.e. lie close under) the Circaean walls."
Telegonus, son of Circe and Ulysses, was supposed to have founded Tusculum.

15.   A. **haud paravero** = "I shall not have amassed"; fut. perf. because before the money denoted by the *quod* clause (without expressed antecedent) can either be buried (*terra premam*) or wasted (*perdam*), it has to be acquired.   B. **avarus ut Chremēs**: though Greek New Comedy and its Roman imitations by Plautus and Terence show many old men named Chremes, no surviving one is a miser.   C. **discinctus . . . nepos** = "or (like) a dissolute (lit. ungirded) grandson"; many manuscripts read *ut* before *nepos* but this is easily understood from the previous verse. Although Romans wore the toga for formal occasions, the tunic alone was worn in the house or informally elsewhere; to wear the tunic loose (ungirded) was a sign of careless living, suited to a wastrel. Roman comedy and satire frequently present the son or grandson of a miser as spending on riotous living the carefully hoarded wealth of his sire.

16.   A. **nunc etc.**: in the 1st stanza, *nunc* is repeated three times to mark the emphatic contrast with *antehac* at the opening of the 2nd; each *nunc* is followed by a different construction to indicate suitable rejoicing.   B. **pede libero** = "with foot unrestrained," i.e. with joy and drink, perhaps with a suggestion of freedom from fear and threat.   C. **pulsanda**: supply *est*; for ancient dancing compare 60 n. 27B.

17.   A. **Saliāribus . . . dapibus** = "to adorn the couch(es) of the gods with Salian feasts." The *lectisternium*, or public offering of a banquet for the gods, each on his or her *pulvinar* (see 42 n. 8A), was the responsibility of the *septemviri epulonum* (originally only three; see in 56 n. 2A). Hence "Salian feasts" does not mean those offered by *Salii* but simply like theirs. The *Salii* were a priestly college sacred to Mars, and their banquets were proverbially lavish.   B. **ornare**: *tempus est* is regularly followed by an inf. ("complementary") rather than by the gen. of the gerund or gerundive; the connotation of the latter construction is different in 62 n. 8B.   C. **erat**: the imperf. denotes something just now realized but true for a while back; see 71 n. 9 (and 84 n. 24B).   D. **sodales**: connoting closer friendship than *amici*.

18.   A. **antehac nefas**: to celebrate while Rome was still threatened might have tempted the wrath of the gods; compare 8 n. 7B (and 77 n. 12B).   B. **antehac** = "heretofore"; it is not inconsistent with the imperf. *erat* but looks even further back than the immediately past victory; see nn. 16A and 17C above. For the internal elision see 57 n. 10B.   C. **depromere . . . avitis** = "to decant Caecuban (wine) from ancestral (wine) cellars"; although *depromere* generally refers to pouring from a jar or amphora, the concept is here transferred generally to wine cellars in which some ancestor had laid down a good vintage.   D. **Caecubum**: i.e. Caecuban wine. When a place was famous for its wine, an adjectival form was used with *vinum* understood; compare n. 23B below, and for a similar usage with *praedium* see 44 n. 3. The *Caecubus ager* was a fertile plain south of Rome which in antiquity produced an especially choice vintage.

19.   A. **Capitōlio**: dat. of reference (disadvantage); for the Capitoline hill see 8 n. 9C (and 50 n. 1B).   B. **regina**: i.e. Cleopatra, for whom see 33 n. 17 (and 46). Kings were traditionally hated at Rome (see 5; 42 nn. 10A, 11C, and 28C; and the 1st par. of 46), but queens were notoriously even more violent and ominous; compare the story of Tullia and Tarquinius in 53 and 54, especially 54 nn. 5A and 6A.   C. **dementes**: by hypallage (see n. 12 above) the epithet (for which compare 57 n. 11A) is transferred from the queen to the ruins which in her madness she was planning. The attack of Cleopatra is described in four stages, each with some such term: first her plans, with *dementes*; then her advance to Actium, with *ebria*; next her defeat, with *furorem* and *mentem lymphatam*; and finally her flight, with *fatale monstrum*; compare n. 27B below.   D. **et**: postponed; see n. 6C above.

20.   **contaminato . . . virorum**: the Romans thought that Eastern courts were staffed either with eunuchs or with perverts, both types constituting a "polluted horde of men foul with (or, in respect to) disease"; *virorum* thus becomes ironical.

21.   A. **quidlibet . . . sperare** = "(she herself so) lacking (in) self-control (as) to hope (for) anything whatsoever," i.e. to have unlimited ambitions.   B. **impotens**: here =

"powerless"; see 74 n. 20. The use of the inf. after adjs. is imitated by Lat. poets from a regular Greek construction; contrast 61 n. 34B.   C. **fortunaque dulci ebria** = "drunk with sweet fortune"; *dulci* suggests not only the sweetness of success but sweet new wine, which makes one intoxicated imperceptibly.

22. **vix . . . ignibus** = "(the fact that) scarcely a single ship (escaped) safe from burning." Actually, although after his victory Octavian burned the captured or surrendered ships, Cleopatra withdrew at the beginning of the battle with her 60 Egyptian *quinqueremes* (see n. 1B above), and Antony himself soon followed her. Their withdrawal or flight has never been satisfactorily explained. Horace glosses over it, as if Cleopatra had shared in the defeat, and he does not mention Antony at all, as if Octavian's victory had been solely over the hated foreign queen and not also over fellow Romans; see pref. above.

23. A. **lymphatam:** = "maddened." This adj. is here used freely with *Mareotico* (*vino*) since it was invented to correspond to the Greek *numphoplektēs* = "struck by a (water) nymph," i.e. deranged by beholding one, according to a popular superstition. It was apparently formed from *lympha* = "water" (for similar formations compare 6 n. 12B and 80 n. 20C), which was probably in some Italian dialect identified with Greek *numphē* = "maiden" (in the special meaning of water nymph).   B. **Mareōtico:** understand *vino*; see n. 18D above. Mareotis was a shallow lake in the Nile delta near Alexandria around which was produced a heady wine.   C. **Caesar:** i.e. Octavian, not yet called Augustus; see n. 2A above.

24. A. **Ītalia:** for the initial long *i-* compare 59 n. 16B (and contrast 55 n. 2B).   B. **remis adurgens** = "driving (her) on with his oars," i.e. closely pursuing. The object is *eam* to be understood with *volantem*; compare 43 n. 6 (and 52 n. 10A). In fact, Octavian did not pursue Cleopatra and Antony immediately, but passed the winter after Actium in the Aegean and went to Egypt only in the summer of 30; see the last par. of 46. Horace heightens the rapidity of Cleopatra's downfall and Octavian's success; compare n. 22 above.

25. A. **accipiter etc.:** the first simile, of the hawk (compare n. 9A above), is suggested by *volantem*; it is found as early as Homer. *Adurgens* is to be understood with both *accipiter* and *venator*.   B. **nivalis Haemoniae:** a district in Thessaly (northeast Greece) which afforded good hunting in the winter snow.

26. A. **fatale** = either "sent by fate (to harass Rome)" or "fraught with fate (either for Rome or for herself)." The adj. is suited to the original supernatural connotation of *monstrum*, for which see the following note.   B. **monstrum:** derived from *monere* and originally signified a prodigy or omen which "warned" that the gods were angry; later it came to mean any unusual or unnatural person, event, or object; for its use of Cleopatra see 46 n. 5A (and compare 78 n. 6B).

27. A. **quae:** fem. because it agrees with the sense, rather than with the grammatical gender, of its antecedent *monstrum*.   B. **generosius perire** = "to die more nobly," i.e. than in chains. At this point Cleopatra begins to stir Horace's admiration, and the rest of the terms applied to her are generally complimentary, except that the last two (*ferocior* and *non humilis*) imply that even her bravery had a touch of overweening pride; compare n. 19C above.   C. **nec . . . ensem:** Plutarch *Ant.* 79 says that Cleopatra tried to stab herself on the news that Octavian was nearing Alexandria.   D. **muliebriter:** compare Velleius' *expers muliebris metus* in 46 n. 18.   E. **nec . . . oras:** Plutarch earlier (*Ant.* 69) says that Cleopatra thought of drawing swift ships across the Isthmus of Suez and fleeing down the Red Sea "to distant (lit. hidden) shores."   F. **reparavit:** given by all the manuscripts, though some editors try to emend; its exact meaning is uncertain. The analogy of *vina Syra reparata merce* (= "wines purchased with [i.e. in exchange for] Syrian merchandise") in *Odes* I 31.12 suggests: "she did not seek hidden shores in exchange," i.e. for her lost kingdom.

28. A. **ausa et ... fortis et:** since there is no main verb in this and the following stanzas, perhaps *ausa* should be taken as = *ausa est* and the first *et* as = *etiam*, in which case only the second is postpositive (see nn. 6C and 19D above), connecting *fortis* (*fuit*) with *ausa* (*est*). Perhaps, however, Horace meant to conclude by piling up a series of descriptive modifiers of Cleopatra, without any main verb; if so, both *ets* are postpositive and mean "both ... and"; compare in 85 p. 3 v. 7. B. **regiam:** supply *domum*; = "palace"; see 54 n. 10C (and 78 n. 12C).

29. A. **fortis ... tractare** = "brave (enough) to handle"; for the inf. with the adj. compare n. 21B above; for Cleopatra's courage compare n. 27B above. B. **corpore combiberet** = "she drained to the full with her body"; *combiberet* is more forceful than simple *biberet*. The reference is to the common, but even in antiquity not surely attested, story that at the end, after hearing of Antony's suicide and finding Octavian implacable, Cleopatra poisoned herself with an asp which a maid smuggled in to her in a basket of fruit; see the end of 46.

30. **deliberata ... ferocior** = "more courageous, once death was decided upon," i.e. even more courageous than she had been before.

31. A. **saevis etc.:** the general sense of these lines is clear: Cleopatra refused to be taken to Rome to appear in Octavian's triumph. The grammar, however, as often in Horace's condensed and interwoven style, is disputable. B. **saevis Liburnis:** may be abl. of means with *deduci* (compare n. 1B above) or it may be dat. with *invidens,* = "begrudging (to) the war ships (which she regards as) cruel." C. **scilicet:** this adv. = "of course" or "evidently"; from *scire licet* ("one may know"). It can be either ironical or, as here, simply emphatic, stressing the obvious fact that Cleopatra's refusal was to be expected from her character and position. Various imperial writers cite Livy for the statement that when Octavian tried to persuade her to surrender she said that she would never adorn his triumph. In the event, Octavian showed a statue of her in his triumph in 29. D. **deduci:** depends in any case on *invidens*, but with a difference depending on the case of *Liburnis*; if that is abl. of means, the inf. is the normal construction with *invideo* = "be unwilling" or "refuse." If *Liburnis* is dat. after *invidens*, the inf. expresses what she begrudges the ships, namely to be led off (in them). In both these renderings, *deduci*, as often, means "to be led off," i.e. as a prisoner, as in the 1st sentence of 22. E. **superbo ... triumpho:** if *deduci* = "to be led off" (see the preceding note), this is, as in 46 n. 15A, dat. of purpose. But *deduci* may also connote "to be led in procession," and, if this be the meaning here, *triumpho* may be either instrumental or loc. ("by" or "in") abl. with it. If so, the thought is elliptical: "begrudging to the ships that she (be taken in them to Rome in order to) be led in a proud triumph."

32. **privata ... non humilis mulier:** may = "(though) deprived (of her royal dignity, still) not (a) humbled woman" or "(a) private (i.e. a queen no longer) (but) not (a) lowly woman"; for *privata* compare 54 n. 7A (and 71 n. 11D). Through Horace's mastery of interlocking order and juxtaposition of contrasting words, not only are these two descriptions of Cleopatra set against each other but *superbo ... triumpho* is split to provide a further contrast within each of the final 2 verses of the poem.

87

To represent the many moods and meters of Horace's four books of *Odes* (see 86 pref.) in a selection as limited as this is impossible. Any reader familiar with Horace will doubtless prefer other favorites to the five odes given below. That to Pyrrha (A) illustrates the light and humorous tone of Horace's love poetry, which, unlike that of Catullus (see 74), probably represents a literary treatment of imaginary affairs. The next two odes are Epicurean in tone, at least in the popular debasement of this philosophy; see 69 pref. The first of them (B) urges enjoyment of the moment because the future is uncertain; the second (C) prefers simple pleasure to overelaborate self-indulgence. The fourth (D) is one of many in which Horace evinces an appreciation of the rustic scene and religion which recalls that of Vergil in the *Eclogues* (see 84) and *Georgics*. In the last ode (E), Horace, a highly self-conscious artist, expresses his confidence that he has achieved enduring fame as a poet.

The meters of four of the following five *Odes*, namely A, B, D, and E, are called Asclepiadic after a minor Greek lyric poet, Asclepiades, of the third century. They are based on trochees with the substitution of spondees or dactyls in certain feet. A and D are in the Asclepiadic strophe or stanza of four verses while B affords a series of "greater" Asclepiadics and E one of "lesser" Asclepiadics. C is in the Sapphic strophe, named for the poetess of Lesbos of about 600; see 74 pref. Sappho's favorite strophe is, next to that of her contemporary Alcaeus (see 86 pref.), the most common in Horace's *Odes*. It is based on trochees, with the substitution of spondees and dactyls in patterns different from those of the Asclepiadics. For the metrical schemes of these meters, see the pages following the selections.

Horatii carmina varia

A.   *Ad Pyrrham*[1]

Quis multa gracilis te puer in rosa
perfusus liquidis urget odoribus
    grato, Pyrrha, sub antro?[2]
      Cui flavam religas comam,

simplex munditiis?[3] Heu quotiens fidem
mutatosque deos flebit,[4] et aspera
    nigris aequora ventis
      emirabitur insolens,[5]

qui nunc te fruitur credulus aurea,[6]
qui semper vacuam, semper amabilem
   sperat, nescius aurae
      fallacis.[7] Miseri quibus

intemptata nites;[8] me tabula sacer
votiva paries indicat uvida
   suspendisse potenti
      vestimenta maris deo.[9]

B.   *Carpe diem*

Tu ne quaesieris—scire nefas—quem mihi, quem tibi
finem di dederint, Leuconoë,[10] nec Babylonios
temptaris numeros.[11] Ut melius quicquid erit pati,[12]
seu plures hiemes, seu tribuit Iuppiter ultimam
quae nunc oppositis debilitat pumicibus mare
Tyrrhenum.[13] Sapias, vina liques, et spatio brevi
spem longam reseces.[14] Dum loquimur, fugerit invida
aetas;[15] carpe diem, quam minimum credula postero.[16]

C.   *Paucis contentus* [17]

Persicos odi, puer, apparatus;[18]
displicent nexae philyra coronae;[19]
mitte sectari rosa quo locorum
   sera moretur.[20]

Simplici myrto nihil adlabores
sedulus, curo;[21] neque te ministrum
dedecet myrtus neque me sub arta
   vite bibentem.[22]

D.   *Fons Bandusiae* [23]

O fons Bandusiae, splendidior vitro,[24]
dulci digne mero non sine floribus,[25]
   cras donaberis haedo,[26]
      cui frons turgida cornibus

primis et venerem et proelia destinat—[27]

frustra; nam gelidos inficiet tibi

    rubro sanguine rivos

        lascivi suboles gregis.[28]

Te flagrantis atrox hora Caniculae

nescit tangere;[29] tu frigus amabile

    fessis vomere tauris

        praebes et pecori vago.

Fies nobilium tu quoque fontium,[30]

me dicente cavis impositam ilicem

    saxis,[31] unde loquaces

        lymphae desiliunt tuae.[32]

E.   *Non omnis moriar*

Exegi monumentum aere perennius[33]

regalique situ pyramidum altius,[34]

quod non imber edax, non Aquilo impotens[35]

possit diruere aut innumerabilis

annorum series et fuga temporum.

Non omnis moriar, multaque pars mei

vitabit Libitinam;[36] usque ego postera

crescam laude recens;[37] dum Capitolium

scandet cum tacita virgine pontifex,[38]

dicar, qua violens obstrepit Aufidus[39]

et qua pauper aquae Daunus agrestium

regnavit populorum, ex humili potens,[40]

princeps Aeolium carmen ad Italos

deduxisse modos.[41] Sume superbiam

quaesitam meritis et mihi Delphica

lauro cinge volens, Melpomene, comam.[42]

---

1. **Ad Pyrrham:** perhaps the most frequently translated of all Horace's odes; Milton's version remains outstanding. *Pyrrha* is Greek for "red-haired"; compare King "Pyrrhus" in sel. 9. The fact that in the 4th verse she binds up *flavam comam* does not

necessarily indicate that her name is not to be taken literally, because Latin and Greek words for color were often imprecise; hence *flavus* might be used of blonde, light brown, or auburn hair; compare 49 n. 2B.

2. A. **quis etc.**: highly interlocking order of words for: *Pyrrha, quis gracilis puer, perfusus liquidis odoribus, te multa in rosa grato sub antro urget*; compare 86 n. 3B. For the convention of addressing rhetorical questions to a faithless girl, compare the end of 74 E.   B. **multa . . . in rosa**: generally taken as = "on a thick (bed) of rose (petals)"; but since a "bed of roses" seems somewhat extravagant for this lad (*puer*), it may mean "in (a garland of) many roses."   C. **urget**: generally taken as = "woos" or "courts" (Milton); but perhaps physical, = "presses (on)," i.e. embraces.   D. **grato . . . sub antro**: a "bucolic" touch; compare 84 n. 21A (and n. 31B below).

3. **simplex munditiis**: Milton renders "plain in thy neatness." Horace is fond of such collocations of words of contrasting connotation (compare 86 n. 32), a rhetorical device called in Greek oxymoron, for which see 57 n. 9C. Pyrrha, realizing that true elegance consists in flawless simplicity, shows Horace's own artistry in contrast to the overornate "style" of her young man, with his flowers and perfumes.

4. **fidem**: the following *mutatosque* (= "and altered"; compare 85 n. 28G) gives this the connotation of a "faithlessness" pledged by gods who, immutable in protecting other oaths, wink at lovers' broken promises.

5. A. **nigris . . . ventis**: to achieve an interlocking word order, Horace transfers the blackness of the rough seas to the winds which roughen them; for similar hypallage compare 86 nn. 12 and 19C. The metaphor of the changeable sea for a fickle mistress is old; compare Catullus in 74 B.   B. **emirabitur** = "will wonder greatly at"; an intensive compound (for intensive *e-* compare 74 n. 9D) used only by Horace in classical Lat., and rare even thereafter.   C. **insolens** = "inexperienced," i.e. unaccustomed to such fickleness, as the landlubber is to the variety of the sea. For *insolens* in this original meaning, rather than in the derived ones of "immoderate" or "insolent," compare 35 n. 22A.

6. **credulus aurea**: the masc. nom. adj. is cleverly juxtaposed to the fem. abl. adj. *aurea* modifying *te*, abl. after *fruitur*. In the *Ars Poetica* 47–48, Horace himself recommends giving words new force by such *callida iunctura*. Here the young man finds from his credulity that "all that glitters is not gold"; see n. 8B below.

7. A. **vacuam** = "free," i.e. devoted only to him.   B. **aurae fallacis**: i.e. of her favor; for this use of *aura*, lit. = "breeze," compare 77 n. 18. Here it carries on the nautical metaphor.

8. A. **miseri**: exclamatory nom. (see 59 n. 20A, and compare 78 n. 20A); with it understand *sunt*.   B. **quibus . . . nites** = "for whom you shine (while you are) untried"; i.e. carrying on the two preceding metaphors, she seems loving and beautiful to those who have not experienced fickleness, just as gilding seems gold to a *credulus* (see n. 6 above) or the sea sparkling to one ignorant of its treacherous squalls (*nescius . . . fallacis*).

9. A. **tabula . . . paries**: interlocking order of words in chiasmus, for which see 17 n. 2. A sacred (temple) wall would show, by a votive tablet, the gratitude of a seafarer who had been saved from shipwreck; Horace, keeping up the metaphor of the fickle sea, humorously and metaphorically has dedicated, with an appropriate inscription, the garments still wet from the shipwreck of his affair with Pyrrha, to show his gratitude to Neptune (Venus might have been expected) for saving him from such a storm of emotion.   B. **maris**: gen. after *potenti* (see 33 n. 25A and 70 n. 19A) rather than with *deo*, as is shown by such phrases as *diva potens Cypri* in *Odes* I 3.1 or *lyrae Musa potens* in I 6.10.

10. A. **tu ne quaesieris**: the *tu* is emphatic; the perf. subj. is more usual than the pres. subj. in negative exhortations and is more colloquial (and more peremptory) than the

polite use of *noli* + inf., for which see 62 n. 9A. In this use, the perf. subj. does not indicate either past or completed action, but simply the action viewed in its entirety, without temporal content.   B. **scire nefas:** parenthetical; understand *est*; for the phrase see 77 n. 12B.   C. **dederint:** perf. subj. in the indirect question in primary sequence since the command is present in sense and the gods (or Fates; compare 85 n. 31A) have already fixed the future end before the command is given.   D. **Leuconoē:** a Greek name = "white-minded"; it is not clear whether the word originally meant "pure-minded" or "empty-minded" and whether Horace used the name with reference to either of these meanings or simply because it sounded well and fitted his meter. The *-ŏē* form two syllables; compare 79 n. 23A.

11.   A. **Babylōnios . . . numeros:** astrologers (*mathematici*) derived the "science" of their calculations (*numeros*) from ancient Babylonia. Though there was frequent legislation against them, confidence in their prognostications was widespread among all classes in Rome.   B. **temptaris:** not 2nd pers. sing. pres. ind. pass., but = *temptaveris* (see 1 n. 4B), hortatory perf. subj. connected rather irregularly to *quaesieris* (see n. 10A above) by *nec* rather than by *neu* (*neve*), as in 74 n. 19D (compare 83 n. 19B).

12.   A. **ut melius . . . pati** = "how (much) better (it is) to endure whatever will be"; *ut* is exclamatory.   B. **erit:** the fut. (rather than a potential subj.) connotes the fixity of the future; compare 71 n. 18 (and 86 nn. 1A and 6A).

13.   A. **tribuit:** either simple pres. or perf. of something already decided (fated) by *Iuppiter*; for the perf. compare n. 10C above.   B. **quae etc.:** i.e. "the winter (with its storms) breaks up the (waves of) the Tyrrhenian Sea by (dashing them against) the opposing rocks."   C. **pumicibus:** lit. = "by pumice rocks" (abl. of means), but here used for any rocks.   D. **Tyrrhēnum** = "Etruscan"; see 49 n. 6B (and 66 n. 18).

14.   A. **sapias, vina liques:** coordinate (paratactic; see 23 n. 1A) hortatory subjs. without connective (in asyndeton; see 4 n. 5B), where prose might have had a fut. condition: "if you are wise, you will strain your wine etc."   B. **liquēs:** 2nd pers. sing. pres. act. subj. from *lĭquō, -āre* = "make liquid" or "clarify" (of a liquid); a trans. verb derivative from the intrans. *lĭquĕō, -ēre* = "be liquid or, clear," for which see 73 n. 20B. Wine was strained through a cloth or sieve to clear it of sediment before drinking. Leoconoë was probably a slave girl, and this would be one of her tasks, which Horace uses by metonymy (compare 49 n. 4 and 85 n. 25A) for the rest; i.e. she should tend to her household chores (or pleasures) and not worry about the future.   C. **spatio brevi:** effectively juxtaposed to *spem longam* (i.e. hope that reaches too far into the future); the abl., whether abs. or instrumental (cause or means), gives the reason why she should cut short her hope; i.e. "because life (is) brief."

15.   **fugerit:** fut. perf. ind., i.e. "invidious time will already have passed on before we finish speaking."

16.   A. **carpe** = "pluck" (as a flower) or "snatch" (as time rushes by); from either connotation, *carpo* came to suggest "I enjoy a fleeting pleasure." *Carpe diem* has become proverbial for the sentiment expressed in Herrick's couplet: "Gather ye rosebuds while ye may, / Old time is still a-flying."   B. **credula:** i.e. foolishly credulous; see n. 6 above. But the adj. is here used as a part. = "trusting." And it is followed (like the verb *credo*) by the dat. *postero* = "the next (day)," i.e. the future. It is also modified by the adverbial phrase *quam minimum* = "as little as possible."

17.   **paucis contentus:** a phrase from Horace's *Sat.* I 3.16, where, however, it is used satirically of one who, pretending to asceticism, will waste a fortune if only he can get it.

18.   A. **Persicos . . . apparatus:** the Persians (and easterners generally) were proverbial for the trappings of luxury; for *apparatus* compare 68 n. 10B.   B. **puer:** here = "slave boy"; see 84 n. 14A (and contrast in n. 2B above).

19.   **nexae philyra coronae** = "garlands (chaplets) bound with bark," i.e. elaborate ones in which flowers had to be tied with strips of the inner bark of the linden tree, as

perhaps were those of Pyrrha's dandy in n. 2B above. They are contrasted with a simple wreath of myrtle; see the 5th and 7th verses.

20. A. **mitte**=*omitte* (compare 73 n. 31B) and here followed by the objective inf. *sectari*, for which see in n. C below.   B. **rosa:** precedes the rel. clause in which it is subject of *moretur* and modified by *sera*; compare *mulier* in 74 n. 8A. In prose it might well have been *rosam* as object of *sectari*, which is here followed by an indirect question; see the following note. A "last rose of summer" would be a fittingly recherché ornament for such a dandy as Pyrrha's (see n. 19 above) but too elaborate for simple Horace. C. **quo locorum**="where"; compare *quo viai*="whither" in 57 n. 11B. It is interrog. for *in quo loco* in an indirect question after *sectari*=*quaerere*, as the subj. *moretur* shows.

21. A. **nihil . . . curo**="may you sedulous(ly) labor in addition not at all, I am anxious," i.e. I do not want you to labor any more over.   B. **simplici myrto:** dat. after an intrans. verb compounded with *ad*; see 59 n. 10 (and 78 n. 1B).   C. **nihil:** an adverbial (or "inner") acc. with *adlabores*; compare 20 n. 4A (and 71 n. 3A). Its negative force is more readily rendered, however, with *curo*, leaving only an intensive force with *adlabores*;="at all."   D. **adlabores:** hortatory subj. (compare nn. 10A and 11B above) in coordinate (paratactic; compare n. 14A above) relation with *curo* (compare the translation above), but may be rendered as if it were subordinate thereto; the usual construction after *curo* is a substantive *ut* clause of purpose. The compound *adlaboro* occurs only here and once again in Horace and is intrans.   E. **sedulus:** adj. modifying the subject of *adlabores*, i.e. the slave, but best rendered in Eng. by an adv.; compare 11 n. 12A.   F. **curo:** some editors, finding the transition from *adlabores* to *curo* harsh, read the imperative *cura* and, keeping *nihil* with *adlabores*, translate: "labor not at all, see to it," i.e. "see that you do not labor at all etc."

22. A. **ministrum:** a more friendly word than *servum*, and Horace does not balance it by any word for himself as *dominum*. This well fits the tone of familiarity that might exist between master and slave in a small household like Horace's Sabine farm, for which see 86 n. 11B.   B. **arta**="close," i.e. closely trained on an arbor. For the Mediterranean custom of providing leafy shelters from the sun, compare 40 n. 15C. Here the arbor served a practical use, since in antiquity, as in parts of Italy today, wine-producing grapevines were trained on trees, often elms, and presumably Horace's shelter also produced his beverage.

23. **fons Bandusiae:** the gen. is probably limiting, giving the name of the fountain (instead of voc. in apposition; compare 68 n. 16A), rather than possessive, indicating to what town it belonged. It may well have been a real fountain with this name, either near his farm beyond Tivoli or near his birthplace, Venusia in Apulia; compare 86 pref.

24. **splendidior:** here has its literal meaning of "brighter" or "clearer"; water may still be called "crystal clear."

25. A. **dulci digne mero:** *digne* is masc. voc. sing. agreeing with *fons* and followed by the abl. (as regularly; see 21 n. 12B). Wine when drunk was normally mixed with water but for libations was used pure (*merum*).   B. **non sine floribus:** Varro (see 28 n. 23A) says that at the "Feast of Fountains," the *Fontanalia* on Oct. 12, flowers were thrown into springs and garlands placed on wells. In antiquity, waters were regularly associated with a god or nymph and hence were worshiped with libations, flowers, and offerings of various kinds, such as the kid sacrificed in the next verses.

26. **donaberis haedo:** since *dono* often takes the acc. of the person to whom a gift is given (see 73 n. 3A), in the pass., when the person becomes the subject, the gift remains in the abl. of means.

27. **cui:** dat. of reference, both of possession with *frons* and of advantage with *destinat*="destines"; compare 43 n. 6 (and 70 n. 13B).

28. A. **inficiet:** basically="will dip in"; but this verb is regularly used of dyeing or staining, with the thing stained as object. The subject is the kid, supplied from *cui*

above and resumed by *suboles* 2 verses below.   B. **lascivi:** basically = "playful"; and only derivatively = "wanton" or "lascivious."

29.   A. **flagrantis . . . Caniculae:** for the Dog Star as harbinger of summer heat compare 86 n. 13c. The next stanza explains that the fountain is shaded by an ilex tree; see n. 31B below.   B. **nescit:** here, as often, equivalent to *nequit.*

30.   **fies . . . fontium** = "you also will become (one) of the well-known fountains." The partitive gen. occurs in Lat. after *esse*, but with *fieri* it seems to imitate a Greek construction. Horace has in mind famous fountains sacred to the Muses such as Castalia at Delphi (below Mount Parnassus), Dirce near Thebes, Hippocrene near Mt. Helicon, also in Boeotia, and Pirene on the hill above Corinth.

31.   A. **me dicente** = "when (or, as) I sing"; the abl. abs. gives both the time when and the means whereby the fountain will become famous, and the pres. part. of *dico* here takes *ilicem* as direct object; compare 85 n. 2B.   B. **cavis . . . saxis:** either dat. after a verb composed with *in-* (see 6 n. 13 and 85 n. 20F), or abl. of place where without a prep. "Hollow rocks" means a grotto, from which the fountain gushes forth; compare those in n. 2D above and in Vergil's *First Eclogue* in 84 n. 21A.   C. **impositam:** i.e. "planted."

32.   A. **loquaces:** the adj. expresses the result of *desiliunt*, i.e. "the waters of the spring bubble as they leap down the rocky face of the overhang."   B. **lymphae** = "water"; see 86 n. 23A.

33.   A. **exegi:** lit. = "I have driven forth"; here = "I have carried to completion," i.e. built; some common meanings are "I have demanded," "I have required," and also "I have spent (time)," as in 5 n. 16B.   B. **monumentum:** lit. = "a reminder," and may be used of writings (see 37 n. 4c), but here Horace metaphorically calls his poems a physical monument or memorial. In this concluding ode of the first three books, Horace asserts that his literary reputation will endure; ancient convention did not object to assertions of their own value by artists or others whose achievement justified such self-confidence; compare for Cicero 32 A and 37.   C. **aere** = "than bronze," which was a common material for such memorials as statues and tablets; compare in 80 n. 8.

34.   A. **regalique . . . altius:** *situs* probably has here its literal meaning of "place, site," and hence of a structure on a site, i.e. "loftier than the royal structure of the pyramids." Since, however, *situs* has a derivative connotation of staying in one place, i.e. "sloth, inactivity," some make this phrase figuratively connote "magnificent ineffectiveness."   B. **pyramidum:** gen. plur.; the three pyramids at Ghizeh constituted one of the "Seven Wonders" of the ancient world, and the pyramid of Cheops, about 480 feet high, was taller than any other monument in the Mediterranean world.

35.   A. **Aquilo impotens** = "the mighty (i.e. raging) north wind," which brings winter storms; contrast Favonius/Zephyrus in 69 n. 11A (and 73 n. 12c).   B. **impotens:** here = "powerful" rather than "powerless"; see 74 n. 20 (and contrast 86 n. 21B).

36.   A. **omnis:** nom. sing. modifying the subject of *moriar* but best rendered in Eng. by the adv. "wholly"; compare *sedulus* in n. 21E above.   B. **multaque pars mei:** i.e. his poetry and his reputation; *multa* is equivalent to *magna.*   C. **Libitinam:** the goddess of death, used by metonymy (compare in n. 14B above, and see 85 n. 20c) for "death, funeral rites, etc." In her temple were kept funeral records, equipment for funerals, etc.

37.   A. **usque:** for its use alone as an adv. see 77 n. 25B.   B. **recens** = "(ever) fresh," modified by the abl. of specification (or means) *postera laude* = "later fame," i.e. reputation among posterity; compare *postero* in n. 16B above.

38.   **dum . . . scandet:** for *dum* = "so long as" with the fut. ind. see 20 n. 1B (and 82 n. 6A). The *pontifex* (probably *maximus*) and one (probably the chief) of the six Vestal Virgins symbolize the expected durability of Roman religion as a guarantee of the lasting Roman state and civilization, a sentiment which made opposition to Christianity strongest in the city of Rome.

39.   A. **dicar** = "I shall be said"; followed, after the long parenthesis *qua . . . potens*, by the indirect statement *princeps . . . deduxisse modos*. Eng. idiom might render "it will be said that I etc."   B. **qua:** rel. adv. = either "where" (as here) or "by what way"; it is the fem. sing. abl. of the interrog. or rel. adj. with *parte* or *via* or some similar fem. noun understood. It here introduces a long parenthetical clause defining where Horace will enjoy fame as a poet, namely in his native Apulia, on the northern border of which lay his birthplace, Venusia; see n. 23 above.   C. **Aufidus:** a rushing (*violens*) mountain stream in Apulia.

40.   A. **pauper aquae** = "poor of (or, in) water"; Apulia lacks good streams. The gen. is used with the adj. *pauper* as equivalent to a word of "want"; words of fullness and want may take an objective gen. or, in the case of a word of want, an abl. of separation; compare 13 n. 7.   B. **Daunus:** the mythical ancestor of the *Daunii*, the chief tribe of Apulia, which was therefore often called *Daunia*. The king is used here by metonymy (compare in nn. 14B and 36C above) for his country.   C. **agrestium . . . populorum:** gen. instead of acc. with *regnavit*, either in a rare Lat. imitation of the Greek construction with verbs of ruling, or on the analogy of the gen. with *potior*, for which see 26 n. 9A (and compare *potens* in n. 9B above).   D. **ex humili potens** = "powerful (although) from humble (origin)"; as punctuated in the text above, this modifies the subject of *dicar*, i.e. Horace, whose father was a freedman; see 86 pref. Some, however, make it modify *Daunus*, who, according to legend, rose from being a refugee from Illyria to be king of Apulia; see n. B above. Horace may have meant the ambiguity to draw a parallel between himself and Daunus.

41.   A. **princeps . . . deduxisse** = "first (or, foremost) to have introduced"; the inf. does not depend on *princeps* but is in indirect discourse after *dicar* and, since this is pass., *princeps* is nom. in agreement with its subject; see 80 n. 9A.   B. **princeps:** used instead of *primus* (where Eng. would use an adv.; compare 11 n. 12A), perhaps because Horace was not by any means the first Roman author to have used Greek lyric meters (see, e.g. for Catullus, 73 pref.) but felt himself to be the foremost (for this connotation of *princeps* see 19 n. 3C and 48 n. 6) to have adapted so many so successfully.   C. **Aeolium carmen:** used for Greek lyric poetry in general, since Horace particularly admired Alcaeus and Sappho, from the island of Lesbos in the area known as Aeolia; see 86 pref. and pref. above.   D. **Ítalos:** for the initial long *i-* compare 86 n. 24A (and contrast 55 n. 2B). It = *Latinos*, since by Horace's time Lat. had become the common language of Italy, although the other Italic dialects probably continued to be spoken locally in more remote districts.   E. **deduxisse:** i.e. "to have introduced"; contrast in 86 n. 31D. From the basic meaning of "to lead down to," it is followed by *ad* + acc. rather than by a dat.   F. **modos** = either "meters" or "rhythmical patterns."

42.   A. **superbiam . . . meritis** = "the credit gained by (my) merits"; Horace invokes the Muse to take the proud honor (not here pejorative) for the success in poetry which she had bestowed on him; compare Ennius' invocation of the Muses in 60 n. 27A and Vergil's in 85 n. 2A, and Lucretius' hymn to Venus in 69, especially n. 1B.   B. **mihi:** dat. of reference, both of advantage with *cinge* and of possession with *comam*; compare n. 27 above.   C. **Delphica lauro:** for the gender compare 61 n. 3 (and 84 n. 2A). Apollo, one of whose chief shrines was at Delphi (see 9 n. 1B), was the god of poetry and music and leader of the Muses. Since the laurel tree was sacred to him, a laurel wreath became the symbol of poetic fame; in C above, Horace was satisfied with the simple myrtle.   D. **volens** = "willing(ly)," i.e. with full recognition of my merits; a regular formula in prayers. For the adverbial rendering compare nn. 21E and 36A above.   E. **Melpomenē:** this one of the nine Muses was chiefly identified with tragedy, but her name means in Greek "songstress" and thus could be applied generally to patronage of poetry; ancient poets do not strictly differentiate the Muses by function. The -*ē* is a Greek fem. sing. nom. (and voc., as here) ending.

88

Vergil's *Aeneid* describes in five books Aeneas' adventures in bringing the remnant of the Trojans to Italy (see 1), in the sixth book his descent to the lower world under the guidance of the Cumaean Sibyl (see 85 n. 4) to visit the shade of his father Anchises (see 1 n. 2b), and in the last six books his war with the natives to establish a new settlement for his Trojans; see 2 and 3. It is, moreover, full of references to Rome's future history and greatness, as, for instance, in the scenes on the Shield of Aeneas; see 55. The high point of this involvement of the future in the past, and, indeed, the turning point at which Aeneas passes from being a Trojan fugitive to becoming the founder of Rome's future, is his interview with Anchises, who permits him to review (not in historical sequence) the souls of Rome's future heroes as they await rebirth by the river Lethe, in accordance with a theory of metempsychosis even older than Plato's elaboration of it in the last book of his *Republic*.

The following selected verses in dactylic hexameter give Anchises' prophetic tribute to Augustus, his condemnation of the civil war between Pompey and Caesar, his comments on some of the famous Republican leaders, and his famous verses on Rome's imperial destiny.

Expedit Anchises Itala de gente nepotes
illustrisque animas Romanum in nomen ituras[1]

Huc geminas nunc flecte acies,[2] hanc aspice gentem
Romanosque tuos. Hic Caesar et omnis Iuli
progenies, magnum caeli ventura sub axem.[3]
Hic vir, hic est, tibi quem promitti saepius audis,
Augustus Caesar, Divi genus,[4] aurea condet
saecula qui rursus Latio regnata per arva
Saturno quondam,[5] super et Garamantas et Indos
proferet imperium;[6] iacet extra sidera tellus,
extra anni solisque vias, ubi caelifer Atlas
axem umero torquet stellis ardentibus aptum.[7]
Nec vero Alcides tantum telluris obivit,[8]
fixerit aeripedem cervam licet, aut Erymanthi
pacarit nemora, et Lernam tremefecerit arcu;[9]

nec qui pampineis victor iuga flectit habenis
Liber, agens celso Nysae de vertice tigris.[10]
Et dubitamus adhuc virtutem extendere factis,[11]
aut metus Ausonia prohibet consistere terra?[12]

Illae autem, paribus quas fulgere cernis in armis,
concordes animae nunc et dum nocte premuntur;[13]
heu! quantum inter se bellum, si lumina vitae
attigerint, quantas acies stragemque ciebunt,[14]
aggeribus socer Alpinis atque arce Monoeci
descendens, gener adversis instructus Eois![15]
Ne, pueri, ne tanta animis adsuescite bella,[16]
neu patriae validas in viscera vertite viris;[17]
tuque prior, tu parce, genus qui ducis Olympo;[18]
proice tela manu, sanguis meus![19]

Ille triumphata Capitolia ad alta Corintho
victor aget currum, caesis insignis Achivis.[20]
Eruet ille Argos Agamemnoniasque Mycenas[21]
ipsumque Aeaciden, genus armipotentis Achilli,[22]
ultus avos Troiae, templa et temerata Minervae.[23]
Quis, te, magne Cato, tacitum aut te, Cosse, relinquat?[24]
Quis Gracchi genus aut geminos, duo fulmina belli,
Scipiadas, cladem Libyae,[25] parvoque potentem
Fabricium vel te sulco, Serrane, serentem?[26]
Quo fessum rapitis, Fabii?[27] Tu Maximus ille es,
unus qui nobis cunctando restituis rem.[28]

Excudent alii spirantia mollius aera,[29]
(credo equidem); vivos ducent de marmore voltus;[30]
orabunt causas melius; caelique meatus
describent radio et surgentia sidera dicent.[31]
Tu regere imperio populos, Romane, memento[32]—
hae tibi erunt artes—pacisque imponere morem;[33]
parcere subiectis et debellare superbos.[34]

---

1. A. **expedit** = "expounds." These 2 verses of the title are based on *Aen.* VI 757–
758, the opening of Anchises' presentation to Aeneas of the souls of Rome's future

heroes; see pref.   B. **Anchīsēs**: see 1 n. 2B; the final *-ēs* is a Greek nom. ending; compare *Aenēās* in 49 n. 1 (but contrast *Persēs* in 15 n. 6).   C. **Itala**: the initial *i-* is here scanned short as in 55 n. 2B; it is long in 59 n. 16B and 87 n. 41D.   D. **Rōmānum in nomen**: for the use of *nomen* to indicate a people compare 41 n. 11B.

2.   **acies**: here = "eyes" (lit. lines of sight), not "battle-line" as it does 20 verses below.

3.   A. **hīc**: adv. here in the 2nd verse; see 10 n. 18B (and 84 n. 13A). But *hǐc* is nom. masc. sing. pronoun both times in the 4th verse.   B. **Ǐūli**: always three syllables in Vergil. Iulus was the son of Aeneas, also called Ascanius, through whom the *gens Iulia* traced its descent from Aeneas' mother Venus; see 55 n. 4.   C. **magnum etc.** = "(who are) about to pass beneath the great vault of the sky," i.e. go up into life.   D. **ventura**: nom. fem. sing. of the fut. act. part. modifying *progenies*.   E. **axem**: lit. = "axle" or "axis" but may be used by metonymy (compare 49 n. 4 and in 87 n. 14B) for the whole wagon or the sphere turning on its axis; compare *axem* 7 verses below.

4.   A. **Augustus Caesar**: antecedent of *qui* in the following verse; the spondees give this name (for which see 83 n. 12B) solemn emphasis.   B. **Dīvi genus** = "son (lit. race) of the Deified (i.e. Julius)"; after Caesar's assassination (see 43), the senate recognized that he had been translated to heaven, as had Romulus (see 60 n. 2) and various early Greek heroes; see 80 pref.

5.   A. **qui**: the rel. pronoun is placed after the verb of which it is the subject; the object is *aurea . . . saecula*.   B. **Latio**: abl. of place where without the prep.; see 85 n. 9E (and contrast the dat. in 49 n. 6A). An adjectival form *Latio* (from *Latius*) which would modify *Saturno* (= Lat. Saturnus) does not occur elsewhere in Vergil, though used by Ovid.   C. **Saturno**: dat. of reference (agent) with the past part. *regnata*; see 21 n. 15C (and 74 n. 18B). For this early Italic deity, presumed to have ruled in the Golden Age, see 85 n. 7A.

6.   A. **super**: here = "beyond," not "over."   B. **et . . . et**: the first is postpositive (see 86 nn. 6C and 19D) and connects *condet* (2 verses above) with *proferet* (in the following verse). The second is merely subordinate, to connect *Garamantas* and *Indos*. Some editors, however, punctuate with a semicolon after *quondam*, in lieu of a main connective, and take *et . . . et* as correlative with the two nouns, = "both . . . and."   C. **Garamantās**: Greek acc. plur. of the 3rd decl.; see 85 n. 21B. These were an African tribe in the Libyan desert which, perhaps in 20, sent an embassy to Augustus, who regarded this as "submission." They were shortly thereafter defeated by Cornelius Balbus, nephew of Caesar's engineer, for whom see 35 n. 8B. The younger Balbus triumphed for this victory in 19 and was the last person other than an emperor or member of the imperial family to celebrate a triumph. Since, however, Vergil died in Sept. 19, on his return from a trip to Greece, it is unlikely that he referred to this conquest in a last-minute revision.   D. **Indos**: in 25 and 20, two Indian kings sent embassies to Augustus; Vergil may well have wanted to compare Augustus' conquests to those of Alexander, who actually entered northwestern India (Pakistan). These references are the latest identifiable in the *Aeneid*.

7.   A. **iacet . . . tellus**: Anchises speaks vaguely of a region (*tellus*) which Augustus might conquer, lying beyond the stars known to the Romans and outside the yearly course of the sun (i.e. the Zodiac).   B. **caelifer Atlās etc.**: the legend of Atlas supporting the vault of heaven is as old as Hesiod. He was located either in the extreme west (the garden of the Hesperides) or in the Atlas mountains. Accordingly, Vergil means that Augustus may expand into Britain in the unknown West (see 84 n. 16) or south into unexplored Africa. He imitates Ennius *Ann.* frag. 59 (Loeb): *qui caelum versat stellis fulgentibus aptum.*   C. **caelifer**: a rare compound adj., apparently first used by Vergil; compare his *Ignipotens* for Vulcan in 55 n. 3B.

8.   A. **Alcīdēs**: Hercules, grandson of Alceus; for the patronymic compare 9 n. 2B (and 69 n. 21C). Hercules was a hero who devoted his life to ridding the world of various

monsters hostile to civilization. Curiously, Vergil does not cite those labors which he performed by distant travel, e.g. to get the girdle of the Queen of the Amazons, the oxen of the Spanish Geryon, or the apples of the western Hesperides. The three of his twelve labors mentioned here were all performed in the Peloponnese, the southern part of Greece. In Greek the nom. sing. of patronymics ends in -*ēs* (compare n. 1B above), and so probably here, though the syllable is in any case long by position.   B. **obivit:** here ="he went through" or "traversed"; contrast the contracted *obit*="he died" in 70 n. 27B.

9.   A. **fixerit ... pacarit ... tremefecerit:** perf. subjs. in coordinate (paratactic) construction after *licet*="(even) granted that"; see 23 n. 1A (and 75 n. 11).   B. **aeripedem cervam**="bronze-hooved hind" (female deer); in the usual version, Hercules captured rather than simply pierced this pet of the goddess Artemis; probably Vergil meant the piercing to mean capturing.   C. **Erymanthi ... nemora:** Hercules slew a great boar which had been laying waste the woods around Mt. Erymanthus.   D. **pacarit**=*pacaverit*; see 1 n. 4B (and 87 n. 11B).   E. **Lernam ... arcu:** in the usual version, Hercules did not make Lerna tremble with his bow, but beat the many heads of the Hydra with his club; the snakelike Hydra dwelt in a marsh near Lerna and ravaged the surrounding country; see 9 n. 9.

10.   A. **iuga:** here="teams"; contrast the literal meaning, "yokes," in 85 n. 26B. The chariot of Dionysus might be drawn by tigers, as here, or by lynxes, as in *Georg.* III 264. In his well-known painting, Titian shows what are identified as "pards," but it is uncertain whether he meant these to be leopards or panthers.   B. **Liber:** in origin the name of an Italic divinity but regarded later as an epithet of the Greek god of wine, Dionysus. Dionysus is also known as Bacchus, an epithet apparently derived from the outcry of his drunken worshipers. The meaning of *Liber* is uncertain; the ancients connected it either with *libō*="pour" or with *liber*="free"; the second would refer to the releasing effect of intoxication. Dionysus is here cited as a civilizer of mankind because he spread the cultivation of the vine in his triumphal progress to Greece from India, where Vergil locates the legendary place of his birth, Mt. *Nȳsa*.

11.   A. **et dubitamus etc.:** Anchises exhorts Aeneas to occupy Italy boldly, but Vergil may well be exhorting his contemporaries to pursue boldly the imperial aims of Augustus.   B. **virtutem ... factis:** "to extend bravery by deeds" is a rather violent inversion, which has led some manuscripts and editors to read *virtute extendere vires*.

12.   A. **Ausonia:** adj. derived from the name of an indigenous people of Campania, called by the earliest Greek settlers *Ausones* and perhaps the same as those called by the Romans *Aurunci*. The Greeks extended the term to the whole of Italy, just as the Romans applied to the Hellenes the name *Graeci*, apparently derived from some inhabitants of western Greece with whom the Italians first came into contact.   B. **consistere:** for Aeneas, ="to settle"; perhaps Vergil also urged his contemporaries "to remain" in Italy and not to desert it, in the mood of discouragement given by Horace in *Epode* 16, or to found a new capital in Troy, as it was rumored that Caesar had planned to do.

13.   A. **illae autem etc.:** Anchises points to the souls, as yet unborn, of Pompey and Caesar. With this passage compare 77.   B. **paribus:** both because Pompey and Caesar were evenly matched and because both used similar Roman arms.   C. **nocte:** the darkness of the lower world is contrasted with the light of life (compare 74 n. 3B), although earlier (640–641) Vergil has described Elysium as luminous and having its own sun.

14.   A. **si ... attigerint:** the protasis of the fut. more vivid condition is equivalent to a temporal clause; ="if ever," i.e. when once.   B. **lumina vitae:** the plur. for "the light of life (above)" is unusual enough for some manuscripts to read the more familiar, but less poetic, *limina vitae*="thresholds of life"; compare, however, 60 n. 5B, 69 nn. 6D and 19B, and 70 n. 24A.

15.   A. **socer ... gener:** for Pompey's marriage to Caesar's daughter see 35 pref. and

n. 7 (and 77 n. 3A).   B. **aggeribus ... Alpīnis:** Caesar would normally have crossed the Alps to enter Italy from Gaul; see following note.   C. **Monoeci:** modern Monaco, so called from the Greek epithet of Hercules *Monoecus*, "of the single (i.e. solitary) house," with reference to his temple on what for the Greeks was a lonely and remote citadel. Caesar was, of course, actually in Cisalpine Gaul when he determined to cross the Rubicon in 49 (see 39 pref.), and more probably had come down from Transalpine Gaul by one of the inland passes rather than along the Riviera and by the Maritime Alps.   D. **adversis etc.** = "arrayed with Eastern (forces) against (him, i.e. Caesar)." Pompey withdrew before Caesar's advance from Italy to Greece, to secure support from the east; see 40 pref.   E. **Ĕōīs:** the Greek noun *Ēōs* = Dawn has both vowels long, but in Lat. verse the adj. formed from it, *Eous* = Eastern, may have an initial short, as here, or long *e*-; the adj. is here used as a noun, with the implication of some such word as *armis, viribus, viris,* or the like.

16.   A. **ne ... adsuescite:** in prohibitions in early Lat. and in poetry, *ne* (here repeated for emphasis) + the imperative may be used instead of the usual prose constructions, for which see 62 n. 9A. The connective "and not" is *neu* (as in the next verse) or *neve*; compare 52 n. 9A (and contrast in 87 n. 11B).   B. **pueri:** Anchises thinks of the souls as children compared with himself; he may mean generally "my children," though only Caesar, as he says 3 verses below, was a direct descendant. Contrast the use of *puer* by a superior to an inferior in 84 n. 14A (and to a slave in 87 n. 18B).   C. **animis ... bella:** a bold inversion of thought, like *virtutem extendere factis* in n. 11B above.

17.   **vīris:** fem. acc. plur. of *vīs*. Vergil might be expected to have said "do not turn your weapons against (into) your country's entrails"; but instead he uses the abstract "forces," i.e. "violence."

18.   A. **tu parce etc.:** if Vergil does not mean to imply that Caesar was the aggressor in the Second Civil War (see 38, 39, and 77), at least he suggests that as the nobler (and more nobly born), Caesar should have made the first effort to preserve peace and the Republic. Vergil's attitude reflects the ambivalence in Augustus' pose as at once "Restorer of the Republic" (see 46, 47, and 86) and heir to the dictator Caesar; compare Tacitus in sel. 48.   B. **genus ... Olympo:** Caesar and the *gens Iulia* traced their descent from Venus (see 33 pref. and 69 n. 1B) and Anchises (hence *sanguis meus* in the next verse) through Iulus; see n. 3B above.

19.   **prōĭcĕ:** *prō-* retains its length before a following vowel because -*ĭ*- stands for consonantal and vowel -*ĭĭ*- (from original -*ĭă*-). This verse is one of the several incomplete (or "half") verses in the *Aeneid*. Scholars differ as to whether these were intentionally meant to give effect by a sudden pause in speech, i.e. by a rhetorical device known as "aposiopesis" (Greek; = silencing off), or whether they represent the slightly unfinished condition in which Vergil left the *Aeneid* at his unexpected death in 19. Vergil was such a perfectionist that on his deathbed he asked that the poem be burned rather than given to the public without his final polish, but Augustus instructed his literary executors to publish it with the minimum of editing, and they clearly felt that these verses, whether deliberate or unfinished, should not be completed.

20.   A. **ille etc.:** Lucius Mummius destroyed and triumphed over Corinth in 146; see 15 pref.   B. **triumphata ... Corintho:** abl. abs. expressing cause; place names, even if masc. in form, are generally fem., though *Veii* in 8 n. 11 is masc. plur. and *Saguntum* in 10 n. 3A is neut. sing.   C. **Capitōlia ad alta:** with *aget currum*; for the neut. acc. "poetic" plur. see 55 n. 13B. Roman triumphs went through the Forum by the *sacra via* and climbed the *clivus Capitolinus* (see 18 n. 14D) to the temple of Jupiter Optimus Maximus (see 12 n. 4), where the victorious general dedicated part of the spoils.   D. **caesis ... Achīvis:** abl. of specification (or cause) with *insignĭs*.

21.   A. **eruet ille etc.:** these verses are generally taken to refer to L. Aemilius Paullus, who defeated Perseus, last king of Macedon and supposedly a descendant of Aeacus, the grandfather of Achilles, at the battle of Pydna in 168; see 15 pref. and B. But the

statement that Paullus "overthrew" Argos and Mycenae (see following note) is a rhetorical exaggeration. Paullus' victory in Macedon opened the way to Roman power in Greece, but neither he nor even Mummius (see n. 20A above) actually destroyed these cities.   B. **Argōs Agamemnoniasque Mycēnas:** *Argōs* is masc. acc. plur. of the plur. *Argi, -orum,* which is used for both the city and its inhabitants. The neut. sing. Greek *Argŏs* occurs in Lat. as a nom. and acc. but not in Vergil. Agamemnon ruled both Argos and Mycenae, though here the adj. *Agamemnonias* applies only to the latter.

22.   A. **Aeacidēn:** here presumably Perseus (see n. 21A above); the *ipsum* suggests victory not only over the cities of Agamemnon but over Achilles, the very hero of the *Iliad*; see 85 n. 22B. The reference is less probably to Pyrrhus, though he also claimed descent from Aeacus through Achilles; see 9 n. 2B (and 60 n. 26A). In Greek, nouns in *-ēs* have *-ēn* in the acc. sing.; compare n. 8A above.   B. **armipotentis:** for this compound see 69 n. 25 (and for similar ones see 55 n. 3B, 60 n. 26B, and n. 7C above).   C. **Achilli:** gen. sing. In early Lat., names in *-ĕs* (for Greek *-eus*; see 15 n. 6 and 85 n. 22B) had a 3rd decl. gen. sing. in *-ĭs.* But confusion with noms. in *-ēs* (see nn. 1B and 8A above) led to the use of a 5th decl. gen. sing. in *-ēi*; for which compare 69 n. 10C. The *-ĭ-* here may be contracted from such an *-ēi* or from a 2nd decl. gen. *-ĕī* from the Greek nom. in *-eus,* which is a diphthong in Greek but might be treated as 2 syllables in Lat.; indeed one good early manuscript reads the diphthong *-eî.*

23.   A. **ultus:** past part. of the dep. *ulciscor*; it is act. and trans. (compare 83 n. 10A, and contrast 1 n. 6B); hence the acc. plur. objects *avos* and *templa.*   B. **avos Troiae:** for these see nn. 1A and 3B above.   C. **templa:** collective neut. acc. plur.; compare 49 n. 10B (and contrast *iuga* in 85 n. 26B).   D. **et:** postpositive; compare n. 6B above.   E. **temerata** = "desecrated"; see 77 n. 29B.   F. **Minervae:** the Greek goddess Athena, from the sanctuary of whose altar, at the sack of Troy, the Greek Ajax wrenched the prophetic daughter of Priam, Cassandra. Earlier during the siege, Odysseus and Diomedes had stolen from the same temple a tutelary statue of "Pallas" Athena called the *Palladium,* so as to deprive the Trojans of its magical protection.

24.   A. **Catō:** the Elder, conservative leader of Rome from the end of the Second Punic War until his death in 149; see 13 and 14.   B. **Cosse:** A. Cornelius Cossus (of disputed rank) in 437 or 426 slew the general of Veii with his own hand and dedicated his armor as *spolia opima* in the temple of Jupiter Feretrius. Livy IV 20 discusses this story in some detail because Augustus, when restoring the temple, said that he read an inscription on the linen corselet dedicated by Cossus. Vergil may well mention Cossus because of this interest on Augustus' part.   C. **relinquat:** deliberative (or dubitative) subj.; contrast the fut. ind. in 67 n. 1A (and 86 n. 6A) and the pres. ind. *rapitis* 4 verses below. It is to be supplied with the following *quis.*

25.   A. **Gracchi:** not merely (or perhaps not so much) the famous revolutionary brothers of the period 133–121 (see 18–20 and 62) but also (or especially) their father, distinguished in the wars in Spain in the mid-2nd cent. (see 16 pref. and 18 n. 1A), and their great-uncle, distinguished in the Second Punic War; see 10 n. 13C (and genealogical chart I following 15). No Gracchus is known between the brothers and the period of Augustus, when the family reappears to play a prominent part under him and his successors; this re-emergence may have led Vergil to select the earlier Gracchi for mention.   B. **duo . . . Scīpiadās:** the ending *-ās* is here acc. plur. of a masc. of the 1st decl.; contrast the Greek 3rd decl. acc. plur. ending *-ăs* in n. 6C above. The reference is both to Scipio Africanus the Elder, who defeated Hannibal (see 10, 12, and 58), and to Scipio Aemilianus (*Africanus Minor*), who destroyed Carthage and Numantia; see 16. Vergil here recalls the verse in which Lucretius mentioned only Scipio the Elder as (nom.) *Scipiadas, belli fulmen, Carthaginis horror*; see 70 n. 25.

26.   A. **parvo:** probably abl. of cause, meaning that he was great both as a general and because he preferred poverty to dishonesty; some would take it as abl. of means and render "great (i.e. wealthy) with small (resources)." However, the adjectival part. *potens* takes the gen. (see 33 n. 25A and 87 n. 9B), though the related verb *potior* more often

takes the abl.; see 46 n. 12A (and 49 n. 3B; for the gen. see 26 n. 9A and 38 n. 4B). For the thought compare *ex humili potens* in 87 n. 40D.   B. **Fabricium**: Fabricius, "great because of little," refused the bribes of Pyrrhus (see 9 A), despite his limited means, and eventually defeated him.   C. **Serrāne**: an epithet of C. Atilius Regulus, consul in 257 during the First Punic War. The epithet was probably derived from his town of origin, but later tradition connected it with the verb *serere* (compare 84 n. 19B) and supposed that he received the news of his election while sowing his grain, just as two centuries earlier in 458, T. Quinctius Cincinnatus had been called from his plough to become dictator against the Aequi. Serranus was apparently often confused with the more famous Marcus Atilius Regulus (perhaps a brother), the suffect consul of 256 who, when later captured by the Carthaginians, refused ransom; see 9 B. This wrong identification may have induced Vergil to mention Regulus Serranus, rather than the more famous Cincinnatus, as an example of the Roman ideal of distinction in public virtue and modest simplicity in private life.

27. **quo . . . Fabii** = "whither, O Fabii, are you hastening (me already) exhausted," i.e. to review even rapidly the numerous heroes of the *gens Fabia* would take Anchises, who is already tired (with talking), too far afield, so he mentions only one.

28. A. **Maximus**: Hannibal's great adversary; see 10 n. 13A.   B. **unus qui etc.**: this verse is paraphrased from Ennius as given in 61 B (see nn. 13–16). The foregoing list of Roman worthies does not appear to have any particular order, chronological or of significance, and is perhaps meant to suggest that the Roman spirits appeared more or less haphazardly. It opens with Mummius and Paullus who, in the 2nd cent., avenged Troy, a topic presumably dear to Anchises. Cato and Cossus combine the 2nd and the 5th cents., but perhaps represent typically Roman worthies. The Gracchi and the Scipios cover from the Punic Wars to the 130's and may belong together as related families; see the genealogical charts following 15. Fabricius and Serranus are again typical early Roman worthies, and the Fabii were a distinguished family throughout Roman history; see 8 n. 1A. It is interesting, however, that Vergil chose to conclude on Fabius Maximus and with the echo of Ennius.

29. A. **excudent alii**: the fut. verbs in these deservedly famous verses are both prophetic and concessive: "others (i.e. the Greeks) will," with the suggestion of "although others will" or "let others"; compare 71 n. 18 (and 86 n. 6A; and contrast n. 24C above). Superiority in arts and sciences is conceded to the Greeks as a foil for the assertion of Roman superiority in making war and imposing peace; see n. 32A below.   B. **spirantia mollius aera** = "more gracefully breathing bronzes," i.e. graceful bronze statues which seem to breathe; for *aera* see 80 n. 8 (and 87 n. 33C).

30. A. **credo equidem** = "(as) I at least believe"; this parenthetical remark emphasizes the concessive force of the fut. verbs.   B. **ducent** = "will mold"; *duco* is strictly used of working soft materials such as wax, clay, or molten metal; here it suggests the marvelously soft and lifelike appearance of Greek marble statues.

31. A. **orabunt causas** = "plead cases"; for *causa* in this sense see the 1st sentence of the 3rd par. of 14 (and 37 n. 25A). In spite of Cicero, Vergil here considers the Romans as still inferior to the Greeks in rhetoric.   B. **radio** = "with a pointer"; the ancients drew geometrical or astronomical diagrams in sand with a stick.   C. **surgentia sidera**: contrast Lucretius' *labentia signa* in 69 n. 4C.   D. **dicent** = "will (fore)tell." The rising of stars served the ancients to mark the seasons for beginning various agricultural or seafaring activities; compare 86 n. 13C.

32. A. **tu . . . Rōmāne**: in view of the preceding concessions, this general apostrophe is adversative: "(but) you, Roman(s)"; compare n. 29A above.   B. **imperio**: abl. of means with *regere*.   C. **memento**: 2nd sing. imperative of *memini*, "fut." in form but regularly used as a pres.; compare *scito* in 32 n. 6B. On it depend *regere* and the three infs. in the following 2 verses.

33. A. **hae . . . artes**: parenthetical; compare n. 30A above.   B. **pacisque imponere**

morem = "to impose the habit of peace"; in this famous verse, the ancient commentator Servius (see 55 n. 12A) read the gen. *pacis*, but the best manuscripts have the dat. *paci*, which is preferred by many modern editors as after a verb compounded with *in-* (see 46 n. 20A, and compare 87 n. 31B), = "to impose (orderly) behavior on peace," i.e. following pacification came the task of civilization of the barbarian tribes. It becomes a matter of taste which one feels Vergil really wrote.

34.   A. **parcere . . . debellare:** since these infs. are without connective to the preceding *imponere*, they are probably in explanatory apposition to it, rather than coordinate.   B. **subiectis:** past part. used as a noun (compare *evocatum* in 45 n. 6); dat. after *parcere*; see 47 n. 7 (and 81 n. 11A).   C. **debellare:** the force of *de-* in composition may be literal, = "down" (from or to; as in *deduxisse* in 87 n. 41E), or metaphorical, = "utterly" (as here). These final 2 verses serve as an *ex post facto* justification for Roman "imperialism" and a program for the rule of Augustus, as indeed does the whole *Aeneid*.

89

The first thirty-nine chapters of the biblical book of Isaiah contain utterances of a Hebrew reformer of the late eighth century B.C. In the seventh chapter there is reference to the birth of a child as a sign of deliverance, verses which the early Christians applied to the birth of Jesus. The opening of the eleventh chapter has "Messianic" prophecies of the return of a "Golden Age" under a new king; the prophet probably had no specific king in mind, though some would identify the king with Hezekiah, who came to the throne about 715. Later Jews regarded Isaiah as the herald of a Redeemer of their people from captivity, and the early Christians saw in him the principal Old Testament witness to the coming of Christ. They therefore took these verses as showing that under Christ a Golden Age would return. Moreover, they saw the work of Divine Providence in the establishment of peace by Augustus (see 47 and 88) as a preparation for the birth and ministry of Christ. Finally they observed the resemblance of Isaiah's language to that of Vergil's *Fourth Eclogue*, which describes the return of the Golden Age under the auspices of a child about to be born; see 85. Thus at least as early as A.D. 300, Vergil was held to have been inspired in this *Eclogue* by the Cumaean Sibyl to prophesy the birth of Christ.

The prophet Micah, almost contemporary with Isaiah, likewise combines rebuke of corruption, threat of disaster, and hope of redemption. A passage in the fifth chapter, which relates the birth of David at Bethlehem to the coming salvation of Israel, was taken by early Christians, who regarded Jesus as the Messiah born of David's line, as prophetic evidence for his birth in Bethlehem.

The following versions of these prophetic passages from Isaiah and Micah are those of the Vulgate Bible, a translation made about A.D. 400 by St. Jerome (see 82 pref.) into the spoken, or "vulgar," Latin of his day. They show how literally he rendered into Latin idioms more suited to the Hebrew and also the changes of vocabulary and grammar which were taking place in late Latin before its transformation into the Romance languages.

A.   *Vaticinationes Isaiae*

Dabit Dominus ipse vobis signum.[1] Ecce virgo concipiet et pariet filium.[2] Et vocabitur nomen eius Emmanuel.[3] Butyrum et mel comedet, ut sciat reprobare malum et eligere bonum.[4]

*   *   *

Et egredietur virga de radice Iesse,[5]
    et flos de radice eius ascendet,[6]

et requiescet super eum spiritus Domini:[7]
spiritus sapientiae et intellectus,
    spiritus consilii et fortitudinis,
spiritus scientiae et pietatis;
    et replebit eum spiritus timoris Domini.
Non secundum visionem oculorum iudicabit[8]
    neque secundum auditum aurium arguet,
sed iudicabit in iustitia pauperes
    et arguet in aequitate pro mansuetis terrae[9]
et percutiet terram virga oris sui[10]
    et spiritu labiorum suorum interficiet impium,[11]
et erit iustitia cingulum lumborum eius,
    et fides cinctorium renum eius.[12]
Habitabit lupus cum agno,
    et pardus cum haedo accubabit;[13]
vitulus et leo et ovis simul morabuntur,[14]
    et puer parvulus minabit eos.[15]
Vitulus et ursus pascentur; simul requiescent catuli eorum;[16]
    et leo quasi bos comedet paleas.[17]
Et delectabitur infans ab ubere super foramine aspidis,[18]
    et in caverna reguli qui ablactatus fuerit manum suam mittet.[19]
Non nocebunt et non occident in universo monte sancto meo,[20]
    quia repleta est terra scientia Domini, sicut aquae
    maria operientes.[21]

B.   *Vaticinatio Michaeae*

Et tu, Bethlehem Ephrata, parvulus es in milibus Iuda.[22] Ex te mihi egredietur qui sit dominator in Israel;[23] et egressus eius ab initio, a diebus aeternitatis.[24] Propter hoc dabit eos usque ad tempus in quo parturiens pariet et reliquiae fratrum eius convertentur ad filios Israel.[25] Et stabit et pascet in fortitudine Domini, in sublimitate nominis Domini Dei sui.[26] Et permanebunt, quia nunc magnificabitur usque ad terminos terrae.[27] Et erit iste pax.[28]

1. **dabit . . . signum:** Isaiah's 7th chap. is a warning to King Ahaz (*ca.* 735–715?) that unless he corrects his ways, God will not help him against the Syrians. The prophet indicates that God will give him a sign but expects Ahaz to neglect it and to suffer accordingly.

2. **virgo concipiet:** the Hebrew word translated in the Septuagint Greek, the Vulgate Lat., and the King James Eng. as "virgin" means a young marriageable girl, whether wed or unwed. The birth may be a general reference to children about to be born who will see the day of repentance and redemption, or may point to a particular birth, perhaps by a young wife of Ahaz. The translation "virgin" accorded with, or even engendered, the belief that the Messiah would issue from a "virgin birth."

3. A. **nomen . . . Emmanuel:** in the act. these would constitute a double acc., as in the King James Eng.: "(she) shall call his name Emmanuel"; in the pass. here, *nomen* becomes the subject of *vocabitur*, and *Emmanuel* is predicate nom.   B. **Emmanuel:** also spelled *Immanuel*, = "God be (or, is) with us."

4. A. **butyrum et mel** = "curds and honey"; the simple food of the unspoiled nomad, as against the urban plenty of Ahaz's courtiers. The child, freed by the coming disaster from corrupting luxury, will know how to choose the good.   B. **butyrum:** from Greek *bouturon* = "cow's cheese"; source of Eng. "butter"; it is probably here not cow's butter, which the Near Eastern nomad would not have had, but curds of goat's or sheep's milk.   C. **mel:** either bee honey or a sweet made from dates.   D. **reprobare:** here = "to reject" or "refuse"; elsewhere = "to reprove" or "condemn"; the verb is rare but classical.

5. A. **virga . . . Iesse** = "a scion from the root (i.e. trunk) of Jesse," i.e. a new king (namely the Messiah) from the line of David.   B. **virga:** like Eng. "scion," lit., = "a shoot (for grafting)"; hence "a descendant."   C. **Iesse:** gen. It is not declined in Lat., as many Hebrew names are not. This second passage is in Hebrew verse, which consists of balanced repetitive phrases, every pair of which forms in Hebrew a musical phrase of equal value.

6. **flos** = "flower"; but the Hebrew means rather "twig."

7. A. **super eum** = "upon him"; classical Lat. would use *in*.   B. **spiritus Domini** = "the spirit of God"; but in Lat. the basic literal meaning of *spiritus* = "breath" is also present; see n. 11 below (and contrast 58 n. 13B).

8. **secundum . . . oculorum** = "according to the sight of (his) eyes"; classical Lat. would use *visus* or *sensus* in the abl. (of means).

9. **pro . . . terrae** = "on behalf of the humble of the earth."

10. A. **virga oris sui** = "with the rod of his mouth," i.e., apparently, "the strict judgments which he will utter."   B. **virga:** compare n. 5B above.   C. **oris:** probably a limiting gen., = "the rod (which is) his mouth," rather than possessive, = "the rod (belonging to, or, coming forth from) his mouth"; compare 87 n. 23.

11. **spiritu:** abl. of means; here lit. = "breath"; see n. 7B above.

12. **cingulum lumborum . . . cinctorium renum:** synonyms, = "the girdle of his loins . . . the binding of his reins (lit. kidneys)."

13. **pardus** = "leopard" or, perhaps, "panther"; compare in 88 n. 10A.

14. A. **vitulus** = "calf"; with the implication of "fatted calf."   B. **morabuntur** = "will sojourn together"; this meaning is "silver" Lat.

15. **minabit** = "will lead." The act. forms of *minor* (= "I threaten") are postclassical and perhaps reflect a popular use for the herdsman (here a child) who "leads" his cattle by threatening them with his shouts.

16. A. **pascentur:** probably here an intrans. dep., = "they will graze," rather than the pass. of the act. verb, = "they will be fed."   B. **simul** = "together" rather than "at the same time"; it should probably be taken with *pascentur* as well as with *requiescent*.

17. A. **quasi bos** = "like (lit. as if) an ox." B. **paleas** = "chaff"; usually rendered "straw."

18. A. **delectabitur** = "will play"; from the meaning "take pleasure in." B. **infans ab ubere** = "the infant at (lit. hanging from) the breast." C. **super . . . aspidis** = "above the hole of the asp"; *foramen* = "a drilled or bored hole," as against a natural *cavum* or *caverna* = "den."

19. A. **caverna reguli** = "the den of the basilisk" (a poisonous serpent, also called "cockatrice"). *Regulus* and the Greek *basiliskos* both mean "little king," being the diminutives of words for "king," in Lat. *rex*, in Greek *basileus*. In mythology even the glance and breath of the basilisk were fatal, but here presumably a real though venomous reptile is meant; indeed, in the Greek version *aspis* is repeated. B. **qui . . . fuerit** = "who shall have been weaned"; *ablacto* is a late Lat. word meaning "I take from the mother's milk."

20. **in . . . meo:** i.e. in the mount of Jerusalem; and, by extension, in all Judaea.

21. A. **repleta est:** Hebrew does not distinguish between pres. and fut.; the Eng. versions render this as fut. whereas Jerome took it as perf. of completed action, i.e. denoting pres. state. B. **maria:** the Vulgate text reads *maris*; since the Greek has an acc. plur. and the Eng. translation renders "as the waters cover the sea," *maria* (or *mare*) is a better reading.

22. A. **Ephrata:** possessive gen. of the indeclinable (see n. 5c above) name of the district in which Bethlehem (also indeclinable) lay, 5 miles southwest of Jerusalem; it is given to distinguish this village from others of the same name. B. **milibus Iuda:** Micah thinks that though in David's prosperous times Palestine was thickly populated, yet the insignificant Bethlehem was chosen for the King's birth and the founding of the Hebrew kingdom. C. **Iuda:** gen. sing.; it is indeclinable, as is *Israel* (also gen.) in the next sentence; compare nn. A above and 25c below.

23. A. **mihi:** dat. of reference ("ethical"; see in 43 n. 23 and 82 n. 21), indicating that God, who speaks through the mouth of the prophet, is indirectly concerned in the appearance of David, the savior-king who is to represent him on earth; = "before me" or "on my behalf." B. **egredietur:** Micah, having envisaged God as addressing Bethlehem in a timeless present (*es*), now makes him prophesy the birth of David with a fut.; this naturally encouraged the later belief that another, coming Messiah would be born in Bethlehem. C. **qui sit etc.:** this rel. clause is subject of *egredietur* without an expressed antecedent; it is subj. because it is indefinite or potential rather than specifying some actual individual; compare 21 n. 20c (and 84 n. 6e).

24. **egressus:** not the past part. of *egredior*, but nom. sing. of the 4th decl. noun; supply *est*. Micah shifts to his own time and speaks of the birth of David as having taken place at the (very) beginning of Hebrew history, almost an eternal time ago. At the same time, the "coming forth" may mean that of a new Messiah, from the ancient lineage of David.

25. A. **dabit eos** = "he will give them (up)," i.e. into captivity. Micah again looks forward from the past and envisages the Hebrews in exile until a woman in travail (probably Israel herself) gives birth to a deliverer. This birth easily lent itself to identification with that prophesied by Isaiah; see n. 2 above. B. **reliquiae . . . Israel:** i.e. the remnants of the (Hebrew) "brethren" of the deliverer (*eius*), namely those still in exile, will return to (him and) those "sons (or, children) of Israel" who are already established in Palestine. C. **Israel:** gen. (compare n. 22c above) rather than abl. of place where, since the combination *filii Israel* is very common in the Old Testament and *Israel* usually indicates the people (or their ancestors), and, even when used for the country, has the connotation of the people in it.

26. A. **et stabit etc.:** the *in* phrases apparently refer to characteristics of the Messiah rather than to the place in which he will stand etc., i.e. "in the strength of the Lord etc.,

he will stand firm and feed (his flock)." For this meaning of *stabit* compare 60 n. 25A (and 77 n. 21B).   B. **pascet:** used transitively without expressed object; compare *me pascente* at the end of Meliboeus' last speech in 84 and contrast *pascentur* = "(animals) will graze" in n. 16A above.

27. A. **permanebunt:** the Vulgate here repeats *convertentur*, but the Hebrew verb (which may have been interpolated by some copyist) probably means "they will endure" rather than "they will dwell secure," as it is sometimes rendered.   B. **nunc magnificabitur etc.** = "he shall be made great (or, extolled, magnified) to the ends of the earth," i.e. the new king shall now (i.e. at the time of deliverance) bring the whole earth under his glorious sway. This Messianic sentence well illustrates Micah's combination of comment on the present with recall of the past and hope for the future.

28. **et ... pax** = "and he will be peace," i.e. the Messiah will bring peace or, since the Hebrew word is the same, salvation. Though Micah continues "when the Assyrian shall come into our land etc.," the early Christians generalized the prophecy to foretell a "Prince of Peace."

90

The birth of Jesus during the Augustan peace (see 47) seemed to the early Christians the fulfillment both of the prophecies of the Old Testament, notably of Isaiah (see 89), and also of the *Fourth Eclogue* of Vergil; see 85. The earliest Gospel, Mark, and the latest, John, begin their accounts with the opening of Jesus' ministry in connection with John the Baptist. The Gospel of Matthew opens with the stories of the Wise Men, of Herod's slaughter of the "Innocents," and of the flight into Egypt. Only Luke relates the Annunciation and the Nativity. Luke is accepted as an author who, toward the end of the first century A.D., combined Mark's account with traditions and sayings drawn from other sources. He was probably also the author of Acts and therefore either was himself a companion of Paul or used the diary of such a companion. He wrote in Greek for a non-Jewish Christian audience, perhaps in Rome, and tried to show that the new religion was not subversive. His Greek is the most correct and elegant of the three "synoptic" Gospels. However, his account of the birth and early years of Jesus is more markedly Hebrew in tone than are later portions of his Gospel. Thus the story of the Nativity presumably reproduces the tradition of early Jewish Christianity rather than an adaptation of such parallel tales as the raising of Romulus and Remus by the shepherd Faustulus (see 4) or the similar Iranian story that Mithras was nurtured by herdsmen.

The following account of the birth of Jesus comes from St. Jerome's revision of earlier "vulgate" Latin translations of Luke's Greek; see 89 pref.

Iesu Nativitas[1]

Factum est autem, in diebus illis exiit edictum a Caesare Augusto, ut describeretur universus orbis.[2] Haec descriptio prima facta est a praeside Syriae Cyrino.[3] Et ibant omnes, ut profiterentur singuli in suam civitatem.[4] Ascendit autem et Ioseph a Galilaea de civitate Nazareth in Iudaeam in civitatem David, quae vocatur Bethlehem (eo quod esset de domo et familia David), ut profiteretur cum Maria desponsata sibi uxore praegnante.[5] Factum est autem, cum essent ibi, impleti sunt dies ut pareret,[6] et peperit filium suum primogenitum et pannis eum involvit et reclinavit eum in praesaepio, quia non erat eis locus in deversorio.[7]

Et pastores erant in regione eadem vigilantes et custodientes vigilias noctis super gregem suum.[8] Et ecce angelus Domini stetit iuxta illos, et claritas Dei circumfulsit illos, et timuerunt timore magno.[9] Et dixit illis angelus: "Nolite timere.[10] Ecce enim evangelizo vobis gaudium magnum, quod erit omni populo; quia natus est vobis hodie Salvator, qui est Christus Dominus, in civitate David.[11] Et hoc vobis signum: invenietis infantem pannis involutum et positum in prae-saepio." Et subito facta est cum angelo multitudo militiae caelestis, laudantium Deum et dicentium:[12]

"Gloria in altissimis Deo,

et in terra pax hominibus bonae voluntatis."[13]

Et factum est, ut discesserunt ab eis angeli in caelum, pastores loquebantur ad invicem:[14] "Transeamus usque Bethlehem et videamus hoc verbum quod factum est, quod Dominus ostendit nobis."[15] Et venerunt festinantes et invenerunt Mariam et Ioseph et infantem positum in praesaepio. Videntes autem cognoverunt de verbo quod dictum erat illis de puero hoc. Et omnes qui audierunt mirati sunt et de his quae dicta erant a pastoribus ad ipsos.[16] Maria autem con-servabat omnia verba haec, conferens in corde suo.[17] Et reversi sunt pastores glorificantes et laudantes Deum, in omnibus quae audierant et viderant, sicut dictum est ad illos.[18]

Et postquam consummati sunt dies octo, ut circumcideretur puer, vocatum est nomen eius Iesus, quod vocatum est ab angelo priusquam in utero conciperetur.[19]

1. A. **Iesu:** the Greek gen. in *-ou* is retained in Lat. as *-u*; compare n. 19C (and contrast n. 5A) below.   B. **Nativitas:** a postclassical derivative from *natus*.

2. A. **factum est:** here perf. of *fio*, = "it became," i.e. it came to pass; contrast n. 12A below. After this impersonal opening, the following verb *exiit* is coordinate, not subordinate, without any connective equivalent to "that"; compare nn. 6A and 14A below (and the paratactic subj. after *licet* in 23 n. 1A and 88 n. 9A).   B. **in diebus illis:** i.e. at the time of the birth of John the Baptist, which has just been related; Luke 1.26 implies that Jesus was born about 6 months after his cousin John. Even in classical Lat., *in* with the abl. is sometimes used to indicate time when or within which.   C. **de-scriberetur:** *describo* is used occasionally in classical Lat. and regularly later for listing for tax purposes, and also the noun *descriptio* rather than *census*; they translate the Greek *apographō* and *apographē*. The census of the Roman Republic had been a listing of citizens for military service. Augustus, following the practice of the Hellenistic monarchies, began a survey of the Roman provinces for taxation, but at different times in different provinces; there is no evidence in the early Empire for any general survey such as was regular every 15 years under the later Empire.   D. **orbis:** used without

terrarum by St. Jerome to translate the Greek *oikoumenē* = "the inhabited (world)"; like the writer in 83 n. 18A, the author of Luke felt that the Roman Empire included all of the world that mattered; compare Vergil on Augustus' conquests in sel. 88.

3. A. **praeside Syriae:** *praeses* is the regular term in the later Empire for "governor." When Pompey settled the East in 63 (see 35 pref.), he left Judaea technically independent under a king-high priest of the "Hasmonaean" house descended from the Maccabees. But he installed as civil governor Antipater, a Jew by religion but an Arab by blood from Idumaea, a district of southern Palestine. He also charged the senatorial proconsul of Syria with general oversight. About 37, Antipater's son, Herod "The Great," removed the last Hasmonaean and made himself king. When he died in 4, Augustus divided the kingdom among his sons, giving the central portion, Judaea, to Archelaus. When Archelaus died about A.D. 6, Augustus placed Judaea under an imperial procurator of equestrian rank. The procurator at the time of the crucifixion of Jesus, about A.D. 33, was Pontius Pilate. In A.D. 41 Claudius restored as king a great-grandson of Herod called Herod Agrippa. When he died in A.D. 44, Judaea again became procuratorial. During the ministry of Paul in the 50's, the successive procurators were Felix and Festus. B. **Cyrino:** a misspelling for (Publius Sulpicius) Quirinius, a *novus homo* (see 13 pref.) who attained the consulship in 12 and later campaigned both in Cilicia and, in A.D. 2, with Augustus' grandson Gaius against the Parthians. He then became legate of Syria. Josephus, Jewish historian of the late 1st cent. A.D., says that on the annexation of Judaea in A.D. 6, Quirinius, still governor of Syria, initiated the first registration for taxes, which resulted in serious riots. The date A.D. 6 for the birth of Jesus is inconsistent with both Luke 1.5 and Matthew 2.1 and 15, who place it "in the days of Herod the king," shortly before his death in 4 B.C. This conflict of tradition cannot be harmonized. The beginning of the Christian era, which agrees with neither, was fixed in the early 6th cent. by a monk at Rome called Dionysius Exiguus, who calculated not from these dates but from a presumed age for Jesus of thirty-three at the time of his crucifixion. Dionysius began his 1st year with the Annunciation, which had been fixed to March 25, 6 months before the Nativity; see in n. 8B below. When later the Church generally accepted the Roman civil year from January 1 (see 22 n. 6), the 1st year was made to begin on the January 1 following the Nativity, with consequent confusion of dating. It should also be remembered that in civil reckoning, the year 1 B.C. immediately precedes A.D. 1, with no year 0 (though astronomers use a year 0 to facilitate their calculations).

4. A. **ut profiterentur:** "so that they might (go and) register"; followed by *in* + acc. (motion), not abl. (place). B. **singuli:** regularly used in the plur. as a distributive for *unus*, i.e. every one to his own city. *Quisque* with a sing. verb would emphasize each individual ("each one") separately. C. **in suam civitatem:** there is no evidence that the Roman tax registration was done in the place of family origin rather than of residence; Luke sought to reconcile diverse traditions that Jesus was born in Bethlehem but began his ministry from Nazareth.

5. A. **et Ioseph:** here *et* = *etiam*. The Hebrew names (*Ioseph, Nazareth, David*, and *Bethlehem*) are not declined, like many of those in 89. B. **eo quod** = "for the reason that"; a classical construction in which *eo* is abl. of cause anticipating the causal *quod* clause with the subj. C. **de ... familia:** late Lat. increases the use of prepositional phrases instead of case constructions, perhaps here for the rare gen. of source with forms of *esse*, as in 65 n. 7B. The use of *de* + abl. here may be an extension of its use with numerals instead of a partitive gen., for which compare 7 n. 5. D. **desponsata sibi uxore:** the Gospels' accounts of Jesus' later life represent Joseph and Mary as his parents; Luke tries to harmonize this with the prophetic tradition that the Messiah would be born of a virgin; see 89 n. 2.

6. A. **factum est ... impleti sunt:** coordinate without connective (paratactic); see n. 2A above. B. **ut pareret:** since the Greek here uses a purpose construction of the gen. of the definite article with the inf. of the verb "to bear," this is probably a purpose

clause in lieu of a rel. clause of characteristic expressing purpose (see 7 n. 8A and 83 n. 17), such as *in quibus pareret*.

7.   A. **pannis** = "with pieces of cloth," i.e. "in swaddling clothes."   B. **reclinavit:** this verb is usually trans. in Lat. (as against intrans. in Eng.) and may mean "to put down," as here.   C. **praesaepio:** from nom. *praesaepium*, though *praesaepe, -is,* also occurs. Basically it means an enclosure for animals, as a pigsty or sheepfold; hence it may mean a stall or stable and even a crib (manger) for feeding animals. The ox and ass were introduced into representations of the Nativity from Isaiah 1.3: *cognovit bos possessorem suum et asinus praesaepe domini sui; Israel autem me non cognovit etc.* The cave over which Constantine in the early 4th cent. erected the Church of the Nativity at Bethlehem presumably had long been identified in local tradition as the scene of the Nativity.   D. **in deversorio** = "in an (or, the) inn" or "guest room."

8.   A. **custodientes . . . noctis:** while *custodire* is trans. more often than intrans. and may connote not only "to guard" but "to preserve" or "to observe (a law, custom, etc.)," its extension here to the abstract "watches of the night" seems farfetched, and *vigilias* should probably therefore be regarded as a cognate acc.   B. **super gregem:** a figurative extension of the use of *super* = "above" with the acc.; compare 88 n. 6A. The fact that the shepherds were watching over their flocks in the fields indicates that the original tradition placed the Nativity between April and November, when in Palestine flocks are kept out of doors. Many ancient calendars began the year in March, as did the Romans originally (see 22 n. 6) and the Christians for many centuries; see n. 3B above. By the 4th cent., however, the Christians had identified the Nativity with the festival on December 25 of the "rebirth" of the sun after the winter solstice, which fell in the festive period called by the Romans the feast of the *Saturnalia*; see 61 pref.

9.   A. **angelus:** this Greek noun, = "messenger," became a term for a supernatural agent of God.   B. **iuxta:** used only as an adv. in Cicero and Sallust but already as a prep. in Caesar and Nepos; this phrase, however, sounds postclassical.

10.   **nolite timere:** for this common form of negative command compare 62 n. 9A (and contrast 88 n. 16A).

11.   A. **evangelizo:** a Greek 1st pers. sing. pres. act. ind. verb from the noun *euangelos* = "messenger of good (news)" (see n. 9A above), which also yields the abstract *euangelia*, which the Anglo-Saxons translated as "go(d)spel(l)" = "good (rather than God's) news."   B. **Christus Dominus** = "the Anointed Lord," a Greek translation of a Hebrew description of the Messiah; in Hellenistic Greek the verbal adj. *christos* = "anointed" came to be pronounced like the verbal adj. *chrēstos* = "good."

12.   A. **facta est:** the impersonal pass. (see n. 2A above) is here made personal, = "a multitude was made" or "came to be."   B. **militiae:** abstract sing. for concrete plur. *militum* = "soldiery" (Eng. "host"); compare *iuventus* in 8 n. 9A (and 72 n. 14).   C. **laudantium . . . dicentium:** agree with the plur. implied in *militiae*.

13.   A. **altissimis:** probably = "in the highest places," i.e. heaven, rather than "among the highest," i.e. the angels.   B. **pax . . . voluntatis:** this translates the Greek of the better manuscripts; it does not mean "men of good will" but "men of (God's) good favor," i.e. men whom God favors. Inferior Greek manuscripts make "good will" nom., coordinate with "peace"; whence the King James Eng. "and on earth peace, good will towards men." The Hebrew for "peace" may also mean "salvation"; compare 89 n. 28.

14.   A. **ut discesserunt:** *ut* is here temporal, = "when" (see 24 n. 17A); it is not dependent on *factum est*, with which the coordinate verb without connective is *loquebantur*; see n. 2A above.   B. **ad invicem:** a postclassical colloquialism here translating a Greek phrase meaning "to one another."

15.   A. **usque:** this adv. is used, as here, in classical Lat. with names of towns in the acc. of place to which without a prep.; its use without *ad* with other than names of towns is post-Augustan.   B. **verbum:** here translates the Greek noun *rhēma*, which in turn

presumably represents a Hebrew (or Aramaic) noun which meant not simply "word" but "subject of speech" or "matter"; hence the Eng. translators rendered this phrase: "this thing which has come to pass." Below, however, in the phrases *de verbo quod dictum erat* and *omnia verba haec*, *verbum* (and in Greek, *rhēma*) means "word" in the sense of "prophecy."   C. **factum est** = "happened" (as in n. 2A above); it here has a subject (as in n. 12A above), namely the rel. pronoun *quod* referring to *verbum*.

16. **et de his:** since here the Greek has no connective, *et* probably here = *etiam*, as in n. 5A above.

17. A. **omnia verba haec:** the placing of the demonstrative last reflects the Greek idiom.   B. **conferens:** translates a Greek part. meaning basically "throwing together" and hence, among various derivative senses, "comparing" or "pondering."

18. A. **in omnibus** = "in respect to everything"; a postclassical extension of the use of *in* to denote the circumstance in which something occurs; compare n. 2B above. B. **dictum est:** impersonal (compare n. 2A above); the meaning is that what they had seen and heard fulfilled the angels' prophecy to them.

19. A. **ut circumcideretur:** the substantive clause (probably of purpose; compare n. 6B above) is used to indicate a legal requirement.   B. **vocatum est nomen:** in this pass. construction *nomen* is subject and *Iesus* is predicate nom.; compare 89 n. 3A. C. **Iesus:** the Greek equivalent of Hebrew Joshua (*Yehoshua*) = "Saviour," the name which earlier Luke 1.31 said was prescribed by the angel of the Annunciation: *ecce concipies in utero et paries filium et vocabis nomen eius Iesum.*

Appendices

I. Metrical Schemes

The following symbols are used to indicate metrical (syllabic, not vowel) quantity and stress:

- — for a long syllable (whether long by nature or by position)
- ◡ for a short syllable (always short by nature)
- ◡̱ for a syllable which may be either long or short at the end of a verse (called *syllaba anceps*), and for syllables within a verse which may be either long or short
- ◡̱◡̱ for cases where a single long syllable or two shorts may occur in a verse
- ∧ for a pause created by the omission of an expected syllable (syncopation).
- ′ for the stress called *ictus* and indicating metrical or musical stress, not word accent; it normally falls on one syllable in each foot (but note the choriamb below) and is placed over the mark of quantity.

The Greeks and Romans normally paused slightly for breath at some point in speaking longer verses. This variable pause, called *caesura* (a "cutting") when it falls within a foot or *diaeresis* (Greek; a "tearing apart") when it comes between 2 feet, has not been indicated in the following patterns except for the fixed syncopated pause in the 2nd verse of the elegiac couplet (no. 2 below), which is shown by ‖ in place of |.

The following are the names and patterns of quantity of the metrical feet (or measures) used in the selections in Part II:

Dactyl	Anapaest	Spondee	Iamb	Trochee	Choriamb
ꞌ◡◡	◡◡ꞌ	ꞌ—	◡ꞌ	ꞌ◡	ꞌ◡◡ꞌ

The following are the names and patterns of quantity of the meters (metrical verses) used in the selections in Part II:

1. Dactylic hexameter; a verse of 6 dactylic feet:

   A spondee may be substituted for any foot except normally the 5th, where the rare presence of a spondee makes the verse "spondaic"; see 59 n. 13. The last (6th) foot is always a spondee or, with a final *syllaba anceps*, a trochee.

Used in selections 49, 55, 59 B, 60, 61, 64 B, 66, 69, 70 A and B, 77, 78, 79 B, 80, 84, 85, 88

2. Elegiac couplet or distich, consisting of a dactylic hexameter verse and a syncopated dactylic hexameter verse improperly called a pentameter because comprising two halves of two and a half hexameters each.

$$\text{–́ ⏖ | –́ ⏖ | –́ ⏖ | –́ ⏖ | –́ ⏑⏑ | –́ ⏓ |}$$
$$\text{–́ ⏖ | –́ ⏖ | –́ ∧ ‖ –́ ⏑⏑ | –́ ⏑⏑ | ⏓ ∧}$$

In the first half of the pentameter, a spondee may be substituted for either or both of the 2 dactyls; in the second half spondees are not allowed. The 3rd foot is always a single long syllable with a pause (syncopation) after it; the last (6th) foot is a single *syllaba anceps* (long or short), also with a pause after it.

Used in selections 51, 52, 54, 73 A, D, and F, 74 B, C, and D

3. Hendecasyllabic (i.e. comprising 11 syllables) or Phalaecian (from a Greek poet who employed it), containing 5 feet, basically trochaic but always with a dactyl in the 2nd foot:

$$\text{⏓ ⏓ | –́ ⏑⏑ | –́ ⏑ | –́⏑ | –́ ⏓ |}$$

The 1st foot is normally a spondee (see 73 n. 12B), but may be either a trochee or, rarely, an iamb (see 73 n. 36B); the last foot, with a final *syllaba anceps*, may be either a trochee or a spondee.

Used in selections 73 B and E, and 74 A

4. Choliambic ("limping" iambic) or scazon (also meaning "limping"), containing 6 feet, basically iambs; the last (6th) foot is either a trochee or, by *syllaba anceps*, a spondee and bears the ictus on the first, not the second, syllable. The conjunction of the final ictus of the 5th foot and the initial ictus of the 6th foot gives the verse its metrical "limp."

$$\text{⏓ –́ | ⏑ –́ | ⏓ –́ | ⏑ –́ | ⏑ –́ | –́ ⏓ |}$$

A spondee may be substituted for the iamb in the 1st or 3rd foot.
Used in selections 73 C and 74 E

5. Epodic couplet (distich) or iambic strophe, containing 2 verses, the first of which is an iambic trimeter (three pairs, or dipodies, of 2 iambic feet each), called in Lat. an iambic senarius (6 feet), and the second is an iambic dimeter (two pairs, or dipodies, of 2 iambic feet each):

$$\text{⏓ –́ | ⏑ –́ | ⏓ –́ | ⏑ –́ | ⏓ –́ | ⏑ –́ |}$$
$$\text{⏓ –́ | ⏑ –́ | ⏓ –́ | ⏑ –́ |}$$

A spondee may be substituted for the iamb in the 1st, 3rd, or 5th foot in the trimeter, and in the 1st or 3rd foot of the dimeter.

Used in selection 86 A

The following metrical schemes (6–10) as used by Horace are not divided into feet because it is uncertain how he regarded them. The descriptions are based on traditional analysis; recent metricians would divide on a choriambic base of ‿ ⏑⏑ ‿ with alterations of longs and shorts and other substitutions.

6. Alcaic strophe; apparently in the initial 2 verses basically iambic with the substitution of an anapaest; the 3rd verse iambic with an incomplete (syncopated) final foot; and in the 4th verse 2 dactyls and 2 trochees (or in the last foot a spondee):

   ◡ ⏌ ◡ ⏌ _ ⏌ ◡ ◡ ⏌ ◡ ◡
   ◡ ⏌ ◡ ⏌ _ ⏌ ◡ ◡ ⏌ ◡ ◡
       ◡ ⏌ ◡ ⏌ _ ⏌ ◡ ⏌ ◡
           ⏌ ◡ ◡ ⏌ ◡ ◡ ⏌ ◡ ⏌ ◡

Used in selection 86 B

7. Sapphic strophe; apparently in the initial 3 verses trochaic with the substitution of a dactyl in the 3rd foot (instead of in the 2nd as in the Hendecasyllabic, no. 3 above) and in the 4th verse a dactyl and a trochee (or spondee):

     ⏌ ◡ ⏌ _ ⏌ ◡ ◡ ⏌ ◡ ⏌ ◡
     ⏌ ◡ ⏌ _ ⏌ ◡ ◡ ⏌ ◡ ⏌ ◡
     ⏌ ◡ ⏌ _ ⏌ ◡ ◡ ⏌ ◡ ⏌ ◡
       ⏌ ◡ ◡ ⏌ ◡

Used in selection 87 C

8. Asclepiadic strophe; the initial 2 verses are lesser Asclepiadic, traditionally of 6 basically trochaic feet; see par. 10 below. The 3rd comprises a spondee, a dactyl, and a spondee (never a trochee); and the 4th a spondee, a dactyl, a trochee, and an incomplete (syncopated) trochee:

    ⏌ _ ⏌ ◡ ◡ ⏌ ⏌ ◡ ◡ ⏌ ◡ ◡
    ⏌ _ ⏌ ◡ ◡ ⏌ ⏌ ◡ ◡ ⏌ ◡ ◡
      ⏌ _ ⏌ ◡ ◡ ⏌ _
      ⏌ _ ⏌ ◡ ◡ ⏌ ◡ ◡

Used in selections 87 A and D

9. Greater Asclepiadic verse, traditionally regarded as a trochaic verse of 8 feet, with the substitution of a spondee in the 1st, of

dactyls in the 2nd, 4th, and 6th, and with syncopation after the 3rd, 5th, and 8th, where the stresses either adjoin or fall on the final syllable.

◡́ _ ◡́ ◡ ◡ ◡́ ◡́ ◡ ◡ ◡́ ◡́ ◡ ◡ ◡́ ◡ ◡̆

Used in selection 87 B

10. Lesser Asclepiadic verse, traditionally regarded as a trochaic verse of 6 feet, with the substitution of a spondee in the 1st, of dactyls in the 2nd and 4th, and with syncopation after the 3rd and 6th, where the stresses either adjoin or fall on the final syllable.

◡́ _ ◡́ ◡ ◡ ◡́ ◡́ ◡ ◡ ◡́ ◡ ◡̆

Used in selection 87 E

The terms Alcaic, Sapphic, and Asclepiadic derive from Greek poets who used these meters.

II. List of Sources

Authors and works have generally been abbreviated in accordance with the *Oxford Classical Dictionary* (ed. 1, 1949, pp. ix–xix; 2nd ed. in preparation). References are according to the subdivisions of the texts in the Loeb Classical Library except for texts not therein included. For full names, titles, and dates, consult the Index of Authors and Works following this list.

PART I

Selections 1–48: Prose

Sel.	*Sources*
1.	*Origo* 9.1, 4.
2.	*Origo* 13.1–4.
3.	*Origo* 13.5–7.
4.	*Liber* 1.
5.	*Liber* 9; 10.1; 8.5; 10.4–5.
6.	*Liber* 11; 12.
7.	*Liber* 21.
8.	*Liber* 23.5–9; 24.4; 23.10.
9 A.	*Liber* 35.1–7.
B.	*Liber* 40.
10.	Composed from *Liber* 42; Eutropius III 8.2; 9; 10.1.
11 A.	Composed from Cic. *Sest.* 142; *Off.* I 108; *Am.* 28.
B.	Livy XXI 4.3–9.
12.	*Liber* 49.
13.	Composed from Quint. XII 11.23; Cic. *Brut.* 65–66; Nepos XXIV (*Hist. Lat.*) 3; Pliny *Nat. Hist.* VIII 5.11.
14.	Cic. *Sen.* 32; 17–19; 38.
15 A.	Val. Max. IV 8.5.
B.	Vell. I 9.1, 3, 4, 5; 10.3–5.
16 A.	Composed from Vell. I 12.3–5; II 4.2–3; Livy XLIV 44.2.
B.	Composed from Cic. *Off.* I 116; *de Or.* II 154; Gellius VI 12.4; II 20.5; Vell. I 13.3.
17 A.	Sall. *Cat.* 9.1–3; 10.1–4, 6.
B.	Vell. II 1.1.
C.	Tac. *Hist.* II 38.1.
18.	Composed from Vell. II 2.1–3; 3.1–3; 4.4; Val. Max. III 2.17.
19.	Vell. II 6.1–4, 6–7; 7.3, 1.

Sel.	*Sources*
20 A.	Composed from Cic. *Off.* II 43; *Har. Resp.* 41; *Leg. Agr.* II 10; *Sest.* 103.
B.	Sall. *Iug.* 41.10–42.5.
21.	Sall. *Iug.* 63.1–2, 4–7; 64.1–5.
22.	Composed from Sall. *Iug.* 113.6–114; Vell. II 12.2–6.
23.	Composed from Florus II 6 (III 18) 1–5; Vell. II 15.1–2, 3; 16.4.
24.	Composed from Vell. II 18.1, 4; 19.1; Florus II 9 (III 21) 1, 6, 7.
25.	Composed from Vell. II 20.2–5; 22.1–5; 23.1, 3; 24.5; Florus II 9 (III 21) 10–11.
26.	Vell. II 25.1–3; 27.5; 28.2–3, 4.
27 A.	Cic. *Har. Resp.* 54.
B.	Composed from Cic. *Cat.* III 24; *Phil.* XI 1.1; *Att.* IX 10.3 (How, *Select Letters of Cic.* no. 53; from Formiae, March 18, 49).
C.	Sen. *Clem.* I 12.1–2.
28.	Composed from Vell. II 29.1; 30.1, 5, 6; Florus II 11 (III 23) 2, 6–8; II 10 (III 22) 2, 6, 9; Gellius XIV 7.1–2.
29.	Cic. *Leg. Man.* 28; 31; 32; 33; 34; 35.
30.	Cic. *Leg. Man.* 60–62.
31.	Cic. *Planc.* 63(end)–66.
32 A.	Cic. *Fam.* V 7.1–3 (How no. 3; from Rome, April/June 62).
B.	Cic. *Att.* I 19.6(end)–7, 10 (How no. 7; from Rome, March 15, 60).

Sel.	Sources
33.	Composed from Vell. II 41.1, 2; Suet. *Iul.* 7.1; 45.1; 50; 52.1–2; 53; 71; 72; 73.
34 A.	Cic. *Mur.* 60; 61; 62; 64; 65.
B.	Sall. *Cat.* 53.6–54.
35 A.	Vell. II 44.1–3.
B.	Cic. *Att.* II 3.3–4 (not in How; from Tusculum, December 60).
C.	Composed from Cic. *Att.* II 18.1, 2, 3 (How no. 10; from Rome, June/July 59); II 17.2 (not in How; from Formiae, May 59); II 21.3 (not in How; from Rome, July/October 59).
36 A.	Cic. *Marc.* 4; 5; 6; 8; 9.
B.	Vell. II 45.1–3.
C.	Cic. *Sest.* 49; 50.
37.	Cic. *Fam.* V 12.1, 2–4, 8, 9 (How no. 22; from Antium, May/June 56).
38 A.	Cic. *Fam.* VIII 14.2–3, 4 (How no. 40; Caelius from Rome, early August 50).
B.	Caesar *Bell. Civ.* I 4.4–5; 22.5.
39.	Composed from Vell. II 48.1, 5; 49.2, 3, 4; Suet. *Iul.* 30.1–5; 31.1, 2; 32.
40.	Caesar *Bell. Civ.* III 94.5–96.

Sel.	Sources
41.	Composed from Cic. *Fam.* VII 3.2 (How no. 64; from Rome, May 46); *Att.* XI 6.5 (How no. 60; from Brundisium, November 27, 48); Vell. II 53.1–3; Florus II 13 (IV 2) 70–73; Sen. *Dial.* IX (*Tranq. An.*) 16.1.
42 A.	Suet. *Iul.* 75.1, 4; 76.1; 78.1; 79.2.
B.	Cic. *Phil.* II 84; 85–87.
43 A.	Suet. *Iul.* 80.4; 82.1–3; 87.
B.	Cic. *Fam.* VI 15 (How no. 78; at Rome, March 15?, 44); *Att.* XIV 4 (not in How; from Lanuvium, April 9, 44).
44.	Sen. Rh. *Suas.* VI 17; 22 (from Livy's lost bk. CXX).
45.	Composed from Vell. II 69.5, 6; 70; 72.1–2; 74.1; Suet. *Aug.* 10.1; 13.1, 3.
46.	Composed from Eutropius VII 7.2; Vell. II 82.4; 85.1, 3; 87.1, 2; 88.1; Suet. *Aug.* 17.2, 3, 4; Florus II 21 (IV 11) 1–3, 4, 9–11.
47 A.	Aug. *Mon. Anc.* (*Res Gestae*; ed. J. Gagé) (I) 1.1, 3; 2; 3.1–2; 6.1–2; (VI) 34–35.1; 35.2.
B.	Vell. II 89.1–5.
48.	Tac. *Ann.* I 1–2; 3.6–7.

PART II

Selections 49–90: Prose and Verse

Sel.	Sources
49.	Ovid *Met.* XIV 447–455, 568–574 (16 verses).
50.	Composed from late descriptions of Rome given by G. Lugli in *Fontes ad topographiam veteris urbis Romae pertinentes* I pp. 5–6.
51.	Ovid *Fasti* IV 809–826 (18 verses).
52.	Ovid *Fasti* IV 827–848 (22 verses).
53.	*Liber* 7.1–8; 15–18.
54.	Ovid *Fasti* VI 587–592, 595–610 (22 verses).
55.	Vergil *Aen.* VIII 626–634, 646–650, 652–653, 655–662 (24 verses).
56.	Livy VI 42.2–4, 7, 9–12.
57.	Composed from Livy IX 29.5–8; Cic. *Sen.* 15–16; 37.
58.	Livy XXX 30.1–3, 10–12, 15–16, 19.
59 A.	Livy XXXIX 51.7–10, 12.
B.	Juv. X 147–167 (21 verses).

Sel.	Sources
60.	Ennius *Ann.* (30 verses as numbered in the Loeb ed.):
A.	117–121 (p. 40) from Cic. *Rep.* I 61.
B.	186–193 (pp. 70, 72) from Cic. *Off.* I 38.
C.	258–259, 262–268 (pp. 96, 98) from Hor. *Sat.* I 4.60–61; Gellius XX 10.1.
D.	366–368 (p. 136) from Gellius VI 2.3.
E.	467 (p. 174) from St. Augustine *Civ. Dei* II 21.3, who quotes Cic. *Rep.* V 1.
F.	175–176 (p. 68) from Cic. *Div.* II 116.
G.	1 (p. 2) from Varro *Ling. Lat.* VII 19.
H.	108 (p. 36) from the late grammarian Priscian.

Sel.   Sources

I. 306 (p. 114) from the 2nd cent. grammarian Festus.

61. Ennius *Ann.* (16 verses as numbered in the Loeb ed.) paralleled with Vergil *Aen.* (15 verses) (in all, 31 verses).

A. 181–185 (p. 70) from Macrobius *Sat.* VI 2.27 paralleled with *Aen.* VI 179–182.

B. 360–362 (p. 132) from Cic. *Off.* I 84; also in Macrobius *Sat.* VI 1.23 paralleled with *Aen.* VI 845–846.

C. 409–416 (pp. 154, 156) from Macrobius *Sat.* VI 3.1 paralleled with *Aen.* IX 803–811; Macrobius also cites Homer *Iliad* XVI 102–111.

62. Composed from Quint. I 1.6; Cic. *Brut.* 211; 103–104; 125–126.

63. Sall. *Iug.* 84.1, 3, 5; 85.10, 13, 14, 17, 28–30; 86.1, 2, 4.

64 A. Cic. *Off.* III 79.

B. Lucan II 69–76, 77–83, 88–92 (19 verses).

65. Sall. *Iug.* 95–96.

66. Lucan II 139–142, 143–151, 160–162, 201–222 (36 verses).

67. Cic. *Verr.* II v 180–182.

68 A. Vell. II 33.1–4.

B. Cic. *Leg. Man.* 20–21.

69. Lucr. I 1–34, 38–43 (40 verses).

70 A. Lucr. III 894–911 (18 verses).

B. Lucr. III 1024–1035, 1042–1049 (20 verses).

71. Cic. *Cat.* I 1–3; 32–33.

72. Cic. *Cael.* 12–14.

73. Cat. 101 (A: 10 verses); 46 (B: 11 verses); 31 (C: 14 verses); 96 (D: 6 verses); 49 (E: 7 verses); 93 (F: 2 verses) (in all, 50 verses).

74. Cat. 5 (A: 13 verses); 70 (B: 4 verses); 85 (C: 2 verses); 72 (D: 8 verses); 8 (E: 19 verses) (in all, 46 verses).

75. Cic. *Prov. Cons.* 19, 32–35.

76. Cic. *Sest.* 96–98.

77. Lucan I 104–105, 111–116, 119–140, 143–151, 153–154 (41 verses).

Sel.   Sources

78. Lucan VIII 536–538, 559–560, 550–551, 538, 541–542, 561–567, 571–581, 582, 595–600, 610–619, 676–677, 701–703 (42 verses).

79 A. Composed from Quint. X 1.114; Tac. *Dial.* 21.5, 6; Cic. *Brut.* 262; Hirtius (Caesar) *Bell. Gall.* VIII praef. 4–5.

B. Quint. X 1.109–112; Juv. X 118–125 (8 verses).

80. Ovid *Met.* XV 762–764, 780–802, 843–846, 746–751, 760–761, 858–860 (39 verses).

81. Cic. *Fam.* XI 28.2–4, 5, 8 (How no. 88; Matius from Rome, end of August 44).

82 A. Vell. II 66.2–5.

B. St. Jerome *Ep.* 22.30 (Loeb ed. pp. 124–128).

C. Petrarch *Ep. ad Fam.* XXIV 2 middle (ed. A. F. Johnson p. 135 lines 47–57).

83 A. Vell. II 67.1–2.

B. *Laudatio funebris, dicta Laus Turiae* (ed. Durry & Gordon) col. I lines 27–28, 30–32; col. II lines 2a–8a, 12–16, 19; Gordon frag. lines 0–3; col. II lines 25, 54–55, 58–60, 69.

84. Vergil *Ecl.* I 1–13, 18–25, 42–46, 64–65, 66, 70–83 (42 verses).

85. Vergil *Ecl.* IV 1–12, 18–47 (42 verses).

86 A. Hor. *Epode* 1 (34 verses).

B. Hor. *Odes* I 37 (32 verses).

87. Hor. *Odes* I 5 (A: 16 verses); I 11 (B: 8 verses); I 38 (C: 8 verses); III 13 (D: 16 verses); III 30 (E: 16 verses) (in all, 64 verses).

88. Vergil *Aen.* VI 788–797, 801–807, 826–853 (45 verses).

89 A. *Vulgate Bible: Prophetia Isaiae* 7.14–15; 11.1–9.

B. *Vulgate Bible: Prophetia Michaeae* 5.2–5.

90. *Vulgate Bible: Evangelium secundum Lucam* 2.1–21.

III. Index of Authors and Works

Authors and works are listed under the abbreviation or name used in the List of Sources. This is usually the abbreviation and name under which they appear in the *Oxford Classical Dictionary* (*OCD*). Texts have been drawn (with some changes) from the editions in the Loeb Classical Library except where other editions are indicated below. Dates are B.C. except where A.D. is given. The selections in which the works are used are listed after each. The sources of the passages from Ennius in 60 and 61 are not listed here but may be found under Ennius in the preceding index.

Aug.: Augustus (63 B.C.–A.D. 14). By birth Gaius Octavius, he became in 44 (on adoption in Caesar's will) Gaius Julius Caesar Octavianus, and, after 27, Imperator Caesar Augustus:

Mon. Anc.: Monumentum Ancyranum (more properly, *Res Gestae*; composed between 2 B.C. and A.D. 14; cited from the ed. by J. Gagé, Paris, Les Belles Lettres, ed. 2, 1950; also available at the end of the Loeb *Velleius Paterculus*): 47 A.

Aulus Gellius: see Gellius.

Bible: see *Vulgate Bible*.

Caesar: Gaius Julius Caesar (102 or 100–44):

Bell. Civ.: Bellum Civile (written between 49 and 44): 38 B, 40.

Bell. Gall.: Bellum Gallicum (7 books probably completed by 52; the 8th added by Aulus Hirtius after 50): 79 A.

Cat.: Gaius Valerius Catullus (*ca.* 84–*ca.* 54):

Carmina: 73 A–F, 74 A–E.

Cic.: Marcus Tullius Cicero (106–43):

Essays

Am.: de Amicitia (written in 44): 11 A.

Brut.: Brutus (written in 46): 13, 62, 79 A.

Off.: de Officiis (written in 44): 11 A, 16 B, 20 A, 64 A.

de Or.: de Oratore (written in 55): 16 B.

Sen.: de Senectute (written in 44): 14, 57.

Letters

(Where these are included in W. W. How, *Cicero: Select Letters*, Oxford, Clarendon Press, 1925, the number is given in parentheses in the Index of Sources, where the dates are also given):

Att.: Epistulae ad Atticum: 27 B, 32 B, 35 B and C, 41, 43 B.

Fam.: Epistulae ad Familiares: 32 A, 37, 38 A, 41, 43 B, 81.

Speeches

Cael.: pro Caelio (delivered in 56): 72.

Cat. I: in Catilinam I (delivered in 63): 71.

Cat. III: in Catilinam III (delivered in 63): 27 B.

Har. Resp.: de Haruspicum Responso (delivered in 56): 20 A.

Leg. Agr.: de Lege Agraria (*contra Rullum*) II (delivered in 63): 20 A.

Leg. Man.: pro Lege Manilia (*de Imperio Gnaei Pompei*; delivered in 66): 29, 30, 68 B.

Marc.: pro Marcello (delivered in 46): 36 A.

Mur.: pro Murena (delivered in 63): 34 A.

Phil. II: *Oratio Philippica* II (written in November 44, but not delivered): 42 B.

Phil. XI: *Oratio Philippica* XI (delivered in 43): 27 B.

Planc.: pro Plancio (delivered in 54): 31.

Prov. Cons.: de Provinciis Consularibus (delivered in 56): 75.

Sest.: pro Sestio (delivered in 56): 11 A, 20 A, 36 C, 76.

Verr. II v: *in Verrem actio* II *oratio* v (*de Suppliciis*; delivered in 70): 67.

Cornelius Nepos: see Nepos.

Ennius: Quintus Ennius (239–169):

Ann.: Annales (verses numbered as by E. H. Warmington in the Loeb ed. of *Remains of Old Latin* I, at the end of which is a concordance with Vahlen's numbers; the sources are listed in the preceding list of sources): 60, 61.

Eutropius (late 4th cent. A.D.):

Breviarium (ed. F. Ruehl, Teubner, 1887): 10, 46.

Florus: Lucius Annaeus Florus (early 2nd cent. A.D.):

Epitomae de Tito Livio bellorum omnium annorum DCC Libri II: 23, 24, 25, 28, 41, 46.

Gellius: Aulus Gellius (*ca.* A.D. 123–*ca.* A.D. 165):

Noctes Atticae: 16 B, 28.

Hirtius: see Caesar *Bell. Gall.*

Hor.: Quintus Horatius Flaccus (Horace, 65–8):

Epodes (published in 30): 86 A.

Odes (*Carmina*; first 3 books published in 23): 86 B, 87 A–E.

Jerome (St.): Eusebius Hieronymus (*ca.* A.D. 345–*ca.* A.D. 420):

Ep.: Epistulae (Loeb ed. of *Select Letters of St. Jerome*): 82 B.

See also *Vulgate Bible*.

Juv.: Decimus Iunius Iuvenalis (Juvenal; *ca.* A.D. 50–*ca.* A.D. 127):

Satires (published in early 2nd cent. A.D.): 59 B, 79 B.

Laudatio funebris, dicta Laus Turiae (ed. M. Durry, Paris, Les Belles Lettres, 1950, with a supplementary fragment published by A. E. Gordon in the *American Journal of Archaeology* LIV, 1950, pp. 223–226): 83 B.

Liber: Liber de viris illustribus urbis Romae (author unknown; late 4th cent. A.D.; ed. F. Pichlmayr with *Sextus Aurelius Victor: de Caesaribus*, Teubner, ed. 2, 1961): 4, 5, 6, 7, 8, 9 A and B, 10, 12, 53.

Livy: Titus Livius (*ca.* 59 B.C.–*ca.* A.D. 17):

ab Urbe condita libri: 11 B, 16 A, 44 (from Sen. Rh.), 56, 57, 58, 59 A.

Lucan: Marcus Annaeus Lucanus (A.D. 39–A.D. 65):

Bellum Civile (or, *Pharsalia*): 64 B, 66, 77, 78.

Lucr.: Titus Lucretius Carus (*ca.* 94–*ca.* 55):

de Rerum Natura libri VI: 69, 70 A and B.

Lugli: G. Lugli, *Fontes ad topographiam veteris urbis Romae pertinentes* I (Rome, 1952): 50.

Nepos: Cornelius Nepos (in *OCD* under *Cornelius* 2; *ca.* 99–*ca.* 24):

Hist. Lat.: de Historicis Latinis (part of *de Viris Illustribus*, 2nd ed. published before 27): 13.

Origo: Origo gentis Romanae (author unknown; late 4th cent. A.D.; ed. F. Pichlmayr with *Sextus Aurelius Victor: de Caesaribus*, Teubner, ed. 2, 1961): 1, 2, 3.

Ovid: Publius Ovidius Naso (43 B.C.–*ca.* A.D. 17):

Fasti (mainly written after A.D. 8): 52, 54.

Met.: Metamorphoses (mainly written between 2 B.C. and A.D. 8): 49, 80.

Petrarch: Francesco Petrarca (A.D. 1304–A.D. 1374):

Ep. ad Fam.: Epistulae ad Familiares (as selected and edited by A. F. Johnson: *Francisci Petrarcae Epistulae Selectae*, Oxford, Clarendon Press, 1923): 82 C.

Pliny: Gaius Plinius Secundus (in *OCD* under *Pliny the Elder*; *ca.* A.D. 23–A.D. 79):

Nat. Hist.: Naturalis Historia (dedicated in A.D. 77): 13.

Quint.: Marcus Fabius Quintilianus (Quintilian; *ca.* A.D. 40–*ca.* A.D. 100):
    Institutio oratoria (published *ca.* A.D. 95): 13, 62, 79 A and B.
Sall.: Gaius Sallustius Crispus (Sallust; 86–*ca.* 34):
    Cat.: Bellum Catilinae (published *ca.* 43): 17 A, 34 B.
    Iug.: Bellum Iugurthinum (published *ca.* 41): 20 B, 21, 22, 63, 65.
Sen.: Lucius Annaeus Seneca (Seneca *Philosophus*, or, the Younger; *ca.* 5 B.C.–A.D. 65):
    Clem.: ad Neronem de Clementia (probably written *ca.* A.D. 55): 27 C.
    Dial. IX (*Tranq. An.*): *Dialogus* IX: *ad Serenum de Tranquillitate Animi* (date uncertain): 41.
Sen. Rh.: Lucius (or, Marcus) Annaeus Seneca (Seneca Rhetor or, the Elder; *ca.* 55 B.C.–*ca.* A.D. 40):
    Suas.: Suasoriae (written late in life): 44 (a passage quoted from Livy).
Suet.: Gaius Suetonius Tranquillus (*ca.* A.D. 69–*ca.* A.D. 140):
    From *de Vita Caesarum* (published *ca.* A.D. 121):
        Aug.: Divus Augustus: 45, 46.
        Iul.: Divus Iulius: 33, 39, 42 A, 43 A.
Tac.: Gaius (or, Publius) Cornelius Tacitus (*ca.* A.D. 55–*ca.* A.D. 130):
    Ann.: Annales (written *ca.* A.D. 115–130): 48.
    Dial.: Dialogus (date and attribution uncertain): 79 A.
    Hist.: Historiae (written *ca.* A.D. 100–115): 17 C.
Val. Max.: Valerius Maximus (early 1st cent. A.D.):
    Factorum ac Dictorum memorabilium libri (published *ca.* A.D. 31; ed. C. Kempf, Teubner, 1888): 15 A, 18.
Vell.: Gaius Velleius Paterculus (*ca.* 19 B.C.–*ca.* A.D. 32):
    Historiae Romanae (dedicated in A.D. 30): 15 B, 16 A and B, 17 B, 18, 19, 22, 23, 24, 25, 26, 28, 33, 35 A, 36 B, 39, 41, 45, 46, 47 B, 68 A, 82 A, 83 A.
Verg.: Publius Vergilius Maro (in *OCD* under *Virgil*; 70–19):
    Aen.: Aeneid (composed 29–19): 55, 88.
    Ecl.: Eclogues (composed 42–*ca.* 37): 84, 85.
Vulgate Bible (translated by St. Jerome *ca.* A.D. 400): 89 A and B, 90.

Vocabulary

NOTE TO THE VOCABULARY

The vocabulary includes not only words occurring in the selections but also some others from which these are derived or with which they might be confused. Proper names and proper adjectives are not listed in the vocabulary but explained in the notes. Vowel *u* and consonantal *v* are alphabetized separately but vowel and consonantal *i* together.

Verb forms differing markedly in spelling from their first principal part are entered separately with cross-references. For the fourth principal part of verbs, the perfect passive participle (called in the vocabulary "past part.") is given for verbs for which one is attested; otherwise, also only if attested, the supine in *-um* or the future participle in *-urus* appears. The writing out of principal parts has been reduced to the minimum necessary to show stem changes. In particular, for regular active verbs of the first and fourth conjugations only the first two principal parts are given; these verbs should be assumed to be complete. The lack of one or more principal parts in any verb is indicated by a dash or dashes.

For nouns, the genitive ending and an abbreviation of gender (m., f., or n.) are given. Adjectives identified as such by three or two terminations are not followed by "(adj.)," as are those of one termination, which also have their genitive terminations. Other parts of speech are followed by appropriate abbreviations in parentheses.

In the vocabulary, a long mark is placed over vowels long by nature, whether final in syllables or "hidden" by consonants following in the same syllable. Diphthongs and short vowels bear no marks. These are, of course, signs of vowel, not of syllabic, quantity. Where the presence or absence of long marks over vowels (particularly over those whose quantity is "hidden") and the indication by dashes of the lack of principal parts do not correspond to those given in Lewis' *Elementary Dictionary*, these differences reflect consultation of the *Thesaurus Linguae Latinae* and of A. Ernout and A. Meillet, *Dictionnaire étymologique de la langue latine* (ed. 4, 1959). The former has been published only through most of *I* and for part of *M*, and the latter affords full principal parts only for basic verbs, under which compounds and derivatives are listed.

References are given to notes in which words are translated or discussed; for many words occurring only once or twice which are not in the notes, references are given to the selection, paragraph (if any), and sentence (not line) or verse.

The abbreviation conj. refers to conjunction (not conjugation), neg. to negative; other obvious abbreviations are used as in the notes. In addition, the following single letters are employed:

f. = feminine	p. = paragraph (not page)
m. = masculine	s. = sentence
n. = neuter or, between numbers, note	w. = with
	v. = verse

Additions to the vocabulary are listed on page 461.

VOCABULARY

ā (before consonants), *ab* (before vowels and some consonants), *abs* (before *tē* and in some compounds) (prep. w. abl.): from, away from; by (followed by noun of agent); from the vicinity of (with a town: 1 n. 5c)

abdicō, -āre: disown; resign office before the term expires (w. *se* and abl.: 7 n. 15A, 57 n. 4B)

abdō, -ere, -idī, -itus: conceal, hide

abdūcō, -ere, -ūxī, -uctus: lead away, arrest; separate

abeō, -īre, -iī (or *-īvī:* 1 n. 4B), *-itūrus:* depart; turn out, end

abhinc (adv.): before now, ago, since

abhorreō, -ēre, -uī, —: shrink back from, abhor; be averse to

abiciō, -ere, -iēcī, -iectus: throw, throw (or cast) down (35 n. 21, 42 n. 17A)

abiēs, -etis (f.): silver fir tree (61 n. 3)

ablactō, -āre: wean (89 n. 19B)

ablātus, -a, -um: past part. of *auferō*

abnuō, -ere, -ī, -itūrus (or *-nutūrus):* refuse, deny

aboleō, -ēre, -ēvī, -itus: destroy, abolish

abrogō, -āre: repeal (a law); cancel (the office of a magistrate: 18 n. 7D)

abs: see *ā*

abscindō, -ere, -idī, -issus: tear away, cut off; divide

absēns, -entis (adj.): absent

absentia, -ae (f.): absence

absterreō, -ēre, -uī, -itus: frighten off; deter

abstinēns (pres. part. of *abstineō* as adj. w. dat.: 31 n. 6c): moderate

abstinentia, -ae (f.): abstinence, starvation; self-restraint

abstineō, -ēre, -uī, -entus: keep off, hold back; refrain from (w. *sē*)

abstrahō, -ere, -xī, -ctus: drag away, detach

abstulī: perf. of *auferō*

absum, abesse, āfuī, āfutūrus: be away from, be absent; be free from

absūmō, -ere, -psī, -ptus: use up, waste; destroy

abundē (adv.): abundantly, amply

abundō, -āre: overflow; abound in (in 61 n. 22A)

abūtor, -tī, -sus (dep. w. abl. 71 n. 1c, 81 n. 8A): use up, abuse

ac: see *atque*

acanthus, -ī (m.): acanthus (in 85 n. 13B)

accēdō, -ere, -essī, -essūrus: draw near to, approach, reach; be added (62 n. 15c, 66 n. 1c); *accēdit:* there is added (34 n. 2A); w. *quod* or *ut*: there is added the additional fact that (37 n. 24, 57 n. 6; in pass.: 26 n. 16A)

accendō, -ere -ī, -ēnsus: set on fire, inflame, excite

acceptus: past part. of *accipiō*

accidō, -ere, -ī, —: befall, happen, occur; *accidit ut* (w. subj.): it happens (happened) that

accīdō, -ere, -dī, -sus: cut down (or, back), prune (75 n. 14); impair

acciō, -īre: call, summon

accipiō, -ere, -ēpī, -eptus: accept (of a law, i.e. pass: 56 n. 11A, 68 n. 5A); receive (of news, i.e. hear: 11 n. 5c, 41 n. 17A, 57 n. 16c); submit to, endure

accipiter, -tris (m. and f.): the "seizer," i.e. hawk (86 n. 25A)

accīsus: past part. of *accīdō*

accommodō, -āre: fit, adapt

accumbō, -ere, -ubuī, -ubitus: lie down (or beside); recline at table

accurrō, -ere, -ī (or *-cucurrī*), *-rsus:* run to, hasten to

accūsātor, -ōris (m.): accuser, prosecutor

accūsō, -āre: accuse, bring a charge against in court

ācer, ācris, ācre: piercing, sharp, fierce, keen

acerbus, -a, -um: harsh, bitter; rude, unripe (75 n. 14)

acervus, -ī (m.): heap (27 B s. 3)

acētum, -ī (n.): vinegar (59 n. 15)

aciēs, -iēī (f.): line of battle; *aciē* (loc. abl.): in battle (26 n. 6A, and often); eye (lit. line of sight; 88 n. 2)

acinacēs, -is (m.): scimitar (46 n. 6c)

acq-: see *adq-*

āctiō, -ōnis (f.): action; lawsuit; (plur.): conduct (20 n. 14D)

āctum, -ī (n. as noun of past part. of *agō*): deed, accomplishment (59 n. 17); decree (often in plur. in either sense, as "achievements" in 15 B p. 2 s. 3)

āctus: past part. of *agō*

āctus, -ūs (m.): act, performance

acūmen, -inis (n.): sharpness, acuteness, keenness

acuō, -uere, -uī, -ūtus: whet, sharpen

acūtus, -a, -um (past part. of *acuō* as adj.): sharp, keen; intelligent

ad (prep. w. acc.): to, toward; to the neighborhood of (with towns: 3 n. 6A); against

adāctus, -a, -um: past part. of *adigō*

addīcō, -ere, -īxī, -ictus: give assent; sentence, adjudge

addō, -ere, -idī, -itus: add, join

addūcō, -ere, -ūxī, -uctus: lead to, bring to; induce

adēmptus: past part. of *adimō*

adeō (adv.): to such an extent, to this point, thus far; so much, so; indeed (emphatic: 85 n. 11B)

adeō, -īre, -iī (or *-īvī:* 1 n. 4B), *-itus:* go to, approach (w. direct object: 80 n. 2A), visit; attack

adeptus, -a, -um: past part. of *adipīscor*

adf-: also written *aff-*

adfectō, -āre: strive after, aspire to

adferō, adferre, attulī, adlātus: bring, take; report; bring forth

adficiō, -ere, -ēcī, -ectus: affect, do something to, work upon; treat; *aliquem dolōre, laetitiā:* cause someone pain, joy, etc.; i.e. punish (25 p. 2 s. 4)

adfīnitas, -ātis (f.): connection by marriage (35 A s. 5, in 38 n. 18)

adfirmō, -āre: make firm, confirm

adflīgō, -ere, -īxī, -īctus: strike down, overthrow, dash to the ground; damage

adfuī, adfutūrus: perf. and fut. part. of *adsum*

adg-: see *agg-*

adhibeō, -ēre, -uī, -itus: apply, bring to bear, employ; treat

adhūc (adv.): hitherto; up till now, as yet

adiciō, -ere, -iēcī, -iectus: throw (or fling) to; put near, add to

adigō, -ere, -ēgī, -āctus: drive, force

adimō, -ere, -ēmī, -ēmptus: take away, deprive of

adipīscor, -ī, adeptus (dep.): get, obtain, attain

aditus: past part. of *adeō*

aditus, -ūs (m.): approach (68 nn. 19B and 21B), access, way of approach (75 n. 10A)

adiūdicō, -āre: award; decide in one's favor

adiungō, -ere, -xī, -ctus: join to, add, fasten to; attach

adiuvō, -āre, -iūvī, -iūtus: help, support, sustain; i.e. increase (in 66 n. 22A)

adlābor, -ābi, -apsus (dep.): glide, flow toward

adlabōrō, -āre: toil at, add to with toil (87 n. 21D)

adlevō, āre: relieve, alleviate, lessen

adliciō, -ere, -ēxī, -ectus: attract, entice

administrātiō, -ōnis (f.): administration; aid

administrō, -āre: administer, manage, direct

admīrābilis, -e: worthy of admiration, wonderful; i.e. paradoxical (72 n. 10B)

admīrātiō, -ōnis (f.): admiration, wonder

admīrātor, -ōris (m.): admirer

admīror, -ārī, -ātus (dep.): wonder at; admire

admodum (adv.): very much; no more than, merely (18 n. 8C)

admoneō, -ēre, -uī, -itus: remind, bring to mind; warn, admonish; urge

admoveō, -ēre, -ōvī, -ōtus: move to, bring near; direct to

adolēscō, -ere, -ēvī, adultus: grow up, mature

adoptiō, -ōnis (f.): adoption

adorior, -īrī, -tus (dep.): attack; undertake; accost

adōrnō, -āre: provide, furnish; embellish

adp-: see *app-*

adq-: also written *acq-*

adquiēscō, -ere, -ēvī, -ētum: be still; acquiesce in, feel satisfaction in; feel relieved by (or, at; w. abl.)

adr-: also written *arr-*

adrigō, -ere, -ēxī, -ēctus: raise up; arouse

adripiō, -ere, -uī, -eptus: grasp (in 43 n. 9C), seize; seize upon, learn

adrogō, -āre: appropriate; add to

ads-: also written *ass-*

adsentiō, -īre, -ēnsī, -ēnsus: assent to, approve

adsequor, -ī, -cūtus (dep.): follow up, overtake (34 n. 21B), attain *adsideō, -ēre, -ēdī, -essum:* sit down by, i.e. nest (86 n. 9B)

adsiduē (or, rarely, n. abl. sing., *adsiduō;* adv.): constantly

adsiduitās, -ātis (f.): constant attention, persistence

adsimulō, -āre: make (something) like (something else), imitate; pretend, simulate (72 p. 3 s. 1)

adst-: see *ast-*

adsuēfaciō, -ere, -ēcī, -actus: habituate, accustom, train

adsuēsco, -ere, -ēvī, -ētus: accustom, make familiar; be accustomed to

adsum, -esse, -fuī, -futūrus: be here, be present; attend, aid

adsūmō, -ere, -psī, -ptus: take up; obtain in addition

adt-: see *att-*

adūlātiō, -ōnis (f.): flattery, cringing courtesy

adulēscēns, -entis (m. and f.): young man, girl

adulēscentia, -ae (f.): youth

adulēscentulus, -ī (m.): youngster, very young man

adulter, -era, -erum (adj.): adulterous, unchaste; as substantive (m. and f.): adulterer, adulteress

adultus: past part. of *adolēscō*

adumbrō, -āre: sketch in outline; represent vaguely

adundō, -āre: come as a wave, roll in upon (an emendation in 61 n. 22A)

adurgeō, -ēre, —, —: press closely, pursue closely

advehō, -ere, -xī, -ctus: bring in, bring hither

advena, -ae (m. and f.): newcomer, stranger (in 2 n. 2A), foreigner

adveniō, -īre, -ēnī, -entum: come to, arrive at, reach

adventus, -ūs (m.): arrival (68 n. 21B), coming, approach

adversārius, -ī (m.): opponent, antagonist

adversor, -ārī, -ātus (dep.): resist, oppose

adversum (-vor-; n. acc. sing. of *adversus* as adv.; ending also *-us*): oppositely, toward; (prep. w. acc.): against, toward, facing

adversus, -a, -um (-vor-; past part. of *advertō* as adj.): opposite, hostile, adverse; in front (lit. turned toward, of wounds: 9 n. 4); (n. plur. as noun): disaster, misfortune; also *adversae (rēs)*

adversus (-vor-): = adversum

advertō (-vor-), -ere, -ī, -sus: turn toward; for *animum advertō* see *animadvertō*

advocātus, -ī (m. as noun of past part. of *advocō*): advocate, lawyer

advocō, -āre: call upon, summon, invoke

advolvō, -ere, -ī, -lūtus: roll toward

aedificium, -ī (n.): building, edifice

aedīlis, -is (m.): an aedile (i.e. a magistrate responsible for the care of markets, food supply, public works, etc.)

aedīlitās, -ātis (f.): the office of aedile (16 n. 1B)

aedis (or *-ēs), -is* (f.): temple; (plur.): house

aeger, -gra, -grum: ill

aemulus, -a, -um (w. dat.): rivaling, vying with; emulous of; (as noun with gen.): rival (17 nn. 7, 19D); follower (34 n. 4C)

aeneātor, -ōris (m.): trumpeter (39 n. 21A)

aequālis, -e: equal, comparable; of the same age

aequinoctiālis, -e: of or pertaining to the equinox (73 n. 12B)

aequitās, -ātis (f.): uniformity; equality, fairness; moderation; w. *animī:* equanimity

aequō, -āre: make equal or even, raze (w. dat.: 16 n. 7); to be equal to (w. dat.)

aequor, -ōris (n.): level surface (esp. of the sea; 69 n. 9); sea (66 n. 21B)

aequus, -a, -um: equal, fair

āēr, āĕris (m.): air, atmosphere (in 69 n. 12A, 77 n. 24, 80 n. 16D)

aerārium, -ī (n.): the public treasury

aerātus, -a, -um: fitted with bronze

aeripēs, -edis (adj.): brazen-footed (88 n. 9B)

āĕrius, -a, -um: of the air, aerial (69 n. 12A)

aerumna, -ae (f.): hardship, distress

aes, aeris (n.): copper, bronze (87 n. 33C); bronze plate (plur.: 61 n. 29A); bronze statue (88 n. 29B); money; *aes aliēnum:* debt

aestās, -ātis (f.): summer

aestimō, -āre: estimate (45 p. 2 s. 1), value (74 A v. 3)

aestuōsus, -a, -um: hot (73 n. 14)

aestus, -ūs (m.): heat, boiling; surge of sea (78 n. 10B), tide

aetās, -ātis (f.): age, period of life; i.e. generation, time (16 n. 11C)

aeternitās, -ātis (f.): eternity

aeternus, -a, -um: eternal, everlasting

aetherius, -a, -um: bright, heavenly, celestial

aevum, -ī (n.): never-ending time; lifetime, generation, period

aff-: see *adf-*

āfuī, āfutūrus: perf. and fut. part. of *absum*

ager, agrī (m.): field, land; territory (2 n. 2c, 28 n. 6c); *agrī cultūra* (f.): agriculture (when written as one word, the *-i-* is short)

agger, -eris (m.): heap, mound; earthwork, causeway

aggredior, -dī, -essus (dep.): advance toward, attack; attempt

agitō, -āre: arouse; put in violent motion, toss

āgmen, -inis (n.): line, column on march; *novissimum āgmen:* the rear guard

āgnōscō, -ere, -ōvī, -itus: recognize, identify

āgnus, -ī (m.): lamb

agō, -ere, ēgī, āctus: drive; do, carry on, accomplish (81 n. 17; compare *āctum* above); *āctum est:* it is accomplished (in 59 n. 17); *āctum esse:* to be done for (41 n. 20); discuss (81 n. 4A, 82 n. 22); pass (time; 5 n. 16B, 12 n. 16, 14 n. 1); *grātiās agere:* give thanks, thank; *causam agere:* plead a case

agrārius, -a, -um: pertaining to the land, agrarian

agrestis, -e: rural, of the country (84 v. 10), boorish

agricola, -ae (m.): farmer

agricultūra, -ae (f.): see *ager*

āiō (defective verb): say; say "yes," affirm

alacer, -cris, -cre: alert, eager, ready

alacritās, -ātis (f.): eagerness, alacrity

albus, -a, -um: white, light (e.g. in complexion: 73 n. 39)

ạlea, -ae (f.): a die for playing at dice (39 n. 23)

aliās (adv. from *alius*): otherwise, at other times (17 n. 11c, 28 n. 9B)

aliēnus, -a, -um: belonging to another; foreign; out of place, irrelevant

aliquamdiū (adv.): awhile, for some time

aliquandō (adv.): now and then, on certain occasions (as opposed to never); at some time; finally, at last

aliquantum, -ī (n.): a little, some, something, a good deal

aliquī, aliqua, aliquod (indefinite adj.) and *aliquis, aliquid* (indefinite pronoun): someone, something, some; anyone, anything, any

aliquō (adv.): to some place; somewhere, anywhere

aliquot (indeclinable adj.): some, a few; several

aliquotiēs (adv.): several times; at different times

aliter (adv.): otherwise, differently

alius, alia, aliud (pronoun and adj.): another, other; *aliī . . . aliī:* some . . . others; gen. usually *alterīus* and only occasionally *alīus,* dat. *aliī*

almus, -a, -um: nourishing, bountiful (epithet of Venus: 69 n. 3, 80 n. 15D)

alnus, -ī (f.): alder; alder-wood, i.e. a boat made thereof (78 n. 23A)

alō, -ere, -uī, -tus (or *-itus*): sustain, nourish; encourage

altāria, -ium (n. plur.): altars

alter, -era, -erum (pronoun and adj.): the other (of two: 10 n. 7B); the second; gen. *alterīus,* dat. *alterī*

altitūdō, -inis (f.): height, altitude

altus, -a, -um (adj.; distinct from the past part. of *alō*): high; deep; *altum, -ī* (n. as noun): i.e. the sea (44 n. 6, 70 n. 21c)

alveus, -ī (m.): hollow; hold of ship

amābilis, -e: lovable (87 A v. 10)

amāns, -antis (pres. part. of *amō*): fond, loving

amārus, -a, -um: bitter (70 n. 15A); i.e. severe (54 n. 14)

ambigō, -ere, —, —: waver, feel doubt; argue about

ambiguē (adv.): equivocally, ambiguously

ambiō, -īre, -iī (or *-īvī:* 1 n. 4B), *-itus:* go around or about; surround

ambitiō, -ōnis (f.): soliciting of votes (usually by lawful means); ambition

ambitiōsus, -a, -um: surrounding; ambitious

ambitus: past part. of *ambiō*

ambitus, -ūs (m.): going around; canvassing for votes (usually by unlawful means)

ambō, -ae, -ō (numeral used as adj. or noun; compare *duo*): both (of two taken together; contrast *uterque*)

āmēns, -entis (adj.; = *ā + mēns*): out of one's mind, mad

āmentia, -ae (f.): madness (46 s. 5)

amīca, -ae (f.): see *amīcus*

amiciō, -īre: wrap

amīcitia, -ae (f.): friendship (2 n. 6, 32 n. 14c); political friendship (38 n. 17A, 72 n. 11B); love (73 n. 31c)

amictus, -a, -um (past part. of *amiciō*): covered, veiled

amictus, -ūs (m.): a throwing around; style of dress; outer garment

amīcus, -a, -um (adj.): friendly; (commonly as a noun; m.): a friend; (f.): a mistress (74 n. 11c)

amittō, -ere, -īsī, -issus: send away; let go, lose

amnis, -is (m.): river

amō, -āre: love

amōmum, -ī (n.): an aromatic shrub (85 n. 15c)

amor, -ōris (m.): love (in 73 n. 31c); friendship (often political, as in 37 n. 13A, 38 n. 8A)

amplē (adv.): generously, abundantly

amplector, -ī, -xus (dep.): encircle, embrace; comprehend; discuss

amplexus, -ūs (m.): embrace; encirclement

amplius (adv.): more, further, in addition, besides

amplus, -a, -um: spacious, abundant, great

an (conj.): or (sometimes only the sign of a question, best omitted in translation)

anceps, -ipitis (adj.): two-headed; doubtful

ancilla, -ae (f.): maidservant

angelus, -ī (m.): messenger (90 n. 9A)

angor, -ōris (m.): suffocation; anguish

angustus, -a, -um: narrow, cramped; short; difficult

anhēlitus, -ūs (m.): quick breathing, panting (61 n. 35)

anima, -ae (f.): breeze; breath (78 n. 27B; i.e. soul (70 n. 24B, 80 n. 16E)

animadvertō (or, *animum advertō*; also *-vort-*), *-ere, -ī, -sus:* turn one's attention to, notice; punish (w. *in* and acc.)

animal, -ālis (n.): living being, animal

animāns, -antis (pres. part. of *animō* as adj.): living; (m. as noun): living being, animal

animō, -āre: give life to, enliven, animate

animus, -ī (m.): rational soul; reason, mind (19 n. 3B); spirit (21 n. 13c and in n. 16, 39 n. 3B); feeling (32 n. 11c, 67 n. 23A); *animum habēre:* have an intention, intend (in 18 n. 17A)

annālis, -is (m.): record, chronicle

annōna, -ae (f.): the year's produce; crop, grain; provision of grain by the state (48 n. 16B; compare 19 n. 7, 20 n. 11c, 42 pref.)

annus, -ī (m.): year

annuus, -a, -um (adj.): yearly (4 n. 1B)

ānser, -eris (m.): goose (8 s. 5, 55 v. 17)

ante (adv.): before, previously; (prep. w. acc.): before, in front of

anteā (adv.): formerly, once, aforetime

antehāc (adv.; for pronunciation see 57 n. 10B, 86 n. 18B): formerly, hitherto

antepōnō, -ere, -osuī, -ositus: place before; prefer (w. acc. and dat.)

antequam (or *ante . . . quam*; conj.): before

anteveniō, -īre, -ēnī, -entum: come before, anticipate; surpass

antiquitās, -ātis (f.): age, antiquity; early times

antīquitus (adv.): in former times, long ago

antīquus, -a, -um: former, ancient

antrum, -ī (n.): cave (55 n. 5B); grotto (84 n. 21A, 87 n. 2D)

ānulus, -ī (m.): signet ring (10 p. 2 s. 6)

aperiō, -īre, -uī, -tus: open, disclose

apertus, -a, -um (past part. of *aperiō* as adj.): open, uncovered

apparātus, -ūs (m.): preparation; implements, supplies; luxuries (68 n. 10B, 87 n. 18A)

appāreō, -ēre, -uī, -itūrus: appear, be evident

apparō, -āre: prepare, put in order

appellātiō, -ōnis (f.): name, title, appellation

appellō, -āre: name, call by name, address

appellō, -ere, -ulī, -ulsus: move to; bring a ship to land

appetō, -ere, -iī (or *-īvī:* 1 n. 4B), *-ītus:* seek, strive for, long for

apprehendō, -ere, -ī, -ēnsus: seize, take hold of

appropinquō, -āre: approach (w. *ad* and acc., or w. dat.)

aptus, -a, -um: fitted, appropriate; adapted, trained; *stellis aptus:* "studded" with stars (88 v. 10)

apud (prep. w. acc.): at, among; in (a person: 72 n. 4); with (a person: 81 n. 8E); at (the house of: 35 n. 8A, 43 n. 21c); in (a temple: 33 n. 6c); in (the works of: 43 n. 19B) *aqua, -ae* (f.): water

āra, -ae (f.): altar

arātor, -ōris (m.): ploughman (85 p. 5 v. 5)

arātrum, -ī (n.): plough (51 n. 11B)

arbitrium, -ī (n.): award (of a judge), decision, choice

arbitror, -ārī, -ātus (dep.): think, form a personal judgment

arbor, -ōris (f.): tree

arbustum, -ī (n. as noun of adj. *arbustus, -a, -um:* wooded): grove (sing. in 61 n. 7, but commonly plur. as in 61 n. 1B, 85 n. 3B)

arca, -ae (f.): chest, box (9 B last s.); sarcophagus (10 last s.)

arceō, -ēre, -uī, —: confine; keep at a distance

arcus, -ūs (m.): bow (88 n. 9E)

ārdeō, -ēre, ārsī, ārsum: be on fire; burn with desire, be eager

arduus, -a, -um: difficult; *ardua* (n. plur. as noun): difficulty, tribulation

ārea, -ae (f.): ground, space, court, area

arēna: = harēna

argenteus, -a, -um: of silver (in 55 n. 14)

argentum, -ī (n.): silver

arguō, -uere, -uī, -ūtus: declare; discuss; accuse

argūtus, -a, -um (past part. of *arguō* as noun): expressive; witty; crafty

ariĕs, -etis (m.): ram (85 n. 28C)

arista, -ae (f.): grain stalk, ear of corn (85 p. 4 v. 3)

arma, -ōrum (n. plur.): weapons, arms, armor

armātus, -a, -um (past part. of *armō*): armed, equipped; (m. as noun): armed man, soldier (58 n. 1B)

armentum, -ī (n.): herd

armipotēns, -entis: powerful in arms, warlike (epithet of Mars: 69 n. 25; of Achilles: 88 n. 22B)

armō, -āre: arm, equip; strengthen

arō, -āre: plough, cultivate

arr-: see *adr-*

ars, artis (f.): art; skill; (plur.): qualities (16 n. 11A); tricks (65 n. 26B); *optimae artēs:* culture; *bonae artēs:* good moral habits (17 n. 14)

artus, -a, -um: fitted; close (of a clinging vine: 87 n. 22B); dense; narrow

artūs, -uum (m. plur.): joints; limbs

arvum, -ī (n.): ploughed field, land under cultivation

arx, arcis (f.): citadel (in 24 n. 8, 55 n. 12D)

ās, assis (m.): as (a small Roman copper coin: 74 n. 2B)

ascendō, -ere, -ī, -ēnsus: go up, ascend

aspectus, -ūs (m.): sight, view; aspect, appearance

asper, -era, -erum: rough, harsh; hard, difficult; *aspera, -ōrum* (n. plur. as a noun): adversity, "rough going"

asperitās, -ātis (f.): roughness, unevenness; harshness, fierceness

āspernor, -ārī, -ātus (dep.): spurn, reject

aspiciō, -ere, -exī, -ectus: look at; consider

aspis, -idis (f.): asp (46 p. 3 s. 6)

ass-: see *ads-*

astringō, -ere, -nxī, -ictus: draw tight, bind fast; put under obligation

astrum, -ī (n.): star

astūtē (adv.): craftily

at (conj.): but; at least

āter, ātra, ātrum: black; dark (e.g. of complexion: 73 n. 39); gloomy

atque or *ac* (conj.): and, as well as, together with, what is more; than (after a comparative); *īdem atque:* same as; *simul ac:* as soon as (69 n. 10A); *proinde ac:* just as (70 n. 26A, 81 n. 3A); *aequē ac:* just as much as (81 n. 11B)

atrōx, -ōcis: savage, cruel, harsh

att-: also written *adt-*

atterō, -ere, -trīvī, -trītus: rub against, wear away; weaken, diminish

attineō, -ēre, -uī, -entus: hold on to; pertain to

attingō, -ere, -igī, -āctus: touch, seize; arrive at, attain to

attollō, -ere, —, —: lift up; exalt

attonō, -āre, -uī, -itus: thunder at; stun, terrify

attulī: perf. of *adferō*

auctor, -ōris (m.): author; producer (81 n. 16A), father; promoter (16 n. 13A); confirmer (in 56 n. 13B)

auctōritās, -ātis (f.): influence (57 n. 19), prestige (47 n. 14); right of confirmation (in 56 n. 13B)

auctus, -a, -um: past part. of *augeō*

audācia, -ae (f.): boldness, courage

audāx, -ācis (adj.): bold

audeō, -ēre, ausus sum (semi-dep.): dare, be bold

audiō, -īre: hear, listen to; *dictō audiēns:* i.e. obedient (w. dat.: 53 n. 3B)

audītus, -ūs (m.): hearing
auferō, auferre, abstulī, ablātus: carry off, remove, steal
augeō, -ēre, auxī, auctus: enlarge, augment; honor, enrich (14 n. 7B, 33 n. 19B, 48 n. 20).
augur, -uris (m.): augur, interpreter of omens (in 52 n. 3)
augurium, -ī (n.): augury; omen (4 n. 8, 52 nn. 3 and 6)
augurius, -a, -um (adj.): of augury, augural (*iūs augurium* in 14 n. 15)
auguror, -ārī, -ātus (dep.): predict; suppose
aura, -ae (f.): breeze, air; i.e. favor (77 n. 18, 87 n. 7B)
aurātus, -a, -um: covered with gold, gilded (55 n. 14)
aureus, -a, -um: golden, of gold (55 n. 17A, 87 n. 6)
aurīga, -ae (m.): charioteer (54 v. 17)
auris, -is (f.): ear
aurum, -ī (n.): gold
auspex, -icis (m. and f.): augur, soothsayer (52 n. 3)
auspicium, -ī (n.): divination from birds, auspice (in 52 n. 3, 71 n. 16C, 76 n. 22B)
ausus, -a, -um: past part. of *audeō*
aut (conj.): or; *aut . . . aut:* either . . . or
autem (conj.): but; however; now; moreover
auxī: perf. of *augeō*
auxilium, -ī (n.): help, aid
avāritia, -ae (f.): greed, avarice (17 n. 2)
avārus, -a, -um: greedy, miserly (86 n. 15B)
avē (imperative of *aveō*): hail!
avēna, -ae (f.): wild oat; oaten pipe (84 n. 2D)
aveō, -ēre, —, —: long for, crave
āvertō, -ere, -ī, -sus: avert, turn away (43 n. 8B); (pass.): be alienated from
avidus, -a, -um: desirous, eager, greedy
avis, -is (f.): bird
avītus, -a, -um: of one's grandfather, ancestral
āvocō, -āre: call away, call off; divert, remove
avunculus, -ī (m.): maternal uncle; great-uncle (45 n. 1B)
avus, -ī (m.): grandfather
axis, -is (m.): axis, pole of the heavens; i.e. vault of heaven (88 n. 3E)

baccar, -aris (n.): foxglove (in 85 n. 13B)

baculum, -ī (n.): staff; scepter (46 n. 6A)
barbarus, -a, -um: foreign, barbarous; (m. as noun): barbarian, i.e. soldier (84 n. 18)
bāsiō, -āre: kiss
bāsium, -ī (n.): kiss (74 n. 4B)
beātus, -a, -um: blessed, fortunate; i.e. rich (in 34 n. 15, 76 n. 18B)
bellātor, -ōris (m.): warrior
bellicōsus, -a, -um: warlike
bellicus, -a, -um: of war, military
belligerō, -āre: wage war (60 B v. 2)
bellipotēns, -entis: mighty in war (60 n. 26B)
bellō, -āre: wage war
bellum, -ī (n.): war; *bellum gerere:* wage war (9 n. 1C); *bellum indīcere:* declare war on (w. dat.); *bellum cōnficere* (22 n. 4, 29 nn. 7B, 17A) or *patrāre* (28 n. 19A): to finish a war (successfully)
bellus, -a, -um: pretty, handsome (74 n. 25)
bēlua, -ae (f.): wild beast (59 n. 21A)
bene (adv.): well
beneficium, -ī (n.): kind deed, service, favor
benevolentia, -ae (f.): good will
benīgnitās, -ātis (f.): kindness, friendliness, courtesy
benīgnus, -a, -um: kindly, friendly, favorable
bibliothēca, -ae (f.): library (82 B s. 1)
bibō, -ere, -ī, —: drink
biennium, -ī (n.): period of two years
bimaris, -e: between two seas (78 n. 10B)
birēmis, -e (adj.): two-oared; (f. as noun, w. *nāvis* understood): a two-oared boat (78 n. 8B)
bis (adv.): twice (84 n. 13C); twofold
blandus, -a, -um: flattering, seductive, agreeable
bonus, -a, -um: good; *bonus, -ī* (m. as noun): a good man (20 n. 17A), in plur.: good (i.e. right-minded) people or conservatives (18 n. 5C, 20 n. 5B, in 65 n. 24); *bonum, -ī* (n. as noun): the good (philosophically): 17 n. 3; compare *prō bonō pūblicō*), in plur.: goods (i.e. property: 26 n. 16B); (comp.) *melior;* (sup.) *optimus*
bōs, bovis (m. and f.): ox, bull, cow (in 51 n. 17)
bracchium, -ī (n.): forearm, arm (in 43 n. 9A)
brevis, -e: short, brief, small; *brevī* (abl. w. *tempore* understood as adv.): in a

little while, soon (9 n. 6B); briefly

breviter (adv.): briefly, concisely

būbō, -ōnis (m.): owl (80 n. 7C)

būstum, -ī (n.): funeral pyre (70 n. 12A)

būtyrum, -ī (n.): butter, curds (89 n. 4B)

cachinnus, -ī (m.): laughter (73 n. 28)

cacūmen, -inis (n.): extremity, summit

cadāver, -eris (n.): corpse

cadō, -ere, cecidī, cāsūrus: fall, fall down (i.e. politically: 27 n. 3B); fall in battle, fall dead (in 66 n. 10A)

caecus, -a, -um: blind; directionless (44 n. 7B); hidden

caedēs, -is (f.): slaughter

caedō, -ere, cecīdī, caesus: cut, cut down; kill (8 n. 5B, and often); beat, cudgel

caelestis, -e: heavenly, from heaven; divine

caelifer, -era, -erum: supporting the heavens (88 n. 7B)

caelum, -ī (n.): sky, heaven; climate

caeruleus (or *caerulus:* 80 n. 6A), *-a, -um:* sky-blue (66 n. 24C)

caesariēs, -ēī (f.): hair, locks (55 v. 21)

caespes, -itis (m.): turf (in 40 n. 16A)

caesus: past part. of *caedō*

calamister, -trī (m.): curling iron (in 79 n. 11)

calamitās, -ātis (f.): misfortune, calamity

calamitōsus, -a, -um: ruinous; (m. as noun): ruined man (41 n. 8)

calamus, -ī (m.): reed; reed pipe (84 nn. 2D and 6F)

callidus, -a, -um: shrewd, skillful; crafty

calor, -ōris (m.): heat, warmth

calvitium, -ī (n.): baldness (33 end of 2nd p.)

calx, calcis (f.): lime (in 25 n. 10B)

campus, -ī (m.): field, plain

candeō, -ēre, -uī, —: be brilliantly white, shine (in 86 n. 14A)

candidus, -a, -um: white, shining; beautiful; clear; sincere

canis, -is (m. and f.): dog

canō, -ere, cecinī, cantum: sing (in 85 n. 2B)

cantus, -ūs (m.): song; singing

capella, -ae (f.): she-goat (84 n. 8B)

caper, caprī (m.): goat

capessō, -ere, -iī (or *-īvī:* 1 n. 4B), *-itūrus:* seize eagerly, snatch at; strive to reach; take up, undertake

capiō, -ere, cēpī, captus: take, capture; get; contain (59 n. 9A, in 77 n. 2); *cōnsilium capere:* see *cōnsilium*

capitulātim (adv.): by headings, summarily

captīvus, -ī (m.): captive

captō, -āre: snatch at, chase, strive for, catch

captus: past part. of *capiō*

caput, -itis (n.): head; i.e. life (63 n. 16, 76 n. 21B); lobe (of a liver: 80 n. 10C)

carcer, -eris (m.): prison (9 B s. 4, 24 p. 3 s. 3)

careō, -ēre, -uī, -itūrus: be without, be deprived of, lack (w. abl.)

carīna, -ae (f.): keel; i.e. ship (78 n. 9C)

cāritās, -ātis (f.): esteem, affection; dearness (i.e. high price: 31 n. 5B)

carmen, -inis (n.): song; poem, poetry (57 n. 13C, 87 n. 41C); incantation

carō, carnis (f.): flesh

carpentum, -ī (n.): two-wheeled cart (53 n. 13B, 54 n. 12A)

carpō, -ere, -psī, -ptus: pluck, take; i.e. enjoy (87 n. 16A)

cārus, -a, -um: dear, precious

cassus, -a, -um: empty; vain (70 B last v.)

castanea, -ae (f.): chestnut tree; chestnut (84 v. 40)

castrō, -āre: cut off (82 n. 8B)

castrum, -ī (n.): fort; *castra, -ōrum* (plur.): military camp

castus, -a, -um: chaste; guiltless

cāsus, -ūs (m.): fall, downfall, destruction; chance happening; accident

catēna, -ae (f.): chain

caterva, -ae (f.): crowd, troop

catulus, -ī (m.): puppy (84 v. 18); young of any animal (89 A line 23)

caupōnor, -ārī, -ātus sum (dep.): barter (60 n. 7A)

causa, -ae (f.): cause, reason; occasion, opportunity; lawsuit (14 p. 3 s. 1, 37 n. 25A, 88 n. 31A); *causā* (w. gen.): for the sake of, for the purpose of

causidicus, -ī (m.): pleader at law

caveō, -ēre, cāvī, cautus: be cautious, be on one's guard against (w. acc.); care for, protect (w. dat.: 39 s. 4)

caverna, -ae (f.): cave; den (89 n. 19A)

cavus, -a, -um: hollow (61 n. 28C); concave

cecidī: perf. of *cadō* (27 n. 3B, 78 n. 4A, 80 n. 5)

cecīdī: perf. of *caedō*

cēdō, -ere, cessī, cessum: withdraw from (in 85 n. 24C), retreat, go away; fall to (66 n. 9); yield (78 n. 14), give way; comply with (w. dat.)

celeber, -bris, -bre: crowded, much visited; famous

celebrō, -āre: crowd; celebrate; make known; do frequently

celer, -eris, -ere: swift, rash

celeritās, -ātis (f.): speed

cella, -ae (f.): storeroom; sanctuary (12 n. 4)

cēlō, -āre: conceal; keep secret (11 A s. 3)

celsus, -a, -um: lofty

cēna, -ae (f.): dinner (i.e. the principal meal of the day, whether at noon or in the evening)

cēnseō, -ēre, -uī, -us: think, express a judgment or opinion (e.g. in the senate); list (or, rate: 63 n. 16)

centum (indeclinable numeral): a hundred; many, countless

centuria, -ae (f.): a century (originally probably comprising 100 men, but later more, as a voting group, in 53 n. 4, or fewer, as one of 60 units in a legion)

centuriō, -ōnis (m.): centurion (a noncommissioned officer commanding a century)

cernō, -ere, crēvī, crētus (rare): separate, distinguish; perceive; understand; decide, decree (i.e. the senate, in 18 n. 9)

certāmen, -minis (n.): struggle; decisive contest

certō, -āre: contend, combat

certus, -a, -um: certain; *certiōrem facere:* to inform; *certior fierī:* to be informed (43 n. 25)

cerva, -ae (f.): hind, deer (88 n. 9B); also m. *cervus, -ī:* a stag

cervix, -īcis (f.): neck (often including the shoulders or head)

cessō, -āre: stop, cease from; be idle (14 p. 2 s. 2); hesitate

cēterī, -ae, -a (as adj.): the remaining, the other; (as pronoun): the rest, the others; (m. or n. plur. as noun): everybody, everything else

cēterum (n. acc. sing. of *cēterī* used as adv.): otherwise, for the rest, furthermore; but, yet, on the other hand

cibus, -ī (m.): food, victuals

cicātrix, -īcis (f.): scar

cieō (or *ciō*), *-ēre, cīvī, citus:* arouse, stir up, agitate; excite

cinctōrium, -ī (n.): sword-belt; girdle (89 n. 12)

cinefactus, -a, -um (unique past part. of a verb not found: *cinefaciō*): turned to ashes (in 70 n. 12A)

cingō, -ere, -xī, -ctus: gird, encircle, surround

cingulum, -ī (n.): girdle, belt (89 n. 12)

cinis, -eris (m.; f. in 73 n. 4): ashes

circā (adv.): around, surrounding, nearby; (prep. w. acc., for *circum*):

circiter (adv.): about, approximately, not far from

circum (prep. w. acc.): around, about; (adv.): all round, round about

circumagō, -ere, -ēgi, -āctus: drive in a circle, turn around

circumcīdō, -ere, -dī, -sus: cut around, circumcise (90 n. 19A)

circumdō, -are, -edī, -atus: put around, surround

circumeō, -īre, -iī (or *-īvī*: 1 n. 4B), *-itus:* go around, travel around, visit, inspect

circumfluō, -ere, -xī, —: flow around; overflow (35 n. 22B)

circumfulgeō, -ēre, -sī, -sus: shine around (90 p. 2 s. 2)

circumfundō, -ere, -ūdī, -ūsus: pour around (in 69 n. 27A), flow around, surround; encompass

circumscrībō, -ere, -psī, -ptus: encircle; limit, hinder; draw up in writing

circumsistō, -ere, -stetī (or *-stitī*), —: stand around; surround

circumveniō, -īre, -ēnī, -entus: surround; oppress; cheat

citerior, -ius (comp. adj.): hither, nearer; (sup.) *citimus, -a, -um:* nearest

cito (archaic: *-ō*; adv.): quickly, soon; (comp.) *citius:* more quickly; sooner, rather

citō, -āre: set in rapid motion; excite; call forth

citrā (adv.): on this side; (prep. w. acc.): on this side of, within, before; except

citrō (adv.): to this side, hither; *ultrō citrōque:* back and forth, to and fro

cīvīlis, -e: civil, civic; polite, urbane; *iūs cīvīle:* law for Roman citizens (14 p. 3 s. 1)

cīvīliter: in the manner of a citizen

cīvis, -is (m. and f.): citizen

cīvitās, -ātis (f.): citizenship (19 n. 6B, 23 n. 3A); community of citizens, state (19 n. 3C); town (90 n. 4C) *clādēs, -is* (f.): disaster (i.e. misfortune; 25 n. 6A), harm

clāmō, -āre: shout aloud; proclaim

clāmor, -ōris (m.): shouting, outcry (15 n. 4); applause; hostile cry

clangor, -ōris (m.): noise, clang

clāreō, -ēre, —, —: be clear, shine; be illustrious

clārus, -a, -um: bright, shining; famous; manifest

classicum, -ī (n.): trumpet call to battle (in 39 n. 21B)

classis, -is (f.): class (i.e. a political division of the people: 53 s. 5); fleet (9 B s. 1)

claudō, -ere, -sī, -sus: close, shut in; restrict

clāvus, -ī (m.): nail (9 n. 19A)

clēmentia, -ae (f.): mercy

cliēns, -entis (m.): client (7 n. 7, 14 n. 6C, 59 n. 24A)

clientēla, -ae (f.): one's clients (28 n. 6D, 57 n. 17B)

clipeus (or *clupeus*), *-ī* (m.): round shield (47 n. 12A, 61 n. 26B)

clīvus, -ī (m.): slope; *clīvus Capitōlinus:* the road up to the Capitol (18 n. 14D)

clupeus: see *clipeus*

coāctus: past part. of *cogō*

cōdex, -icis (m.): book (82 B s. 6)

cōdicillī, -ōrum (m. plur.): small tablet; short note

coēgī: perf. of *cogō*

coeō, -īre, -iī (or *-īvī*: 1 n. 4B), *-itus:* go or come together, unite, ally oneself

coepī, -isse, -tus (defective; usually past rather than pres. in connotation): began, commenced

coetus, -ūs (m.): meeting; company (73 n. 17)

cōgitātiō, -ōnis (f.): thought, deliberation; opinion

cōgitō, -āre: think, ponder; plan, intend

cōgnātiō, -ōnis (f.): relationship

cognitus: past part. of *cōgnōscō*

cōgnōmen, -inis (n.): family name (as against gentile *nomen*)

cōgnōscō, -ere, -ōvī, -itus: learn (by inquiry), recognize; investigate

cōgō, -ere, coēgī, coāctus: bring together, collect; force, compel

cohors, cohortis (f.): cohort (a body of 400–600 soldiers, of which there were 10 in a legion)

cohortor, -ārī, -ātus (dep.): encourage; incite, exhort

coll-: also written *conl-*

collātus, -a, -um: past part. of *conferō*

collēctīcius, -a, -um: gathered together hastily (41 n. 5B)

collēga, -ae (m.): colleague (in a magistracy), associate

colligō, -ere, -ēgī, -ēctus: collect; acquire; deduce

collis, -is (m.): hill

collocō, -āre: set into place, arrange; erect; set right

colloquium, -ī (n.): conference, colloquy (or talk: 7 n. 11)

collum, -ī (n.): neck

colō, -ere, -uī, cultus: cultivate, care for (83 n. 6B); tend (or worship) (77 n. 25C); esteem; i.e. inhabit

colocāsia, -ōrum (n. plur.; a f. sing. is found): marsh lilies (in 85 n. 13B); Egyptian beans

colōnia, -ae (f.): colony, settlement

color, -ōris (m.): color

columba, -ae (f.): dove, pigeon

coma, -ae (f.): hair; leaves, foliage

comāns, -antis (adj.): hairy (of a comet: 80 n. 20C)

combibō, -ere, -ī, —: drink up (86 n. 29B), absorb

comedō, -ēsse (or *-edere*), *-ēdī, -ēsus* (or *-ēstus*): eat, devour

comes, -itis (m. and f.): companion

cōmis, -e: courteous, friendly, obliging

cōmitās, -ātis (f.): kindness, courtesy, friendliness

comitātus, -ūs (m.): retinue; crowd

comitiālis, -e: of an assembly; *comitiālis morbus:* i.e. epilepsy (33 n. 11A)

comitium, -ī (n.): place of assembly; (plur.): an assembly (of the people)

comitō, -āre: accompany

commemorō, -āre: call to mind; relate (15 n. 13C, 30 n. 5A, in 31 n. 18A)

commendō, -āre: entrust; recommend

commentārius, -ī (m.): memorandum (28 n. 23E); brief factual account (32 n. 19A, 79 n. 6A)

comminus (adv.): hand to hand, in close contest; close by

committō, -ere, -īsī, -issus: bring together, join; *proelium committere:* to join or begin battle (10 n. 6A); entrust something to someone (w. acc. and dat.)

commodō, -āre: accommodate, supply; please, be obliging

commodus, -a, -um: convenient; pleasant

commoveō, -ēre, -ōvī, -ōtus: move, excite, remove

commūnicō, -āre: share, communicate (w. *cum*+abl. of the person); share in

commūnis, -e: common; public

compāctus, -a, -um: past part. of *compingō*

comparātiō, -ōnis (f.): comparison

compāreō, -ēre, -uī, —: be evident, appear; be present, exist

comparō, -āre: prepare; establish; procure, purchase

compellō, -ere, -ulī, -ulsus: drive together, collect; compel, incite

compēscō, -ere, -uī, —: restrain, repress

compingō, -ere, -ēgī, -āctus: join together; confine

compleō, -ēre, -ēvī, -ētus: fill up; complete; satisfy

complūrēs, complūra (or *complūria):* several; very many

compōnō, -ere, -osuī, -ositus: put together, unite; compare; compose, construct, arrange; settle, pacify

compos, -potis (adj.): possessing fully (w. gen.: 44 n. 24c)

comprehendō, -ere, -ī, -ēnsus: seize, arrest; perceive; express

comprimō, -ere, -essī, -essus: press together; embrace (4 n. 4b); restrain; suppress

comprobō, -āre: approve; prove

concēdō, -ere, -essī, -essus: go away, retire (5 n. 15b); yield, concede, allow, consent

concelebrō, -āre: attend in numbers, frequent; fill (with offspring: 69 n. 5c); celebrate, honor

concertō, -āre: strive zealously; debate

concessī, -us: perf. and past part. of *concēdō*

concidō, -ere, -ī, — (from *con*+*cadō*): fall utterly, collapse; be slain

conciliō, -āre: bring together, conciliate; obtain; cause

concilium, -ī (n.): assembly (of the *plebs:* in 21 n. 11a, 76 n. 6); council

concipiō, -ere, -ēpī, -eptus: take, receive; perceive, comprehend; conceive (offspring: 69 v. 5; a wish: 47 n. 17a)

concitātiō, -ōnis (f.): excitement, violent passion; agitation

concitō, -āre: stir up; instigate

conclāmātiō, -ōnis (f.): shouting (27 C s. 3)

conclāmō, -āre: cry out together, shout

conclūdō, -ere, -sī, -sus: shut up, enclose; conclude, finish

concordia, -ae (f.): harmony, concord

concors, -cordis (adj.): agreeing, harmonious

concupīscō, -ere, -piī (or *-īvī:* 1 n. 4b), *-pītus:* desire

concurrō, -ere, -ī (or *-cucurrī*), *-rsum:* run together, run to the rescue

concursus, -ūs (m.): a running together; gathering; assault

condemnō, -āre: convict, condemn

condiciō, -ōnis (f.): condition, term (of an agreement: 9 n. 18, 26 n. 2, 38 n. 7a, 56 n. 14b); status (67 n. 5, 82 n. 10b)

conditor, -ōris (m.): founder; i.e. author (13 n. 1b)

condō, -ere, -idī, -itus: establish, found; store away, conceal; construct, compose

cōnferō, -ferre, -tulī, collātus (or *conl-):* bring together, compare (90 n. 17b); contribute; (w. *se*): betake oneself (35 n. 23, 40 nn. 2 and 6); *signa cōnferre:* bring battle flags together, i.e. join battle (41 n. 5a, 56 n. 8)

cōnfertus, -a, -um: packed close together, in close order

cōnficiō, -ere, -ēcī, -ectus: make ready, accomplish; *bellum cōnficere:* see *bellum; prōvinciās cōnficere:* establish provinces (29 n. 4); *exercitum cōnficere:* raise an army (30 n. 8b); *corpus cōnficere:* to compose a body (of writing: in 37 n. 15b); (pass.): be exhausted, be overcome; (past part.): exhausted, done in (40 n. 11b)

cōnfīdō, -ere, -īsus sum (semi-dep.): trust completely, rely on (w. dat.: in 40 n. 1b, 41 n. 3b)

cōnfīgo, -ere, -ixī, -ixus: fix, nail together; transfix, pierce (61 C v. 2)

cōnfīrmō, -āre: establish, strengthen, reassure; affirm, declare

cōnflātus, -a, -um: past part. of *cōnflō*

cōnflīgo, -ere, -xī, -ctus: strike together; struggle

cōnflō, -āre: blow up, kindle; fuse together (72 n. 7e)

cōnfluō, -uere, -uxī, —: flow together; come in crowds

cōnfodiō, -ere, -ōdī, -ossus: dig up; pierce, stab (43 A s. 5)

cōnfugiō, -ere, -ūgī, —: flee, take refuge

congerō, -ere, -essī, -estus: heap up (66 vv. 14, 23), collect

congressus, -ūs (m.): meeting, interview

cōniciō, -ere, -iēcī, -iectus: throw, throw together; unite; guess, conjecture

coniugium, -ī (n.): marriage

coniūnctiō, -ōnis (f.): union, agreement; partnership (35 B s. 3, 38 n. 8A)

coniungō, -ere, -iūnxī, -iūnctus: join together, connect; (past part.): related, intimate

coniūnx, -iugis (m. and f.): consort (husband or wife)

coniūrātiō, -ōnis (f.): conspiracy (71 s. 6)

coniūrō, -āre: take an oath together (5 n. 13B, 6 n. 16B)

conl-: see *coll-*

cōnor, -ārī, -ātus (dep.): attempt, endeavor, try

conquīrō, -ere, -sīvī, -sītus: seek for carefully, collect

cōnscelerātus, -a, -um: utterly wicked, depraved (72 n. 16A)

cōnscendō, -ere, -ī, -ēnsus: mount, ascend; embark

cōnscrībō, -ere, -īpsī, -īptus: levy, enroll; put together in writing; *patrēs cōnscriptī:* see *pater*

cōnsector, -ārī, -ātus (dep.): follow after, hunt down

cōnsecūtus: past part. of *cōnsequor*

cōnsēnsiō, -ōnis (f.): agreement; conspiracy

cōnsēnsus, -ūs (m.): a common feeling, agreement; conspiracy

cōnsentiō, -īre, -ēnsī, -ēnsus: agree together, make an agreement; unite; conspire

cōnsequor, -ī, -cūtus (dep.): follow upon; earn, gain

cōnserō, -ere, -ēvī, -itus: sow, plant (84 n. 19B)

cōnserō, -ere, -uī, -tus: bring together, join; *proelium cōnserere:* join battle (11 n. 12C)

cōnservātor, -ōris (m.): preserver

cōnservō, -āre: protect, preserve

cōnsīdō, -ere, -ēdī, -essum: sit down; subside (75 n. 11)

cōnsilium, -ī (n.; see 71 n. 13B): advice, counsel; plan; advisory body (i.e. the senate: 76 n. 6); wisdom; *cōnsilium capere:* to adopt a decision, decide (in 38 n. 9C); *eō cōnsiliō ut* (and subj.): with the intention of

cōnsistō, -ere, -stitī (39 n. 17A, 40 n. 21B, 80 n. 15C), *-stitus:* stand still, halt (39 n. 17A); place oneself (80 n. 15C), settle (88 n. 12B); be firm; consist in

cōnsōbrīnus, -ī (m.): cousin, cousin-german (5 n. 2A)

cōnsōlor, -ārī, -ātus (dep.): encourage, console

cōnspectus, -ūs (m.); sight, view; countenance

cōnspiciō, -ere, -exī, -ectus: get sight of, catch a glimpse of; gaze upon; perceive

cōnspīrātiō, -ōnis (f.): agreement; conspiracy

cōnspīrātus, -ī (m. as noun of past part. of *cōnspīrō*): conspirator

cōnspīrō, -āre: combine; plot together, conspire (43 n. 1A)

cōnstāns, -antis (pres. part. of *cōnstō* as adj.): firm, steadfast; persistent; faithful

cōnstantia, -ae (f.): constancy, firmness

cōnstat (or *cōnstitit*; pres. or perf. of *cōnstō*): it is (was) agreed, it is (was) evident (w. acc. + inf.: 15 n. 5A, and often)

cōnsternō, -ere, -strāvī, -strātus: bestrew (in 40 n. 16A); spread out

cōnstituō, -uere, -uī, -ūtus: set up, station; appoint, determine, decide; arbitrate, judge

cōnstitūtum, -ī (n. as noun of past part. of *cōnstituō*): agreement, compact

cōnstō, -āre, -itī, -atūrus: stand firm; be fixed (or agreed on: see *cōnstat* above); consist of (w. simple abl. or *ex* + abl.)

cōnstringō, -ere, -nxī, -ictus: bind, restrain

cōnsuēscō, -ere, -ēvī, -ētus: accustom, accustom oneself; (perf.): be accustomed, be in the habit of

cōnsuētūdō, -inis (f.): habit, custom; familiarity, companionship

cōnsul, -is (m.): consul (term for the two chief magistrates of Rome)

cōnsulāris, -e: of a consul, consular, of consular rank; (m. as a noun): ex-consul (44 p. 2 s. 5)

cōnsulātus, -ūs (m.): consulship (21 n. 11B); consul's term of office

cōnsulō, -ere, -uī, -tus: deliberate, consult (w. acc., for a magistrate consulting the senate: 28 last s.); decide on (65 n. 11C); act in the interests of (w. dat.)

cōnsultor, -ōris (m.): adviser; consulter

cōnsultum, -ī (n. as noun of past part. of *cōnsulō*): decree; *senātūs cōnsultum:* decree of the senate (30 n. 17A, and often); *s.c. ultimum:* a decree of the senate which authorized the consuls to protect the state (in 18 n. 9, and often)

cōnsummō, -āre: bring to completion, perfect

cōnsūmō, -ere, -psī, -ptus: take all at once, consume, waste, exhaust

contāgiō, -ōnis (f.): contact, contagion

contāminō, -āre: bring into contact, mingle; defile, stain

contemnō, -ere, -psī, -ptus: value little, despise, disregard

contemptor, -ōris (m.): despiser, disregarder (as adj.: 21 n. 16)

contendō, -ere, -ī, -tus: fight, contend; assert; strive; pursue; hasten

contentiō, -ōnis (f.): contest, dispute

contentus, -a, -um (past part. of *contineō* as adj.): satisfied, content (w. abl.)

conterō, -ere, -trīvī, -trītus: wear away; waste; destroy

conterreō, -ēre, -uī, -itus: frighten, subdue by terror

conticēscō, -ere, -ticuī, —: become silent

contineō, -ēre, -uī, -entus: keep together, keep in, contain; restrain; *sē continēre* (w. abl.): to remain on (or in)

contingō, -ere, -igī, -āctus: touch (64 n. 12 B), touch on; concern; occur

continuō, -āre: continue, extend; pass (time)

continuō (n. abl. sing. of *continuus* as adv.): immediately, forthwith

continuus, -a, -um: unbroken, uninterrupted

cōntiō, -ōnis (f.): meeting (of the people to hear discussion: 29 pref.); speech (at such a meeting: 15 B p. 2 s. 3, in 63 n. 5A)

cōntiōnor, -ārī, -ātus (dep.): address a meeting, harangue (42 n. 22B)

contrā (prep w. acc.): against; (adv.): on the other side (20 n. 9, 26 n. 15B, 33 n. 26)

contrahō, -ere, -xī, -ctus: draw together, collect, contract, make less

contrārius, -a, -um: contrary, hostile

contremō, -ere, —, —: tremble, quake

contribuō, -uere, -uī, -ūtus: enroll together (or, in: 25 n. 1c); contribute

contrucīdō, -āre: put to the sword (27 C s. 2)

contubernium, -ī (n.): sharing a tent with; i.e. comradeship (on military service: 5 n. 2c, 21 n. 23B)

contumēlia, -ae (f.): insult (38 B s. 2, 45 n. 21B), invective

conturbō, -āre: confuse, throw into disorder (74 n. 5B)

convellō, -ere, -ī, -ulsus (or *-ol-*): tear away, rend; tear to pieces, shatter

convenienter (adv.): suitably, consistently

conveniō, -īre, -ēnī, -entum: come together, meet; *convenit:* it is agreed upon

convertō (or *-vort-*), *-ere, -ī, -sus:* turn around, turn back; change, convert

convīctus, -ūs (m.): banquet

convīvium, -ī (n.): entertainment, banquet (5 n. 3B)

convocō, -āre: call together, summon

cōpia, -ae (f.): fullness, abundance, fluency (of style: 36 n. 1D); (plur.): resources, wealth (36 n. 5); supplies; troops (of soldiers: 1 s. 2, in 68 n. 15B)

cor, cordis (n.): heart (60 n. 23c)

cornū, -ūs (n.): horn; flank, wing (of an army: 45 s. 4)

corōna, -ae (f.): garland (87 n. 19); crown

corōnātus, -a, -um (past part. of *corōnō*): garlanded (42 B s. 2)

corōnō, -āre: wreathe, crown

corpus, -oris (n.): body; structure, mass, collection (of literary work: 37 n. 15c)

corripiō, -ere, -uī, -eptus: seize, carry off; reprove

corrumpō, -ere, -ūpī, -uptus: destroy, corrupt, seduce; spoil

coruscō, -āre, —, —: vibrate, brandish (in 55 n. 20A); gleam, flash

cotīdiē (adv.): daily, each day

crās (adv.): tomorrow (87 D v. 3)

crēber, -bra, -brum: thick, close, crowded; frequent, at short intervals; numerous

crēdō, -ere, -idī, -itus: believe, trust; be of the opinion, imagine

crēdulus, -a, -um: trustful, credulous (i.e. too much so: 87 nn. 6 and 16B)

cremō, -āre: burn

creō, -āre: create, make; elect (a magistrate: 5 n. 17B, and regularly)

crepitō, -āre, —, —: rattle, clash

crēscō, -ere, crēvī, crētus: grow, increase

crīmen, -inis (n.): accusation (46 n. 13, in 67 n. 16A)

crīminor, -ārī, -ātus (dep.): bring a charge against, accuse *croceus, -a, -um:* saffron, yellow (85 p. 5 v. 8)

crūdēlis, -e: cruel

crūdēlitās, -ātis (f.): cruelty, harshness

cruentus, -a, -um: bloody; bloodthirsty

cruor, -ōris (m.): blood; bloodshed

crūs, crūris (n.): leg (in 43 n. 11)

cubiculum, -ī (n.): bedchamber (5 s. 8)

culmen, -inis (n.): summit, roof; pinnacle (78 v. 41)

culpō, -āre: blame, reproach, complain of

culter, -trī (m.; also *cultrum, -ī,* n.): knife (5 s. 9)

cultus, -a, -um (past part. of *colō*): cultivated; polished, elegant

cultus, -ūs (m.): cultivation (of crops: 47 B s. 3, 85 n. 13A); care, attention; respect, worship; culture, manner of life (65 n. 4A); clothing, attire (46 n. 5c)

cum (conj.): when; whenever (w. indicative); since, because (w. subj.); although (w. subj.); *cum prīmum:* as soon as; *cum . . . tum:* not only . . . but also (21 n. 24, 42 n. 1, 72 n. 15)

cum (prep. w. abl.): with, together with (regularly placed after and attached to 1st and 2nd sing. and plur. personal pronouns)

cumulō, -āre: accumulate; overload

cūnābula, -ōrum (n. plur.): cradle (85 nn. 14A and c)

cunctātiō, -ōnis (f.): delay, hesitation

cunctor, -ārī, -ātus (dep.): delay, hesitate

cūnctus, -a, -um: all, entire, in a body

cuneus, -ī (m.): wedge (61 n. 10); wedge-shaped body of troops

cupiditās, -tātis (f.): desire, greed

cupīdō, -inis (m. or f.): desire (in 17 n. 12, and often), greed, cupidity

cupidus, -a, -um: desirous (72 n. 17c), avaricious (m. dat. sing. distinguishable from *cupīdō* by the long *-ī-*)

cupiō, -ere, -īvī, -ītus: long for, be eager for, desire; favor

cupressus, -ī (f.): cypress (84 n. 12)

cūr (adv.): why?

cūra, -ae (f.): care, worry; diligence; anxiety; loved object

cūrātor, -ōris (m.): overseer (47 n. 9), guardian

cūria, -ae (f.): the senate house (14 n. 6A, 47 n. 12B, 80 n. 14)

cūrō, -āre: take care of, administer; see to, have something done (w. acc. and gerundive); be anxious (87 n. 21A)

currō, -ere, cucurrī, cursum: run

cursus, -ūs (m.): a running, way; course (of action: 35 n. 13A); speed (17 n. 20B); *cursus honōrum:* sequence of magistracies (in 31 pref., compare 12 n. 10B)

curūlis, -e: of a chariot; *sella curūlis:* folding seat of a magistrate (8 n. 8B); *aedīlis curūlis:* a curule aedile (i.e. entitled to a curule seat and originally a patrician)

custōdia, -ae (f.): guard, protection, custody; (plur.): guard, sentinel, watch

custōdiō, -īre: guard, preserve (or keep: 90 n. 8A); hold captive

custōs, custōdis (m.): guard, protector; jailer

cytisus, -ī (m.): clover (84 n. 23)

daedalus, -a, -um: skillful; artfully contrived, intricate, variegated (69 n. 8B)

damnō, -āre: find guilty, condemn; blame

damnum, -ī (n.): harm, loss; fine

daps, dapis (f.): feast; sacrificial feast (86 n. 17A)

datus, -a, -um: past part. of *dō*

dē (prep. w. abl.): from, away from, down from; about, concerning

dēbellō, -āre: fight out, finish a war; subdue (88 n. 34c)

dēbeō, -ēre, -uī, -itus: owe; ought (w. inf.)

dēbilitō, -āre: enfeeble, debilitate; break up (in 87 n. 13B)

dēcēdō, -ere, -essī, -essum: go from, withdraw (31 n. 8B); disappear, die

decem (indeclinable cardinal numeral): ten

decemvir, -ī (m.): a decemvir (one of a commission of ten magistrates: 7 s. 1, 56 n. 2A)

decemvirālis, -e: of the decemvirs

deceō, -ēre, -uī, —: be seemly, befit; see *decet* below

dēcernō, -ere, -crēvī, -crētus: decree (especially used of the senate: 18 n. 9), resolve; decide, determine; decide by combat, contend

dēcertō, -āre: struggle fiercely, fight a decisive battle

dēceptus: past part. of *dēcipiō*

decet, decuit (impersonal pres. and perf. act. ind. 3rd pers. sing. of *deceō*): it becomes (became); it is (was) fitting *dēcidō, -ere, -dī, —* (from *dē + cadō*): fall down (15 A last s.) or, away; fall down dead; fail, perish

dēcīdō, -ere, -dī, -sus (from *dē + caedō*): cut off; decide, come to an agreement

decimus, -a, -um: tenth

dēcipiō, -ere, -ēpī, -eptus: ensnare, deceive

dēclāmātiō, -ōnis (f.): declamation (59 n. 29B)

dēclārō, -āre: reveal; declare; demonstrate

dēclīnō, -āre: turn away, deflect, let sink, decline (of age: 13 s. 5)

decor, -ōris (m.): adornment; grace, comeliness (some forms are likely to be confused with like ones of *decōrus*)

decōrus, -a, -um: suitable; adorned; comely

dēcrētum, -ī (n. as noun of past part. of *dēcernō*): decision, decree (especially of the senate; compare *cōnsultum*); resolve, plan

dēcrēvī: perf. of *dēcernō*

decumānus, -a, -um: of the tenth part; *decumāna porta:* the main gate of a Roman camp (in 40 n. 3)

decumus: = decimus (56 n. 1B)

dēcurrō, -ere, -cucurrī, -cursum: run down, hasten down; run over; march (of troops)

decus, -oris (n.): ornament, splendor (or glory: 85 n. 11C); moral dignity, worth (some forms like those of *decōrus* and *decor, -ōris,* may be distinguished by the short *-o-*)

dēdecet, -ēre, -uit, — (impersonal): it is unseemly, unsuitable

dēdecus, -oris (n.): disgrace

dēditiō, -ōnis (f.): surrender

dēdō, -ere, -idī, -itus: give up, abandon, surrender; dedicate

dēdūcō, -ere, -ūxī, -uctus: lead down (or away; as a prisoner: 22 s. 1, 86 nn. 31D and E); introduce (87 n. 41E); *dēdūcere nāvem:* launch a ship

dēfendō, -ere, -ī, -ēnsus: repel; defend

dēfēnsiō, -ōnis (f.): defending, defense

dēfēnsor, -ōris (m.): defender, protector, advocate

dēferō, -ferre, -tulī, -lātus: remove; report; confer (an office: 31 n. 8C, 42 n. 27B, 47 n. 10); *nōmen dēferre:* indict

dēficiō, -ere, -ēcī, -ectus: fail, desert, be wanting

dēfīniō, -īre: define, limit, determine

dēflectō, -ere, -exī, -exus: bend aside, divert; lead astray; deviate

dēfleō, -ēre, -ēvī, -ētus: weep over, mourn

dēfōrmis, -e: ill-formed, hideous; disgracing (78 n. 20C)

dēfōrmitās, -ātis (f.): ugliness, deformity; vileness

dēfōrmō, -āre: disfigure; dishonor

dēfuī, dēfutūrus: perf. and fut. part. of *dēsum*

dēgener, -eris (adj.): unworthy of one's ancestors, degenerate (78 v. 39)

dēgō, -ere, -ī, —: spend or pass (of time: 18 n. 15B)

dehinc: thereafter, thence

dēiciō, -ere, -iēcī, -iectus: throw down, hurl down, destroy; lay low, kill; disappoint

deinde or *dein* (adv.): thereupon, then, next (for pronunciation see 74 n. 4C)

dēlātus, -a, -um: past part. of *dēferō*

dēlectātiō, -ōnis (f.): delight, pleasure

dēlectō, -āre: delight, please; (pass.): take pleasure in (w. abl.)

dēlēctus: past part. of *dēligō*

dēlēgō, -āre: give in charge, assign, delegate

dēleō, -ēre, -ēvī, -ētus: delete, destroy

dēlīberātiō, -ōnis (f.): deliberation

dēlīberō, -āre: deliberate, take counsel; resolve, decide upon (86 n. 30)

dēliciae, -ārum (f. plur.): delight, pleasure, favorite, darling

dēlictum, -ī (n. as noun of past part. of *dēlinquō*): fault, offense

dēligō, -ere, -ēgī, -ēctus: pick out, choose

dēlinquō, -ere, -īquī, -ictus: fail, be wanting; do wrong, transgress

dēmēns, -entis (adj.; from *dē + mēns*): out of one's mind, insane (57 n. 11A, 86 n. 19C)

dēminuō, -uere, -uī, -ūtus: make smaller, diminish

dēminūtiō, -ōnis (f.): lessening, decrease

dēmissē (adv. from past part. of *dēmittō*): humbly, with humiliation (in 35 nn. 18A and B)

dēmittō, -ere, -īsī, -issus: let down, lower; depress, humble

dēmō, -ere, -psī, -ptus: take away

dēmum (adv.): at length, at last, finally

dēnegō, -āre: reject, deny

dēnique (adv.): then, thereupon; finally, at last; at least

dēnotō, -āre: point out, indicate

dēns, dentis (m.): tooth; tusk (in 13 n. 13)

dēnsus, -a, -um: close, crowded

dēnūntiō, -āre: announce; denounce

dēpellō, -ere, -ulī, -ulsus: drive away; remove

dēpendeō, -ēre, —, —: hang down

dependō, -ere, -ī, -ēnsus: pay, spend, expend

dēpōnō, -ere, -osuī, -ositus: lay aside, give up; entrust, deposit

dēportō, -āre: carry away; bring home

dēpōscō, -ere, -popōscī, —: demand, request

dēpositum, -ī (n. as noun of past part. of *dēpōnō*): deposit (64 n. 8c)

dēposuī: perf. of *dēpōnō*

dēprehendō, -ere, -ī, -ēnsus: seize upon, catch; surprise

dēprimō, -ere, -essī, -essus: press down, depress

dēprōmō, -ere, -psī, -ptus: draw forth, decant (wine: 86 n. 18c), take out

dēpūgnō, -āre: fight out, combat; quarrel

dērigō, -ere, -ēxī, -ēctus: lay straight; direct (often confused with *dīrigō*); aim; define, limit

dērigui (perf. of an unattested pres. *dērigescō:* 64 n. 10c): grew stiff

dēscendō, -ere, -ī, -ēnsus: go down; have recourse, resort

dēscrībō, -ere, -ipsī, -iptus: write down, enroll (90 n. 2c); describe; preside

dēscīscō, -ere, -ivī, -itum: leave, desert (17 n. 20c, and often)

descrīptiō, -ōnis (f.): enrollment; listing (in 90 n. 2c)

dēserō, -ere, -uī, -tus: desert, forsake

dēsertor, -ōris (m.): a deserter

dēsīderium, -ī (n.): longing (73 n. 30a, w. gen. in 83 n. 19a), desire; object of desire

dēsīderō, -āre: long for, desire; miss, feel need of (14 p. 1 near end); demand

dēsidia, -ae (f.): idleness, sloth (46 p. 3 s. 2)

dēsīgnō, -āre: mark out; elect or designate (for an office; of the office, in 28 n. 20b)

dēsiliō, -īre, -uī, -sultus: leap down, dismount

dēsinō, -ere, -sivī or *-siī* (both rare), *-situs:* cease, stop

dēsistō, -ere, -stitī, -stitus: cease, desist from

dēspērātiō, -ōnis (f.): hopelessness, despair

dēspērō, -āre: give up hope, despair of

dēspiciō, -ere, -exī, -ectus: look down upon; despise

dēspondeō, -ēre, -ī, -ōnsus: pledge, promise in marriage

dēstinō, -āre: make firm, determine (74 n. 28), appoint, destine (in 87 n. 27)

dēsum, -esse, -fuī, -futūrus: be absent, fail, be wanting, be lacking (w. dat.)

dēterreō, -ēre, -uī, -itus: frighten away; deter, prevent

dētrahō, -ere, -xī, -ctus: pull down; remove

dētrīmentum, -ī (n.): something worn away; damage, harm

dētulī: perf. of *dēferō*

deus, -ī (m.): god; nom. plur.: *deī, dii, dī* (13 n. 2b, 58 n. 15d); gen. plur.: *deōrum* or *deum* (11 n. 14b); dat. or abl. plur.: *deis, diīs,* or *dīs* (12 n. 15d, 60 n. 4b)

dēversōrium, -ī (n.): inn (90 n. 7d), guest room

dēvertō (-vort-), -ere, -ī, -sum: turn away; go to; digress

dēvincō, -ere, -īcī, -ictus: overcome, subdue completely (69 n. 26c)

dēvorō, -āre: devour (52 n. 14); suffer; accept eagerly

dexter, -tra, -trum: on the right; skillful; favorable; *dextra* (f. as noun w. *manus* understood: in 6 n. 13): right hand

dī: = deī (from *deus*)

diadēma, -atis (Greek n.): royal headband, diadem (42 n. 13c, 46 n. 6a)

diciō, -ōnis (f.): rule, authority

dīcō, -ere, dīxī, dictus: say, tell, speak; call, name, appoint (8 n. 10c, 56 n. 7c); foretell (88 n. 31d); *iūs dicere:* pronounce law (in 56 n. 15)

dictātor, -ōris (m.): dictator (8 n. 10b, in 26 n. 13a)

dictātūra, -ae (f.): dictatorship

dictitō, -āre: declare, assert repeatedly (81 n. 16b)

dictiō, -ōnis (f.): saying, speaking, declaring

dictum, -ī (n. as noun of past part. of *dīcō*): saying, assertion, remark; *dictō audīre:* obey (w. dat.: 53 n. 3b)

dictus: past part. of *dīcō*

didicī: perf. of *discō*

dīdūcō, -ere, -ūxī, -uctus: lead apart; open up

diēs, diēī (m.): day; (f.): (specific) day (12 n. 8B); *ad diem:* in time, promptly

differō, -erre, distulī, dīlātus: differ (intrans.); scatter; postpone (43 n. 6)

difficilis, -e (adj.): difficult, laborious, perilous

diffīdō, -ere, -īsus sum (semi-dep.): despair; distrust (w. dat.: 40 n. 1C)

diffugiō, -ere, -ūgī, —: flee in different directions, scatter, disperse

diffundo, -ere, -ūdī, -ūsus: pour forth, diffuse, scatter

dignātiō, -ōnis (f.): honor, rank

dignitās, -ātis (f.): dignity, rank, esteem, eminence (personal: 20 n. 3B, 25 n. 6C, 34 n. 13, 38 n. 16C; political: 19 n. 14C, 25 nn. 2A and B, 38 n. 21C; general: 76 n. 18C)

dignus, -a, -um: worthy, worthy of (w. abl.: in 21 n. 12B, and often)

dīgredior, -ī, -essus (dep.): depart, go aside, digress

diī, diīs: nom. plur. and dat. or abl. plur. of *deus*

diiungō: see *disiungō*

dīlātus: past part. of *differō*

dīlēctus: past part. of *dīligō*

dīligēns, -entis (adj.): industrious, diligent, careful

dīligenter (adv.): diligently, industriously

dīligentia, -ae (f.): carefulness, industry, diligence

dīligō, -ere, -ēxī, -ēctus: single out; esteem highly, be fond of

dīmicō, -āre: fight, contend

dīmittō, -ere, -īsī, -issus: send away, dismiss, abandon

dīrigō, -ere, -ēxī, -ēctus: distribute; arrange in rows; direct (often confused with *dērigō;* cf. *cursum dīrēxit* in 24 end)

dīripiō, -ere, -uī, -eptus: tear apart; seize; plunder

diruō, -uere, -uī, -utus: destroy

dīrus, -a, -um: fearful, awful

dīs:= deīs (from *deus*)

discēdō, -ere, -essī, -essum: depart

discernō, -ere, -crēvī, -crētus: separate, distinguish, discern

discerpō, -ere, -sī, -tus: tear into pieces

discessus, -ūs (m.): departure, parting

discinctus, -a, -um (past part. of *discingō*): loosely girded, i.e. dissolute (86 n. 15C)

discingō, -ere, -xī, -ctus: ungird

disciplīna, -ae (f.): education, training, discipline

discō, -ere, didicī, —: learn, be taught; become acquainted with

discordia, -ae (f.): disagreement, discord

discrēvī, discrētus: perf. and past part. of *discernō*

discrīmen, -inis (n.): crisis, danger, decisive moment

discutiō, -ere, -ssī, -ssus: shatter, break up, dispel

disertus, -a, -um: fluent, eloquent

dīsiciō, -ere, -iēcī, -iectus: drive asunder, break up; disperse, rout

disiungō (or *diiungō*), *-ere, -iūnxī, -iūnctus:* unyoke, separate

dīspergō, -ere, -sī, -sus: scatter, disperse

displiceō, -ēre, -uī, -itus: displease, be unsatisfactory to (w. dat.)

dispōnō, -ere, -osuī, -ositus: place apart, dispose, arrange

disputō, -āre: examine, discuss; explain

dissēdī: perf. of *dissideō*

dissēnsiō, -ōnis (f.): dissension, disagreement

dissentiō, -īre, -ēnsī, -ēnsum: disagree, differ (w. *ā*+abl.; also w. *cum*+abl.: 27 A s. 2)

disserō, -ere, -uī, -tus: discuss, harangue

dissideō, -ēre, -ēdī, —: sit apart; disagree (w. *cum*+abl.: 27 A s. 3)

dissimilis, -e (adj.): unlike

dissimilitūdō, -inis (f.): unlikeness, difference

dissimulō, -āre: keep secret, conceal (53 n. 3A), dissemble (11 A s. 3)

dissolvō, -ere, -ī, -lūtus: dissolve, destroy; release

dissuādeō, -ēre, -sī, -sus: advise against, object, dissuade

distendō, -ere, -ī, -tus: stretch out, distend; fill

distribuō, -uere, -uī, -ūtus: divide, distribute

distulī: perf. of *differō*

dītō, -āre: enrich

diū (adv.): for a long time; (comp.) *diūtius:* longer; (sup.) *diūtissimē:* for a very long time

dīus, -a, -um: godlike, divine (60 n. 2)

diūtinus, -a, -um: lasting, long

diūturnitās, -ātis (f.): length of time, long duration

diūturnus, -a, -um: lasting, enduring

dīversitās, -ātis (f.): disagreement; variety, diversity

dīversus, -a, -um: turned different ways, opposite; different

dīves, -itis (adj.): rich, costly

dīvidō, -ere, -īsī, -īsus: divide; distribute

dīvīnus, -a, -um: divine

dīvitiae, -ārum (f. plur.): riches

dīvortium, -ī (n.): separation, divorce (in 83 n. 3)

dīvus,-a, -um: divine, deified (of a human recognized after death as a divinity: in 47 title, in 60 n. 2, in 80 pref.); (m. as noun): god, a deified human (i.e. Caesar in 88 n. 4B: *Dīvī genus* used of Augustus)

dīxī: perf. of *dīcō*

dō, dare, dedī, datus: give; i.e. say (84 n. 9)

doceō, -ēre, -uī, -tus: teach, inform

doctrina, -ae (f.): learning (13 n. 11c, 34 n. 2); training

doctus, -a, -um (past part. of *doceō* as adj.): learned, cultured

doleō, -ēre, -uī, -itūrus: grieve, grieve for; afflict

dolor, -ōris (m.): grief, anguish, indignation

domesticus, -a, -um: of the family, domestic; personal

domicilium, -ī (n.): home, abode, domicile

domina, -ae (f.): mistress, lady

dominātiō, -ōnis (f.): mastery, rule, domination

dominātor, -ōris (m.): master, ruler

dominātus, -ūs (m.): mastery, sovereign rule, tyranny

dominor, -ārī, -ātus (dep.): have dominion, rule

dominus, -ī (m.): master, owner, ruler

domō, -āre, -uī, -itus: subdue, master

domus, -ūs (f.): house, home; *domum* (acc.): homeward; *domī* (loc.): at home, in the house; *domī et mīlitiae:* at home and on service (or in the field, i.e. in civil and military spheres: 13 n. 5A, and often)

dōnec (conj.): until (in 6 n. 3); while, as long as

dōnō, -āre: present, give (73 n. 3A, 87 n. 26)

dōnum, -ī (n.): gift

dormiō, -īre: sleep

dōs, dōtis (f.): dowry

dōtālis, -e: pertaining to (i.e. as) a dowry (49 n. 10B)

dracō, -ōnis (m.): large snake (in 12 n. 2A), dragon

dubitō, -āre: be uncertain, be in doubt, doubt; hesitate, delay

dubius, -a, -um: doubtful, uncertain, critical; *dubium, -ī* (n. as noun): a matter of doubt

ducentī, -ae, -a: two hundred

dūcō, -ere, dūxī, ductus: lead; i.e. mould (88 n. 30B); prolong (41 n. 2, 64 n. 3c); consider, regard as (in 74 n. 16c)

ductus, -ūs (m.): leadership, command

dulcēdō, -inis (f.): sweetness, charm

dulcis, -e (adj.): sweet, pleasant

dum (conj.): until; as long as, while (with pres. in 6 n. 8, 28 n. 16, 53 n. 10B; with perf. in 79 n. 10A)

dummodo (or *dum . . . modo*; conj.): so long as, if only, provided that

dūmōsus, -a, -um: covered with brambles (84 n. 21c)

dūmus, -ī (m.): bramble (55 n. 15A)

duo, duae, duo (cardinal numeral): two; both

duodecim (indeclinable cardinal numeral): twelve

duodēsexāgēsimus, -a, -um: fifty-eighth (41 p. 2 s. 7)

duplex, -icis (adj.): double, twofold

dūrus, -a, -um: hard

duumvir, -ī (m.): duumvir (the two chief magistrates of a colony: 24 n. 15)

dux, ducis (m.): leader, commander, general

ē or *ex* (prep. w. abl.): out of; i.e. of (with numerals: 7 n. 5, 8 n. 2A); from, away from; because of; as a prefix occasionally intensive or almost neg. (73 n. 11B)

ēbrius, -a, -um: intoxicated, drunk (46 n. 3)

ebur, -oris (n.): ivory (80 n. 8)

ecce (interj.): behold!

ecquī, ecquae (or *ecqua*), *ecquod* (interrog. adj.): any?

ecquis, ecquid (interrog. pronoun): anyone, anything?

edāx, -ācis (adj.; from *edō:* eat): devouring, consuming

ēdīcō, -ere, -īxī, -ictus: declare, proclaim; order

ēdictum, -ī (n. as noun of past part. of *ēdīcō*): proclamation, edict

ēdisserō, -ere, -uī, -tus: set forth in full, explain, relate

ēdō, -ere, -idī, -itus: give out, bring forth, publish; (past part.): lofty (forms may be distinguished from like forms of pres. *edō* by the initial long *ē*-)

edō (2nd and 3rd pers. sing.: *ēs*, *ēst*), *edere* (or *ēsse*), *ēdī*, *ēsus:* eat

ēdoceō, -ēre, -uī, -tus: teach thoroughly, show

ēducō, -āre (probably not derived from *dūcō, -ere*): train, bring up, educate

efferō, -ferre, extulī, ēlātus: carry up (or away: 76 n. 20B); *sē efferō:* i.e. revive (75 n. 14)

efficāx, -ācis (adj.): effective, efficient

efficiō, -ere, -ēcī, -ectus: make, cause, bring about

efflāgitō, -āre: demand urgently, insist

effrēnātus, -a, -um: unbridled, unrestrained (71 n. 2C)

effundō, -ere, -ūsī, -ūsus: pour forth, extend, lavish

effūsus: past part. of *effundō*

ēgelidus, -a, -um: chilly; lukewarm, tepid (73 n. 11B)

ego (sing. 1st pers. pronoun): I; declined *meī, mihi* or *mī, mē, mē*

egomet: intensive for *ego* (63 n. 8C)

ēgredior, -ī, -essus (dep.): go out, come forth

ēgregius, -a, -um: distinguished, remarkable, illustrious

ēgressus: past part. of *ēgredior*

ēgressus, -ūs (m.): coming or going forth (89 n. 24), departure

ēiciō, -ere, -iēcī, -iectus: cast or drive out, expel, exile

ēiectiō, -ōnis (f.): banishment

ēiulātiō, -ōnis (f.): lamentation

ēiulātus, -ūs (m.): lamentation, moaning (24 p. 3 s. 4)

ēiulō, -āre: wail, moan, lament (82 B s. 5)

ēlanguēscō, -ere, -guī, —: grow faint, slacken, relax

ēlātus: past part. of *efferō* (from *extollō*)

ēlegāns, -antis (adj.): select, tasteful, elegant

elephantus, -ī (m.): elephant (9 A s. 3, in 13 n. 13, 59 n. 11A)

ēlidō, -ere, -īsī, -īsus: crush, destroy

ēligō, -ere, -ēgī, -ēctus: pluck out; choose

ēloquentia, -ae (f.): eloquence

ēloquium, -ī (n.): speech; eloquence

ēlūctor, -ārī, -ātus (dep.): struggle out, force a way through

ēlūdō, -ere, -sī, -sus: play, make sport of (i.e. frustrate: 71 n. 2B): elude, avoid

ēmendō, -āre: correct, revise

ēmētior, -īrī, -mēnsus (dep.): measure out; pass over (1 n. 6B)

ēmicō, -āre, -uī, -ātus: leap forth (77 v. 40); shine forth

ēminēns, -entis (adj.): projecting, prominent, lofty

ēmineō, -ēre, -uī, —: project, jut out, be prominent

ēmīror, -ārī,— (dep.): wonder greatly at (87 n. 5B)

ēmittō, -ere, -īsī, -issus: send out, release; utter

emō, -ere, ēmī, ēmptus: buy

ēn (interj.): behold! (84 n. 8A)

ēnārrō, -āre: explain (or relate) in full

ēnervō, -āre: enervate, weaken

enim (conj.): for; namely, that is to say; assuredly, certainly

ēnitēscō, -ere, -tuī, —: shine forth, display itself

ēnsis, -is (m.): sword

eō, īre, iī (or *īvī:* 1 n. 4B), *itūrus:* go

eō (abl. of *is*): therefore, on that account (20 n. 14B)

eō (adv.; case uncertain: in 21 n. 13B): there, in that place; thither, thereto

eōdem (adv.): to the same place (21 n. 13B)

epistula, -ae (f.): letter, epistle

eques, -itis (m.): horseman, cavalryman; knight, i.e. an equestrian (a well-to-do person: 17 pref.)

equester, -tris, -tre: equestrian, of the cavalry

equidem (adv.): indeed, truly; for my part, as far as I am concerned

equitātus, -ūs (m.): cavalry (65 n. 2B)

equus, -ī (m.): horse

era, -ae (f. of *erus*): mistress (of a house: 60 n. 9B)

ērēxī, ērēctus: perf. and past part. of *ērigō*

ergā (prep. w. acc.): in respect to, toward

ergō (conj.; in Ovid the final *-o* is short; compare in 59 n. 29B): therefore

ērigō, -ere, -ēxī, -ēctus: raise up, erect; arouse

ēripiō, -ere, -uī, -eptus: snatch away; rescue

errō, -āre: wander; make a mistake, err

error, -ōris (m.): wandering, going astray; error

ērudiō, -īre: educate

ērudītus, -a, -um (past part. of *ērudiō* as adj.): erudite, learned *ērumpō, -ere, -ūpī, -uptus:* burst or break out, erupt

ēruō, -uere, -uī, -utus: tear up, overturn

erus, -ī (m., compare f. *era*): master, owner (73 n. 26)

ēscendō, -ere, -ī, -ēnsus: climb up, mount, ascend

esse: inf. of *sum*

et (conj.): and; *et . . . et:* both . . . and (8 .n. 12; compare 85 n. 6A)

etenim (conj.): for, for truly, and indeed

etiam (conj.): and also, also, even, yet; *nōn modo . . . sed etiam:* not only . . . but also

etiamsī (conj.): even if, although

etsī (conj.): albeit, even if, although

eunt-: stem of oblique forms of *iēns,* pres. part. of *eō*

ēvādō, -ere, -sī, -sus: go out, leave behind; escape, get away

ēvangelizō, -āre: bring good news (90 n. 11A)

ēveniō, -īre, -ēnī, -entus: come out, turn out, happen; *ēvenit ut* (w. subj.): it happens that

ēventus, -ūs (m.): occurrence, event, result

ēvertō, -ere, -ī, -sus: overturn, destroy

ēvītō, -āre: avoid, shun

ēvocātus, -ī (m. as noun of past part. of *ēvocō*): a re-enlisted soldier (45 n. 6)

ex: see *ē*

ex(s)-: see *exs-*

exaequō, -āre: make equal; place on a level, regard as equal; become equal

exagitō, -āre: rouse, disturb; excite, i.e. obsess (21 n. 4B)

exanimis, -e (adj.): breathless; lifeless, dead (43 n. 15A)

exārdēscō, -ere, -ārsī, -ārsus: blaze out, flame up

exarmō, -āre: disarm

exaudiō, -īre: hear clearly, understand, heed

excēdō, -ere, -essī, -essum: go out, withdraw, retire; go beyond, exceed

excellēns, -entis (pres. part. of *excellō* as adj.): eminent, excellent

excellō, -ere, -uī (rare), *-lsus:* excel, surpass, be eminent

excelsus, -a, -um (past part. of *excellō*): high, eminent

excidium, -ī (n.): destruction

excīdō, -ere, -dī, -sus: cut off, cut down, raze

excipiō, -ere, -ēpī, -eptus: take on, receive; incur

excitō, -āre: arouse, summon forth, excite

exclūdō, -ere, -sī, -sus: shut out, exclude; hinder, prevent

excōgitō, -āre: contrive, invent, excogitate

excruciō, -āre: torture, excruciate

excūdō, -ere, -ī, -sus: hammer out, forge

exedō, -ere, -ēdī, -ēsus: eat up, devour (64 B v. 5)

exemplum, -ī (n.): example, precedent, pattern (36 n. 17B)

exeō, -īre, -iī (or *-īvī:* 1 n. 4B), *-itus:* go out, depart, leave

exerceō, -ēre, -uī, -itus: train, practice; manage

exercitus, -ūs (m.): army; *exercitum cōnficere:* raise an army (30 n. 8B)

exhauriō, -īre, -sī, -stus: draw out, empty, exhaust

exhibeō, -ēre, -uī, -itus: present, exhibit

exhortor, -ārī, -ātus (dep.): exhort, encourage

exigō, -ere, -ēgī, -āctus: push forth; drive out; require, exact; spend (of time); complete (i.e. build: 87 n. 33A)

exiguus, -a, -um: small, scanty

exiliō and *exilium:* see *exs-*

eximius, -a, -um: outstanding, choice

exinde (adv.): after that, then

exīstimō, -āre: think, consider, judge (43 n. ʾ7n.) estimate

exitiābilis, -e (79 B s. 5): deadly, fatal

exitiālis, -e (75 p. 2 s. 7): = *exitiābilis*

exitium, -ī (n.): destruction, disaster (5 n. 13B)

exitus, -ūs (m.): departure (in 19 n. 13D), exit; end (19 n. 13A, 59 n. 7), outcome (59 n. 22)

exoptō, -āre: desire greatly

exōrdior, -īrī, -sus (dep.): begin

exorior, -īrī, -tus (dep.): come forth, arise

exōrnō, -āre: adorn, embellish

expavēscō, -ere, -pāvī, —: be terrified, dread (86 B v. 23)

expediō, -īre: free; arrange; expound (88 n. 1A); *expedit:* it is expedient

expedītiō, -ōnis (f.): campaign, expedition

expellō, -ere, -pulī, -pulsus: drive out, expel

expendō, -ere, -ī, -pēnsus: weigh out; expend; ponder

experior, -īrī, -tus (dep.): try, test, experience

expers, -tis (adj., from *ex + pars*): having no part in, free from (w. gen.: 28 n. 22E, 46 n. 18)

expertus, -a, -um (past part. of *experior* as adj.): experienced (pass. sense: 16 n. 6A); tried, expert

expīrō: see *exspīrō*

expleō, -ēre, -ēvī, -ētus: fulfill, satisfy; accomplish

explōrō, -āre: search, investigate, explore

expōnō, -ere, -osuī, -ositus: set out; reveal, expose, explain

exprimō, -ere, -essī, -essus: press out, model; represent; express

exprobrō, -āre: reproach, upbraid

exprōmō, -ere, -psī, -ptus: bring forth, exhibit, expound, express (24 n. 17B)

expūgnātiō, -ōnis (f.): taking by storm, storming (23 s. 3)

expūgnō, -āre: take by storm, subdue (i.e. violate: 5 s. 8)

expulī, expulsus: perf. and past part. of *expellō*

exquīrō, -ere, -sīvī, -sītus: seek out, search, enquire

exquīsītus, -a, -um (past part. of *exquīrō* as adj.): carefully sought out; choice, exquisite

exs-: also spelled *ex-*

exsanguis, -e: bloodless, pale; lifeless

exscindo, -ere, -idī, -issus: extirpate, annihilate

exsecror, -ārī, -ātus (dep.): curse, execrate, abhor

exsecūtor, -ōris (m.): prosecutor, avenger

exsequor, -ī, -cūtus: (dep.): follow out, perform, execute

exsiliō, -īre, -uī (or *-īvī* or *-iī:* 1 n. 4B), —: leap forth

exsilium, -ī (n.): exile

exsistō, -ere, -stitī (72 n. 16C), —: stand forth, appear, exist

exspectātiō, -ōnis (f.): awaiting, expectation

exspectō, -āre: wait, await, expect

exspīrō, -āre: breathe out, breathe one's last, expire

exstimulō, -āre: goad, incite, stimulate

exstinguō, -uere, -xī, -ctus: put out, extinguish; destroy

exstō, -āre, -itī, -ātūrus: stand out, be visible; be extant

exsul (or *exul*), *-ulis* (m.): exile, banished person

exta, -ōrum (n. plur.): entrails (as examined for taking omens in 80 n. 10C)

extendō, -ere, -ī, -tus (or *-ēnsus*): stretch out, extend

extenuō, -āre: diminish, weaken, extenuate

externus, -a, -um: foreign, external

exterreō, -ēre, -uī, -itus: frighten thoroughly, terrify

exterus, -a, -um: outside; (comp.) *exterior:* outer, exterior; (sup.) *extrēmus* (or *extimus*): outermost, farthest, extreme, last

extollō, -ere (perf. and past part. used with *efferō*): raise up, extol

extorqueō, -ēre, -sī, -tus: wrench away, extort

extrā (adv. and prep. w. acc.): outside, outside of, beyond

extrahō, -ere, -xī, -ctus: drag out, pull out, extract

extrēmus: sup. of *exterus*

extulī: perf. of *efferō* (from *extollō*)

exturbō, -āre: drive (or, thrust) out

exul: see *exsul*

exundō, -āre: flow out (or, over)

exuō, -uere, -uī, -ūtus: put off; get rid of

exuviae, -ārum (f. plur.): something stripped off; clothing; spoils (77 n. 22)

fabricō, -āre: construct, build, fabricate

fābula, -ae (f.): tale, story, fable; play

faciēs, faciēī (f.): appearance, face

facile (n. of *facilis* as adv.): easily, readily

facilis, -e: easy; quick, affable, courteous

facilitās, -ātis (f.): ease, facility; affability, good nature

facinerōsus, -a, -um: criminal, villainous

facinus, -oris (n.): achievement, deed; misdeed, crime (72 n. 18A)

faciō, -ere, fēcī, factus: make; produce; do; elect (in 56 n. 1A, 63 n. 1D, 64 n. 4B); *iter facere:* to march; *factum est* (impersonal): it came to pass (90 n. 2A), it happened (90 n. 15C)

factiō, -ōnis (f.): faction, political party (34 n. 19C, 38 n. 22A, in 47 n. 2)

factiōsus, -a, -um: factious, seditious

factum, -ī (n. as noun of past part. of *faciō*): deed (21 n. 8), achievement; event

facultās, -ātis (f.): capability, means, opportunity; supply, goods, riches

fācundus, -a, -um: eloquent, fluent

faex, faecis (f.): dregs, refuse

fāgus, -ī (*f.*): beech tree (in 84 n. 2A)

fallāx, -ācis (adj.); deceptive (87 n. 7B), fallacious

fallō, -ere, fefellī, falsus: trip, cause to fall; trick, deceive; fail; escape notice

falsus, -a, -um (past part. of *fallō* as adj.): false, supposed; deceived, mistaken

falx, falcis (f.): pruning knife, sickle (85 p. 5 v. 4)

fāma, -ae (f.): rumor, report, reputation (good or bad)

famēs, famis (f.): hunger, famine; violent longing, avidity

familia, -ae (f.): household (in 28 n. 23B), family (65 n. 8A); = *gens* (33 n. 1B)

familiāris, -e: belonging to the household; *familiāris, -is* (m. as a noun): close friend (28 n. 23B, 35 n. 8C); servant (44 n. 9A); *rēs familiāris* (f.): property, estate (81 n. 9A)

familiāritas, -ātis (f.): intimacy

famul, -is (archaic; 70 n. 26B) or *famulus, -ī* (m.): household slave, servant (66 n. 8, 78 n. 3B)

farciō, -īre, -sī, -tus (-*sus*, late Lat. *farcītus*): stuff, cram

fās (n., only nom. and acc. sing.): divine law; justice, equity, that which is proper or permitted (in 8 n. 7B, 42 n. 28C, 64 n. 12A)

fascis, -is (m.): bundle (of rods containing an axe, symbol of the *imperium:* in 8 n. 8C)

fāstī, -ōrum (m. plur.): calendar; register of events, annals; register of higher magistrates (42 n. 26A)

fastidiōsus, -a, -um: disdainful; loathsome

fastigium, -ī (n.): elevation, height; high rank

fātālis, -e: fateful (86 n. 26A); fated, fatal

fateor, -ērī, fassus (dep.): admit, acknowledge

fatigō, -āre: tire, fatigue

fatīscō, -ere (in archaic Lat. also dep.: *-or, -ī*), —, —*:* gape open (61 n. 29B); grow weary, be exhausted

fātum, -ī (n. as noun of past part. of *fātur*): fate, destiny; i.e. death

fātur (in pres. and fut., only in 3rd pers. sing. and plur.), *fārī, fātus* (dep.): speak, say

faveō, -ēre, fāvī, fautūrus: be favorable, favor, befriend (w. dat.)

fax, facis (f.): torch; i.e. cause of ruin (23 n. 5, 26 n. 8C)

febris, -is (f.): fever

fefelli: perf. of *fallō*

fēlīcitās, -ātis (f.): happiness, felicity, good fortune

fēlix, -īcis: lucky, fortunate (65 n. 13, 79 n. 15C)

fēmina, -ae (f.): woman

fera, -ae (f.): see *ferus*

fērālis, -e: funereal (in 77 n. 3D), of the dead

ferē (adv.; but not of *ferus*, whose adv. is not used): quite, entirely, just; usually, mostly, nearly, almost, about

fēriae, -ārum (f. plur.): holidays, festivals

ferō, ferre, tulī, lātus (perf. and past perf. borrowed from *tollō*): bear, carry, endure; bring, report (news, etc.; 4 n. 13, 21 n. 21B, 80 n. 3B); *sē ferre:* present oneself as (48 n. 15B), conduct oneself; *ferre* + adv.: regard as + adj. (3 n. 2A, 33 n. 12, 63 n. 6, 81 n. 2C); *ferre pedem:* stir one's foot (i.e. go)

ferōx, -ōcis (adj.): fierce, cruel, savage

ferrātus, -a, -um: fitted with iron (in 60 n. 16A)

ferre: inf. of *ferō*

ferreus, -a, -um: made of iron

ferrūgō, -inis (f.): iron-rust

ferrum, -ī (n.): iron; iron tool, sword

fertilis, -e: fertile, fruitful

ferus, -a, -um: wild, fierce; (f. as a noun): wild beast (69 n. 13B)

fervēns, -entis (pres. part. of *ferveō* as adj.): hot, boiling; violent

ferveō, -ēre, —, —: boil, be very hot

fervidus, -a, -um: boiling, hot; impetuous, raging

fessus, -a, -um: weary; weak

fēstīnō, -āre: hasten, hurry

fētus, -a, -um: having just given birth (55 n. 5A)

fētus, -ūs (m.): offspring

fibra, -ae (f.): fiber, vein; segment of liver (80 n. 10B)

fictus: past part. of *fingō*

fidēlis, -e: faithful, trustworthy, loyal

fidēs, fidei (f.): faith, reliance; trustworthiness (51 n. 6, and often); i.e. (lack of) faith (87 n. 4); promise

fidūcia, -ae (f.): confidence, trust

fīdus, -a, -um: loyal, trustworthy, faithful

fīgō, -ere, fīxī, fīxus: fasten, attach; pierce, transfix

fīlia, -ae (f.): daughter

filius, -i (m.): son

fingō, -ere, -xī, fictus: shape (in 55 n. 8B); contrive, devise; pretend, feign

finiō, -īre: set limits to, bound, define

finis, -is (m.): boundary, limit, border; land, territory; termination, end

fiō, fierī, factus sum (as pass. of *faciō*): become, be made

firmitās, -ātis (f.): strength, firmness; endurance

firmō, -āre: make firm, strengthen, fortify; encourage

firmus, -a, -um: strong, firm, stable, faithful

fissilis, -e: split; easy to split (61 n. 11)

fixī, fixus: perf. and past part. of *figō*

flagrō, -āre: flame; be inflamed, excited

flāmen, -inis (m.): priest (42 n. 8B)

flamma, -ae (f.): flame, blaze

flāvēscō, -ere, —, —: become golden yellow (85 p. 4 v. 3)

flāvus, -a, -um: yellow, blond (49 n. 2B, in 87 n. 1)

flectō, -ere, -ēxī, -exus: bend, turn, curve

fleō, -ēre, -ēvī, -ētus: weep

flōrēns, -entis (pres. part. of *flōreō* as adj.): in bloom, flowering; flourishing

flōreō, -ēre, -uī, —: be in flower, flourish

flōs, -ōris (m.): flower

fluctus, -ūs (m.): wave, swell (44 n. 7B); turbulence

flūmen, -inis (n.): river

fluō, -uere, -uxī, -uxus: flow, flow away; i.e. vanish

fluvius, -ī (m.): river

focus, -ī (m.): fireplace, hearth (51 n. 15A)

foederātus, -a, -um: confederated, allied (10 n. 3B)

foedus, -a, -um: loathsome, repulsive; disgraceful, base

foedus, -eris (n.): treaty, alliance

fōns, fontis (m.): fountain

(for): found only in 3rd pers.; see *fātur*

forāmen, -inis (n.): opening, hole (in 89 n. 18C)

fore, forem, etc.: for *futūrum esse, essem, etc.* (21 n. 26C, and often)

fōrma, -ae (f.): form, shape; appearance, beauty

formīdō, -inis (f.): fear, terror; something feared

formīdolōsus, -a, -um: frightful; timid

formōsus, -a, -um: finely formed, beautiful, handsome

fors, fortis (f.): chance, accident

fortasse (adv.): perhaps, possibly

forte (abl. of *fors* as adv.): by chance, accidentally (5 n. 3A, and often)

fortis, -e: strong; brave

fortiter (adv.): strongly, bravely

fortitūdō, -inis (f.): strength, bravery

fortūna, -ae (f.): luck, fortune (personified: 64 n. 8D, 77 v. 3, 78 n. 32A); condition

fortūnātus, -a, -um: lucky, fortunate (79 n. 21B), prosperous

forum, -ī (n.): forum, market place, public square; specifically: the Roman Forum (e.g. in 66 n. 11A, 80 v. 19)

fossa, -ae (f.): ditch (51 n. 13A), moat

frāctus: past part. of *frangō*

frāgmen, -inis (n.): fragment, broken piece (18 p. 2 s. 4)

frangō, -ere, -ēgī, -āctus: break

frāter, frātris (m.): brother

frāternus, -a, -um: of a brother, fraternal

fraus, fraudis (f.): deception, fraud; crime; harm

fraxinus, -ī (f.): ash tree (in 61 n. 3)

frēgī: perf. of *frangō*

fremitus, -ūs (m.): a dull roaring sound

frēnum, -ī (n.; usually plur.): bridle, curb; restraint (66 n. 5B)

frequēns, -entis (adj.): frequent (i.e. often: 14 n. 18B); in great numbers, crowded

frequenter (adv.): frequently

fretum, -ī (n.): strait, channel (distinguishable from the n. of *frētus* by the short -e-)

frētus, -a, -um: relying on, trusting in (w. abl.)

frigus, -oris (n.): cold

frondifer, -era, -erum: leafy, leaf-bearing

frondōsus, -a, -um: leafy, full of leaves

frōns, frontis (f.): brow, forehead; front

frūctus, -ūs (m.): fruit, produce; proceeds, income: enjoyment

frūgēs, -um (f. plur.): fruits of the earth, crops

frūgifer, -era, -erum: fruitful, fruit-bearing

frūmentārius, -a, -um: relating to grain (20 n. 11A, 29 n. 15A); *rēs frūmentāria:* grain supply (compare 29 n. 15A)

frūmentum, -ī (n.): grain

fruor, -ī, -ūctus (dep.): enjoy, delight in (w. abl.: in 87 n. 6)

frustrā (adv.): in vain, to no purpose

frustror, -ārī, -ātus (dep.; also a rare act. *frustrō*): deceive, frustrate *fūdī:* perf. of *fundō*

fuga, -ae (f.): flight

fugiō, -ere, fūgī, —: flee, escape; flee from (69 n. 7B); escape the notice of (37 n. 22A, 38 n. 11B)

fugitīvus, -a, -um: runaway, fugitive; (m. as a noun): runaway slave, fugitive

fugō, -āre: put to flight, rout

fuī: perf. of *sum*

fulgeō, -ēre, -lsī, —: flash, shine

fulmen, -inis (n.): lightning, thunderbolt (77 n. 33B)

fulmineus, -a, -um: of lightning, lightning-swift; sparkling; destructive, murderous

fulsī: perf. of *fulgeō*

fūmō, -āre, —, —: smoke

fūmus, -ī (m.): smoke

fūnctus, -a, -um: past part. of *fungor*

funda, -ae (f.; not from root of *fundō, -ere*): sling

fundāmen, -inis (n.): foundation

fundātor, -ōris (m.): founder

funditor, -ōris (m.; from *funda*): slinger

funditus (adv. from noun *fundus*): to the bottom; completely

fundō, -āre: found, establish

fundō, -ere, fūdī, fūsus: pour, pour out, pour forth; put to flight, scatter in rout (of armies)

fundus, -ī (m.): bottom; farm, estate

fūnestus, -a, -um: deadly, calamitous

fungor, -ī, fūnctus (dep.): perform, execute, discharge (w. abl.: 51 n. 15B, 56 n. 10B); (past part.): having held (an office, etc.: 23 n. 12B)

fūnus, -eris (n.): funeral procession, funeral; death

furiōsus, -a, -um: mad, insane, raging

furō, -ere, —, —: be mad, rave

furor, -ōris (m.): fury, rage (i.e. political extremism: 19 n. 1C, 22 n. 13C, 71 n. 2A); i.e. stormy weather (73 n. 12A)

fūsus, -a, -um (past part. of *fundō* as adj.): stretched out, prostrate; extended, broad; put to flight; diffuse (of style)

fūsus, -ī (m.): spindle (85 n. 30B; distinguishable only by the context from the m. of *fūsus, -a, -um*)

futūrus: fut. part. of *sum*

gaesum, -ī (n.): heavy iron javelin (55 n. 20C)

galea, -ae (f.): helmet (plur. in 61 n. 20B)

gaudeō, -ēre, gāvīsus (semi-dep.): be glad, rejoice (w. abl.: 73 n. 26, 77 n. 19)

gaudium, -ī (n.): joy, delight; source of pleasure

gelidus, -a, -um: icy cold, frosty

geminus, -a, -um: twin; double

gemitus, -ūs (m.): sigh, groan (in 43 n. 13)

gemma, -ae (f.): bud; jewel (in 46 n. 6A)

gemō, -ere, -uī, —: groan, lament; bemoan, bewail

gener, -erī (m.): son-in-law (53 s. 3, 88 n. 15A)

generātim (adv.): by species (69 n. 17B)

generōsus, -a, -um: of noble birth; noble-minded, magnanimous; (comp. adv.) *generōsius:* more nobly (86 n. 27B)

genetrīx, -īcis (f.): ancestress (69 n. 1B, 80 n. 1A)

genitābilis, -e: procreative (69 n. 11B)

genitor, -ōris (m.): father, sire, begetter (60 A v. 4)

genitus: past part. of *gignō*

gēns, gentis (f.): race; tribe; species; gens (a group of families connected by common ancestry; in 65 n. 7C)

genuī: perf. of *gignō*

genus, -eris (n.): genus, family (34 n. 12B); i.e. descent (33 n. 1D); class, type (37 n. 22C)

gerō, -ere, gessī, gestus: carry, have; perform, do, manage; *bellum gerere:* wage war (9 n. 1C); *negōtī gerentēs:* businessmen (76 n. 10); *gesta* (n. plur. of past part. as noun) or *rēs gestae* (47 title): deeds, achievements

gestiō, -īre, -īvī, —: leap, exult; desire eagerly

gestō, -āre: bear, have, wear

gestus: past part. of *gerō*

gestus, -ūs: (m.): motion, gesture

gignō, -ere, genuī, genitus: beget, produce; cause; (past part.): born or descended (w. abl.: 5 n. 2B, in 33 n. 1A)

gladiātōrius, -a, -um: gladiatorial (28 p. 4 s. 1)

gladius, -ī (m.): sword

gliscō, -ere, —, —: swell or spread gradually, grow imperceptibly

glōria, -ae (f.): glory, renown; ambition, thirst for glory

glōrificō, -āre: glorify (90 p. 3 s. 6)

glōriola, -ae (f.): a little glory (37 n. 27B)

glōrior, -ārī, -ātus (dep.): glory, boast (w. abl.)

glōriōsus, -a, -um: glorious; braggart

gracilis, -e: slight, slender (87 A v. 1)

gradus, -ūs (m.): step, degree, grade

grandis, -e: large; great, dignified

graphium, -ī (n.): stylus (43 n. 9D)

grassor, -ārī, -ātus (dep.): go; loiter

grātia, -ae (f.): favor, grace, kindness; influence; thanks; *grātiā* (w. gen.): on account of; *in grātiam redīre:* return to favor (35 n. 11, 38 n. 17B); *grātiās agere:* to thank; *grātiam habēre:* to feel grateful; *grātiam referre:* to return a favor

grātīs (abl. plur. as adv.: 12 n. 13C): through kindness; without recompense

grātulātiō, -ōnis (f.): rejoicing; congratulation

grātulor, -ārī, -ātus (dep.): show joy, be glad; congratulate (w. dat. of person: 43 n. 23)

grātus, -a -um: pleasing, acceptable

gravis, -e: heavy; burdensome, oppressive; weighty, grave

gravitās, -ātis (f.): weight, heaviness, oppressiveness; gravity (i.e. of speech or manner: 34 A s. 1)

gremium, -ī (n.): bosom, lap (in 69 n. 27A)

grex, gregis (m.): herd, flock; clique

gubernātor, -ōris (m.): steersman, pilot; governor, director

gubernō, -āre: steer, pilot; direct, guide, govern

gurges, -itis (m.): whirlpool; eddies (of a river: 66 n. 18)

gutta, -ae (f.): drop (of a liquid: 80 v. 11)

habēna, -ae (f.): rein, bridle

habeō, -ēre, -uī, -itus: have, hold, possess; consider (17 n. 15B, 22 n. 3A); *orātiōnem habēre:* to deliver a speech; *animum habēre:* to intend (18 n. 17A)

habilis, -e: easily handled, manageable; suitable, nimble; expert

habitō, -āre: dwell, live

habitus, -ūs (m.): condition; appearance, dress; quality, character

haedus, -ī (m.): young goat, kid (87 n. 26)

haereō, -ēre, -sī, -sūrus: cling, hold fast; stay close, adhere; abide, keep to

harēna, -ae (or *arēna*; f.): sand (in 25 n. 10B, 49 n. 2B); beach; arena

harundinētum, -ī (n.): thicket of reeds (24 n. 14A)

haruspex, -icis (m.): soothsayer (by consultation of entrails; 21 n. 3B, in 52 n. 3)

hasta, -ae (f.): spear (61 n. 32A, 63 n. 13C)

hastīle, -is (n.): spear, javelin (61 n. 19B)

haud (adv.): not, not at all, by no means

hauriō, -īre, -sī, -stus: drain, drink up; breathe in (in 25 n. 12B); consume, exhaust

hedera, -ae (f.): ivy (in 85 n. 13B)

herba, -ae (f.): grass

hercule (67 n. 2; or *mē hercule*, 31 n. 4; interj.): by Hercules!; assuredly

hērēditās, -ātis (f.): inheritance

hērōs, -ōis (m.): hero, demi-god (43 n. 30A, 85 nn. 16B and 21B)

hesternus, -a, -um: of yesterday

heu (exclamation): alas (in 82 n. 21)

hīc (in early Lat. *hĭc*), *haec, hoc* (demonstrative pronoun): this, this . . . here; he, she, it; often correlative of *ille, illa, illud:* that; gen. *hūius,* dat. *huic*

hīc (adv.: 10 n. 18B, 84 n. 13A, 88 n. 3A): here, in this place, now, at this time

hiems, hiemis (f.): winter

hinc (adv.): hence, from this place; thereafter, next (85 n. 23)

historia, -ae (f.): history

hodiē (adv.): today

homō, -inis (m.): man; human (man or woman)

honestās, -ātis (f.): reputation, respectability; integrity, honesty

honestus, -a, -um: honored; deserving honor, respectable

honōs (or *honor*), *-ōris* (m.): honor; public office (8 n. 8C, and often); public mark of honor (33 n. 25C, 42 nn. 5B and 9B); *cursus honōrum:* see *cursus*

hōra, -ae (f.): hour

horreō, -ēre, -uī-, —: bristle; tremble; shrink from

horribilis, -e: horrible, fearful

horridus, -a, -um: bristling (in 60 n. 29), rough; uncouth; horrifying

horrificō, -āre, —, —: make rough, make terrifying (in 25 n. 6B); cause terror

horrificus, -a, -um: terrifying, frightful

hortātiō, -ōnis (f.): encouragement, exhortation

hortātus, -ūs (m.): encouragement, exhortation

hortor, -ārī, -ātus (dep.): urge, encourage, exhort

hospes, -itis (m.): host; guest; stranger

hostia, -ae (f.): victim, sacrifice (in 21 n. 2G)

hostilis, -e: of an enemy, hostile

hostis, -is (m.): enemy, the enemy

hūc (adv.): to this place, hither

hūiuscemodī (gen. of *hīc modus*): of this sort, of such a nature

hūmānitās, -ātis (f.): humanity; kindliness; civilization, refinement

hūmānus, -a, -um: human, of man; civilized

humilis, -e: on the ground, low; small, slight; lowly, meek

humus, -ī (f.): earth, ground

hydra, -ae (f.): water serpent, hydra (as a proper name: 9 n. 9)

ī, īs:=eī, eīs (from *is*)

iaceō, -ēre, -uī, —: lie; lie low; be cast down; be obscure (64 n. 1C)

iaciō, -ere, iēcī, iactus: throw; throw down (foundations, i.e. establish: 52 v. 9)

iactātiō, -ōnis (f.): tossing (44 p. 1 s. 3); boasting

iactō, -āre: throw, toss about; boast (lit. throw oneself about)

iactus: past part. of *iaciō*

iam (adv.): now; already; at last; presently; *nōn iam* or *iam nōn* or *neque iam:* no longer; *iam vērō:* furthermore, and besides

iānitor, -ōris (m.): doorkeeper, janitor

iānua, -ae (f.): door

ibi (or *ibī*; adv.): there, in that place

ibīdem (adv.): in the same place

īctus, -a, -um (common past part. of a verb *īcō, īcere, īcī, īctus,* which is archaic in the pres. and rare in the perf.): hit, struck, smitten (44 n. 20A)

īctus, -ūs (m.): stroke, stab (43 A p. 1 s. 5), cut; (metrical) stress

idcircō (adv.): for this reason, therefore

īdem, eadem, idem (pronoun and adj.): same; nom. m. and dat. or abl. plur.: *iīdem, iīsdem* (13 n. 10A)

identidem (adv.): again and again, repeatedly

ideō (adv.): for this reason, therefore

idōneus, -a, -um: suitable, fit, apt

iēiūnō, -āre: fast, abstain from (82 n. 9A)

iēns, euntis: pres. part. of *eō*

igitur (conj.): therefore, consequently

ignārus, -a, -um: ignorant, inexperienced, unaware; unknown

ignāvia, -ae (f.): slothfulness (65 n. 8C); cowardice

ignipotēns, -entis (adj.): controlling fire (as noun, i.e. Vulcan: 55 n. 3B)

ignis, -is (m.): fire

ignōminia, -ae (f.): disgrace, degradation

ignōrō, -āre: not know, be unacquainted, be ignorant; to ignore (in late Lat.: 52 n. 11A)

ignōscō, -ere, -ōvī, -ōtus: pardon, excuse, overlook

ignōtus, -a, -um (adj., from neg. *in-* + past part. of *[g]nōscō*): not known, unknown

iī, iīs:=eī, eīs (from *is*)

iīdem, iīsdem:=eīdem, eīsdem (from *īdem*)

īlex, -icis (f.): "live" or evergreen oak (in 61 n. 3)

īlicō (adv.): on the spot, there; immediately

ill-: also written *inl-*

illabōrātus, -a, -um: not labored over, spontaneous (79 n. 14D)

illātus: past part. of *īnferō*

ille, illa, illud (demonstrative pronoun and adj.): that, that yonder; the further, or, the former (in correlation w. *hīc*); the well-known (as a postpositive demonstrative adj.); gen. *illīus,* dat. *illī*

illecebra, -ae (f.): allurement, enticement

illīc (adv.: 55 n. 2A, 66 n. 12B): there, in that place, yonder

illiciō, -ere, -exī, -ectus: allure, persuade, entice

illigō, -āre: bind on, fasten

illō (adv.): thither, to that place

illūc (adv.): thither, to that place; to that end, thereto

illūminō, -āre: bring into light, illuminate

illūstris, -e: brilliant; illustrious; distinct (of style: 79 n. 9C)

illūstrō, -āre: make bright (or clear: 71 p. 3 s. 1); explain; illustrate; make famous

imāgō, -inis (f.): copy, image (i.e. ancestral image or mask: 63 n. 13B); semblance, appearance

imbellis, -e: unwarlike, peaceful

imber, imbris (m.): rain

imbuō, -uere, -uī, -ūtus: wet, stain (84 n. 5B); saturate; instruct, imbue

immānis, -e: enormous, monstrous; savage

immānitās, -ātis (f.): enormity, excess (72 p. 3 s. 2, 75 n. 10B); savageness, barbarism

immātūrus, -a, -um: unripe, untimely, premature

immēnsus, -a, -um (adj.; from neg. *in-* + past part. of *mētior*): immeasurable, immense

immineō, -ēre, —, —: lean toward, hang over; threaten, be imminent

immittō, -ere, -īsī, -issus: send in, throw in; let loose

immō (adv.): no indeed; by all means (according to context: 71 n. 7A)

immoderātē (adv.): without measure; immoderately

immodicus, -a, -um: excessive, unbounded

immortālis, -e: undying, immortal

immortālitās, -ātis (f.): immortality

immōtus, -a, -um (adj.; from neg. *in-* + past part. of *moveō*): unmoved, motionless; firm

immūnis, -e: free from, untaxed

immūtō, -āre: change, alter

imp-: rarely written *inp-*

impatiēns, -entis (adj.; from neg. *in-* + pres. part. of *patior*): impatient; intolerant

impavidus, -a, -um: fearless

impedīmentum, -ī (n.): hindrance; (plur.): baggage

impediō, -īre: entangle; delay; prevent

impedītus, -a, -um (past part. of *impediō* as adj.): hindered; burdened; obstructed (i.e. hard of access)

impellō, -ere, -ulī, -ulsus: strike against; urge forward, impel

impendō, -ere, -ī, -ēnsus: pay out, expend; devote

impēnsa, -ae (f.): cost, expense

impēnsus, -a, -um (past part. of *impendō* as adj.): (freely) expended; ample; intense

imperātor, -ōris (m.): commander-in-chief, general

imperātōrius, -a, -um: of a general

imperitō, -āre: command, rule over (w. dat.)

imperium, -ī (n.): order; military authority, supreme command (in 52 n. 3, 57 n. 19); empire

imperō, -āre (w. dat.): order; rule, be master; (w. acc.): requisition, demand

impertiō, -īre: share with, bestow, impart

impetrō, -āre: gain one's end; obtain by entreaty

impetus, -ūs (m.): attack; vehemence (in 34 n. 10A)

impleō, -ēre, -ēvī, -ētus: fill up, make full; complete, fulfill

implūmis, -e: without feathers (i.e. unfledged: in 86 n. 9B)

impolītus, -a, -um (adj.; from neg. *in-* + past part. of *poliō*): unpolished, inelegant; unfinished (in 75 n. 14)

impōnō, -ere, -osuī, -ositus (w. acc. of object placed and dat. of place on which): place upon (6 n. 13, 43 n. 16A, 51 n. 14); impose (in 46 n. 20A; i.e. establish: 88 n. 33B)

impotēns, -entis (adj.; from *in-* either neg. or prep. + *potēns*): powerless (86 n. 21B); uncontrolled (87 n. 35B); the meaning is uncertain in 74 n. 20

improbō, -āre: disapprove, blame, condemn

improbus, -a, -um: wicked, unprincipled; vile

imprōvīsus, -a, -um: unforeseen, unexpected, sudden

impudēns, -entis (adj.): shameless, impudent

impudenter (adv.): shamelessly, impudently

impulī, impulsus: perf. and past part. of *impellō*

impūnitās, -ātis (f.): freedom from punishment, safety, impunity

impūnitus, -a, -um (adj.; from neg. *in-* + past part. of *pūniō*): unpunished, unrestrained

īmus (or *infimus*): sup. of *inferus*

in (prep.): in, among, on (w. abl.); into, toward, against (w. acc.)

in-: as a prefix may be either the prep. = to, in; or a neg. = not, un-

inānis, -e: empty; useless, vain; inane

inaudītus, -a, -um (adj.; from neg. *in-* + past part. of *audiō*): unheard-of, incredible

incautus, -a, -um: reckless; unsuspicious, incautious

incēdō, -ere, -essī, -essum: go, proceed, walk; happen

incendō, -ere, -ī, -ēnsus: set fire to, burn; inflame

incertus, -a, -um: uncertain; hesitating, doubtful; untrustworthy

incessus, -ūs (m.): walking, gait; approach, attack

incestus, -a, -um: impure, polluted, incestuous; (n. as noun): incest

incipiō, -ere, -ēpī, -eptus: take in hand, begin; originate

incitō, -āre: set in rapid motion, arouse, incite

inclīnō, -āre: bend, divert; incline, decline

inclūdō, -ere, -sī, -sus: shut in, confine; include

inclutus, -a, -um (or *inclitus*): celebrated, glorious (69 n. 28c)

incōgnitus, -a, -um (adj.; from neg. *in-* + past part. of *cōgnōscō*): not investigated, unknown

incohō, -āre: begin, commence

incolō, -ere, -uī, —: inhabit, dwell

incolumis, -e: uninjured, safe, sound

incōnstāns, -antis (adj.; from neg. *in-* + pres. part. of *cōnstō*): changeable, fickle

incorruptus, -a, -um (adj.; from neg. *in-* + past part. of *corrumpō*): unspoiled, uncorrupted, genuine, pure

incrēdibilis, -e: unbelievable, incredible

incultus, -a, -um (adj.; from neg. *in-* + past part. of *colō*; it is not past part. of *incolō*): uncultivated, barren; unkempt, unpolished

incumbō, -ere, -ubuī, -ubitus: lay oneself upon, lean on; burden

incunctanter (adv.): without delay (82 n. 23)

incūsō, -āre: accuse, complain of

incutiō, -ere, -ussī, -ussus: strike into, inspire

inde (adv.): thence, from that place; thenceforth, after that; *inde . . . hinc:* on the one hand . . . on the other (in 77 n. 6A)

indemnātus, -a, -um (adj.; from neg. *in-* + past part. of *damnō*): uncondemned, unsentenced

indīcō, -ere, -īxī, -ictus: declare publicly, proclaim; appoint

indignātiō, -ōnis (f.): displeasure, indignation

indignor, -ārī, -ātus (dep.): be indignant at (w. acc.), resent; despise

indignus, -a, -um: unworthy (w. abl.); *indignē ferre:* to consider unworthy (3 n. 2A)

indūcō, -ere, -ūxī, -uctus: lead in, conduct; induce; *in animum indūcere:* resolve

induō, -uere, -uī, -ūtus: put on, dress in

industria, -ae (f.): diligence, activity, industry

industriē (adv.): diligently, industriously

ineō, -īre, -iī (or *-īvī:* 1 n. 4B), *-itus:* go into, enter; enter upon (w. a direct object or *in* + acc.: 2 n. 6); undertake, commence (intrans.: 29 n. 17D, 85 n. 11D); *cōnsilium inīre:* form a plan

ineptiō, -īre, —, —: act absurdly (74 n. 15c)

ineptus, -a, -um: silly, inept; unsuitable, unfit

inermis, -e: unarmed (59 n. 5A)

inesse: inf. of *insum*

inexplēbilis, -e: insatiable (24 n. 5)

infacētus, -a, -um: dull, without wit

īnfāmia, -ae (f.): ill fame, dishonor, disgrace

īnfāmis, -e: disreputable, disgraceful, infamous

īnfandus, -a, -um: unutterable, monstrous (66 n. 7); shocking

īnfāns, -fantis (adj.): not able to speak, young; (m. and f. as noun): little child, infant

īnferior: comp. of *īnferus*

īnferō, -ferre, -tulī, inlātus (or *illātus*): bring in, bring against, inflict; *bellum īnferre:* wage war (w. dat.)

īnferus, -a, -um: low, under; (comp.) *īnferior:* lower; (sup.) *īnfimus* (or *īmus*): lowest

īnfestus, -a, -um (adj.; from prep. *in-* + *-festus,* as in *manifestus*): hostile, dangerous

īnficiō, -ere, -ēcī, -ectus: dye, stain (87 n. 28A); corrupt, infect

īnfimus (or *īmus*): sup. of *īnferus*

īnfindō, -ere, -idī, -issus: cleave, split open

īnfinītus, -a, -um (adj.; from neg. *in-* + past part. of *fīniō*): unlimited, boundless, infinite

īnfinitās, -ātis (f.): boundlessness, infinity

īnfirmus, -a, -um: weak, infirm

īnflammō, -āre: set on fire; inflame

īnfrā (prep. w. acc.): below, beneath

īnfuī: perf. of *insum*

īnfundō, -ere, -ūdī, -ūsus: pour in, pour on

ingeminō, -āre: redouble (in 61 n. 32A)

ingemō, -ere, -uī, —: groan over, lament

ingeniōsus, -a, -um: endowed with natural abilities, clever, ingenious

ingenium, -ī (n.): innate quality, nature, character; natural gifts, talent (36 n. 1c) *ingēns*, *-entis* (adj.): unnatural, huge, prodigious; great, powerful

ingrātus, *-a*, *-um:* unpleasant, ungrateful

ingredior, *-ī*, *-essus* (dep.): advance, proceed; enter upon, i.e. undertake

inhospitālis, *-e:* inhospitable

inhūmānus, *-a*, *-um:* barbarous, inhuman: uncivil

iniciō, *-ere*, *-iēcī*, *-iectus:* throw into, put in, place on; infuse (w. acc. of the thing and dat. of the person)

iniī (or *inīvī*: 1 n. 4B): perf. of *ineō*

inimīcitia, *-ae* (f.): enmity (often political: 60 n. 19, 67 n. 1B)

inimīcus, *-a*, *-um:* unfriendly, hostile; (m. as a noun): personal (or political) enemy (29 n. 2, 33 n. 22B, 35 n. 25)

inīquitās, *-ātis* (f.): injustice, unfairness

inīquus, *-a*, *-um:* uneven; unequal; unfair; hostile

initium, *-ī* (n.): entrance, beginning

initus, *-ūs* (m.): entrance (69 n. 12C)

iniungō, *-ere*, *-iūnxī*, *-iūnctus:* join, attach to; inflict

iniūria, *-ae* (f.): wrong, injustice; outrage, injury; *iniūriā* (abl. as adv.): wrongly, unfairly

iniūstus, *-a*, *-um:* unreasonable, unjust

inl-: see *ill-*

innectō, *-ere*, *-ēxuī*, *-exus:* entwine, twist, weave about

innocēns, *-entis* (adj.; from neg. *in-* + pres. part. of *noceō*): harmless, guiltless, innocent

innocentia, *-ae* (f.): harmlessness, innocence; integrity

innumerābilis, *-e:* countless, innumerable

inopia, *-ae* (f.): need, want, lack

inopīnātus, *-a*, *-um* (adj.; from neg. *in-* + past part. of *opīnor*): unexpected

inops, *-opis* (adj.): without means, poor, wretched

inp-: see *imp-*

inquam, *inquit* (defective verb, found only in certain forms of pres., imperf., fut., and perf.): I say, he says, etc. (used only within direct quotations: 9 n. 5)

inquinātus, *-a*, *-um* (past part. of *inquinō*): foul, filthy, polluted

inquinō, *-āre:* pollute, make filthy

inr-: also written *irr-*

inrīdeō, *-ēre*, *-īsī*, *-īsus:* laugh at, jeer, mock

inrumpō, *-ere*, *-ūpī*, *-uptus:* break in

inruō, *-uere*, *-uī*, —: rush in, invade

insānus, *-a*, *-um:* of unsound mind, insane; absurd

insatiābiliter (adv.): insatiably (70 n. 12B)

inscius, *-a*, *-um:* ignorant, unknowing

inscrībō, *-ere*, *-ipsī*, *-iptus:* write on, inscribe

inscriptiō, *-ōnis* (f.): inscription (47 n. 13A)

inserō, *-ere*, *-sēvī*, *-situs:* graft (in 84 n. 19B; to be distinguished from the following)

inserō, *-ere*, *-uī*, *-tus:* implant; insert; introduce

insideō, *-ēre*, *-ēdī*, —: sit on; settle on, occupy

insidiae, *-ārum* (f. plur.): ambush; snare, plot

insidior, *-ārī*, *-ātus* (dep.): lie in ambush; plot against

insigne, *-is* (n. of *insignis* as noun): sign, symbol, decoration (8 n. 8D)

insignis, *-e:* distinguished, famous, remarkable

insitus, *-a*, *-um* (past part. of *inserō* [1]): implanted (i.e. inborn: in 17 n. 21A, 57 n. 5B)

insolēns, *-entis* (adj.; from neg. *in-* + pres. part. of *soleō*): unaccustomed (35 n. 22A, 87 n. 5C); unusual; immoderate, insolent

insolentia, *-ae* (f.): strangeness; excess; arrogance, insolence

insolitus, *-a*, *-um* (adj.; from neg. *in-* + past part. of *soleō*): unfamiliar, unaccustomed; unusual, strange

insōns, *-ontis* (adj.): guiltless, harmless

instar (n., indeclinable): likeness (w. gen.); (as if adj.): as good as (49 n. 9A)

instinctus, *-a*, *-um* (past part.; only form found of *instinguō*): incited, impelled, instigated

instituō, *-ere*, *-uī*, *-ūtus:* set up, establish; arrange; determine on

institūtum, *-ī* (n. as noun of past part. of *instituō*): purpose; habit; decree

instō, *-āre*, *-itī*, *-ātūrus:* stand upon or near, be at hand; urge on, press on

instruō, *-uere*, *-ūxī*, *-ūctus:* equip, prepare, set in order

insuētus, *-a*, *-um* (adj.; from neg. *in-* + past part. of *suēscō*; not past part. of *insuēscō*): unaccustomed, unused; strange, unusual

insula, *-ae* (f.): island

insultō, *-āre:* leap (or prance) upon (70 n. 23A); insult; triumph over *insum, inesse, infuī, infutūrus:* be in, be present (w. dat.: in 21 n. 15A; or w. *in* and abl.)

insuper (adv.): above, overhead; moreover, besides

insurgō, -ere, -rēxī, -rēctus: rise up, revolt, insurrect

intāctus, -a, -um (adj.; from neg. *in-+* past part. of *tangō*): untouched, uninjured, intact

integer, -gra, -grum: whole, unimpaired; fresh

integritās, -ātis (f.): soundness; innocence, integrity

intellēctus, -ūs (m.): perception, discernment

intellegō, -ere, -ēxī, -ēctus: understand, know, realize, learn

intempestus, -a, -um: unseasonable, unpropitious, dark; *intempestā nocte:* in the dead of night (12 n. 3A)

intemptātus, -a, -um (adj.; from neg. *in-* +past part. of *temptō*): untouched, untried (in 87 n. 8B)

intendō, -ere, -ī, -tus (or *-ēnsus):* stretch out, extend; aim, direct

intentus, -a, -um (past part. of *intendō*): attentive, intent, eager

inter (prep. w. acc.): among, between, in the midst of

intercēdō, -ere, -essī, -essum: come between, intervene; intercede (especially of a tribune interposing his veto: 18 n. 7C, 39 n. 7)

intercessiō, -ōnis (f.): mediation; protest, veto

interdīcō, -ere, -īxī, -ictus: forbid, interdict

interdum (adv.): at times, now and then, occasionally

intereā (adv.): meanwhile; nevertheless

interemō: see *interimō*

intereō, -īre, -iī (or *-īvī:* 1 n. 4B), *-itūrus:* perish, die

interesse: inf. of *intersum*

interest (impersonal; from *intersum*): it concerns, it interests (w. gen. of person)

interficiō, -ere, -ēcī, -ectus: kill, destroy

interfuī, -futūrus: perf. and fut. part. of *intersum*

interim (adv.): meanwhile, in the meantime

interimō (or *interemō*), *-ere, -ēmī, -ēmptus* (or *-ēmtus):* take away; do away with, kill

interior, -ius (comp. adj.): inner, interior; (sup.) *intimus:* innermost

interitus, -ūs (m.): ruin, annihilation, death

interminātus (adj.; from neg. *in-+*past part. of *terminō:* 68 n. 6C; it is not past part. of *inter-minor*): endless, boundless

interminor, -ārī, -ātus (dep.; from *inter+ minor*): threaten, forbid by threats

intermittō, -ere, -īsī, -issus: leave off, interrupt, neglect, intermit

interpellō, -āre: interfere with, hinder

interpōnō, -ere, -osuī, -ositus: place between, interpose, insert, interfere

interpres, -etis (m.): interpreter

interritus, -a, -um (adj.; from neg. *in-+* past part. of *terreō*): undismayed, unterrified

interrogō, -āre: ask, question, interrogate

interrumpō, -ere, -ūpī, -uptus: break apart, break off; interrupt

intersum, -esse, -fuī, -futūrus: lie between; differ, be different; be present at, take part in, assist; see *interest*

intimus: sup. of *interior*

intolerandus, -a, -um: insupportable, intolerable

intrā (prep. w. acc.): within, inside; into

intrepidus, -a, -um: unshaken, not hurried or excited, calm

intrō, -āre: go into, enter, penetrate

introeō, -īre, -iī (or *-īvī:* 1 n. 4B), —*:* go into, enter

intrōrsum (or *intrōrsus;* adv.): inwards, within

intueor, -ērī, -itus (dep.): look upon, gaze at; examine, consider

intulī: perf. of *inferō*

inūrō, -ere, -ūssī, -ūstus: burn in; crimp (hair: 79 n. 11)

inūsitātus, -a, -um (adj.; from neg. *in-+* past part. of *ūsitor*, a frequentative of *ūtor*): unusual, novel

inūtilis, -e: useless; injurious

invādō, -ere, -sī, -sus: enter, invade

invalidus, -a, -um: weak, inadequate, invalid

invectiō, -ōnis (f.): a bringing in; invective (42 B title)

invehō, -ere, -xī, -ctus: carry in, introduce; drive over; attack, inveigh against (71 title)

inveniō, -īre, -ēnī, -entus: come upon, find, meet with; invent, discover, ascertain *inventum, -ī* (n. as noun of past part. of *inveniō*): invention, device, i.e. doctrine (34 n. 4ʙ)

invicem (adv., originally prep. *in+vicem*, acc. of *vicis*): by turns, alternately; mutually; *ad invicem:* to one another (90 n. 14ʙ)

invictus, -a, -um (adj.; from neg. *in-+* past part. of *vincō*): unconquered, unconquerable

invideō, -ēre, -īdī, -īsus: look askance at, cast an evil eye on (74 n. 6); envy, hate

invidia, -ae (f.): envy; unpopularity, ill will

invidiōsus, -a, -um: envious, invidious; hateful

invidus, -a, -um: envious, jealous

inviolātus, -a, -um (adj.; from neg. *in-+* past part. of *violō*): unhurt, inviolate

invīsō, -ere, -īsī, —: go to see, visit; see (73 n. 21ʙ)

invīsus, -a, -um (past part. of *invideō* as adj.): hateful, detested; hostile

invītus, -a, -um (adj.; from neg. *in-+*a derivative of *volō, vīs*): unwilling, reluctant, against one's will

involvō, -ere, -ī, -lūtus: roll upon; wrap up, envelop; overwhelm

iocōsus, -a, -um: humorous, facetious

iocus, -ī (m., but n. plur. *ioca*): joke, jest

ipse, -a, -um (intensive pronoun or adj.): self; very, precisely; i.e. of one's own accord (85 nn. 14ʙ, 24ʙ, 28ʙ); gen. *ipsīus,* dat. *ipsī*

īra, -ae (f.): anger, rage

īrācundia, -ae (f.): irascibility, wrath

is, ea, id (demonstrative pronoun or adj.): this, that; he, she, it; the; gen. *ēius,* dat. *eī;* nom. m. and dat. or abl. plur. *iī, iīs* (16 n. 9ᴇ)

iste, ista, istud (demonstrative pronoun or adj.): that (of yours: 34 n. 8ʙ), that (which is at hand); that (awful; pejoratively: in 71 n. 2ᴀ); gen. *istīus,* dat. *istī*

istūc (adv.): in that direction, thither

ita (adv.): so, thus, in this way

itaque (conj.): and so, accordingly, therefore

item (adv.): likewise, furthermore; in like manner

iter, itineris (n.): way, journey; road, path; *iter facere:* to march

iterō, -āre: repeat

iterum (adv.): again, a second time; in turn

iuba, -ae (f.): mane; crest of a helmet (in 61 n. 30ᴀ)

iubeō, -ēre, iussī, iussus: order, tell, command; wish, bid

iūcunditās, -ātis (f.): pleasantness, charm; delight, enjoyment

iūcundus, -a, -um: pleasant, agreeable, delightful

iūdex, -icis (m.): judge (i.e. God: 82 B s. 3); juror; decider

iūdicium, -ī (n.): trial, judicial process; court; judgment, verdict; power of judging, discernment

iūdicō, -āre: judge, determine, decide; think

iugulō, -āre: cut the throat, murder

iugulum, -ī (n.): throat, neck

iugum, -ī (n.): yoke (51 last v., 85 n. 26ʙ); i.e. a yoked pair of animals (88 n. 10ᴀ)

iūnior: comp. of *iuvenis*

iūre (abl. of *iūs* as adv.): rightly (18 n. 17ʙ)

iūrgium, -ī (n.): quarrel, strife

iūrō, -āre: take an oath, swear; see *iūs iūrandum*

iūs, iūris (n.): law (see for types 14 p. 3 s. 1); right, justice; legal prerogative (or authority)

iūs iūrandum, iūris iūrandī (n.): oath (2 n. 7ᴀ; often written as one word but still declined in both parts, as in 9 n. 17ᴀ)

iussī, iussus: perf. and past part. of *iubeō*

iussū (abl. sing.; only form used of *iussus, -ūs*): by order, by decree

iussum, -ī (n. as noun of past part. of *iubeō*): order, command

iūstitia, -ae (f.): justice, equity

iūstus, -a, -um: honorable, just, right

iūtus: past part. of *iuvō*

iuvenca, -ae (f., or m. *iuvencus, -ī*): heifer (or young bullock: 86 n. 12)

iuvenis, -is (adj.): youthful, young; (m. and f. as a noun): young person, youth; (comp.) *iūnior:* younger; (no sup.)

iuventa, -ae (f.): season of youth, youth

iuventūs, -ūtis (f.): time of youth, young manhood; young persons (62 n. 16ʙ, 72 n. 14), young men (of military age: 8 n. 9ᴀ)

iuvō, āre, iūvī, iūtus: help (in 86 n. 7ʙ); benefit (54 n. 2ʙ); please (85 n. 3ᴄ)

iūxtā (adv.): close, near by; equally (65 n. 9ʙ), alike; (prep. w. acc.): near, close to (90 n. 9ʙ) *labefactō, -āre:* cause to totter, shake; weaken; overthrow

labellum, -ī (n.): little (i.e. dainty) lip

labium, -ī (n.): lip

labō, -āre: totter (66 n. 14B), waver

lābor, -ī, lapsus (dep.): slip, slide; sink, begin to fall; go to ruin

labor, -ōris (m.): labor, effort; hardship, suffering (differentiated from the preceding by the short -a-)

labōrō, -āre: work, strive; be hard pressed, suffer

lāc, lactis (n.): milk; *lāc pressum:* i.e. cheese (84 n. 25)

lacerna, -ae (f.): cloak (military: in 45 n. 10A)

lacerō, -āre: tear to pieces, rend

lacessō, -ere, -īvī, -ītus: provoke, annoy; arouse

lacrima, -ae (f.): tear

lacrimō, -āre: shed tears, weep (i.e. drip: 80 n. 8)

lacteus, -a, -um: milk-white (55 n. 19)

lacūna, -ae (f.): pit, hole; lake, pool (70 n. 22 C)

lacus, -ūs (m.): lake, pool

laedō, -ere, -sī, -sus: injure, vex

laetor, -ārī, -ātus (dep.): be glad, rejoice (w. abl.: 78 n. 2)

laetus, -a, -um: fruitful (of fields: 69 n. 13C); rich; glad (in 52 n. 6); pleasing, delightful

laevus, -a, -um: on the left (i.e. favorable: 52 n. 5A)

lambō, -ere, —, —: lick, lap (55 n. 7)

lāna, -ae (f.): wool

languēscō, -ere, -guī, —: grow weak or languid (57 p. 3 s. 2); sink

lānificium, -ī (n.): spinning, weaving (5 n. 8, 83 n. 5B)

lapideus, -a, -um: of stone (10 p. 2 last s.)

lapis, -idis (m.): stone; milestone (10 n. 14A)

lār, lăris (m.): household god; i.e. home (73 n. 24B)

largē (adv.; from *largus*): generously

largior, -īrī, -ītus (dep.): give lavishly, bestow, impart; bribe

largitiō, -ōnis (f.): a giving freely, bestowing, generosity; bribery

largitor, -ōris (m.): generous giver, squanderer; briber

largus, -a, -um: plentiful; liberal, generous

lascivus, -a, -um: sportive (87 n. 28B); wanton

lassitūdō, -inis (f.): weariness, lassitude

lateō, -ēre, -uī, —: lie hid, escape notice

lātrō, -āre: bark, bark at (w. direct object in 12 n. 3B)

latrō, -ōnis (m.): bandit, robber (distinguishable from the preceding by the short -a- and in the oblique forms)

lātus, -a, -um: past part. from *tollō* but used for *ferō*

lātus, -a, -um: broad, wide (distinguishable from the preceding only by the context)

latus, -eris (n.): side (46 n. 6B, 78 n. 29A; distinguishable from the two preceding by the short -a- and in the oblique forms)

laudātiō, -ōnis (f.): praise, eulogy (83 B title)

laudātor, -ōris (m.): praiser, eulogizer

laudō, -āre: praise, commend, laud

laurea, -ae (f.): laurel tree, i.e. war (in 32 n. 20B)

laurus, -ī (f.): laurel (87 n. 42C)

laus, laudis (f.): praise; fame, reputation (76 n. 22F), merit

lautus, -a, -um: splendid, sumptuous; *lautissimī* (n. of sup. as a noun): the wealthy (in 31 n. 9B)

laxus, -a, -um: loose, open, spacious

lectīca, -ae (f.): litter (43 n. 16A; derived from *lectus* below)

lēctiō, -ōnis (f.): a selecting; a reading aloud (see *legō, -ere*); *lēctiō senātūs:* a making up of the senate (by selecting those qualified to be senators: 57 n. 3)

lēctus: past part. of *legō*

lectus, -ī (m.): couch, bed (the short -e- shows that its root is different from the preceding)

lēgātiō, -ōnis (f.): ambassadorship; embassy (10 n. 17)

lēgātus, -ī (m. as noun of past part. of *lēgō, -āre*): envoy, ambassador (9 B s. 5); deputy, legate (i.e. a senatorial commander of a legion under the higher command of a magistrate: in 14 n. 4A, 21 n. 2D)

legiō, -ōnis (f.): a levy (of troops); legion (the main military unit of the Romans)

lēgitimus, -a, -um (adj.; from *lēx, lēgis*): fixed by law, lawful, legitimate

lēgō, -āre: to send as a deputy (or envoy); to bequeath

legō, -ere, lēgī, lēctus: collect; select (for the senate: 47 n. 18); read (29 n. 3, and often)

lēniō, -īre: make mild, pacify
lēnis, -e: soft, gentle, mild; gradual
lēnitās, -ātis (f.): softness, gentleness
lentus, -a, -um: pliant (84 n. 12); slow (i.e. at ease: 84 n. 3A)
leō, -ōnis (m.): lion
lepōs, -ōris (m.): charm, grace (69 nn. 14B, 23B); wit
lepus, -oris (m.): hare (distinguishable from the preceding by the short *-o-*)
lētālis, -e: deadly, fatal
lētum, -ī (n.): death
levis, -e: light, trivial
lēx, lēgis (f.): law; contract (or agreement: 26 n. 2, in 67 n. 5); *lēgem ferre:* pass a law (20 n. 7, 24 n. 10, 45 n. 2B)
libēns, -entis (pres. part. of *libet* as adj.): willing; glad
libenter (adv.): gladly, willingly
liber, librī (m.): book (distinguishable from the following by the short *-i-* and by the loss of *-e-* in the oblique cases)
līber, -era, -erum: free; unrestrained (5 n. 3B)
līberālis, -e: of freedom; of free persons; liberal
līberī, -ōrum (m. plur.): children (9 n. 14A, 15 n. 16A, 19 n. 13B; distinguishable from the m. plur. of *līber* above only by the context)
lībertās, -ātis (f.): liberty, freedom
lībertīnus, -ī (m.): freedman (76 n. 11)
lībertus, -ī (m.): freedman (in 76 n. 11)
libet, -ēre, -uit (or *-itum est*; impersonal): it pleases, is agreeable
libīdinōsus, -a, -um: licentious, lustful
libīdō, -inis (f.): longing, desire; wantonness, lust
licentia, -ae (f.): lack of control, license
licet, -ēre, -uit (or *-itum est*; impersonal): it is permitted (w. dat. of person); it is lawful; granted that, although (w. subj., w. or without *ut* as a connective: 23 n. 1A, and often)
ligneus, -a, -um: wood, wooden (9 B last s.)
līmen, -inis (n.): threshold
līmōsus, -a, -um: muddy, slimy (64 n. 7B)
līmus, -ī (m.): slime, mud (24 p. 3 s. 3)
lineāmentum, -ī (n.): line, outline (72 n. 2); feature, lineament
lingua, -ae (f.): tongue; language, speech
linquō, -uere, līquī, (lictus in compounds): leave, depart from (73 nn. 13A, 22C)
liqueō, -uēre, -uī, —: flow, be liquid (73 n. 20B)

liquēscō, -ere, —, —: become fluid, liquefy, melt
liquidus, -a, -um: liquid, fluid, flowing
liquō, -āre: make liquid; clarify (87 n. 14B)
līquor, līquī, — (dep.): run liquid (61 n. 33B)
liquor, -ōris (m.): liquid, fluid
litō, -āre: offer acceptable sacrifice; give favorable omens (80 n. 10A)
littera, -ae (f.): letter of the alphabet; (in plur): letter (32 n. 3A); also "letters" or literature
lītus, -oris (n.): shore, beach
līvor, -ōris (m.): bruise (83 n. 13C)
locuplēs, -ētis (adj.): rich in lands (20 n. 10C); wealthy
locuplētō, -āre: enrich, adorn
locus, -ī (m.); plur.: *loca, -ōrum* (n.): place, spot, locality; situation, place in an order (of time: 43 n. 17B; for rank: 77 n. 10D)
longē (adv. of *longus*): far away, by far
longus, -a, -um: long, extended; remote
loquāx, -ācis (adj.): loquacious, babbling (87 n. 32A)
loquella, -ae (f.): speech, word (69 n. 28A)
loquor, -uī, -cūtus (dep.): speak, say, tell
lōrum, -ī (n.): leather strap (24 p. 3 s. 3)
lūceō, -ēre, -xī, —: be light, shine, glow
lucerna, -ae (f.): lamp (41 n. 18C)
lūctus, -ūs (m.): mourning, grief, lamentation
lūcus, -ī (m.): sacred wood; grove (49 v. 1, 80 n. 9B)
lūdō, -ere, -sī, -sus: play, amuse oneself; make sport of, mock; elude
lūdus, -ī (m.): game, sport; school (28 p. 4 s. 1); (plur.): public games, exhibitions
lumbus, -ī (m.): loin (89 n. 12)
lūmen, -inis (n.): light (60 n. 5B, and often); i.e. life (70 n. 24A); eye (77 n. 34B, 78 n. 27A); glory (i.e. famous man: 27 n. 10)
lūna, -ae (f.): moon
lūnāris, -e: of the moon, lunar (in 80 n. 6A)
luō, luere, luī, —: loose, free; pay off; atone for
lupa, -ae (f.): she-wolf (55 n. 5A)
lupercal, -ālis: a grotto sacred to Faunus; (plur.): ceremony to Faunus (42 nn. 12A, 26B)
lupercus, -ī (m.): priest of Faunus (42 n. 8C)

lupus, -ī (m.): wolf
lūridus, -a, -um: pale, sallow, ghastly, lurid (80 v. 9)
luscus, -a, -um: one-eyed (59 n. 21B)
lūtum, -ī (n.): plant yielding yellow dye, yellow (85 n. 28I)
lūx, lūcis (f.): light, brightness (i.e. safety: 29 n. 12); *prīma lūx:* dawn
lūxuria, -ae (f.): luxury, profusion
lūxuriōsus, -a, -um: luxurious, exuberant
lūxus, -ūs (m.): luxury, debauchery; pomp
lympha, -ae (f.): water (in 86 n. 23A, 87 n. 32B)
lymphātus, -a, -um: distracted, maddened (86 n. 23A)

māchinor, -ārī, -ātus (dep.): devise, contrive, plot
mactō, -āre: extol, honor; sacrifice; punish (71 n. 19c)
maculō, -āre: spot; pollute
madeō, -ēre, -uī, —: be wet, be sodden
maeror, -ōris (m.): grief, sorrow
magis (adv.): more, in a higher degree; rather, in preference
magister, -trī (m.): master; teacher (34 A s. 3)
magistrātus, -ūs (m.): magistracy
māgnificō, -āre: esteem highly; praise, magnify (89 n. 27B)
māgnificus, -a, -um: great, elevated; magnificent, rich
māgnitūdō, -inis (f.): magnitude, size, greatness
māgnopere (or *māgnō opere;* abl. as adv.: 14 n. 17): very much, exceedingly; earnestly
māgnus, -a, -um: large, big, great; (comp.) *māior;* (sup.) *māximus*
māiestās, -ātis (f.): greatness, grandeur; dignity, majesty
māior, māius (comp. of *māgnus*): larger, greater; *māior nātū:* i.e. older (15 n. 11A)
māiōres, -rum (m. plur. of *māior* as noun): fathers, ancestors (16 n. 9B); *mōs māiōrum:* ancestral customs (15 n. 13B)
male (adv. of *malus*): badly, wrongly, adversely
maledīcō, -ere, -dīxī, -dictus: say ill of, curse
maledictum, -ī (n. as noun of the past part. of *maledīcō*): abusive word, curse

maleficium, -ī (n.): misdeed; harm
malīgnus, -a, -um: ill-natured, malignant
mālō, mālle, māluī, —: wish more, choose, prefer
malus, -a, -um: bad, not good; (comp.) *pēior:* worse; (sup.) *pessimus:* worst
manceps, -ipis (m.): purchaser; contractor (in 31 n. 5B)
mancipium, -ī (n.): a taking possession, legal purchase; property; slave
mandō, -āre: send; send word, order; entrust
māne (n. acc. sing. of an adj. found only in this form and used as adv.): in the morning
maneō, -ēre, mānsī, mānsum: remain, stay; endure
mānēs, -ium (m.): the spirits of the dead; *ad mānēs:* i.e. to the underworld (77 n. 4A)
manifestus, -a, -um (adj.; from *manus*+ *-festus,* perhaps = taken, or, aimed): manifest, obvious
mānō, -āre: drip, distill
mānsuēscō, -ere, -ēvī, -ētus (from *manus* + *suēscō*): to accustom, train, habituate
mānsuētūdō, -inis (f.): mildness, gentleness
mānsuētus, -a, -um (past part. of *mānsuēscō* as adj.): tamed, mild, humble (in 89 n. 9)
manus, -ūs (f.): hand; handful (i.e. group: 78 n. 8D); *manū* (abl.): in hand-to-hand fighting (24 n. 2A), in action (65 n. 25); *manus ultima* (46 n. 20A) or *extrēma* (62 n. 15B): i.e. the finishing touch
mapālia, -ium (n. plur.): huts (64 n. 14B)
mare, -is (n.): sea
margarīta, -ae (f.): pearl (33 p. 3 s. 2)
marmor, -oris (n.): marble; shining surface of sea
māter, -tris (f.): mother
māteria, -ae (or *māteriēs, -ēī;* f.): matter, substance; timber, wood, material
mātrimōnium, -ī (n.): marriage
mātrōna, -ae (f.): married woman, wife; woman of rank
mātūrus, -a, -um: ripe, mature; seasonable; early
mausōlēum, -ī (n.): splendid tomb, mausoleum (46 n. 16A)
māximē (adv. of *māximus*): especially, exceedingly, very

māximus, -a, -um (sup. of *māgnus*): largest, greatest, chief

mē: acc. and abl. of *ego*; *mē hercule:* see *hercule*

meātus, -ūs (m.): a going, path (88 p. 4 v. 3)

medicīna, -ae (f.): healing art, medicine; remedy

medicus, -ī (m.): doctor

mediocris, -e: middle, average; mediocre, inferior

meditor, -ārī, -ātus (dep.): ponder; plan; rehearse

medius, -a, -um: in the middle of (12 n. 7B, 54 n. 12C); mid

meī: gen. of *ego*; also m. or n. gen. sing. or m. nom. plur. of *meus*

mel, mellis (n.): honey (89 n. 4C; often plur.: 85 n. 18B); sweetness

melior, melius (comp. of *bonus*): better

membrum, -ī (n.): member, limb; part

meminī, -isse (defective): remember; recollect; mention

memor, -oris (adj.): remembering, mindful; reminiscent, commemorative

memorābilis, -e: memorable, remarkable

memoria, -ae (f.): memory; remembrance; historical account, record

memorō, -āre: mention, relate

mēns, mentis (f.): mind, feeling, character; intellect; intention, purpose (12 n. 5, 20 n. 5D); *bona mēns:* good sense (58 n. 15C)

mēnsis, -is (m.): month

mentiō, -ōnis (f.): a calling to mind, mention

mentior, -īrī, -ītus (dep.): lie, pretend; lie about, feign, counterfeit (85 n. 27)

mercātor, -ōris (m.): trader (in 31 n. 5B), merchant; buyer

mercēnārius, -a, -um: serving for pay, mercenary (9 B s. 4)

mercēs, -ēdis (f.): wages, recompense

mercor, -ārī, -ātus (dep.): trade, deal in, purchase (33 p. 3 s. 2)

mereō, -ēre, -uī, -itus: deserve; earn, merit

mereor, -ērī, -itus (dep.): deserve, merit; be meritorious; *stipendia merērī:* serve in the army; *bene merērī dē* (w. abl.): deserve well of, serve well

merīdiēs (m.): midday, noon; the south

meritum, -ī (n. as noun of past part. of *mereō*): something deserved, merit, desert; (by contrast): demerit, fault

merum, -ī (n. of *merus* as noun): unmixed wine (i.e. not diluted with water: 87 n. 25A)

merus, -a, -um: pure, unmixed; plain, mere

merx, -cis (f.): goods, merchandise (often plur.: 85 n. 25C)

mētior, -īrī, mēnsus (dep.): measure

metuō, -uere, -uī, —: fear, be apprehensive

metus, -ūs (m.): fear; cause of fear

meus, -a, -um: my, mine

mī: = mihī

migrō, -āre: depart, migrate

mihī (or *mihi*): dat. of *ego*

miles, -itis (m.): soldier

milia (n.): plur. of *mille*

mīlitāris, -e: of a soldier, military

mīlitia, -ae (f.): soldiering, military service, warfare; i.e. soldiers (90 n. 12B); *mīlitiae* (loc.) . . . *domī:* in the field . . . at home (13 n. 5A)

mīlitō, -āre: serve as a soldier (7 n. 6B, 82 n. 8C)

mille (adj.): thousand; *mille passūs:* a thousand paces (i.e. a Roman mile); (plur. as noun): *milia* w. gen., e.g. *duo milia passuum:* i.e. 2 miles

minimē (adv. of *minimus*): least of all, very little, not at all, no

minimus, -a, -um (sup. of *parvus*): least, littlest

minister, -trī (m. of adj. as noun): servant, attendant (87 n. 22A)

minitor, -ārī, -ātus (dep.): threaten, menace (with dat. of person in 30 n. 4B)

minō, -āre: drive (of animals; late Lat. from *minor*: 89 n. 15)

minor, -ārī, -ātus (dep.): threaten

minor, minus (comp. of *parvus*): less, smaller; *minor nātū:* i.e. younger (15 B p. 2 s. 2)

minuō, -uere, -uī, -ūtus: make small, lessen; diminish, ebb; mitigate, abate

mīrābilis, -e: wonderful, marvelous, strange (see 72 n. 10B)

mīror, -ārī, -ātus (dep.): wonder; wonder at (21 n. 17B); admire, esteem

mīrus, -a, -um: strange, astonishing

misceō, -ēre, -uī, mīxtus: mix, unite (23 n. 2A); confuse, confound (17 n. 9, 18 n. 6B, 59 n. 26C)

miser, -era, -erum: poor (in money: 34 n. 15), wretched

misereor, -ērī, -itus (dep.): pity, commiserate (w. gen.: 24 n. 18A, 82 n. 13)

miseria, -ae (f.): misery, wretchedness

misericordia, -ae (f.): pity, compassion

misericors, -cordis (adj.): compassionate, tenderhearted, merciful

miseror, -ārī, -ātus (dep.): lament, deplore, commiserate

missiō, -ōnis (f.): a sending; liberation; discharge (21 n. 14B, 33 n. 8A), dismissal

missus: past part. of *mittō*

mītigō, -āre: soften; soothe; mitigate

mītis, -e: mild, ripe; lenient

mittō, -ere, mīsī, missus: send, send away, dismiss; let go (40 n. 12, 73 n. 31B); produce; omit

moderātiō, -ōnis (f.): regulation; self-control, restraint, moderation

moderātus, -a, -um (past part. of *moderor* as adj.): moderate, restrained

moderor, -ārī, -ātus (dep.): moderate, restrain; regulate

modestia, -ae (f.): modesty; discretion, propriety of conduct

modestus, -a, -um: modest, discreet

modicus, -a, -um: moderate, little, scanty

modo (adv.; from abl. of *modus*, w. iambic shortening of the final -ō, for which compare 59 n. 29B); only, merely; recently, just now; see *dummodo*

modus, -ī (m.): means, manner; measure, meter (in verse: 87 n. 41F)

moenia, -ium (n. plur.): fortifications, city walls (49 n. 8)

moenus: see *mūnus* (69 n. 24C)

mōlēs, -is (f.): bulk, mass; massive structure, dam

mōlior, -īrī, -ītus (dep.): strive; set in motion; attempt, endeavor

mollis, -e: soft, tender (85 n. 17), gentle; flexible, supple

moneō, -ēre, -uī, -itus: warn, advise; predict

mōns, montis (m.): mountain; mountain range

mōnstrum, -ī (n.): portent, divine sign; monster (of Cleopatra in 46 n. 5A, 86 n. 26B; of Catiline in 72 n. 6); monstrous deed (78 n. 6B); monstrous person (78 n. 24B)

monumentum, -ī (n.): that which brings to mind (37 n. 4C); memorial, monument (87 n. 33B); i.e. tomb

mora, -ae (f.): delay; cause of delay; lapse of time

morbus, -ī (m.): disease

mordeō, -ēre, momordī, morsus: bite

moribundus, -a, -um: dying, moribund

morior, -ī (or *-īrī*), *-tuus:* die, die out, expire

moritūrus: dep. fut. part. of *morior*

moror, -ārī, -ātus (dep.): delay, remain; sojourn (late Lat.: 89 n. 14B)

mōrōsus, -a, -um: fretful, hypercritical; (comp.) *mōrōsior:* overfastidious (33 p. 2 s. 3)

mors, mortis (f.): death

morsus, -ūs (m.): biting, bite; pain, vexation

mortālis, -e: subject to death, mortal

mortuus: past part. of *morior*

mōs, mōris (m.): custom, manner, habit, precedent; (plur.): conduct, behavior, manners, morals, character; *mōs māiōrum:* ancestral or traditional custom or behavior (15 n. 13B), = also *mōs patrius* (57 n. 21) and *mōs parentum* (73 n. 8A)

mōtus: past part. of *moveō*

mōtus, -ūs (m.): motion; commotion, turmoil, uprising

moveō, -ēre, mōvī, mōtus: move, set in motion; stir, disturb

mox (adv.): soon, presently; thereupon, afterward

mucrō, -ōnis (m.): edge, point; sword's point

mulceō, -ēre, -sī, -sus: stroke, caress (55 n. 8B)

mulcō, -āre: beat, maltreat

muliebris, -e: of a woman, feminine (46 n. 18); effeminate

muliebriter (adv.): like a woman (86 n. 27D)

mulier, -eris (f.): woman; wife; mistress (74 n. 7B)

mūliō, -ōnis (m.): mule driver (53 n. 13A)

multa, -ae (f.): a money penalty, fine

multiplex, -icis (adj.): multiple, manifold

multiplicō, -āre: multiply, increase

multitūdō, -inis (f.): large number, crowd, multitude; i.e. "the masses"

multō, -āre: punish (by a *multa*), fine

multō (n. abl. sing. of *multus* as adv.): by much, greatly

multum (n. acc. sing. of *multus* as adv.): much, very, greatly, especially, often; (comp.) *plūs:* more; (sup.) *plūrimum:* most

multus, -a, -um: much, many; i.e. continually (63 n. 3B, 65 n. 23B); (comp.) *plūs, plūris:* more; (sup.) *plūrimus, -a, -um:* most; *multā nocte:* late at night (also *intempestā nocte,* 12 n. 3A) *munditia, -ae* (f.): cleanliness, neatness, elegance (usually in plur.: 87 n. 3)

mundus, -a, -um: clean, neat, elegant

mundus, -ī (m.): world (82A last s., 85 n. 9E), universe (80 n. 24B)

mūnia, -ōrum (n. plur.): duties, functions

mūnicipālis, -e: municipal, of a provincial town; m. as noun: a townsman (76 n. 9)

mūnificentia, -ae (f.): liberality, munificence

mūniō, -īre: wall, fortify, strengthen

mūnitus, -a, -um (past part. of *mūniō*): fortified, protected

mūnus, -eris (n.; archaic spelling *moenus,* 69 n. 24C): service, duty, task, rite (73 n. 8B); gift (73 n. 3B)

mūnusculum, -ī (n.): little gift (85 n. 13B)

mūrex, -icis (m.): shellfish from which purple dye came; purple (85 n. 28F)

murmur, -uris (n.): murmur, roaring

mūsa, -ae (or *M-*; f.): muse (60 n. 27A, 85 n. 2); i.e. music (84 nn. 2B and C)

mutilō, -āre: cut off, mutilate

mūtō, -āre: change; move in exchange (85 n. 25B), exchange (86 n. 13E); alter (85 n. 28G, in 87 n. 4)

mūtuus, -a, -um: borrowed, lent; mutual, reciprocal; *aes mūtuum:* a loan (65 n. 20B)

myrica, -ae (f.): tamarisk (85 v. 2)

myrtus, -ī (f.): myrtle, myrtle tree (87 n. 21B)

nam (conj.): for; *namque* (emphatic): for truly, for indeed

nanciscor, -ī, nactus (or *nanctus*; dep.): obtain, find

nārēs, -ium (f. plur.): nostrils, the nose (24 p. 3 s. 3)

nārrō, -āre: tell, relate; describe

nāscor (originally *gnāscor*), *-ī, nātus* (dep.): be born; begin, grow, arise (43 n. 21B)

nāta, -ae (f.): see *nātus* below

nātālis, -e: of birth, natal; (m. as noun): birthday (in 41 n. 13B)

nātiō, -ōnis (f.): race, tribe, people, nation

nātivitās, -ātis (f.): nativity, birth (90 n. 1B)

nātūra, -ae (f.): nature

nātūrālis, -e: natural, by birth, according to nature

nātus, -a, -um (past part. of *nāscor*): born; (m. or f. as noun): son, daughter

nātū (m. abl. of specification, either of supine of *nāscor* or of a nom. *nātus, -ūs*): in birth; *māior* or *minor nātū, etc.*: i.e. older or younger, etc. (15 n. 11A)

nauta, -ae (m.): sailor

nauticus, -a, -um: of sailors, nautical

nāvālis, -e: of ships, naval

nāviger, -era, -erum: ship-bearing, navigable (69 v. 3)

nāvigō, -āre: sail, cruise

nāvis, -is (f.): ship; *nāvis longa:* i.e. warship (9 n. 12B)

nāviter (adv. of *nāvus*): energetically, diligently, wholeheartedly

nāvus, -a, -um: energetic, busy

nē (neg. conj. w. subj.): that . . . not, in order that . . . not, lest; (neg. adv. w. hortatory and jussive subj.): not; *nē . . . quidem* (adv.): not even

ne- (in compounds) or *-ne* (as enclitic): the original, weak, form of *nē*; *-ne* indicates a question to which the answer may be "yes" or "no"

nē (affirmative interj. with a similar form in Greek and not related to neg. *nē*; used only with personal or demonstrative pronouns): verily, indeed, really

nec (neg. conj.): see *neque*; = *et non* (80 n. 16C, 83 n. 19B)

necessārius, -a, -um: necessary; connected by natural ties, related; (m. as noun): close friend (81 n. 2B)

necesse (n. adj.; only in nom. and acc. with *esse* or *habēre*): necessary, unavoidable

necessitūdō, -inis (f.): necessity, need; close relationship, friendship (32 n. 10B)

necis, -em: gen. and acc. sing. of *nex*

necne (conj.): or not (used in indirect questions)

necō, -āre: kill, murder

nectō, -ere, nexuī, nexus: bind, tie together

nefārius, -a, -um: wicked

nefās (n., indeclinable): wicked deed, abomination, something contrary to divine law (in 8 n. 7B, 66 n. 7, 77 n. 12B, 87 n. 10B)

nefāstus, -a, -um: contrary to religion, impious (8 n. 7B)

neglegēns, -entis (pres. part. of *neglegō* as adj.): negligent, careless

neglegentia, -ae (f.): carelessness, negligence

neglegō, -ere, -ēxī, -ēctus: neglect, be indifferent to

negō, -āre: say no, refuse, deny; say . . . not

negōtiātor, -ōris (m.): wholesaler dealer, financier (31 n. 6B)

negōtium, -ī (n.): business; trouble; *negōtī gerentēs:* businessmen (76 n. 10)

nēmō (m. and f. pronoun used of persons only): no man, no one; gen. and abl. usually from *nūllus,* i.e. *nūllīus, nūllō;* dat. *nēminī,* acc. *nēminem*

nemorōsus, -a, -um: wooded, full of trees

nempe (conj.): certainly, indeed, forsooth

nemus, -oris (n.): grove

nepōs, -ōtis (m.): grandson; descendant

neque, nec (neg. conj.): neither, and . . . not; *neque . . . neque,* or *nec . . . nec:* neither . . . nor

nequeō, -īre, -īvī, —: be unable, cannot

nēquīquam (adv.; from *nē*+abl. of *quisquam*): in vain

nēsciō, -īre: not know, be ignorant of

nēscius, -a, -um: ignorant, unaware

nēve, neu (conj.): and not, nor

nex, necis (f.): murder, death

niger, -gra, -grum: black, dark

nihil or *nīl* (n., indeclinable): nothing; no, none of (w. gen.); (as adv.): not at all (20 n. 4A, 71 n. 3A, 87 n. 21C)

nihildum (n., indeclinable): nothing yet

nihilōminus (adv.): none the less, notwithstanding

nihilum, -ī (n.; original form of *nihil*): nothing

nīl: = *nihil*

nimis (adv.): too much, excessively

nimium (adv.): too much, too

nimius, -a, -um: very great, very much, excessive

nisi (conj.): if not, except, unless

niteō, -ēre, -uī, —: gleam, shine

nitor, -ī, nīxus (or *nīsus;* dep.): lean on; depend on; press forward; strive

nivālis, -e: snowy (86 n. 25B)

niveus, -a, -um: snowy, snow-white (in 51 n. 17)

nōbilis, -e: well known, distinguished, noble (used of senators of consular families as adj. or noun: 18 pref., 36 n. 6B)

nōbilitās, -ātis (f.): high birth (particularly from a consular family: 63 n. 14B), nobility; (collectively): the *nōbilēs* (in 20 n. 14A, and often)

nōbīs: dat. and abl. of *nōs*

noceō, -ēre, -uī, -itūrus: injure, hurt (w. dat.)

noctū (old loc. abl. found only in this case as adv.): by night (1 n. 3)

nocturnus, -a, -um: nocturnal

noenum (neg. adv., from *ne-*+*oinom*=*ūnum*): archaic form of *nōn* (61 n. 14A)

nōlō, nōlle, nōluī, —: be unwilling, not wish

nōmen, -inis (n.): name (in particular, the gentile or middle name of a Roman); reputation (in 77 n. 21A, 78 n. 5); i.e. a people (41 n. 11B, 88 n. 1D)

nōminō, -āre: name

nōn (neg. adv.; see also *noenum* above): not; *nōn sōlum* (or *nōn modo*) . . . *sed etiam:* not only . . . but also

nōndum (neg. adv.): not yet

nōnne (double neg. interrog. adv.): introduces a question expecting the answer "yes"

nōnnūllus (or *nōn nūllus:* 37 n. 20B, 40 n. 16C), *-a, -um:* some (lit. not none); (plur.): several (33 n. 21; contrast 42 n. 9A)

nōnus, -a, -um: ninth

nōs (plur. 1st pers. pronoun): we; also, I (32 n. 12B, and often); declined *nostrum* or *-trī, nōbīs, nōs, nōbīs*

nōscō (originally *gnōscō*), *-ere, nōvī, nōtus:* learn; know (in perf.); knew (in pluperf.)

nōsmet: intensive for *nōs* (37 n. 27A)

nōsse: contracted perf. inf. of *nōscō*

noster, -tra, -trum: our, ours; (m. plur. as noun): our soldiers, our men

nostrī: gen. of *nōs;* also m. and n. gen. sing. or m. nom. plur. of *noster*

nostrum: gen. of *nōs;* also n. nom. sing. or m. or n. acc. sing. of *noster*

nota, -ae: (f.): mark (54 n. 16D)

notō, -āre: mark, indicate

nōtus, -a, -um (past. part. of *nōscō* as adj.): known, well known

novāle, -is (n. of *novālis* as noun): ploughed field (84 n. 17)

novālis, -e (adj., from *novus*): newly ploughed

novem (indeclinable cardinal numeral): nine

novitās, -ātis (f.): newness, novelty

novus, -a, -um: new, novel, strange; (sup.) *novissimus, -a, -um:* newest; most recent

nox, noctis (f.): night

noxia, -ae (f.): harm; offense

noxius, -a, -um: harmful; guilty

nūbēs, -is (f.): cloud

nūbilus, -a, -um: cloudy, darkened (49 n. 2A)

nūbō, -ere, -psī, -ptus: marry (only of the woman; lit. veil oneself for, w. dat.: 74 n. 7C)

nūdus, -a, -um: bare, naked, stark (of style: 79 n. 7A)

nūllus, -a, -um (pronoun and adj.): not any, no, none; gen. nūllīus, dat. nūllī

num (interrog. particle): sign of question expecting answer "no"; whether, if (in indirect question)

nūmen, -inis (n.): divine power or spirit; divinity (in 73 n. 24B, 77 nn. 22, 30B)

numerus, -ī (m.): number; i.e. calculation (87 n. 11A)

numquam (adv.): not ever, never

nunc (adv.): now, at this time

nūntiō, -āre: report, announce

nūntius, -ī (m.): messenger; message

nūper (adv.): recently, lately

nūptiae, -ārum (f. plur.): marriage

nurus, -ūs (f.): daughter-in-law

ob (prep. w. acc.): on account of, for

obdūrō, -āre: be firm against, persist

obeō, -īre, -iī (or -īvī: 1 n. 4B; -īt: 70 n. 27B), -itus: go to meet; traverse (88 n. 8B); attend to; mortem obīre (15 B s. 3; or diem suum obīre): meet death, die

obiciō, -ere, -iēcī, -iectus: throw against; place opposite; reproach someone (dat.: 40 n. 19B) for something (acc.)

oblātus: past part. of offerō

oblīquus, -a, -um: slanting (77 n. 34A), crosswise; indirect

oblīvīscor, -ī, -lītus (dep.): forget (w. gen.)

oborior, -īrī, -tus (dep.): arise, spring up

obruō, -uere, -uī, -utus: overwhelm, overthrow, hide, bury

obscūrus, -a, -um: dark, obscure

obsequium, -ī (n.): compliance, obedience

obsequor, -ī, -cūtus (dep.): yield to, submit to (w. dat.)

obses, -idis (m. and f.): hostage

obsideō, -ēre, -ēdī, -essus: besiege

obsidiō, -ōnis (f.): siege

obsistō, -ere, -stitī, -stitus: place oneself in the way, oppose (w. dat.: in 3 n. 5)

obstinātus, -a, -um (past part. of obstinō): resolved, stubborn, obstinate

obstinō, -āre: resolve; be determined

obstō, -āre, -itī, -ātūrus: stand in way of, oppose (w. dat. or w. quōminus and subj.)

obstrepō, -ere, -uī, —: roar at, resound

obstringō, -ere, -nxī, -ictus: confine, bind, hamper

obticeō, -ēre, —, —: be silent

obtineō, -ēre, -uī, -entus: hold fast, occupy, possess; obtain, acquire (57 n. 5E)

obtingō, -ere, -igī, —: happen, occur

obtrectātiō, -ōnis (f.): detraction, disparagement; bickering (38 n. 8B)

obtrectō, -āre: disparage; oppose (35 n. 3)

obtulī: perf. of offerō

obveniō, -īre, -ēnī, -entum: go to meet; befall, happen

obviam (adv.; originally prep. ob+viam, acc. of via: 20 n. 14F): in the way; toward, against; īre obviam (w. dat.): meet; oppose (20 n. 14E)

obvius, -a, -um (adj.; formed from obviam: 20 n. 14F): in the way of; over against; exposed to (not in Lat. "obvious")

obvolvō, -ere, -ī, -lūtus: wrap around, cover

occāsiō, -ōnis (f.): opportunity, fit time, occasion

occāsus: past part. of occidō

occāsus, -ūs (m.): a falling, going down; w. sōlis: sunset, west

occidō, -ere, -dī, -āsus (from ob+cadō): fall down (70 n. 19B); set (used of the sun: 74 A vv. 4, 5)

occīdō, -ere, -dī, -sus (from ob+caedō): strike down, cut down, kill (5 n. 12, and often)

occiduus, -a, -um: going down, setting

occīsus: past part. of occīdō

occulō, -ere, -uī, -tus: cover up, hide, conceal

occultus, -a, -um (past part. of occulō as adj.): hidden, secret, occult

occupātiō, -ōnis (f.): a taking possession, seizure; employment, occupation

occupātus, -a, -um (past part. of occupō as adj.): busy, employed, occupied

occupō, -āre: seize, win, occupy; fall upon, attack

occurrō, -ere, -ī, -rsum: go to meet, meet (83 n. 20), fall in with (w. dat.: 10 n. 5B, or w. ad or in+acc.)

ocellus, -ī (m.): lit. little eye; i.e. something or someone precious, darling (73 n. 19C)

octō (indeclinable cardinal numeral):
eight

octōgēsimus, -a, -um: eightieth (14 n. 1)

oculus, -ī (m.): eye

ōdī, ōdisse, ōsūrus (defective: 11 n. 6):
hate

odium, -ī (n.): hatred

odor, -ōris (m.): smell, odor; perfume,
scent (87 A v. 2)

offendō, -ere, -ī, -ēnsus: strike against,
hit; stumble, blunder; come upon,
find; *animum offendere:* to hurt the
feelings

offēnsa, -ae (f.): displeasure, enmity;
offense, affront

offēnsiō, -ōnis (f.): a stumbling against;
mishap, disaster; displeasure, dislike

offerō, -ferre, obtulī, oblātus: bring
before, offer, give

officium, -ī (n.): obligation (67 n. 20),
duty (43 n. 4); *in officiō esse:* to
remain loyal

ōlim (adv.): once, formerly, at any past
time (73 n. 31A)

ōmen, -inis (n.): sign, omen

omnīnō (adv.): wholly, altogether, in all;
in general

omnis, -e: every, every kind of; all

onerārius, -a, -um: of burden, freight-
carrying

onerō, -āre: load, burden

onus, -eris (n.): burden

opācus, -a, -um: in the shade, shaded,
opaque

opera, -ae (f.): effort, assistance; *operam
dare:* i.e. try (35 n. 9E; nom. distinguishable from n. and acc. plur.
opera of *opus* by the context)

operiō, -īre, -uī, -tus: cover, cover over

operōsus, -a, -um: industrious; done
with much labor

opertus, -a, -um (past part. of *operiō* as
adj.): hidden

opīmus, -a, -um: rich

opīniō, -ōnis (f.): opinion, supposition,
conjecture; belief, expectation (in 34
n. 9, in 37 n. 4A)

opīnor, -ārī, -ātus (dep.): think, conjecture, suppose

oportet, -ēre, -uit, —: (impersonal): it is
necessary, it behooves

oppetō, -ere, -iī (or *-īvī:* 1 n. 4B), *-ītus:* go
to meet; *oppetere mortem:* to die

oppidum, -ī (n.): town, city

oppōnō, -ere, -osuī, -ositus: set against,
oppose, place in the path of

opprimō, -ere, -essī, -essus: press down,
oppress; overwhelm, fall upon

oppūgnātiō, -ōnis (f.): attack, assault,
siege

oppūgnō, -āre: attack, assault, siege

ops, opis (f.): help; (plur.: 1 n. 5B):
riches, resources, possessions

optābilis, -e: desirable

optimātēs, -ium (m.): adherents of the
patricians, conservatives (i.e. supporters of the *nōbilēs:* 18 n. 13A, 76
n. 2B)

optimē (adv. of *optimus*): in the best way,
most fortunately

optimus, -a, -um (sup. of *bonus*): best;
optimī virī: aristocrats, "best people"
(compare 72 n. 17B, 76 n. 3)

optō, -āre: choose, prefer; wish for,
welcome

opus, -eris (n.): work, task; *opus est* (w.
abl.): there is need of (25 n. 5A, 51 n. 5)

ōra, -ae (f.): shore, coast

ōrāculum, -ī (n.): oracle, prophecy

ōrātiō, -ōnis (f.): speech, oration;
eloquence (79 nn. 7C, 15A)

ōrātor, -ōris (m.): orator

orbis, -is (m.): ring, circle; orb; *orbis
terrārum* (*orbis* alone in 90 n. 2D): i.e.
earth, world (9 n. 6C, and often)

orbō, -āre: deprive, bereave

ōrdinō, -āre: set in order

ōrdior, -īrī, -sus (dep.): begin, undertake

ōrdō, -inis (m.): row, rank, order (i.e.
account: 15 n. 13C); station, class (of
society: in early Rome, the patricians
and plebeians: 7 pref., 56 n. 16; in
Cicero's time, the senators and
equestrians: in 32 n. 9A, 76 n. 8A)

orīgō, -inis (f.): beginning, source, origin

oriēns, -entis (pres. part. of *orior* as m.
noun): the rising (sun), the East

orior, -īrī, -tus (dep.): arise, appear, come
forth, be born from

ōrnāmentum, -ī (n.): equipment; adornment; distinction

ōrnātus, -ūs (m.): decoration, embellish-
ment

ōrnō, -āre: adorn, decorate, embellish

ornus, -ī (f.): mountain ash (in 61 n. 3)

ōrō, -āre: entreat, pray

ortus: past part. of *orior*

ortus, -ūs (m.): rising (especially of the
sun); source, origin

ōs, ōris (n.): mouth; face

os, ossis (n.): bone

ōsculum, -ī (n.): kiss

ostendō, -ere, -ī, -tus (or *-ēnsus*): show, reveal; declare

ostentō, -āre: show, parade, boast

ostentum, -ī (n. as noun of past part. of *ostendō*): portent (39 n. 19B)

ōtiōsus, -a, -um: at leisure, disengaged, idle (not in Lat. "otiose")

ōtium, -ī (n.): leisure (i.e. peace: 32 n. 4B), freedom (from business: 76 n. 18C, 86 n. 4C)

ovīle, -is (n.): sheepfold

ovis, -is (f.): sheep

pābulum, -ī (n.): fodder; (plur.): pastures (69 v. 14)

pacīscor, -ī, pactus (dep.): make a bargain or contract, pledge

pācō, -āre: make peaceful, pacify (83 B p. 2 s. 1)

pactiō, -ōnis (f.): agreement (i.e. compromise: 39 n. 5B); treaty, compact

pactum, -ī (n. as noun of *pactus*): agreement (51 n. 10), contract, pact

pactus, -a, -um: past part. of *pacīscor* (see also *pangō*)

paedor, -ōris (m.): filth (64 B v. 5)

paene (adv.): nearly, almost

paenitentia, -ae (f.): repentance, regret, penitence

paenitet, -ēre, -uit, — (impersonal): it causes regret, makes one sorry for (w. acc. of person, and gen. of thing: in 22 n. 12B, and often)

palam (adv.): openly

palea, -ae (f.): chaff, hay (89 n. 17B)

palleō, -ēre, -uī, —*:* be (or look) pale

pallidus, -a, -um: pale

palma, -ae (f.): palm (of hand); palm tree, palm branch (as a symbol of victory: 14 n. 13B)

palūs, -ūdis (f.): marsh, swamp (24 n. 14B)

pampineus, -a, -um: vine-wreathed

pangō, -ere, pepigī (or *pēgī; panxī* rare), *panctus* (or *pactus,* as also for *pacīscor*): fasten, agree on, make a bargain; compose (a literary work: 69 n. 21B)

pannus, -ī (m.): cloth, rag (90 n. 7A)

pār, paris (adj.): equal, like, similar, a match for

parātus, -a, -um (past part. of *parō* as adj.): ready, equipped

parcius (comp. adv. of *parcus*): more sparingly (i.e. more mercifully: 82 n. 18)

parcō, -ere, pepercī, parsus: spare, show mercy to (w. dat.: 47 n. 7, and often); be sparing of (in 77 n. 29A)

parcus, -a, -um: frugal, scanty

pardus, -ī (m.): pard (leopard or panther: 89 n. 13)

parēns, -entis (m. or f.; not the pres. part. of *pariō,* though related to it and not to *pāreō*): parent

pāreō, -ēre, -uī, —*:* appear; obey (w. dat.; lit. to appear at someone's command)

pariēs, -etis (m.): wall

pariō, -ere, peperī, partus (fut. part. *paritūrus*): produce (i.e. acquire: 21 n. 9, 31 n. 19A); create, give birth to

pariter (adv.; from *pār*): equally, at the same time

parma, -ae (f.): a small round shield (61 n. 18)

parō, -āre: prepare, make ready; furnish, equip

parricīdālis, -e: parricidal, murderous (24 n. 4B)

parricīdium, -ī (n.): parricide; murder

pars, partis (f.): part; i.e. others; direction; (plur.): political party (25 n. 5B, and often), role (43 n. 5B)

particeps, -cipis (m.): participant

partim (adv.): partly, to some extent; *partim . . . partim:* some . . . others (27 n. 8B, 29 n. 16A)

parturiō, -īre, -īvī (or *iī:* 1 n. 4B), —*:* be in travail, be in labor

partus: past part. of *pariō*

partus, -ūs (m.): birth

parum (adv. and indeclinable noun): little, too little; not enough

parvulus, -a, -um (diminutive of *parvus*): very little

parvus, -a, -um: little, small; (comp.) *minor;* (sup.) *minimus*

pāscō, -ere, pāvī, pāstus: feed, nourish; (pass. as dep.: 89 n. 16A): feed (oneself); graze

pāscuum, -ī (n.): pasture (in 86 n. 13D)

passim (adv.): in every direction, widespread, at random, indiscriminately

passus, -ūs (m.): pace (5 Roman feet); *mille passūs:* mile, *mīlia passuum:* miles

pāstor, -ōris (m.): shepherd (90 p. 2 s. 1)

patefaciō, -ere, -ēcī, -actus: lay open (10 n. 4B), expose

pateō, -ēre, -uī, —*:* lie or be open, extend

pater, -tris (m.): father; *patrēs cōnscrīptī:* senators (27 n. 16B, 71 n. 14A, 75 n. 1A) *paternus, -a, -um:* of one's father(s)

patientia, -ae (f.): patience, endurance

patiēns, -entis (pres. part. of *patior* as adj.): enduring, patient

patior, -ī, passus (dep.): allow, put up with; suffer, endure

patria, -ae (f.): native land, country

patricius, -a, -um: patrician (7 pref., 56 n. 13A)

patrius, -a, -um: of a father, paternal (53 n. 9B, in 54 n. 6A); *patria potestās:* a father's power over his household (in 57 n. 19)

patrō, -āre: bring to pass; accomplish, complete (28 n. 19A)

patrōnus, -ī (m.): legal protector, patron (in 7 n. 7, 73 n. 37)

patulus, -a, -um: spreading (84 n. 2A)

paucī, -ae, -a (plur. adj.; the sing. is rare): few; (as noun): few, a few; (m. as noun): the select (i.e. the optimates: 20 n. 13C, 38 n. 22A)

pauculī, -ae, -a (plur.): very few

paulātim (adv.): little by little

paulisper (adv.): for a little while

paulō (abl. of *paulus* as adv.): a little, somewhat, slightly

paulum (n. acc. sing. of *paulus* as adv.): = *paulō*

paulum (n. of *paulus* as noun): a little, a trifle

paulus, -a, -um (rare except in n.): small

pauper, -eris (adj.): poor (i.e. lacking in, w. gen.: 87 n. 40A)

paupertās, -ātis (f.): poverty

paveō, -ēre, pāvī, —: be terrified

pāx, pācis (f.): peace (88 n. 33B, 89 n. 28, 90 n. 13B)

pectus, -oris (n.): breast (60 n. 22B)

pecūnia, -ae (f.): money

pecus, -oris (n.): cattle (collectively)

pedes, -itis (m.): foot soldier, infantryman

pelagus, -ī (n.): sea

pelliciō, -ere, -exī, -ectus: entice, coax

pellō, -ere, pepulī, pulsus: drive, beat, rout

penātēs, -ium (m. plur.): deities of the household stores (*deī penātēs:* 1 n. 2A); i.e. house (54 n. 12B)

pendeō, -ēre, pependī, —: hang, hang down

penes (prep. w. acc.): within; within possession of (28 n. 19B)

penetrō, -āre: enter, penetrate

pēnsitō, -āre: weigh carefully, estimate (39 n. 15B)

pēnsō, -āre: weigh, ponder, estimate (44 n. 25B)

pepercī: perf. of *parcō* (47 n. 7)

peperī: perf. of *pariō* (21 n. 9)

pepigī: perf. of *pangō*

per (prep. w. acc.): through, throughout, across; by means of (instrumental or agent: 5 n. 16A, 47 n. 2); as a prefix it often connotes thoroughness or completeness

perāctus: past part. of *peragō*

peradulēscēns, -entis: very young

peragō, -ere, -ēgī, -āctus: go through, complete

peragrō, -āre: travel through, traverse (75 n. 4B)

percellō, -ere, -culī, -culsus: strike, beat down; smite (i.e. upset: 15 n. 3A, 20 n. 14C, 69 n. 12D)

percutiō, -ere, -ssī, -ssus: strike through, strike

perdō, -ere, -idī, -itus: ruin; lose

perdūcō, -ere, -ūxī, -uctus: lead through; prolong; spend

perēgī: perf. of *peragō*

peregrīnus, -a, -um: foreign

perennis, -e: everlasting

pereō, -īre, -iī (or *-īvī:* 1 n. 4B; *-it:* 79 n. 19C), *-itūrus:* perish, die

perfero, -ferre, -tulī, -lātus: carry through

perficiō, -ere, -ēcī, -ectus: complete, finish, perfect

perfidia, -ae (f.): treachery (in 11 n. 14C)

perfodiō, -ere, -ōdī, -ossus: pierce through, transfix

perfruor, -ī, -ūctus (dep.): to enjoy fully (w. abl.)

perfugiō, -ere, -ūgī, —: flee for refuge

perfugium, -ī (n.): refuge, shelter from

perfundō, -ere, -ūdī, -ūsus: pour over, drench (87 A v. 2)

perfungor, -ī, -ūnctus (dep.): perform, discharge one's office (w. abl.)

pergō, -ere, perrēxī, perrēctus: proceed, hasten

perīculōsus, -a, -um: dangerous

perīculum, -ī (n.): trial; danger, peril

perimō, -ere, -ēmī, -ēmptus: destroy, kill

perītus, -a, -um: experienced, skilled (w. gen.: 13 n. 1C)

perlātus: past part. of *perferō*

permaneō, -ēre, -ānsī, -ānsūrus: stay through to the end, continue; persist, be permanent *permisceō, -ēre, -uī, -ixtus:* mingle together; throw into confusion (28 n. 11c)

permittō, -ere, -īsī, issus: allow, permit (w. dat.)

permixtiō, -ōnis (f.): mixture, mixing together (20 n. 12b)

permoveō, -ēre, -mōvī, -mōtus: move thoroughly, affect, influence

permultī, -ae, -a (plur. adj.; the sing. is rare): very many

permūtō, -āre: change completely; exchange

perniciēs, -ēī (f.): ruin, destruction

perniciōsus, -a, -um: ruinous, pernicious

perpellō, -ere, -pulī, -pulsus: impel, force

perpetior, -ī, -pessus (dep.): bear patiently, endure (to the end)

perpetuus, -a, -um: perpetual, continuous, unbroken

perpoliō, -īre: polish thoroughly, make perfect

perpolītus, -a, -um (past part. of *perpoliō*): plastered with (25 p. 2 s. 7)

persequor, -ī, -cūtus (dep.): pursue, persecute; follow through to the end (i.e. recount fully)

persevērō, -āre: persist, continue resolutely

persuādeō, -ēre, -sī, -sus: persuade (w. dat. of person and either acc. of the matter or an *ut* clause of purpose)

persultō, -āre: gambol, leap across (or, over, w. acc.: 69 v. 14)

pertaedet, -ēre, -sum est (impersonal and semi-dep.): it wearies, it disgusts; (personal pass.): be disgusted with (w. acc.: 33 n. 7)

pertendō, -ere, -ī, -tum (or *-ēnsum*): stretch on (toward a goal); go straight on

perterreō, -ēre, -uī, -itus: frighten thoroughly

pertimēscō, -ere, -timuī, —: become very frightened, be very fearful

pertināx, -ācis: persevering, obstinate, pertinacious

pertineō, -ēre, -uī, —: reach, belong, affect, pertain to (w. *ad*)

pertrahō, -ere, -xī, -ctus: draw along, drag

pertulī: perf. of *perferō*

perturbō, -āre: disturb, upset

perveniō, -īre, -ēnī, -entum: come to, arrive

pervertō (-vort-), -ere, -ī, -sus: overturn, throw down, pervert

pēs, pedis (m.): foot

pessimus, -a, -um (sup. of *malus*): i.e. the worst of (24 n. 9c, 28 n. 14c)

pestilentia, -ae (f.): plague, pestilence

pestis, -is (f.): plague; destruction

petītor, -ōris (m.): striver for; candidate for office

petō, -ere, -iī (or *-īvī:* 1 n. 4b; *-īt:* 78 n. 32b), *-ītus:* seek, aim at (1 n. 4b); ask for; seek (an office: 21 n. 14a, 64 n. 2); woo (74 n. 7d)

phalerae, -ārum (f. plur.): metal plaques worn as military insignia (63 n. 13c)

philyra, -ae (f.): inner bark of linden tree (87 n. 19)

picea, -ae (f.): spruce tree, pitch pine (in 61 n. 3)

piceus, -a, -um: made of pitch; pitch black (61 n. 34a)

pietās, -ātis (f.): devotion to duty; piety (in 23 n. 13a, in 62 n. 11b, 83 n. 11)

piget, -ēre, -uit (or *-itum est*; impersonal): it annoys, causes dislike (w. gen. of the cause of feeling and acc. of the person)

pignus, -oris (or, *-eris;* n.): pledge, guarantee (77 n. 3a)

pīlum, -ī (n.): javelin (66 n. 11c, 78 n. 20e)

pīnus, -ūs (f.): pine tree (in 61 n. 3)

pīrāticus, -a, -um: of pirates, piratical

pirus, -ī (f.): pear tree (in 84 n. 20a)

pius, -a, -um: devout, dutiful (in 23 n. 13a)

placeō, -ēre, -uī, -itus: be pleasing to, please (w. dat.)

plācō, -āre: calm; appease, placate

plāga, -ae (f.): blow, stroke

plānē (adv.; from *plānus*): plainly, distinctly; wholly, entirely

plangor, -ōris (m.): beating the breast, lamentation

plānus, -a, -um: flat, plane; distinct, plain

plausus, -ūs (m.): clapping, applause (77 n. 19)

plēbēius, -a, -um: of the plebs

plēbs, plēbis (f.): plebs (7 pref.); common people (18 n. 14a, 21 n. 11a)

plēctor, -ī, — (dep.): be beaten, punished

plēnus, -a, -um: full; rounded (of a face; 33 n. 9)

plērīque (nom. plur. of adj. *plērusque* as noun): the greater part, the majority

plērumque (n. acc. sing. of *plērusque* as adv.): generally, usually; for the most part; very often

plērusque, -aque, -umque: the greater part, most

plūrimus: sup. of *multus*

plūs, plūris: comp. of *multus, -a, -um:* n. acc. sing. as comp. adv. of *multum*

plūsculus, -a, -um: a little more

pōculum, -ī (n.): cup (59 A s. 4)

poēma, -atis (Greek n.): poem (32 n. 20B, 79 n. 23A)

poena, -ae (f.): punishment, penalty, requital

poēta, -ae (m.): poet

poliō, -īre: polish

polītus, -a, -um (past part. of *poliō* as adj.): polished, accomplished, refined, cultivated

polliceor, -ērī, -itus (dep.): promise

polus, -ī (m.): pole (of sky: 52 n. 5C)

pōmum, -ī (n.): piece of fruit (i.e. apple: 84 v. 39)

pondus, -eris (n.): weight

pōnō, -ere, posuī, positus: place, set, put; pitch (camp); lay aside (48 n. 15A, 78 n. 20E)

pōns, pontis (m.): bridge

ponticulus, -ī (m.): little bridge (39 p. 3 s. 2)

pontifex, -ficis (m.): pontifex (or pontiff; member of a civil board in charge of religion, whose head was called *pontifex maximus:* in 14 n. 15, and often)

pontificius, -a, -um: of a pontifex (w. *iūs:* 14 n. 15)

pontus, -ī (m.): sea (in 69 n. 9)

populāris, -e: of the people, popular; (m. plur. as a noun): i.e. politicians who sought the support of the *populus* in the tribal assembly rather than that of the senatorial *optimātēs* (28 pref.; 76 n. 2B)

populus, -ī (m.): people, esp. the Roman citizen body, including both plebeians and patricians

porta, -ae (f.): gate (40 n. 3), door (60 n. 16A)

portendō, -ere, -ī, -tus: indicate, reveal; predict, portend (21 n. 3A, 80 title)

portentum, -ī (n. as noun of past part. of *portendō*): omen, portent

porticus, -ūs (f.): colonnade (55 n. 14)

portō, -āre: carry

portus, -ūs (m.): harbor, port

pōscō, -ere, popōscī, —: demand

positus, -a, -um: past part. of *pōnō*

possessiō, -ōnis (f.): possession; seizing

possideō, -ēre, -ēdī, -essus: own, possess, occupy

possum, posse, potuī, —: can, be able; be powerful (81 n. 8D); *plūrimum posse:* to have great influence, be very powerful

post (adv.): after, afterward (of time: 14 n. 3, 73 n. 35A); behind, after (of place); (prep. w. acc.): after (of time); behind, next to, inferior to (of place)

posteā (adv.): later, after this, afterward

posterior: comp. of *posterus*

posteritās, -ātis (f.): succeeding generations, posterity

posterum (n. of *posterus* as noun): the following; *in posterum:* in (or, for) the future

posterus, -a, -um: following, next, after; (comp.) *posterior:* further back; (sup.) *postrēmus* (or *postumus*): last

posthāc (adv.): hereafter

postis, -is (m.): doorpost; door

postquam, post . . . quam (conj.): after, when

postrēmō (abl. of *postrēmus* as adv.): at last, finally

postrēmum (n. acc. sing. of *posterus* as adv.): for the last time, last of all

postrēmus (or *postumus*): sup. of *posterus*

postulō, -āre: demand, claim (by right)

postumus (or *postrēmus*): sup. of *posterus*

potēns, -entis: (pres. part. as adj. from a verb stem also yielding *potuī:* 33 n. 25A): powerful; (as equivalent to a pres. part. of *potior*): master of (w. gen.: 87 n. 9B; contrast 88 n. 26A); *rērum potēns:* i.e. master of the state (33 n. 25A, and often)

potentia, -ae (f.): power, influence

potestās, -ātis (f.): legal or legitimate authority or power; possibility, opportunity

potior, -ius (comp. of *potis*): more able; preferable

potior, -īrī, -ītus (dep.): become master of, obtain, capture (w. abl.: 46 n. 12A, 49 n. 3B; or w. gen.: 26 n. 9A, 38 n. 4B)

potis, -e: capable (61 n. 21B); (comp.) *potior, -ius;* (sup. adv.) *potissimum*

potissimum (n. acc. sing. of sup. of *potis* as adv.): chiefly, most of all, especially *potius* (comp. adv. of *potis*): rather

potō, -āre: drink, carouse

potui: perf. of *possum*

prae (prep. w. abl.): in comparison with; by reason of, because of; as a prefix, often intensive, = very

praebeō, -ēre, -uī, -itus: offer, furnish; exhibit

praecellō, -ere, —, —: surpass, excel (16 n. 13c)

praeceps, -cipitis (adj.): headlong (25 p. 2 s. 8)

praeceptum, -ī (n. as noun of past part. of *praecipiō*): maxim, rule, precept (in 34 n. 4B)

praecīdō, -ere, -īdī, -īsus (*prae* + *caedō*): cut off, cut short, destroy

praecipiō, -ere, -ēpī, -eptus: instruct, advise, order

praecipuus, -a, -um: special, particular

praeclārus, -a, -um: famous, distinguished

praecō, -ōnis (m.): crier, herald

praecurrō, -ere, -cucurrī (rarely *-currī*), *-cursum:* run on in advance (83 n. 18B); anticipate

praeda, -ae (f.): booty, plunder, spoil

praedicō, -āre: proclaim; speak before; predicate

praedīcō, -ere, -īxī, -ictus: say in advance ("editorially": 23 n. 11, 26 n. 8A, 28 n. 3B); predict

praedictus, -a, -um (past part. of *praedīcō* as adj.): aforementioned

praeditus, -a, -um (adj.; probably from *prae* + past part. of *dō*): gifted, endowed with (w. abl.); (in late Lat.): put in charge of

praedium, -ī (n.): farm, estate (in 44 n. 3)

praedō, -ōnis (m.): pirate, robber

praeesse: inf. of *praesum*

praefātiō, -ōnis (f.): a saying beforehand, preface

praefectūra, -ae (f.): office of prefect

praefectus, -ī (m. as noun of past part. of *praeficiō*): one placed in charge of, prefect (w. gen. or dat.)

praeferō, -ferre, -tulī, -lātus: bear before; offer, prefer

praeficiō, -ere, -ēcī, -ectus: put in command of (w. acc. of person and dat. of thing or responsibility: 4 n. 3)

praefui, praefutūrus: perf. and fut. part. of *praesum*

praegnāns, -antis (adj.): with child, pregnant (90. s. 4)

praegravō, -āre: weigh down, burden; outweigh

praemium, -ī (n.): reward (i.e. pleasure: 70 n. 5D)

praemoneō, -ēre, -uī, -itus: forewarn (in 80 n. 3)

praemonitus: past part. of *praemoneō*

praemonitus, -ūs (m.): warning (80 n. 12), premonition

praemūniō, -īre: fortify beforehand

praenōmen, -inis (n.): first (or personal) name

praeparō, -āre: prepare, provide with

praepes, -etis (adj.): flying (61 n. 24B)

praepōnō, -ere, -osuī, -ositus: put before, place first

praeripiō, -ere, -uī, -eptus: snatch away, forestall, anticipate

praerumpō, -ere, -ūpī, -uptus: break (or tear) off in front

praeruptus, -a, -um (past part. of *praerumpō* as adj.): steep, abrupt, rugged

praesaepium, -ī (n.; also *praesaepe, -is*): crib, manger (90 n. 7c)

praesāgium, -ī (n.): presentiment, foreboding; prediction (78 v. 14)

praescrībō, -ere, -īpsī, -īptus: write before; prescribe, direct

praesēns, -entis (pres. part. of *praesum* as adj.): present, in person

praesentia, -ae (f.): presence; *in praesentiā:* for the present

praesertim (adv.): especially, particularly

praeses, -idis (m.): ruler, governor (90 n. 3A)

praesidium, -ī (n.): guard, garrison (29 n. 15B); protection (29 nn. 8D, 11A)

praestābilis, -e: pre-eminent, excellent

praestō (adv.): at hand, ready

praestō, -āre, -itī, -itus: be superior, excel (w. dat. of person and abl. of specification for the quality: 16 nn. 9c and D, 62 n. 4); perform; show, evince (62 n. 11B)

praestringō, -ere, -nxī, -ictus: bind fast, compress; confuse, dazzle (in 77 n. 34A)

praesum, -esse, -fuī, -futūrus: preside over, command (w. dat.)

praeter (prep. w. acc.): beyond, past; contrary to, in addition to; besides, except

praetereā (adv.): besides this, moreover

praetereō, -īre, -iī (or *-īvī:* 1 n. 4B), *-itus:* pass by, pass over *praeteritus, -a, -um* (past part. of *praetereō* as adj.): past, gone by

praetermittō, -ere, -mīsī, -missus: let go by, let pass, let go; omit, neglect

praeterquam (adv.): except, besides; *praeterquam quod:* except that, besides that

praetexō, -ere, -uī, -tus: to weave (a border) on; to cover, conceal

praetextātus, -a, -um (adj.; from *praetextus*): wearing the *toga praetexta* (of freeborn boys: 15 n. 12A; also of magistrates: compare 8 n. 8c)

praetextum, -ī (n. as noun of past part. of *praetexō*): pretext, pretense

praetextus, -a, -um (past part. of *praetexō*): with a (purple) border woven on (of the *toga* worn by children and magistrates: 8 n. 8c, 15 n. 12A)

praetor, -ōris (m.): (originally) name of chief magistrate(in 59 n. 24B); (later) praetor (judicial magistrate: 56 n. 15)

praetōrium, -ī (n. of *praetōrius* as noun): headquarters in a camp; (plur.): i.e. palace (59 n. 24B)

praetōrius, -a, -um: of a praetor; *porta praetōria:* gate nearest to headquarters (40 n. 3)

praetrepidāns, -antis (pres. part. of a verb not otherwise attested): trembling in advance (i.e. eager: 73 n. 15)

praetūra, -ae (f.): office of praetor, praetorship

praevalidus, -a, -um: very strong, of superior strength

prātum, -ī (n.): meadow

prāvus, -a, -um: wicked, vicious

precor, -ārī, -ātus (dep.): beg, beseech

premō, -ere, -ssī, -ssus: press (i.e. lie on: 64 n. 16); oppress; force in; compress (i.e. close: 78 n. 27A); visit frequently; *lāc pressum:* i.e. cheese (84 n. 25)

pretium, -ī (n.): price, cost; value

prex, precis (f.): prayer, request; imprecation

prīdem (adv.): long ago; *iam prīdem:* now for a long time

prīdiē (adv.): on the day before

prīmō (n. abl. sing. of *prīmus* as adv.):= *prīmum*

prīmōgenitus, -a, -um: first-born (90 s. 5)

prīmum (n. acc. sing. of *prīmus* as adv.): first, at first, for the first time; *quam prīmum:* as early as possible; *ut prīmum:* as soon as

prīmus, -a, -um (sup. of *prior*): first; *in prīmīs:* especially, chiefly

prīnceps, -cipis (adj. or m. noun): first (11 n. 12B); leader (1 n. 1G), foremost man (19 n. 3c, and often; of Augustus: in 48 n. 6)

prīncipātus, -ūs (m.): leadership (35 n. 6A; of Augustus: 48 n. 11A)

prīncipium, -ī (n.): beginning

prior, prius (comp. adj.): former, previous; (sup.) *prīmus*

prīscus, -a, -um: of former times, ancient

prīstinus, -a, -um: former, original

prius (adv. of *prior*): before, sooner, previously

priusquam (or *prius . . . quam*; conj.): sooner than, before (w. subj.: 2 n. 3B); until

prīvātus, -ī (m. as noun of past part. of *prīvō*): a private individual, citizen (as opposed to a magistrate: in 30 n. 8A, 54 n. 7A, 71 n. 11D; of Cleopatra: 86 n. 32)

prīvō, -āre: deprive (w. acc. of person and abl. of separation of thing: 4 n. 2B)

prō (prep. w. abl.): before, in front of; instead of, in place of; in behalf of

prō (interj. of wonder or grief): Oh, Alas (w. nom.: 78 n. 20A, or w. acc.: 26 n. 8c)

probābilis, -e: likely, credible, probable

probitās, -ātis (f.): uprightness, honesty

probō, -āre: approve; prove

prōcēdō, -ere, -cessī, -cessum: move forward, advance, come forth

procerēs, -um (m. plur.): leading men, chiefs

prōcērus, -a, -um: high, tall (61 A v. 4)

prōcōnsul, -is (m.): proconsul, governor of a province

prōcōnsulāris, -e: of a proconsul, proconsular

procul (adv.): at a distance, away; from afar

prōcumbō, -ere, -ubuī, -ubitum: sink down, fall forward

prōdesse: inf. of *prōsum*

prōdō, -ere, -idī, -itus: put forth, reveal; relate; hand over (to the enemy: i.e. betray: 1 n. 1B)

prōdūcō, -ere, -ūxī, -uctus: lead forth; prolong

proelior, -ārī, -ātus (dep.): fight

proelium, -ī (n.): battle, combat; *proelium cōnserere* (or *committere*): join battle (11 n. 12c) *profectiō, -ōnis* (f.): departure (71 n. 14c)

profectō (adv.; from *prō* + abl. of *factum*): certainly, doubtless, in fact

prōferō, -ferre, -tulī, -lātus: carry out, bring forward, proffer; reach forth

proficīscor, -ī, -ectus (dep.): set out, start, depart

profiteor, -ērī, -essus (dep.): declare publicly, profess; register (90 n. 4A)

prōflīgō, -āre: dash to the ground; destroy; finish

profugiō, -ere, -fūgī, —: flee, run away, escape

prōfuī, prōfutūrus: perf. and fut. part. of *prōsum*

profundō, -ere, -fūdī, -fūsus: pour out, burst forth

prōgeniēs (f.; only nom., acc., and abl. sing.): descendants, progeny

prōgredior, -ī, -gressus (dep.): go forth, advance

prōgressus, -ūs (m.): advance, progress

prohibeō, -ēre, -uī, -itus: hold back, restrain; prohibit; prevent, keep from (w. acc. of person and abl. of separation of that from which)

prōiciō, -ere, -iēcī, -iectus: throw forth, throw away; give up

proinde ut (or *ac*)*:* just as, like (70 n. 26A, 81 n. 3A)

prōlātus: past part. of *prōferō*

prōmineō, -ēre, -uī, —: hang forward, lean out (44 n. 12); extend, project

prōmittō, -ere, -īsī, -issus: promise, assure

prōmptus, -a, -um: brought forward, at hand, ready, prompt; inclined to

prōmulgō, -āre: propose openly, promulgate

prōmunturium, -ī (n.): headland, promontory (46 p. 1 last s.)

prōnūntiātiō, -ōnis (f.): proclamation, pronouncement

prōnus, -a, -um: bent over; leaning forward, i.e. ready (22 n. 3B); prone to (33 n. 13)

prŏpāgō, -āre (-ŏ- in 69 v. 20): extend, propagate; preserve

prŏpāgō, -inis (f; -ŏ- in 69 v. 39): shoot (of a plant); offshoot, offspring

prope (prep. w. acc.): near, close to; (adv.): almost, nearly, recently

prōpendeō, -ēre, -ī, -pēnsus: hang down; be inclined to

prōpēnsus, -a, -um (past part. of *prōpen-*

deō as adj.): hanging down; inclining toward; disposed, willing, propense

properō, -āre: hasten

properus, -a, -um: speedy, hasty

propinquitās, -ātis (f.): nearness; relationship

propinquus, -a, -um: near, neighboring; related

propior, -ius (comp. adj.): nearer; (sup.): *proximus*

prōpōnō, -ere, -osuī, -ositus: put forward, present; propose, expose

prōpositum, -ī (n. as noun of past part. of *prōpōnō*): plan, intention (18 n. 3B), project (36 n. 6C), aim (76 n. 17A), point at issue (38 n. 4A), proposal

propter (prep. w. acc.): near, next to; because of, on account of

proptereā (adv.): therefore, on this account; *proptereā quod:* because, in as much as

prōpūgnāculum, -ī (n.): rampart; (defensive) bulwark (on a ship: 86 n. 1c)

prōpūgnātor, -ōris (m.): defender, champion

prōrogō, -āre: prolong, extend, prorogue (a magistracy or command)

prōrumpō, -ere, -ūpī, -uptus: burst forth, rush forth

prōscrībō, -ere, -īpsī, -īptus: proclaim, publish; proscribe (83 A s. 2)

prōscrīptiō, -ōnis (f.): public notice of sale; proscription (66 title, 83 A title)

prōsiliō, -īre, -uī (rarely -iī or -īvī: 1 n. 4B), —: spring up, start up

prosperus, -a, -um: favorable, fortunate; (n. plur. as noun): good fortune

prōspiciō, -ere, -ēxī, -ectus: look forward, look out upon, see

prōsternō, -ere, -strāvī, -strātus: strew before, spread out; cast down, destroy

prōsum, -desse, -fuī, -futūrus: be of advantage (w. dat.)

prōtegō, -ere, -tēxī, -tēctus: cover, protect

prōtendō, -ere, -ī, -tus (or -ēnsus)*:* stretch out

prōtinus (adv.): forward; continuously; immediately

prōtrahō, -ere, -xī, -ctus: draw forth, drag out, protract

prōtulī: perf. of *prōferō*

prōvehō, -ere, -xī, -ctus: carry forward, convey, carry out (i.e. to sea: 44 n. 6)

prōvidentia, -ae (f.): foresight; forethought, providence

prōvideō, -ēre, -vīdī, -vīsus: foresee; see to, care for, provide

prōvincia, -ae (f.): public office; province (29 n. 4)

prōvolvō, -ere, -ī, -lūtus: roll forward; overturn

proximus, -a, -um (sup. of *propior*): nearest, next; last

prūdēns, -entis (adj.): foreknowing, knowledgeable, prudent

prūdentia, -ae (f.): prudence, foresight; good sense

pūblicē (adv.): i.e. at the public expense (9 B s. 3)

pūblicus, -a, -um: public, of the people

pudeō, -ēre, -uī (or *-itum est*): feel shame; (usually impers.) *pudet* (79 n. 13): it shames, it makes (one feel) ashamed (w. acc. of person and gen. of cause of shame)

pudīcitia, -ae (f.): modesty, chastity (5 s. 8)

pudīcus, -a, -um: modest, chaste (5 s. 7)

pudor, -ōris (m.): shame, sense of shame, modesty, decency

puella, -ae (f.): girl; mistress (in 74 n. 7B)

puer, -erī (m.): boy (84 n. 14A, in 87 n. 2B, 88 n. 16B); slave (87 n. 18B)

pūgiō, -ōnis (m.): dagger (43 A s. 4)

pūgna, -ae (f.): fight, battle

pūgnō, -āre: fight

pulcher, -chra, -chrum: beautiful

pulchritūdō, -inis (f.): beauty

pullus, -ī (m.): nestling (86 n. 9C)

pulsō, -āre: strike, beat

pulsus: past part. of *pellō*

pulvīnar, -āris (n.): couch, sacred couch (42 n. 8A, in 86 n. 17A)

pulvis, -eris (m.): dust

pūmex, -icis (m.): pumice stone; any porous rock (87 n. 13C)

pungō, -ere, pupugī, pūnctus: prick: vex, disturb (35 n. 20B)

pūniō, -īre: punish

puppis, -is (f.): stern of ship; i.e. ship (78 n. 16B)

pupugī: perf. of *pungō*

purpurātus, -ī (m. of adj. as noun): a person dressed in purple (6 n. 12B)

purpureus, -a, -um: purple, dark

pūrus, -a, -um: clean, unspotted, pure; straightforward (of style: 79 n. 9B)

pusillus, -a, -um: little, petty

putō, -āre: think, consider, believe

putris (or *puter, -tris*), *-e:* rotten, decaying

pȳramis, -idis (f.): pyramid (87 n. 34B)

quā (adv.: 87 n. 39B): by what way, where

quadriennium, -ī (n.): a period of four years (14 n. 3)

quaerō, -ere, -sīī (or *-sīvī:* 1 n. 4B), *-sītus:* seek, look for, inquire, ask

quaesō: older form of *quaerō*

quaestiō, -ōnis (f.): inquiry, investigation (19 n. 12); a jury court (19 pref.)

quaestor, -ōris (m.): quaestor (junior magistrate serving as financial assistant to a consul or governor: in 14 n. 2C; compare 31)

quaestūra, -ae (f.): quaestorship (31 s. 2)

quālis, -e (adj.): of which kind, what sort of; (w. *tālis*): as

quāliter (adv.): just as, like

quam (conj.): than, as; *quam* w. sup.: as ... as possible (33 n. 8C, 65 n. 21C); how

quamquam (conj.): although

quamvīs (adv.): however, however much; (conj.): although

quandō (temporal or interrog. adv. or conj.): because, since; when

quandōquidem (conj.; *-ŏ-* in 73A v. 5): since indeed

quantum (n. acc. sing. of *quantus* used as adv.): (interrog.) how much?; (rel.) as much as

quantus, -a, -um (correlative or interrog. adj. or pronoun): how great

quārē (adv.; from abl. *quā rē*): why, wherefore

quartus, -a, -um: fourth

quasi (=*quamsi*; adv. and conj.): as if (67 n. 21, 82 n. 22)

quatiō, -ere, —, quassus: shake

quattuor (indeclinable cardinal numeral): four

quattuordecim (indeclinable cardinal numeral): fourteen

-que (enclitic): and (1 n. 1F); but (in 77 n. 20B)

queō, quīre, quīvī, quitus: be able, can

quercus, -ūs (f.): (Italian) oak (61 n. 3)

queror, -ī, -stus (dep.): complain

quī, qua, quod (indefinite adj.): any

quī, quae, quod (rel. pronoun): who, which, what, that

quī, quae, quod (interrog. adj.): what? which? what kind of?

quī (old abl. as interrog. adv.): how (74 n. 13B)

quia (conj.): because, since

quicumque, quaecumque, quodcumque (indefinite pronoun): whoever, whatever

quidam, quaedam, quiddam (or *quoddam*; indefinite pronoun and adj.): a certain one, someone

quidem (adv.): indeed, at any rate; on the other hand; *nē . . . quidem:* not even (referring to the word contained)

quiēs, quiētis (f.): quiet, rest

quiēscō, -ere, -ēvī, -ētus: to become quiet, to rest

quiētus, -a, -um (past part. of *quiēscō* as adj.): quiet, at rest

quilibet, quaelibet, quodlibet (indefinite adj.): any (you wish)

quin (conj.; =*quī+nōn* or *nē:* 21 n. 12A, 75 n. 6C): that not, but that; (as a coordinating conj.: 19 n. 9A) rather, on the contrary

quīnquāgintā (indeclinable cardinal numeral): fifty

quīnque (indeclinable cardinal numeral): five

quīntus, -a, -um: fifth

quippe (adv.): of course, obviously; for indeed (78 n. 12A); (conj.) as of course

quis, quid (interrog. pronoun; or adj., as in 87 A v. 1): who? what? *quid* (as adv.): why?

quis, quid (indefinite pronoun): anyone, anything (after *sī, nisi, nē,* and *num:* 4 n. 11B, and often; after *quantō:* 48 n. 19B)

quislibet, quidlibet (indefinite pronoun) anyone or anything (you wish)

quisnam, quaenam, quidnam: who (what) in the world?

quisquam, quidquam (or *quicquam*; indefinite pronoun): anyone (regular after a universal neg.: 61 n. 21C, 62 n. 9B; after a universal *sī:* 62 n. 16A)

quisque, quaeque, quidque and *quodque* (indefinite pronoun and adj.): each one, each; everyone, all

quisquis, quicquid (or *quidquid*; indefinite rel. pronoun): whoever, whatever

quō (interrog. adv.; case uncertain: 21 n. 13B): where? whither?; (rel. adv.) where, whither (76 n. 17B)

quoad (adv.): as long as, as far as; until (in 6 n. 3)

quod (conj.): because; that, the fact that (82 n. 1B), as to the fact that; *quod sī:* but if (37 n. 20A, and often)

quōminus (conj.): by which the less, so that not, from (after verbs of hindering, preventing, etc.)

quondam (adv.): formerly; some day

quoniam (conj.): since, because

quoque (connective adv.): also

quot (adj., plur. indeclinable): how many?; (rel.) as many (as; see *tot*)

quotannīs (abl. plur. as adv.: (84 n. 13B): every year

quotiēns (connective adv.; interrog. or correl. or, in 87 A v. 5, exclamatory): how many times; as often as, whenever

quotus, -a, -um: which in order; *quotus quisque:* i.e. how few (48 n. 24)

radius, -ī (m.): staff, pointer (88 n. 31B)

rādīx, -īcis (f.): root

rāmus, -ī (m.): branch, bough

rapacitās, -tātis (f.): greed, rapacity

rapāx, -ācis (adj.): grasping, greedy

rapīna, -ae (f.): plundering, pillage

rapiō, -ere, -uī, -tus: snatch, seize; i.e. hurry (someone) (in 88 n. 27); hasten (in pass.: 68 n. 18E)

rapsō, -āre: seize, drag about (83 n. 13A)

rārus, -a, -um: scattered, far apart, few at a time, rare

raster, -trī (m.; also *rastrum, -trī,* n.): rake (4 last s., 85 p. 5 v. 4)

ratiō, -ōnis (f.): reckoning, account (12 n. 14B); consideration; plan, reason; theory, system

ratis, -is (f.): raft, boat

ratus, -a, -um (past part. of *reor*): fixed, agreed upon

recēdō, -ere, -essī, -essum: go back, retreat, vanish

recēns, -entis (adj.): fresh, new

recidō (recc-), -ere, -dī, -cāsūrus (re-+ cadō): fall back on, be reduced to

recīdo, -ere, -īdī, -īsus (re-+caedō): cut back (or off)

recipiō, -ere, -ēpī, -eptus: take or get back, recover; accept, permit (18 n. 4B); *sē recipere:* betake oneself (46 n. 16B); return (3 n. 6B), retreat (45 n. 5)

recitō, -āre: read aloud, recite

reclīnō, -āre: lay down (90 n. 7B), recline

recordātiō, -ōnis (f.): recollection, remembrance, record

recordor, -ārī, -ātus (dep.): bring back to mind, recall

rēctē (adv. of *rēctus*): rightly, correctly

rēctor, -ōris (m.): guide, controller

rēctus, -a, -um (verbal adj. from *regō*): upright, straight; correct (of style: 79 n. 7A)

recubō, -āre, —, — (rare): lie on one's back, recline (69 v. 35, 84 v. 1)

recumbō, -ere, -ubuī, —: lie back; sink down

recuperō, -āre: regain, get back, recuperate

recūsō, -āre: refuse

redāctus: past part. of *redigō*

reddō, -ere, -idī, -itus: give back, restore; render; *ratiōnem reddere:* render an account

redēgī: perf. of *redigō*

redeō, -īre, -iī (or *-īvī:* 1 n. 4B), *-itus:* return

redigō, -ere, -ēgī, -āctus: drive back; reduce, render

rediī, reditus: perf. and past part. of *redeō*

redimō, -ere, -ēmī, -ēmptus: buy back, redeem, pay for

reditus, -ūs (m.): return; interest (on an investment), revenue (from a property)

redūcō, -ere, -dūxī, -ductus: lead or bring back

redundō, -āre: overflow

refectus: past part. of *reficiō*

referō, referre, rettulī, relātus: bring back; repay (6 n. 15); report, relate

rēfert (from abl. *rē+fert*), *-ferre, -tulit, —* (impersonal): it is of advantage to; it profits (w. gen. of person depending on *rē-*)

refertus, -a, -um (re-+ past part. of *farciō*): stuffed, filled with (w. abl.: 13 n. 7, 28 n. 6D; or w. gen.: 29 n. 9C)

reficiō, -ere, -ēcī, -ectus: repair, restore; re-elect (56 n. 1A)

reflectō, -ere, -ēxī, -exus: bend or turn back (55 n. 8A)

reformīdō, -āre: shun (through dread), shrink (from), fear (greatly)

refringō, -ere, -ēgī, -āctus: break open

refugiō, -ere, -ūgī, —: flee back

refūtō, -āre: drive back; refute, disprove

rēgālis, -e: royal, of a king

rēgia, -ae (f.): palace (probably f. adj. w. *domus* understood: 54 n. 10C, 78 n. 12C)

rēgīna, -ae (f.): queen

regiō, -ōnis (f.): region, part of the world; district, direction

rēgius, -a, -um: kingly, royal, of the king (5 n. 2C, and often)

rēgnō, -āre: reign, rule (w. gen.: 87 n. 40C); be pre-eminent in (79 n. 16)

rēgnum, -ī (n.): kingdom, kingly power; (collective, or poetic, plur.): rule (49 n. 10B, 54 n. 5D), kingdom (64 n. 15C, 78 nn. 4C, in 9A)

regō, -ere, rēxī, rēctus: rule, be king; guide, direct

regredior, -ī, -essus (dep.): go back, return

rēgulus, -ī (m.): the basilisk (i.e. a poisonous serpent: 89 n. 19A)

rēiciō, -ere, -iēcī, -iectus: throw back, repel, reject

relātus: past part. of *referō*

relēgō, -āre: send away, banish, relegate

religiō, -ōnis (f.): superstition; religious feeling; religion

religiōsus, -a, -um: sacred, religious

religō, -āre: tie back

relinquō, -ere, -īquī, -ictus: leave, abandon

reliquiae, -ārum (f. plur.): remains, relics

reliquus, -a, -um: remaining, the rest or remainder of (41 n. 1B, 81 n. 8C); *reliquum tempus:* the future (compare *reliquum vītae tempus:* 5 s. 12)

remissus, -a, -um (past part. of *remittō* as adj.): slack; mild, gentle

remittō, -ere, -mīsī, -missus: send back; slacken, relax

remoror, ārī, -ātus (dep.): stay or linger behind

removeō, -ēre, -mōvī, -mōtus: take away, move back, remove

rēnēs, -um (m. plur.): kidneys (89 n. 12)

renovō, -āre: renew, renovate

renuo, -uere, -uī, —: deny by a motion of the head; refuse

reor, rērī, ratus (dep.): reckon, think

reparō, -āre: acquire anew, renew (in 77 n. 20A), repair; seek in exchange (see 86 n. 27F)

repellō, -ere, reppulī, repulsus: drive back, repel

rependō, -ere, -ī, -ēnsus: repay, recompense

repēns, -entis (adj.): sudden, unexpected

repēnsō, -āre: compensate (22 n. 12C)

repente (abl. of *repens* as adv.): suddenly

repentīnus, -a, -um: sudden, hasty, unexpected

reperiō, -īre, repperī, repertus: find

repetō, -ere, -iī (or *-īvī:* 1 n. 4B), *-ītus:* seek or ask again, ask back; repeat; *poenās repetere ab aliquō:* inflict punishment on someone; *rēs repetundae:* property to be recovered (at law: in 12 n. 14A)

repleō, -ēre, -ēvī, -ētus: fill again, fill up

repōnō, -ere, -osuī, -ositus: put back, replace

reportō, -āre: bring back

repraesentō, -āre: show; represent; accomplish

reprehendō, -ere, -ī, -ēnsus: hold back, restrain; blame, reprove, reprehend

reprobō, -āre: disapprove, reject (89 n. 4D); reprove, condemn

repudiō, -āre: reject, repudiate

repūgnō, -āre: fight back, oppose

repulsus: past part. of *repellō*

reputō, -āre: reckon

requiēs, -ētis (f.): rest, repose

requiēscō, -ere, -ēvī, -ētus: find rest, repose

requīrō, -ere, -sīī (or *-sīvī:* 1 n. 4B), *-sītus:* ask, look for, miss

rēs, reī (f.): thing (variously translated according to context); *rēs familiāris:* property; *rēs frūmentāria:* grain supply; *rēs militāris:* warfare; *rēs pūblica:* commonwealth; *rēs gestae:* history, achievements; *rēs novae:* revolution; *rēs secundae:* prosperity

rescindō, -ere, -scidī, -scissus: cut down, destroy; rescind (a law)

resecō, -āre, -uī, -tus: cut back, cut short

reserō, -āre: unbolt, unlock

reservō, -āre: keep back, save up, reserve

resideō, -ēre, -sēdī, —: sit back, sit (i.e. in judgment: 82 n. 11); remain, reside

resistō, -ere, -stitī, —: be opposed to, resist (w. dat.)

resolvō, -ere, -ī, -lūtus: loose, untie, unfasten; melt; resolve

resonō, -āre: re-echo, resound

respiciō, -ere, -exī, -ectus: look back; take notice of, consider; respect

respīrō, -āre: breathe

respondeō, -ēre, -ī, -ōnsus: reply, respond; correspond to (16 n. 6B)

respōnsum, -ī (n. as noun of past part. of *respondeō*): answer, response

restinguō, -ere, -xī, -ctus: put out, extinguish

restituō, -ere, -uī, -ūtus: set up again; renew, restore

restitūtiō, -ōnis (f.): restoration, reinstating, restitution

restō, -āre, -itī, —: stand firm, withstand; be left

retineō, -ēre, -uī, -entus: restrain, control

retrō (adv.): backward, back

reus, -ī (m.): defendant, one accused of or condemned for a crime; *reum agere:* bring to court as a defendant

revertor (*-vort-*), *-ī, -sus* (dep.; the act. is rare): go back, return

revirēscō, -ere, -ruī, —: grow green again

revocō, -āre: recall, revoke

rēx, rēgis (m.): king

rīdeō, -ēre, -rīsī, -rīsus: laugh; laugh at

rīpa, -ae (f.): bank (of a river)

rīvus, -ī (m.): brook, small stream

rōbur, -oris (n.): oak (in 61 n. 3); strength, vigor

rōbustus, -a, -um: hard, strong

rogātiō, -ōnis (f.): request; law (18 n. 7B, 56 n. 11B)

rogō, -āre: ask, beg (i.e. court: 74 n. 22); propose (a law: in 56 n. 11B)

rōs, rōris (m.): dew

rosa, -ae (f.): rose (87 nn. 2B, 20B)

rōscidus, -a, -um: dewy

rōstrum, -ī (n.): beak (of a bird); ram (reinforced prow of a ship); (plur.): the Rostra (the speaker's platform in the Forum, decorated with the rams of ships captured from the Antians in 338 B.C.: 14 n. 6B, and often)

rota, -ae (f.): wheel (54 n. 15)

rubeō, -ēre, —, —: be red, grow red

ruber, -bra, -brum: red

rudis, -e: rough, rude, uncultivated

ruīna, -ae (f.): a tumbling down, ruin

ruitūrus: fut. part. of *ruō*

rūmor, -ōris (m.): hearsay, report, murmur

rumpō, -ere, rūpī, ruptus: break

ruō, ruere, ruī, rutus (fut. part. *ruitūrus*): rush, tumble

rūpēs, -is (f.): a rock, cliff (84 n. 21B)

rursus (adv.): again (56 n. 6C); backward (59 n. 11B)

rūs, rūris (n.): country; (loc.) *rūrī:* in the country

rūsticus, -a, -um: of the country (m. as noun, i.e. country folk: in 76 n. 9)

rūtrum, -ī (n.): spade (52 n. 12A)

rutus: past part. of *ruō*

sacer, -cra, -crum: sacred; i.e. accursed

sacerdōs, -ōtis (m. and f.): priest, priestess

sacrō, -āre: consecrate, devote

sacrum, -ī (n. of *sacer* as a noun): holy thing; sacred place; rite

saeculāris, -e: pertaining to a *saeculum*; secular (82 n. 14A)

saeculum (or *saeclum* in 69 n. 17C, in 85 n. 1), *-ī* (n.): century, age (82 n. 5), lifetime (i.e. = *genus:* 69 n. 17C)

saepe (adv.): often; (comp.) *saepius*; (sup.) *saepissimē*

saeviō, -īre: be furious, rage

saevus, -a, -um: cruel; i.e. rough (of the sea)

sagulum, -ī (n. diminutive): military cloak (55 n. 18)

sagum, -ī (n.): military cloak; *ad saga īre:* i.e. go to war (23 n. 15)

salix, -icis (f.): willow (84 n. 23)

salsus, -a, -um: salty

salūbris (salūber), -e: healthful, sound

salūs, salūtis (f.): safety, health; *salūtem dīcō:* send greeting to (abbrev. S.D. w. dat.: 32 n. 1B, 37 title)

salūtō, -āre: greet, salute

salvātor, -ōris (m.): savior

salvus, -a, -um: safe, well

sanctum, -ī (n. of *sanctus* as noun): holiness (11 n. 14A)

sanctus, -a, -um: sacred, holy

sandyx, -icis (f.): red color, scarlet (85 n. 29)

sānē (adv. of *sānus*): reasonably, soberly; certainly, indeed

sanguinolentus, -a, -um: bloody (52 v. 18, 54 v. 14)

sanguis, -inis (m.): blood (i.e. family: 15 n. 15B, 33 n. 3A), slaughter

sānus, -a, -um: healthy

sapiēns, -entis (pres. part. of *sapiō* as adj.): wise; (m. as a noun): wise man, philosopher (34 n. 6, 41 n. 17C)

sapientia, -ae (f.): wisdom, good sense

sapientipotēns, -entis: mighty in wisdom (60 n. 26B)

sapiō, -ere, -iī (or *īvī:* 1 n. 4B), —: taste of, have discernment, be wise, have sense

sarcophagus, -ī (m. as noun of a Greek adj. = flesh-devouring): coffin, sarcophagus (46 n. 17B)

satelles, -itis (m.): attendant, bodyguard (78 n. 20D)

satis (adv. and indeclinable adj.): enough, sufficient(ly); (comp.) *satius:* more satisfying, better, preferable

sata, -ōrum (n. plur. as noun of past part. of *serō*): standing crops, planted fields

saxum, -ī (n.): rock, stone

scandō, -ere, —, —: climb, mount (87 n. 38)

scelerātus, -a, -um: accursed, crime-stained (53 n. 14B, 54 n. 16B, 78 n. 8E)

scelus, -eris (n.): crime, sin

scēptrum, -ī (n.): regal staff, scepter; (collective, or poetic, plur.): rule (54 n. 9C, 78 n. 12D)

scidī: perf. of *scindō*

sciēns, -entis (pres. part. of *sciō* as adj.): knowing

scientia, -ae (f.): knowledge, science

scīlicet (adv.; from *scīre licet*): of course (86 n. 31C)

scindō, -ere, -idī (early: *scicidī*), *-issus:* cut, tear, split

sciō, -īre: know, know how to (w. inf.)

scītō (fut. imperative of *sciō*): be assured (32 nn. 6B, 12A)

scopulus, -ī (m.): rock, crag

scrībō, -ere, -īpsī, -īptus: write

scriptor, -ōris (m.): writer, author

scriptum, -ī (n. as noun of past part. of *scrībō*): anything written, book

scūtum, -ī (n.): shield

sē (acc. and abl. sing. and plur. of *sui*): himself, herself, itself, themselves

sēcernō, -ere, -crēvī, -crētus: set apart, divide

sēcessiō, -ōnis (f.): secession, revolt

sēcrētum, -ī (n. as noun of past part. of *sēcernō*): hidden thing, mystery, secret; hiding place

secta, -ae (f.): path; way of life; philosophical school (67 n. 13B); i.e. political party (76 n. 7)

sector, -ārī, -ātus (dep.): follow, run after eagerly (74 n. 21); look for (in 87 n. 20)

secundum (n. acc. sing. of *secundus* as prep. w. acc.): according to

secundus, -a, -um (gerundive of *sequor* as adj.): following; second; favorable, prosperous; *rēs secundae:* prosperity

secūris, -is (f.): axe (61 n. 2)

sēcūritās, -ātis (f.): unconcern; safety

sēcūrus, -a, -um (*sē- = sine + cūra*): free from care, safe, secure

secus (adv.): otherwise, differently

sed (conj.): but; *nōn modo . . . sed etiam:* not only . . . but also

sedeō, -ēre, sēdī, sessum: sit; remain sitting

sēdēs, -is (f.): seat, throne; fixed abode, building; temple *sēditiō, -ōnis* (f.): civil discord, sedition

sēditiōsus, -a, -um: full of discord, turbulent, seditious

sēdō, -āre: calm, settle, allay

sēdulus, -a, -um: diligent, sedulous (87 n. 21E)

seges, -etis (f.): field of grain, crop

sēgnis, -e: slow, tardy, slack; *sēgniter* (adv.): slackly; *nōn sēgnius:* i.e. no less actively (or bravely: 19 p. 2 s. 2)

sēiungō, -ere, -iūnxī, -iūnctus: separate, disjoin, sever

sēligō, -ere, -ēgī, -ēctus: separate, select, choose out

sella, -ae (f.): chair, seat; *sella curūlis:* the official folding stool of a magistrate (8 n. 8B)

semel (adv.): once

sēmen, -inis (n.): seed

sēmita, -ae (f.): footpath, path (metaphorical: 75 n. 5)

semper (adv.): always

sempiternus, -a, -um: everlasting

senātor, -ōris (m.): senator

senātōrius, -a, -um: of a senator

senātus, -ūs (m.): senate

senectūs, -ūtis (f.): old age

senēscō, -ere, -nuī, —: grow old (14 n. 20)

senex, senis (adj.; gen. plur. *senum:* 8 n. 8A, 74 n. 2A): old; (m. as a noun): old man; (comp.) *senior, -ius:* older

sēnī, -ae, -a: six each (84 n. 13C)

senīlis, -e: aged, senile

senior: comp. of *senex*

senium, -ī (n.): old age (77 n. 16B)

sēnsim (adv.): gradually, little by little (14 n. 20)

sēnsus: past part. of *sentiō*

sēnsus, -ūs (m.): perception, consciousness; opinion; understanding; sense

sententia, -ae (f.): feeling, opinion (i.e. wish: 43 n. 18C); decision; sentence, saying

sentiō, -īre, sēnsī, sēnsus: be aware of, feel; think; realize

sentis, -is (m.; usually plur.): bramble, brier bush (85 p. 4 v. 4)

sepeliō, -īre, -iī (or *-īvī:* 1 n. 4B), *-pultus:* bury

septem (indeclinable cardinal numeral): seven

septimus, -a, -um: seventh

septuāgēsimus, -a, -um: seventieth

sepulchrum, -ī (n.): grave, tomb

sepultūra, -ae (f.): burial

sepultus: past part. of *sepeliō*

sequor, -ī, -cūtus (dep.): follow, pursue

seriēs (f.; only acc. and abl. sing.: *-em, -ē*): chain, row, succession

sērius, -a, -um: grave, serious

sermō, -ōnis (m.): talk; discourse (62 n. 1), conversation (43 n. 21A, 62 n. 2); language; diction, style (79 n. 3C)

serō, -ere, sēvī, satus: sow (in 88 n. 26C, compare 84 n. 19B), plant

serō, -ere, -uī (rare), *-tus:* bind together, sew, join (in 84 n. 19B)

serpēns, -entis (m. or f.): snake (12 s. 2)

serta, -ōrum (n. plur. as noun of past part. of *serō* = bind): wreathes

sērum (n. acc. sing. of *sērus* as adv.): late (at night)

sērus, -a, -um: late; *in sērum:* until late (in the day: 46 n. 10)

servīlis, -e: of slaves, servile (83 B s. 7)

serviō, -īre (w. dat.): be slave to, serve

servitium, -ī (n.): slavery, servitude

servitūs, -ūtis (f.): slavery

servō, -āre: preserve, save, maintain, guard

servolus (-vu-), -ī (m.): young (or, insignificant) slave (43 n. 16C)

servus, -ī (m.): slave, servant

sēscentī, -ae, -a: six hundred

sēsē: = sē

sēstertius, -ī (m.; from *sēmis + tertius* = a half less than three): sestertius (or sesterce; a small coin, originally silver and worth 2½ asses; later bronze and worth 4 asses); the archaic gen. plur. *sēstertium* came to be regarded as a n. sing. noun and yielded a n. plur. *sēstertia, -iōrum* (33 n. 16B)

seu: = sīve

sevēritās, -ātis (f.): sternness, severity

sevērus, -a, -um: strict, severe; impartial

sex (indeclinable cardinal numeral): six

sexāgiēns (adv.): sixty times

sexāgintā (indeclinable cardinal numeral): sixty

sextus, -a, -um: sixth

sī (conj.): if; *quod sī:* but if

sibi (sing. and plur. dat. of *suī*): to himself, herself, itself, themselves

sīc (adv.): thus

siccus, -a, -um: dry; (n. as noun): dry land

sīcut (adv.): even as, just as, as; just as if

sīdus, -eris (n.): star; i.e. the dog star (86 n. 13C); group of stars, constellation

significātiō, -ōnis (f.): sign, signification; sign of assent, applause *significō, -āre:* mean, signify; express, report

signō, -āre: mark, indicate

signum, -ī (n.): sign

silentēs, -um (m. plur. as noun of pres. part. of *sileō*): the silent ones, i.e. the dead (80 n. 11c)

silentium, -ī (n.): silence

sileō, -ēre, -uī, —: be silent

silēscō, -ere, —, —: become silent; i.e. grow calm (73 n. 12c)

silva, -ae (f.): wood, forest

silvestris, -e: of the woods, sylvan (84 n. 2b), wooded

similis, -e: like, similar (w. dat.: 19 n. 2, or w. gen.: 81 n. 21)

similitūdō, -inis (f.): likeness, resemblance, similitude

simplex, -icis (adj.): simple, unadorned, plain (87 n. 3)

simul (adv.): at once, together, at the same time; *simul ac* (conj.: 69 n. 10a) or *atque* or *ac prīmum* (39 n. 11b), or *simul* alone (85 n. 16a): as soon as, as well as

simulācrum, -ī (n.): likeness, image; statue

simulō, -āre: copy; assume the appearance of, feign (65 p. 2 s. 1), simulate

simultās, -ātis (f.): rivalry, animosity (17 A s. 2, 33 last s.)

sin (or *sī nōn;* conj.): but if, if however

sine (prep. w. abl.): without

singulāris, -e: alone, single, solitary; unique, singular, extraordinary

singulī, -ae, -a: each (individually: 90 n. 4b), one at a time; separate, individual

sinister, -tra, -trum: left, on the left; auspicious; inauspicious, adverse (in 52 n. 5a)

sinō, -ere, sīvī, situs: put, place (i.e. bury: 10 last s.); allow, permit

sinus, -ūs (m.): a curved surface, fold; bosom, lap; bay

sistō, -ere, stitī, status: cause to stand, place

sitiō, -īre: thirst, be thirsty

sitis, -is (f.): thirst

situs, -a, -um (past part. of *sinō*): placed, situated; buried

situs, -ūs (m.): site (i.e. building: in 87 n. 34a)

sīve (or *seu;* conj.): or if; *sīve ... sīve:* if ... or if; whether ... or; either ... or

sīvī: perf. of *sinō*

sōbrius, -a, -um: sober (33 p. 4 s. 2), temperate

socer, -erī (m.): father-in-law (54 n. 5b, 88 n. 15a)

sociālis, -e: of allies, allied, confederate, "social" (23 s. 1)

societās, -ātis (f.): fellowship; alliance, society

socius, -ī (m.): a partner, ally, comrade; (as adj.): allied with, joined to (69 v. 24)

sodālis, -is (m. and f.): comrade (86 n. 17d)

sōl, sōlis (m.): sun

sōlācium, -ī (n.): solace, comfort, consolation

soleō, -ēre, -itus (semi-dep.): be wont, be accustomed

solidus, -a, -um: whole; sound, solid

solium, -ī (n): throne (54 n. 7a)

sollers, -ertis (adj.): skillful, clever

sollicitō, -āre: disturb, stir up

sollicitus, -a, -um: agitated, disturbed

sōlum (n. acc. sing. of *sōlus* as adv.): only

solum, -ī (n.): ground (distinguishable from the preceding by the short -*o*-)

sōlus, -a, -um: alone, only, single, sole; gen. *sōlīus,* dat. *sōlī*

solvō, -ere, -ī, -lūtus: loosen, untie, free; pay a debt; fulfill; *nāvem solvere:* to set sail

somnium, -ī (n.): dream

somnus, -ī (m.): sleep

sonitus, -ūs (m.): sound

sonō, -āre, -uī, -itus: make a noise, sound, resound

sonus, -ī (m.): noise, sound

sōpiō, -īre: put to sleep

sōpītus: past part. of *sōpiō* (70 A v. 11)

soror, -ōris (f.): sister

sors, sortis (f.): lot, decision by lot; chance; sort, kind

sortior, -īrī, -ītus (dep.): cast lots; obtain by lot, take as one's share

sōspes, -itis (adj.): safe, unhurt

spargō, -ere, -sī, -sus: strew, scatter; spread, disperse

spatium, -ī (n.): space, extent, distance; period of time

speciēs (f.; only in acc. and abl. sing.: -*em,* -*ē*): sight, look; appearance, aspect

spectāculum, -ī (n.): show, sight, spectacle

spectātor, -ōris (m.): onlooker, spectator

spectō, -āre: look at, watch, inspect, regard

spernō, -ere, sprēvī, sprētus: reject, scorn, spurn

spērō, -āre: hope, hope for, expect

spēs, speī (f.): hope

spīritus, -ūs (m.): breath (25 n. 12B, 89 n. 11), exhalation (25 n. 12B); spirit (89 n. 7B); high spirit, courage (58 n. 13B)

spīrō, -āre: breathe

splendidus, -a, -um: brilliant, glittering, gorgeous, illustrious

spoliō, -āre: despoil, strip (w. acc. of person and abl. of separation of thing: 15 n. 15A)

sponte (f. abl. sing. as adv. of obsolete *spōns*): of one's own accord, voluntarily

stabiliō, -īre: make firm, confirm

stabilis, -e: firm, fixed, stable (in 85 n. 31A)

stabilītus, -a, -um (past part. of *stabiliō*): stabilized, established

stabulum, -ī (n.): standing-place, fixed abode, lair (61 n. 9B); stable

stāgnum, -ī (n.): standing water; swamp

statim (adv.): at once, immediately

statiō, -ōnis (f.): post, station

statua, -ae (f.): image, statue

statuō, -ere, -uī, -ūtus: set up, erect; establish, fix; decree, decide

statūra, -ae (f.): stature, height

status: past part. of *sistō*

status, -ūs (m.): position; condition, state, status

stella, -ae (f.): star; *stella cōmāns:* i.e. comet (80 nn. 20A and C)

sterilitās, -ātis (f.): bareness, sterility, unfruitfulness

sternō, -ere, strāvī, strātus: spread out, strew; spread over, cover; lay low, overthrow

stertō, -ere, stertuī (rare), —: snore (70 B v. 19)

stetī: perf. of *stō*

stimulus, -ī (m.): goad, spur

stīpendium, -ī (n.): tax; pay, stipend; (in plur.): military service (29 n. 5)

stirps, -pis (m. or f.): stem; stock, race, family

stīva, -ae (f.): plough handle (51 n. 16A)

stō, stāre, stetī, stātūrus (the *-a-* is lengthened in the fut. part. and in the supine *stātum* but short in derivatives formed directly on the root; see *statim, etc.* above): stand (57 n. 10A, and often), stand firm (in 60 n. 25A); make to stand (i.e. stop: in 71 n. 17)

stolidus, -a, -um: stupid, stolid

stomachor, -ārī, -ātus (dep.): be irritated, be angry

strāgēs, -is (f.): massacre, carnage

strāvī, strātus: perf. and past part. of *sternō*

strēnuus, -a, -um: active, vigorous, strenuous

strepō, -ere, -uī, —: make a noise, clatter

stringō, -ere, -nxī, -ictus: draw together, compress; bind; unsheathe (a weapon: 24 n. 4C, and often)

struō, -ere, -ūxī, -ūctus: heap up, pile; build, erect; arrange

studeō, -ēre, -uī, —: be eager for, desire; pursue, engage in; be zealous for (w. dat.: 72 n. 1)

studiōsus, -a, -um: eager, zealous

studium, -ī (n.): enthusiasm, zeal (often partisan: 68 n. 18C); study, pursuit; eagerness, desire (in 73 n. 16)

stultus, -a, -um: foolish, stupid

stuprum, -ī (n.): defilement, debauchery

suādeō, -ēre, -sī, -sus: urge, persuade (w. dat.)

suāsor, -ōris (m.): adviser, persuader

suāvis, -e: sweet, pleasant, agreeable

sub (prep. w. acc.): under, beneath, up to (w. verbs of motion); (of time): before (44 n. 1), about, until; (w. abl.): under, below, near to, behind; (of time): during, within, in the time of

subeō, -īre, -iī (or *-īvī:* 1 n. 4B), *-itus:* go under, enter, come up to; undergo, endure

subiciō, -ere, -iēcī, -iectus: throw under, put under, cast below; subject, conquer; put up; substitute

subiectus, -a, -um (past part. of *subiciō*): subjected; (m. as noun): the conquered (88 n. 34B)

subigō, -ere, -ēgī, -āctus: overcome, conquer; compel

subinānis, -e: rather empty, rather vain

subinde (adv.): just after, thereupon; from time to time, frequently

subitō (abl. of *subitus* as adv.): suddenly, at once, unexpectedly

subitus, -a, -um (past. part. of *subeō*): sudden, surprising

sublātus: past part. of the rare compound *sustollō* but used for both *tollō* and *sufferō* (16 n. 3B)

sublevō, -āre: raise up, assist; alleviate

sublimitās, -ātis (f.): loftiness, height, sublimity

subm-: also written *summ-*

submitto, -ere, -īsī, -issus: put under, put down, drop; submit; send up (from below; i.e. raise: of flowers: 69 n. 8c, of bulls: 84 n. 14B); provide a substitute for

submoveō, -ēre, -ōvī, -ōtus: remove, separate (in 58 n. 1A)

subolēs, -is (f.): sprout; offspring, issue

subōrnō, -āre: fit out, supply, equip; employ as a secret agent

subsellium, -ī (n.): bench (18 n. 15A)

subsidium, -ī (n.): reserve force, auxiliary troops; help, aid (29 n. 15A)

subsistō, -ere, -stitī, —: stand still, halt; hold out, resist; last, abide

subsum, -esse, —, —: be behind, be under, be at hand

subter (adv. or prep. w. acc.): below, beneath (69 n. 4B)

subtīlis, -e: delicate, fine; subtle

subvertō (-vort-), -ere, -ī, -sus: upset, overthrow, subvert

succēdō, -ere, -essī, -essus: go or come under, come up to, approach; be next to, succeed; be successful, prosper

successus: past part. of *succēdō*

successus, -ūs (m.): advance, approach; success

succlāmō, -āre: call out in answer

succumbō, -ere, -ubuī, -ubitum: fall down, sink; yield, succumb

succurrō, -ere, -ī, -rsum: run up under, run to assist; help, succor (w. dat.)

sūdō, -āre: sweat, exude (85 n. 18A)

sūdor, -ōris (m.): sweat (61 n. 23)

suēsco, -ere, suēvī, suētus (rare in the uncompounded form): become accustomed to

sufferō, -ferre, sustulī, sublātus (perf. and past part. also used for *tollō*): undergo, endure, submit to

sufficiō, -ere, -ēcī, -ectus: supply; suffice

suffodiō, -ere, -ōdī, -ossus: dig up, dig under, undermine

suī (sing. and plur. gen. 3rd pers. reflexive pronoun; no nom., dat. *sibi*, acc. and abl. *sē* or *sēsē*): of himself, herself, itself, themselves; also m. or n. gen. sing. or m. nom. plur. of *suus*

sulcus, -ī (m.): furrow (51 v. 17)

sum, esse, fuī, futūrus: be, exist

summ-: see *subm-*

summa, -ae (f. of *summus* as noun): top, summit; main thing, total, whole

summus, -a, -um (or *suprēmus*; sup. of *superus*): highest, upmost

sūmō, -ere, -psī, -ptus: take, assume

sūmptuōsus, -a, -um: expensive; extravagant, lavish

sūmptus: past part. of *sūmō*

sūmptus, -ūs (m.): expense, outlay

super (prep. w. acc.): over, on top of, beyond (88 n. 6A); on; (w. abl.): above, on, concerning; (adv.): above, from above (69 n. 27B); in addition, besides (70 n. 7A)

superbia, -ae (f.): pride (87 n. 42A); haughtiness

superbus, -a, -um: proud, haughty; (m. as noun): the proud (88 last v.)

superior, -ius (comp. of *superus*): higher, former, previous

supernus, -a, -um: upper, celestial, supernal

superō, -āre: go over, surmount, overcome; excel, surpass; abound, be in excess

superstes, -itis (adj.): standing by; remaining alive (86 n. 3c); surviving

superstitiō, -ōnis (f.): superstition

supersum, -esse, -fuī, -futūrus: be left over, remain, survive

superus, -a, -um: over, above, upper, higher; (comp.) *superior*; (sup.) *suprēmus* (or *summus*)

superveniō, -īre, -ēnī, -entus: come in addition, arrive, follow

supervolō, -āre: fly over (15 A last s.)

suppeditō, -āre: furnish generously, provide

supplex, -icis (adj.): kneeling, entreating, suppliant

supplicium, -ī (n.): punishment; death penalty; supplication (17 s. 3)

supplicō, -āre: beseech, beg, supplicate (w. dat.; 12 n. 15D)

suprā (adv. or prep. w. acc.): above, beyond

suprēmus, -a, -um (or *summus*; sup. of *superus*): highest, utmost, last

surgō, -ere, -rēxī, -rēctus: raise up (trans. rarely); arise, get up

sūrsum (adv.): upwards, on high, high above (82 B s. 3)

suscēnseo, -ēre, -uī, —: be angry (w. dat.)

suscipiō, -ere, -ēpī, -eptus: undertake, undergo, take up, receive; adopt *suspendō, -ere, -ī, -ēnsus:* hang up, suspend; hang; keep in suspense; interrupt

suspiciō, -ere, -exī, -ectus: look up at; respect; suspect

sustineō, -ēre, -uī, -entus: hold up, sustain; hold back, restrain; withstand, endure

sustulī: perf. of the rare compound *sustollō* and used for both *tollō* and *sufferō* (16 n. 3B)

suus, -a, -um (sing. and plur. 3rd pers. reflexive adj.): of or belonging to himself, herself, etc., his own, their own; his, hers, its, theirs; (nom. plur. m. as a noun): one's own men (3 n. 6C, and often)

tabella, -ae (f.): picture (on a wooden tablet)

tabernāculum, -ī (n.): tent, hut (40 n. 16A)

tābēscō, -ere, -buī, —: melt away; waste away (70 A last v.)

tabula, -ae (f.): tablet (for writing), placard, panel (for a painting: 87 n. 9A)

taceō, -ēre, -uī, -itus: be silent

tacitus, -a, -um (past part. of *taceō*): silent, in silence

tactus: past part. of *tangō*

taeda, -ae (f.) pine; marriage torch (of pine wood; 77 n. 3B)

taedium, -ī (n.): weariness

taeter, -tra, -trum: foul-smelling; foul

tālis, -e (adj.): such; *tālis . . . quālis:* such . . . as

tam (adv.): so, so greatly

tamen (adv.): yet, nevertheless; however

tamquam (adv.): just as, like; as if

tandem (adv.): at last; (in questions) pray, then (71 n. 1A)

tangō, -ere, tetigī, tāctus: touch; hit, strike

tantopere (or *tantō opere;* abl. as adv.): so greatly, so much

tantum (adv.): so much, so far; only (26 n. 15A), merely; *tantum modo:* only (21 n. 6C, 24 n. 13)

tantus, -a, -um: so much, so great

tarditās, -ātis (f.): slowness, tardiness

tardō, -āre: make late, or, slow; check

tardus, -a, -um: late, slow

taurus, -ī (m.): bull (84 v. 25, 85 n. 26A)

tē (acc. and abl. of *tū*): thee, you

tēctum, -ī (n. of *tēctus* as noun): covered place, dwelling, house

tēctus, -a, -um: past part. of *tegō*

tegmen, -inis (n.): cover, shade (84 v. 1)

tegō, -ere, tēxī, tēctus: cover

tellūs, -ūris (f.): earth, land

tēlum, -ī (n.): weapon; missile, dart

temerārius, -a, -um: thoughtless, heedless (78 n. 18A)

temerē (adv.): without good reason, rashly; *nōn temerē:* not easily, not readily

temeritās, -ātis (f.): rashness (45 n. 14D)

temerō, -āre: blacken; defile, desecrate (77 n. 29B, 88 n. 23E)

temperāns, -antis (pres. part. of *temperō* as adj.): moderate, temperate

temperantia, -ae (f.): moderation, self-control, temperance

temperō, -āre: control, stop

tempestās, -ātis (f.): weather; storm, tempest; time (48 n. 22); i.e. crisis (22 n. 7)

tempestīvus, -a, -um: timely, seasonable; i.e. calm (of the sea: 29 n. 14)

templum, -ī (n.): temple

temptāmentum, -ī (n.): attempt, trial

temptō (or *tentō*), *-āre:* make an attempt upon (85 n. 20B); try, test; try to win over

tempus, -oris (n.): time, occasion; (plur.): i.e. emergency (30 n. 3B, 37 n. 18, 72 n. 12)

tempus, -oris (n., usually plur.; from a different root than the preceding): temple (of the head: 61 n. 28B)

tendō, -ere, tetendī (3 n. 3), *tentus* (or *tēnsus*): stretch, stretch out, extend; move, march

tenebrōsus, -a, -um: dark, gloomy

teneō, -ēre, -uī, -tus: hold, possess, keep; seize, grasp

tener, -era, -erum: tender, young

tenor, -ōris (m.): uninterrupted course, tenor

tentō: = temptō

tenuis, -e: meager, slight; poor; (m. as a noun): a poor person; (plur.): the poor

tepēns, -entis (pres. part. of *tepeō* as adj.): warm (59 n. 10)

tepeō, -ēre, —, —: be warm

tepor, -ōris (m.): gentle warmth (73 n. 11B)

teres, -etis (adj.): rounded, smooth, well-turned, well-formed (33 p. 2 s. 1, 55 n. 8A)

tergum, -ī (n.): back; *tergum vertere:* to flee (lit. to turn the back)

terminō, -āre: end; put a limit (or end) to

terra, -ae (f.): earth, land, country; *orbis terrārum:* (inhabited) world (see *orbis*)

terreō, -ēre, -uī, -itus: frighten

terribilis, -e: terrible, dreadful

tertius, -a, -um: third

testimōnium, -ī (n.): evidence, proof, testimony

testis, -is (m.): witness

testor, -ārī, -ātus (dep.): call as a witness; show, declare; bear witness to

tētē: intensive for *tē* (73 n. 5)

tetulī: = tulī

tēxī: perf. of *tegō*

theātrum, -ī (n.): theater (77 n. 19)

thēsaurus, -ī (m.): treasure (82 B s. 4); treasure house

tibi (dat. of *tū*): to thee, to you

tigris, -is (or *-idis,* m. or f.): tiger (in 88 n. 10A)

timeō, -ēre, -uī, —: fear, be afraid, dread

timidus, -a, -um: afraid

timor, -ōris (m.): fear

tingō (or *tinguō:* 54 n. 6B), *-ere, -xī, -ctus:* dip, soak

tinniō, -īre: ring (61 n. 19A)

tinnītus, -ūs (m.): ringing (of metals: 61 C p. 2 v. 4)

tīrō, -ōnis (m.): recruit, young soldier; (as adj.): untrained (41 n. 5C)

toga, -ae (f.): toga (outer garment worn by a citizen); i.e. peace (27 n. 13B, and often); *toga praetexta:* toga with a purple border (in 8 n. 8C, compare 15 n. 12A)

tolerō, -āre: bear, endure; sustain, relieve

tollō, -ere, sustulī, sublātus (perf. and past part. also used for *sufferō*): raise up; take away; destroy

tonitrus, -ūs (m.): thunder (52 n. 5A)

torpeō, -ēre, —, —: be numb, be made numb

torqueō, -ēre, -sī, -tus: turn, twist

torreō, -ēre, -uī, tostus: roast, scorch, burn

tot (adj., indeclinable): so many; *quot . . . tot, tot . . . quot:* as many *(tot)* . . . as *(quot)*

totidem: just as many, just so many

tōtus, -a, -um: the whole, the whole of; entire, all; gen. *tōtīus,* dat. *tōtī*

trabs, trabis (f.): timber, beam

tractō, -āre: handle, manage, treat

tractus: past part. of *trahō* (83 n. 13A)

trādō, -ere, -idī, -itus: hand over, give up; relate

trahō, -ere, traxī, tractus: draw, attract

trāiciō, -ere, -iēcī, -iectus: hurl across; transfer; pierce (43 n. 9E)

trānō, -āre: swim across (69 v. 15)

tranquillus, -a, -um: peaceful, quiet, tranquil

trāns (prep. w. acc.): across, over

trānscendō, -ere, -ī, -ēnsus: climb or step over, transcend

trānscurrō, -ere, -ī (or *-cucurrī*), *-rsus:* run across, pass

trānseō, -īre, -iī (or *-īvī:* 1 n. 4B), *-itus:* go across, cross

trānsferō, -ferre, -tulī, -lātus: carry or bring over, transfer; translate

trānsfīgō, -ere, -ixī, -ixus: pierce through, transfix

trānsfugiō, -ere, -ūgī, —: flee to the other side, desert (6 n. 10A)

trānsiliō, -īre, -uī, —: leap across

trānslātus: past part. of *trānsferō*

trānsmarīnus, -a, -um: beyond the sea, overseas

trānsmittō, -ere, -īsī, -issus: send across (w. 2 accs.: 39 n. 24); (intrans.): cross over (39 n. 25A)

transtulī: perf. of *transferō*

trānsversus, -a, -um: crosswise; cross-country (44 n. 4A)

trecentī, -ae, -a: three hundred

tredecim (indeclinable cardinal numeral): thirteen

tremefaciō, -ere, -ēcī, -actus: make tremble (in 88 n. 9E)

tremō, -ere, -uī, —: quake, tremble

tremor, -ōris (m.): shaking, trembling

trepidus, -a, -um: agitated, anxious

trēs, tria (cardinal numeral): three

trēsvirī: = triumvirī

tribūnal, -ālis (n.): raised platform, tribunal (82 B s. 3)

tribūnātus, -ūs (m.): office of tribune

tribūnicius, -a, -um: of a tribune

tribūnus, -ī (m.): *(plebis)* tribune of the plebs (7 s. 5, and often); *tribūnus mīlitāris:* tribune of a legion (a junior officer: 14 n. 4A, and often)

tribuō, uere, -uī, -ūtus: assign; grant; render

tribus, -ūs (f.): tribe (usually one of the thirty-five "tribes" into which the *populus* was subdivided: in 21 n. 11A, 25 n. 1B, 53 n. 4)

tricēsimus, -a, -um: thirtieth

trichila, -ae (f.): bower, arbor (40 n. 15C)

trifōrmis, -e: having three forms, threefold (80 n. 24B)

trīgintā (indeclinable cardinal numeral): thirty

tristis, -e: sad

triumphō, -āre: triumph, celebrate a triumph (9 n. 10c); (pass.) be triumphed over (i.e. defeated: in 64 n. 14A)

triumphus, -ī (m.): triumphal procession, celebration of a victory; triumph

triumvir, -ī (m.; plur. also *trēsvirī*): a triumvir (one of three commissioners: 18 s. 5, 44 pref., 47 n. 4A, compare 35 pref.)

trucīdō, -āre: slaughter, massacre

truncus, -ī (m.): trunk, body

tū (2nd pers. sing. pronoun; gen. *tuī*, dat. *tibi*, acc. and abl. *tē*): thou, you

tuba, -ae (f.): trumpet

tueor, -ērī, tūtus (dep.): look at, consider; watch over, protect

tugurium, -ī (n.): hut, hovel (24 last s.)

tuī: gen. of *tū;* also m. or n. gen. sing. or m. nom. plur. of *tuus*

tulī (or *tetulī*): perf. of *tollō* and used for *ferō*

tum (adv.): then; *cum . . . tum:* see *cum*

tumultuor, -ārī, -ātus (dep.): make a disturbance

tumultus, -ūs (m.): uprising, disturbance, tumult

tumulus, -ī (m.): mound, hill (45 p. 3 s. 1); tomb-mound

tunc (adv.): then; now

turba, -ae (f.): disorder; crowd, mob

turbō, -āre: disturb, throw into confusion

turbulentus, -a, -um: stormy, disordered, turbulent

turgidus, -a, -um: swollen

turpis, -e: disgraceful, shameful

tūte: intensive form of *tū* (60 n. 28B, 70 n. 16B)

tūtēla, -ae (f.): protection

tūtor, -ārī, -ātus (dep.): watch over, protect (83 n. 10A)

tūtor, -ōris (m.): protector, guardian (often legal; not in Lat. an academic "tutor")

tūtus, -a, -um (past part. of *tueor*): safe

tuus, -a, -um (2nd pers. sing. possessive adj.): thine, your, or yours

tyrannus, -ī (m.): tyrant (in 59 n. 25A, 78 n. 13C), ruler (60 n. 28C)

ūber, -eris (n.): teat, tit (in 55 n. 6A), udder

ūber, -eris (adj.): rich, fruitful

ubi (or *ubī*; interrog. and rel. adv.): where; (conj.): when, whenever; *ubi prīmum:* as soon as

ubīque (adv.): everywhere

ulcīscor, -ī, ūltus (dep.): avenge; punish, take vengeance on (88 n. 23A)

ūllus, -a, -um: any, anyone, any at all; gen. *ūllīus,* dat. *ūllī*

ulterior, -ius (comp. adj.): farther, more remote; (sup.) *ultimus:* farthest

ultimus: sup. of *ulterior*

ultor, -ōris (m.): punisher, avenger

ultrō (adv.): on the farther side; besides, furthermore; of one's own accord; *ultrō citrōque:* to and fro

ululō, -āre: cry out, howl (in 80 n. 11B)

ulva, -ae (f.): sedge, swamp-grass (64 n. 7B)

umbō, -ōnis (m.): knob; boss of a shield; the shield itself (61 n. 19c)

umbra, -ae (f.): shade (49 n. 2A), shadow

umerus, -ī (m.): shoulder (in 43 n. 6, 88 v. 10)

umquam (adv.): ever, at any time

ūnā (f. abl. sing. of *ūnus* as adv.: 32 n. 3c): together; in the same place, at the same time, as well (70 n. 7B)

unda, -ae (f.): wave

unde (interrog. or rel. adv.): whence, from where

ūndecimus, -a, -um: eleventh

ūndēvīgintī (indeclinable cardinal numeral): nineteen

undique (adv.): from every side (61 n. 21D), all around; utterly, completely

ūnicē (adv.): solely, uniquely

ūniversus, -a, -um: all together, all in one, whole, entire

ūnus, -a, -um (cardinal numeral): one, single, alone; the only one; gen. *ūnīus,* dat. *ūnī*

urbānus, -a, -um: of the city, urban; refined, witty

urbs, urbis (f.): wailed town, city (in 19 n. 6B); i.e. Rome (15 n. 13A, and often)

urgeō, -ēre, ursī (rare), —: press on, push forward, drive, urge (i.e. woo: 87 n. 2c)

ūrō, -ere, ūssī, ūstus: burn, burn up

ursus, -ī (m.): bear

ūsque (adv.): continuously, right on (87 n. 37A), i.e. still (77 n. 25B); as far as, up to (in 71 n. 1A); *ūsque ad:* all the way up to (without *ad:* 90 n. 15A)

ūsūrpō, -āre: seize for use, usurp; make use of (in conversation, i.e. talk of: 36 n. 3D) *ūsus:* past part. of *ūtor*

ūsus, -ūs (m.): use, practice, employment; experience, habit, usefulness, profit

ut (or *utī*; adv., or conj. w. ind.): as, just as; when, after; *ut prīmum:* when first, as soon as; (conj. w. subj.): so that, with the result that; in order that; (w. verbs of fearing): lest, that . . . not

uter, utra, utrum: which of two, which; whichever of two, whichever one; gen. *utrīus,* dat. *utrī*

uterque, utraque, utrumque: each (of two taken separately; contrast *ambō*), either, each one; both

uterus, -ī (m.): womb (90 last s.)

utī: a stronger form of *ut* (28 n. 23D, 63 nn. 5B, 10C; distinguishable from *ūtī,* the inf. of *ūtor,* by the short *-u-;* see 42 n. 27C)

ūtilis, -e: useful, profitable

ūtilitās, -ātis (f.): usefulness, utility, expediency

utinam (adv.): if only, would that

ūtor, -ī, ūsus (dep.; w. abl.: 14 n. 16B, and often): use, employ (i.e. follow: 35 n. 9D); i.e. associate with (72 n. 3); profit by, enjoy

utrum (conj.): whether; *utrum . . . an:* whether . . . or; *utrum . . . annōn, utrum . . . necne:* whether . . . or not

ūva, -ae (f.): grape (85 p. 4 v. 4)

ūvidus, -a, -um: wet, damp

uxor, -ōris (f.): wife

vacca, -ae (f.): cow (51 n. 17)

vacō, -āre: be empty; be free from; be idle, have leisure for

vacuus, -a, -um: empty, unoccupied, free (87 n. 7A)

vādō, -ere, (in compounds:*-vāsī,-vāsum*)*:* go, hurry, rush

vae (interj.): woe on; alas (w. acc.: 74 n. 24, or dat., as in *vae victīs*)

vāgītus, -ūs (m.): crying, squalling

vagor, -ārī, -ātus (dep.): stroll around, wander

vagus, -a, -um: wandering, vagrant, vague

valdē (adv.; contracted form of *validē* from *validus*): strongly; exceedingly, very much

valeō, -ēre, -uī, -itūrus: be strong, be in good health; have influence; *plūrimum valēre:* to be very powerful; *valē,*

valēte (imperatives): farewell, good-by

valētūdō, -inis (f.): state of health; good health; bad health, illness (in 43 n. 19E)

validus, -a, -um: strong, sturdy; healthy

vāllum, -ī (n.): line of palisades, rampart (in 4 n. 12), fortification

vānitās, -ātis (f.): emptiness, aimlessness, untruthfulness; (rarely) vanity

vānus, -a, -um: empty; useless, vain

varietās, -ātis (f.): diversity, variety

varius, -a, -um: diverse, different, manifold, varying

vāstitās, -ātis (f.): empty place, desert; desolation, waste

vāstus, -a, -um: waste, desolate; enormous, monstrous

vātēs, -is (m. and f.): soothsayer (50 n. 8B), prophet; poet

vāticinātiō, -ōnis (f.): prophecy

-ve (enclitic conj.): or (2 n. 4B, and often)

vectīgal, -ālis (n.): tax, tribute; private income, revenue

vector, -ōris (m.): carrier (of goods), trader (85 n. 24D)

vectus: past part. of *vehō*

vegetus, -a, -um: lively, vigorous (33 p. 2 s. 1)

vehemēns, -entis (adj.): violent, impetuous, vehement

vehementer (adv.): violently, impetuously, vehemently

vehō, -ere, vexī, vectus: bear, carry

vel (conj.): or (in 27 n. 1); *vel . . . vel:* either . . . or; (adv.): even (76 n. 21A)

velle: inf. of *volō*

vellō, -ere, vulsī (or *vol-*; in compounds: *-vellī*), *vulsus* (*vol-*)*:* pluck, pluck out; tear down (55 n. 11E)

vellus, -eris (n.): fleece (85 n. 28H)

vēlō, -āre: cover, wrap, cover up, veil

vēlōcitās, -ātis (f.): speed, velocity

vēlox, -ōcis (adj.): quick, swift

vēlum, -ī (n.): sail

velut (or *velutī*; adv.): just as, as, like

vēnālis, -e: for sale, venal

vēnātor, -ōris (m.): hunter (86 B v. 19)

vēndō, -ere, -didī, -ditus (from *vēnum dare*; in 26 n. 16C): to sell

venēnum, -ī (n.): poison (59 A s. 1, 85 n. 15A)

veneror, -ārī, -ātus (dep.): respect, venerate (8 n. 8F)

vēneō, -īre, -iī (or *-īvī:* 1 n. 4B), *vēnitum* (from *vēnum īre:* 26 n. 16C); go for sale, be sold (as pass. of *vēndō*) *venia, -ae* (f.): favor, indulgence

veniō, -īre, vēnī, ventum: come

ventitō, -āre, —, —: come repeatedly, visit frequently (74 n. 18A)

ventus, -ī (m.): wind

venus, -eris (f.): loveliness, charm; (name of a goddess): Venus (in 69 n. 1B, and often), i.e. love.

venustus, -a, -um: lovely, charming, graceful

vēr, vēris (n.): spring (29 n. 17D)

verbum, -ī (n.): word, talk; prophecy (90 n. 15B)

vērē (adv. of *vērus*): truly (the abl. of *vēr* has a final short -*e*: 29 n. 17D)

verēcundia, -ae (f.): modesty, bashfulness, reserve

verēcundus, -a, -um: reserved, modest, shy

vereor, -ērī, -itus (dep.): fear, be afraid

vergō, -ere, —, —: turn, slope; lie, be situated

vēritās, -ātis (f.): truth, truthfulness, verity

vērnus, -a, -um: of spring

vērō (n. abl. sing. of *vērus* as adv.): truly, indeed; however; *iam vērō:* moreover

versō (vor-), -āre: turn often

versor, -ārī, -ātus (pass. of *versō*): engage in, be active in

versus, -a, -um: past part. of *vertō*

versus, -ūs (m.): turning; line, row; a line (i.e. verse) of poetry

versus (adv. and prep. w. acc.): toward, facing

vertex (vortex), -icis (f.): whirl, whirlpool; top, summit (of a mountain: 88 v. 15); head

vertō (archaic *vortō*), *-ere, -ī, -sus:* turn, change into (80 n. 20B)

vērum (n. acc. sing. of *vērus* as adv.): but, but also (25 p. 2 s. 3); = *vērō*

vērum, -ī (n. sing. of *vērus* as noun): truth (in 11 n. 14A)

vērus, -a, -um: true, real, genuine

vester, -tra, -trum: your, yours

vestimentum, -ī (n.): garment; (plur.): clothes (in 87 n. 9A)

vestiō, -īre: clothe, cover

vestis, -is (f.): clothing

vestrī: gen. of *vōs*; also m. and n. sing. or m. nom. plur. of *vester*

vestrum: gen. of *vōs*; also m. acc. sing. and n. nom. and acc. sing. of *vester*

veterānus, -ī (m.): veteran

vetō, -āre, -uī, -itus: forbid, veto

vetus, -eris (adj.): old, of long standing, old and still existing; (comp.) *vetustior:* older; (sup.) *veterrimus:* oldest

vetustās, -ātis (f.): old age; long duration

vexī: perf. of *vehō*

vēxillum, -ī (n.): military standard, ensign (63 n. 13C)

via, -ae (f.): road, way, journey; *via Appia:* the Appian Way (from Rome to Brundisium: in 57 n. 2A)

viāticum, -ī (n.): traveling money (24 p. 3 s. 5)

viburnum, -ī (n.): viburnum (a shrub: in 84 n. 12)

vicēsimus, -a, -um: twentieth

vīcīnus, -a, -um: neighboring, nearby

vicis (f. gen.; no nom., acc. *vicem*, abl. *vice*, plur. nom. and acc. *vicēs*, dat. and abl. *vicibus*): change, interchange, alternation, turn (4 n. 1B); (acc. as prep.) *vicem:* in place; *invicem:* in turn; (abl.) *vice:* in place of (w. gen.); *vice versā:* turn reversed; i.e. just the contrary

vicissitūdō, -inis (f.): change, alternation, vicissitude

victor, -ōris (m.): conqueror, victor; (as adj.): conquering, victorious (21 n. 6B, 30 n. 13)

victōria, -ae (f.): victory

victrīx, -īcis (f.): conqueress; (as adj.): victorious (49 n. 12, 77 n. 14)

victus: past part. of *vincō* (not of *vīvō*)

victus, -ūs (m.): sustenance, food (20 n. 11C): way of life (46 n. 5C)

vīcus, -ī (m.): village; district of a city, quarter, alley (53 n. 14A, 54 n. 16B)

videō, -ēre, vīdī, vīsus: see, discern, perceive; (in pass.): seem

vigeō, -ēre, -uī, —: flourish, prosper

vigilia, -ae (f.): wakefulness (9 n. 19B), lying awake; sentry duty (65 n. 23A), watch (in 90 n. 8A); time of keeping watch (a fourth part of the night: 41 p. 3 s. 4)

vigilō, -āre: be awake, be watchful (90 p. 2 s. 1)

vīgintī (indeclinable cardinal numeral): twenty

vigor, -ōris (m.): vigor, force

vīlis, -e: cheap

vīlla, -ae (f.): country house, villa

vīmen, -inis (n.): pliant twig, osier

vinciō, -īre, -xī, -ctus: bind, fasten, fetter (22 n. 1B)

vincō, -ere, vīcī, victus: conquer; win (an argument); i.e. prove (81 n. 3A); win (a case: 7 n. 9)

vinctus: past part. of *vinciō*

vinculum, -ī (n.): bond, fetter

vindex, -icis (m. and f.) defender, champion (26 n. 1B), protector; avenger

vindicō, -āre: claim, claim at law (as free; 20 n. 13B, 38 n. 22B, 47 n. 2); i.e. liberate; avenge (7 n. 13, 19 n. 4B); punish (17 n. 16B)

vīnea, -ae (f.): vineyard

vīnum, -ī (n.): wine

violēns, -entis (adj.): impetuous, rapid (in 87 n. 39C), violent

violentia, -ae (f.): violence

violō, -āre: violate, do violence to, profane

vir, virī (m.): man (specifically, as against *homō*); husband; man of courage; *vir optimus:* gentleman

vireō, -ēre, -uī, —: grow green, be verdant

virēs: see *vīs*

virga, -ae (f.): slender green branch, rod (89 nn. 5B, 10A and B)

virgātus, -a, -um: made of twigs; striped (55 n. 18)

virginitās, -ātis (f.): virginity

virgō, -inis (f.): maiden, girl

viridis, -e: green

virtūs, -ūtis (f.): manliness, strength, courage, virtue, excellence; good character, moral perfection; merit, worth; (in plur.): good qualities

vīs, vīs (f.): force, strength, energy, violence, power; (in plur.): strength, force (in 14 n. 2A)

viscus, -eris (n.; usually plur.): entrails, viscera

visiō, -ōnis (f.): act of seeing (in 89 n. 8), vision

vīsō, -ere, -sī, -sus: look at attentively, survey, view; go to see, visit, keep seeing (30 n. 15D)

vīsus: past part. of *videō* or *vīsō*

vīsus, -ūs (m.): sight, vision

vīta, -ae (f.): life

vītis, -is (f.): vine, grapevine (87 C v. 8)

vitium, -ī (n.): fault, flaw; vice

vitō, -āre: avoid, shun

vitrum, -ī (n.): glass, crystal (87 D v. 1)

vitulus, -ī (m.): calf (89 n. 14A)

vituperō, -āre: blame, vituperate

vīvō, -ere, vīxī, vīctum: live

vīvus, -a, -um: alive

vix (adv.): with difficulty, hardly, barely, scarcely

vixdum (adv.): scarcely, barely

vīxī: perf. of *vīvō*

vōbīs: gen. and abl. of *vōs*

vocābulum, -ī (n.): designation, name

vocō, -āre: call, summon, invite; name

volgus: = *vulgus*

volitō, -āre: fly back and forth, flit about

voln-: = *vuln-*

volō, -āre: fly

volo, velle, voluī, —: wish, be willing

volt-: = *vult-*

volucer, -cris, -cre: winged, swift; (f. as a noun w. *avis* understood): bird (51 n. 9B)

voluntārius, -a, -um: willing, voluntary

voluntās, -ātis (f.): will, wish, desire; good will

voluptās, -ātis (f.): pleasure (69 n. 2B), enjoyment

volvō, -ere, -ī, -lūtus: cause to roll, revolve, turn about

vōmer, -eris (m.): ploughshare (52 n. 9C)

vort-: = *vert-*

vōs (2nd pers. plur. pronoun; gen. *vestrum* or *vestrī,* dat. and abl. *vōbīs,* acc. *vōs*): you

vōsmet: intensive for *vōs* (27 n. 7C)

vōtivus, -a, -um: promised in a vow, votive

vōtum, -ī (n.): vow, solemn pledge; wish, prayer

vōx, vōcis (f.): voice, sound, tone, utterance, cry; speech, saying

vulgus (or *volgus*), *-ī* (n.): the public, the common people (74 n. 11B, 77 n. 17); a crowd

vulnerō (voln-), -āre: wound

vulnus (voln-), -eris (n.): wound (metaphorical: in 67 n. 16A), injury; i.e. misfortune (44 n. 20B)

vultur (volt-), -uris (m.): vulture (4 s. 8)

vultus (volt-), -ūs (m.): face, features, expression, looks

Additions to the Vocabulary

adloquor, -uī, -cūtus (dep.): address (73 n. 4)

citus, -a, -um: swift (86 n. 27E)

dēhortor, -ārī, -ātus (dep.): dissuade (60 n. 22c)

flētus, -ūs (m.): a weeping, tears (73 n. 9)
frōns, frondis (f.): a leafy branch, foliage (77 v. 30)

indicō, -āre: show, indicate (87 n. 9)
indomitus, -a, -um: indomitable (77 v. 34)
īnferiae, -ārum (f. plur.): funeral rites (73 n. 2B)
interceptus, -a, -um: past part. of *intercipiō* (77 v. 6)
intercipiō, -ere, -cēpī, -ceptus: cut off, intercept

molestē (adv.): badly, with vexation (72 n. 19B)
mūtus, -a, -um: silent, dumb, mute (73 n. 4)

pecus, -udis (f.): head of cattle, animal (69 n. 13B)
placidus, -a, -um: quiet, placid (69 n. 28B)

rapidus, -a, -um: swift, rapid (74B v. 4)
rēmus, -ī (m): oar (86 n. 24B)

scelestus, -a, -um: wicked; (as noun): wretch (74E v. 15)
sublīmis, -e: sublime, on high, lofty (77 v. 26)
suspīciō, -ōnis (f.): distrust, suspicion (72 p. 3 s. 4)

ultrā (adv. and prep. with acc.): beyond (48 line 3), besides

vestīgium, -ī (n.): footstep; trace, vestige (85 n. 19)
vigēscō, -ere, —, —: to become vigorous, eager (73 n. 16)

DATE DUE